BY THE EDITORS OF CONSUMER GUIDE®

1000s
OF FREE*
THINGS

*or almost free.

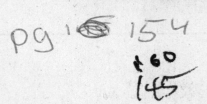

BEEKMAN HOUSE
New York

CONTENTS

Manufactured in the United States of America
10 9 8 7 6 5 4 3 2 1

Library of Congress Catalog Card Number: 86-6088

ISBN: 0-517-60412-4

Cover Design: Michael Johnson
Art: Steve Boswick
Photography: Sam Griffith

The prices and availability of the items listed in this book have been thoroughly checked and to the best of our knowledge are valid at the time of publication. However, the Editors of Consumer Guide® and Publications International, Ltd., take no responsibility for changes or substitutions made by a source, or for a source's failure to comply with the stated terms of an offer. Consumer Guide® and Publications International, Ltd., are in no way associated with anyone who is offering items that are listed in this book, nor does the inclusion of an item in any way imply endorsement of a manufacturer, product, organization, or cause.

CONTENTS

CONTENTS

FREE THINGS FOR PARENTS 198

FREE THINGS TO HELP YOU STAY HEALTHY 238

FREE THINGS TO HELP YOU LOOK GOOD 284

FREE THINGS FOR THE WAY YOU LIVE 294

CONTENTS

ALL ABOUT THIS BOOK

About This Book:

What's in It and How to Use It

Nothing is for nothing? If it's "free" there must be a catch? Not so. All over the country manufacturers, organizations, and associations are giving things away. They're giving away how-to and do-it-yourself guides, project plans, cookbooks and recipes, garden seeds and planting guides, product samples, know-how for parents with kids of all ages, posters and bumper stickers, car care manuals, wall charts and maps, health care information, advice on managing your money, fashion advice and free cosmetic samples, copies of magazines, and kids' stuff like games, projects, and coloring books.

The list could go on and on. And that's why we've put together this book. It's a real treasure chest of freebies—good, valuable stuff that you can get free, or nearly free, just for the asking. Some of the items are fun, like glow-in-the-dark jewelry or a scarf juggling kit. Some are practical—a cookbook crammed with recipes using turkey, for instance, or a rundown on doing your own car maintenance. Some, like a guide to buying or sewing clothes specially designed for handicapped people, fill a little-recognized need. There are panic preventers, such as a new parent's handbook on baby care, and lots of money-saving guides on how to buy everything from an automobile to a wristwatch. You'll find oddball things like a catalog full of boomerangs, and necessary things like first-aid ointment. You'll find all these, and *hundreds* of others, in the pages of this book.

What Does "Free" Really Mean?

Now for some practical points, and the first one is price. How free are these free things? A very good proportion of the items in this book *are* free. They cost you nothing more than the stamp that goes on your request. Lots more are "free with an SASE." An SASE is a self-addressed, stamped envelope that the company or organization can use to send you your item. A long SASE is a particular *size* envelope—business size or #10, about 9½ inches long and 4½ inches wide. You address the envelope to *yourself*, with your name and *full* address including your zip code, and you stamp it with (unless otherwise directed) a first-class stamp. Then you fold it up and send it to the company along with your request for your freebie. Other items in this book cost 25 cents, 50 cents, or $1.00. *Nothing* in this book costs more than $2.00, and that $2.00 always includes postage and handling.

Will the Price Stay the Same?

Every price in this book has been checked, and is good *at the time of publication*. And most manufacturers have assured us that the prices quoted in *1000s of Free Things* will be good through December 1986. You have to remember, though, that nothing is really certain. Financial pressures force organizations to raise their prices; government departments may be cut or eliminated; if postal rates go up, so will the prices of sample items and information. But even if a company or organization charges you more than the price listed here, be patient—you'll probably still be getting a bargain.

ALL ABOUT THIS BOOK

How Long Will These Free Things Be Available?

Most manufacturers and organizations have promised to honor requests for the items listed in this book through December 1986. A few qualified that assurance by saying that they *expect* to be able to fill requests through that date. Some federal and other major organizations, including the American Medical Association, could only promise that orders would be filled as long as supplies lasted, and where the item seemed important or interesting enough to be included here, we have used it. So, with these few reservations, you should be able to get any of the items listed in this book as long as your request arrives before December 31, 1986, and you'll get it at the listed price. But don't forget that things can go wrong. A company may go out of business, or a huge demand for a certain item may mean that the supply runs out sooner than the company expected. We've done our best, but we cannot be responsible for unforeseen problems that may occur.

How Do You Get Your Free Things?

We've made it as easy as possible for you. All you do is send the required materials or money (if any) to the listed address. The listed price *includes* postage and handling. If an item costs 50 cents plus 50 cents postage and handling, we've listed it as $1.00. So don't worry about extras. But to make the best of this book, *do* follow the few simple rules given below.

Follow a Few Simple Rules

1. *Don't send for things you don't want.* Think before you send for one of these free things. Do you really want it? Remember, your request will cost you at least the price of your postage stamp.

2. *Don't ask for more than one of each item.* Our listings are made on the basis of *one* request per person. In many cases only the single item is free—there's a charge for more than one. In other cases, there's a reduced rate for multiple copies. If you send for an item and find when you get it that it would be perfect for your club, class, or friends, write to the source and ask for details of multiple rates. (Often you won't even need to do this—the price list and rates will be included with the material sent to you.)

3. *Do obey the instructions.* For every item, under "cost," you'll see precise instructions on what the sender wants from you—50 cents, a long SASE, a postcard request. All these instructions mean something. An organization that asks you to write on a postcard probably doesn't have the staff to open hundreds or thousands of letters. If you don't use a postcard, you probably won't get a response. If the item calls for a *long* SASE, it usually means that the item won't fit in a small one, so send the right size—if you don't, the organization doesn't have to send you the item.

4. *Use the correct postage.* When you're sending an SASE, use one first-class stamp unless the directions say something else. Sometimes you'll be asked for two first-class stamps, or 39¢ postage, or two *loose* first-class stamps. Send *exactly* what's asked for.

5. *Send the correct money.* If you don't send the right money the source doesn't have to answer your letter. If you're sending cash through the mail, tape it securely between two pieces of cardboard or two 3'' x 5'' cards. That way it won't rattle around, and would-be thieves won't know there's money in the envelope. Occasionally—although we've tried to avoid this—you'll be asked to send a check or money order. Do so; the source will not accept coins or stamps.

6. *Send complete information.* Tell the source exactly what you want and where to send it. This may sound elementary, but you'd be astonished how many people don't do it. Complete information means: your name, your full address *including* your zip code, and the name or names of the freebies you want, as they appear in this book. If you're sending a letter, include your name, address, and zip code on *both* the envelope *and* the letter—in the mailing room of a big organization it's very easy for one to get separated from the other and lost for good.

7. *Write legibly.* One more thing—make sure you write so that your information is easy to read. Your best friends may have learned to decipher your handwriting, but a stranger won't be able to. Write in ink. If in doubt, type or print.

ALL ABOUT THIS BOOK

How Were These Free Things Chosen?

The editors of CONSUMER GUIDE®chose the items for this book out of a regular flood of freebies that arrived in our offices day after day from the time we made manufacturers and organizations aware of our plans for this book. Our editors personally inspected each item. If we thought it was worth the effort you'll make sending for it—and worth the charge if there is one—we put it in. If we didn't, we left it out.

Among the things we have *not* included are straight advertising "sells," literature that seems to pressure the reader to join its cause or subscribe to its funds, and product brochures that contain no useful information. We've included product brochures that *do* have some solid information, and a few that qualify as "idea books" on the strength of their illustrations.

One point to keep in mind: People who send you free things aren't always disinterested. Most of them want you to buy their product, support their cause, join their organization, subscribe to their magazine. You don't *have* to do any of these things, unless you want to. If you receive application or subscription forms, you can ignore them. You may also find yourself on other mailing lists—companies often share mailing lists of possible customers. This may not bother you. If it does, you can get yourself taken *off* mailing lists, and we've got a freebie that tells you how. It's *How Did They Get My Name?* and you'll find it in the section on "Consumer Services."

What Do the Star Ratings Mean?

We've tried to give you an idea of what you'll be getting by rating each item on a four-point scale of one to four stars—and we were careful not to judge by appearances only; looks aren't everything. A big, glossy brochure that we describe as an "idea book," meaning that it contains little practical information, will rate lower than a copied sheet that gives you really great how-to instructions for a home repair project. A four-star item is one we consider a real steal at the price; a one-star item is worth having but may be very small, have limited appeal, or offer less information than other things in the same category. A five-recipe leaflet, for instance, may rate one star, where a 50-page cookbook will rate four. But who knows? That one-star leaflet may contain a recipe that will become an all-time family favorite. So be flexible.

How Long Will You Have To Wait?

It could be anything from a few days to eight weeks before you get your freebie. Many sources quote a time period of four to six weeks. A few pride themselves on responding to requests the day they get them—but only a few. Don't be disappointed if you do have to wait six weeks or so. Remember that your item has probably been mailed the least expensive way, so even after it leaves the sender it may still take a while to reach you.

How Do You Write to a Freebie Source?

Suppose you want to write to the people who sent your freebie—or didn't send it, in which case you want to complain. What do you do?

- First of all, *don't* write to a box number. It's often the fulfillment house that handles bulk requests for special offers, not the source itself.
- If the address of the company or manufacturer that sent your freebie is *not* on the item or the envelope it came in, call the reference department of your local library. They'll usually be able to find it as long as you have a company name—even a brand name will do.
- If you're writing for information, send your letter to a specific person—like the Director of Public Relations or the Director of Consumer Relations. Sometimes you'll have the person's name or title. If not, either of those titles should get your letter to the right department. Specify the information you want: a catalog, a price list, a publications list, resources in a particular area, accredited professional sources.
- If you have a complaint, address it—by name if possible—to the president of the company. Explain why you're writing and give all the relevant information: the name of the item or product, the price, the date you ordered the item, the date you received it (if you did receive it), and why you aren't satisfied. Enclose a self-addressed, stamped envelope for a reply.

How This Book Works

So that you'll find your way easily through the huge number of items in this book, we've divided it into

ALL ABOUT THIS BOOK

major sections: *Free Things for Your Home, Free Things for Parents, Free Things to Help You Stay Healthy,* and so on. Within each major section there's a breakdown into smaller categories. The parents' section, for instance, groups items for expectant parents first, then for parents of babies, next for parents of growing children, then moves on to parents of teenagers. So, first check out the *Table of Contents* and find the chapter that's most likely to contain the things you're looking for. Start there.

Start there—but don't stop there. You'll miss a lot of terrific free things if you do. For instance, you're worried that your teenager has a problem with drugs or alcohol. You check out *Free Things for Parents,* and sure enough, there's a promising booklet on children and drugs and what parents can do about the situation. So far so good. Now try the chapter on health. You'll find a section on health hazards that has more information about drug and alcohol abuse. Great. Keep going. Flip through the *Free Things for Teens* chapter. It lists several publications on these "tricky topics" that are written for teenagers from their point of view. Maybe one of them is just what you need to help get your teen off drugs.

One Thing Leads to Another

That's the way this book works—one thing leads to another. Take another idea. There's a special chapter of *Free Things for Kids,* and it's written in kids' language so your youngsters can send off for their own free things. But you'll find good things for children in the section for parents, too—things that you can do with your children, teaching aids that develop a child's skill through play, things a young

child would need your help with. What's more, there's probably stuff for *you* in the children's section—maybe you'd love the popcorn ball maker listed for kids.

One thing leads to another in more ways than one. Many of the items included here come from major organizations and associations that have access to other information that can be useful to you—what you're getting here is a direct line to the people who know. Large health organizations put out literature on dozens of different health-related matters. A pamphlet on a particular health problem—arthritis, perhaps—will usually include addresses of other organizations that deal with that specific condition. So a 22-cent freebie can open the door to specialized information and assistance you didn't know was available—or that you suspected was available without knowing just how to go about finding it.

Have Fun With 1000s of Free Things

All in all, what you have in *1000s of Free Things* is nearly 400 big pages of super stuff on every subject you can think of, and all at the best possible price—free, or almost free. It's a book to have fun with, to browse in, to flip through—chances are that almost any page you light on will have something that gets you reaching for your pen and an envelope. Use this book to help you find out new things, explore new ideas, try new activities. There's so much great stuff here that you could keep your mailman busy for months—and all these good things will be a nice change from all the unwanted mail that lands on your welcome mat. Happy hunting.

FREE THINGS
for the
HOME

Buying, Building, or Renting a Home

HOW TO BUY A HOUSE
★★★★

Any time mortgage rates fall, more people look into the possibility of buying their first house. If that's the position you are in right now, *Tips on Buying a Home,* a free 14-page brochure by the Better Business Bureau can save you a lot of time, trouble, and probably money. It tells you everything from how to decide on the size and floor plan of your home to how to budget for the purchase to how to inspect a new or older house. And after you've found the house you want, the leaflet takes you through the steps in contract negotiations. Different types of mortgages are explained in short, simple terms, and you learn all about closing costs, including "points" and various fees. A handy checklist keeps you from forgetting to ask other important questions before you buy a house.

Write for:
Tips on Buying a Home (No. 24-154)

Cost: Free

Send to:
Council of Better Business Bureaus
1515 Wilson Blvd.
Arlington, VA 22209

Tips on Buying a Home

BUYING OR SELLING A HOME?
★★★

Purchasing a home involves many factors, from calculating what you can afford and arranging financing, to closing the sale. A new four-page report from the Bank of America helps you make these kinds of decisions more wisely and easily, taking you through

the home-buying process from choosing a house to figuring out the monthly payments for mortgage and other expenses, through to the closing. Another booklet tells how to sell your home, whether you plan to sell it on your own or let a real estate agent handle the sale. These two helpful guides can save you time and money and provide answers to many of the questions that arise in buying or selling a home.

Write for:
Steps to Buying a Home
A Guide to Selling Your Home

Cost: $1.00 (U.S. check or money order only)

Send to:
Bank of America, Dept. 3120
Box 37128
San Francisco, CA 94137

THE PLACE YOU CALL HOME
★★★★

This booklet is intended as a first step toward making a housing choice that suits your needs and resources. You'll examine the affordability of available housing, housing as an investment, and alternate investments if you're going to rent. The booklet looks at housing choices and compares them for costs, liability, tax benefits, and maintenance responsibilities. Three worksheets help you decide what's important to you in housing and how much you can comfortably invest in it.

Write for:
The Housing Market: A Guide to Sensible Choices

Cost: $1.25

Send to:
Distribution Center
7 Research Park
Cornell University
Ithaca, NY 14850

HOW TO AFFORD YOUR HOME
★★★★

Whatever your age or lifestyle, keeping a roof over your head is one of your major expenses. *Your Housing Dollar,* a 42-page book put out by the Money Management Institute, condenses a great deal of information into handy, readable form. Whether you're renting a one-room apartment or building a retirement home, it will guide you in making the most of your housing dollar.

continued

HOME

Thoughtful questions, suggestions, and worksheets aid you in determining your housing needs — where you want to live, how much you can spend, and whether to rent, buy, or build. It also advises on how to preplan your move to save time, energy, and money, and offers checklists to take some of the guesswork out of judging apartments and houses. The four pages evaluating a potential home's heating, wiring, plumbing, sewage disposal, water pipes, and air conditioning are alone worth the $1.00 price of the book.

Write for:
  Your Housing Dollar

Cost: $1.00

Send to:
  Money Management Institute — Dept. PI
  Household International
  2700 Sanders Rd.
  Prospect Heights, IL 60070

Your Housing Dollar

FOR PROSPECTIVE HOME BUYERS
★★★★

Each year in this country three million families buy a house. Another three million start thinking about it. This 190-page paperback is the complete home buyer's guide. You'll learn, first of all, if you can benefit from this book and how. You'll learn about location of a home, how to deal with a real estate broker or a developer, how to finance your home, how to protect that massive investment, and how to close the deal. You'll also learn the elements of good design and good construction. There's a glossary of real estate terms that takes the mystery out of real estate transactions. This book is in its fourth edition, and it's a real bargain — it only costs you $1.00 instead of the $2.25 cover price.

Write for:
  Lawyers Title Home Buying Guide

Cost: $1.00

Send to:
  Lawyers Title Insurance Corp.
  P.O. Box 27567
  Richmond, VA 23261

Lawyers Title Home Buying Guide

FIGURING THE COST OF HOME OWNERSHIP
★★★★

Can you afford to buy your own home? For many, home ownership is a questionable undertaking because of high interest rates and the increasing cost of maintaining a home once you've bought it. If you're pondering whether your financial position will permit you to buy a home, perhaps this publication from the University of Illinois will help. *Financing Your Home* is designed to help prospective home buyers determine in dollars and cents whether they can afford to take on the high cost of home ownership.

Learn how to figure how much you can afford in purchase price and monthly housing costs, and how to negotiate contracts and mortgages, understand real estate terminology, and check out the fine print. Forms are provided which you can fill out to discover just how much your new home may cost you. A payment table tells you how much your monthly repayments will be on various interest rates. There's also a helpful home mortgage guide describing the various types of mortgages available such as fixed rate, owner financed, balloon, graduated payment, adjustable zero interest, blended wrap, rollover, VA, and FHA. A good way to get to the practicalities involved in the complex and costly business of buying a home.

Write for:
  Council Notes A1.3 Financing the Home

Cost: $1.00

A SASE is a self-addressed stamped envelope.

Send to:
Small Homes Council—Building Research Council
University of Illinois at Urbana-Champaign
One E. St. Mary's Road
Champaign, IL 61820

A NEW HOME IN YOUR FUTURE?

★★★★

One of the most confusing and, possibly, most costly things about buying a new home is shopping for the right mortgage. One type of mortgage, the adjustable rate mortgage or ARM, is discussed here. This booklet provides useful basic information about ARMs, explaining how they work, some of their risks and advantages, how to reduce the risks, and how to get information from mortgage lenders. ARM terms are defined in a handy glossary, and there is a checklist to help you ask lenders the right questions and decide whether an ARM is a good option for you.

Write for:
Consumer Handbook on Adjustable Rate Mortgages (No. 129P)

Cost: Free

Send to:
Consumer Information Center
P.O. Box 100
Pueblo, CO 81002

Consumer Handbook on Adjustable Rate Mortgages

MODERN HOMESTEADING

★★★★

In years past, thousands of Americans acquired their land and homes under "homesteading" laws. The Federal government still sells public land to give you a start on a place of your own, and this eight-page brochure tells about the two types of property the Federal government makes available for sale:

real property and public lands. Real property is mainly developed land, such as a military base or office building. Public land is undeveloped land with no improvements, mostly in the western states and Alaska. To learn more about public land you can buy and build on, send for this brochure from the U.S. Department of the Interior Bureau of Land Management.

Write for:
Are There Any Public Lands for Sale? (No. 128P)

Cost: $1.00

Send to:
Consumer Information Center
P.O. Box 100
Pueblo, CO 81002

FANTASIZING ABOUT A NEW HOME

★

If you're planning a custom-built home, these two full-color glossy booklets will whet your appetite for a beautifully designed house in the country. *Vacation Homes* is a 14-page album of full-color photos of custom-designed homes built with red cedar shakes and shingles. *Timeless Beauty* also offers 14 pages of color photos showing family homes, beach houses, country estates, and mountain hideaways. These attractive booklets are strictly for fantasy—there's very little in the way of practical home-building information.

Write for:
Vacation Homes
Timeless Beauty

Cost: 35¢ for each title

Send to:
Red Cedar Shingle & Handsplit Shake Bureau
Suite 275
515 116th Ave., N.E.
Bellevue, WA 98004

WORKING WITH A HOMEBUILDER

★★★★

This booklet describes the business dealings and procedures involved when you, as a prospective homeowner, engage the services of a contractor or an architect. You'll find how to obtain plans and specifications for your building or house, how to prepare contract documents, how to select a contractor, and some rules for trouble-free building.

This eight-page publication tells about the architect's and contractor's services, fees, and payments, and sets out a digest of some of the provisions of the General Conditions of the Contract, published by the American Institute of Architects. You'll find out how to change orders during construction and how to terminate the contract if necessary. It's must reading if you're going to build.

Write for:
Business Dealings With the Architect and the Contractor

Cost: $1.00

Send to:
University of Illinois at Urbana-Champaign
Small Homes Council
One E. St. Mary's Rd.
Champaign, IL 61820

FAINT HEART NEVER BUILT FAIR HOME
★

Beware—here are all the dire pitfalls of trying to build your own home, listed by the Home Builders Association of Indiana. This inconsequential diary with cartoons presents information that is, to say the least, discouraging. You might want to give this to a *very* good friend who is considering acting as his own builder, or if your marriage is secure, to an overambitious spouse! That's a one-laugh warning against overestimating your talents as a do-it-yourselfer from an association that would like to do it for you.

Write for:
Diary of a Mad Home Builder

Cost: 50¢

Send to:
William Carson
Home Builders Association of Indiana
143 W. Market St.
Indianapolis, IN 46204

BUILD YOUR OWN HOME
★★★

Would you like to build your own dream home? Then you'll need floor plans, and here are some offered by

the Home Building Plan Service. These magazines retail for $2.95 each, but you can get them for $2.00 to cover postage and handling. Each publication features renderings of homes with descriptions and sketches of floor plans on each page. (The actual blueprints are sold by the organization.) The eight titles available are: *Solar & Energy-Saving All-American Homes for the 80s* (48 pages); *Recreation & Holiday Homes* (96 pages); *Hillside Homes* (96 pages); *Duplexes, Townhouses and Condominiums* (64 pages); *Contemporary and Traditional Homes* (82 pages); *Contemporary Masonry Homes* (48 pages); *Thermal Energy Designs for 21st Century Homes* (48 pages); and *Homes for the 80s*.

Write for:
Title of magazine required

Cost: $2.00 each

Send to:
Home Building Plan Service, Inc.
2235 N.E. Sandy Blvd., Studio 213
Portland, OR 97232-2884

YOUR VACATION HIDEAWAY
★★★★

Dreaming of that comfortable vacation home, neatly tucked in the woods or next to a well-stocked lake? Here's an opportunity to own a complete set of detailed blueprints for an ultra-modern, four-level house that, when completed, will provide 1200 square feet of living space. Even if you're not an architect or builder, the blueprints should fascinate you. Included are full electrical and plumbing specifications, and a materials list. This is especially appropriate for a youngster interested in architecture.

Write for:
L-P Vacation Home Plans

Cost: $1.00

Send to:
Louisiana-Pacific Corporation
1300 S.W. Fifth Ave.
Portland, OR 97201

L-P Vacation Home Plans

A SASE is a self-addressed stamped envelope.

THIS OLDER HOUSE

★★★★

It's got potential, but the old house needs lots of work. You might just turn it into your dream home, if only you could be sure it won't be an impossible task to fix it up to suit you. Cornell University researchers tell you what to look for when you inspect an older house. You'll learn how to inspect the building site, roof, electrical service, basement, plumbing, heating system, insulation, and walls. Illustrations show what to look for in the various stages of inspection. A handy checklist helps you keep track of just how much work may be needed in remodeling. A very practical guide, and a must for the smart shopper who's thinking of buying an older house.

Write for:
How to Inspect the Older House

Cost: $1.00

Send to:
Distribution Center
7 Research Park
Cornell University
Ithaca, NY 14850

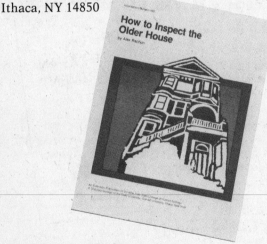

How to Inspect the Older House

A CONDO: TO BUY OR NOT TO BUY?

★★

This booklet may be able to answer your questions about whether condominium ownership is right for you. The first step is understanding exactly what a condominium is. This booklet tells you and explains what the "common elements" are and how they're maintained. There's a section on the advantages and responsibilities of condominium ownership and another on the role of title insurance when you buy a condominium. This booklet stresses the point that if you do buy, you'll become part of a community that will make collective decisions affecting everyone in the condominium.

Write for:
Condominiums From the Ground Up

Cost: Free

Send to:
Lawyers Title Insurance Corp.
P.O. Box 27567
Richmond, VA 23261

Condominium From the Ground Up

BUYING A CO-OP OR CONDO

★★★★

Any housing purchase is a major one, but buying a cooperative or a condominium merits special considerations. That's what this booklet is about: the definition of these two different kinds of ventures and the responsibilities involved. You'll learn the principles of cooperative housing and condominiums and the advantages and disadvantages of each. You'll learn about the legal aspects, standard practices and procedures, and questions you should ask yourself and the seller before you buy either. There's a good list of definitions here, too, and a list of other books on housing decisions.

Write for:
Cooperative Housing and Condominiums

Cost: $1.25

Send to:
Distribution Center
7 Research Center
Cornell University
Ithaca, NY 14850

HOME

CONDOS AND CO-OPS
★★★★

Want to own a home but not a house? The answer could be buying either a condominium or a co-operative. What are they and what's the difference between them? You can quickly learn all about them in a free 12-page booklet, *Tips on Condos and Co-ops*, from the Better Business Bureau. Both condos and co-ops are good alternatives to buying a single detached family home and can better suit the childless couple, single person, or senior citizen. They also can make excellent investment property. This booklet tells you what to look for when purchasing either a newly-built condominium unit, a townhouse, a rental apartment that is being converted into a condominium, or a co-op.

Write for:
Tips on Condos and Co-ops (No. 24-193)

Cost: Free

Send to:
Council of Better Business Bureaus
1515 Wilson Blvd.
Arlington, VA 22209

FINDING THE PERFECT PAD
★★★

Apartment hunting can be hard work these days, so here's a tiny booklet you can stash in your purse or pocket to help rate the units you see. *A Guide to Renting an Apartment* gives straightforward information about setting priorities, what to look for in both new and old units, moving expenses, leases, and renters' insurance. Take along a pencil—much of the 36 pages consists of charts and forms to fill out along the way, including four pages of grids to sketch the apartment layouts you see. Most helpful is an apartment rating system based on five categories—appearance, special services, location, layout, and price. If your approach to apartment hunting is methodical, rather than haphazard, this free guide is worth taking along when you're ready to hit the pavement and find that perfect place.

Write for:
A Guide to Renting an Apartment

Cost: Free

Send to:
State Farm Insurance Companies
Public Relations Department—DH
One State Farm Plaza
Bloomington, IL 61701

APARTMENT HUNTING TIPS
★★★

To rent or not to rent? That may be the big question when you're looking over a choice of apartments. It's a hard enough task to find the "right" apartment in a city you know, but what if you've just moved to a city new to you? The Better Business Bureau's free 10-page booklet, *Tips on Renting an Apartment*, can help make your search for the best apartment a lot easier. You learn how to fill out applications for renting an apartment, what to look for in inspecting an apartment, and what to be aware of in signing a lease. The booklet also describes significant tenant rights and what to include in a security deposit agreement. Finally, you learn about subletting and what is expected when you plan to move out.

Write for:
Tips on Renting an Apartment (No. 146)

Cost: Free

Send to:
Council of Better Business Bureaus
1515 Wilson Blvd.
Arlington, VA 22209

Tips on Renting an Apartment

BUYING A MOBILE/ MANUFACTURED HOME?
★★★★

Mobile/manufactured homes are usually less expensive to buy and maintain than traditional homes. For that reason, many young couples, senior citizens, and singles prefer buying a mobile/manufactured home. If you're in the market for either, you can learn a lot from the Better Business Bureau's free 14-page booklet *Tips on Buying a Mobile/ Manufactured Home*. It tells about single- and multi-section units, what the basic price should include, what extras you'll need to look for, and offers advice on financing and insurance. You also learn about

A SASE is a self-addressed stamped envelope.

mobile/manufactured home communities and what to look for beyond just appearance. There may be rules and regulations that prohibit children or pets, or the community may have special parking regulations. Finally, there are tips on relocating the home.

Write for:
Tips on Buying a Mobile/Manufactured Home (No. 311-03227)

Cost: Free

Send to:
Council of Better Business Bureaus
1515 Wilson Blvd.
Arlington, VA 22209

DON'T LEAVE HOME WITHOUT IT
★★★★

For many American families, mobility is a way of life. If a move is on the horizon for you, the American Movers Conference has a very good free foldout to help you negotiate successfully with a mover and keep track of the innumerable details that make for a nontraumatic, trouble-free move.

The best thing about this five-page pamphlet is that it is so specific; starting about eight weeks ahead of moving day, use the "countdown checklist" to take you methodically through tasks like getting estimates from several moving companies, sorting and packing your possessions, filling out and mailing change-of-address cards, sending drapes or carpets out for cleaning before the move, arranging for cash or traveler's checks to pay the mover, and even checking your car tires for the final trip to your new home. An excellent aid to coping with a move without losing your mind.

Write for:
Guide to a Satisfying Move

Cost: Free with a long SASE

Send to:
American Movers Conference
2200 Mill Road
Alexandria, VA 22314

PROFIT FROM YOUR GARAGE SALE
★★★★

A garage sale is a great idea if you're moving or just if you want to clear away some of the clutter that's accumulated around the house. Here's a booklet of 101 ideas to make a garage sale successful. The tips are highly practical; for example, you'll learn that it's quantity rather than quality that attracts customers to stop in and browse. There are also lots of good rules for pricing and displaying your merchandise. One suggestion: display low-cost items together under one sign—"Everything on this table 35¢"—to save yourself a lot of tagging. This booklet is well worth the $2.00 cost. In fact, it's a bargain in itself to *Free Things* readers—it usually costs $3.00 plus 50¢ for postage.

Write for:
Garage Sales—101 Ideas to Make Your Sale Easy, Fun, Successful

Cost: $2.00

Send to:
Treasure Cove Specialties
P.O. Box 67
Lombard, IL 60148

CUT DOWN ON MOVING COSTS
★★

Instead of paying a professional mover to transport your earthly belongings from one location to the other, you can do the job yourself. And if you do some sensible planning, you'll spare yourself a lot of frustration. *Your Guide for a Safe Move* is a free four-page foldout from the American Rental Association that really packs a lot of good advice into its few pages. Here's where you'll learn to make an inventory of your goods in order to figure out how big a rental truck you'll need—there's a simple formula to help you do this, plus a chart showing the average cubic feet of space needed for various household items. Use the helpful tips for packing and loading the truck to give maximum protection to all your valuables.

Write for:
Your Guide for a Move

Cost: Free

Send to:
American Rental Association
1900 19th St.
Moline, IL 61265

ICC ADVISES ON MOVING
★★★★

This straightforward, no-nonsense booklet from the Interstate Commerce Commission tells exactly what
continued

the consumer's rights and responsibilities are in a move, as well as the mover's. Material is broken into categories like estimates (binding and nonbinding), inventory, weights, pick-ups and deliveries, the mover's liability for loss and damage, and payment and filing of claims. You'll also learn where to go for more help from local ICC offices if you need it. If you move, you're asked to fill out a questionnaire that's included in the book and return it to the ICC.

Write for:
   When You Move: Your Rights and
      Responsibilities

Cost: Free

Send to:
   Interstate Commerce Commission
   Office of Compliance and Consumer Assistance
   Washington, DC 20423

When You Move: Your Rights and Responsibilities

MOVING OUT OF STATE?
★★★★

Moving from one city or state to another can present monumental problems and cost a small fortune, unless you plan properly for such a major move. The Better Business Bureau's free 20-page brochure, *Tips on Interstate Moving*, can relieve you of a lot of long-distance moving headaches. You learn what the best time of year is to make an interstate move, how to choose a mover, what should be included in an estimate, how to lighten your moving load, and how to arrange for a "binding" price agreement. Learn all about weights such as tare weight, gross weight, and net weight. Also learn about storing your things if they have to be shipped later. Three basic liability plans are described, and a handy moving checklist reminds you of major steps to take in making the big move.

Write for:
   Tips on Interstate Moving (No. 24-160)

Cost: Free

Send to:
   Council of Better Business Bureaus
   1515 Wilson Blvd.
   Arlington, VA 22209

Home Improvements and Interior Design

DON'T MOVE, IMPROVE!
★★★★

Need an extra bedroom or want a newer, bigger kitchen? Want your old house converted into a new, more energy-efficient solar-heated home? Many homeowners are discovering it's a lot smarter—and cheaper—to enlarge or add-on to their present home than to move and buy a new one. The Better Business Bureau's free six-page brochure, *Tips on Home Improvements*, tells you what to look for, and what to look out for, in dealing with building contractors before hiring them for a remodeling job. Advice is offered on getting several bids from different contractors, requesting "full" or "limited" warranties, and being aware of interest and service charges on work done. These and other important points covered can help make your home improvement safe and budget-sound.

Write for:
   Tips on Home Improvements (No. 205)

Cost: Free

Send to:
   Council of Better Business Bureaus
   1515 Wilson Blvd.
   Arlington, VA 22209

MAKING HOME IMPROVEMENTS?
★★★

Whether you want to increase your home's energy efficiency or simply add space and comfort, home improvements involve careful planning. A four-page report from the Bank of America can help you decide how to finance your project, find professionals to do the work, and avoid pitfalls. It tells how to get various estimates for the work, what energy conservation tax benefits you may take advantage of, and how to find and work with a reliable contractor. You'll also learn all about liens, ways to protect yourself in a contract, and shopping for credit to pay for the work.

Write for:
   Planning Home Improvements

Cost: $1.00 (U.S. check or money order only)

Send to:
   Bank of America, Dept. 3120
   Box 37128
   San Francisco, CA 94137

SELECTING A QUALIFIED CONTRACTOR

★★★

Your home represents a large investment, and its proper care and maintenance is essential. Also important is the fact that your home must suit your present needs and lifestyle. Just because you may need an additional bedroom, or a more modern kitchen, is no reason to uproot your family and move; remodeling may be the answer. Home improvements can update your home and increase the value of your investment, but planning is vital. *Selecting a Professional Remodeling Contractor* is a great little pamphlet that tells you how to go about getting the job done the way you want it. Published by the National Association of the Remodeling Industry, the brochure covers guidelines for selecting a contractor, determining the improvements you want made, and complying with specifications and building codes. There is a checklist to help you determine your priorities and a copy of the association's code of ethics.

Write for:
   Selecting a Professional Remodeling Contractor

Cost: Free

Send to:
   National Association of the Remodeling Industry
   1901 North Moore Street
   Suite 808
   Arlington, VA 22209

HOW TO DESIGN AN INTERIOR

★★★★

This booklet is designed to help you make the interior of your home more livable and attractive. You'll focus on the various elements of design—space, furnishings for that space, arrangement, color, and form. The eight-page booklet solves a typical decorating problem with before and after illustrations, and there's a discussion of whether to concentrate on contemporary or traditional furniture and the pros and cons of each. And throughout you'll find

good do's and don'ts to keep in mind as you plan your interior design.

Write for:
   Interior Design

Cost: $1.00

Send to:
   University of Illinois at Urbana-Champaign
   Small Homes Council
   One E. St. Mary's Rd.
   Champaign, IL 61820

PLANNING A ROOM

★★★

Before you buy furniture or move existing pieces around, some room planning is in order. Here's a brochure on how to plan a room for an apartment, home, vacation home, or retirement home. Diagrams give the size (in inches) of furniture commonly found in living, dining, and bedrooms, together with layout plans. You select the furniture for a specific room from the illustrations provided, cut them out, and place them on graph paper which is also provided. This allows you to see a scale model of a room before you buy or move a stick of furniture. You save time and money, and you don't get a sore back.

Write for:
   Room Planning Guide

Cost: 50¢ and a long SASE (44¢ postage)

Send to:
   American Furniture Manufacturers Association
   P.O. Box HP-7
   High Point, NC 27261

Room Planning Guide

HOME

PLANNING EFFICIENT BEDROOMS

★★★

The word "efficient" as defined in this booklet means the smallest bedroom that will accommodate the necessary furniture and allow access to it, and still leave adequate floor space for dressing, sleeping, and cleaning. This booklet lists typical furniture sizes for currently manufactured dressers, nightstands, beds, and chairs—remember that older furniture may be larger. There are several bedroom floor plans to show the most efficient placement of a double bed, two twin beds, and one twin bed in a room, plus planning suggestions for architects and builders on bedroom area layouts and notes on how to evaluate an existing bedroom plan. Good ideas for using space to the best advantage.

Write for:
Bedroom Planning Standards

Cost: $1.00

Send to:
University of Illinois at Urbana-Champaign
Small Homes Council
One E. St. Mary's Rd.
Champaign, IL 61820

SMART SHOPPING FOR A GOOD NIGHT'S SLEEP

★★

Your mattress and foundation play a big part in how well you sleep at night. If it's time to get a new sleep set (or you're wondering if it is), *Good Night America: A Guide to Better Sleep* will help you make the right decision. In this 16-page booklet, the Better Sleep Council provides a primer on sleep (with tips on getting to sleep and sleeping better) and tells you how to judge your mattress and foundation to find out if they should be retired. It also tells you what to look for when shopping for a new set. Always lie down and roll about a bit before you buy, advises the Council. And don't try to put a spanking new mattress on an old, worn out foundation—buy the set.

There's some interesting trivia here, too. Did you know that Charles Dickens always arranged his guests' bedrooms so that the headboard pointed north? Or that Benjamin Franklin had several beds so he could move from one to another whenever the sheets got too warm? Well, you know now!

Write for:
Good Night America: A Guide to Better Sleep

Cost: 50¢

Send to:
The Better Sleep Council
P.O. Box 275
Burtonsville, MD 20866

PLANNING A CONVENTIONAL KITCHEN

★★★★

The purpose of this booklet is to provide standards for designing and judging plans of kitchens using conventional equipment. You'll learn an easy way to determine how much counter space and cabinet space you'll need and where it should be, how to plan the kitchen arrangement for efficient operation, and how to evaluate a kitchen by a scoring plan that you can adapt to any residential kitchen that uses ordinary storage cabinets. Using the knowledge in this booklet, you should come out with the best possible plan in a kitchen that's equipped with conventional equipment—not custom-designed extravaganzas.

Write for:
Kitchen Planning Standards

Cost: $1.00

Send to:
University of Illinois at Urbana-Champaign
Small Homes Council
One E. St. Mary's Rd.
Champaign, IL 61820

A KITCHEN FOR THE KITCHEN WORKER

★★★★

A kitchen that looks like it's out of *House & Garden* means nothing to the person who works in it if the workspace isn't efficient. And efficiency means forethought in planning and design. This solid booklet will help you plan a new kitchen, remodel an existing one, reorganize your present kitchen, or adapt an apartment kitchen—all to make it functional and efficient. There are work flow plans (all illustrated), height considerations, floor plans with furniture and appliance cut-outs to scale, and even plans for designing a kitchen for wheelchair workers. The whole idea of designing a kitchen is to conserve energy—yours, and that required by the appliances you'll be using. Lots of great information in these 30 big (8½″ × 11″) pages. An excellent buy.

Write for:
Functional Kitchens

A SASE is a self-addressed stamped envelope.

Cost: $1.50

Send to:
Distribution Center
7 Research Park
Cornell University
Ithaca, NY 14850

FURNISHING THE NURSERY

★★★

A new baby means all sorts of new purchases—new crib, new mattress, and new baby furniture. This pleasant 30-page booklet put out by a juvenile products manufacturer is designed to help new parents furnish the nursery. The booklet's best feature is that it shows you how to tell well-made, durable furniture from the shoddy stuff by checking features like drawer construction, the types of joints used, and whether nails or screws hold everything together. There's a lot of advertising, but it doesn't overwhelm some good practical information.

Write for:
How to Select Your Baby's Major Needs

Cost: 25¢

Send to:
Simmons Juvenile Products Co., Inc.
613 E. Beacon Ave.
P.O. Box 287
New London, WI 54961

How to Select Your Baby's Major Needs

PLANNING A BETTER BATHROOM

★★★

Two eight-page booklets here and both focus on the bathroom. One deals with the bathroom equipment that's available, with diagrams and explanations of properties and specifications. All the equipment is discussed on the basis of safety and wearability. The other booklet is important to read when bathrooms are being planned so you choose fixtures and equipment according to their intended use and the space available; so the bathroom itself is in the best location; and so you can determine the most effective use of plumbing to serve the fixtures and equipment you plan to install. Very practical information.

Write for:
Bathroom Equipment
Bathroom Planning Standards

Cost: $2.00 for both

Send to:
University of Illinois at Urbana-Champaign
Small Homes Council
One E. St. Mary's Rd.
Champaign, IL 61820

EVERYBODY INTO THE POOL!

★★★★

The long, hot summer can be a lot more pleasant—and cooler—with a family swimming pool. If you're in the market for one, you can learn a lot about pools from the Better Business Bureau's free 8-page booklet, *Tips on Buying a Swimming Pool.* Should your pool be above-ground or in-ground? How much will it cost? How can you finance the cost? Which pool builder should you choose? These questions are answered, and tips are offered on how to work with a pool builder, what to look for in a contract, and what energy-saving features should be considered. Pool safety and maintenance advice finishes the booklet.

Write for:
Tips on Buying a Swimming Pool (No. 24-151)

Cost: Free

Send to:
Council of Better Business Bureaus
1515 Wilson Blvd.
Arlington, VA 22209

A POOL FOR YOU

★★★

If a swimming pool is in your family's future, here's a good way to plan the big event—send for this packet of three booklets that tell you how to plan a swimming pool, how to get the most pleasure out

continued

of it, and how to maintain it. Planning requires you to consider size and shape—depending on what you want to use the pool for—wading and floating, swimming laps, or diving. Learn about swimming aerobics, which could be a great new health routine for the family, and about aqua dynamics, a series of simple to advanced exercises that are performed in the water. The maintenance booklet gives important safety tips and discusses pumps, filters, heaters, chemicals, and covering or storing the pool in winter. A lot of good tips here, and a bargain at $1.00.

Write for:
  Pool Planning Kit

Cost: $1.00

Send to:
  Dept. PI
  National Spa and Pool Institute
  2111 Eisenhower Ave.
  Alexandria, VA 22314

Pool Planning Kit

MAKING YOUR WATER SAFER
★★★★

Most communities' tap water is safe to drink, but few would disagree that it could be even safer. Improving your water for drinking or cooking can be done simply and economically by installing a water conditioner in your home. The Better Business Bureau's free eight-page brochure, *Tips on Water Conditioners*, can clear up the cloudy home-water picture for you. Learn the difference between hard and soft water, the three ways you can get softened water, and solutions to the problems of iron, sulfur, acidity, and bad taste in your home's water supply. These and other tips guide you when you look to buy a water conditioner. A handy checklist offers overall and last-minute purchasing safeguards.

Write for:
  Tips on Water Conditioners (No. 311-02266)

Cost: Free

Send to:
  Council of Better Business Bureaus
  1515 Wilson Blvd.
  Arlington, VA 22209

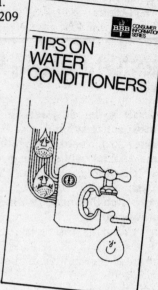

Tips on Water Conditioners

WOOD MOULDING—A TO Z
★★★★

As a skilled do-it-yourselfer, you'll not only tap this plentiful source of ideas for using moulding in your home, you'll also learn fascinating lore about moulding, like how lumber becomes trim. Next come basic profiles of 27 different types of wood mouldings, illustrated with detailed, easy-to-read drawings that show dozens of uses. Some of them? Chair rail, ceiling trim, beamed ceilings, paneled walls, garage door designs.

There's good information on how to work with wood mouldings and jambs, and even how to install a prehung door. A handy conversion chart converts linear measurements to the metric system. This booklet is well worth $2.00—it even gives you something interesting to read while you take a break from your labors.

Write for:
  From Tree to Trim

Cost: $2.00

Send to:
  Wood Moulding & Millwork Producers
    Association
  P.O. Box 25278
  Portland, OR 97225

A SASE is a self-addressed stamped envelope.

WORKING WITH WOOD MOULDING

★★★★

A lot of essential information has been condensed into this handy foldout pamphlet. Clear illustrations show profiles of a couple of dozen types of wood moulding and ideas for their use, and there's information on how to measure how much you'll need, and how to miter and cope mouldings. There's also guidance on the tools you'll need to do the job. You can probably do fairly simple moulding jobs by consulting this pamphlet. For larger, more complicated work, you'll want the $2.00 booklet *From Tree to Trim,* put out by the same people.

Write for:
How to Work With Wood Mouldings

Cost: 40¢

Send to:
Wood Moulding & Millwork Producers
   Association
P.O. Box 25278
Portland, OR 97225

How to Work With Wood Moldings

HOW TO PRETTY UP A PLAIN ROOM

★★★

Want to turn a plain room into one with detail and charm? This publication suggests you do it by using decorative wood mouldings. The eight-page color booklet shows how specific moulding patterns were used to create various room designs, some modern, others in a Colonial or country style. Drawings of the specific mouldings used accompany color pictures of moulding used in various rooms of a home. From parlor to bathroom, wood mouldings can make a decorative difference and transform an ordinary room

into a showplace on a minimum budget, and this 8″ × 11″ publication proves it handsomely.

Write for:
Design and Decorate With Wood Mouldings

Cost: 75¢

Send to:
Wood Moulding & Millwork Producers
   Association
P.O. Box 25278
Portland, OR 97225

Design and Decorate with Wood Moldings

MOULDING FINISHES

★★

Paint it or stain it? Shellac, varnish, oil, or wax it? This brochure suggests various ways of finishing wood mouldings in the home. Opaque paint finishes, clear or natural finishes, and semi-transparent color finishes are described along with finishing products such as bleach, primer, sealer, filler, and antiquing color. A list of tools is given along with tips on how to use them. You even get tips for cleanup.

Write for:
How to Finish Wood Mouldings

Cost: 40¢

Send to:
Wood Moulding & Millwork Producers
   Association
P.O. Box 25278
Portland, OR 97225

CEILING DECORATION

★★★

Ceiling mouldings not only cover the seams where the walls meet the ceiling, but can be decorative

continued

HOME

elements in their own right. Here's an eight-page brochure that gives ideas on how to use ceiling mouldings to decorate a room, and how to cut and install them. As any home handyman knows, cutting moulding can sometimes be a puzzling task. This brochure helps solve the mystery. Drawings also show various ceiling mouldings to choose from. There's a lot of solid, finely detailed information in this little leaflet. The drawings are small, but impressively clear.

Write for:
    How to Install Ceiling Mouldings

Cost: 40¢

Send to:
    Wood Moulding & Millwork Producers
        Association
    P.O. Box 25278
    Portland, OR 97225

How to Install Ceiling Molding

FOR LATTICE LOVERS
★★

You may be surprised to learn how many ways there are of decorating with lattice wood moulding. Here is a 32-page idea book showing many traditional and untraditional uses, and the booklet is profusely illustrated with ideas for both interior and exterior application of lattice. Projects suggested include accent walls, decks, fences, furniture trim, lighting fixtures, mail boxes, picture frames, room dividers, and more. A decorator's delight, and a steal for 75¢.

Write for:
    How to Work With Lattice

Cost: 75¢

Send to:
    Wood Moulding & Millwork Producers
        Association
    P.O. Box 25278
    Portland, OR 97225

ALL ABOUT WINDOWS
★★★★

Home planners, builders, and owners selecting windows will appreciate the information on windows offered by the University of Illinois in their new publication. Tips are offered on the three basic types of windows—sliding, swinging, and fixed—as well as a variety of combinations. Subjects discussed include double-hung windows, horizontal sliding windows, casement windows, awning and jal-awning windows, jalousie windows, bottom-hinged windows, top-hinged windows, fixed windows, patio doors and window walls, and skylight and roof windows. There are some good tips as to what kind of windows work best in certain locations—for instance, a sliding window positioned over a sink or a large piece of furniture can be awkward to open and close; and a window controlled by a hand crank is a better choice in such a position. Lots of other equally good information, too.

Write for:
    Council Notes F11.1 Selecting Windows

Cost: $1.00

Send to:
    Small Homes Council—Building Research Council
    University of Illinois at Urbana-Champaign
    One E. St. Mary's Rd.
    Champaign, IL 61820

Selecting Windows

HANDYMAN DOOR SPECIAL
★★★

Step-by-step installation procedures for interior jambs and exterior door frames are contained in a brochure from the Wood Moulding & Millwork Producers Association. Instructions are given for assembling and installing jambs and frames in either "knockdown" or "prehung" form. Drawings offer helpful illustrations along with short instructions.

A SASE is a self-addressed stamped envelope.

Illustrations of various types of wood moulding are included. A useful guide for the home handyman.

Write for:
How to Install Interior Jambs & Exterior Door Frames

Cost: 40¢

Send to:
Wood Moulding & Millwork Producers
  Association
P.O. Box 25278
Portland, OR 97225

LIGHTING FOR THE WAY YOU LIVE
★★★

Home lighting shouldn't be a matter of placing a lamp where it might look good, but where it can best suit the needs, life-styles, and activities of a home's occupants. According to the American Home Lighting Institute, home lighting should be planned to take into account the way we live, work, and play. In this colorful, informative 20-page booklet The Institute gives guidelines to good home lighting along with lots of tips for both interior and exterior lighting. See how to light foyers and entrance halls, living areas, dining areas, kitchens, bedrooms, and bathrooms. There's information, too, on accent, recessed, and track lighting; types of lighting fixtures, and light sources.

Write for:
Guidelines to Good Lighting

Cost: $2.00

Send to:
Public Information Services
American Home Lighting Institute
435 N. Michigan Ave.
Chicago, IL 60611

FURNITURE BUYING TIPS
★★★

Furniture costs keep spiraling, but one way to keep them under control is to heed this alert and practice the wise buying practices suggested by the American Furniture Manufacturers Association in these three little brochures, which are all designed to help you get the most out of your furniture buying dollars.

Do's and Don'ts When You Buy Furniture tells you how to be a smart furniture shopper and what to do if you have a problem with a purchase. You're cau-

tioned about buying furniture "close outs" or "as is" items, and warned of the dangers of "truck buying." Line drawings help you recognize basic styles of chairs, hutches, chests, desks, tables, and other furniture.

When You Buy Upholstered Furniture tells how to measure and plan before you shop, why solid frames are important for chairs or couches, and how to check for good tailoring. You learn about different upholstery fabrics and what to look for when you're choosing fabrics. Illustrations show basic upholstered styles of chairs and sofas, and there's a helpful list of fabric definitions.

When You Buy Wood Furniture tells about construction details such as veneers, grain, and finishes, and explains how to care for fine wood furniture. A list of definitions is included.

Write for:
Do's and Don'ts When You Buy Furniture
When You Buy Upholstered Furniture
When You Buy Wood Furniture

Cost: $1.00 and a long SASE (44¢ postage) for all three

Send to:
American Furniture Manufacturers Association
P.O. Box HP-7
High Point, NC 27261

Do's and Dont's When You Buy Furniture

A CHAIR IS JUST A CHAIR?
★★★★

When you buy one piece of furniture at a time, without regard to how it will look with the rest of your home furnishings, you can be in big trouble. A chair may not be just a chair when it conflicts with the rest of a room. It can be a big, expensive white elephant. So can a couch, end table, lamp, or other piece. To tune in to the fine art of furnishing your

continued

HOME

home or apartment, check out the Better Business Bureau's new 10-page brochure, *Tips on Buying Furniture*. It tells how to plan before you buy — what you'll need, how items will be used, how much space there is to work with, and how much to budget. It also tells about furniture types and terms, finishes, and upholstered furniture.

Write for:
Tips on Buying Furniture (No. 24-153)

Cost: Free

Send to:
Council of Better Business Bureaus
1515 Wilson Blvd.
Arlington, VA 22209

THE WELL-DRESSED WINDOW
★★★

Window draperies can add beauty to your home, and they are usually essential for privacy. They can also be expensive, particularly if your home has a lot of windows or ones of unusual sizes. If you've ever thought about simply buying fabric and sewing your own draperies, this helpful 16-page booklet may be just what you're looking for. The booklet offers advice tailored to different window styles, and has plenty of useful information about the proper hooks, brackets, bolts, and suchlike needed to hang the drapes properly. You'll learn how to measure, cut, and construct drapes, and how to make drape linings. You'll even pick up helpful hints about making pinch pleats. The publisher also offers sample fabric swatches to help you match your drapes to your decor.

Write for:
How to Sew Draperies
Sample fabric swatches

Cost: Free

Send to:
Triblend Mills, Inc.
4004 Anaconda Rd.
Tarboro, NC 27886

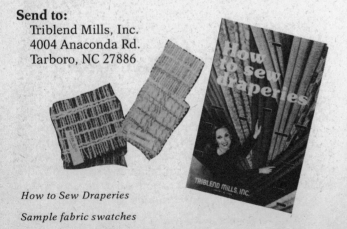

How to Sew Draperies

Sample fabric swatches

MAGIC OF CARPET AND RUG BUYING
★★★★

If there is any magic to the art of buying the right carpets and rugs for the home or apartment, it is in knowing more about them. Carpets can add beauty, color, sound-proofing, and value to your home, but they can be a rather bewildering thing to shop for. There is a wide variety of constructions, textures, colors, and fibers to choose from, so it could be worth your while to send for this free 12-page brochure, *Tips on Carpet and Rugs*, from the Better Business Bureau. It answers the most-often-asked questions about carpets and rugs. It describes carpeting terms, warranties, contracts with dealers, and offers simple tests you can make on carpets and rugs to be sure they are all they're supposed to be. Decorating hints and a helpful buying checklist are also included.

Write for:
Tips on Carpet and Rugs (No. 311-02230)

Cost: Free

Send to:
Council of Better Business Bureaus
1515 Wilson Blvd.
Arlington, VA 22209

Tips on Carpet and Rugs

BEFORE YOU PAINT
★★★

It's time to paint the outside of the house, or maybe just the living room or kitchen. To make the job smoother and get the most out of your next home paint job, you can use the information given here about painting inside and outside the home. This 26-page publication from the U.S. Department of Agriculture's Science and Education Administration includes tips on how to prepare the surface, select the right paint, and employ the best and newest

A SASE is a self-addressed stamped envelope.

methods of applying paint, safety precautions, and a fact-filled section on how to paint interiors and exteriors. The booklet also contains information on finishes and stains, whitewashing, and clean-up.

Write for:
Painting Inside and Out (No. 139P)

Cost: $1.50

Send to:
Consumer Information Center
P.O. Box 100
Pueblo, CO 81002

Painting Inside and Out

A PERFECT COVERUP

★★★★

Be sure to check out *The Wallcovering How-To Handbook* before you start your next wallpapering project. This free 16-page booklet from the Wallcovering Information Bureau makes the job much easier with its step-by-step approach. From fabrics to vinyls to strippable wallcoverings, you'll learn how to select the product that suits both your home's architecture and personality. You'll receive ideas on different ways to use wallcoverings, how to measure out the amount you'll need, and how to buy it. You'll learn about the tools you will need and what must be done to prepare the walls before applying the cover. Illustrated directions give advice on hanging, matching patterns, and dealing with corners and ceilings. There are also tips for making room accessories from remnants, and a glossary of terms you need to know.

Write for:
The Wallcovering How-To Handbook

Cost: Free

Send to:
Wallcovering Information Bureau, Inc.
66 Morris Avenue
Springfield, NJ 07081

DECORATING THE NATURAL WAY

★★

If your dream home is decorated in earth tones and natural fiber fabrics, you should check out this wallcovering catalog and sample kit. Shibui Wallcoverings offers unusual patterns and designs, each constructed from plant fibers from around the world. Rush, jute, cotton yarn, cork, and leaves are a few of the materials actually used to form rich, beautifully textured wall decoration. You'll find a wide variety of weaves and colors, from elegant to rustic. Shibui Wallcoverings also offers a paper hanging tool kit, adhesive, and protective coating spray. There are directions for determining the amount of wallcovering you will need, although the company will do it for you if you wish. The $2.00 cost includes 80 or so swatches, a price list, tips for ordering and measuring, and a $2.00 gift certificate good on your first order.

Write for:
Catalog and samples

Cost: $2.00

Send to:
Shibui Wallcoverings
P.O. Box 1638
Rohnert Park, CA 94928

Shibui catalog and samples

HOME

YE OLDE TAVERN NOTICES ON PARCHMENT
★★★

These truly amusing, quaint old tavern notices have been reprinted on parchment to give them the look and feel of historical documents. You get two notices, one 11″ × 14″ and the other 9″ × 15″, and either of them could be framed or attached to an old wood block and then varnished. Copy for one of these notices announces "4 pence a night for bed," and stipulates, "no more than five to sleep in one bed... no razor grinders or tinkers taken in...organ grinders to sleep in the washhouse." The other is a wine and victual list for a Colonial inn—cash down, no credit, just like today.

Write for:
Rules of the Tavern poster
Fare of the Tavern poster

Cost: $1.00 for both (no stamps)

Send to:
Historical Documents Co.
Dept. E
8 N. Preston St.
Philadelphia, PA 19104

PICTURE THAT
★★★

Newlyweds and apartment dwellers often find themselves long on wall space and short on cash for decorating. In fact, almost everyone you know has a bare nook or corner that could use some cheerfulness. For one dollar, you can receive a framed picture—a six-inch square with frame from a random selection by the manufacturer. The photographic prints are happy, colorful, homey scenes—shells, flowers, fruit, and so forth. One that we previewed was of a basket of lemons, a juicer, and a pitcher of lemonade, matted and tucked inside a chrome-colored plastic frame. A bright way to spend a buck.

Write for:
Framed Picture

Cost: $1.00

Send to:
IMC Management, Inc.
IMC Plaza
1 Bridge Street
Garnerville, NY 10923

Chrome Framed Picture

Maintaining Your Home

KEEPING YOUR HOME IN SHAPE
★★★★

Even given the advances made in techniques and materials during the last few years, there's no such thing as a maintenance-free house. This brochure is a combination primer/checklist on just what you must do to keep your home in top shape. You'll learn to check the foundation, doors and windows, exterior walls, and roof for water and structural damage. Then there are the mechanical, electrical, and heating and cooling systems to be inspected regularly. Finally, you must keep the grounds and yard in good shape. This maintenance checklist should keep you free of sudden surprise repairs.

Write for:
Maintaining the Home

Cost: $1.00

Send to:
University of Illinois at Urbana-Champaign
Small Homes Council
One E. St. Mary's Rd.
Champaign, IL 61820

WHY IS THE NEW LAWN A LAKE?
★★★★

Each year, thousands of new homeowners learn about drainage and erosion the hard way. Ideally, a home should be built on a well-drained knoll—but with the pressure for urban development, less desirable sites are often used for building. This no-nonsense booklet explains basic home drainage, how basement seepage happens and how you can correct it, and some of the other problems of poor drainage systems. It tells how you or a professional can correct your problems, and you'll learn a lot here about different soils and their draining capacities, proper land use to control erosion, and the best types of drainage materials to use. Good illustrations, too.

Write for:
Drainage Around the Home

Cost: $1.00

Send to:
Distribution Center
7 Research Park
Cornell University
Ithaca, NY 14850

PLUMBING THE MYSTERIES OF PLUMBING
★★★★

This circular is intended to guide you, as a home-owner, in the selection of plumbing fixtures and accessories and to help you understand the problems connected with household water supply and waste-disposal systems. If you're buying a home, there's a checklist of things to look for in the kitchen and bathroom. There are excellent diagrams of a typical home water distribution and drainage system and detailed explanations of what goes on when the plumbing is installed in a new house. There's a guide to different kinds of plumbing fixtures and notes on plumbing codes and prefabricated plumbing units. Solid stuff.

Write for:
Plumbing

Cost: $1.00

Send to:
University of Illinois at Urbana-Champaign
Small Homes Council
One E. St. Mary's Rd.
Champaign, IL 61820

WISHING FOR A WELL?
★★

It may surprise you to learn that less than 3 percent of the fresh water in this country is found in lakes and streams, and that more than 97 percent is found underground. If you own a well, you can tap into this naturally safe and clear system of underground wa-

ter and, at the same time, avoid depending on "city water" and the increasing bills that you get for using it. This 12-page booklet from the Water Systems Council discusses private wells and water systems. You'll find information on the three popular types of wells (machine-drilled, driven, and bored), the two types of centrifugal pumps (jet and submersible), and the workings of the complete system.

Write for:
Understanding Underground Water—A Guide to Private Wells and Water Systems

Cost: $1.00

Send to:
Water Systems Council
221 N. LaSalle St.
Chicago, IL 60601

WELL DONE WATER
★★

If you need information on installing a well or locating a water system, the Water Systems Council can provide you with 28 pages of straight facts on the subject in this mini-manual. This booklet, which is in its seventh printing, covers locating and constructing water wells; sizing the water system; and a note on water quality and its management. You'll read about safe and unsafe places to drill, the minimum recommended distances between water supplies and various sources of contamination, and the type of equipment available. Diagrams and tables accompany the information.

Write for:
Order Your Water Well Done

Cost: $2.00

Send to:
Water Systems Council
221 N. LaSalle St.
Chicago, IL 60601

WHAT TO DO IF THE PLASTER IS PEELING
★★★

The first in a new series of publications on old house restoration from the University of Illinois covers the subject of plaster. A 16-page publication with drawings tells how damaged, sagging plaster can often be repaired. Options for what to do if plaster is too badly damaged to be repaired are also offered. Also

continued

included: a history of plastering, a glossary of plaster terms, and explanations of the most frequent causes of plaster failure. Useful information for anyone doing their own home restoration, and from people who should have all the facts—the University's Small Homes Council—Building Research Council.

Write for:
Old House Restoration No. 1—Plaster

Cost: $1.00

Send to:
Small Homes Council—Building Research Council
University of Illinois at Urbana-Champaign
One E. St. Mary's Rd.
Champaign, IL 61820

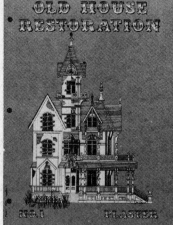

Old House Restoration No. 1—Plaster

NEW LOOK FOR OLD BUILDINGS
★★★

Owners, developers, and managers of historic wood frame buildings can be thankful for this advice on how to rehabilitate the exteriors of homes or other buildings using substitute materials such as aluminum or vinyl siding. The information assists in assuring that the resurfacing is appropriate for the preservation of historic wood frame buildings. Text and photos show various restoration solutions to problems.

Write for:
Aluminum & Vinyl Siding on Historic Buildings (No. 135P)

Cost: $1.00

Send to:
Consumer Information Center
P.O. Box 100
Pueblo, CO 81002

REPAIRING HISTORIC WOODEN WINDOWS
★★★

If you own or manage an historic building you may be faced with the problem of having to keep the wooden windows in proper repair. Here's what you need to know in order to evaluate the architectural or historical significance of windows, and then how to maintain, repair, or replace them. The advice here is also good for any owner of an older home with wooden windows who wants to repair or replace them.

Write for:
Repair of Historic Wooden Windows (No. 140P)

Cost: $1.00

Send to:
Consumer Information Center
P.O. Box 100
Pueblo, CO 81002

ALL ABOUT CRAWL SPACES
★★★★

Some crawl spaces are open; some are closed and heated; some are susceptible to moisture and if untreated will cause problems in the home; some contain the furnace and must be kept thoroughly ventilated; others provide access to plumbing fixtures, but the fixtures themselves must be insulated to protect them from freezing. If you have a crawl space instead of a basement, this eight-page publication will put you in touch with the problems you may have and don't know about, or those you have and don't know what to do about. Either way, there are answers and plenty of diagrams to help you understand what's going on beneath your feet.

Write for:
Crawl-Space Houses

Cost: $1.00

Send to:
University of Illinois at Urbana-Champaign
Small Homes Council
One E. St. Mary's Rd.
Champaign, IL 61820

KEEP YOUR BASEMENT DRY
★★★★

If your basement is damp or musty, it can damage your enjoyment of a basement recreation room, things stored there, and the home's foundation. A free 10-page brochure from the Better Business Bureau, *Tips on Basement Waterproofing,* can lead you in the right direction toward having a drier, safer, more pleasant basement for work, hobbies, storage, and extra living space. You learn what wet basement problems to look for, what possible solutions there are, and how to assess alternative methods of treating persistent basement wetness. Before signing with a contractor to have major work done, get several estimates and follow the Bureau's contract tips.

Write for:
Tips on Basement Waterproofing (No. 24-170)

Cost: Free

Send to:
Council of Better Business Bureaus
1515 Wilson Blvd.
Arlington, VA 22209

WHY ARE THE BASEMENT WALLS WET?

★

Is the moisture on your basement walls caused by condensation or seepage? A simple piece of aluminum foil taped securely to the wall for several days will give you the answer. (If the side facing the wall is wet, it's seepage; if the side facing the basement is wet, it's condensation.) Though this small booklet is heavy on the ads for the manufacturer's product, there is some sound information about how a homeowner can waterproof masonry walls, along with advice on pinpointing the problem, preparing the surface, and applying a waterproofing sealer.

Write for:
How to Waterproof Masonry Walls

Cost: Free

Send to:
How to Waterproof Masonry Walls
Department PI
UGL PO Box 70
Scranton, PA 18501

WATERPROOF THE BASEMENT

★★

If your problem is a wet basement, this small, 20-page booklet can help you find the causes. These can be as varied as your particular building site, incorrectly installed gutters and sewers, faulty subsurface drainage, or faulty construction of basement walls and floors. Once you pinpoint the cause, you'll learn from this booklet how to alleviate the problem and seal all leaks. There's a glossary of terms that are helpful to know when you're dealing with a wet basement, and photos and illustrations add to the clarity of the text. Not a glamorous little publication, but very competent.

Write for:
Z-Z-Poxy for Painting & Waterproofing

Cost: Free with a long SASE

Send to:
Dur-a-flex, Inc.
221 Park Ave. Box 8122
East Hartford, CT 06108

Z-Z-Poxy for Painting and Waterproofing

SURVIVING YOUR SEPTIC TANK

★★★

If you're a homeowner who's meeting a septic tank for the first time, you need this booklet. It tells how a septic tank works (there's also information on cesspools), and how to prevent minor and major problems by using the proper capacity for your family. You get advice on keeping tree roots where they belong, discouraging cars and trucks from driving over the septic line, and *always* keeping the disposable diapers (and lots of less obvious items of household waste) out of your system. Simple illustrations and good advice are worth your postage stamp.

Write for:
The Worry-Free Way to Care for Septic Tanks and Cesspools

Cost: Free

continued

HOME

THE INS AND OUTS OF SUMP PUMPS
★★★

Need help with a sump pump? This $2.00 *Home Sump Pump Kit* offers guidance on installation, trouble shooting, and maintenance. Included is a four-page leaflet full of clearly written information on what to look for before installing a sump pump, a description of the sump pit, as well as step-by-step procedures and a diagram for installation.

There's also a four-page homeowner's notebook describing four types of sump pumps and two types of installation, and giving maintenance tips, along with several photos and diagrams. A trouble shooting chart lists trouble symptoms and their corresponding possible causes and corrections.

Write for:
Home Sump Pump Kit

Cost: $2.00

Send to:
Sump and Sewage Pump Manufacturers
  Association
211 N. LaSalle St.
Chicago, IL 60601

WHEN THE HEATING FAILS
★★★★

This booklet offers guidelines to preparing for home heating emergencies. First it suggests an energy audit to help you plan for back-up heating by understanding what your central heating system will offer and how well your home will retain heat. There's a discussion of multi-fuel furnaces, generators, and secondary heating devices (freestanding fireplaces, stoves, and so on), plus hints on stowing fuel for your secondary system safely and planning an emergency heating area. There's information on retaining body heat in a cold home, safety measures to take in this emergency, and related problems.

Write for:
Home Heating in an Emergency

Cost: $2.00

PLAYING IT COOL
★★★★

A power failure can be caused by an act of nature or a man-made blackout, but whatever the cause the natural inclination is to panic. Don't. You can protect your appliances, your heating system, and your water pipes, and if you've taken time before the lights go out to read *What to Do When the Power Fails*, you'll be able to impress everyone around with your cool efficiency.

This handy little book tells you what to do before, during, and after a power failure. There are checklists of emergency supplies of food and equipment to see you and your family through a power cut—for several days, if need be. You get hints on purifying water, finding adequate heat sources, and handling emergency fires. You also find out what to do when the power is restored.

Write for:
What to Do When the Power Fails: Bulletin A-60

Cost: $1.95

Send to:
Garden Way Publishing
Schoolhouse Rd.
Pownal, VT 05261

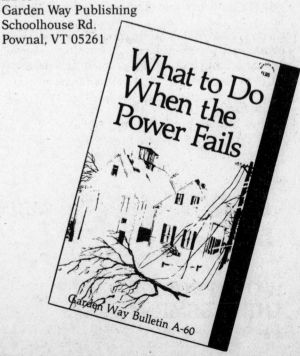

What to Do When the Power Fails

A SASE is a self-addressed stamped envelope.

MAINTAINING YOUR SWIMMING POOL

★★★

If you have an indoor or outdoor swimming pool, you could probably use this free booklet on how to keep a pool clean and in good working condition. You'll learn about different types of disinfectants such as liquid chlorine, calcium and lithium hypochlorite, bromine, and other chemicals; how to balance the alkaline level of your pool's water, and how to control algae. There's lots of good advice for a pool manager, too.

Write for:
Residential Pool Chemical Guide

Cost: Free

Send to:
Dept. PI
National Spa and Pool Institute
2111 Eisenhower Ave.
Alexandria, VA 22314

Residential Pool Chemical Guide

Do-It-Yourself Projects and Repairs

HANDYMAN'S HOW-TO GUIDE

★★★

This abundantly illustrated, 31-page booklet offers solid, commonsense advice for the handyman or woman around the house. It covers step-by-step directions for various projects, the equipment you'll need, and safety and cleanup. Especially thorough are the instructions for bricklaying work in the yard or garden, and for removing old wallpaper and then repapering. There's also a handy, full-page drawing of a house to help you inspect the exterior of your home from time to time in order to catch and correct minor repairs before they escalate into full-blown and costly problems. In addition to much good advice and information, there's lots of hype to get you to buy the company's tools. You can make your own decision as to whether you fall for the hype.

Write for:
The Hyde How-To Guide

Cost: $2.00

Send to:
Hyde Manufacturing Co.
54 Eastford Rd.
Southbridge, MA 01550

The Hyde How-To Guide

RENT IT AND SAVE MONEY

★★★

Why buy it, if you can rent it? Want to clean the carpets, till the backyard, trim a tree, spray-paint the house, go camping or canoeing, motorbike on a mountain, or cut floor tile? All these undertakings require equipment that you won't be using on an everyday basis and therefore you may not want to spend big bucks on. The alternative to buying such items is to rent them.

This catalog proves that at U-Haul you can do a lot more than rent a truck for a cross-town or cross-country move; in fact, they can rent you just about anything from a videocassette recorder to a recreational vehicle. The *U-Haul Center Catalog* is a free guide to hundreds of items and pieces of equipment you can rent to make life easier and less costly. The full-color, 112-page catalog has a cover price of $2.95 but is offered here free for the asking. It will open your eyes to just how broad your rental options are.

Write for:
U-Haul Center Catalog

continued

HOME

Cost: Free

Send to:
U-Haul Center Catalog
Department PI
P.O. Box 21503
Phoenix, AZ 85036

U-Haul Center Catalog

FILL UP THE TOOL BOX
★★

Many of the folks who live and work in the Pacific Northwest states make tools and related handyman items and sell them through Shannon Marketing. A new free tabloid sales newspaper tells you what you can buy, from gas-saving torches for tough cutting and welding jobs to equipment for smaller farm or home projects. Socket sets, sanders, grips, vices, air hoses, impact drills, even leather bibs are available. Some of the major items such as the Dillon torch, said to be "the perfect welder for small jobs and the first significant improvement in oxygen/acetylene welding in 65 years," come with free use of a VHS videocassette showing how the item is used—a nice plus.

Write for:
Shannon Marketing Catalog

Cost: Free

Send to:
Shannon Marketing, Inc.
P.O. Box 378
Welches, OR 97067

WORKING WITH RENTED TOOLS
★★

Need a tall extension ladder or blower to put insulation in the attic? Installing new carpeting or sanding the floor? Want to spray-paint the house? The American Rental Association offers four free brochures about equipment you can rent for those jobs around the house that require specialized equipment you won't use often enough to justify buying. You can get almost any piece of equipment you need at your local A.R.A. Rental Center's "Can-Do Store," and the brochures, all free, show diagrams of each item and explain its use. Write for the brochures that deal with your specific project plans.

Write for:
Working With Grinding, Sanding, and Polishing Tools
Working With Painting and Decorating Tools
Working With Flooring Tools
Working With Building and Remodeling Tools

Cost: Free

Send to:
American Rental Association
1900 19th St.
Moline, IL 61265

TOOLING UP FOR ACTION
★★

"Sure You Can!" is the optimistic message conveyed in four free booklets from the American Rental Association. The idea is that if you rent the right tools you can do major repair jobs yourself. One booklet covers working with concrete and shows 24 tools and accessories for building a sidewalk, a patio, or a driveway. Another shows plumbing tools and equipment needed to thread a pipe, clean a drain, or install a new plumbing fixture. The third illustrates 28 tools for maintenance work on your car—charging a battery, doing a tune-up, rebuilding an engine, changing a tire, and so on. The fourth covers lawn and garden equipment and tells how to pick the right tool for the job. It's good to know that rental tools are available, but if you're skilled enough to do your own major repairs, it probably pays to *own* your own equipment.

Write for:
Working With Concrete
Working With Plumbing Tools
Working With Automotive Tools
Working With Lawn/Garden Tools

Cost: Free

Send to:
American Rental Association
1900 19th St.
Moline, IL 61265

A SASE is a self-addressed stamped envelope.

Working With LawnGarden Tools

BE YOUR OWN BEST REPAIRMAN

★★★★

Broken window? Leaky faucet? Wouldn't you rather fix it yourself than pay someone else to do it? *Simple Home Repairs* is an explicit, illustrated booklet that shows you how to take care of all those annoying household problems. Easy-to-follow directions take you step by step through fixing leaking faucets, frayed electrical cords, loose tile, plaster holes, and much more. Another special feature is a section on how to use basic tools. You'll find lots of useful advice on how to diagnose a problem and what to use to remedy the situation. Home repair is simpler than it looks, and a lot less costly than hiring outside help. And you'll have the satisfaction of doing it yourself.

Write for:
Simple Home Repairs: Bulletin A-28

Cost: $1.95

Send to:
Garden Way Publishing
Storey Communications, Inc.
Schoolhouse Road
Pownal, VT 05261

Simple Home Repairs

DON'T CALL THE PLUMBER

★★★★

Clogged drains, leaking faucets and dripping toilets don't have to mean expensive plumbing repair bills. Fix them yourself. While many problems do require professional help, there are a number of remedies you can apply yourself and this handy 12-page booklet from Clorox tells you how. With illustrated step-by-step instructions, you'll learn how to rid your home of many irritating plumbing malfunctions. You'll know what parts and tools you'll need, how and where to shut off the water, and more. Doing it yourself will save you money and time, and give you the satisfaction of accomplishment.

Write for:
Home Plumbing Repairs

Cost: 25¢

Send to:
The Clorox Company
Department CC-FT
P.O. Box 24305
Oakland, CA 94623

Home Plumbing Repairs

OUTSIDE REPAIRS MADE EASY

★★★★

Getting outside help for most home repair jobs can be costly and frustrating. Often it's hard even to find anyone interested in some of the work you need to have done. You can learn how to do many of the common exterior home maintenance jobs yourself and save headaches and money. Here's a 40-page booklet that shows in simple words and drawings how to repair roofs; repair and install storm or screened doors and windows; caulk exteriors; repair or replace metal gutters and downspouts; rebuild or replace wood steps or porch flooring; fix cracks in concrete sidewalks; and paint the exterior of a house, barn, or garage. With good information on exterior home maintenance from chimney to sidewalk, this is a helpful book for any homeowner or handy person.

Write for:
Simple Home Repairs—Outside (No. 142P)

Cost: $2.00

continued

HOME

Send to:
Consumer Information Center
P.O. Box 100
Pueblo, CO 81002

Simple Home Repairs Outside

TROWELING TECHNIQUES

★★★★

This booklet is meant to be an aid to homeowners, apprentices, and students, although even old pros may find it useful for quick reference. Detailed illustrations coupled with well-written instructions form this primer for laying and finishing concrete slabs, doing small concrete repairs, laying concrete block, building gable ends, and installing gypsum wallboard. For each job you'll find a list of tools and supplies necessary, as well as hints on cutting bricks, cleaning them after mortaring, and making patches and repairs.

Write for:
Troweling Tips and Techniques

Cost: $1.00

Send to:
Marshalltown Trowell Co.
P.O. Box 738
104 S. 8th Ave.
Marshalltown, IA 50158

WRECK-IT-YOURSELF REMODELING

★

Here's a comic look at do-it-yourself remodeling from the Home Builders Association of Indiana. The message is that the amateur is more likely to wreck the place than remodel it, and the treatment is amusing. It may discourage the fainthearted from remodeling, but your true do-it-yourselfer will grin and forge ahead. This little publication, you will note, is put out by people who make money if you *don't* do it yourself.

Write for:
Diary of a Mad Remodeler

Cost: 50¢

Send to:
William Carson
Home Builders Association of Indiana
143 W. Market St.
Indianapolis, IN 46204

WHAT KIND OF ROOF OVER YOUR HEAD?

★★★

Your roof must offer weather protection, fire resistance, durability, and beauty. This booklet discusses the various types of roofing there are, and the in-place cost, durability, and maintenance of each—note that the slope of your roof automatically limits the selection available to you. You'll learn how roofing is applied, and some common problems that occur when it hasn't been properly applied. There's a table of all roofing materials with sizes, weights, and fire ratings, and a section on gutters and downspouts.

Write for:
Roofing Materials

Cost: $1.00

Send to:
University of Illinois at Urbana-Champaign
Small Homes Council
One E. St. Mary's Rd.
Champaign, IL 61820

UP ON THE ROOF

★★

This pamphlet says you can cover your old roof with cedar and shows you precisely how to do it, but unless you are an accomplished do-it-yourselfer you should probably let a roofer handle the job. If you are handy, you'll learn how to lay cedar shingles or handsplit shakes over your existing roof. The pamphlet tells how to prepare your roof, how much roofing to order, and exactly what kinds of nails and

A SASE is a self-addressed stamped envelope.

tools to use. Detailed cartoons show each step, along with clearly written instructions. There are excellent before-and-after color photos.

Write for:
Put a New Cedar Roof Right Over Your Old Roof

Cost: 10¢

Send to:
Red Cedar Shingle & Handsplit Shake Bureau
Suite 275
515 116th Ave., N.E.
Bellevue, WA 98004

BUT WHERE WILL I PUT IT?
★★★

From attic to (wine) cellar, the common complaint is heard: "I don't know where I can put all this stuff!" This 24-page booklet comes up with some answers. It shows you how to use brackets to build bookshelves, tables, wall shelves, desks, plant stands, greenhouses, even wine racks. There are also good ideas for expanding basement or garage storage space by the simple addition of shelves. The basic explanation of how to use the brackets is clear, and the plan booklet is chock-full of creative ideas. No carpentry I.Q. required.

Write for:
SISU Designer's Guide

Cost: 25¢

Send to:
SISU Shelving Corp.
P.O. Box 8366
Fort Collins, CO 80525

GETTING DOWN TO FLOORS
★★★

From the looks of this manual, installing a wood floor is not a job for the beginner. However, the experienced do-it-yourselfer will welcome this detailed, illustrated guide to installing wood flooring in a variety of conditions: over a concrete slab, over a plywood subfloor over concrete, on screeds (sometimes called sleepers), or over wood joists. There are also specific instructions on how to lay plank flooring, parquet, block, and herringbone floors, and how to lay a new strip floor over an old one. There's even information on laying gymnasium floors over a concrete slab and how to put strip flooring on walls and ceiling. Definitely not for the totally inexperienced.

Write for:
Hardwood Flooring Installation Manual

Cost: 50¢

Send to:
National Oak Flooring Manufacturers' Association
8 N. Third St.
Suite 810, Sterick Bldg.
Memphis, TN 38103

FINISHING HARDWOOD FLOORS
★★

Make no mistake, sanding and refinishing a hardwood floor is a difficult, messy job. But it can be done by the careful do-it-yourselfer, and these detailed, illustrated directions for every phase of the operation will help. You'll learn exactly how to prepare the floor for refinishing, the kinds of equipment you'll need, the sanding process for both new and old floors, and how to finish the job with sealers, stains, or varnish. There's special information for sanding strip, plank, parquet, and other fancy floors; and how to bleach, lacquer, and stencil wood floors for interesting and unusual effects.

Write for:
Hardwood Flooring Finishing/Refinishing Manual

Cost: 50¢

Send to:
National Oak Flooring Manufacturers' Association
8 N. Third St.
Suite 810, Sterick Bldg.
Memphis, TN 38103

PLAY WITH A FULL DECK
★★

This booklet is full of plans and ideas for outdoor living and storage that the skilled do-it-yourselfer can make out of wood. Here are building plans with photos and detailed drawings for a garden house/cabana with deck, a combination firewood rack and bike storage shed, and a neat enclosure for garbage cans or compost. Sharp, detailed black-and-white photographs show other ideas—arbors, screens, a patio counter and entertainment center, gazebos, an above-ground pool structure, and a firepit deck. You order the plans separately.

continued

HOME

Write for:
Garden Living and Storage, Form P-15

Cost: 35¢

Send to:
Western Wood Products Association
1500 Yeon Building
Portland, OR 97204

Garden Living and Storage

PRESSURE-TREATED WOOD PROJECTS

★★★★

Pressure-treated wood products have been deeply impregnated with long-lasting preservatives that eliminate the food source (wood) that permits rot, decay, and insect attack. The four booklets in this *Great Plans* series contain ideas and plans for outdoor projects using pressure-treated wood. Each booklet offers step-by-step instructions and *lots* of illustrations. In *Great Gazebos,* you'll learn how to make both square and hexagonal gazebos. *Great Decks* has plans for building several types of backyard decks and a flight of stairs. *Great Fences* shows you how to build a gate and several different styles of fences. It also discusses how to build a fence on sloping land. The booklet on weekend projects promises you can "do-it-yourself" in one weekend and includes instructions on constructing a garden walkway, a wood planter, a garden bench, an arbor, a picnic table, a child's play area, and more.

Write for:
Great Decks
Great Fences
Great Gazebos
Great Weekend Projects

Cost: 50¢ each

Send to:
Osmose Wood Preserving, Inc.
P.O. Drawer O
Griffin, GA 30224-0249

Great Projects brochures

GREAT OUTDOOR LIVING

★★★

Wouldn't you love to have a multi-tiered deck for the yard? How about a gazebo for summer evening get-togethers? Or perhaps the gardener in the family would enjoy a bonsai pavilion for growing and displaying flowers. Ideas such as these are in a new publication crammed with photos and plans for a gazebo with storage area, wooden entry decks, benches, planters, and a bonsai work and display pavilion. Builders' sketches and dimensions and building tips are included for each project. A lot of ideas here for a few nickels.

Write for:
Outdoor Ideas

Cost: 35¢

Send to:
Western Wood Products Association
1500 Yeon Building
Portland, OR 97204

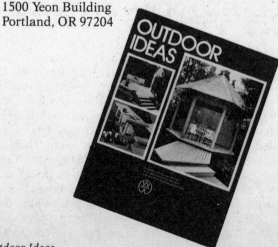

Outdoor Ideas

A SASE is a self-addressed stamped envelope.

BUILD YOUR OWN LOG CABIN

★★

The Lumbermaker is a chain saw accessory from Haddon Tools that you can use to make your own boards, beams, and lumber pieces. *The Chain Saw and the Lumbermaker* is an illustrated instruction booklet that tells you how to do everything from making stair steps and patio stones from tree trunks to felling trees and cutting poles. There are even step-by-step directions for building a simple log cabin. The Lumbermaker, however, isn't really a tool for the home hobbyist but for the home carpenter with some experience.

Write for:
   The Chain Saw and the Lumbermaker

Cost: $2.00

Send to:
   Haddon Tools
   4719 W. Route 120
   McHenry, IL 60050

SITTING ON A PROBLEM?

★★★★

Can't find anyone to repair the broken seat of Grandma's old cane rocker? Why not do it yourself? According to Garden Way's booklet *Chair Caning*, a 32-page step-by-step guide for both beginners and skilled craftspeople, the materials are inexpensive, the steps easy to follow, and the results satisfying. You'll learn traditional and modern techniques of seat-weaving from these detailed, illustrated instructions. Included are six-way and four-way patterns for restoring cane seating, and directions for weaving beautiful rush and splint seating.

Write for:
   Chair Caning: Bulletin A-16

Cost: $1.95

Send to:
   Garden Way Publishing
   Schoolhouse Rd.
   Pownal, VT 05261

Chair Caning

YES, YOU CAN REFINISH THAT ROCKER!

★

Geared to both nervous novices and more experienced woodworkers, this little guide to wood refinishing gives you some tips on tackling the sometimes messy process. You'll learn the basics of how to evaluate the condition of the wood, how to test for shellac or lacquer, how to remove old finishes, how to select and apply stain or a clear finish. There's a color chart of stains and finishes, and color photographs to keep you on course. Safety tips, too.

Write for:
   The Finishing Touch

Cost: Free

Send to:
   The Finishing Touch
   United Gilsonite Laboratories
   Dept. CG
   Box 70
   Scranton, PA 18501

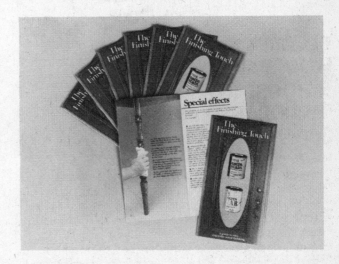

The Finishing Touch

OUT-THINKING A THIEF

★★★

The Adventures of Surelocked Homes is a free booklet from State Farm Fire and Casualty Company that provides some good advice about protecting your home from burglars. Illustrated with simple cartoon drawings, the 16 pages present six things you can do to prevent theft and break-in, and a straightforward section on how to act if you come face to face with a thief. There's a sample inventory form for listing

continued

HOME

theft-prone items. Though the material seems to cover all the bases, most of the tips offered are of the commonsense variety. But a reminder never hurts, and that's basically what this booklet provides.

Write for:
The Adventures of Surelocked Homes

Cost: Free

Send to:
State Farm Insurance Companies
Public Relations Department — DH
One State Farm Plaza
Bloomington, IL 61701

The Adventures of Surelocked Homes

CHOOSING A BURGLAR ALARM
★★★

Seven million homes are burglarized each year. Though it may hurt to admit that it's a necessary measure, more and more people are relying on burglar alarm systems to protect themselves and their property. This pamphlet, put out by the National Burglar and Fire Alarm Association, discusses the alarm systems that are available, and the strengths and weaknesses of each. It also covers sensory devices that supplement an alarm system (pressure mats, ultrasonic devices, infrared and proximity detectors), do-it-yourself alarms, and how to locate reputable alarm companies.

Write for:
Considerations When Looking for a Burglar Alarm System

Cost: $1.00 with a long SASE

Send to:
National Burglar and Fire Alarm Association, Inc.
1101 Connecticut Ave., N.W.
Washington, DC 20036

OUTSMARTING BURGLARS
★★

Burglaries occur in the United States, on an average, once every ten seconds. These two small leaflets are written to help you burglar-proof your business and home. Business owners will not only be advised of the alarms, lights, and noise systems that will discourage burglars, but they'll also learn a few tricks. One that clothing stores can use: Reverse alternating hangers on racks, making it impossible for a thief to sweep a line of merchandise off the rod. Homeowners will learn a dozen burglar-proofing tips that use noise and light.

Write for:
How to Burglar-Proof Your Business
How to Keep Your Family Burglar Unhappy

Cost: Free with a long SASE

Send to:
Insurance Information Institute
Dept. BB/FB
110 William St.
New York, NY 10038

How to Burglar-Proof Your Business
How to Keep Your Family Burglar Unhappy

HOME SECURITY BASICS
★★

The comforting message of this small leaflet from the Insurance Information Institute is that nine out of ten household burglaries are preventable. A homeowner's chief allies (light, time, and noise) are the burglar's chief enemies. This leaflet tells you how to use all three to slow a burglar down and make him give up and try another, less difficult location. You'll also learn some good home security habits to develop and practice, and what to do if you should encounter a thief in your home.

Write for:
Home Security Basics

Cost: Free with a long SASE

Send to:
Insurance Information Institute
Dept. HSB
110 William St.
New York, NY 10038

PROTECTING THE HOME AGAINST FIRE AND BURGLARS

★★★★

A homeowner's best friend may not be a dog or a mortgage lender but something that protects the home and family from fire or burglars. Fire and smoke alarms are required by law in many areas, and more home and business owners are seriously installing burglar alarm systems. The Better Business Bureau's free 14-page brochure, *Tips on Residential Alarm Systems*, walks you through a short course in fire alarms, including ionization smoke alarms and photoelectric alarms. It tells you how the different alarms work, where to locate them, and offers maintenance and testing tips. Burglar alarm systems such as wired screens, pressure mats, photoelectric beams, ultrasonic sensors, and microwave sensors are also described. Whether you opt for a do-it-yourself burglar alarm system or contract with an alarm company to have a system installed, these tips can save you headaches and money.

Write for:
Tips on Residential Alarm Systems (No. 24-159)

Cost: Free

Send to:
Council of Better Business Bureaus
1515 Wilson Blvd.
Arlington, VA 22209

HOME SWEET BURGLAR-PROOF HOME

★★★

Every ten seconds in this country a home is burglarized, yet few people do much to protect their personal treasures or themselves. Nearly half of all home robberies are committed without the use of force to gain entry. *Bless This House*, an informative 12-page booklet published by Aetna Life and Casualty, leads the consumer through a home audit with useful advice for securing valuables and entryways. Recommendations are given for installing locks, insuring possessions, and thwarting unwant-

ed visitors while you are away. Every home should have a copy of this inspection guide to enable the family to evaluate its defenses.

Write for:
Bless This House

Cost: Free

Send to:
Resources
Aetna Life and Casualty
151 Farmington Avenue
Hartford, CT 06156

FIRE SAFETY PACKET

★★

Here's a packet of four leaflets about fire safety. *Tips for Travelers* lists 15 ways you can protect yourself in a hotel or motel fire—any one of them could save your life. *Fire Safety for High Rise Apartment Dwellers* stresses fire drills, escape routes, and what to do if a fire occurs. *Tips for Meeting Planners* advises people who plan business meetings to put fire safety on the agenda and to check the safety of the facility where the meeting is to be held. *Tips for Home Owners and Renters* stresses eliminating potential fire hazards, installing smoke detectors, and developing a family escape plan.

Write for:
Be Fire Smart:
Tips for Home Owners and Renters
Tips for Travelers
Fire Safety for High Rise Apartment Dwellers
Tips for Meeting Planners

Cost: Free with a long SASE

Send to:
Insurance Information Institute
Dept. BFS
110 William St.
New York, NY 10038

Be Fire Smart Tips

HOME

FIGHT FIRE BEFORE IT HAPPENS

★★★★

Here's a frightening thought: Fire fighters tell us that a whopping 70 percent of home fires needn't happen; they are caused by sheer carelessness. *The Legend of Fire* shows you how to protect your family, your home, and yourself by identifying and correcting potential fire hazards now.

There's a concise description of each of the 11 major causes of fatal home fires (sloppy smoking habits is number one) and clear directions for their prevention. Striking full-color drawings of a Promethean fire fighter accompany the text. A good house-cleaning, suggests this booklet, will prevent fires caused by collections of unnecessary combustibles. Also included are advice on emergency fire fighting if a fire develops while you're cooking on the stove, cautionary measures for cooking in a fireplace, and a practical look at family fire escape drills.

Write for:
The Legend of Fire

Cost: Free

Send to:
State Farm Insurance Companies
Public Relations Department — DH
One State Farm Plaza
Bloomington, IL 61701

The Legend of Fire

HOME FIRE SAFETY

★★★★

More than 6,000 Americans die each year because of fires in their homes. Many of these fires could have been prevented, especially those that resulted from carelessness such as smoking, faulty or improperly used heating systems, faulty electrical wiring and equipment, and cooking-stove accidents. The Better

Business Bureau's free eight-page brochure, *Tips on Home Fire Protection*, tells about the major causes of fires in the home and offers suggestions on how to prevent them. One section is devoted to a description of smoke detectors, fire detectors, and extinguishers. Another suggests an escape plan for the family in case of a fire. Survival tips are offered in case a fire breaks out in your home. This is an important safety brochure no home should be without, and the price is certainly right.

Write for:
Tips on Home Fire Protection (No. 311-02216)

Cost: Free

Send to:
Council of Better Business Bureaus
1515 Wilson Blvd.
Arlington, VA 22209

USEFUL SAFETY REMINDERS

★★

Did you know that when you're away on vacation, highly flammable hydrogen gas can build up in your home's hot water system? To avoid possibility of an explosion, after returning from vacation and before using the dishwasher or clothes washer, you should turn on all hot water faucets and let the water flow from each for two minutes. You'll learn safety tips such as this from one of these three free brochures. Another is about safety in discarding an old refrigerator or freezer, the third about safe use of a portable electric heater.

Write for:
Caution When Returning From Vacation
Stop! Help Save a Child's Life
Follow These Safety Tips When Using Your
    Portable Electric Heater

Cost: Free with a long SASE

Send to:
Assocation of Home Appliance Manufacturers
20 N. Wacker Dr.
Suite 1500
Chicago, IL 60606

HOW SAFE IS YOUR HOME?

★★★

Did someone slip on the bathroom rug last week? Do you know how to shut off the main gas valve in your home? Do you keep a few unused pills in a prescription drug bottle after they are no longer needed?

How safe is the "jungle gym" the kids play on in the back yard? And do you know that each year more than 20,000 Americans are killed, and another 3 million disabled in home accidents? If you want to make sure your home is an accident-free one, send for this free checklist from the National Easter Seal Society. You may discover your home isn't as safe as you thought it was, but once you recognize the hazards, you can correct them. A valuable freebie for any family.

Write for:
A Safe Home Is No Accident

Cost: Free with a long SASE

Send to:
National Easter Seal Society
2023 Ogden Ave.
Chicago, IL 60612

A Safe Home Is No Accident

PROTECTING YOURSELF AGAINST CRIME
★★★

Beyond barricading yourself in your home and never going out, there are ways to protect yourself, both as an individual and as a community, against crime. This booklet begins with the home by telling you what kinds of locks work best, then discusses dealing with pickpockets and purse-snatchers, taking precautions against car thefts, whether or not guns are effective protection, and how to be a less-likely victim.

The rest of the booklet is devoted to what communities can do to prevent crime and bring concerted influence to bear on the criminal justice system. This booklet deals primarily with crime against property, not people.

Write for:
Protecting Yourself Against Crime (#564)

Cost: $1.00

Send to:
Public Affairs Pamphlets
381 Park Ave. South
New York, NY 10016

TORNADO SAFETY
★★

Tornadoes can occur at any time of the year, but they most frequently happen during April, May, and June. And though Texas suffers more tornadoes than any other, no state in the United States is entirely free of the threat. This brief, to-the-point leaflet tells you what to do before, during, and after a tornado. It stresses that you should work out an emergency plan in case a tornado strikes and tells what you should do during a tornado—don't try to flee it in a car or other vehicle. The third section tells what you should be alert for after a tornado—broken power lines and shattered glass, for example.

Write for:
Tornado Safety...Before, During, After

Cost: Free with a long SASE

Send to:
Insurance Information Institute
Dept. TS
110 William St.
New York, NY 10038

Tornado Safety...Before, During, After

OH, RATS!
★★

Nobody likes to think about them, but the statistics are frightening. About 100 million rats roam the United States, and they carry 35 diseases dangerous to humans and animals (so do mice). Rats also damage $500 million to $1 billion worth of property

continued

HOME

every year. This booklet, put out by The d-CON Company, gives information on how to keep rats from moving in, how to detect them if they do move in (by locating droppings, runways, holes, and burrows), and how to kill them. The three basic methods of extermination are briefly discussed, along with rat control methods your community can implement.

Write for:
Rats

Cost: Free

Send to:
The d-CON Co., Inc.
225 Summit Ave.
Montvale, NJ 07645

Saving Energy in the Home

SMART HOME INSULATION
★★★★

Is your home an energy guzzler? Do your windows and walls leak cold air in winter? Do your air conditioners work overtime in summer to keep the house cool? Like many other homes, yours may not have enough insulation. Two free publications from the Better Business Bureau may help solve the problem. The free 18-page brochure, *Facts on Home Insulation,* is a simple minicourse on insulating the home. You learn how much insulation is needed for ceilings, walls, floors, and attics, and the types of insulation used in the various spaces. Tips also are offered on window insulation, caulking, and weatherstripping. This booklet offers good advice on making your home insulation more efficient. A companion brochure, *Consumer Tips on Home Insulation,* is a one-page, small, double-sided fact sheet that offers basic, common sense advice about properly insulating your home.

Write for:
Facts on Home Insulation (No. 04-135)
Consumer Tips on Home Insulation (No. 01-141)

Cost: Free

Send to:
Council of Better Business Bureaus
1515 Wilson Blvd.
Arlington, VA 22209

ESTIMATING ENERGY SAVINGS
★★★★

These two publications provide data for estimating the energy you can save by the insulation of ceilings, walls, foundations, doors, and windows. You'll learn the R-value of insulated parts of your home (the higher the R-value, the better the insulating properties of the material or component); you'll learn how to determine the degree-days for your locality and how much heat is lost in insulated and noninsulated walls, foundations, and ceilings. You'll be surprised at the amount of heat that goes out the door and unweatherproofed windows. The good eight-page booklets also tell you how to figure if the return on your insulation is worthwhile.

Write for:
Savings by Insulating Doors and Windows
Savings by Insulating Ceilings, Walls and
Foundations

Cost: $2.00 for both

Send to:
University of Illinois at Urbana-Champaign
Small Homes Council
One E. St. Mary's Rd.
Champaign, IL 61820

WINDOW DRESSINGS FOR WINTER
★★★★

Even double-glazed windows can rob a tight, well-insulated house of up to 45 percent of its expensive heat during winter months. Fortunately you can make very effective window coverings from a wide range of materials at moderate cost. It's especially easy after reading *Make Your Own Insulated Window Shutters.* Because shutters are so efficient in saving heat, experts predict these thermal treatments will become standard home equipment in the near future. Air conditioning expense, too, will be lessened. This informative booklet covers the three major types of insulating window covers—quilted curtains, multiple shades, and thermal shutters—as well as materials used for each. Six simple and attractive plans are included, with step-by-step instructions and illustrations.

Write for:
Make Your Own Insulated Window Shutters:
Bulletin A-80

Cost: $1.95

A SASE is a self-addressed stamped envelope.

Send to:
> Garden Way Publishing
> Storey Communications, Inc.
> Schoolhouse Road
> Pownal, VT 05261

Make Your Own Window Shutters

SAVING ENERGY: ALL YOU NEED TO KNOW

★★★★

This exhaustive, 93-page report will tell you just about everything you need to know about why Americans must conserve energy, and how they can do it if they want to. The projects listed in this book are wide-ranging—from home heating and cooling to energy conservation in recreation. Every facet of life is covered from using energy in different forms to winterizing your wardrobe to conserve heat and furnishing your home to do the same. Tables, charts, and illustrations graphically underscore ways and means of becoming energy conscious. There's a three-page checklist for energy maintenance in your home. A terrific book.

Write for:
> Save Energy, Save Dollars

Cost: $1.50

Send to:
> Distribution Center
> 7 Research Park
> Cornell University
> Ithaca, NY 14850

STOP HEATING THE OUTDOORS

★★★★

Did you know the greatest source of heating loss is your windows? Generally, doors and windows cover 20 to 25 percent of the sidewalls of a house, accounting for as much as 50 percent of your fuel bills. This can be quite surprising to the homeowner who thought his or her house was well insulated. *Window Heat Loss: How to Stop It Cold!* is an informative manual for inexpensive elimination of costly energy leaks. The booklet thoughtfully explains insulation values, types of storm windows and how to build your own, weatherstripping, and caulking. Interior window coverings are also discussed in detail, with illustrated instructions for making your own insulated shades, curtains, and shutters.

Write for:
> Window Heat Loss: How to Stop It Cold!:
>   Bulletin A-43

Cost: $1.95

Send to:
> Garden Way Publishing
> Storey Communications, Inc.
> Schoolhouse Road
> Pownal, VT 05261

Window Heat Loss: How to Stop It Cold!

SLASHING HOME ENERGY COSTS

★★★★

Opportunities for energy conservation and waste-cutting abound in every home, without expensive renovations. The booklet *Cut Those Energy Costs* gives the consumer practical information for cutting back on home energy consumption in comfort. Heating and cooling, appliance usage, fireplace care, insulation, and auto maintenance are covered. You'll also find pertinent illustrations which aid in carrying out hundreds of energy-efficient ideas. Some of these steps don't cost a cent; others may require dollar expenditures that will quickly be recouped. You'll be surprised how much difference a few hours of work can make in those energy bills.

continued

HOME

Write for:
Cut Those Energy Costs: Bulletin A-46

Cost: $1.95

Send to:
Garden Way Publishing
Storey Communications, Inc.
Schoolhouse Road
Pownal, VT 05261

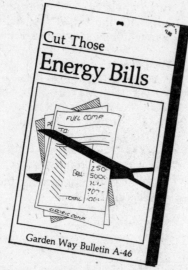

Cut Those Energy Costs

SAVING ENERGY = SAVING MONEY
★★★★

If you walked through your house right now looking at how much energy you're using and, in some cases, wasting, you might not be so surprised the next time you get your utility bills. The Better Business Bureau's free 12-page brochure, *Tips on Saving Energy*, takes you on a room-by-room tour of your home for examples of saving energy and dollars. Special seasonal tips are offered on how to reduce your energy consumption—and energy bills—in summer and winter, hot-water-use tips, and cooking and laundry energy-saving advice. A list tells you what various home appliances use in average electrical wattage and how many kilowatts per hour they consume annually. Here is home energy advice that makes sense and saves dollars.

Write for:
Tips on Saving Energy (No. 311-02217)

Cost: Free

Send to:
Council of Better Business Bureaus
1515 Wilson Blvd.
Arlington, VA 22209

WISE ENERGY USE
★★★★

Saving energy means saving money, we are reminded by the U.S. Office of Consumer Affairs. It also means preserving our limited domestic energy resources for future generations. Seventy percent of residential energy is used for heating and cooling our homes and apartments, 20 percent for heating water, and the remaining 10 percent for lighting, cooking, and running small electric and gas appliances. Here is a fact-filled 24-page government booklet with tips on how to save energy at home, from setting up an energy budget to taking advantage of energy tax credits. It's all aimed at helping you become a wiser energy consumer and save money at the same time.

Write for:
Your Keys to Energy Efficiency (No. 584P)

Cost: Free

Send to:
Consumer Information Center
P.O. Box 100
Pueblo, CO 81002

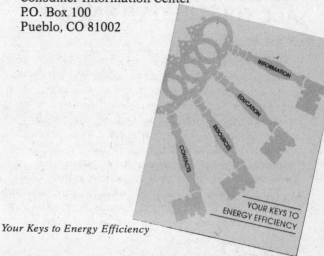

Your Keys to Energy Efficiency

FOR APARTMENT DWELLERS
★★★★

Whether you own, rent, or manage an apartment, you know how high energy bills have gone in recent years. Heating and cooling apartments and using electric appliances and hot water means high utility bills, but following some proven energy-saving practices can help bring costs down. In this U.S. Department of Energy booklet, you'll find 22 pages of tips on how to make an apartment more energy-efficient. The information covers heating, air conditioning, lighting, water, and use of appliances such as refrigerators, freezers, ranges, washers, dryers and dishwashers. Learn how to make your radiators work more efficiently; how to weatherproof windows and doors and install inexpensive storm windows; and make your air conditioner work more efficiently.

A SASE is a self-addressed stamped envelope.

Write for:
Tips for an Energy Efficient Apartment (No. 133P)

Cost: $1.00

Send to:
Consumer Information Center
P.O. Box 100
Pueblo, CO 81002

DOE/CE/24423-1

TIPS FOR AN
ENERGY EFFICIENT APARTMENT

U.S. Department of Energy
Office of Conservation and Renewable Energy
Building Energy Research and Development
Building Services Division
Under Contract No. DE-AC01-83CE24423

Tips for an Energy Efficient Apartment

SOLAR ENERGY SIMPLIFIED
★★★★

You're too late to get in on the Federal solar energy tax credit, which expired at the end of 1985, but you may still be able to take advantage of state or local tax incentives if you install some sort of solar energy system in your home. The Better Business Bureau's free 12-page brochure, *Facts on Solar Energy for Your Home*, takes you through a short, simple course on home solar energy systems. These systems collect the sun's energy and use it for domestic hot water use and/or to heat or cool homes. Learn how solar collectors work, and the difference between "passive" solar and "active" solar systems. You don't have to convert your whole house into a solar energy home, but can add partial solar conversions for heating hot water or the swimming pool.

Write for:
Facts on Solar Energy for Your Home (No. 24-142)

Cost: Free

Send to:
Council of Better Business Bureaus
1515 Wilson Blvd.
Arlington, VA 22209

SOLAR ENERGY: WOULD IT WORK IN YOUR HOME
★★★

You've heard and read a lot about solar energy and how it can save you money heating or cooling your home. The U.S. Department of Energy has two free publications that may tell you all you need to know on the subject of solar energy use in the home. Among the questions answered: Is solar feasible for your home? Can you afford to have a solar system installed? Is solar legally feasible in your area because of zoning requirements? If you buy a solar system, what do you buy? How about a solar greenhouse or solar "sunspace"? If you're considering any kind of solar energy installation, these publications are for you.

Write for:
Solar Energy Systems Consumer Tips
Sunspaces and Solar Greenhouses

Cost: Free

Send to:
Conservation and Renewable Energy Inquiry and
Referral Service
P.O. Box 8900
Silver Spring, MD 20907

GREENHOUSE RUNS ON THE SUN
★★

Thinking of building a room addition? Need to cut down on heating bills? The Vegetable Factory suggests that a self-installed solar greenhouse might be the answer to both problems. This 16-page brochure is full of color photos and product information describing energy-efficient, add-on greenhouses that are manufactured from shatter-proof double panels of fiber glass or Plexi-DR supported by aluminum beams and can be installed, the manufacturer claims, in less than a day. A wide variety of glazing panels with blueprints are also available for do-it-yourselfers. Also they may qualify for available federal or state energy tax credits.

Write for:
The Sun at a Down-to-Earth Price

Cost: $2.00

Send to:
Vegetable Factory, Inc.
P.O. Box 2235, Dept. FT-87
New York, NY 10163

HOME

YOUR HOUSE AND THE SUN
★★

Solar orientation means the placement of your house on a site with respect to compass directions, so that the rooms are correctly related to sun position, wind direction, views, or other desirable surroundings. This booklet discusses the benefits of solar orientation and the successful uses of it—you'll need to know the changing position of the sun throughout the year. The diagrams here are true for latitude 40°N, and nearly true over a band of about 5° on either side.

Write for:
Solar Orientation

Cost: $1.00

Send to:
University of Illinois at Urbana-Champaign
Small Homes Council
One E. St. Mary's Rd.
Champaign, IL 61820

SUN POWER
★★

The idea of harnessing the sun's energy to supplement the world's dwindling supply of fossil fuels is widely discussed today. But how do you do it? *Solar Energy Facts* explains the types and practical applications of solar heating units now available. The glossary is a layman's guide to a number of important solar energy terms, such as retrofit, tilt angle, and solar friction, and this readable 14-page booklet also has a fascinating section on design details that can improve the efficiency of a solar heating system.

Write for:
Solar Energy Facts

Cost: Free

Send to:
Research Products Corp.
1015 E. Washington Ave.
Madison. WI 53701

RENEWABLE ENERGY
★★★

Renewable energy technologies use energy from endless suppliers such as sunlight, water flow, and vegetation. Renewable energy devices for heating the home include solar collectors, windmills, and wood-burning stoves. The U.S. Department of Energy's publication on renewable energy offers a simplified look at solar heating and cooling, wind machines, and other systems.

Another publication on passive cooling tells how this low-energy method can keep a home cool in warm weather. A third describes low-cost passive solar add-ons for the home, such as pumps, thermostats, and rooftop solar collectors. The three are free and offer a lot of good advice on alternative methods of heating and cooling the home.

Write for:
Renewable Energy: An Overview
Passive Cooling
Low-Cost Passive Solar Retrofits

Cost: Free

Send to:
Conservation and Renewable Energy Inquiry and
  Referral Service
P.O. Box 8900
Silver Spring, MD 20907

IDEAS FOR SUMMER COOLING
★★★★

Keeping the heat out of the house is the most important step toward achieving summer comfort. This booklet tells how to do it with solar orientation of the house (before it's built) and sun controls like overhangs and tall plantings—to name but two of the many ideas included here. You'll learn how to pull heated air out of your home with attic and window fans and how to cool air (when all else fails) with air conditioners or evaporative coolers. There's information on cooling mobile homes, too.

Write for:
Summer Comfort

Cost: $1.00

Send to:
University of Illinois at Urbana-Champaign
Small Homes Council
One E. St. Mary's Rd.
Champaign, IL 61820

ENERGIZED BY THE SUN
★★★

One way to combat increasing energy costs and increase your home's market value is to add—or retrofit—a solar energy heating system. Up to 60 percent of the nation's homes receive enough sunlight for a solar retrofit. Solar space heating can be either active or passive. Passive systems use building components such as floors, walls, and sun-spaces to collect and store heat. Active systems rely on hardware and mechanical means such as roof-top collectors to harness and distribute heat. The U.S. Department of Energy offers three illustrated pamphlets with lots of good advice to the home-owner considering such a renovation. Discussed are factors which affect the feasibility of a retrofit, types of solar systems, cost and savings compari-sons, and compatibility of existing heat distribution systems with various solar methods. Also included are bibliographies for further reading.

Write for:
Converting a Home to Solar Heat
Passive Solar Heating
Space Heating With Active Solar Energy
Systems

Cost: Free

Send to:
Conservation and Renewable Energy Inquiry and
Referral Service
P.O. Box 8900
Silver Spring, MD 20907

Landscaping for Energy Conservation

FENCES NO, TREES YES!

★★★★

One tree provides the cooling equivalent of five 10,000 BTU air conditioners, according to University of Illinois researchers, which is one good reason for looking into this eight-page publication on land-scaping for energy conservation, prepared by the University's Small Homes Council—Building Research Council. Suggestions are offered for plant-ing trees, bushes, vines, and other plants to provide windbreaks and shade to make a home cooler in summer but warmer in winter. Line drawings show how these natural energy conservation techniques work.

Write for:
Council Notes B3.1 Landscaping for Energy
Conservation

Cost: $1.00

Send to:
Small Homes Council—Building Research
Council
University of Illinois at Urbana-Champaign
One E. St. Mary's Road
Champaign, IL 61820

SAVE ON COOLING COSTS

★

With electricity costs rising annually, any advice on lowering air conditioning costs can make a satisfy-ing difference in the checkbook. Research Products Corporation offers a free booklet about precoolers, which can be attached to air conditioners to save up to 20 percent in energy costs and cut down on wear and tear on the appliances. Precoolers, invented only a few years ago, are devices that cool the air before it enters the air conditioner's condenser. This eight-page, pocket-sized brochure tells how precool-ers work and what to consider before buying one.

Write for:
Facts About Precoolers

Cost: Free

Send to:
Research Products Corporation
P.O. Box 1467
Madison, WI 53701-1467

NATURE'S HOT WATER HEATER

★★

People in some parts of the country use geothermal hot water to heat their homes inexpensively. They use modern methods of distributing underground heat to homes and office buildings. A new publica-tion by the U.S. Department of Energy tells all about geothermal energy (such as energy from active vol-canoes or steam-spouting geysers). Some lucky home-owners, especially in western states, may be able to heat and cool their homes by using geothermal ener-gy. This interesting six-page publication includes a

continued

HOME

remarkable amount of information, complete with maps and diagrams, about the geological, environmental, and economic aspects of geothermal energy.

Write for:
Geothermal Energy

Cost: Free

Send to:
Conservation and Renewable Energy Inquiry and Renewal Service
P.O. Box 8900
Silver Spring, MD 20907

WARM AND COZY WITH HYDRONIC HEATING
★★

When the time comes to buy a new home or make major alterations in your present one, why not make your own decision about which type of heating system best suits your needs? *Selecting a Heating System* has some interesting facts to help you decide, but the booklet's title is misleading. This 14-page publication focuses primarily on hydronic heating, otherwise known as steam and hot water heating. For $1.00, you'll learn the advantages of hydronic heating for both comfort and energy conservation, and you'll get a quick course on how boilers operate, how hot water baseboards function, and how hydronics can be combined with the use of solar energy.

Also available for a SASE is a great little three-page foldout called *Fuel Cost Facts,* which you can use to determine how much heat you get for your fuel dollar, whether you have electric, oil, or gas heating in your house.

Write for:
Selecting a Heating System
Fuel Cost Facts

Cost: $1.00 for Selecting a Heating System
Fuel Cost Facts—free with a SASE

Send to:
Better Heating-Cooling Council
35 Russo Place, P.O. Box 218
Berkeley Heights, NJ 07922

IF YOU'RE HEATING WITH WOOD
★★★

Do you have a wood-burning stove or fireplace, or are you considering either as an alternative or sup-

plemental heating source for your home? The high cost of gas and oil has prompted thousands of people to turn to stoves or fireplaces that burn cheap, old-fashioned wood. Heating with wood can be a good idea, but you should know all you can about using this natural heat source. This 24-page government publication has information on how to buy wood, what woods are best for home heating use, how to buy and operate a wood-burning stove or fireplace, and safety precautions. A fine summary, with sketches to help anyone heat with wood more efficiently.

Write for:
Heating with Wood (No. 131P)

Cost: $1.00

Send to:
Consumer Information Center
P.O. Box 100
Pueblo, CO 81002

Heating With Wood

FACTS ON FIREWOOD
★★★★

This practical, down-to-earth booklet was written by a homesteader who cooks his meals on a wood stove and heats his home with wood fires—so does the illustrator. They tell where even city folks can find free wood (call your local Streets Department, for a start), how to select the best pieces, how to cut and transport it, "limb it," and split the logs. There's stacking and seasoning information, and a section on the most efficient fireplaces and wood stoves. A firewood rating chart, good illustrations of the best firewood trees around and how to identify them, an extensive reading list on the subject, and how to select the right chain saw complete the data in this extensive, inexpensive booklet.

Write for:
How to Select, Cut, and Season Good Firewood

A SASE is a self-addressed stamped envelope.

Cost: 50¢

Send to:
 Stihl, Inc.
 Dept. B
 536 Viking Dr.
 Virginia Beach, VA 23452

WOOD FOR FUEL

★★★★

As a result of the energy crunch, wood is making a comeback as a popular home heating fuel. Interest in wood-burning stoves has boomed in the last ten years, but if you use one you also need to know where to get firewood, how to select it, and where to store it. You can be guided in these matters by *Wood—Use It Wisely*, a 16-page booklet from the Wood Heating Alliancee. In addition to advising you on your wood needs, there's sound advice on choosing a wood-burning appliance for your home. Safety is your first consideration; efficiency runs a close second. There's information on using, maintaining, and caring for your appliance, chimney, and stove pipe, and on what to do in case of a chimney fire.

Write for:
 Wood—Use It Wisely

Cost: Free with a long SASE

Send to:
 Wood—Use It Wisely
 Wood Heating Alliance
 1101 Connecticut Ave, NW
 Washington, D.C. 20036

WOOD FIRES AND WOOD STOVES

★★★★

America's forebears got along very nicely without automatic appliances, and today more and more people are returning to wood fires and wood stoves in an effort to cut down on energy bills. This handbook is a wonderful, detailed guide on how to live with a wood stove. It begins with what to wear in a home heated by a wood fire and what home furnishings will keep heat in. Different kinds of woods are listed according to burning quality. You'll learn how to build a fire, cook on an open fire and a wood stove, and care for your cooking stoves and heating stoves. You'll even find some recipes for successful stovetop cooking and oven baking. Twenty cheerful pages.

Write for:
 The Warmth of Woodfires

Cost: $1.25

Send to:
 Distribution Center
 7 Research Park
 Cornell University
 Ithaca, NY 14850

WOOD STOVE SAFETY

★★

Wood stoves are coming back into use and with them can come fire hazard. This brochure, put out by the Insurance Information Institute, lists 11 safety tips to remember when you're using a wood stove. It also tells how to select a new or used stove—be sure to check for cracks or other defects—where and how to install the stove, which National Fire Protection Association standards pertain, chimney requirements, and about stove pipes and dampers.

Write for:
 Wood Stove Safety

Cost: Free with a long SASE

Send to:
 Insurance Information Institute
 Dept. WSS
 110 William St.
 New York, NY 10038

ALL ABOUT KEROSENE HEATERS

★★★

From 10 to 12 million kerosene heaters are now in use in America, as more people turn to them to supplement their central heating systems. Kerosene heaters can quickly warm a small room, basement, workshop, or garage, or be helpful in emergency heating situations. But before you buy or use a kerosene space heater, you should learn all you can about their safe use. Some people become ill because of kerosene fumes or the reduction of oxygen they can cause. The government offers this free publication explaining how kerosene heaters work and how to use them safely.

Write for:
 Kerosene Heaters (No. 583P)

Cost: Free

Send to:
 Consumer Information Center
 P.O. Box 100
 Pueblo, CO 81002

HOME

DEVICE TO SAVE WATER

★★★

This water-saving device is nothing more than a little stainless steel disc, ¾ inch in diameter, with a ⅛-inch hole bored in the center. You install it in your shower head (it fits most conventional types), and according to the manufacturer it can save an average family of four up to $75 annually in water bills and water-heating costs. For your dollar you'll receive two flow conservers, as they're called, and illustrated directions for installation—it's as easy as installing a new washer.

Write for:
Stainless Steel Water Conserver (2)

Cost: $1.00 and a long SASE

Send to:
National Homeowners Association
1906 Sunderland Place, N.W.
Washington, DC 20036

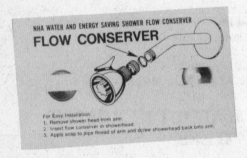

Stainless Steel Water Conservers

MAKE LIGHT BULBS LAST LONGER

★★

Here's a new way to save money on light bulbs: Inserting a little pressure-sensitive device called "The Cup" onto the base of a light bulb can increase its life 60 to 100 times. The manufacturer claims that this translates into about eight years of extended life for a new bulb used 24 hours a day. You can send for a sample of the UL-listed "Cup" for $2.00. If you order a dozen (for $21.50) you'll get two free pairs of cardboard "rainbow" glasses for the kids.

Write for:
"The Cup" Sample (specify candelabra base or regular base)

Cost: $2.00

Send to:
Mr. Rainbows
P.O. Box 27056
Philadelphia, PA 19118

"The Cup" Sample

Home Appliances and Equipment

BEFORE YOU MAKE A SERVICE CALL...

★★★★

The Association of Home Appliance Manufacturers claims that 40 percent of all service calls are unnecessary, wasting about $80 million yearly. This wonderful booklet is a checklist for individual appliances in your home. Read it *before* you call for service and you may be able to identify and correct the problem yourself. There's an electrical checklist—for starters, is the plug firmly inserted into the wall outlet? Then there's a list of problems for each appliance, with possible causes and remedies for each. Only when you've exhausted these should you call for service.

This booklet also tells where to write if you're not satisfied with the service you get, and if the dealer won't cooperate. An invaluable standby for any appliance-owner—which means practically everyone. You can get it from your local electric company. Tell them in your letter that the booklet is published by the Edison Electric Institute.

Write for:
How To Avoid Unnecessary Service Calls on Your Electric Appliances (publication of Edison Electric Institute)

Cost: Free

A SASE is a self-addressed stamped envelope.

Send to:
Your local electric company

PROBLEMS WITH AN APPLIANCE?

★★

The toaster burning your breakfast? Your washing machine sounding like a jet plane ready to take off? Your television set on its last legs? Before you call a repairman or think of tossing out the appliance, check out the suggestions in the Better Business Bureau's free booklet, *Consumer Tips on Appliance Service*. You learn about checking into warranties so you may not have to pay for parts and labor to have an appliance repaired. It tells what to check for if an appliance doesn't work properly before calling for service and, if repair is needed, how to be prepared for the service call.

Write for:
Consumer Tips on Appliance Service (No. 245)

Cost: Free

Send to:
Council of Better Business Bureaus
1515 Wilson Blvd.
Arlington, VA 22209

GETTING ACQUAINTED WITH HOME APPLIANCES

★★★

Here are two helpful booklets for use in the laundry room and kitchen. *Knowing Your Home Appliances* is a 24-page guide to ranges, refrigerators, freezers, dishwashers, washers, and dryers, and it's designed for those in the market for these appliances as well as those who already own them and want to know more about how they work and how to use them wisely. Information is offered on installation requirements, average life expectancy, available models, basic construction points, and buying hints. The glossary of appliance terms can help you know how to separate the facts about major appliances from the salesperson's hype. It's a useful booklet about costly appliances that need care to keep running efficiently.

The second guide, the 16-page *Porcelain Enamel Questions & Answers*, tells you about uses for and care of porcelain, which is used on over 200 products, most of them major home appliances. Can you put hot pans on porcelain enamel surfaces? How can you clean stains off them? How can you repair a damaged porcelain surface or a chip in a porcelain enamel pot? Short, helpful tips answer these and other questions.

Write for:
Knowing Your Home Appliances
Porcelain Enamel Questions & Answers

Cost: 50¢ each (coins only)

Send to:
Porcelain Enamel Institute, Inc.
Consumer Services Dept.
1111 N. 19th St.
Arlington, VA 22209

FEATHERING YOUR NEST

★★★

Looking for home appliances? Need a bedroom suite or living room rug? This brand new booklet, *Home Furnishings and Equipment*, from the Money Management Institute of Household International, covers the basics from wicker to washers, as well as household extras like computers and VCRs. Developed for first-timers, the book's 40 illustrated pages contain buying guidelines for wood and upholstered furniture, bedding and floor coverings, major appliances and telephones. In addition, readers are helped to identify needs and wants, establish buying priorities, and set up a long-term purchase plan. You'll also learn the ins and outs of cash versus credit, furniture rental, and buying used furniture.

Write for:
Home Furnishings and Equipment

Cost: $1.00

Send to:
Money Management Institute—Dept. PI
Household International
2700 Sanders Road
Prospect Heights, IL 60070

Home Furnishings and Equipment

HOME

SAVING ENERGY IN THE KITCHEN
★★

Do you open the oven door frequently to check on a meal baking inside? Do you leave the oven open while basting? Do you cook foods at higher temperatures than necessary? What color is your gas flame? Are you using less energy running the dishwasher than doing the dishes by hand? Do you always use the drying cycle or let the dishes dry overnight in the machine? You'll learn more about energy-efficient use of ranges and dishwashers in these two six-page booklets that tell you how to save both time and money in the kitchen.

Write for:
Saving Energy With Your Range
Saving Energy With Your Dishwasher

Cost: 50¢ each

Send to:
Association of Home Appliance Manufacturers
20 N. Wacker Dr.
Suite 1500
Chicago, IL 60606

WHICH APPLIANCES ARE ENERGY GUZZLERS?
★★

Does a room air conditioner use more energy than a home freezer? You may be surprised to learn that a freezer is the greater energy user of the two. And refrigerators use up more energy in the home than hot water heaters. A free booklet tells which major home appliances are the biggest energy users and how improved energy efficiency can reduce the amount of money you pay on utility bills. Another booklet tells how to read the energy guide labels found on major appliances.

Write for:
Facts on Major Home Appliance Energy
    Consumption and Efficiency Trends
Communicating With Consumers About the
    Energy Guide Appliance Labeling Program

Cost: Free (Facts on Energy Consumption)
60¢ (Communicating With Consumers)

Send to:
Association of Home Appliance Manufacturers
20 N. Wacker Dr.
Suite 1500
Chicago, IL 60606

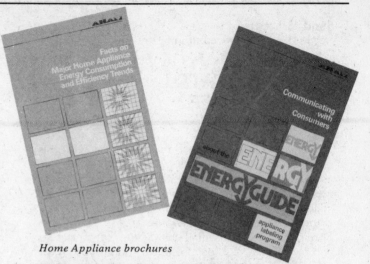
Home Appliance brochures

MARVELOUS MICROWAVES
★★

Microwave ovens save time, cook or defrost rapidly, and preserve the taste and nutritional value of foods. And microwave ovens are clean, cool, and safe. So says the Association of Home Appliance Manufacturers, which invites you to learn more about how microwaves cook by sending for a folder that explains radiant energy cooking. If you own a microwave oven or are thinking of buying one, this brochure can reassure you about the safety of microwave cooking—federal health officials state that there "hasn't been a documented case of human injury" from microwaves emitted by ovens.

Write for:
The Microwave Oven: How It Works, Why
    It's Safe

Cost: 25¢

Send to:
Assocation of Home Appliance Manufacturers
    20 N. Wacker Dr.
Suite 1500
Chicago, IL 60606

DIRECTIVES ON DISHWASHERS
★★★

Once considered a luxury, dishwashers are virtually a necessity today—and a practical one, too. According to this 16-page booklet from Maytag, 16.2 hours a month can be saved by using a dishwasher instead of washing dishes by hand. *How to Buy a Dishwasher* will be a welcome guide for anyone planning to make this major appliance purchase. Careful shopping will allow you to purchase yours with the features you want plus long life and dependability.

A SASE is a self-addressed stamped envelope.

You'll learn that the initial price is only one factor to consider. Others include performance, service-free use, energy usage, and convenience features. The booklet discusses construction materials and warranties, washing and racking systems, and details many of today's available convenience features. There is also a checklist to use to evaluate the models you are considering purchasing for your home.

Write for:
   How to Buy a Dishwasher

Cost: 25¢

Send to:
   Consumer Information Center
   How-To-Buy Booklets
   Dept. FT
   The Maytag Company
   Newton, IA 50208

How to Buy a Dishwasher

COOL NEWS ON REFRIGERATORS

★★★

How full do you keep the freezer part of your refrigerator? Do you keep it too full, or block the air vents? How often do you defrost your manual or partially automatic freezer? How often do you clean the condenser coils? If you're in the market for a new refrigerator or freezer, which models are more energy efficient? Here are two guides to help you use your refrigerator and freezer wisely or shop for the models that offer the best value for the money.

Write for:
   Saving Energy With Your Refrigerator and Freezer
   1985 Consumer Selection Guide for Refrigerators
      and Freezers

Cost: 25¢ (Saving Energy)
         $1.00 (Selection Guide)

Send to:
   Association of Home Appliance Manufacturers
   20 N. Wacker Dr.
   Suite 1500
   Chicago, IL 60606

THIS IS THE WAY WE WASH OUR CLOTHES

★★★

Home laundry today is certainly easier than it was in the era of wringer washers and outdoor clotheslines. Most modern homes and even apartments are equipped with laundry rooms or, at the very least, closet space for a washer and dryer. Selection of these major appliances is a serious investment, one which can be confusing within the present market of numerous special features. Two booklets from Maytag, *How To Buy a Dryer* and *How To Buy an Automatic Washer,* sort out the facts so you can make a wise decision. The 16-page booklets tell you to consider price, operating costs, service-free use, performance, and convenience features. Construction, cycles, and controls are also discussed. Each booklet has a handy checklist in the back for you to evaluate the models you choose.

Write for:
   How to Buy a Dryer
   How to Buy an Automatic Washer

Cost: 50¢

Send to:
   Consumer Information Center
   How-To-Buy Booklets
   Dept. FT
   The Maytag Company
   Newton, IA 50208

LAUNDRY ROOM TIPS

★★★

Do you use cold water rinses for all your clothes washing loads? Do you rewash loads if you're not satisfied they're clean enough? Do you pack too many items in the washer? Do you mix heavy and light clothing together in the clothes dryer? Do you toss lint-collecting towels in with synthetic or permanent press articles? You'll learn how to use your clothes washer and dryer more efficiently if you look at a new eight-page guidebook that can save you lots more than the two quarters it costs.

Write for:
   Saving Energy With Your Home Laundry
      Equipment

continued

HOME

Cost: 50¢

Send to:
Association of Home Appliance Manufacturers
20 N. Wacker Dr.
Suite 1500
Chicago, IL 60606

NEW CHOICES FOR TELEPHONE BUYERS

★★

With the divestiture of AT&T and the emergence of local telephone companies, many consumers are still confused about whether it's best for them to buy or to lease their phones. If you decide to buy, you'll get some guidance from this pamphlet put out by the Electronic Industries Association. In question and answer format, this buyer's guide gives tips on the comparative costs of buying or leasing, and what you should do with your old phone if you purchase your own. It also enlightens you regarding "tone" and "pulse" phones and what kinds of telephones are available, including cordless phones.

Write for:
How to Buy a Telephone

Cost: Free with a long SASE

Send to:
Electronic Industries Association
Consumer Electronics Group
P.O. Box 19100
Washington, D.C. 20036

How to Buy a Telephone

TO BUY OR NOT TO BUY

★★★

You now have the option of renting your telephone or buying it from your phone company, one of its competitors, or an independent manufacturer. It may

sound like a bargain to buy a less-expensive phone instead of one from the telephone company, but that may not be the case. There are a lot of considerations to make before a decision can be made to rent or to buy, and from whom to get a phone. The Better Business Bureau's free six-page booklet, *Tips on Buying Your Own Phone,* answers your questions about renting or buying a phone, and it explains what equipment is available. Shopping guidelines are included to show you how to compare purchase and rental prices, warranty and repair arrangements, and other considerations.

Write for:
Tips on Buying Your Own Phone (No. 24-187)

Cost: Free

Send to:
Council of Better Business Bureaus
1515 Wilson Blvd.
Arlington, VA 22209

SMART LONG-DISTANCE CALLING

★★★★

It's fun to talk to someone in another city, state, or country—until the phone bill arrives. Then you wonder how you could have spent so much money talking long-distance for so few minutes. The Better Business Bureau's free seven-page booklet called *Tips on Long-Distance Telephone Services* plugs you in to the many alternatives available for long-distance calling. You learn what "equal access" is, what a "primary carrier" is, and how to choose one of the discount long-distance services. It suggests several questions you should ask before choosing a service. For example, how large is the company's service coverage? Is there a subscription fee, a monthly fee, or a minimum monthly usage charge? Are there any additional costs or discounts? The company offering the lowest rates may not necessarily offer the best all-around service, nor offer features best suited to your individual needs. This is a helpful guide for any long-distance caller.

Write for:
Tips on Long-Distance Telephone Services
(No. 24-199)

Cost: Free

Send to:
Council of Better Business Bureaus
1515 Wilson Blvd.
Arlington, VA 22209

A SASE is a self-addressed stamped envelope.

A HELPFUL PHONE BOOK

★★★★

Confused about telephones and telephone service since the break-up of AT&T? Not sure whether to buy your phone or rent it? Befuddled by the variety of long-distance phone companies and the services they offer? If so, take a look at The Federal Communications Commission's free 20-page booklet, which is designed to help answer your telephone questions. It tells about local calling options, leasing or buying a telephone, how to install a phone in your home, how to get repair service, and where to go for help and more information. It also describes the major long-distance services and gives pointers on choosing a long-distance company.

Write for:
A Consumer's Guide to Telephone Service (No. 588P)

Cost: Free

Send to:
Consumer Information Center
P.O. Box 100
Pueblo, CO 81002

Consumer's Guide to Telephone Service

LONG DISTANCE OPTIONS

★★

To vie for your business, long distance phone companies are offering a variety of rates, bonuses, and special features. To help consumers compare these features and make an informed choice, the Telecommunications Research and Action Center has prepared a residential comparison chart. The chart, which is regularly updated, lists rates and nineteen other features for eight major companies. It also gives information on how to obtain a personalized, computer-generated printed comparison of rates for long-distance calls you actually make.

Write for:
Tele-Tips Long Distance Comparison Chart

Cost: $2.00 with a SASE

Send to:
TRAC
P.O. Box 12038
Washington, DC 20005

COMMON SENSE ABOUT AIR CONDITIONERS

★★★

Room air conditioners can be real energy guzzlers and cost small fortunes to run. It's smart to keep older models in good running order or replace them with newer, more energy-efficient models. Here are three booklets to help you solve your room air conditioner problems. Suggestions are given for choosing a new air conditioner and using and caring for those you already own and intend to keep. Learn what Btuh and EER stand for, and how to take simple steps to ensure that your air conditioner doesn't cost you money by working harder than it needs to.

Write for:
Saving Energy With Your Room Air Conditioner
Cooling Load Estimate Form for Air Conditioners
Consumer Selection Guide for Room Air Conditioners

Cost: 25¢ (Saving Energy)
35¢ (Cooling Load)
$1.00 (Consumer Guide)

Send to:
Association of Home Appliance Manufacturers
20 N. Wacker Dr.
Suite 1500
Chicago, IL 60606

ALL ABOUT AIR CONDITIONING

★★★★

Air conditioning is a lot more than just cooling the air. A good system or unit also treats the air to control simultaneously its temperature, humidity, cleanliness, and distribution. Whether you're in the market for a central air-conditioning system for your entire house, or you are just considering buying an individual air-conditioning unit to cool part of the house or an apartment, this free 16-page booklet from the Better Business Bureau, *Facts About Central Air Conditioning,* can offer some good advice. The information-loaded booklet explains what air conditioning is, how it works, and what its benefits

continued

are. It describes the different types of central systems, including "total comfort" climate control systems, and offers tips on finding a reliable contractor and taking bids on installation of a central air conditioning system. Tips on operating and servicing your unit are included.

Write for:
Facts About Central Air Conditioning
(No. 311-03201)

Cost: Free

Send to:
Council of Better Business Bureaus
1515 Wilson Blvd.
Arlington, VA 22209

IT'S IN THE AIR
★★

These days it's hard to escape polluted air. But special air filters and cleaners can help clean the air in your home. If you have a health problem that's caused or aggravated by contaminants in the air, you may want to send for this free leaflet. Although it's basically a promotion for the manufacturer's air cleaning machine, the brief discussion of the merits and efficiency of different devices will give you enough background to know what you're looking for when you shop for an air cleaner.

Write for:
Cleaning Facts

Cost: Free

Send to:
Research Products Corp.
1015 E. Washington Ave.
Madison, WI 53701

THE HIGH COST OF HEATING
★★★★

If you're a home owner, you know all about high heating bills. One way you can make your home more comfortable and reduce your gas bill is to consider having a new energy-efficient furnace or boiler installed. The Better Business Bureau offers a free eight-page booklet called *Tips on Central Heating Systems* that lists the types of central home heating systems and tells how the different systems work. The booklet also describes automatic controls that can save you money while keeping your home heated comfortably. Suggestions are given to help you choose a reliable contractor to install a new home heating

system. It's all valuable advice if you're in the market for a new furnace or boiler.

Write for:
Tips on Central Heating Systems

Cost: Free

Send to:
Council of Better Business Bureaus
1515 Wilson Blvd.
Arlington, VA 22209

CHOOSING A HOME COMPUTER
★★★

The Electronic Industries Association offers this solid guide to help take the confusion out of buying a home computer. This illustrated booklet will fit into your pocket for "in-store" reference. First, it stresses the importance of knowing, before you buy, just what you want your computer to do—are you, for instance, going to use it for household budget management, catalog buying, addresses, recipes, games? Learn how to understand computer language and to select software. This is an excellent publication for the first-time computer purchaser.

Write for:
How to Buy a Home Computer

Cost: Free with a 6″ × 9″ SASE (56¢ postage)

Send to:
Electronic Industries Association
Consumer Electronics Group
P.O. Box 19100
Washington, D.C. 20036

How to Buy a Home Computer

DO YOU NEED A HOME COMPUTER?

★★★★

A few years ago, the latest thing in home technology was the microwave oven. After that, it was the video cassette recorder. Today it's a home computer. If you're considering buying one, check out the Better Business Bureau's free eight-page booklet *Tips on Buying a Home Computer*. It offers a short, "user friendly" course in computer jargon, explains what the different components are, and tells you what a home computer can do. Smart shopping and price comparison advice that can help you decide which computer will do the most for you—at the best price.

Write for:
Tips on Buying a Home Computer (No. 24-183)

Cost: Free

Send to:
Council of Better Business Bureaus
1515 Wilson Blvd.
Arlington, VA 22209

Tips on Buying a Home Computer

SEWING MACHINE CHECKLIST

★★★

Will the machine you're considering sew through at least six layers of coating? Will it sew chiffon or other sheer fabric without puckering? How about sewing over two layers of flatfell seams on jeans denim (16 layers)? Does the seam stretch at least 50 percent on stretch stitches? These questions and 32 others need "yes" answers before you buy a new sewing machine. This folder, put out by the Bernina sewing machine people, suggests that you take along six sample fabrics of your own and try to sew them on each machine, using the checklist, and that you take the time to consider a number of brands. The

test will clearly reveal the quality of the stitch delivered by each machine you consider. A useful guide.

Write for:
How to Buy a Sewing Machine

Cost: Free

Send to:
Swiss-Bernina, Inc.
534 W. Chestnut
Hinsdale, IL 60521

Hassle-Free Home Cleaning

HOW CLEAN IS A CLEAN HOUSE?

★★★★

This wonderful booklet asks some very basic questions. One of them—do you and your spouse or partner agree on standards of housekeeping? That's the important first step in this booklet on housecleaning basics and home care. Once you've agreed on acceptable standards, consider the ways this booklet offers to simplify house care (prevent unnecessary cleaning, for one thing). This detailed information covers not only the basics of cleaning specific areas and appliances, but also lampshades, marble, window shades, and other hard-to-clean areas and surfaces.

Write for:
Basics of Housecleaning and Home Care

Cost: 85¢

Send to:
Distribution Center
7 Research Park
Cornell University
Ithaca, NY 14850

TAKING THE HASSLE OUT OF HOUSECLEANING

★★★

You hate housework, although you know it has to be done. You're the most disorganized person in the world, and the state of your house shows it. Then you might not be interested in this booklet, either. But, if you can stand *reading* about cleaning, you'll find *Hassle-Free Cleaning for Singles and Other Busy*

continued

HOME

People both entertaining and helpful. Did you know you can make your bed while you're still in it? Did you know that ash trays *can* be easy to clean? Have you even considered doing the cleaning using the "buddy" system? Find out how to march through cleaning the kitchen or bathroom, keep the furniture dust-free, speed through the laundry, or combat insects—whether "crawlers" or "fliers." All this information might even take a bit of the hassle out of housework.

Write for:
Hassle-Free Cleaning for Singles and Other Busy People

Cost: Free (postcard requests only)

Send to:
Johnson Wax
Consumer Services Center
P.O. Box 567—Dept. W-85
Racine, WI 53403

HOUSEKEEPING TIPS
★

"Where will I find the time to clean my house top to bottom?" "Where do I start?" "Is there a way to clean quickly so there's more time for fun?" These are some of the questions answered in a helpful little foldout brochure called the *No Time for Cleaning Guide*. It's a straight sell for Tackle cleaner disinfectant, but the housecleaning tips are helpful. Get your unenthusiastic teens to read it—maybe they'll be prompted to help more around the house. Or, of course, maybe they won't. Some of the tips included here: Use moderate heat when cooking to minimize grease splatters; do the jobs you hate first—it will make the rest seem easier.

Write for:
No Time for Cleaning Guide

Cost: 25¢

Send to:
Free Things
The Clorox Company
Corporate Communications Dept.
P.O. Box 24305
Oakland, CA 94623

FREE AIR FRESHENER
★★★

Want to freshen up the laundry hamper, diaper pail, lingerie drawer, or vacuum cleaner bag? You can get a free sample of the Hoover Company's air freshener, a white tablet about the size of a quarter, just by sending for it. The tablets are sold four in a package at Hoover dealers, but you might like this free sample to try in your home before you buy the package.

Write for:
Hoover Air Freshener Tablet

Cost: Free with a long SASE

Send to:
The Hoover Company
Home Institute—Dept. F
101 E. Maple St.
North Canton, OH 44720

Hoover Air Freshener Tablet

PUTTING ON THE SHINE
★★★

Can't get the crayon marks off your dining room table? Or the water rings off your antique hutch? Here—compliments of Johnson Wax—is all you need to know about paste, wax, and spray furniture polish. In this 28-page booklet that's handy to have around any well-kept home you'll find good, practical advice on cleaning, polishing, waxing, and dusting various wood surfaces, plastic furniture, vinyl and leather upholstery, even genuine antiques.

A section on furniture care problems gives remedies for scratches, cloudiness, burns, blemishes, mars, hairline cracks, and water rings. Get the last word on removing nail polish, candle wax, and paint stains, even spilled milk, plus tips on cleaning pianos and organs, carved wood surfaces, and window sills. An attractive publication for anyone who loves good furniture.

Write for:
Furniture Care

A SASE is a self-addressed stamped envelope.

Cost: Free (postcard requests only)

Send to:
Johnson Wax
Consumer Services Center
P.O. Box 567—Dept. U-85
Racine, WI 53403

POLISHING IT OFF

★★★★

Nevr-Dull Magic Wadding Polish is an ingenious product—specially treated cotton wadding that can be used to clean and polish jewelry, car chrome, aluminum doors, brass door knobs, copper pans, silverware, fishing equipment, boating hardware, and so on. It's easy to use—no mess to clean up afterwards—and the manufacturer claims that it won't scratch or corrode metal surfaces. You can try it for yourself. Send 50¢ for a small sample tin.

Write for:
Nevr-Dull Sample

Cost: 50¢

Send to:
The George Basch Co., Inc.
P.O. Box 188
Freeport, NY 11520

Use the Ultimate Metal Polish and Cleaner

NEVR-DULL

The original magic wadding polish

Nevr-Dull Sample

UPHOLDING YOUR UPHOLSTERY

★★

This little ten-page pamphlet contains a wealth of information about your upholstered furniture. Before you even buy, you ought to read the information on what's inside upholstered pieces, which fabrics wear and clean well, and how to read furniture labels.

Once you've bought the piece, this pamphlet will tell you how to care for it and maintain it (shampoo at least twice a year). A special section is devoted to spot and stain removal, and a stain chart tells you which cleaning method to use for removal of common stains. You'll learn also about the cleanability code that the furniture industry has adopted and the proper cleaning method for all types of upholstery fabric.

Write for:
Guide to Complete Upholstery Care

Cost: 25¢

Send to:
Bissell, Inc.
c/o Advertising Dept.
P.O. Box 1888
Grand Rapids, MI 49501

GETTING THE LOWDOWN ON CARPETS

★★★★

Before you buy new carpeting or a new rug, you would do well to read this thorough booklet put out by Cornell Cooperative Extension Service. The booklet advises making a long-range plan for the room in which your floorcovering will be used, and points out several factors that should affect your color choice. You'll learn about fiber characteristics from a helpful fiber chart and about different carpet construction, durability, padding, labels, and flammability regulations. There's good information on kitchen, bathroom, and patio carpeting, and there's a large section devoted to carpet care. A very good publication.

Write for:
The Selection and Care of Rugs and Carpets

Cost: 65¢

Send to:
Distribution Center
7 Research Park
Cornell University
Ithaca, NY 14850

CARING FOR CARPETS

★

This little folder is heavy on brand name promotion, but it does have some sound information on carpet care and vacuum cleaner selection depending on your cleaning needs. It discusses both wool and the man-made fibers used in carpets today, and the

continued

durability, soil resistance, and resilience of each type. There's some information on cleaning techniques, plus tips on such problems as cleaning carpeted stairs, loss of color and luster, fuzzing, and more. You also learn why it's so hard to get animal hair off the rug—the oil in the hair makes it cling.

Write for:
Consumer Guide to Carpet Cleaning

Cost: Free with a long SASE

Send to:
The Hoover Co.
Home Institute—Dept. C
101 East Maple St.
North Canton, OH 44720

LIQUID WAX SAMPLE
★★★

A cup of this wax, used with a gallon of water and applied to your car, will keep it waxed and polished for two to four months. Used full strength, the wax will preserve and lubricate shop, lawn, and garden tools. Along with these claims, the makers of Par-Fé concentrate liquid wax say Par-Fé is safe for all hard surfaces (i.e., wood paneling, floors, furniture, Formica, aluminum, etc.). Send for this 1-oz. sample package and try it for yourself. The company has been making this wax for 50 years.

Write for:
1-oz. sample of Par-Fé Concentrate Liquid Wax

Cost: 75¢

Send to:
Par-Fé Wax Corp.
207 W. 72nd St.
Kansas City, MO 64114

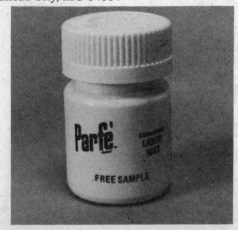

Par-Fé Concentrate Liquid Wax

WOOD FLOOR CARE
★★★★

First you must know exactly what kind of wood floor you have and whether or not it has a surface finish or a penetrating seal. Then you'll be able to care for it properly following these detailed instructions from the Oak Flooring Institute. You'll find an excellent section on removing 12 different kinds of stains, including that unsightly one caused by standing water.

There are sections on small floor repairs you can make without professional help, total floor refinishing, and what to do about cracks and squeaks. If you still have problems with your wood floor, the Institute invites your questions, to which they promise free advice. A lot of information in this small booklet.

Write for:
Wood Floor Care Guide

Cost: 25¢

Send to:
National Oak Flooring Manufacturers' Association
8 North Third Street
Suite 810 Sterick Bldg.
Memphis, TN 38103

BEYOND THE BLACK HEEL MARKS
★★★★

If you want sparkling, shiny-clean floors, just like on the TV commercials, get some how-to tips from this free 36-page booklet, which is full of advice on cleaning, waxing, and polishing. There's information on flooring types, floor care products, how to use floor polishes and how to remove them, and why you should wax certain types of flooring. Detailed advice on regular daily, weekly, and periodic care, too. You'll learn how to care for no-wax, vinyl, asphalt, wood, cork, and stone floors, as well as for various types of carpeting. There's information on floor and carpet problems and how to solve them, and a full section on dealing with spots and stains.

Write for:
Floor Care

Cost: Free (postcard requests only)

Send to:
Johnson Wax
Consumer Services Center
P.O. Box 567—Dept. V-85
Racine, WI 53403

FREE THINGS
for Your
GARDEN

GARDEN

Outdoor Gardening

NEW FOR THE GARDEN
★★★

A sweeter variety of corn, a golden-yellow bush bean, a compact bush-type watermelon, red and orange cosmos, and a clear lemon-colored tomato are among the new-for-1986 vegetables, fruits, and flowers described in the 1986 Catalog from Earl May Seed and Nursery of Iowa. The catalog offers tips on where, when, and how to plant, and tells you which plants are particularly suited to the climate in your area. It recommends good cutting flowers, and tells you which bloom best in full sun and which do well in the shade. The catalog is free, but if you send 25¢, the company will send you a sample package of seeds worth approximately one dollar. We received a package of Summer Poinsettia seeds, but types will vary.

Write for:
1986 Earl May Seed & Nursery Catalog
Sample package of seeds and catalog

Cost: Catalog free
25¢ for seeds and catalog

Send to:
Earl May Seed and Nursery Co.
Shenandoah, IA 51603

Earl May 1986 Seed & Nursery Catalog and sample package of seeds

TOMATO BIG AS THE RITZ?
★★★

Would you believe tomatoes the size of grapefruits, so large you need two hands to carry one? Up to six and a half pounds each, claims Spring River Nurseries, Inc. The amazing hybrid produces delicious, meaty, juicy tomatoes so large a single slice covers a plate, with 10 to 15 slices per tomato. For 50¢ you will receive a packet of these tomato seeds, complete with planting directions. You'll also receive a full-color, 32-page catalog of the nursery's other blue-ribbon plants. They offer extra-large all-season strawberries; jumbo red raspberries; mammoth cabbages; and giant white sweet corn, to name a few. Won't your summer salads be tasty?

Write for:
Tomato Seeds and Catalog

Cost: 50¢

Send to:
Spring River Nurseries, Inc.
Dept. FT8
Spring River Road
Hartford, MI 49057

Spring River Nurseries seeds and catalog

AN ABUNDANCE OF BLOOMS
★★★

Annuals are delightfully versatile flowers, blooming until fall in cold climates and even longer where the weather's warmer. They're easy to grow, and they offer a wonderful way to landscape a new home, shade a patio or terrace, or dress up a rock garden. Use *Annuals*, a free bulletin from Burpee, as a reliable guide to starting annuals indoors or outdoors, transplanting them, and caring for the growing plants. There are also creative plans for attractive "garden pictures"; imagine, for example, blue morning glories on a fence behind large flowered zinnias, with dwarf yellow marigolds and white or lavender alyssum in front.

Burpee also offers a free bulletin on biennials, which bloom the second year after planting, and perennials, which reward your initial labor by reappearing year after year with minimal attention from you.

A SASE is a self-addressed stamped envelope.

Write for:
Annuals
Biennials and Perennials

Cost: Free with a long SASE

Send to:
Customer Service
W. Atlee Burpee Co.
3300 Park Ave.
Warminster, Pa 18974

COMING UP ROSES

★★★★

A successful rose garden does need lots of tender loving care, but even a beginning gardener can grow these most gorgeous and romantic blooms. *Roses Are for You!* is a generously illustrated folder which lets the amateur gardener in on tips and know-how accumulated over the years by the experts. Since AARS growers are the people who help develop new rose hybrids in test gardens and each year honor the best of these roses, their advice is probably the last word on the subject. It's a friendly and encouraging publication; there's even a wonderfully lucid series of drawings showing *exactly* how to prune a rose bush—the task that baffles many a hopeful rose grower.

Write for:
Roses Are for You!

Cost: Free with a long SASE

Send to:
All-America Rose Selections
Publicity Office
RR 1, P.O. Box 740
Palmara, IN 47164

REAP WHAT YOU SOW

★★★

How to Sow Seeds Indoors and Out, a free four-page booklet from the Burpee people, is a convenient and valuable guide to when, how, and where to plant dozens of the most popular vegetable and flower seeds. You'll learn which seeds should be started indoors, and which should be sown directly in your garden because they take poorly to transplanting. You'll discover that you get more plants from expensive hybrid seeds if you start them indoors, and that fast-germinating vegetables like leaf lettuce and mustard greens will do best planted from seed in the garden. Handy timetables tell when to plant.

Write for:
How to Sow Seeds Indoors and Out

Cost: Free with a long SASE

Send to:
Customer Service
W. Atlee Burpee Co.
300 Park Ave.
Warminster, PA 18974

A GARDENFUL OF IDEAS

★★★★

Some of the most beautifully illustrated and helpful books on gardening are the Burpee catalogs which you can get free through the mail. Three different catalogs are offered. The *Burpee Gardens Catalog* lists about 1800 products for the home gardener, including flower and vegetable seeds, plants, roots, bulbs, trees, and garden tools. It's published in December/January each year. The *Burpee Spring Bulb Catalog,* which comes out in March, includes scores of spring-flowering bulbs shipped direct from Holland. And *Burpee's Fall Garden Catalog* includes spring-flowering bulbs for fall planting as well as perennial plants, fruit trees, and berries. It's published each July. Send for the current catalog and enjoy a gardenful of planting ideas.

Write for:
(according to season) Burpee Gardens Catalog; Burpee Spring Bulb Catalog; Burpee's Fall Catalog

Cost: Free

Send to:
Customer Service
W. Atlee Burpee Co.
300 Park Ave.
Warminster, PA 18974

GARDENING MADE EASY

★★★★

Everything you need to know about starting flowers and vegetables from seeds is yours in this handy color folder—it opens into a poster that could hang attractively in your basement or gardening room. It's free from Jiffy Products, along with a free sample of their famous Jiffy-7 plant starter pellets—just soak the pellet in water and it expands to form a miniature "pot," complete with soil in which you plant two or three seeds. When the strongest seedling is the right size, you transplant it, pellet and all;

continued

GARDEN

the mesh coating allows the roots free movement, and eventually breaks away as the plant grows.

This brochure-poster also offers tips on rooting and growing cuttings and on transplanting seedlings from seed flats. A double offer you can't lose on, and the price is certainly right: All it costs is the postage.

Write for:
Starter Pellet and "How-to" Brochure

Cost: Free with a long SASE (39¢ postage)

Send to:
Jiffy Products of America, Inc.
Attn: Free Jiffy-7 Offer
P.O. Box 338
West Chicago, IL 60185

Starter Pellet

HOW TO HAVE AN EVER-BLOOMING GARDEN
★★★

Have you ever planned a garden only to find that all your flowers burst into bloom at the same time, leaving you with nothing but lush greenery for the rest of the season? Make sure it doesn't happen again by heeding the words of wisdom in Cornell University's 14-page guide to selecting flowering plants to give your garden a continuous display of blooms from early spring to late frost. Many exotic flowers are suggested, along with familiar favorites like daffodils, tulips, iris, peonies, and so on. Charts tell you how tall plants grow and when they bloom, so that you can plan your flower beds to best effect. For the gardener who loves an all-season display of flowers, this is a valuable guide...not glamorous, but packed with solid information.

Write for:
Sequence of Bloom of Perennials, Biennials, and Bulbs

Cost: $1.60

Send to:
Distribution Center
7 Research Park
Cornell University
Ithaca, NY 14850

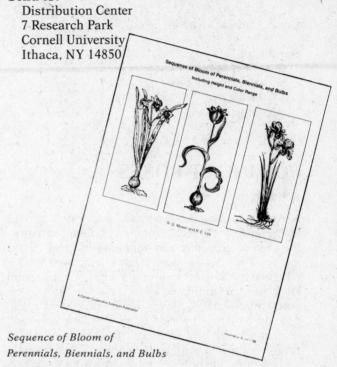

Sequence of Bloom of Perennials, Biennials, and Bulbs

WATER LILIES CAN BE FOR YOU, TOO
★★

Water lilies afloat on a quiet pond delight the eye and calm the spirit. If you'd like to start your own— even if it's only a four-gallon tub garden—send $2.00 for a copy of *Water Visions*. It's a full-color catalog from Van Ness Water Gardens, and it's got lots of practical planning and planting information along with irresistible color photos. With it comes an attractive how-to pamphlet. There's a booklist, too, but with all this information you'll probably need no further reading to start you off. You've already got instructions for cleaning and maintaining a water garden, building fountains and waterfalls, and landscaping the area around your water garden or tub garden. The maintenance checklist suggests a monthly program for keeping your pond, plants, and fish in top form.

Write for:
Water Visions

Cost: $2.00

Send to:
Van Ness Water Gardens
2460 N. Euclid Ave.
Upland, CA 91786

A SASE is a self-addressed stamped envelope.

Water Visions

GOOD GOURD!

★★★

Anyone who can grow squashes, cucumbers, melons, and pumpkins will have no trouble with beautiful gourds. The growing interest in gourds has prompted activity not only among gardeners, who are planting horticultural displays across the country, but also among hobbyists who have crafted the colorful varieties into planters, bird feeders, and other decorative items. A packet of 12 information sheets, available from the American Gourd Society, contains useful and interesting information on sprouting, harvesting, and caring for this inedible fruit. One sheet outlines standard exhibition and judging rules. Another gives directions for making hanging baskets. There is also advice for preserving the color of ornamentals and for growing uncommon varieties such as lagenarias and luffas.

Write for:
12 Gourd Bulletins

Cost: $1.65

Send to:
American Gourd Society
Box 274
Mount Gilead, OH 43338

NEWS FOR GARDENERS

★★★★

National Gardening, the monthly magazine of the National Gardening Association, is a full-color periodical serving both indoor and outdoor gardeners. Sample copies are available for $1.00. Recent issues included features on house plant care, how to grow sweet potatoes, holiday decorating with fruit, and the effects of acid rain on gardens. Recipes and readers' tips are also included. A seed swap col-

umn enables readers to seek out special seeds or give away their bounty. A very attractive magazine, *National Gardening* gives the public practical help in their gardens, keeps people in touch with other gardeners countrywide, and provides the latest information on developments of interest to gardeners.

Write for:
National Gardening Magazine Sample

Cost: $1.00

Send to:
National Gardening Magazine Sample
National Gardening Association
Department PI
180 Flynn Avenue
Burlington, VT 05401

National Gardening Magazine sample

THE GARDENER'S COMPANION

★★★★

Whether you want to grow orchids, clematis, azaleas, or herbs, you'll probably want to read up a bit on it first, and here's a good place to start. *Capability's Books for Gardeners*, an annually updated mail order catalog of almost 600 books, is more than just another catalog. Capability's has put together a sourcebook offering a wider selection of gardening books than can be found in local garden centers or bookstores, and all the listings are also screened for quality.

No matter what your gardening interest, you'll love browsing through these 60 illustrated pages. If you've always wanted a perennial flower border, maybe you'll be inspired to design one. If you do fine with lettuce but feel that roses are too rarefied for you, there's bound to be a book to broaden your horizons and develop your confidence. Don't miss the sec-

continued

GARDEN

tions on landscaping, wildflowers, and famous gardens, either.

Write for:
Capability's Books for Gardeners

Cost: $1.00

Send to:
Capability's Books for Gardeners
Box 114FT
Highway 46
Deer Park, WI 54007

ORCHARD-FRESH FRUIT
★★★

Dwarf fruit trees reward you two ways—in spring with bright blossoms and in fall with ripe fruit. *Planting Your Dwarf Fruit Orchard* tells you how to reap this double reward. It's a very good gardener's handbook that takes you through every step from planting to pest control. Especially good are the directions and suggestions for shaping and training your dwarf trees. Pruning is more an art than a science, and since dwarf fruit trees aren't pruned as heavily as full-size trees, the illustrations for how to make your cuts, pinchings, and croppings are very valuable.

Write for:
Planting Your Dwarf Fruit Orchard: Bulletin A-8

Cost: $1.95

Send to:
Garden Way Publishing
Schoolhouse Rd.
Pownal, VT 05261

Planting Your Dwarf Fruit Orchard

TREES FOR SPECIAL OCCASIONS
★★★

Sending flowers is an old custom, but the beauty of flowers quickly fades. Planting a tree for a special occasion, however, gives you a permanent reminder of the event. Trees add beauty, provide shade and homes for birds, cool and clean the air, and act as a buffer against noise. You don't even need a country estate; trees can be grown on an apartment balcony or even in a tub. The checklist in this foldout will help you choose the right tree for your purpose and your location. Instructions for planting and care are included so that your special-event tree will flourish. A lovely idea.

Write for:
Plant a Tree for Your Special Occasion (FS-363)

Cost: Free

Send to:
USDA Forest Service
P.O. Box 2417
Washington, D.C. 20013

UNDER THE SPREADING SHADE TREE
★★★★

Trees do more than just shade your home. They beautify, protect against the elements, attract birds, and add value to your property. But shopping for a good shade tree isn't easy. A new four-page brochure from the Better Business Bureau, *Consumer Tips on Mail Order Shade Trees*, cautions against mail order firms that tout the sale of "quality" shade trees for bargain prices. Some exaggerate the worth, size, or health of the trees they offer for sale, and you wind up buying an inferior variety or even a common weed. The Bureau suggests buying shade trees from reputable mail order gardening companies or from your local tree nursery.

Write for:
Consumer Tips on Mail Order Shade Trees
(No. 286)

Cost: Free

Send to:
Council of Better Business Bureaus
1515 Wilson Blvd.
Arlington, VA 22209

A SASE is a self-addressed stamped envelope.

FIRST AID FOR TREES
★★★

Pruning and repairing are two important steps in the overall care of your shade and landscape trees. If you remove unwanted twigs and branches at the right time and repair minor injuries throughout the year, you can help your trees grow beautiful, shapely, and strong. That means many hours of enjoying your personal outdoor environment. *Pruning Shade Trees and Repairing Their Injuries* is an illustrated 16-page booklet published by the U.S. Department of Agriculture. You'll learn all about what to clip and when to do it. There is advice on developmental and maintenance pruning for both young and mature trees, and the appropriate pruning season for various types of trees. You'll learn the techniques required for both deciduous trees and evergreens. First aid remedies for bark injuries, lightning damage, insect infestation, and splits are also given.

Write for:
Pruning Shade Trees and Repairing Their Injuries
(No. 116P)

Cost: $1.00

Send to:
Consumer Information Center
P.O. Box 100
Pueblo, CO 81002

CRABGRASS AND OTHER EARTHLY DELIGHTS
★★★★

If your crabgrass and dandelions prosper to the point where you're thinking about entering them in a horticultural display at the county fair, this booklet belongs in your library. *Weed Control in Lawns and Other Turf* is put out by a pretty good source—the U.S. Department of Agriculture. The best defense against weeds is a dense, vigorously growing turfgrass, in which the weeds will have difficulty gaining a foothold. In 41 information-packed pages you'll learn turf care, herbicide treatments and weed types, turf renovation, and spot treatments. Twenty-one common lawn weeds are illustrated and their growing habits described. One chart equates common, chemical, and trademark names of herbicides, and another cites the response of various lawn weeds to herbicide treatments.

Write for:
Weed Control in Lawns and Other Turf
(No. 118P)

Cost: $2.00

Send to:
Consumer Information Center
P.O. Box 100
Pueblo, CO 81002

Vegetable and Herb Gardening

PLOTTING YOUR VEGETABLE GARDEN
★★★★

All you need for a home vegetable garden is a sunny plot of land where the soil is fairly good and water doesn't stand. And whether you've got space for only a few tomato plants or a plot big enough to supply all your vegetable needs, start planning early with help from these excellent free gardening guides. *Vegetables* is a two-page booklet that shows you how to draw up a plan to keep your garden producing all season long. An illustrated leaflet on tomatoes, peppers, and eggplant explains how to grow these popular plants in the garden or in pots or planters set on a sunny patio, balcony, or roof-top. Similar illustrated guides give you basic gardening information for onions, root crops, and leafy greens and celery.

Write for:
Vegetables
Tomatoes, Peppers, and Eggplant
Onions
Root Crops
Leafy Greens and Celery

Cost: Free with a long SASE

Send to:
Customer Service
W. Atlee Burpee Co.
300 Park Ave.
Warminster, PA 18974

EARLY BIRD GARDENING
★★

Every home gardener knows that winter is really over when the first young lettuce and spinach is ready to harvest. A raised bed garden means you can savor the first delicious yields from your own plot

continued

GARDEN

earlier than if you plant in a regular garden. Raised bed gardening allows you to plant earlier and harvest earlier, and can also increase your yields. What's more, you don't have to till your garden before you plant. If you want to know more, write for a copy of *How to Maximize Garden Yields With Raised Beds*, eight copied pages from Butterbrooke Farm that include directions for preparing a raised bed, techniques for improving productivity, planting tips, and soil maintenance suggestions.

Write for:
   How to Maximize Garden Yields With
      Raised Beds

Cost: $1.25

Send to:
   Butterbrooke Farm
   78 Barry Rd.
   Oxford, CT 06483

YOUR WINTER VEGETABLE GARDEN
★★★★

You'll find it hard to believe how easy it is to build a cold-frame from boards and an old storm window. And once you've done it you can enjoy homegrown lettuce, onions, radishes, and tomatoes for up to three months after the growing season officially ends. *Building & Using Cold Frames* tells you exactly how to do it. There's no extra filler in this little book—just the information, instructions, and illustrations you need to construct a dependable cold frame.

Write for:
   Building & Using Cold Frames: Bulletin A-39

Cost: $1.95

Send to:
   Garden Way Publishing
   Schoolhouse Rd.
   Pownal, VT. 05261

Building and Using Cold Frames

GROW WELL WITH YOUR GARDEN
★★★★

You can grow fresher, better-tasting, more nutritious vegetables in your back yard after you read *Your Nutritious Garden*. You'll reap healthful produce with the satisfaction of knowing you've done it yourself. This detailed, illustrated 44-page book, published by The National Gardening Association, includes a garden plan with recommendations for fruits and vegetables that act as cancer inhibitors. There's also advice for the patio gardener. You'll find vitamin charts, dietary recommendations, growing tips for popular vegetables, and even recipes for delicious veggie dishes. A chapter on pest control tells you how to get the bugs out effectively, and a planning chart explains when and how to plant your crops.

Write for:
   Your Nutritious Garden

Cost: $1.00

Send to:
   Your Nutritious Garden
   National Gardening Association
   Department PI
   180 Flynn Avenue
   Burlington, VT 05401

Your Nutritious Garden

GROWING A VEGETABLE GARDEN
★★★★

Growing your own vegetables is not difficult, it's fun, and you'll be growing delicious food for much less than you can buy it. This detailed booklet with photographs and diagrams will tell you exactly how to do it. You'll start by finding out what equipment you'll need (nothing elaborate), how to prepare your soil, and how to choose what to plant (some vegetables are difficult to grow, and you'll do better buying them). You'll learn about thinning, mulching, and weed control, and the booklet also lists some good perennial crops, bulb crops, legumes, potherbs (spinach, chard), potatoes, root, and salad crops. You get a list of suggested varieties of 32 different vegetables. An excellent publication.

Write for:
The Home Vegetable Garden

Cost: $2.00

Send to:
Distribution Center
7 Research Park
Cornell University
Ithaca, NY 14850

STARTING FROM SEED
★★★★

Without seeds, you'll have no garden—so start now with a free packet of vegetable seeds from Butterbrooke Farm. Just send them 50¢ to cover postage and handling, and they'll send you a sample packet of the variety you select. All their seeds are open-pollinated, chemically untreated, and pure line, so you can save seed from your harvest for use next year. Seeds are packed by hand in a manila envelope. Butterbrooke Farm currently offers 58 popular varieties from which to choose, ranging from asparagus to watermelon seeds. Also available are basil, dill, marigold, nasturtium, and sunflower seeds.

Write for:
Sample packet of vegetable seeds (state the packet you prefer)

Cost: 50¢

Send to:
Butterbrooke Farm
Dept. CG
78 Barry Rd.
Oxford, CT 06482

Sample packet of vegetable seeds

FRUIT OF THE VINE
★★★★

Homegrown cucumbers, watermelons, squash, and pumpkins make beautiful and delicious additions to your garden. And don't forget gourds—they make an attractive display, and they're fun to fashion into ornaments, utensils, or even a birdhouse. This free booklet is a guide to growing, harvesting, and serving these interesting plants. You'll learn how to judge when a watermelon is ripe, how to combat cucumber beetles and squash bugs, how to pollinate the female flowers on a vine plant, and how to harvest cucumbers. A well-written freebie from Burpee.

Write for:
Vine Crops

Cost: Free with a long SASE

Send to:
Customer Service
W. Atlee Burpee Co.
300 Park Ave.
Warminster, PA 18974

EXTEND YOUR PLANTING SEASON
★★★

If you're still in the mind-set that tells you spring is the only time to plant your vegetables, don't miss Burpee's helpful planting guide for fall crops. The late planting dates for more than 45 popular vegetables are listed according to the average dates of first frost countrywide. You'll learn how to extend your harvest with fall plantings of vegetables that need cooler weather in which to mature. Some even taste better after being exposed to frost.

Write for:
Planting Guide for Fall Crops

Cost: Free with SASE

Send to:
Customer Service
W. Atlee Burpee Co.
300 Park Ave.
Warminster, PA 18974

A HILL OF BEANS
★★★★

You don't have to be an expert gardener to grow beautiful, bountiful rows of beans, peas, and other

continued

GARDEN

legumes. What's more, legumes will work for your garden by increasing the nitrogen content of the soil in which they grow. To become better acquainted with the legume family, send for this free four-page booklet. It offers step-by-step directions for growing snap, lima, and shell beans, and peas with or without edible pods. And don't forget peanuts—the kids will be fascinated by the way the stalks, or pegs, grow downward into the soil; underground, the stalks produce clusters of peanuts.

Write for:
Beans, Peas and Other Legumes

Cost: Free with a long SASE

Send to:
Customer Service
W. Atlee Burpee Co.
300 Park Ave.
Warminster, PA 18974

SEEDS OF GOOD TASTE
★★★★

Eight little sample packets of herb seeds will introduce you to the delights of homegrown fresh basil, chervil, dill, caraway, chives, roquette (rocket), sorrel, and savory. Accompanying the sample packets is a fascinating catalog of seeds from all over the world (France, primarily), and gourmet food items ranging from tea to such exotica as truffles, snails, lobster paste, couscous, anchovies, and caviar. You'll also receive several gourmet recipes for cooking with shallots, plus planting instructions for shallot bulbs. All for a dollar.

Write for:
8 Sample Seed Packets

Cost: $1.00

Send to:
LeJardin du Gourmet
P.O. Box 177
West Danville, VT 05873

SEASON TO TASTE
★★★★

Most people can chop, dice, and sauté, but the real craft of cooking comes from enhancing the flavors of your ingredients. That often means cooking with herbs. But herbs do more than flavor food; they have medicinal uses and pleasing fragrances. The best way to learn about using herbs is to grow your own. This illustrated booklet teaches you through step-by-

step directions everything you need to know to harvest 15 of the most popular kitchen herbs. Most herbs may be planted indoors or out, and may be transplanted and propagated. Although freshly picked herbs have a more delicate flavor than dried herbs, you'll find good advice for both drying and freezing your crop. There are recipes for *bouquet garni*, herb vinegar, and herb teas. There is also a comprehensive chart listing each herb with compatible culinary suggestions, medicinal uses, and gift ideas.

Write for:
Grow 15 Herbs for the Kitchen: Bulletin A-61

Cost: $1.95

Send to:
Garden Way Publishing
Storey Communications, Inc.
Schoolhouse Road
Pownal, VT 05261

ALL YOU NEED NOW IS A SPICE RACK
★★★

If you like to garden but have little space, why not try an herb garden—indoors or out? Pinetree Garden Seeds offers seven herbs—basil, dill, fennel, oregano, sage, savory, and thyme—for $2.00. The seeds are packaged separately in small envelopes (a little goes a long way) and included in each is a brief information sheet. All the seeds are germination tested and guaranteed, and they haven't been treated with chemicals. This is a practical offer both for the home gardener and the adventurous cook. Ask for the company's free seed catalog as well.

Write for:
Seven Herbs

Cost: $2.00

Send to:
Pinetree Garden Seeds
New Gloucester, ME 04260

Pinetree Garden catalog and seeds

A SASE is a self-addressed stamped envelope.

Small-Space and Indoor Gardening

SMALL-SPACE GARDENING
★★★★

You love flowers and trees but don't have room for a garden? Then try container gardening, which lets you enjoy the pleasures of a garden in a miniyard or on a porch, patio, terrace, or balcony. Cornell University horticulturists have put together this 14-page publication telling how to get into container gardening. There's information on types of containers, growing mediums, mulching and watering (plants in containers often need more frequent watering then those in an open bed), wintering over, and more. The photos will make you want to rush out and find a tub or barrel to start planting in. This lavishly illustrated black-and-white booklet shows you how container gardening can enhance anyone's home or yard. Very attractive.

Write for:
Container Culture of Trees and Shrubs for
Gardens and Terraces

Cost: $1.50

Send to:
Distribution Center
7 Research Park
Cornell University
Ithaca, NY 14850

*Container Culture of Trees and Shrubs
for Gardens and Terraces*

GOOD THINGS IN SMALL SPACES
★★★

Even if you don't have a backyard, you can have homegrown vegetables. Grow them in pots, boxes, buckets, hanging baskets—just about any container that's handy. Or grow an herb garden or a pot of small-fruit tomato plants close enough to the kitchen door for last minute picking. *Container Gardening Outdoors* provides instructions and illustrations for planting a 3' × 4' planter with radishes, lettuce, spinach, beets, bush beans, baby carrots, and kale.

This free bulletin also tells you how to grow vegetables "in the air" by providing trellises for your box gardens of cucumber, pole bean, or tomato plants—it saves space and the vegetables are easy to pick. There are tips on replanting for maximum production, and a list of vegetables recommended for outdoor containers. Another free bulletin gives you lots of information on growing vegetables in a greenhouse.

Write for:
Container Gardening Outdoors
Growing Vegetables in the Home Greenhouse

Cost: Free with a long SASE

Send to:
Customer Service
W. Atlee Burpee Co.
300 Park Ave.
Warminster, PA 18974

RETHINKING HOUSEPLANTS
★★★

The premise of this information-packed leaflet is you should choose houseplants not just for their looks or color, but according to what your home can offer them in the way of humidity, light, and water. The leaflet lists 65 houseplants and their environmental needs, and it also lists plants in three night temperature categories. You'll learn about common houseplant diseases and how most of them are related to environment. The leaflet also talks about potting soils, sterilizing soil, pots, fertilizers, and insects, and it lists plants that will withstand dry conditions or neglect. There are good suggestions for plants to use in tubs and hanging baskets, and for trailing effects.

Write for:
Houseplants: An Environmental View

Cost: Free with a long SASE

Send to:
West Virginia Dept. of Agriculture
State Capitol Building
Charleston, WV 25305

GARDEN

IN-HOME HORTICULTURE
★★★★

The knack for cultivating lush greenery indoors depends just as much on careful selection of the plants as on providing optimum growing conditions, as you will learn in this 32-page booklet from the U.S. Department of Agriculture. *Selecting and Growing House Plants* identifies in words and pictures hundreds of succulents, foliage, and flowering plants for you to consider inviting into your home. It lists characteristics, cultivation, and special requirements. You'll also learn about potting, watering and fertilizing, lighting, propagation, and seasonal care. There are directions for constructing a terrarium, and for tending to the florist's plant you received as a gift. There is also a glossary of terms used throughout the book. For novices and green thumbs, the book is worth the $1.00.

Write for:
   Selecting and Growing House Plants (No. 117P)

Cost: $1.00

Send to:
   Consumer Information Center
   P.O. Box 100
   Pueblo, CO 81002

GROWING GREAT GESNERIADS
★★

A sunny window, regular watering, average warmth and humidity—that's the formula for growing happy African violets, gloxinia, and other exotic members of the gesneriad family. To learn more about these beautiful houseplants, send a SASE to the American Gloxinia and Gesneriad society for their free guide to caring for, fertilizing, and doctoring your favorite gesneriads. Since these plants must have a humid environment, you'll welcome practical suggestions for supplying that extra bit of moisture that may be missing from the air in your home during the fall and winter months.

Write for:
   Gesneriads, Exotic House Plants

Cost: Free with a long SASE

Send to:
   Lois N. Russell
   American Gloxinia and Gesneriad Society
   5320 Labadie
   St. Louis, MO 63120

THE MOST POPULAR FLOWERING PLANT
★★★★

The first specimen came to the United States in 1936, and since then local, state, and national societies have dedicated themselves exclusively to the culture and improvement of this one plant. It's the African violet, which is actually not a violet nor even related to one. This excellent booklet discusses a bit of the history of this lovely houseplant and tells how to grow it—incorrect light is the most common reason for lack of bloom. You'll learn how to divide it, propagate it, water it, fertilize, and rejuvenate an old plant. Detailed black-and-white photos illustrate all these steps, and also show some problems you can overcome with the help of the information here.

Write for:
   Growing African Violets

Cost: $1.00

Send to:
   Distribution Center
   7 Research Park
   Cornell University
   Ithaca, NY 14850

BLOOMING CACTUS
★★★

Indoor gardeners will be dazzled by *Flowering Jungle Cacti*, which catalogs more than 350 varieties available from California Epi Center, a mail-order nursery specializing in flowering cacti. Printed on high-gloss paper with dozens of rainbow-color photographs accompanying the cacti descriptions, this 32-page booklet will surely whet your desire to grow delicate "Fair Annet," sensational "Pegasus," exotic "Clarence Wright," or just about any other of the scores of varieties pictured. The $1.00 charge for this handsome catalog can be deducted from your first order.

Write for:
   Flowering Jungle Cacti

Cost: $1.00

Send to:
   California Epi Center
   P.O. Box 1431
   Vista, CA 92083

A SASE is a self-addressed stamped envelope.

GARDEN

Flowering Jungle Cacti

Cactus and Succulent Catalog

THAT CURIOUS CACTUS

★★

Hundreds of species of flowering desert and jungle cacti and other succulents are listed in this catalog from K & L Cactus Nursery. The diverse selection will appeal to all levels of cactus gardeners, from the novice to the advanced collector. From the larger, spiny desert cacti to the free-flowering South American varieties, each item is carefully described and many are pictured in full color. Care instructions are also included. The booklet covers orchid cacti, agaves, crassulas, euphorbias, and more, and the K & L Cactus Nursery will fill special requests whenever possible. Also listed are seed packets, gardener's accessories, handcrafted pottery, insecticides, and books. The $2.00 cost is refunded with your first order.

Write for:
Cactus and Succulent Catalog

Cost: $2.00

Send to:
K & L Cactus Nursery
12712 Stockton Blvd.
Galt, CA 95632

GROW AN EGG FULL OF CACTUS

★★★★

What a super way to watch the miracle of nature! Along with this two-part transparent plastic "egg," you get a portion of soil mix and a capsule with about 50 mixed cactus seeds. You plant the seeds by pressing them firmly into the soil mix in the bottom portion of the egg, then add water, attach the top portion of the egg, and let nature take its course. Keep the egg in a shaded area, away from direct sunlight. The seeds will sprout within three to 28 days. When the seedlings are about half an inch tall, you can transplant them into a sandy, well-drained soil mix in small pots. Kids will love this. So will invalids and shut-ins. In fact it's a sure winner for anyone who loves plants and Mother Nature.

Write for:
Cactus Egg

Cost: $1.25

Send to:
K & L Cactus Nursery
12712 Stockton Blvd.
Galt, CA 95632

Cactus Egg

GARDEN

PLANTS ON DISPLAY
★★

A plant column under glass is the showpiece of terrariums. A plant column is an appealing decoration, and according to this booklet it's easy to assemble and care for. A two-page plant list gives you a wide variety of plants to choose from, and all the necessary instructions are here for choosing soil, planting, and caring for the finished column. *How to Make a Plant Column* has all the information to help you turn your home into a showcase of greenery, and the attractive photographs will make you want to start right away.

Write for:
    How to Make a Plant Column

Cost: $2.00

Send to:
    The Terrarium Association
    P.O. Box 276
    Newfane, VT 05345

How to Make a Plant Column

PLANTS IN BOTTLES
★★★

A terrarium can be the perfect answer for the forgetful gardener or the traveler who loves houseplants but can't seem to give them the TLC they need. *Q. & A.* and *Planting the Big Ones* tell all about the care

and feeding of a terrarium. Like putting ships in bottles, there is a trick for putting plants in those large glass bottles, and these pamphlets will tell you how it's done. You'll learn how to choose plants that will do well in the light, water, and temperature conditions you can offer, and you'll find out about the most common terrarium problems and their solutions. It will look like you have a green thumb—even if you and your past houseplants know the truth.

Write for:
    Q. & A.:
    Planting the Big Ones

Cost: 75¢ each

Send to:
    The Terrarium Association
    P.O. Box 276
    Newfane, VT 05345

GARDEN IN A GLASS
★★

Want to learn how to make terrariums, hanging glass ball planters, or partridgeberry bowls? Miniature gardening in bowls can be a fun hobby and you can learn all you need to know about it in this instruction folder offered by The Terrarium Association. The slim, eight-page folder is a bit high-priced but has photos and easy-to-follow instructions on what you need and how you put together these pretty little glass-enclosed gardens—they could make wonderful gifts. If you're looking for a creative hobby that could also solve your gift-giving problems, this could be for you.

Write for:
    How to Make Partridgeberry Bowls, Hanging Glass Ball Planters, and Terrarium Trees

Cost: $2.00

Send to:
    The Terrarium Association
    P.O. Box 276
    Newfane, VT 05345

FREE THINGS
about
FOOD

FOOD

Food Shopping and Food Safety

KEEPING ABREAST OF YOUR FOOD BUDGET
★★★★

Next time you're convinced that the cashier made a mistake ringing up your groceries (those three bags couldn't *possibly* have cost $45.00), turn for help to *Your Food Dollar*, a bright, cheery, 32-page booklet from the Money Management Institute. Presented in a readable style with pleasant line drawings is practical information on planning a food budget, making shopping lists, nutrition and the four food groups, storing and preparing food, food and drug laws, grading, and labeling.

There are pointers on how to shop for food (Do you dare to read labels? Do you even glance at unit pricing? Do you take advantage of seasonal buys?), but the greater portion of this guide is devoted to food buying guides—detailed advice on sorting through, judging, selecting, and storing foods. There's a cost-per-serving chart for various meat and poultry cuts, a food spending plan to fill in, and a table listing cheeses and their uses. An excellent way to spend $1.00.

Write for:
  Your Food Dollar

Cost: $1.00

Send to:
  Money Management Institute
  Dept. PI
  Household International
  2700 Sanders Rd.
  Prospect Heights, IL 60070

Your Food Dollar

LOST IN WONDERLAND?
★★

Do you feel like Alice in a supermarket, a little lost in a wonderland of food and possible bargains? Chuck vs. sirloin—which is better? Jumbo, large, medium, or small—which is the best buy? Do the best buys always come in the biggest boxes? Are generic foods the bargains they appear to be? Why do you always seem to end up with more items in the shopping cart than you intended putting there? Is coupon clipping worth the effort? These and other dilemmas of supermarket shopping are answered in a pamphlet that can teach you some good food shopping habits. Here's something that makes good sense, especially for only 20 cents.

Write for:
  Supermarket Survival

Cost: 20¢

Send to:
  National Dairy Council
  6300 N. River Rd.
  Rosemont, IL 60018-4233

Supermarket Survival

HELP FOR THE SINGLE COOK
★★★

Plenty of recipes can help you prepare a meal for four or more people, but what do you do if you're cooking only for yourself, or yourself and one other person? This 16-page booklet—hosted by Maytag's "lonely repairman"—offers day-by-day menu suggestions aimed at one or two people, complete with shopping lists and daylong schedule tips. You may not be turned on by all of the menu ideas, but the booklet's emphasis on preplanning and smart shopping is helpful in general terms.

Write for:
  Ol' Lonely's Guide to Cooking Alone

A SASE is a self-addressed stamped envelope.

Cost: 50¢

Send to:
Ol' Lonely Cookbook
Dept. FT
The Maytag Company
Newton, IA 50208

Ol' Lonely's Guide to Cooking Alone

SMART FOOD SHOPPING & FREEZER FOOD PLANS

★★★★

Organize your meal planning. Peruse the newspaper food ads. Plan your shopping trips. Spend only what you budget. These and other smart food shopping tips are offered by the Better Business Bureau in a free 16-page brochure, *Facts on Shopping for Food.* A second brochure, *Tips on Freezer Food Plans & Buying Beef in Bulk,* explains what freezer foods are, how they work, what they cost, what you'll get (and won't get) if you buy beef in bulk quantities. Some ads you see that promise big savings if you join freezer food clubs or buy a whole side of beef may not prove to be bargains at all. Helpful checklists in each brochure guide you toward smart and economical food buying.

Write for:
Facts on Shopping for Food (No. 235)
Tips on Freezer Food Plans & Buying Beef in Bulk (No. 24-200)

Cost: Free

Send to:
Council of Better Business Bureaus
1515 Wilson Blvd.
Arlington, VA 22209

BELOW FREEZING

★★★★

From the moment you purchase a frozen food item to the time you serve it, you play an important role in preserving the quality of the product. What you do to the food on the journey from store to home to freezer to table can affect the way it looks and tastes. By following a few simple practices, you can preserve the flavor, texture, and color of frozen foods and avoid needless waste. This handy 8½" × 14" chart-style *Frozen Food Storage Guide* from Pillsbury features hints on buying, storing, and using frozen foods; a list of foods and the length of time they may be stored; and tips on what to do with frozen foods during a power failure.

Write for:
Frozen Food Storage Guide

Cost: Free with a long SASE

Send to:
The Pillsbury Company
Consumer Response
P.O. Box 550
Minneapolis, MN 55440-0550

FOOD: HOW TO KEEP IT SAFE

★★

Jokes about getting food poisoning from school lunches or the food at the local greasy spoon restaurant stop being jokes when they happen to you or someone in your family. And even home cooking can cause food poisoning if food isn't carefully stored and prepared. *Foodborne Illness — The Consumer's Role in Its Prevention* explains about botulism, salmonella, staphylococcus, and C. perfringens, all of which are microorganisms that are found in food and can cause poisoning. There are valuable tips for consumers on buying, storing, and preparing foods to prevent contamination, and the emphasis of this three-page foldout is on cleanliness, consumer awareness, and common sense. The foldout is available while supplies last.

Write for:
Foodborne Illness — The Consumer's Role in Its Prevention

Cost: 75¢

Send to:
Order Department, OP-048
American Medical Association
P.O. Box 10946
Chicago, IL 60610

FOOD

CLEANING UP YOUR (KITCHEN) ACT

★★★

It's unlikely that Food and Drug Administration officials will ever show up at your door to inspect your kitchen for proper food storage. And maybe it's just as well—chances are your kitchen might not pass the test. For instance, do you store foods under the sink? What if the pipes start leaking, or an army of bugs decides to take up residence in this dark, damp spot? And how often do you clean the dust off the canned goods in your pantry? You should do it, otherwise harmful bacteria can easily be pushed into the food when you open the can. These and other important suggestions for cleaning up your storage act are included in this free booklet. Do you dare read it? The booklet is available while supplies last.

Write for:
Can Your Kitchen Pass the Food Storage Test?

Cost: Free (postcard requests only)

Send to:
FDA/Office of Consumer Affairs, HFE-88
5600 Fishers Lane
Rockville, MD 20857

Can Your Kitchen Pass the Food Storage Test

STORING FOOD SAFELY

★★

In this day of inflation, it's imperative to control food waste. You can do it with good food handling practices, and this folder from Pillsbury tells you how. You'll learn how to purchase and transport food from a safety standpoint and then how to store it properly—leftovers can save money, but unless you handle and store them quickly, the food won't be safe to eat. You'll also learn where in the kitchen germs are liable to be found and how to clean to avoid the risk of contamination. You'll review the four major types of food poisoning, and find out which foods are often involved and how cross-contamination frequently causes poisoning. Ask also for the fact sheet about preventing and eliminating insects in grain-based foods.

Write for:
Food Safety in the Home
Preventing or Eliminating Insects in Grain-Based Foods

Cost: Free with a long SASE

Send to:
The Pillsbury Company
Consumer Response
Box 550
Minneapolis, MN 55440-0550

KEEP COOL

★★★★

Meat and poultry is kept fresh for you until the moment you buy it in the store. Then it's up to you to keep it fresh until it's eaten, and that includes the leftovers. The U.S. Department of Agriculture's Food Safety and Inspection Service has a free 32-page book that tells how to keep food—especially meat and poultry—safe at home. Most of the approximately 2 million cases of food poisoning that occur annually are due to improper handling of food in the home, but you don't have to become a statistic if you follow the rules in this book. It tells why food spoils, how to keep food hot or cold enough to avoid spoilage, what to do if the freezer fails, and how to report food illness. A thorough and thoughtful examination of an important subject.

Write for:
The Safe Food Book

Cost: Free

Send to:
FSIS Publications Office
Room 1165-South
Washington, DC 20250

The Safe Food Book

Cooking Equipment and Techniques

PROS AND CONS OF COOKWARE

★★★

If you're about to equip your very own kitchen for the first time, or are looking to replace what you've got, read this foldout pamphlet about the advantages and disadvantages of different kinds of cookware. But read it *before* you buy. The pamphlet discusses the merits of aluminum, stainless steel, stainless steel with different bonded bottoms, porcelain, cast iron, tin, copper, glass, and glass ceramic. It also tells how to recognize quality cookware. There are some good tips for energy-efficient cooking and safety hints for handling cookware and using small appliances.

Write for:
Get a Handle on Cookware and Small Appliances

Cost: Free

Send to:
Farberware
Subsidiary of Kidde, Inc.
1500 Bassett Ave.
Bronx, NY 10461

THE FINE ART OF PEELING AN ORANGE

★★★★

Are you the sort of person who approaches the peeling of an orange as a scientific exercise, or do you always end up with a handful of squished fruit and juice up to your elbows? If you're the messy kind, you'll welcome this neat little gadget from Sunkist. It's a plastic peeler with a point on one end to score neat lines around the orange, and a curved blade at the other to remove the segments of peel. You should wind up with a cleanly skinned, unmessy orange. This little package also includes a lemon faucet for extracting juice from whole lemons. You don't even need to cut the top off the lemon. Just twist the faucet into the stem end of the lemon until the plastic threads are covered. The juice is retained in the top half of the faucet, which has a spout that can be opened for pouring the juice into a container. A handy little pair of kitchen tools.

Write for:
Orange peeler and lemon faucet

Cost: 50¢

Send to:
Sunkist Growers, Inc.
Dept. 9090, Box 4578
Overland Park, KS 66204

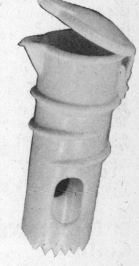

Orange peeler and lemon faucet

HOW TO USE YOUR PRESSURE COOKER

★★

Maybe you've had that pressure cooker stored on the top pantry shelf for years now, or maybe you just got one for a gift and have no idea how to use it. *A Guide for the 80's Cook* is an eight-page foldout that gives step-by-step instructions for pressure cooking and how it works, plus pointers for successful use and a meal-in-one dinner recipe. There are also simple tips on adapting conventional recipes to pressure cookers, quick cooling, use of other dishes and molds in the cooker, and cooking times for various altitudes.

Write for:
A Guide for the 80's Cook

Cost: Free

Send to:
Presto Brochures—CG
P.O. Box 1212
Eau Claire, WI 54702

COOKING UNDER PRESSURE

★★

The title of *Presto! A Party* is deceiving. This isn't about cooking for the impromptu cocktail party or entertaining unexpected guests—it's about cooking with a pressure cooker. Included in this eight-page foldout is brief information about pressure cooking

continued

FOOD

(don't remove the cover until pressure is completely reduced) and seven recipes from around the nation. Try the Midwest's Chicago Steak Rollups, the Creole Cod from the Gulf Coast, or the Southwest's Texas Barbeque Pot Roast. The menu suggestions are helpful.

Write for:
Presto! A Party

Cost: Free

Send to:
Presto Brochures—CG
P.O. Box 1212
Eau Claire, WI 54702

CUTLERY AND CARVING GUIDE

★★★★

Now here's a booklet that tells you how to carve everything! Clear diagrams show the correct (and easy) way to carve standing rib roasts, boneless roasts, pot roasts with bones, hams, leg of lamb, crown roasts, corned beef, and roast turkey or chicken. There are some excellent tips on carving at the table, some carving etiquette, and good information on cutlery care. You'll also find suggestions for which knife or kitchen tool to use for which job. An informative little 36-page book with clear, no-nonsense illustrations.

Write for:
Cutco Use/Care Carving Guide

Cost: $1.00

Send to:
Sales Promotion Dept.
ALCAS Cutlery Corp.
Box 810
1116 E. State St.
Olean, NY 14760

Cutco UseCare Carving Guide

THE CUTTING EDGE

★★★★

It's estimated the American homemaker uses a kitchen knife approximately 10,000 times each year, probably more than any other item in the home. Proper selection, use, and care will allow you to get the best from your cutlery. *Knife Knowledge* is a 24-page booklet that covers what's necessary to keep your knives in shape. You'll learn how to keep knives sharp (there are illustrated directions for using a sharpening steel), and a section on knife safety will encourage you to practice habits that prevent accidents and injuries. You'll also find step-by-step directions on how to bone chicken, fillet fish, and carve a turkey. Soon you will be slicing like a pro.

Write for:
Knife Knowledge

Cost: $1.00

Send to:
Kathleen Conroy
Manager of Public Relations
Chicago Cutlery
5420 North Country Road 18
Minneapolis, MN 55428

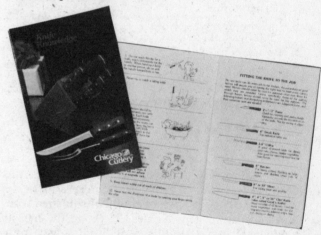

Knife Knowledge

POTS, PANS, AND MUFFIN TINS

★★★

Confused about cookware? Grandma always used cast iron; mom likes copper; you're hooked on the nonstick variety. This guide addresses consumers' frequently asked questions about aluminum, stainless steel, cast iron, copper, tin, chrominum-plated steel, porcelain on metal, and nonstick cookware. There's also a section on nonmetal cookware, and information about microwave oven cookware and accessories.

A SASE is a self-addressed stamped envelope.

In this useful publication you'll also find tips on cooking utensils; energy-saving cooking techniques; safety in the kitchen; healthful cooking; two pages of questions and answers about cookware; a list of terminology concerning finishes and decorations; an eight-page, illustrated metric guide listing cooking utensils and their preferred sizes; and a kitchen metric conversion table. A useful publication for the cook who's conscientious about equipment.

Write for:
Guide to Cookware and Bakeware

Cost: $1.25

Send to:
Cookware Manufacturers Association
P.O. Box J
Walworth, WI 53184

HOWS AND WHYS OF MICROWAVE OVENS

★★★★

One of the most popular convenience appliances for the kitchen today is a microwave oven. Is one for you? Many kinds of foods can be prepared in a microwave oven in a fraction of the time it takes by conventional heating or cooking methods. But is a microwave oven practical for your use? A new eight-page brochure from the Better Business Bureau, *Tips on Microwave Ovens*, tells what they are, how they differ from conventional ovens, what safety precautions they require, and what to look for when you go shopping for a microwave oven. The guide booklet suggests that you only buy the size unit you need and that you select a model that has only the features you'll use.

Write for:
Tips on Microwave Ovens (No. 311-4113)

Cost: Free

Send to:
Council of Better Business Bureaus
1515 Wilson Blvd.
Arlington, VA 22209

DINNER IN TEN MINUTES

★★★

Probably no other cooking appliance has opened up as many options for the consumer as the microwave oven. Foods are cooked faster and, in many instances, better in a microwave than by conventional cooking methods. Another unique benefit is quick defrosting

of foods. Read *How to Buy a Microwave Oven* by the Maytag Company before you purchase your new appliance. You'll learn about the wide range of sizes, types, and styles, as well as the many convenience features offered by today's models. The 16-page booklet covers construction and materials, warranties, cleaning, and programming the settings. Careful shopping will allow you to purchase a microwave oven with the features you want plus long life and dependability. The booklet is geared toward counter-top models and includes an evaluation checklist in the back.

Write for:
How to Buy a Microwave Oven

Cost: 25¢

Send to:
Consumer Information Center
How-To-Buy Booklets
Dept. FT
The Maytag Company
Newton, IA 50208

How to Buy a Microwave Oven

MICROWAVE OVEN RADIATION

★★★

On one hand, zapping your dinner to piping hot doneness in minutes is a marvelous convenience; on the other, how safe is microwave radiation, anyway? Concerned consumers will get the straight facts in this foldout leaflet. The Food and Drug Administration has regulated the manufacture of microwave ovens since 1971. On the basis of current knowledge about microwave radiation, the Agency believes that ovens that meet the FDA standard and are used according to the manufacturer's instructions are safe for use. In addition, you'll learn exactly what microwaves are, microwave oven safety standards, and the effects of microwaves on the body. There are tips and suggestions for safe microwave oven use and checking ovens for leakage.

continued

FOOD

Write for:
Microwave Oven Radiation (No. 533P)

Cost: Free

Send to:
Consumer Information Center
P.O. Box 100
Pueblo, CO 81002

GAS VS. ELECTRIC— THE RANGE FROM WHICH TO CHOOSE

★★★

It's time to outfit the kitchen with a new stove, but which should you buy? An electric or a gas range? There are advantages to both, and two booklets from Maytag—*How to Buy a Gas Range* and *How to Buy an Electric Range*—can help you choose. Whichever you decide, though, you'll find there are more options you'll need to consider before making your purchase. For instance, you can choose from free-standing ranges, eye-level ranges with microwave ovens, slide-ins, drop-ins, wall ovens, and cooktops in a variety of colors, and styles. Another factor to consider is how easy the appliance is to clean. The two 16-page booklets discuss the pros and cons as well as most of the features available on the ranges you'll find in the stores today. There is also a checklist for you to evaluate the models you are considering to make sure you get what your family needs.

Write for:
How to Buy a Gas Range
How to Buy an Electric Range

Cost: 25¢ each

Send to:
Consumer Information Center
How-To-Buy Booklets
Dept. FT
The Maytag Company
Newton, IA 50208

The Best of the Cookbooks

THE MICROWAVE GOURMET

★★★★

The microwave oven is the best-selling appliance in America. Nearly half of all U.S. households own a microwave oven, and experts predict by 1990 there will be one in 90 percent of all homes in this country. Yet the new cooking machine necessitates a few new cooking techniques, as Corning tells you in this colorful 64-page recipe book, *Microwave Cooking*. It's loaded with information along with yummy recipes. You'll learn the advantages of the microwave oven and how it works, and find cooking charts and detailed explanations of microwave cookware. There are recipes for appetizers and soups, eggs and roasts, ethnic foods and desserts. This is a comprehensive, mouth-watering book. Allow four to six weeks for delivery.

Write for:
Microwave Cooking

Cost: $2.00

Send to:
Microwave Cookbook Offer
P.O. Box 375
Big Flats, NY 14814-0375

Microwave Cooking

THIRTY-MINUTE MAIN MEALS

★★★★

Cooking a satisfying meal in 30 minutes is simple, according to the folks who whipped up this collection of a dozen main dish recipes using rice. For instance, why not try Apricot-Glazed Pork Chops and Curried Rice with steamed snow peas, and Strawberries in Brandied Sour Cream? Or how about Sherried Chicken With Golden Rice, Layered Fruit Salad, and French bread? Then there is Jambalaya with Confetti Broccoli, garlic bread, and Icy Pecan Pie. Not to skimp, the book also has recipes for every item suggested on a meal menu. Drawings show how to make each meal not only step-by-step, but minute-by-minute, so that you really do serve the whole meal in 30 minutes or less. Instructions are provided for both conventional and microwave ovens.

The recipe book was printed with two different covers, each book featuring a different rice. One features Mahatma extra long-grain enriched rice, the other Carolina enriched rice. Recipes are the same in both books except for the rice used. Specify if you want the Mahatma or Carolina recipe book.

Write for:
30 Minute Meals (Mahatma Rice)
30 Minute Meals (Carolina Rice)

Cost: 50¢ each

Send to:
Riviana Foods, Inc.
P.O. Box 2636
Houston, TX 77252

30 Minute Meals

BAKER'S DOZEN—DOUBLED

★★★★

Out of 13,000 recipes submitted to the Red Star Yeast's 1st Baking Recipe Exchange, these 26 were chosen as the best. The titles are intriguing, the ingredients unusual, and the short description of each recipe's history makes your fingers itch to try them out. Who can resist Aunt Mabel's Vita-B Bread packed with bran? Or Burlap Bread, an adaptation of an oatmeal bread with natural foods and high nutrition in mind? Yankee Bean Pot Bread is another mouth-waterer—one of its ingredients is bean and bacon soup. Besides the recipes, you'll learn some excellent bread-making and baking techniques. This little book is a winner.

Write for:
Prizewinning Recipes From Red Star's 1st Baking Recipe Exchange

Cost: 75¢

Send to:
1st Recipe Exchange
Universal Foods Corporation
433 E. Michigan
Milwaukee, WI 53201

OLD OR ETHNIC BAKING WINS THE DAY

★★★★

Yet more prizewinners from the Red Star Yeast people's baking contest. The third recipe exchange yielded 30 winners because of the high quality and strong appeal of the recipes. Some are ethnic and old world in origin; for instance, Yaroslav's Snack Bread is Russian and features chopped onion, hard-cooked eggs, bacon, and sour cream. Some are recipes that have been passed on through several generations, like My Sunshine Braid, which includes eggs, shredded carrots, seedless raisins, and grated orange rind. There's a Mexican pizza that combines a pizza crust with taco ingredients, and a sauerkraut rye bread. Tips on good baking are part of this illustrated booklet, which is a festival of unusual baking recipes for the innovative and inquisitive.

Write for:
The Best of Red Star's 3rd Baking Recipe Exchange

Cost: 75¢

Send to:
3rd Recipe Exchange
Universal Foods Corporation
433 E. Michigan
Milwaukee, WI 53201

NOT JUST FOR THANKSGIVING

★★★

Roast turkey is a favorite holiday tradition among many American families, but there's more than one way to cook turkey. *Turkey Made Easier*, a 20-page color-illustrated booklet from the Louis Rich Company, shows you how easy and nutritious it is to cook using boneless breast of turkey. In addition to traditional methods, most of the recipes also offer microwave instructions, making preparation faster and even easier. There are recipes for appetizers, salads, entrees, and sandwich ideas. South Sea Turkey Kabobs, Turkey in Tarragon Cream, Turkey Enchiladas, Basque Turkey—you'll want to gobble up every one.

Write for:
Turkey Made Easier

Cost: 50¢

Send to:
Turkey Made Easier
Louis Rich Company
P. O. Box 3976
Kankakee, IL 60902

FOOD

THE ROQUEFORT STORY

★★★

True Roquefort cheese comes only from Roquefort, France, where it is made of milk from the famous Lacaune sheep. This small, elegant booklet tells how the French eat their Roquefort cheese (just before dessert, with a good red wine), how to recognize and buy genuine Roquefort, and how to preserve and serve it. Then you'll find 49 recipes using Roquefort in appetizers and snacks (like a Roquefort sherry dip), dressing and salads, entrees (try Quiche Roquefort à la Canyon) and desserts. There are several exceptional color photographs in this small, delightful cookbook.

Write for:
Roquefort Recipe booklet

Cost: Free

Send to:
Roquefort Association, Inc.
P.O. Box 2908
Grand Central Station
New York, NY 10017

Roquefort Recipe booklet

DRESSING UP YOUR MENU

★★★★

If your household is like many, preparing meals has become a race against the clock. There just isn't time to experiment with unusual ingredients or recipes that take extra time to fix. This is why Hidden Valley Ranch put together the recipes in this full-color 16-page booklet. You may not have known that Hidden Valley Ranch salad dressings can replace many ingredients commonly used in cooking. Whether it's a dip, appetizer, soup, sauce, vegetable, pasta, seafood, poultry, or meat entree, each recipe gets a kick from the hearty blend of spices used in the dressing mix. You'll find many uses for the dressing, as a dry mix or a prepared sauce. There is calorie and nutrition information, too. And when your family compli-

ments you on the meal, you don't *have* to tell them how easy it was.

Write for:
More Than a Salad Dressing

Cost: 50¢

Send to:
The Clorox Company
Department CC-FT
P.O. Box 24305
Oakland, CA 94623

More Than a Salad Dressing

COUNTRY INN COOKING

★★★★

Country inns across the nation are usually known for their imaginative menus and high-quality food. Selected innkeepers were asked to create recipes using Hidden Valley Ranch dressings and came up with some delicious ideas for salads, entrees, and main dishes. These have been collected in a color-filled recipe book that offers some distinctive recipes from some of the most famous country inns in America. Some examples: Shakertown ham in aspic from Kentucky, grilled salmon from Oregon, roasted quail with liver mousse from New Mexico, chilled chicken salad with fruit and rice from Indiana, and Honey Run Ranch burgers from Ohio. Real taste treats here for the gourmet.

Write for:
Country Inn Recipes

Cost: $1.00

Send to:
The Clorox Company
Dept. CC-FT
P.O. Box 24305
Oakland, CA 94623

A SASE is a self-addressed stamped envelope.

Country Inn Recipes

APPLE ENCYCLOPEDIA

★★★★

You'll find a lot more than just apple recipes in this paperback book. It's literally a mini-encyclopedia about apples, giving you history and folklore, health and nutrition notes, descriptions and color photographs of apple varieties, and information on buying and handling apples. The 450 apple recipes cover appetizers, soups (Creamy Apple Soup), main dishes, salads, sandwiches, breads, beverages, desserts, sauces and toppings, candies and confections, and jellies and preserves. There are canning, freezing, and preserving notes, and quickie uses for apples all day long. A real bargain, too—you can have this $3.95, 220-page book for only $2.00.

Write for:
Apple Kitchen Cook Book

Cost: $2.00

Send to:
New York & New England Apple Institute
Box 768
Westfield, MA 01086

A GRAND (MARNIER) COOKBOOK

★★★★

You may have sipped Grand Marnier liqueur after an elegant meal. But have you thought of cooking with it? James Beard, the noted chef, created 55 recipes specifically using this liqueur in meat and fish dishes—Loin of Pork au Grand Marnier, for example; fruits and vegetables, like Asparagus with Sauce Maltaise and a fresh fruit salad laced with the liqueur; and desserts that go on and on. French pound cake, frozen soufflé, puddings, trifles, mousses of all denominations, tortes, and tarts are all enlivened and graced with this prized liqueur. The color photographs are works of art.

Write for:
The Grand Grand Marnier Cookbook

Cost: $1.50

Send to:
The Grand Marnier Cookbook
P.O. Box 1134
Maple Plain, MN 55348

WHO'S FOR A PEANUT BUTTER OMELET?

★★★★

A St. Louis doctor, looking for an easily digested, high-protein food for his patients, invented peanut butter in 1890. Since that quiet beginning, peanut butter has become a staple food of this nation. Here's a booklet from the Oklahoma Peanut Commission featuring dozens of delicious-sounding recipes and menu ideas using peanut butter and peanuts. You'll be surprised to find them in pies, cakes and frostings, ice cream, puddings, and soups, as well as sandwiches, main dishes, and breads. And don't forget peanut butter omelets and milkshakes.

Write for:
It's Easy to Be a Gourmet With Peanuts

Cost: $1.00

Send to:
Oklahoma Peanut Commission
Box D
Madill, OK 73446

DON'T GO EASY ON THE GARLIC!

★★★★

At last, something special for garlic lovers. The Fresh Garlic Association offers a 16-page booklet with great garlic recipes from great American restaurants. You may not have realized just how versatile fresh garlic is until you've checked out this cookbook. It has recipes for a garlic soufflé from California, Sole Verte with Dill Sauce from Ohio, a Mediterranean garlic sauce from Chicago, Garlic Broccoli Salad from Washington, DC, and other recipes using garlic with pheasant, eggplant, pasta, squab, and rack of lamb. You'll recognize the famous restaurants whose chefs have helped earn their reputations serving these garlic delights.

Write for:
Great Garlic Recipes from Great American Restaurants

continued

FOOD

Cost: $1.00

Send to:
Fresh Garlic Association
P.O. Box 2151
Gilroy, CA 95021

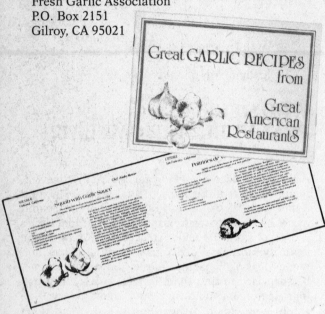

Great Garlic Recipes From Great American Restaurants

NEW TASTES WITH TUNA
★★★★

In 1903, the first 700 cases of tuna were packed commercially at San Pedro, California. Today, the United States packs well over 30 million cases of tuna each year, and Americans eat an average of 3.2 pounds a year each. Tuna, in a word, has been happily accepted in the American diet, and this book of delicious tuna recipes should stimulate even more interest in this high-protein food.

There are appetizers, soups (Tuna Gazpacho Blanco, Tuna Bisque), eight sandwich recipes, skillet meals, wonderful dishes for children (Bird's Nest Tuna Salad, Tuna Kittens, Tuna Party Cones), and lots of salads. There are also hot meals made with tuna, company specials, diet menus, and one-dish dinners. You'll go through your 3.2 pounds of tuna in no time with these 27 pages of terrific ideas.

Write for:
Everybody in the Kitchen With Tuna

Cost: 50¢ (in coin or stamps)

Send to:
Tuna Research Foundation, Inc.
1101 Seventeenth St., N.W.
Suite 910
Washington, DC 20036

QUICKER BAKED GOODS
★★★★

A new quick-rise yeast from Red Star and Universal Foods Corporation can save time while baking—it rises up to 50 percent faster than you're used to. Learn how the new yeast works and what you can do with it from this free brochure, which includes six recipes: cinnamon twists, pecan rolls, onion bread, pizza (with suggestions for sauce and toppings, too), egg twists, and buttermilk pan rolls.

If you want more, the brochure includes an order form for the *Red Star Quick-Rise Yeast Recipes* book. But for starters, the free brochure is a real bargain.

Write for:
The Red Star Quick-Rise Recipe Collection

Cost: Free with a long SASE

Send to:
Quick-Rise Recipe Collection
Universal Foods Corporation
433 E. Michigan
Milwaukee, WI 53201

A CORN SYRUP COOKBOOK
★★★★

The nostalgic cover is a reproduction of a Karo corn syrup cookbook that was published in 1910. Inside are more than 200 recipes, many from the past but updated to meet the modern cook's emphasis on quick main dish cooking. Apart from the main dishes, you'll find out how to use corn syrup in vegetables, salads, desserts, cakes, cookies, and a variety of old and new candy recipes. There are recipes for beverages like Strawberry-Tea Punch, sangría, hot spiced wine, and Irish coffee, together with a section on how to use corn syrup in canning. The spiral-bound booklet includes some mouth-watering color photographs and reproductions of Karo corn syrup ads through the years. An attractive 128-page cookbook.

Write for:
The Karo Cookbook

Cost: $2.00

Send to:
Karo Cookbook
Dept. KCB-X
Box 307
Coventry, CT 06238

A SASE is a self-addressed stamped envelope.

MMMM, MAPLE SYRUP

★★★

Maple syrup lovers who eat pancakes just so they can drown the stacks in pure maple syrup won't be able to resist these two offerings. Every recipe in *The Official Vermont Maple Cookbook* lists maple syrup or maple cream (also known as maple butter) as one of the ingredients. From beverages, breads, and main dishes, through cakes, desserts, and fruit dishes, this booklet has 80 tasty treats. Try the traditional Country Baked Ham or the Butternut Loaf, a Vermont family favorite, or go for the more exotic Broiled and Curried Scallops. If those don't tempt you, you can always look in *Pure Vermont Maple Syrup Recipes*. This little pamphlet has 18 more recipes featuring maple syrup and includes a brief description of how the syrup is made.

Write for:
The Official Vermont Maple Cookbook
Pure Vermont Maple Syrup Recipes

Cost: $1.25

Send to:
Dakin Farm
Route 7
Ferrisburg, VT 05456

HONEY WITH EVERYTHING

★★★★

Here are some delicious ways to introduce honey into your meals—from jams and preserves to main dishes, meats, and vegetables. You'll be intrigued at the unexpected dishes you can dress up with a dollop of honey—like a vegetable borscht, Pasta Primavera, Take Along Lentil Casserole, and Shrimp Singapore. There are breads, butters, jellies, chutneys, and some luscious desserts including Devilish Pecan Pie, Honey and Nut Flutes ("like a baklava without all the bother"), and Strawberry Cream Cheese Pie. Lots of facts about honey, too. Did you know that the most popular honey flavors in California are clover, followed by alfalfa, sage and sage-buckwheat, orange, and a blend of floral honeys? Well, you know now. And if you want to know how to choose a honey to complement a certain meal or dish, remember that the lighter the color of the honey, the milder its flavor.

Write for:
Honey Naturally

Cost: $1.00

Send to:
California Honey Advisory Board
P.O. Box 265
Sonoma, CA 95476

Honey Naturally

Mostly Main Dishes

VERSATILE TURKEY

★★★

Delicious, nutritious, versatile, and economical. That's how the California Turkey Industry Board describes turkey, and they justify their claims with the recipes in this cookbook that they offer for a quarter. Turkey is a smart buy because it's less expensive than most other meats, has the same high-quality protein content, but contains less fat, cholesterol, and calories. Thirty turkey recipes are offered in this attractive 16-page booklet, with black-and-white photos showing many of the dishes. They include Turkey Tenderloin, Almond-Crusted Turkey Steaks, Sherried Turkey Wings, Southern-Style Turkey Drumsticks, Stuffed Turkey Thighs Florentine, and Turkey Tamale Pie. Included are directions for roasting turkey and recipes for half a dozen different turkey stuffings. A lot of turkey talk for a quarter.

Write for:
30 Ways to Serve California Turkey

Cost: 25¢

Send to:
California Turkey Industry Board
814 14th St. #3
Modesto, CA 95354

FOOD

EVERYONE'S SECOND FAVORITE BIG BIRD
★★★

Even if you're no stranger to roasting a turkey, you can learn a trick or two from a new booklet about America's favorite holiday Big Bird. This good-looking publication is stuffed with expert advice on how to handle a turkey from the time you buy it to when you wrap up the leftovers. Easy-to-use charts offer information on thawing, cooking times and temperatures, and recipes to round out your meal. For inexperienced carvers, there is a step-by-step illustrated section on how to carve a turkey. Check out the recipes for savory bread, oyster, cornbread, or fruit stuffing; turkey gravies; turkey-broccoli casserole; turkey salad; and turkey gumbo soup. This free 24-page booklet comes from the U.S. Department of Agriculture's Food Safety and Inspection Service. Most government publications are available while supplies last.

Write for:
Talking About Turkey

Cost: Free

Send to:
FSIS Publications Office
Room 1165-South
Washington, DC 20250

Talking About Turkey

LET'S TALK TURKEY
★★★

Turkey is considered to be one of the most nutritious and healthful meat sources, yet the price of turkey is often a real bargain. If you think turkey is just for **Thanksgiving**, check out this recipe booklet from the **Louis Rich Company**. *Turkey Anytime* is a 32-page pamphlet containing color photos and recipes for over two dozen delicious meals made with fresh turkey cuts, from Turkey Cordon Bleu to a hearty turkey Harvest Soup. The booklet has a section featuring low-cal entrees and one for people who love to barbecue. Singles will appreciate the chapter "For One or Two." It offers tips on storing and reheating leftovers, and scales down recipes for today's smaller households; of course, cooks with larger families can always multiply the proportions to feed as many mouths as they need to. If you love turkey, you'll like this book.

Write for:
Turkey Anytime

Cost: $1.00

Send to:
Louis Rich "Turkey Anytime" Cookbook Offer
3 Stuart Drive
P.O. Box 4448
Kankakee, IL 60902

Turkey Anytime

A CHICKEN IN EVERY POT
★★

Are you bored with your same old chicken recipes? Then maybe you'd like to bring out your pressure cooker and experiment with some of the chicken dishes in this eight-page folder. Here are seven poultry recipes from around the world as well as brief information about pressure cooking. Try Spain's Arroz Con Pollo, Italy's Chicken Cacciatore, the classic French Coq au Vin, or Chicken Paprika from Hungary. Also included are Sweet 'n Sour Chicken from China, Greek Lemon Herbed Chicken, and an Americanized version of an East Indian chicken dish.

Write for:
A Chicken in Every Pot

Cost: Free

Send to:
Presto Brochures—CG
P.O. Box 1212
Eau Claire, WI 54702

90

A SASE is a self-addressed stamped envelope.

FOR FOOD PROCESSOR COOKS
★★★

If you use your food processor a lot and are running short of recipes to try, here's an attractive little book from KitchenAid to help you out. Entrees include Portugese Stew, Spring Scallops and Fruit Salad with Ginger Dressing, and Thai Curry Beef (with this one you also get the recipe for homemade curry paste). Desserts offer Cold Lime Soufflé, Walnut Mandarin Torte, and Chocolate Cappuccino Pie—cappuccino custard in a dark cookie crust topped with whipped cream.

Each recipe is accompanied by preparation and cooking times. There's also a good list of do-it-ahead staples that can save time when you actually come to cook, among them some interesting herb butters and a parsley vinaigrette that can double as a marinade for poultry or a sauce for steamed vegetables. Some good, original ideas here.

Write for:
Gourmet Express

Cost: 50¢

Send to:
Consumer Information and Product Publicity
KitchenAid Division
Hobart Corporation
Grant Building South
Troy, OH 45374

Gourmet Express

"THE BUTCHER" SHARES HIS RECIPES
★★

Pressed for recipe ideas for your pressure cooker? In this ten-page foldout, Merle Ellis, a syndicated food columnist, shares some know-how about pressure cooking and offers nine main dish recipes using chicken, beef, and pork. Detailed instructions, accompanied by line drawings, show you how to cut up a chicken, a seven-bone beef pot roast, and a pork roast.

According to Ellis, meat cooks three to ten times faster in a pressure cooker than by any other cooking method, and it's a good way to make efficient use of less expensive cuts. Cut up a chicken, for instance, and use the breast in chicken tarragon; throw the other pieces into the pot for chicken stock; then remove the meat from the bones to make a dish of chicken enchiladas with mole sauce.

Write for:
Puttin' on the Pressure with Merle Ellis

Cost: Free

Send to:
Presto Brochures—CG
P.O. Box 1212
Eau Claire, WI 54702

EMPTY-NESTERS' COOKBOOK
★★

If there are just two of you at the table, it's easy to run out of new recipe ideas, but here is a little brochure with 14 recipes especially tailored for two—like Chicken Marengo, Broccoli Frittata, Comida Mexicana, Hot Monterrey Bake, Pork Chops with Cumin Rice, Virgin Islands Chicken and Rice, Tahitian Ham and Rice, and other delicious meals. Tips are included on how to serve perfect rice for two. A nicely balanced selection of dishes, and a real bargain for anyone who cooks for two on a regular basis.

Write for:
Easy 'n Thrifty Recipes for 2

Cost: Free with a long SASE

Send to:
The Rice Council
P.O. Box 740121
Houston, TX 77274

WELCOME TO DIXIELAND!
★★★

Why do Southern cooks love black-eyed beans or peas? (If it's eaten fresh, it's a pea; if it's left to mature and cured until dry, it's a bean.) Black-eyes are the favorite vegetable of the Deep South because of their rich and robust flavor, and they have nutritional qualities that make them stick to the ribs. Black-eyes are also economical, costing less per serv-
continued

FOOD

ing than most other main-dish ingredients. Here's a recipe book and folder to introduce you to the wonders of black-eyed beans—how to soak and cook them and how to use them in your meals. Recipes include Plantation Black-eyes, New Orleans Black-eye Salad, Texas Black-eye Chili, and Bayou Black-eyed Chicken. Why not try this free entree into the world of Dixie-style cooking?

Write for:
  Favorite Black-eye Recipes from Dixieland

Cost: Free with a long SASE

Send to:
  Californic Dry Bean Advisory Board
  531-D N. Alta Ave.
  Dinuba, CA 93618

THE JOY OF EGGS
★

This little folder from the Georgia Egg Commission celebrates the ease of cooking in small quantities with eggs. The eight recipes are simple, low in calories, imaginative, and often use leftovers. Chicken and Eggs features hard-cooked eggs with the yolks combined with cooked chicken, mayonnaise, and dry mustard to make a kind of chicken-deviled eggs. There's an apple-custard pie that sounds light and delicious and a nutritious strawberry soda hyped with a fresh egg. You'll also learn the correct way to hard-cook—not hard-boil—an egg, and there are hints for storing and using eggs economically. Your dollar will get you these and a selection of other egg recipes.

Write for:
  Eggs Are for Joy (Just Older Youth)

Cost: $1.00 and a long SASE

Send to:
  Free Things
  Georgia Egg Commission
  State Farmers' Market
  Forest Park, GA 30050

CATCHING UP WITH KETCHUP
★★

Ketchup is the stuff kids spread all over hot dogs, hamburgers, and the kitchen table, right? Yes, but here's a pocket-sized leaflet with 22 recipes that include ketchup in such diverse dishes as Paella, Tuna Creole, Old-Fashioned Bean Soup, Meatballs Gingerly Spiced, Bayou Jambalaya, and Sweet &

Spicy Pork Chops. There are some good kid-pleasers, too, like Sloppy Joes and Skillet Spaghetti, along with barbecued chicken, a couple of homemade salad dressings, and a trio of easy party dips. If your kids love anything with ketchup on it, maybe you can expand their culinary horizons by offering one of these dishes with ketchup *in* it.

Write for:
  Put Your Best Foot Forward With Heinz Ketchup

Cost: Free with a SASE

Send to:
  Put Your Best Foot Forward
  c/o Heinz U.S.A.
  P.O. Box 57
  Pittsburgh, PA 15230-0057

MICROWAVE BROWNING
★

If your microwave oven doesn't have a browning element and you wish the meats you cook in the microwave looked browner or crisp on top, check into the things you can do with Kitchen Bouquet microwave browning spray. This little color folder tells about the browning spray and offers seven recipes, including Roast Chicken With Herbs, Roast Beef With Bearnaise Sauce, Garlic-Glazed Leg of Lamb, Browned Pork Chops, and Chicken Cacciatore. There's even a recipe for Teriyaki Fish. Here's an almost-free opportunity to broaden your microwave cooking horizons.

Write for:
  New Microwave Meal Ideas

Cost: 25¢

Send to:
  The Clorox Company
  Corporate Communications Dept.
  P.O. Box 24305
  Oakland, CA 94623

NUTS ABOUT MICROWAVE COOKING?
★★★

Now here's a terrific little cookbook. The 4000 peanut growers of Oklahoma and their families have put together a 32-page booklet of recipes and menu ideas for using peanuts in microwave oven cooking. You may be surprised to discover you can use peanuts and peanut butter in microwaved main dishes, cakes and frostings, cookies, bars, muffins, pies, and candies. You also learn tips about browning agents and other coatings, along with instructions on how to make candy in the microwave oven. Given all these fun recipes with peanuts, you should have no trouble getting the kids to help out in the kitchen.

Write for:
Microwave Magic

Cost: $1.00

Send to:
Oklahoma Peanut Commission
Box D
Madill, OK 73442

Microwave Magic

PLENTY OF PEANUTS
★★★

There's just no knowing where you'll find a peanut. If your family's acquaintance with the ubiquitous nut is limited to peanut butter, peanut brittle, and peanuts straight from the package, educate them with some of these imaginative dishes. There's Peanut Vegetable Soup, Quail with Peanut Dressing, Peanut Chicken with Mustard Sauce, and Peanutty Pesto Sauce for Pasta. Then you get Peanutty Gingerbread, Peanut Butter Chocolate Ice Cream, Peanut Butter Mashmallow Fudge, and a whole slew of delicious-sounding cakes, cookies, and pies. There's even a cheesecake with peanuts. Lots of unusual nutty ideas in this illustrated 14-page publication. You even learn three ways to roast peanuts, along with some tips for using the blender and food processor to make your own peanut butter.

Write for:
People Pleasin' Peanut Treats

Cost: Free with a long SASE

Send to:
Georgia Peanut Commission
P.O. Box 967
Tifton, GA 31793

NEW ANGLE ON HEALTHY EATING
★

For change-of-pace cooking, try using corn germ to bread meat, fish, or vegetables. Or use wheat germ as a delicious thickener, browning agent, or additive to everyday dishes. These two modest recipe folders describe ways to use wheat and corn germ that you never dreamed of—how about Italian dumpling casserole? These are ideas for health food aficionados and cooks who like to experiment with new tastes.

Write for:
Corn Germ Recipes
Raw Wheat Germ Recipes

Cost: 25¢ and a long SASE

Send to:
Fearn Soya Foods
Dept. CC-WC
4520 James Place
Melrose Park, IL 60160

COOKING WITH SOY
★

Soy granules are a good source of protein and can be used as a meat extender or as a base for soup, cookies, or salad dressing. Soy powder is a high-protein base for soy milk, soy yogurt, soy custard, and no-milk ice cream. These two folders from Fearn Soya Foods contain recipes and nutritional information for both soya powder and soya granules, and there are some interesting recipes like vegetable chilis, granule pizza, and wheatless crackers.

Write for:
Soya Granules Recipes
Soya Powder Recipes

Cost: 25¢ and a long SASE

Send to:
Fearn Soya Foods
Dept. CC-SF
4520 James Place
Melrose Park, IL 60160

FOOD

TAKING THE HAM OUT OF THE BURGER

★

These four pamphlets contain a variety of recipes for vegetarian burgers and other meatless dishes. One concentrates on sunflower mix recipes; another on a breakfast patty mix of sesame seeds, oats, and soy; another on sesame mix; and the last on Brazil nut mix recipes. There are 41 recipes in all, which should give you plenty of meatless meals and a better-looking food budget.

Write for:
Vegetarian Burgers Recipes

Cost: 25¢ and a long SASE

Send to:
Fearn Soya Foods
Dept. CC-VB
4520 James Place
Melrose Park, IL 60160

ALL ABOUT ALMONDS

★

What comes in the following varieties: nonpareil, mission, neplus, and peerless? If you don't know, brush up your knowledge of almonds with this eight-page foldout, *Almonds for Goodness Sake.* Learn the various forms in which almonds are sold, and read up on the almond's history, cultivation, and processing. There are also tips on roasting, toasting, blanching, chopping, grinding, and storing, and quick ideas for dressing up all kinds of dishes with almonds.

No recipes in that one, but another folder, *Almonds From California... Every Day,* offers about a dozen ideas for lunches and dinners, snacks and desserts. Among them—Chicken Noodles Almondine, uncooked almond fudge, and almond cheese wafers.

Write for:
Almonds for Goodness Sake
Almonds From California... Every Day

Cost: Free with a long SASE

Send to:
Almond Board
Dept. FT
P.O. Box 15920
Sacramento, CA 95852

NUTTY IDEAS ABOUT ALMONDS

★★

Eat them plain or crush, chop, sliver, toast, blanch, or roast them—or use them in these unusual recipes. This 12-page pamphlet, free from the Almond Board of California, has dinner, breakfast, and brunch ideas, plus suggestions for soups, sandwiches, vegetable dishes, sweets, and snacks—all using almonds. The California Almond Fettucini sounds good, or how about Almond Spinach Bisque, or healthy Bean Sprout Almond Salad? There's a nutrition chart—almonds are good for you—and tips on how to roast, toast, split, blanch, chop, grind, and store almonds.

Write for:
Almonds Add a Lot!

Cost: Free with a long SASE

Send to:
Almond Board
Dept. FT
P.O. Box 15920
Sacramento, CA 95852

Almonds Add a Lot!

SWEET ON SAUERKRAUT

★

Sauerkraut and sole? Why not? Here's a handful of recipes that prove sauerkraut to be more versatile than you may have given it credit for. The sheet of 15 recipes is perforated so that you can tear the recipes apart and file them with other favorites. If you enjoy sauerkraut in a reuben sandwich or with sausage or franks, try it in more sophisticated style, with fillet of sole, braised duck, or even as a stuffing in tomatoes. These recipes are both unusual and simple to follow.

A SASE is a self-addressed stamped envelope.

Write for:
Sauerkraut Recipes

Cost: 50¢

Send to:
J.G. Van Holten & Son, Inc.
P.O. Box 66
Waterloo, WI 53594

SWEET NEWS IS NOT NEW

★★

What has been used as a natural sweetener for centuries in China, India, and Arabia; is rich in calcium, potassium, and phosphorous; and is said to be superior in nutritional value to sugar, honey, maple syrup, or any other sweetener? The answer is molasses. Learn about the many benefits of molasses, how to use it in cooking, and how to avoid a bitter taste by trying high grade, pure, unsulphured molasses made from 100 percent pure, natural sugar cane juice. There are plenty of simple recipes in this free 28-page booklet, as well as lots of information and tips about molasses. Get some new ideas about using molasses in cereals, sandwiches, soups, salad dressings, and meat, poultry, and fish dishes. Free with the booklet is a 25¢ coupon toward a purchase of Grandma's Molasses.

Write for:
The Surprise Natural Sweetener

Cost: Free with a long SASE

Send to:
The Molasses Information Network
Box 9179
Morristown, NJ 07960

GOOD THINGS IN SMALL PACKAGES

★★

Canned shrimp on your pantry shelf is always a useful standby when you haven't had time to get to the store but you want something a bit more special than tuna. *Shrimp in a Hurry,* a useful 16-page booklet available free from Robinson Canning Co., has 28 tempting shrimp recipes for dips, appetizers, soups, salads, main dishes, and collector's items such as Shrimp Toast, Shrimp Soufflé, and Shrimp Perdu. Don't pass up the helpful tips explaining how to get the best taste, texture, and cooking results when you're using canned shrimp. For example, if you chill the unopened cans for a few hours before use, shrimp salad or shrimp cocktail will have extra "bite."

Write for:
Shrimp in a Hurry

Cost: Free

Send to:
Robinson Canning Co., Inc.
P.O. Box 4248
New Orleans, LA 70178

Shrimp in a Hurry

COOKING WITH OYSTERS

★

Oysters are fascinating creatures; they produce pearls, and they're the darlings of the gourmet. *Can-venient Ways With Oysters,* as the unfortunate name suggests, deals with the kind that you get in the can, not on the half-shell. It's a free ten-page recipe leaflet from Robinson Canning Co., Inc., and although it's short on glamour, the recipes are interesting—oyster patties, scalloped oysters, and oyster pie, as well as more familiar favorites like stew and gumbo. There's a Creole touch to these concoctions that may seem exotic to those from other parts of the country. The booklet also tells you how oysters live, breed, and make pearls.

Write for:
Can-venient Ways With Oysters

Cost: Free

Send to:
Robinson Canning Co., Inc.
P.O. Box 4248
New Orleans, LA 70178

Prices are for single items only; prices and information are accurate at time of publication.

FOOD

GRAB A CRAB
★★

Is crabmeat your idea of bliss? If so, you obviously need the recipe for a quiche with the tempting name of Crab Meat Bliss. It's one of the dishes in *Can-venient Ways With Crab Meat,* an unpretentious but endearing (and free) 14-page booklet from Robinson Canning Co., Inc. In addition to the story of how crabs live, where they're found, and what *they* like to eat, there are 13 recipes for crabmeat appetizers, main dishes, and dips. Did you know you can make an unusual omelette with crabmeat and Tabasco sauce, or that crabmeat, shrimp, and cheese can be combined in a baked seafood salad? Or how about getting out the cayenne and green onions for a pan of deviled crab?

Write for:
   Can-venient Ways With Crab Meat

Cost: Free

Send to:
   Robinson Canning Co., Inc.
   P.O. Box 4248
   New Orleans, LA 70178

Pasta, Rice, and Legumes

GIVING GARLIC ITS DUE
★★

What's pasta without garlic? What garlic is to pasta it can also be to vegetables, says the Fresh Garlic Association. Whether it's an Italian-style vegetable and pasta concoction or a Chinese broccoli stir-fry, fresh garlic can lift vegetables out of the ordinary and make them delectable and even the stars of the meal. Two recipe folders introduce you to using garlic in pasta and vegetable dishes such as Garlic Mostaccioli, pesto for pasta, Linguine with Garlic Clam Sauce, Garden Vegetable Fettuccine, Basque-Style Eggplant Casserole, Snow Peas Canton, Garlic Kebabs, and minced garlic in a Bloody Mary Party Soup. Some free garlic goodies here.

Write for:
   Garlic & Pasta Go Together
   Garlic & Vegetables Go Together

Cost: Free with a long SASE

Send to:
   The Fresh Garlic Association
   c/o Caryl Saunders Associates
   2121 Leavenworth St.
   San Francisco, CA 94133

DON'T PASS UP THE PASTA
★

You bought all that macaroni on sale and don't know what to do with it? Try Un-Potato Salad. Want some different hors d'oeuvres? How about Cocktail Meatballs Marinara? Can't think of a thing for dessert? Don't miss Tagliatelle con le Mele Florentina. Even if you can't pronounce it, this marvelous concoction of noodles, apple sauce, almonds, and raisins will make you fluent in Italian cooking at least. This foldout contains 13 recipes that will make your friends wonder where you learned that special Italian touch. They're all easy to prepare, too, from ingredients you probably have on the shelf.

Write for:
   Pasta: Mama DeDomenico's Favorite Recipes

Cost: Free with a long SASE

Send to:
   Golden Grain Macaroni Co.
   P.O. Box 24204
   Oakland, CA 94623

Pasta: Mama DeDomenico's Favorite Recipes

SEVENTEEN RECIPES FOR RICE LOVERS
★

If you can't eat one more forkful of chop suey but would welcome other ideas for rice dishes, here are 17 of them. *Favorite Recipes From the Rice Growing States* gives absolutely no product information, which is surprising since it's published by The Rice Council of America. It simply lists in its six small pages

A SASE is a self-addressed stamped envelope.

some unusual recipe ideas, all of which sound delicious. You can try, for instance, Shrimp Louisiana Casserole, Mincemeat Rice, Texas Hash, Mississippi Rice Salad, or Jambalaya. There's also a classic creamy rice pudding.

Write for:
Favorite Recipes From the Rice Growing States

Cost: Free

Send to:
The Rice Council
P.O. Box 740121
Houston, TX 77274

NICE RICE, OOODLES OF NOODLES

★★

Creative Cooking With Rice-A-Roni® and Noodle Roni® is a tiny foldout with 14 recipes for unusual rice dishes. Wild Curry With Almonds—doesn't that sound good? It's a crunchy, semisweet combination of spices, onion, apple and lemon juice, banana, and slivered almonds. How does Rice-A-Roni Egg Fu Yung sound? Or Fettucine Riviera, with chicken, ham, and mushrooms? There's an interesting Quiche-A-Roni, and Clams Parmesano is a light, tempting idea for seafood lovers. These recipes call for a lot of good, fresh ingredients, and they're very easy and suitable for cooks of all skill levels. Interesting ideas in a mini-size foldout.

Write for:
Creative Cooking with Rice-A-Roni® and
  Noodle Roni® No. 2

Cost: Free with a long SASE

Send to:
Golden Grain Macaroni Co.
P.O. Box 24204
Oakland, CA 94623

BROWN RICE RECIPES

★★

Brown rice is the whole grain rice from which only the inedible hulls have been removed by mechanical action. It isn't milled or polished and therefore retains a natural brown coating of bran. Its flavor is often described as "nutty," and its texture is slightly chewy. For brown rice lovers, here is a small booklet with a dozen recipes, including entrees, side dishes, and desserts. They include Stuffed Zucchini, Herbed

Pork Chops and Brown Rice, a cheeseburger skillet dinner, Cornish Hens Bombay, Shrimp Fried Brown Rice, Sherried Mushroom Rice, Brown Rice Custard, and Rice-and-Peaches-and-Cream. There are actually two cookbooks with the same recipes, but one calls for River Rice natural brown rice and the other for Mahatma long-grain brown rice. Specify which recipe booklet you want when ordering.

Write for:
Your Collection of Special Recipes (River Rice)
Your Collection of Special Recipes (Mahatma Rice)

Cost: 50¢ each

Send to:
Riviana Foods, Inc.
P.O. Box 2636
Houston, TX 77252

COOKING RICE JUST RIGHT

★★

If you want to know more about rice and its place in the family of nutritional foods, or you just can't seem to get your rice as light and fluffy as you'd like, here are two small booklets to help you. *A Rice Primer,* which is free, tells nutritional facts about foods and the vitamins and minerals they provide; explains how to read package labels about enrichment and nutrition; describes the basic food groups; and gives you some facts about rice cookery. *The Success Rice Cooking Guidebook* tells how you can prepare successful rice, offers 24 recipes, and introduces something new: Now you can boil rice in a plastic bag to ensure perfect results. The booklet includes a coupon for 25¢ off your next purchase of Success Boil-in-Bag rice.

Write for:
A Rice Primer
The Success Rice Cooking Guidebook

Cost: Free (Primer)
  35¢ (Guidebook)

Send to:
Riviana Foods, Inc.
P.O. Box 2636
Houston, TX 77252

The Success Rice Cooking Guidebook

FOOD

RICE FOR BEGINNERS

★

Young cooks, in age or experience, won't have to worry about serving semi-cooked or scorched rice if they pick up this free little booklet about cooking perfect rice. *Rice 'n Easy* consists of 14 pages filled with lots of drawings and simple step-by-step recipes for getting rice right every time. Some good recipes here for just the price of a postage stamp.

Write for:
Rice 'n Easy

Cost: Free with a long SASE

Send to:
The Rice Council
P.O. Box 740121
Houston, TX 77274

HEALTHY AND TASTY

★

Rice fits in perfectly with all the changes a lot of people need in their diets to make for better health. Rice is rich in complex carbohydrates, virtually sodium-free, and low in calories. It's also cholesterol-free and contains only a trace of fat. Facts like these will encourage the health-conscious cook to try the eight taste-tempting recipes in this free folder. A sampling of ways to add variety to your rice cooking menus: Caribbean Island Rice, Turkey Oriental Soup, and Rice Salad Milano.

Write for:
Cooking Healthy With Rice

Cost: Free with a long SASE

Send to:
The Rice Council
P.O. Box 740121
Houston, TX 77274

FIVE WITH RICE

★

There's nothing very new here, but if your family eats a lot of rice you may welcome a few new recipe ideas. This brochure is designed to encourage you to "eat right with rice," and offers a Savory Vegetable Rice Medley, Garden Vegetable Rice, Zesty Chicken 'n Rice Italiano, a dill-flavored rice salad, and a raspberry rice dessert flavored with almonds and Kirsch liqueur.

Write for:
Delicious and Nutritious Rice

Cost: Free

Send to:
Delicious and Nutritious Rice
P.O. Box 725 — Dept. 827
Lubbock, TX 79491-0526

RICE MUNCHIES AND CRUNCHIES

★★★

Here are some tempting ways to add versatility to breakfasts and snacks using those crunchy rice cakes you may just have tried with butter or jelly. Dieters will welcome new ideas to liven up a low-calorie meal—a rice cake has only 35 calories to begin with, so you can afford to splurge a bit with the toppings. Recipes here include Swiss Mushroom Toast; Tuna Tempter, with basic tuna dressed up with grated zucchini and carrot mixed with plain yogurt; and Brunch Casserole, which tops the rice cakes with deviled ham and cheese in a cream of celery soup base. If you're not on a diet, try Nutter Scotch Squares with peanut butter and butterscotch morsels, or Candy Coated Treats with a chocolate covering. There are unusual party ideas, too, like Chutney Tidbits — wedges of rice cake spread with a cream cheese and chutney mixture, or Rice Munchies, flavored with garlic, onion, and grated Parmesan cheese. Seventeen ideas in a nicely illustrated pamphlet.

Write for:
Rice Cakes Anytime

Cost: Free

Send to:
Rice Cakes Anytime
c/o Heinz U.S.A.
P.O. Box 57
Pittsburgh, PA 15230-0057

Rice Cakes AnyTime

A SASE is a self-addressed stamped envelope.

FINE IDEAS FOR FRUGAL FARE
★★

This is a guide to basic, simple ways of preparing hearty, humble whole grains and legumes—wheat, rye, corn, oats, rice, barley, millet, buckwheat, soybean, large and small beans, garbanzos, black-eyed peas, split peas (green and yellow), and lentils. You'll learn basic cooking methods for each of the whole grains, what foods complement their taste, and how to cook legumes. There are also directions for sprouting all of these and instructions for stocking your pantry with other interesting frugal fare. And that's really the essence of this booklet—simplicity, frugality as a challenge to creativity, and balance.

Write for:
  Eight Grains/Eight Legumes

Cost: $2.00

Send to:
  Creative Living Center
  P.O. Box 478
  San Andreas, CA 95249

REDISCOVER THE BEAN
★★

Beans are an excellent source of vegetable protein, and you can use them to replace costly meat in your food budget or as part of a nutritionally balanced vegetarian diet. In this ten-page foldout, color photographs of 12 types of beans and information on their best use take the cook well beyond chili. A nutritional guide lists protein and vitamin content of beans—a big health plus is that they have no cholesterol and the cooking and storage tips will help you put together eight dishes like Vegetarian Chowder and Chuck Wagon Bean Pot. A good way to rediscover the bean.

Write for:
  A Primer on Bean Cookery

Cost: Free with a long SASE

Send to:
  California Dry Bean Advisory Board
  531-D N. Alta Ave.
  Dinuba, CA 93618

THE PEANUT STORY
★★★

Contrary to the popular concept, the peanut is not a nut but a legume which belongs to the pea and bean family. Like nuts, however, peanuts are delicious and nutritious; they're high in protein, fats, niacin, thiamine, and phosphorous (but not cholesterol). This fact-filled booklet on the peanut, as grown in North Carolina and Virginia, gives you more information. Did you know peanuts are an ingredient in shaving cream, ink, and plastics? You'll learn about the historical background, the scientific development of the peanut by George Washington Carver, and how the peanut industry functions today. You'll follow the botanical origin of the peanut plant with the enclosed wall chart. Finally, there are some tasty recipes for desserts and peanut soup.

Write for:
  Thoughts on Peanuts

Cost: Free with first-class postage

Send to:
  Growers Peanut Food Promotions
  P. O. Box 1709
  Rocky Mount, NC 27802-1709

Thoughts on Peanuts

HOW TO COOK A PEANUT
★★

Two leaflets from the Oklahoma Peanut Commission pack in a whole lot of information about everyone's favorite snack—they tell how to blanch, French fry, dry or oil roast, sugarcoat, and store peanuts, and then they tell how to make a tempting variety of snacks, candies, and cookies from them. You'll find recipes for peanut brittle, peanut butter fudge, peanut butter ice cream, and peanut butter appetizers. Lots of tempting alternatives to a plain old sandwich for the kids' lunch boxes, too.

Write for:
  How to Cook a Peanut
  Recipes From Your Oklahoma Peanut Commission

Cost: Free with a long SASE

continued

FOOD

Dairy Products

DAIRY PRODUCTS MAKE DISHES SPECIAL
★★★

A glass of milk with lunch or sour cream on a baked potato is as close as some people get to dairy products in their meals. If you're one of them, *The Wonderful World of Milk* will convert you to goodies like chilled Almond Soup, Custard Corn Pie, or Eggnog Baked Custard. This 16-page booklet contains recipes for appetizers, vegetables, main dishes, desserts, and beverages, and the color photos will urge you to start cooking. *The Wonderful World of Real Dairy Foods* shows how real dairy products make recipes special. Why not try Golden Corn Chowder, Snowy Cheese Salad, Oh Boy Casserole, or yummy Orange Eggnog Soufflé with Cranberry Sauce?

Write for:
    The Wonderful World of Milk
    The Wonderful World of Real Dairy Foods

Cost: 35¢ each

Send to:
    Milk World or Real World
    c/o American Dairy Association
    P.O. Box 760
    Rosemont, IL 60018-7760

The Wonderful World of Real Dairy Foods
The Wonderful World of Milk

THE CREAM OF THE CREAM
★★★

Cream has always been held in high regard by poets, writers, and lovers; to describe someone or something as the "cream" of the crop has always been a great compliment. You'll understand why when you try the classic Newburg Sauce, the elegant crepes, or the delightful desserts and beverages in *The Wonderful World of Cream*. Just the photos will have you reaching for the whipped cream, but you'll be missing a lot if you don't try the main dish recipes in this nice 20-page booklet. You'll even learn how to make *crème fraîche*, the current darling of the gourmet set. *The Wonderful World of Sour Cream*, will show you what sour cream can do for the taste of cinnamon coffeecake or the flavor of salads and desserts—it even turns up in Glazed Pot Roast. Twelve pages of ideas that will prove you can do more with sour cream than plop a dollop on a baked potato.

Write for:
    The Wonderful World of Cream
    The Wonderful World of Sour Cream

Cost: 35¢ each

Send to:
    Cream World or Sour Cream World
    c/o American Dairy Association
    P.O. Box 760
    Rosemont, IL 60018-7760

BUTTERING UP YOUR MEALS
★★★

Throw away the diet book before you even open this one. It's a butter-with-everything collection of sauces, spreads, and serving ideas accented throughout with sunny photographs. Learn to make a tempting Frosted Sandwich Loaf—buttering the bread between fillings of salmon, parsley butter, and cheddar cheese keeps the filling from soaking into the bread, thus improving both looks and texture. You'll find out how to make butter curls, roses, and daffodils, along with an assortment of butter sauces and spreads for use on bread and in hors d'oeuvres. Sixteen delightful pages full of ideas.

Write for:
    The Wonderful World of Butter

Cost: 35¢

Send to:
    Butter World
    c/o American Dairy Association
    P.O. Box 760
    Rosemont, IL 60018-7760

A SASE is a self-addressed stamped envelope.

COTTAGE CHEESE GOES GOURMET

★★★

In America's quest for thinness, cottage cheese has acquired a reputation as a great diet food—and not much else. If that's your attitude, this cookbooklet will be an eye-opener. For instance, the Islander Treat Salad, combining cottage cheese with lobster, sour cream, grapes, and pineapple, definitely puts the old standby into the gourmet class. *The Wonderful World of Cottage Cheese* contains 14 pages of such delights. Tuna Chow Mein, Appetizer Ham Balls, Vegetable Chutney Salad, and Chocolate Cheese Pie will make you forget cottage cheese *ever* meant "diet." Color photos give you lots of ideas for dressing up the table with dishes that look delicious.

Write for:
The Wonderful World of Cottage Cheese

Cost: 35¢

Send to:
Cottage Cheese World
c/o American Dairy Association
P.O. Box 760
Rosemont, IL 60018-7760

PLAIN AND PARTY CHEESE TREATS

★★★

From classic Quiche Lorraine through dips, soups, appetizers, and soufflés to an unusual Cheddar Short-bread, *The Wonderful World of Cheese* introduces you to new ways of enjoying cheese. A cheese, wine, and fruit chart solves the question of which go together—nice ideas for easy picnics or impromptu parties. A two-page listing of different cheeses and their flavors, characteristics, and uses will give you new confidence when you're buying and serving cheeses. Color photos let you know that the recipes in this 20-page cookbooklet may be a bit more complicated than cheese and crackers—but they're worth the effort.

Write for:
The Wonderful World of Cheese

Cost: 35¢

Send to:
Cheese World
c/o American Dairy Association
P.O. Box 760
Rosemont, IL 60018-7760

The Wonderful World of Cheese

MORE WAYS TO SAY CHEESE, PLEASE

★★★

Macaroni and cheese is a surefire easy dinner dish, but if that's the extent of your cheese-eating you're missing a lot—like the 22 great ideas in *Cheese Magic*. Morning Muffin, Gourmet Pizza, Blue Cheese Beef Balls and Pineapple Cherry Cheesecake are among these nice alternatives to a cheese sandwich. *Cheese Quickies*, a colorful 14-page booklet, also has cheese suggestions for appetizers, main dishes, sandwiches, and cheese desserts. There are some super "party starters," a meatless spaghetti dinner, and a gorgeous Cheese Crumble Apple Pie.

Write for:
Cheese Magic
Cheese Quickies

Cost: 35¢ each

Send to:
Cheese Magic or Cheese Quickies
c/o American Dairy Association
P.O. Box 760
Rosemont, IL 60018-7760

FOR YOGURT LOVERS

★★

Baked chicken with yogurt and sautéed mushrooms. Yogurt mustard dressing with chopped capers. Yogurt mayonnaise. Red Raspberry Yogurt Mousse. Strawberry Yogurt Pie. Yuummm! Yogurt isn't just for eating out of a cardboard cup, and to prove it you can check out the yogurt recipes suggested in a pocket-sized 12-page booklet from Dannon, the

continued

FOOD

yogurt people. Besides more than a dozen recipes, you get tips on how to freeze yogurt to make some delectable desserts.

Write for:
  Favorite Yogurt Recipes from Dannon

Cost: Free

Send to:
  The Dannon Company, Inc.
  Department "C"
  P.O. Box 1975
  Long Island City, NY 11101

YOGURT: NOT A FUNNY WORD ANYMORE
★★

This booklet is put out by the Dannon yogurt people and is heavy on information about their products, but there's also a lot of material here to interest health-conscious Americans, young and old alike. You'll learn how yogurt is made and the role it plays in diet and weight control and as a source of protein and calcium. When you shop for yogurt, it will help to know how to read and understand what's written on the cup—there is a crucial difference between "natural flavor" and "natural yogurt." You'll find some serving ideas for yogurt and some unusual flavor combinations.

Write for:
  Yogurt and You

Cost: Free (postcard requests only)

Send to:
  The Dannon Company, Inc.
  Dept. "A"
  P.O. Box 1975
  Long Island City, NY 11101

YOGURT FOR EVERY MEAL
★★

This 16-page booklet contains recipes (along with tempting color photographs) for yogurt coolers, soups, dips, salads, entrees, and desserts, as well as tips on cooking with yogurt. Yogurt enhances everything from a peach-almond cooler, horseradish beef dip, and fresh mushroom salad to moussaka, quiche, or pancakes—not to mention Lemon Pound Cake, Strawberry Cheese Torte, and Frozen Raspberry Yogurt. Yogurt, which has been with us since Biblical times, remains one of the favorite health foods of

modern times and these recipes will certainly help you understand why.

Write for:
  The Wonderful World of Yogurt

Cost: 35¢

Send to:
  Yogurt World
  c/o American Dairy Association
  P.O. Box 760
  Rosemont, IL 60018-7760

The Wonderful World of Yogurt

BUTTERMILK BAKING
★★

Real buttermilk, the fluid left over from butter churning, contains a natural emulsifier that gives baked goods a fine, uniform texture—emulsifiers allow the shortening, flour, and liquid to blend more easily in the batter. Here are four sets of recipe cards using Saco cultured buttermilk powder, and they sound wonderful. There's everything from Buttermilk Spice Doughnuts and cinnamon bread to Quiche Lorraine, cakes of all flavors, and an entire bakery of yeast breads. There are 14 recipes in each set of 3″ × 5″ cards, and you order two sets at a time.

Write for:
  Saco Recipe Cards, Sets A and B
  Saco Recipe Cards, Sets C and D

Cost: $1.00 for two sets; $2.00 for four sets

Send to:
  Saco Foods, Inc.
  6120 University Ave.
  P.O. Box 5461
  Madison, WI 53705

A SASE is a self-addressed stamped envelope.

PUTTING ZING INTO A SHAKE
★★

The makers of this 70-calorie shake mix have taken pity on the dieter with a sweet tooth. These delicious-sounding drinks and desserts are based on ALBA/77 Fit n' Frosty shake mix (you whip it up with ice and water) and Sugar-Free Hot Cocoa Mix, both made with nonfat dry milk. You can add simple flavorings and come up with such treats as Berry Peachy Shake, Hot Peppermint Patty, Chocolate Orange Blossom, Scottish Fling (with molasses and ground ginger), Ambrosia Cream (with orange juice and fresh oranges topped with toasted coconut), or Mocha Whip. Party specials include Strawberry Salad Mold, Banana or Fudge Pops, and Choco Blocks. Sounds like a painless way to diet. With the little recipe leaflet you get a foldout on facts about calcium—ALBA's High-Calcium hot cocoa mix is sugar-free and contains more calcium than an 8-ounce glass of milk.

Write for:
Shakes & More (plus 10 Questions & Answers About Calcium)

Cost: Free with a SASE

Send to:
Shakes & More
c/o Heinz U.S.A.
P.O. Box 57
Pittsburgh, PA 15230-0057

Fruits and Vegetables

TAKE AN AVOCADO TO LUNCH
★

If you've never met an avocado you didn't like, you'll love this packet. An attractive, 12-page foldout in fruity colors—lime green on pale yellow—tells you about the avocado's history, growing season and cultivation, and nutritional value (it's high in vitamin C, thiamin, and niacin, among others).

Find out how to plant your own avocado trees (they're nice houseplants but won't bear fruit), and how to choose, prepare, and freeze avocados. Lots of recipe ideas for sandwiches, salads, guacamole, appetizers, even baby food. An accompanying information sheet has more facts on varieties and tells you how to test an avocado for ripeness. More recipes, too.

Write for:
Meet the Florida Avocado
Introducing the A-1 Avocado

Cost: Free with a long SASE

Send to:
Kendall Foods Corp.
P.O. Box 458
Goulds, FL 33170

NEW USES FOR AVOCADOS AND LIMES
★

There's more to an avocado than guacamole, and a lime has more to offer than a pretty garnish for a drink. Those are the messages conveyed in these mini-pamphlets. The one about Florida avocados includes a delicious-sounding recipe for Mexican Chili Avocados and an intriguing Tuna Avocurry. It also gives hints on how to tell if an avocado is ready to eat.

The leaflet on limes reminds you that a lime provides an excellent salt substitute for people on low-sodium diets and can be squeezed on meats, poultry, vegetables, and fish. A squeeze of lime will also keep freshly cut fruit from turning brown and will add an extra touch of flavor. Several nice ideas in these tiny leaflets.

Write for:
Avocado and Lime recipes

Cost: Free with a SASE

Send to:
Recipe Pamphlets
P.O. Drawer 9
Homestead, FL 33090-0009

FOR STRAWBERRY LOVERS
★★★★

You'll find delicious new ways to use the baskets of strawberries you bring home if you send for this free cookbook from the California Strawberry Advisory Board. It's a beautifully designed 14-page color booklet in an odd 8″ × 8″ size, so you have to send either a 9″ × 12″ self-addressed envelope or an adhesive self-addressed label. Both the information about storing and thawing frozen strawberries and the recipes in this delightful book make it worth having. How can you resist chocolate mousse with strawberry cream, strawberry "mudslide" pie, strawberry tarts, or strawberry soup, pudding, parfait, and cheesecake? A charmer all around.

Write for:
Strawberry Sweeties

continued

FOOD

Cost: Free with a 9″×12″ self-addressed envelope or label

Send to:
California Strawberry Advisory Board
P.O. Box 269
Watsonville, CA 95076

Strawberry Sweeties

BEAUTIFUL BLUEBERRIES
★★

Blueberries, which used to be available only in summer, now are available all year around in the freezer section of your supermarket. In fact, blueberries can be enjoyed at any meal and in any season, as this handy little brochure tells you. Learn how to freeze blueberries from the garden, too, or dry them for future use in some of the wonderful recipes provided here. These include blueberry sponge custards, blueberry soup, blueberry-peach coffee cake, blueberry cream cheese fingers, and pinwheel muffins—certainly guaranteed to brighten anyone's day.

Write for:
Blueberry Recipes to Brighten Your Day

Cost: 35¢

Send to:
North American Blueberry Council
Dept. IF
P.O. Box 166
Marmora, NJ 08223

FROM THE GARDEN OF EDEN?
★★★

A relative of the blueberry plant is the oldest thing living on earth today, some 13,000 years old. Some botanists say blueberries may even have grown in the Garden of Eden. Blueberries are known as the all-American fruit because this is the only continent where cultivated blueberries are grown in quantity as a commercial crop. Get to know blueberries better in a delightful little 14-page *Passport to the World of Blueberries*. You'll find more history about the berry, where and when it is harvested throughout the United States, and how to buy blueberries. For good measure, there are recipes for blueberry pie and blueberry streusel muffins with walnut topping. Here is a fun tour through the world of blueberries.

Write for:
Passport to the World of Blueberries

Cost: 35¢

Send to:
North American Blueberry Council
P.O. Box 166
Marmora, NJ 08223

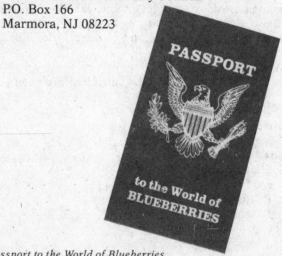

Passport to the World of Blueberries

TART AND TASTY
★★

Cranberries grow in Massachusetts, Rhode Island, New Jersey, Wisconsin, Washington, and Oregon, and are found in the fresh produce section of supermarkets September through November. They freeze well and can be stored for up to nine months. They're rich in vitamin C, contain only 25 calories per half cup, and are low in sodium. Learn even more about cranberries in any or all of five free brochures from Ocean Spray. You'll be sent the brochures that are available at the time you write.

Write for:
Fresh Cranberries—Consumer Tips
Refresh a Better Way with Ocean Spray
Saucy Ideas from Ocean Spray
Nutritional Facts: Cranberry Drinks
Fresh Cranberries Are In!

Cost: Free

A SASE is a self-addressed stamped envelope.

Send to:
Ocean Spray Cranberries, Inc.
225 Water St.
Plymouth, MA 02360

Cranberry brochures

HERE'S SOME GRAPE NEWS
★★

This delightful brochure comes from the California Table Grape Commission and is filled with good grape news. For one thing, a cupful contains only 107 calories, and grapes make a satisfying snack—they're low in sodium, and because they contain fiber and water they make you feel "full" when you're not. You'll learn about 13 different varieties of grapes and when they're in season, and you'll get six grape recipes including Grape and Rice Salad, Picadillo With Grapes, and Grape Shortbread Bars.

Write for:
Grapes: The Natural Snack

Cost: Free with a long SASE

Send to:
California Table Grape Commission
P.O. Box 5498
Fresno, CA 93755

SHORT AND SWEET
★

When you want to "dress up" a meal and you're clean out of ideas, maybe *Recipes Using Prune and Apricot Butters* will tickle your imagination. Barbecued chicken gets an unusual fillip with the addition of apricot sauce, and prune butter folded into an omelet makes a novel lunch dish. The two-page leaflet includes 13 recipes for soufflés, muffins, tarts, sweet breads, cakes, and kipfels all made with apricot or prune butter. There's also a list of unusual

ways you can use fruit butters right from the jar in fruit salads, blintzes, or to liven up a glass of cold milk.

Write for:
Recipes Using Prune and Apricot Butters

Cost: Free (postcard requests only)

Send to:
Globe Products Co., Inc.
Consumer Products Div.
P.O. Box 1927
Clifton, NJ 07012

SOLAR ENERGY FRUIT
★

Here's an ancient fruit that can be used in new ways—in the microwave, in the food processor, freshly stored in a backpacker's knapsack or an office desk drawer. Figs have been around since Adam and Eve, but some fresh ideas about them are offered in this free leaflet. There's brief nutrition information about the "solar energy" fruit— they're completely sun-ripened and sun-dried—and recipe ideas for sandwiches, spreads, appetizers, breakfast dishes, and figs poached in wine, stuffed in baked apples, and baked in cakes and muffins.

Write for:
New Excitement With the Solar Energy Fruit

Cost: Free with a long SASE

Send to:
California Dried Fig Advisory Board
Dept. SE
P.O. Box 709
Fresno, CA 93712

GIVE A FIG!
★★★

Figs are among the most nutritious of all fruits, and chances are you haven't had one since you'd come home from school and Mom was waiting with a plate of chewy Fig Newtons and a glass of milk. Maybe reading these three leaflets from the California Dried Fig Advisory Board will renew your interest in the delicious fruit. Figs' natural sugars pump quick energy into the bloodstream for all the strenuous and fun sports that require high levels of exertion. Figs also rate high in calcium, fiber, and potassium. You'll receive over a dozen recipes, each with dried figs as an important ingredient, such as Three-Grain Muffins and Yam Bake à L'Orange. You'll also learn

continued

FOOD

nutritional information on dried figs, and receive a buyer's guide to the fiber content of over 100 different fruits.

Write for:
California Dried Figs — Recipes, Serving Ideas
Fabulous Figs, the Fitness Fruit
Buyer's Guide to Fruit Fiber

Cost: Free with a long SASE

Send to:
California Dried Fig Advisory Board
Dept. FT
P.O. Box 709
Fresno, CA 93712

HOLD THE MARTINI...
★★★

More than 98 percent of ripe olives consumed in the U.S. are grown in California's warm inland valleys, where the climate is similar to the Mediterranean regions where olives originated thousands of years ago. An attractive 32-page booklet with color photos tells all about ripe olives and contains about two dozen recipes for using olives in appetizers, soups and salads, sandwiches, vegetable dishes, beef and lamb, poultry and seafood. The Mexican Puff Olé, sort of an olive pizza, looks especially tasty.

If the only place you've met an olive is in a martini (and those are the green kind), you'll be surprised how versatile the black olives used in these recipes actually are. Incidentally, California olives are green when they come from the tree and have a very bitter taste. The curing method used dictates the final color.

Write for:
The Itinerant Ripe Olive

Cost: Free

Send to:
California Olive Industry
Dept. 2000
P.O. Box 4098
Fresno, CA 93744

The Itinerant Ripe Olive

PUMPKIN ALL YEAR ROUND
★

If you think pumpkins hibernate until Halloween, why not expand your horizons and experiment with some delicious and undemanding desserts that use canned pumpkin? Of course there's the traditional pumpkin pie, but pumpkin nut bread, cookies, and muffins are also possibilities. You'll find these and several other pumpkin treats in Libby's free little folder *Honest to Goodness Pumpkin Recipes*. There are also serving suggestions and tips for doubling the recipes so that you can freeze a batch for another day.

Write for:
Honest to Goodness Pumpkin Recipes

Cost: Free with a long SASE

Send to:
Libby's Honest to Goodness Pumpkin Recipes
CGP Offer
P.O. Box 43502
Chicago, IL 60643

VINTAGE FRUIT SAUCE
★★★

Several years ago, Red Star Yeast introduced a recipe that used yeast to ferment fruit, thus creating a fruit sauce with a vintage flavor. Here's the recipe for this vintage fruit sauce, along with 22 recipes that use it in main dishes like glazed ham or sauced ribs, as a salad dressing or in a salad ring, in vegetables, breads, and holiday fare (Cranberry Nut Bread, Bohemian Christmas Braid). Try also some of the delicious-sounding desserts, such as Vintage Fruit Sauce Upside-Down Cake, and Vintage Berry Ice Cream. This attractive cookbook also suggests that you bottle extra sauce as gifts for gourmet friends.

Write for:
Vintage Fruit Sauce Recipe Collection

Cost: 50¢

Send to:
Vintage Fruit Sauce
Universal Foods Corporation
433 E. Michigan
Milwaukee, WI 53201

PEACHES APLENTY
★★

If peaches are your hang-up, here are enough peach recipes to satisfy your craving at any meal, any time

A SASE is a self-addressed stamped envelope.

of day. There are beverages like peach nog or peach shake, breakfasts like peach French toast, and lunches—how about a gourmet chicken salad with fresh peaches? There are main dishes—Persian Peach Glazed Chicken, for example—peach soups, peach desserts including a mousse, and some peach dip for a snack between meals. There's also information on how much fresh peaches yield when they're canned, frozen, or dried, and tips on choosing the perfect fresh peach.

Write for:
A Peach Potpourri

Cost: Free with a long SASE

Send to:
West Virginia Dept. of Agriculture
State Capitol Building
Charleston, WV 25305

IPOMOEA BATATA: JUST CALL IT A SWEET POTATO
★★

Sweet potatoes, yams, *Ipomoea batatas*—whatever you call them, they're packed with nutrition, and a 3½-ounce specimen contains only 141 calories. This recipe booklet reminds you that sweet potatoes can be baked, boiled, fried, broiled, microwaved, candied, or frozen. You can use them in breads, salads, pies, custards, and cakes, and here are 36 different ways to prepare them. Consider, for example, Sweet Potato Sausage Casserole, Sweet Potato Soufflé, Peanut-Sweet Potato Patties, Grated Sweet Potato Salad, Pineapple Spiced Sweet Potatoes, and French Fried Sweet Potatoes.

Write for:
Cooking With Sweet Potatoes

Cost: 50¢ and a long SASE

Send to:
Harold H. Hoecker
SPC-CGP3
P.O. Box 14
McHenry, MD 21541

FRESHER IS BETTER
★★

Fresh fruits and vegetables contain fiber, which is important in our diet because it adds bulk that nutrition experts believe can reduce intestinal disorders. Most fresh fruits and vegetables are also low in sodium, and spare you the preservatives (including sugar and salt) common to most canned foods. To learn more about the health benefits of fresh fruits and vegetables, send for three free brochures offered by the United Fresh Fruit and Vegetable Association. Specialty fruits are described, such as cherimoya, coconut, guava, kiwifruit, mango, papaya, even the ever-popular kumquat. Specialty vegetables you'll learn more about include bok choy, celeriac, chayote, daikon, fennel, jicama, salsify, and water chestnuts. You also get some interesting recipes for salads, main dishes, and desserts that use these lesser-known fruits and vegetables.

Write for:
The Joy of Fresh
Specialty Fruits
Specialty Vegetables

Cost: Free with a long SASE

Send to:
United Fresh Fruit and Vegetable Association
727 N. Washington St.
Alexandria, VA 22314

Joy of Fresh, Specialty Fruits, and Specialty Vegetables

ORANGES AND LEMONS ALL WAYS
★★

These three leaflets from Sunkist celebrate lemons and Valencia and navel oranges and tell how to cut them, cook with them, and use them to garnish your favorite dishes. There are some splendid thirst quenchers (Honey Citrus Punch, for example), backyard barbecue basics (Orange Barbecue Sauce and Western Baked Beans), salads (Orange Two-Bean Salad), and sauces (Quick Lemon Hollandaise and Lemon Sesame Butter) that all put these citrus favorites to good use. Besides the recipes, there's nutritional information on all three fruits.

continued

FOOD

Write for:
Pick o' the Crop leaflets

Cost: Free with a long SASE

Send to:
Consumer Services
Sunkist Growers
Box 7888·
Van Nuys, CA 91409

CORNY STORIES

★★

Although corn is the king of American crops, only a small portion of the annual crop ever reaches the store in its original form. If you've ever wondered what happens to the rest of those billions of ears, now you can find out. *Tapping the Treasure in Corn,* a free two-page foldout from the Corn Refiners Association, explains briefly and succinctly how refiners turn corn into starches, sweeteners, feed, oil, and alcohols.

Appropriately printed in yellow and green, the brochure lists hundreds of uses for refined corn products. You'll be fascinated to learn that corn dextrins are used in book bindings and soaps; corn syrup goes into pickles and pickle products; corn dextrose is used to make rayon; and corn oil and free fatty acids are ingredients of rust preventives.

Write for:
Tapping the Treasure in Corn

Cost: Free

Send to:
Corn Refiners Association, Inc.
1001 Connecticut Ave., N.W.
Washington, DC 20036

A TOUCH OF DUTCH

★

Authentic Pennsylvania German potato salad to serve hot or cold. A yummy holiday fruit salad with an open-ended number of fruits to use. Whole wheat pineapple carrot cake. A "heavenly" canned fruit cake. These are some of the recipes in two one-pagers offered from Emily Ann's Down Home Kitchen. Only a handful of recipes here, but some of them are worth collecting.

Write for:
Most Requested Recipes for 1985—Salads
Most Requested Recipes for 1985—Desserts

Cost: 50¢ for both and a long SASE

Send to:
Salads and Desserts
Emily Ann Creations
303 S. 34th St.
Tacoma, WA 98408

Baked Goods and Sweet Desserts

BATCH OF BAKERY PRIZEWINNERS

★★★★

In this collection of winning recipes from Red Star Yeast's 2nd Baking Recipe Exchange are 23 more intriguing recipes with unusual ingredients. Corn-Fetti Bread features dill weed, cream-style corn, and pimento-stuffed olives in a white bread; Savory Jonni Buns are cornmeal buns laced with dry onion soup mix; Raisin Banana Batter Bread is a heavy, nutritious loaf that couples banana bread with raisin-bran cereal. You'll certainly want to try these recipes if you're an enthusiastic baker. You'll also find some good baking tips, whether you're a novice baker or an old pro. Color photographs of some of the recipes appear on the cover.

Write for:
The Best of Red Star's 2nd Baking Recipe Exchange

Cost: 75¢

Send to:
2nd Recipe Exchange
Universal Foods Corporation
433 E. Michigan
Milwaukee, WI 53201

The Best of Red Star's 2nd Baking Recipe Exchange

NEW AND EASY YEAST COOKING

★★★★

Discover how to use Red Star's new quick-rise yeast in this 28-page recipe booklet, which describes how the high-activity yeast rises up to 50 percent faster than regular yeast. You can learn all about active dry yeasts and compressed yeast and about mixing, kneading, rising, and baking. Recipes include White Bread, Easy Egg Braid, French Bread, Honey Whole Wheat Bread, Wheat Germ Bread, Garlic Bubble Loaf, Zucchini Buns, Caramel Crown Coffeecake, Granola Coffeecake, Pecan Caramel Rolls, Cinnamon Rounds, Onion Mustard Buns, and other taste treasures. Also included are holiday recipes for Finnish Easter bread, brioche, kolache, pulla, and other traditional Christmas and Easter baking delights.

Write for:
New and Easy Yeast Recipes

Cost: 75¢

Send to:
New and Easy Recipes
Universal Foods Corporation
433 E. Michigan
Milwaukee, WI 53201

YEAST BREADS FROM YOUR FOOD PROCESSOR

★★★★

Who can resist the warm taste of freshly baked homemade breads or rolls? Now they're a snap to make using your food processor and Red Star's new quick-rise yeast. This new yeast rises up to 50 percent faster than regular dry yeast and is still 100 percent natural. Sunbeam, who teamed up with Red Star on this booklet, says its professional food processor produces a perfectly kneaded yeast dough in only 60 seconds. No hand kneading is necessary and cleanup is simple.

Check out this yeast bread food processor cookbook that tells you how to make Buttermilk Rye Bread, Sweetheart Coffeecake, Chocolate Swirl Coffeecake, Grandma's Cinnamon Rolls, white bread, Mexican pizza, and Chicago-style deep-dish pizza. You also get a coupon worth 10¢ for any Red Star yeast product.

Write for:
Food Processor Cookbook

Cost: 75¢

Send to:
Food Processor Cookbook
Universal Foods Corporation
433 E. Michigan
Milwaukee, WI 53201

STUFF OF THE STAFF OF LIFE

★★

Obscure data: The daily ration of a Roman soldier was two pounds of whole-grain wheat or rye. With a little wine, that was it. Some consider this simple, hearty fare the reason for the success of the Roman Empire. A tiny but informative booklet put out by the Roman Meal people (whose founder copied the soldiers' diet to regain health after an illness) explains just what is in bread, why it's there, what makes up a wheat kernel, and *all* about additives and preservatives. The booklet also tells you where you can send for a newsletter on nutrition, borrow a 16mm film on bread, and send for recipes and a diet scale. Well worth your SASE.

Write for:
Bread on the Table

Cost: Free with a SASE

Send to:
Roman Meal Co.
Dept. F
P.O. Box 11126
Tacoma, WA 98411-0126

BREADS WITH HONEY

★★

You're a bread lover? How does Dutch Double Dill Bread sound? It's a mouth-watering recipe that calls for whole wheat, rye flour, caraway seed, dried dill weed, *and* dill seeds. Or how about Spiced Pineapple Zucchini Bread? There's also Delaware Crackling Bread, carrot and bran muffins, and kneadless bran bread, all in this slim but idea-filled recipe folder from the California Honey Advisory Board. Good hints for better breads and an easy recipe for honey butter, too. Nice.

Write for:
Honey and Bread

Cost: Free with a long SASE

Send to:
California Honey Advisory Board
P.O. Box 265
Sonoma, CA 95476

FOOD

BREAD BASICS
★

If you'd like some new bread and muffin recipes or recipes for apple pectin stock or bread and butter pickles, you'll like what Emily Ann's Down Home Kitchen has to offer. You can send for two two-page sets of recipes. The *Best Breads* recipes include one-hour whole wheat rolls, easy batter bread, easy pocket bread, English muffins, and deep-dish pizza. *End of the Garden Treasures* includes recipes for homemade apple pectin stock, bread and butter pickles, zucchini relish, and green tomato mincemeat.

Write for:
Garden Treasures
Best Breads

Cost: 50¢ each and a long SASE

Send to:
Garden Treasures and Best Breads
Emily Ann Creations
303 S. 34th St.
Tacoma, WA 98408

FRUITY PASTRY DESSERTS
★

If you like to bake, you'll get a few new ideas from these two brief leaflets of recipes that use fruit fillings and glazes. You get about a dozen recipes for such alluring pastries as Blueberry Mini-Cheesecakes, Prune Bars, Raspberry Pecan Torte, and Apricot Parfait Pie.

Write for:
Solo Kitchen Tested Recipes

Cost: 25¢ and a SASE

Send to:
Solo Products
Sokol and Co.
5315 Dansher Rd.
Countryside, IL 60525

RISE TO THE OCCASION WITH YEAST
★★★★

You may not think about yeast on a daily basis, but without it you would not be able to enjoy many baked treats that you take for granted. This booklet-sized cookbook, one of a number offered by Universal Foods' Red Star Yeast Division, packs more than 30 recipes into 28 pages, covering a range of goodies that includes breads and rolls, coffeecakes and sweet rolls, and even main-dish breads. Cooks with a fondness for appealing bread dishes will find this cookbook especially useful.

Write for:
Time-Saving Yeast Breads

Cost: 75¢

Send to:
Universal Foods Corporation
Red Star Yeast Division
433 East Michigan St.
Milwaukee, WI 53201

Time-Saving Yeast Breads

TRADITIONAL POUND CAKES
★

Everyone talks about dieting and good nutrition—but staying with a diet is sometimes easier said than done. When you do go off your diet, go off in a big way with a delicious pound cake from the Georgia Egg Commission.

The Commission's home economists are offering a collection of pound cake recipes that recapture the great flavor our ancestors enjoyed, while at the same time providing the basic goodness of eggs. With your copy you'll get a selection of other tasty recipes using eggs.

Write for:
Eggs. For the Good of Our Country

Cost: $1.00 and a long SASE

Send to:
Georgia Egg Commission
State Farmers' Market
Forest Park, GA 30050-2082

A SASE is a self-addressed stamped envelope.

COOKIES FOR THE CONNOISSEUR

★★★★

Anyone can bake cookies, right? Whipping up a batch of chocolate chip cookies or peanut butter swirls for the office party or school bazaar is no problem—but ordinary cookies are just not contenders when you put them next to the fancy goodies in this attractive little book. When did you last produce a cookie that looked like a pizza, a hamburger, a doughnut, or a ladybug? You can now.

This publication from Wilton, the cake decorating people, gives you lots of good, basic recipes for butter, chocolate, peanut butter, sugar, and shortbread cookies, but that's just for starters. The fun part is in the variations and decorations. Learn how to transform ordinary cookies into Cookie Baskets (fill them with candy), Sandie Snowmen, Caterpillar Crescents, Meringue Mushrooms, Pecan and Chocolate Tartlets, and all sorts of other charming or sophisticated treats. There are illustrated how-to tips on dipping, decorating, molding, and making cut-outs. If one of your pet cold-weather activities is making cookies with the kids, send for this book and you'll have them eating out of your hand.

Write for:
How to Make Great Tasting Fancy Cookies

Cost: $1.99

Send to:
Wilton Enterprises, Inc.
2240 West 75th Street
Woodridge, IL 60517

How to Make Great Tasting Fancy Cookies

CHOCOLATE— THE DIETER'S DOWNFALL

★★

If chocolate is your thing, you'll love the recipes from the Ghiradelli Chocolate Company in San Francisco. Instructions are given for melting chocolate on the stove or in the oven or microwave oven. Then you are treated to favorite chocolate recipes from famous Ghiradelli Square, where chocolate has reigned supreme since 1852. Recipes include Gourmet Chocolate Dipped Strawberries, chocolate "Decadence Cake," Gay Nineties Silk Pie, Chocolate Fondue Dessert, Chocolate Almond Torte, Chocolate Mint Cookies, and Chocolate Sour Cream cake frosting. If you're not prepared to succumb to temptation on the spot, don't even *think* of sending for this little luxury-crammed leaflet.

Write for:
Ghiradelli Chocolate Recipes

Cost: Free with a long SASE

Send to:
Ghiradelli Chocolate Company
P.O. Box 24204
Oakland, CA 94623

GIVING THE LIE TO "THIN IS BEAUTIFUL"

★★★★

Given America's "thin is beautiful" philosophy, this wonderful booklet is positively subversive. It's called *Candy Making for Beginners* and it comes from Wilton, the company that deals in cake decorating and confectionery art—and confectionery art is an apt description of the gorgeous goodies Wilton promises to teach you how to make. You'll learn how to mold, hand-dip, and decorate candies, including those with centers, swirls, and layers of different colors, and how to make candies in stand-up molds (an Easter lamb, for instance). There are step-by-step illustrated directions for candy cups, chocolate roses and pine cones, and delectable special occasion treats for Christmas, Easter, Valentine's Day, and Halloween.

It's hard to believe it's as easy as it looks to produce these do-it-yourself goodies—but this bright and happy little book will convince you that it can't be as difficult as you used to think. The book includes a catalog of Wilton's candy-making supplies. Basic recipes include Dipped Cordial Cherries, Truffles, Marshmallow Caramel Bon-Bons, Rocky Road, and Mints. How can you resist? Anyway, you can always kid yourself that you're only making them as gifts for other people.

Write for:
Candy Making for Beginners

continued

FOOD

Cost: $1.99

Send to:
Wilton Enterprises, Inc.
2240 West 75th Street
Woodridge, IL 60517

Candy Making for Beginners

THE CHOCOLATE ALTERNATIVE
★★★

It was known to the ancients as the honey locust; we call it carob. Because it's naturally sweet, low in fat and calories, and contains no caffeinelike stimulants, carob is being used these days as a nutritious, low-priced alternative to chocolate by people with allergies or the desire to avoid chocolate's high cholesterol, caffeine, and sugar levels.

This informative 32-page book from the Garden Way people tells you everything you wanted to know about carob and more. In a straightforward style, and with a few line drawings, it explains what carob is, how it's grown (and how you can grow it), and how to cook with it. Also included are nutritional content, 24 recipes for carob desserts and frostings, and a list of suppliers of carob in all forms.

Write for:
Cooking With Carob: Bulletin A-48

Cost: $1.95

Send to:
Garden Way Publishing Co.
Schoolhouse Rd.
Pownal, VT 05261

Herbs and Spices

THE SEASONED COOK
★★★★

Among those areas of the world where a combination of cultures, climate, and produce have created a distinctive cuisine, few hold more interest for the gourmet than New Orleans. Since it is not always possible to visit in person, Gazin's has put together the best of Louisiana recipes, food specialties, and gourmet cooking tools to make it easy for you to enjoy that delectable Creole cuisine in your home. For $1.00 you will receive three generous packets of Gazin's Creole Spices, a recipe leaflet of 14 Creole-style dishes, and a 32-page gourmet catalog. You'll find specialty foods as well as the fixings to make your own specialties from soups to sauces. There is also a selection of Creole and Cajun cookbooks.

Write for:
Spices and Recipes

Cost: $1.00

Send to:
Gazin-Robinson, Inc.
Box 19221
New Orleans, LA 70179

Spices and Recipes

A SASE is a self-addressed stamped envelope.

SPICES THROUGH THE AGES

★★

If the only spices you ever see come out of little bottles, the drawings in this 20-page brochure, *A Glossary of Spices,* will introduce you to the reality of herbs and spices as plants. You'll learn where spices come from, how they've been used through history (there's a lot of fascinating folklore attached to herbs), how to use them now, and which ones will grow in this country. Ask also for the one-page *Spicy Butters Chart,* which will open a whole new perspective on simple but out-of-the-ordinary butter seasonings. For instance, add ground nutmeg to softened butter and spread it over spinach, beans, or broccoli. Or make curry butter to add to chicken, fish, or potatoes. Eighteen different butter and spice combinations are presented here.

Write for:
A Glossary of Spices
Spicy Butters Chart

Cost: $1.00 for the glossary
50¢ for the chart

Send to:
American Spice Trade Association, Inc.
580 Sylvan Ave.
P.O. Box 1267
Englewood Cliffs, NJ 07632

THE SPICE OF LIFE

★★

Those aren't weeds in your garden, they're herbs or spices just waiting to become part of your salad or to flavor a roast or some fish. You can learn all about herbs and spices from a clever little 8-page booklet called *The Magic Seasoning Tree.* It tells what families different herbs and spices belong to and what their uses are, and is accompanied by an 8"×11" drawing of what different herbs and spices look like. A nice pair of reference guides to keep handy in the kitchen for the times when you're short of ideas on how to spice up meats, fish, salads, and soups.

Write for:
The Magic Seasoning Tree and Poster

Cost: $1.00 and a long SASE

Send to:
CLC Press
P.O. Box 478
San Andreas, CA 95249

SPICE UP YOUR LIFE WITH SPICES

★★★

Variety is the spice of life, and here's a variety of three spice samples offered free from Modern Products, Inc. You get samples of Instant Spike® Delicious seasoning, a blend of 39 ingredients; Vege-Sal® All Natural salt and vegetable blend, which is an all-purpose vegetized mineral salt seasoning made of earth and sea salt crystals and 14 dried vegetables; and Vegit® Natural low-sodium vegetable seasoning, a combination of natural herbs and vegetables, high-flavor yeast, hydrolized protein from soya beans, and papainenzyme from papayas. These products are available in most health food and specialty food stores.

Write for:
Samples of Instant Spike®, Vege-Sal®, and Vegit®

Cost: Free with a long SASE

Send to:
Modern Products, Inc.
P.O. Box 09398
Milwaukee, WI 53209

Samples of Instant Spike®, Vege-Sal®, and Vegit®

HERBAL ESSENCE

★★★

Through the skillful use of herbs and spices, imaginative flavors can be created and simple foods made into gourmet delights. Herbs and spices are also a tasteful, healthful alternative to salt. *Do Yourself A Flavor* shows you how to put sparkle into your cooking, even if you're a beginner. The four-page pamphlet gives lots of good basic information on cutting and drying your home-grown seasonings, with suggestions for creating your own blends. Preparation methods are different for hot and cold foods, you'll learn. There are listings for strong, medium, and delicate flavors, and suggested blends for various types of foods. You'll learn to make herb butter and vinegars as well as a couple of French combinations.

continued

FOOD

Write for:
 Do Yourself A Flavor (No. 531P)

Cost: Free

Send to:
 Consumer Information Center
 P.O. Box 100
 Pueblo, CO 81002

SAY IT WITH HERBS
★★

Once you've tasted your own home-grown herbs, you'll never want to go back to the packaged variety. Most herbs are easy to grow, and you can grow some of them indoors all winter long. Don't limit yourself to using herbs only as seasonings, either; they're great in jellies, vinegars, cheese, potpourris, teas, cosmetics, and natural dyes. If you've never grown fresh herbs but would like to try, write for a free copy of this valuable four-page guide to growing 27 different herbs. Also included are suggestions for freezing herbs, directions for making fragrant sachets, and a handful of recipes to spice up salad dressings, soups, pasta, and main dishes. You even get a ground plan for an herb garden.

Write for:
 Herbs

Cost: Free with a long SASE

Send to:
 Customer Service
 W. Atlee Burpee Co.
 300 Park Ave.
 Warminster, PA 18974

Do-It-Yourself Foods

A HONEY OF A JAM
★

This brief pamphlet from the California Honey Advisory Board presents seven recipes for sugarless jams and preserves; you use honey to sweeten them. Find out how to make apricot-pineapple jam, pear butter, strawberry jam (by the regular method or in the microwave), lemon-orange marmalade, peach jam, no-cook freezer honey jam, and an intriguing item called fruit leather, which is made of fruit puree and honey that's been dehydrated or dried in the sun. There are a few tips on drying fruit and hints for

preserving, freezing, and canning fruits in honey syrup.

Write for:
 Food Preservation With Honey: Jams and
  Preserves

Cost: Free with a long SASE

Send to:
 California Honey Advisory Board
 P.O. Box 265
 Sonoma, CA 95476

PUTTING UP PRESERVES
★★★

Although your grandmother did it as a matter of course, many modern homemakers have to learn home canning and freezing from scratch—from choosing the right fruit and vegetables to using modern preserving techniques. The *Kerr Home Canning and Freezing Book* includes illustrated step-by-step directions for canning, freezing, and pickling. There are also dozens of recipes for fruit juices, salads, main dishes, jellies, preserves, butters and conserves, and sauces that you can prepare and freeze for later use. A special section on canning for the diabetic shows you how to can without using sugar. A practical book to have in your kitchen.

Write for:
 Kerr Home Canning and Freezing Book

Cost: $2.00

Send to:
 Kerr Glass Mfg. Corp.
 Consumer Products Div.
 P.O. Box 76961
 Los Angeles, CA 90076

WHAT TO DO
WITH ALL THAT FISH?
★★

Catch too many fish? Is your freezer filling up? Then try preserving your fish in one of three exciting ways: smoking, canning, or pickling. Three fish preserving pamphlets from the University of Wisconsin tell you how, with step-by-step instructions on how to safely pickle, can, or smoke fish at home. They also include laboratory-tested, mouth-watering recipes to enhance your fish dinners. Good information, attractively presented. Order one, two, or all three of the booklets.

A SASE is a self-addressed stamped envelope.

Write for:
Home Pickling of Fish
Home Canning of Fish
Home Smoking of Fish

Cost: 42¢ each for Home Pickling and Home
Canning
47¢ For Home Smoking

Send to:
Agricultural Bulletins
30 N. Murray St.
Rm. 245
Madison, WI 53715

PICKLISH SITUATIONS

★★★★

No hamburger or hot dog should be without them.
Whether sweetly piquant, mouth-puckeringly sour,
or flaming hot and pungent, pickles and relishes
bring zest to the table. With modern methods it
takes just a few hours in the kitchen to transform the
bounty of your garden into a year-round supply of
pickled delicacies. Most of the recipes in this 32-page
booklet are for fresh-pack pickles, produce which
has been prepared and packed raw into jars. Some
are for traditional brined pickles. There are recipes
for sweet and sour pickles, dills, and refrigerator
and freezer pickles. You'll want to try your hand at
pickling fruits and vegetables such as cabbage,
squash, and green beans. Rhubarb chutney and
green tomato mincemeat are a couple of the relish
recipes you'll find. This booklet includes loads of
pickling tips and a chart to help you prevent problems that might occur.

Write for:
Favorite Pickles and Relishes: Bulletin A-91

Cost: $1.95

Send to:
Garden Way Publishing
Storey Communications, Inc.
Schoolhouse Road
Pownal, VT 05261

INSTANT PICKLES

★★★★

If the idea of making pickles puts you in mind of
hours of work in the kitchen, here's a real eye-opener
for you. Seventeen of the 51 recipes in this attractive
cookbooklet need only overnight refrigeration (to
blend the flavors) before serving. Among them are
Peach Raisin Chutney, Spicy Orange Beets, an interesting Cauli-Slaw, and Jiffy Spiced Fruit with a base

of peaches or pears. There are lots of good traditional pickle recipes too—sweet, dill, and mixed
pickles; Kosher Dills; Pickles Indienne—along with
relishes and fruit and vegetable preserving ideas.
Better yet, you learn just how to get started with the
right equipment, ingredients, and techniques. There's
a chart of common weights and measures; information on adjusting processing times if you live more
than 1000 feet above sea level; and a trouble-shooting
guide to pickling problems like hollow, soft, or slippery pickles. Lots of good information packed into a
neat, 32-page publication from Heinz. You'll also get
a recipe postcard and a little folder of recipes from
State Fair Blue Ribbon winners.

Write for:
Heinz Guide to Successful Pickling (plus Blue
Ribbon folder and pickle postcard)

Cost: Free with a large SASE (6″ × 9″) with
60¢ postage

Send to:
Heinz Guide to Successful Pickling
Heinz U.S.A.
P.O. Box 57
Pittsburgh, PA 15230-0057

Heinz Guide to Successful Pickling

EGGS IN A PICKLE

★

Pickling eggs is a popular method of preserving
them, and it's done by placing peeled, hard-cooked
eggs in a solution of vinegar, salt, spices, and other
seasonings. This pamphlet tells you which eggs to
use for pickling and how to prepare them for pickling, and it contains six different pickling recipes for
a dozen eggs at a time; choose from Red Beet Eggs,
Sweet and Sour Eggs, Dark and Spicy Eggs, Cidered
Eggs, Dilled Eggs, and Pineapple Pickled Eggs—all
unusual additions to your menu. You'll get other egg
information and recipes along with this brochure.

continued

FOOD

Write for:
Peter Piper Picked a Peck of Pickled Eggs

Cost: $1.00 and a long SASE

Send to:
Georgia Egg Commission
State Farmers' Market
Forest Park, GA 30050

DRYING FOODS AT HOME
★★★

Drying, one of the oldest methods of preserving food, is still useful, convenient, and space-saving. This booklet tells you how to dry vegetables and fruits in your kitchen oven or in a special food dehydrator. You'll learn how to pretreat the food and how sulfuring is one way to preserve color, prevent souring, and retain vitamins A and C—you get thorough instructions for doing it, too. You'll also find out how to pack and store food after it's dried. And there are recipes for making fruit and vegetable leathers, meat jerky, and using dried vegetables and fruits in delicious dishes. Good charts and illustrations.

Write for:
Home Drying of Foods

Cost: $1.50

Send to:
Distribution Center
7 Research Park
Cornell University
Ithaca, NY 14850

SPROUTS: A GARDEN IN THE KITCHEN

Sprouts are vegetables you can grow all year long without a garden of any kind. All you need is an empty jar, untreated seeds, and a few days' growing time. Although sprouting is easy and inexpensive, there are a few tricks to learn, and this free illustrated booklet will teach you to sprout everything from the more familiar alfalfa and mung beans to broccoli, cabbage, and cauliflower seeds. Hang the full-page sprout information chart in your kitchen for easy reference on how to sprout, when to harvest, and how to use your generous crops.

Write for:
Sprouts

Cost: Free with a long SASE

Send to:
Customer Service
W. Atlee Burpee Co.
300 Park Ave.
Warminster, PA 18974

WHEN YOU *REALLY* EAT OUT

Here's a handy leaflet on edible wild plants. There are no sketches of the plants because it's easy to misidentify immature ones, and rather than rely on pictures you should have an expert with you when you go out on your first few collecting trips. Still, here's good information on fresh fruits that you can eat, where you can obtain flour from plants, and lots of spring pot herbs, mushrooms, salad fixings, starchy vegetable substitutes, drinks, and sweets— all found in the wild. Did you know that Queen Anne's lace is the parent of the culinary carrot? Or that some people prefer chickweed to spinach? Interesting stuff in this little foldout.

Write for:
Edible Wild Plants

Cost: Free with a long SASE

Send to:
West Virginia Dept. of Agriculture
State Capitol Building
Charleston, WV 25305

SPROUT YOUR OWN SEEDS

Health food people will tell you that sprouting seeds is a nutritious, self-sufficient way of providing food for oneself in a world where the available food supply is diminishing in quantity and quality. *The Sproutletter*, a 12-page newsletter published six times a year, is devoted to spreading the word about sprouting. It has articles on how to sprout wild and cultivated seeds, recipes using sprouts, and news about what's going on in the world of sprouts, nutrition, and indoor food gardening. You can get a sample copy for $1.50.

Write for:
Sample issue of The Sproutletter

Cost: $1.50

Send to:
Sprouting Publications
P.O. Box 62-V
Ashland, OR 97520

A SASE is a self-addressed stamped envelope.

BE YOUR OWN WINE MAKER

★★

The good news: Even a beginner can make fruit wine, according to *The Vierka Wine Book*, a 32-page encyclopedia of wine-making. The not so good news: This book won't tell you exactly *how* to do it. There's a certain amount of technical information about yeasts, sugars, and handling fruit, and the essentials are included here on pages tightly packed with information in small type. There are also sections on handling disease and other wine-making problems, as well as recipes for apple, apricot, cherry, dandelion, date, elderberry, plum, rosehip, and other delicious fruit wines.

The translation from the German is a bit stilted, but the booklet is readable. If you already know something about wine-making, this nice little encyclopedia is a good addition to your library. If you're brand new to the subject, however, a lot of your beginner's questions will go unanswered.

Write for:
   The Vierka Wine Book

Cost: $1.95

Send to:
   Semplex of U.S.A.
   4805 Lyndale Ave. North
   Minneapolis, MN 55430

BREWING UP
IN THE BASEMENT?

★

Any adult may make wine and beer for personal use — 100 gallons of each per year. A household with more than one adult member may make 200 gallons of each a year. This catalog has everything you'll need to make wine and beer, from concentrated fruit juices to a list of how-to books. There's even extract of root beer, ginger ale, and cola available for home-made soft drinks. The catalog doesn't tell you how to do it, though.

Write for:
   Catalog of Supplies for the Amateur Winemaker
      and Beermaker

Cost: Free

Send to:
   Semplex of U.S.A.
   4805 Lyndale Ave. North
   Minneapolis, MN 55430

MAKING APPLE CIDER

★★★

If you want to encourage the children to cut down their soft drink consumption, let them help you make a healthy substitute. Even if you've never done it before, making your own apple cider is not such an awesome task. This 32-page book includes a good discussion of basic equipment and a fine guide to what constitutes "perfect" cider apples, followed by a step-by-step guide to making your own cider. Also included are recipes and hints for what to do with all the leftover pomace (skins, cores, seeds, stems, and pulp) that you've wrung free of juice. Illustrated with cheerful photographs—the little girl on the cover is a charmer.

Write for:
   Making the Best Apple Cider: Bulletin A-47

Cost: $1.95

Send to:
   Garden Way Publishing
   Schoolhouse Rd.
   Pownal, VT 05261

Making the Best Apple Cider

SWEETER THAN HONEY

★★★

At first, most city dwellers can't tell a sugar maple from a red maple or a Norway maple. But don't be discouraged. This book explains how to recognize each type of maple, and how to make maple sugar if the tree in your yard is the right kind. There's information on the equipment you'll need. You'll learn how to pick the right spring day and start tapping your tree by ten o'clock in the morning—you'll have plenty of sap by suppertime. Next, you boil it, "apron" it, and presto, you've got do-it-yourself maple syrup for home use. By the end of the season, you'll know whether you're interested enough to get into sugar-

continued

FOOD

ing in a bigger way. If so, the later chapters of this 32-page book will tell you how.

Write for:
Making Maple Syrup: Bulletin A-51

Cost: $1.95

Send to:
Garden Way Publishing
Schoolhouse Rd.
Pownal, VT 05261

DO-IT-YOURSELF HONEY
★★★

Now here's an interesting idea for a hobby—and a practical one at that. Beekeeping will give you all the honey you need, and you'll probably have some left over for special gifts to friends. According to this nice manual, beekeeping is a challenging hobby equally suitable for youngsters, active adults, and retired people—you might even earn a few extra dollars by selling some of your honey. *Starting Right With Bees* is a practical 32-page book designed to get the beginner off to a good start. It will answer many of your early questions, offer solutions to common problems, and—of course—teach you to make honey.

Write for:
Starting Right With Bees: Bulletin A-36

Cost: $1.95

Send to:
Garden Way Publishing
Schoolhouse Rd.
Pownal, VT 05261

Starting Right With Bees

ATTITUDES FOR BEEKEEPERS
★★★★

The novice beekeeper will find this hefty information packet a boon. It includes *all* kinds of information on this hobby/business. There are six photo-illustrated booklets on beekeeping equipment, package bees, the honeyflow, spring and fall management of bees, and pollination for the home gardener. You'll also receive a catalog of beekeeping equipment, along with an order form, price list, and some taste-tempting recipes made with golden honey. Lots of information for the money, and it's all updated annually.

Write for:
Beekeeping Information Packet

Cost: $1.00

Send to:
Dadant & Sons, Inc.
Hamilton, IL 62341

Barbecuing and Other Entertainment Ideas

ALL FIRED UP
★★★★

Barbecue is a great American tradition. Americans can't claim to have invented it, but outdoor chefs across the land have perfected charcoal cooking, adding their own touches and making it America's favorite way to cook and entertain. *Kingsford's Best Barbecues: A Tour of American Regional Favorites* is a full-color, 48-page barbecue cookbook you'll want in your collection. It features several creatively different menus and recipes as developed by seven of America's favorite regional barbecue chefs, each sharing their philosophies and cooking experiences. You'll also learn the history of Kingsford charcoal and how to start and maintain an ideal fire. There is a list of tips and general advice for better barbecues.

Write for:
Kingsford's Best Barbecues

Cost: $2.00

Send to:
The Clorox Company
Department CC-FT
P.O. Box 24305
Oakland, CA 94623

A SASE is a self-addressed stamped envelope.

Kingsford's Best Barbecues

BARBECUE, AMERICAN-STYLE

★★★

People who barbecue are always looking for something—and the newest thing in outdoor cooking is mesquite, a wild wood that gives off an aromatic smoke when burned. *New American Barbecue Recipes* is a color-illustrated leaflet that gives tips and recipes for barbecuing with mesquite. It comes from Clorox, the manufacturers of Kingsford charcoal briquets. You'll soon be preparing Grilled Shrimp in Peanut Sauce, Eggplant Parmigiana, and Barbecue Ribs with Mustard-Honey Glaze. All are flavored with the secret ingredient of the Southwest. You'll learn how to build the perfect cooking fire and how to estimate the temperature of the grill surface.

Write for:
New American Barbecue Recipes

Cost: 25¢

Send to:
The Clorox Company
Department CC-FT
P.O. Box 24305
Oakland, CA 94623

BREAK OUT THE BARBECUE

★★★

Twelve new barbecue ideas are offered in this attractive little booklet from Heinz to tempt you to try their Thick and Rich Barbecue Sauce. Along with treatments of such classic barbecue fare as spareribs, short ribs, and steaks, you get interesting dishes with an ethnic flavor—like East-West Chicken, Pei Par Orange Duck, and Haute Creole Barbecue Shrimp. Or try the Double Heroes—hot and sweet Italian sausage with red and green peppers on split rolls, or a Mixed Grill Brochette with boneless lamb

chunks, calves' liver, bacon, and vegetables. You can also try brushing grilled vegetables or fresh corn with barbecue sauce for a different accompaniment to the meal. The dishes can be cooked in the oven when the weather won't allow outdoor dining.

Write for:
Big, Bold Barbecue

Cost: Free with a long SASE (39¢ postage)

Send to:
Big, Bold Barbecue
c/o Heinz, U.S.A.
P.O. Box 57
Pittsburgh, PA 15230-0057

Big, Bold Barbecue

THE GOURMET GRILL

★★★

Barbecues add zest to campouts, beach trips, picnics, tailgate parties and virtually every outdoor activity. They also make weeknight dinners more exciting; and cooking on an outdoor grill is easy. This one-page foldout leaflet from Clorox, manufacturers of Kingsford charcoal briquets, contains six color-illustrated recipes to spark your next barbecue dinner. Try Grilled Sausage with Apples and Onions or Swordfish with Wine Herb Baste tonight. Full-course menu ideas are given along with each recipe. There are also directions for the perfect fire. Invite the whole gang over!

Write for:
Fast and Easy Barbecue Recipes

Cost: Free with a long SASE

Send to:
The Clorox Company
Department CC-FT
P.O. Box 24305
Oakland, CA 94623

FOOD

DECORATIONS TO TAKE THE CAKE

★★★★

Have you ever yearned to squeeze cake frosting out of one of those tubes and create garlands of roses, borders of icing lace, tiny icing flowers, or stars, stripes, and leaves of icing? This beginner's booklet is from the Wilton Cake Decorating Products people and gives you explicit instructions (along with detailed color photographs) for decorating 30 different cakes, including clown cakes, shower cakes, a castle cake for your birthday princess, a baseball cake featuring glove and baseball, and a host of decorating ideas for cookies and cupcakes. The center section of the booklet is a catalog of cake decorating equipment.

Write for:
Wilton Beginners Guide to Cake Decorating

Cost: $1.99

Send to:
Wilton®
2240 W. 75th St.
Woodridge, IL 60517

LIVEN IT UP WITH LIME

★

If you're a versatile bartender or a cook who likes food to look as good as it tastes, check out the tips in this cheery six-page foldout. Learn how to pick a good, fresh lime and how to keep it that way; how to get the most juice out of a lime—keep it at room temperature for at least an hour; and how to make perfect fluted slices, lime curls, lime wedges, lime cartwheels, lime twists, lime boats, even lime ice cubes. An accompanying information sheet gives you ideas for using limes in hot and cold drinks, desserts, main meals, lunches, and brunches. You'll just have to try Lime Scramble—lime juice sprinkled over guess what.

Write for:
How To Make Great Garnishes With Florida Limes
Limes, Limes, Limes . . . Florida's Juicy Fruit

Cost: Free with a long SASE

Send to:
Kendall Foods Corp.
P.O. Box 458
Goulds, FL 33170

CROWD-PLEASING APPETIZERS

★

All of these are quantity recipes for showers, teas, receptions, cocktail parties, and coffees, and all of them make use of the ubiquitous egg. There are some lovely-sounding miniature cream puffs that you can fill with either lemon curd or chicken spread; Date Nut Finger Sandwiches; Stuffed Dill Pickle Slices; Tuna Party Dip; and Chicken Almond Finger Sandwiches. A simple rule of thumb allows two to four appetizers per person. Any of these recipes can easily be doubled or tripled if you're having a really big bash. The Georgia Egg Commission will send other egg recipes along with this brochure.

Write for:
Appetizing Appetizers Using Eggs

Cost: $1.00 and a long SASE

Send to:
Free Things
Georgia Egg Commission
State Farmers' Market
Forest Park, GA 30050

DON'T LET YOUR PARTY THROW YOU

★★

Giving parties is fun when you have everything you need to carry it off. But lots of people just don't have the right equipment—or not in the necessary quantities—for large-scale festivities. There is a solution, however; you can rent everything (and everybody, excluding your guests), from china and table linen to waiters and waitresses. *Your Party Rental Guide* is a free 16-page booklet, illustrated in full color, put out by the American Rental Association to prove that you don't have to live like a Rockefeller to throw an impressive bash.

This handy little booklet promotes the ARA's rental activities, but there are also practical recipes for a good cocktail party, dinner party, graduation party, or class reunion, plus good coverage of how to plan a full wedding reception. All in all, a useful standby for the hopeful host or hostess.

Write for:
Your Party Rental Guide

Cost: Free

A SASE is a self-addressed stamped envelope.

Good Things to Drink

A WINE IS JUST A WINE?

★

You may not have realized it, but most of your favorite wines are probably varietals, a fancy word for varieties. Cabernet Sauvignon, Chardonnay, Chenin Blanc, French Colombard, Pinot Noir, Riesling, and Zinfandel are some varietals. California varietals are produced to capture the distinctive taste of the named grape variety, such as the floral character of Riesling or the spiciness of Zinfandel. They're different from generic and proprietary wines, which are blended to create a consistent taste. There's more about varietals in this snappy little illustrated booklet from Paul Masson Vineyards. There are some recipes, too, calling for varietals wines in veal roast Florentine, swordfish or shark steaks, a sausage casserole, chicken kebabs, and beef medallions. Who said a wine is just a wine?

Write for:
What's a Varietal?

Cost: Free

Send to:
Paul Masson Vineyards
P.O. Box 1852
Saratoga, CA 95070-0199

What's a Varietal?

TRY IT WITH WINE

★★

Whether you sip it from an elegant glass or stir it into a sauce (or both), wine is a wonderful addition to a meal. Even simple everyday cookery perks up remarkably when you add a dash of wine to bring out the flavor. *Wine Cookery Made Easy,* from Meier's Wine Cellars of Cincinnati, has some unusual ideas for drinks, entrees, and desserts, including Mint Julep, One-Pot Chili, Cream Sherry Pie, and Rump Roast Rosé. Nice ways to make routine meals a bit special.

Write for:
Wine Cookery Made Easy

Cost: Free with a long SASE

Send to:
Promotional Dept.
Paramount Distillers
3116 Berea Rd.
Cleveland, OH 44111

A WINE LOVER'S GUIDE

★★

The wines of California have taken their place in the connoisseur's cellar, and Americans no longer have to go to Europe or other far-flung points to visit a vineyard. To help you plan some delightful visits of your own, the Wine Institute of California has prepared *California's Wine Wonderland,* a tour guide to the state's wineries. The 48-page directory lists more than 400 wineries open to the public.

Apart from a brief but clear explanation of wine-making, this little directory provides practical information—addresses and phone numbers, hours, travel directions, picnic facilities, whether you'll get a chance to do some wine-tasting. For easy reference, all the wineries are also indexed alphabetically at the back of the book. This handy booklet is a bargain, but you may also want to do more extensive reading on California wines and wine-making before you make your visit.

Write for:
California's Wine Wonderland

Cost: Free with a long SASE (39¢ postage)

Send to:
Wine Institute
165 Post St.
San Francisco, CA 94108

FOOD

WISING UP TO WINES

★★

According to Plato, "When a man drinks wine at dinner, he begins to be better pleased with himself." If you love wine, too, but are daunted by the mystique that sometimes surrounds it, send for *Ways With Wine*, a free 13-page booklet from Paul Masson Vineyards. It will answer some of your questions about serving temperatures, the correct way to open the bottle, and the proper glass to serve wine in.

Did you know you can make mixed drinks with wine, too? This little booklet includes several, such as champagne punch and sherry flip, as well as some unusual recipes for cooking with wine. Clearly a push for the brand-name wines, but a helpful little guide, and very readable.

Write for:
Ways With Wine

Cost: Free

Send to:
Paul Masson Vineyards
P.O. Box 2292
Saratoga, CA 95070-0199

CHILI AND...

★★

No one is quite sure who invented chili, but one thing's for certain—there are chili lovers all over the place. There's even an International Chili Society, and this little booklet from the Montezuma tequila people includes some of the Society's tempting championship chili recipes, including German Red Oklahoma Championship Chili, Georgia Championship Chili, Colorado Championship Indian Chili, and the 1972 World Championship Chili. Equally tempting Montezuma tequila drink recipes are also featured here. There's even an application form for membership in the International Chili Society—$10.00 a year, or $100.00 for life! The same distributor offers a leaflet introducing you to Sabroso, a coffee liqueur from Mexico, and telling you how to concoct drinks with exotic names like Latin Lover, Brave Bull, and the classic Black Russian.

Write for:
Chili Recipes from Montezuma
Treasures of Sabroso

Cost: Free

Send to:
Barton Brands
P.O. Box 1240
Chicago, IL 60690

HAVE SOME MADEIRA, M' DEAR...

★★

Perk up your meats, poultry, soups, stews, breads, and puddings with wine and see how the lips smack at your table. Starting in the 1700s in Colonial America, Madeira became a standard in preparing delights from New England to New Orleans. In Victorian England, no responsible hostess would dare serve a soup minus a splash of Madeira. Now you can enjoy the delights of Madeira in your meals by exploring the 14 recipes offered in a little folder about cooking with 3 Islands American Madeira wine. Recipes include New England Pork Chops, Boston Baked Chicken, Poached Fish Fillet, Spinach Soup, Hunter's Stew, Spiked Fruit Cocktail, Wine-Baked Apples, Spirited Brown Bread, and Twentieth Century Tipsy Pudding.

Write for:
3 Islands American Madeira in the Kitchen

Cost: Free with a long SASE

Send to:
Promotional Dept.
Paramount Distillers
3116 Berea Rd.
Cleveland, OH 44111

MAKE MINE MELON

★★★

The light, fresh, delicious flavor of ripe honeydew melon has a place in every cook's repertoire. Throughout the pages of this color recipe booklet by the distributors of Midori, you'll discover the versatile mixability of the melon liqueur. Professional bartenders have long found Midori to be a winning ingredient in drink competitions; their recipes, too, are given. The Mellonaire is the winner of the 1983 Bartender's Guild National Cocktail Competition and combines crème de banana, triple sec, sweet and sour, and Midori. Other beverage favorites include the Midori mimosa, and a range of frozen, creamy, and colada drinks. Midori comes to dinner, too, enhancing fruit cups, salad dressings, vegetables, seafood, and chicken. At the back of the book is an order form for glassware imprinted with the Midori logo.

A SASE is a self-addressed stamped envelope.

Write for:
The Midori Story

Cost: Free

Send to:
Midori Recipe Book Offer
P.O. Box 5646
Hamden, CT 06518

The Midori Story

SAMBUCA STYLE
★★★

For dinner tonight let's start with a Sambuca Snowball Slush, then go to the Scambuca (scampi flamed in sambuca) and linger leisurely over Chocolate Sambuca Mousse and coffee. Anything is possible when you stash the Sambuca Romana next to your spice rack. In a delightful four-color recipe book, the makers of this Italian liqueur demonstrate 56 ways to cook with sambuca—besides the traditional manner, of course, which is to drink it straight up with three coffee beans. There are recipes for cocktails, party punches, and after dinner drinks. You'll soon be lacing your desserts and basting your meats with the licorice-flavored liqueur.

Write for:
Sambuca Romana Recipe Book

Cost: Free

Send to:
Palmer & Lord, Ltd.
345 Underhill Blvd.
Syosset, NY 11791
RE: Sambuca Romana Recipe Book

MORE THAN A DRINK
★

"Wow—I Could Have Had a V-8!" Remember the ad? In fact, according to this color pamphlet, V-8 vegetable juice is for more than just drinking. This combination of the juices of eight vegetables can be used in sauces, salad dressings, salads, fish and vegetable dishes, beef kabobs, Oriental Chicken, Vegetarian Lasagna, and Turkey Tostadas. Recipes for these and other dishes using V-8 juice are yours for the asking. And the makers remind you that V-8 has only 35 calories per 6-ounce serving, is high in vitamins A and C, and contains no preservatives.

Write for:
Eat Well, Feel Great With V-8

Cost: Free

Send to:
Communications Center
Campbell Soup Company
Campbell Place
Camden, NJ 01801

A PERFECT POT OF TEA
★

This mini-flyer offers the final word on tea drinking from "just about the oldest tea company in the world" and the only one in England to be operated on a continuing basis by nine generations of the same family. The House of Twining dates back to 1706, and you'll get a description of its full line of teas in this tiny guide. Eighteen tea blends are listed along with their origins, characteristics, and brief serving suggestions. There are directions, too, for brewing the perfect pot of tea.

Write for:
The Twinings Tea Guide

Cost: Free with a SASE

Send to:
Twinings Tea
Box TW
c/o Grossich and Partners
38 E. 29th St.
New York, NY 10016

The Twinings Tea Guide

FOOD

Slimming and Special Diets

CALORIES: YOUR BODY COUNTS THEM

★★

Many fad diets advise you not to count calories. But your body will whether you do or not, and if you want to lose weight you might as well learn to count them accurately. You'll also need to know what nutrients your body needs when you're on a diet. This folder tells you how to cut your calorie intake even while you're eating the same things you've always eaten—for instance, take smaller portions, and put them on a smaller plate to look large. You'll learn how many calories different forms of exercise will burn off. There are 11 great self-help tips for dieting, and the names of organizations that will help if you just can't do it alone.

Write for:
What To Know About a Weight-Control Diet
    Before You Eat One

Cost: 20¢

Send to:
Order Department
National Dairy Council
6300 N. River Rd.
Rosemont, IL 60018-4233

ALL THINGS IN MODERATION

★★★

We all know that good eating is essential to good health, but with the barrage of diets, theories, research, and whims of today's nutritional practitioners, what can you believe? The U.S. Department of Agriculture and the U.S. Department of Health and Human Services combined efforts to publish this colorful 24-page booklet, *Dietary Guidelines for Americans*. Suggesting a seven-point program for presently healthy adults, the guidelines are explored in detail with advice on achieving each one. There is information for starting a new baby on an adequate diet, losing weight, calorie expenditure for various physical activities, avoiding cholesterol and sugar, and more. Food alone cannot make you healthy, but good eating habits based on moderation and variety can keep you healthy and improve your overall health.

Write for:
Dietary Guidelines for Americans (No. 520P)

Cost: Free

Send to:
Consumer Information Center
P.O. Box 100
Pueblo, CO 81002

FOR CALORIE COUNTERS

★★★

This calorie catalog with information on more than 1,200 foods is offered by the National Dairy Council. To make it easy to use, entries are organized around the four food groups: milk products, meats, fruits and vegetables, and grains. Besides making it easier to find a particular food so you can check its calorie count, the catalog's organization helps emphasize the importance of maintaining good health by eating foods from each of the four food groups daily. This 24-page 5″×7″ booklet can help cooks simplify the task of figuring the balance of nutrients the body needs.

Write for:
Your Calorie Counter

Cost: 70¢

Send to:
Order Department
National Dairy Council
6300 N. River Rd.
Rosemont, IL 60018-4233

FOOLING YOUR SWEET TOOTH

★★★

When your doctor, or your figure, tells you it's time to cut back on sugar, you can fool your sweet tooth by using sugar substitutes. For 50¢ to cover postage and handling, the makers of Sweet 'n Low will send you sample packets of their product, which is made from dextrose and saccharine. A one-gram packet of Sweet 'n Low gives you the sweetness of two teaspoons of sugar for only 3½ calories, and you can stash the little packet in your purse or pocket so that you'll always have a supply on hand when you're lunching or dining out, having a cup of coffee at your desk, or visiting a friend.

Write for:
Sweet 'n Low samples

Cost: 50¢

A SASE is a self-addressed stamped envelope.

Send to:
Cumberland Packing Corp.
2 Cumberland St.
Brooklyn, NY 11205

Sweet 'n Low samples

GO TURKEY!

★★★

Here's a new diet built around turkey. Because turkey is one of the lowest calorie meats around, you can indulge in larger portions of turkey than possible with other meats when you follow a special two-week diet plan designed by the director of California's Western Nutritional Services. The recipes sound delicious and filling. And if you decide not to go with the diet plan, the recipes can add variety to your turkey dishes. There are recipes for Turkey Cutlets, Florentine Stuffed Turkey Breast, Ginger Turkey Stir-Fry, Fruited Turkey Mini-Roasts, Turkey Wings Jerusalem made with white wine, and Orange-Cranberry Turkey Slices. The format is a glossy poster you can hang in the kitchen; you even get a turkey magnet to hold it to the refrigerator. A good deal for a dollar—provided, of course, you like turkey.

Write for:
The Two-Week California Turkey Diet

Cost: $1.00

Send to:
Diet
California Turkey Industry Board
P.O. Box 3329
Modesto, CA 95353-3329

DIETING WITH YOGURT

★★

Only seven pages of this pocket-sized 60-page book are devoted to diet menus. The remaining pages talk about a psychological mind-set for dieting, with the emphasis on what you should eat while you diet rather than what you should *not* eat. There's good advice on eating behavior and habits that will help you diet, learning self-discipline, understanding why you sometimes have cravings to eat, and combining exercise with your diet. There's a calorie guide to many common foods and nutritional information on all types of yogurt. This booklet is written by Dr. Morton B. Glenn, former president of the American College of Nutrition.

Write for:
The Yogurt Way to Diet

Cost: 50¢

Send to:
The Dannon Company, Inc.
Dept. "B"
P.O. Box 1975
Long Island City, NY 11101

The Yogurt Way to Diet

BREAD TAKES THE DREAD OUT OF DIETING

★★

If the details of dieting stump you, maybe you need this handy foldout brochure that fits in your pocket or hangs on your fridge. It's small, but filled with dieting data—a weight chart; an excellent though abbreviated calorie counter; 14 days' worth of menus; how to adapt the diet for men, teens, and non-dieters; acceptable substitutions; and best of all, tips on how to outsmart the fatty inside you. You can even eat bread—in fact, this low-fat diet is based on using Roman Meal bread when appropriate.

Write for:
Diet and Nutrition Plan

Cost: Free with a SASE

continued

FOOD

Send to:
Roman Meal Co.
Dept. F
P.O. Box 11126
Tacoma, WA 98411-0126

Send to:
Free Things
Georgia Egg Commission
State Farmers' Market
Forest Park, GA 30050

DIETING WITH RICE

★★

Provided you like rice, here's a week's worth of recipes that look pretty easy to prepare. *Uncle Ben's 7-Day Rice Diet* offers nutritionally balanced plans to let you eat three meals a day for a total count of about 1000 calories (a multivitamin a day is recommended). Preparation time is streamlined because you can cook enough rice at one time to use in several meals— you can cover what's left over and store it in the refrigerator. These dishes are good for low-sodium diets, too, with salt often replaced by lemon juice, herbs, or spices. Monday's menu lets you dine on Curried Orange Chicken, then you progress through the week to a Sunday brunch of Fisherman's Frittata, with soup and a dessert of Mexican Chocolate Rice Cream for dinner. If you hate rice, forget the whole thing.

Write for:
Uncle Ben's 7-Day Rice Diet

Cost: Free with a long SASE

Send to:
Uncle Ben's 7-Day Rice Diet™
P.O. Box 725—Dept. 1200
Lubbock, TX 79491-0526

EGGS-ACTLY 80 CALORIES

★★

If you're trying to diet, keep in mind that one egg is packed with protein and vitamins, yet contains only 80 calories. That's straight from the Georgia Egg Commission, who put out this folder of low-calorie egg recipes designed to stretch budgets and "egg your diet on." There's a 40-calorie lemon curl cookie recipe; coffee fluff at 67 calories per serving; a cottage cheese and egg spread made with Worcestershire sauce, dry mustard, hot pepper sauce, and minced onions at a low 134 calories per serving; and a hearty stay-trim salad that weighs in at just 125 calories. Your copy of *Size Things Up With Eggs* will come with a selection of other egg information and recipes.

Write for:
Size Things Up With Eggs

Cost: $1.00 and a long SASE

DELICIOUS SALAD DRESSINGS

★★★

Many people eat salads regularly because they taste so good and help keep you fit and lean. But the vegetables, fruit, meat, cheese, fish, or eggs you put in your salads can give you a heavy calorie wallop and insufficient nutrients for your body's everyday needs. Here is a new guide to help you mix and match salad ingredients that are low in calories and high in nutrition, along with suggestions for dressings that offer delicious taste with fewer calories per tablespoon. Another brochure with tantalizing color photos offers recipes for a garden salad, cucumber and herb dressing mold, and creamy macaroni and cheese salad using Hidden Valley Ranch dressings. Some mouth-watering salad ideas here to help you reduce your caloric intake.

Write for:
Mix 'n Match Salad Making Calorie & Nutrition
  Guide
Fresh Salad Ideas and Recipes

Cost: 25¢ each

Send to:
The Clorox Company
P.O. Box 24305
Oakland, CA 94623

DELIGHTS OF ALMOND OIL

★★

Almond oil is said to have been one of the ingredients in the cosmetics used by Cleopatra and other noble Egyptian ladies of her time. It was also burned in ancient times to give light. Nowadays, we use it for cooking. Almond oil has no cholesterol, and because it is cold-pressed it is lower in saturated fats than most other cooking oils. In addition to being nutritious it has a mild aroma that gives a light, subtle flavor to food. The Almond Board of California offers a 10-page recipe leaflet on almond oil and its use in cooking. Recipes include Almond Muffins, Oyster Beef Chow Mein, Pesto Pasta Salad, and Chocolate Mousse Pie.

Write for:
Light & Lively Recipes With California
  Almond Oil

A SASE is a self-addressed stamped envelope.

Cost: Free with a long SASE

Send to:
Almond Board of California
P.O. Box 15920
Sacramento, CA 95852

A ROUNDUP OF HEALTHY EATING
★★★

Three recipe leaflets from the Hain Nutrition Bureau are chock-full of tips for reducing cholesterol and sodium and adding fiber in your diet. The first, *Dietary Fiber Tips & Recipes,* explains how to add fiber effectively and deliciously and why it is important to our overall well-being. Included are ten kitchen-tested recipes for such fibrous dishes and foods as fruits, vegetables, salads, dried beans and peas, and whole grains. The second leaflet, *Low-Sodium Tips & Recipes,* contains nutrition information and a series of creative ways to reduce sodium, including seven tested new recipes. *Low-Sodium* also includes a list of 46 no-salt-added, all-natural food products that are available today. *Low-Cholesterol Tips & Recipes* discusses the dangers of cholesterol and gives 17 suggestions for reducing this harmful substance in our bodies. Six great recipes, including Chicken Italiano and New Orleans Gumbo, are given.

Write for:
Dietary Fiber Tips & Recipes
Low-Sodium Tips & Recipes
Low-Cholesterol Tips & Recipes

Cost: Free

Send to:
The Hain Nutrition Information Bureau
c/o Lewis & Neale, Inc.
928 Broadway
New York, NY 10010

TOFU: A TALENTED FOOD
★★★★

What is tofu? It's a delicious, mild-flavored "cheese" made from soybeans. It looks like ricotta cheese pressed into a dense, congealed square. Tofu is a low-calorie, low-sodium, cholesterol-free, protein-rich, inexpensive food. This booklet, *Cooking With Tofu,* is filled with information on how to incorporate tofu into your meal plans, its nutritional values,

and how to make your own from scratch. Tofu goes into eggs, salads, soups, and desserts and can be deep-fried as an appetizer. You'll find recipes for tofu burgers (good hot or cold), lasagna, and egg-free mayonnaise. There is even advice on growing your own soybeans.

Write for:
Cooking With Tofu: Bulletin A-74

Cost: $1.95

Send to:
Garden Way Publishing
Storey Communications, Inc.
Schoolhouse Road
Pownal, VT 05261

Cooking With Tofu

GUILT-FREE BUTTER
★★

Butter Buds are butter-flavored granules that you reconstitute with water to get the taste of melted butter without, the makers assure you, the high cholesterol, high calories, or high cost of real butter. If you'd like to try them, the company will send you a sample half-ounce packet plus a three-page 3″×5″ foldout of recipes using Butter Buds. A 4-ounce portion of liquid Butter Buds has only 48 calories, compared to 800 in a 4-ounce stick of butter, and you can pour it over cooked vegetables; stir it into soups, casseroles, and sauces; or add it to cake mixes, diet dinners, or frozen foods. You can't fry with it, though, since it's a fat-free product.

Write for:
Sample packet of Butter Buds and recipe foldout

Cost: 50¢

continued

FOOD

Sample packet of Butter Buds and recipe foldout

LEMON LIVENS A LOW-SODIUM DIET

★★★

This is one of the best booklets around on planning low-sodium meals and enhancing them with other flavors and herbs. It's from the Sunkist people, and its emphasis is on using fresh citrus fruits—especially lemons—to add zest and flavor to appetizers, soups, salads, meats, poultry, fish, vegetables, desserts, and snacks. There's also a great section on what to order when you eat out if you're avoiding salt; a sodium- and calorie-content chart of popular fresh produce items; and some fresh lemon recipes like Lemon-Lite Creamy Carrot Soup, Turkey Piccata á la Lemon, Fresh Lemon Mayonnaise, and Three-Spice Lemon Chicken Salad. Fifteen practical, lemon-yellow pages.

Write for:
Pass the Salt

Cost: Free with a long SASE

Send to:
Consumer Services
Sunkist Growers
Box 7888
Van Nuys, CA 91409

LOW-SODIUM FRUITS AND VEGETABLES

★★

Did you know that an apple contains only one milligram of sodium per 100 grams, a tomato only three?

So if you're on a sodium-restricted diet or just want to cut down on your salt intake, step up the quantities of fresh fruits and vegetables in your diet. This small recipe folder contains a sodium content chart for most fresh fruits and vegetables plus ten low-sodium recipes for vegetable, salad, chicken, and fish dishes. A useful detail—each recipe gives the sodium content for six servings and for one serving. You'll find some hints for savory salt substitutes, too.

Write for:
Low-Sodium Cooking

Cost: Free with a long SASE

Send to:
United Fresh Fruit and Vegetable Association
727 N. Washington St.
Alexandria, VA 22314

CITRUS FRUITS FOR THE DIABETIC

★★

Diabetics must make careful choices about the types and quantities of carbohydrates they consume. This sensible booklet from the Sunkist people thoroughly explains the role in the diabetic diet of the carbohydrates found in citrus fruits. It also tells how citrus fruits should be eaten or drunk before strenuous exercise, how they can be a great boon when eating out, and how to use them for snacks. There's a chart showing the carbohydrate content of fresh fruits and juices, and dried and canned fruits. You'll also find some delicious-sounding recipes like Tangerine Orange Gel, Orange Biscuits, and Lemon Chicken. This booklet is also available in Spanish.

Write for:
Citrus Fruits in the Diabetic Diet

Cost: Free with a long SASE

Send to:
Consumer Services
Sunkist Growers
Box 7888
Van Nuys, CA 91409

SPICE IT UP!

★★

People on all kinds of diets are finding spices perfectly suited to their needs: They're rich in flavor, yet low in sodium, calories, fat, and cholesterol. The American Spice Trade Association shows how to

A SASE is a self-addressed stamped envelope.

FOOD

make the best use of these advantages in its new *Spice & Diet Cookbooklet*. It features 31 delicious recipes, such as Baked Cranberry Pork Chops, Mediterranean Fish Chowder, Honey and Lime Chicken, and Spiced Orange Chiffon Pie. It also includes a diet spice chart and complete nutritional analysis of the major spices. The recipes are grouped in three sections—low sodium, low calorie, and low carbohydrate—and each recipe shows a count for all three of these factors so that people on combined diet plans will have all the facts they need.

Write for:
Spice & Diet Cookbooklet

Cost: $1.00

Send to:
American Spice Trade Association
580 Sylvan Ave.
Englewood Cliffs, NJ 07632

Spice & Diet Cookbook

NOW CONSIDER LACTAID®
★★★

Not everyone can enjoy milk, ice cream, cheese, or other dairy products. Milk contains complex natural sugar, lactose. To digest lactose, the body has to produce an enzyme called lactase. If your body can't produce lactase, you have trouble digesting milk and its byproducts. Now comes a new product called LactAid®, an enzyme that splits lactose into more easily digestible sugars. To learn more about LactAid®, send for the free brochure, *Why LactAid®?* It could help you or a member of the family who gets sick from regular milk or milk byproducts. It gives a list of the lactose and calcium content of dairy foods, and tells which nondairy foods might contain lactose. The leaf also gives recipes using LactAid® Brand Specially Digestible® dairy products.

Write for:
Why LactAid®?

Cost: Free with a SASE

Send to:
LactAid®, Inc.
P.O. Box 111
600 Fire Rd.
Pleasantville, NJ 08232

TAKING A BREAK FROM SUGAR
★

If you're getting too much sugar in your diet, and most of us are, here's an alternative. Aspartame, which was discovered in 1965 and has become a well-known word in the language of calorie-counters, is a low-cal sweetener that is 180 times sweeter than sucrose. Aspartame is an important component in many reduced-calorie foods and beverages and is consumed regularly by more than 50 million Americans. A free brochure from the Calorie Control Council discusses aspartame and reviews its safety record and approval in 1981 by the Food and Drug Administration. In fact, aspartame was the first low-calorie sweetener to be approved by the FDA in more than 25 years.

Write for:
Aspartame

Cost: Free

Send to:
Calorie Control Council
Suite 500-D
5775 Peachtree-Dunwoody Rd.
Atlanta, GA 30342

SWEETNESS AND LIGHT
★★★

Of the three artifical sweeteners that have whet the palates of millions of Americans over the years, the one souring ingredient common to them all has been controversy. Saccharin, which has no calories yet is 300 times sweeter than sugar, and aspartame, which has the same amount of calories as sugar yet is 200 times as sweet, are currently available to help satisfy Americans' twin cravings for sweets and slimness. Cyclamate, calorie-free yet 30 times sweeter than sugar, was banned by the Food and Drug Administration in 1970 because of concerns over its safety. *Sweetness Minus Calories=Controversy* is a four-page pamphlet put out by the Department of Health

continued

FOOD

and Human Services. It discusses the three artificial sweeteners, their healthful use, test results, and RDA rulings.

Write for:
  Sweetness Minus Calories=Controversy
    (No. 526P)

Cost: Free

Send to:
  Consumer Information Center
  P.O. Box 100
  Pueblo, CO 81002

A LIGHTER FARE
★★

Pickings are no longer slim for dieters these days. The shelves in the diet sections of supermarkets are now groaning under the weight of new products promising good taste but fewer calories. Today's shedders are tempted with everything from salad dressing to cheese, and from gravy to beer. Light foods and beverages are among the fastest growing segments of the American food industry. However, a scorecard to help decipher the labels on these new products would be a useful tool for the shopper. Lite, light, sugarless, sugar free, reduced calorie, low calorie—these are some of the terms used. *That Lite Stuff* is a two-page flyer that explains all of this. Both the Food and Drug Administration and the Bureau of Alcohol, Tobacco and Firearms have labeling guidelines for dietetic foods and beverages. After reading this publication you'll be able to determine whether your shopping choices are actually saving you calories or not.

Write for:
  That Lite Stuff (No. 527P)

Cost: Free

Send to:
  Consumer Information Center
  P.O. Box 100
  Pueblo, CO 81002

Nutrition and Healthy Eating

A MINI-COURSE IN FOOD AND NUTRITION
★★★

Five pamphlets in this packet present vital information on what we eat and where and how we get it.

One concentrates on the "food biz" and suggests a dozen simple ways to outwit the industry and save money. Another discusses the scientific evidence that Americans eat too much fat and tells how to cut down on harmful saturated fat in the diet. The third talks about a nutritious diet of fresh vegetables; whole grains; more beans and low-fat milk; and more lean meat, fish, and poultry. The fourth talks about the dangers of chemical additives and how to eliminate two of the big ones—sugar and salt—from our diet (there's a good list of both safe and questionable additives). Finally, the last pamphlet tells you what's left to eat after you eliminate all the no-no's.

Write for:
  Midget Encyclopedia of Food and Nutrition

Cost: 25¢

Send to:
  Center for Science in the Public Interest
  1501 Sixteenth St., N.W.
  Washington, DC 20036

ARE YOU A SMART EATER?
★★★

Keep healthy by eating foods with the nutrients including vitamins and minerals that are necessary for growth and maintaining good health. A ten-page booklet from Pillsbury tells how to be sure you are getting the necessary nutrients in the right amounts. Learn all about protein, Vitamin A, thiamine, riboflavin, niacin, Vitamin C, calcium, and iron and the foods they are found in. There's a useful nutrition quiz that puts you on the spot about the nutritional content of your own diet and tells you whether or not you're a "smart eater."

Write for:
  Good Nutrition: A Bite in the Right Direction

Cost: Free with a long SASE

Send to:
  The Pillsbury Company
  Consumer Response
  P.O. Box 550
  Minneapolis, MN 55440-0550

DOES YOUR FOOD SCORE NUTRITIONALLY?
★★★

A serving of black beans gets the highest nutrition rating in this booklet, which scores hundreds of

A SASE is a self-addressed stamped envelope.

foods. A chocolate bar gets the lowest rating—minus 42. The booklet breaks down food into such categories as vegetables; grain foods; beans, nuts, and seeds; poultry, fish, meat and eggs; fresh fruits; nondairy beverages; snacks; dairy products; breakfast cereals and foods; and odds and ends. The higher the rating, the higher the nutritional content of the food. It's interesting to find out if what you eat is really good for you...and just *how* good. And if you've got kids who are receptive to nutritional facts, you'll open their eyes with *these* facts. Like a mock ad for pop—"Rips off your body as well as your purse."

Write for:
   Food Scorecard

Cost: $1.00

Send to:
   Center for Science in the Public Interest
   1501 Sixteenth St., N.W.
   Washington, DC 20036

HOW TO EAT RIGHT

★

What's safe to eat and what isn't? How can you enjoy eating and still lose weight? What foods are high in sodium, chemicals, or other preservatives? The Center for Science in the Public Interest has a free color catalog of materials that help you know what foods are safe to eat, what foods provide the most nutritional benefit, and what to avoid. The catalog describes about a dozen posters that cover important nutritional subjects. For instance, there's a "sodium scoreboard" poster, a fat and calorie guide, and another poster that evaluates the safety of dozens of preservatives and other chemicals that are added to our food. For those into regular exercising, there's another poster that tells how many calories various exercises eat up. And if you're concerned about how much sugar you consume, a poster tells the sugar content of more than 200 processed foods. An "Anti-Cancer Eating Guide" poster suggests what foods to eat to lower the risk of developing many types of cancer. The catalog is free (but the posters aren't). Good healthful eating tips from a respected source.

Write for:
   Life Saving Guides About Eating Right

Cost: Free

Send to:
   Center for Science in the Public Interest
   1501 Sixteenth St., NW
   Washington, DC 20036

JUNK OR GEMS?

★★

Everyone loves some junk food some of the time. That's why there are more than 140,000 fast food restaurants in the U.S. Why is fast food so popular? Because it's convenient—you can find a meal almost anywhere, anytime, and it's predictable—you know what you're getting. Moreover, "fast" food usually does live up to its name, which means it fits a busy life-style, and it is usually economical. But is fast food good for you? Here is a little color brochure that takes a closer look at fast food and just how good it is (or isn't) for you. On the plus side: Most fast food meals are good sources of protein and B vitamins. On the minus side: They can be low in calcium, low in vitamins A and C, and high in calories. Especially helpful here are suggestions for substitutes that can add more food value to an otherwise nutritionally inadequate fast food meal. Since the average American eats fast food nine times a month, it makes sense to know just what those nine meals add up to in terms of a total diet.

Write for:
   Fast Food: Junk? Gems? or Just OK?

Cost: 20¢

Send to:
   Order Department
   National Dairy Council
   6300 N. River Rd.
   Rosemont, IL 60018-4233

Fast Food: Junk? Gems? or Just OK?

FOOD

FOR FAST FOOD JUNKIES
★★★

Every day millions of Americans flock to an array of fast food restaurants to devour hamburgers, cheeseburgers, hot dogs, french fries, onion rings, pizza, tacos, shakes, and soft drinks. But are fast foods really nutritious? *What About Nutrients In Fast Foods?* is a four-page pamphlet from the Department of Health and Human Services which says there is no simple yes or no answer to the controversy over convenience dining. The article discusses overall healthful eating while exploring the specific vitamins and minerals found in some favorite fast foods. Tables list nutritive values of foods available at some restaurant chains.

Write for:
What About Nutrients In Fast Foods? (No. 529P)

Cost: Free

Send to:
Consumer Information Center
P.O. Box 100
Pueblo, CO 81002

HOW GOOD ARE FAST FOODS?
★★★

Most of us enjoy a meal at a "fast food" restaurant at least once in a while. Others depend on them regularly for a majority of their meals. Are hamburgers, hot dogs, fried chicken and other "fast foods" good for us? The American Council on Science and Health has prepared a 34-page booklet, *Fast Food and the American Diet*, which discusses the nutritional characteristics of fast foods and describes the actual and potential nutrient contributions of fast food meals to the daily diet. Is eating at a fast food restaurant cheaper than eating at home? Can fast foods be part of a healthy total daily diet? These and other questions are answered, and a handy chart shows the nutritional content of popular fast food.

Write for:
Fast Foods and the American Diet

Cost: $2.00

Send to:
American Council on Science and Health
47 Maple St.
Summit, NJ 07901

NO JUNK FOODS PERMITTED HERE
★★★

What a nice way of telling people that you do not welcome junk foods in your kitchen, office, cafeteria, classroom—or your life. It's a reminder to yourself, too, that junk foods add nothing to your health, but do cost you a lot of money and clutter up your cupboards and refrigerator. The eye-catching design, printed on an 8½" × 11" cardboard poster, shows a hot dog and bottle of soda circled in red and slashed with a heavy red line. The caption reads "Please! No Junk Foods." Indispensible for any household with members under 18—and many more with members *over* 18.

Write for:
Please! No Junk Foods poster

Cost: $2.00

Send to:
Center for Science in the Public Interest
1501 Sixteenth St., N.W.
Washington, DC 20036

HOW FOOD AFFECTS KIDS' SCHOOLWORK
★★★

Johnny had a chocolate bar and a cola for lunch and now he can't concentrate on his math. Why? Because caffeine—found in both the chocolate and the cola—has got him so hyped up he can't sit still and concentrate. And the sugar in the candy bar may be affecting his short-term memory. The message—kids who don't eat right don't learn right—is not new, but it's effectively repeated in this eight-page leaflet from the International Reading Association. Included here are some suggestions to parents for improving their children's diet, beyond making sure they eat right at home. For example, parents can encourage the inclusion of nutrition education in the school curriculum, and can work with school authorities to remove candy and caffeine beverages from school vending machines and replace them with healthier snacks like fruits, nuts, milk, and fruit drinks. Parents can also request that school fund-raising projects not rely on the sale of candy or sweets. Good information here for the concerned parent.

Write for:
Eating Well Can Help Your Child Learn Better

Cost: Free

A SASE is a self-addressed stamped envelope.

Send to:
International Reading Association
800 Barksdale Road
P.O. Box 8139
Newark, DE 19714-8139

TOO MUCH FAT?

★★

If you eat an average American diet, about 40 percent of your calories come from fat. The food may taste good to you, but all that fat could contribute to a heart attack, a stroke, or breast or bowel cancer. A new brochure tells you to eat a good diet based largely on fruits, vegetables, whole grains, low-fat dairy products, and low-fat poultry (without the skin) and fish. Learn about saturated fats, dietary cholesterol, fats, and what foods are best for you.

Write for:
The UN-greasy Spoon

Cost: 25¢

Send to:
Center for Science in the Public Interest
1501 Sixteenth St., N.W.
Washington, DC 20036

FAT FOR GOOD AND BAD

★★★★

To many diet-conscious consumers, fat is a dirty word. It means being overweight or obese and therefore is something to avoid. But the body needs some fat in the diet for good health. Fat also makes food taste better and keeps you from getting hungry just after a meal. A new government publication discriminates between what's good about fat and what's bad and suggests how to deal with fat wisely in the diet. The four-page brochure gets a little technical, but even the person who is not schooled in nutrition can follow most of it and pick up some tips that can help get a handle on how much and what kind of fat to eat.

Write for:
A Compendium on Fats (No. 515P)

Cost: Free

Send to:
Consumer Information Center
P.O. Box 100
Pueblo, CO 81002

CARBOHYDRATE PRIMER

★★

Is honey better for you than sugar? What are starches, and is starch really fattening? Why is dietary fiber important in nutrition? You can learn more about carbohydrates—sugar, starch, and fiber—from this 12-page 8″ × 11″ booklet. Learn what carbohydrates are, what foods they are found in, and how the body uses them. It's useful information even if the price of the brochure is a little steep. And no, starchy foods aren't necessarily fattening and don't really deserve their bad reputation. A baked potato, for instance, is a low-calorie food—but only if you resist the temptation to slather it with high-calorie butter or sour cream.

Write for:
Carbohydrates—The Inside Story

Cost: $1.50

Send to:
Distribution Center
7 Research Park
Cornell University
Ithaca, NY 14850

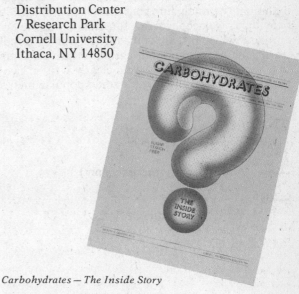

Carbohydrates — The Inside Story

LET'S HEAR IT FOR CARBOHYDRATES

★★

These eight folders make up a packet of materials that extol carbohydrates as a necessary part of the diet—if eaten sensibly and in certain foods. These titles will help you get the gist: *Add a Little Starch to Your Life*, *Controlling the Sweet Tooth With Carrots*, *Enjoy Eating Vegetables*, *The Right Way With Rice*, *Keep a Healthy Balance* (on beans), *The Knack of Snacking* (with oatmeal), *Fighting Fat* (with apples), and *Facts About Fiber* (concentrating on whole wheat bread). This packet should do a lot to re-

continued

FOOD

move the guilt you feel when you're eating a high-carbohydrate snack.

Write for:
The Carbohydrate Connection

Cost: $1.00

Send to:
Distribution Center
7 Research Park
Cornell University
Ithaca, NY 14850

A HIGH-ENERGY DIET
★★

Primer on Three Nutrients studies the respective roles of the three main energy-producing nutrients in your diet—protein, fat, and carbohydrate. You'll discover that a high-protein diet doesn't have to include heavy doses of meat, and learn how to get high-quality protein into your diet. This publication explains how carbohydrates function to provide energy, and which fats are of the highest quality. You'll learn how to include both carbohydrates and fats in a sensible eating plan. This clearly written two-page foldout usefully dispels some popular myths about food.

Write for:
Primer on Three Nutrients

Cost: Free (postcard requests only)

Send to:
FDA/Office of Consumer Affairs, HFE-88
5600 Fishers Lane
Rockville, MD 20857

A PINCH OF SALT
★★★

Fact: One teaspoon of salt contains about 2000 mg of sodium. Fact: Estimates place sodium consumption by adults at 2300 to 6900 mg a day. Fact: The National Research Council indicates that a safe and adequate sodium intake per day is about 1100 to 3300 mg for an adult. It is virtually impossible for people who eat a varied diet to get too little sodium. The trick for most of us is in cutting down. *Sodium: Think About It...* is an attractive 12″ x 18″ foldout poster that will help you plan your diet with sodium content in mind. There is information on the range of sodium in the major food groups, including convenience and snack foods.

Write for:
Sodium: Think About It... (No. 532P)

Cost: Free

Send to:
Consumer Information Center
P.O. Box 100
Pueblo, CO 81002

Sodium, Think About It

NUTRITION NEWS FOR WOMEN
★★

More women than men suffer from calcium and iron deficiencies. Women of child-bearing age have an even greater need for iron in their diet. The type of contraception a woman uses also may affect her needs for specific vitamins and minerals. This eight-page 8″ × 10″ publication from the Food and Drug Administration tells women what vitamins and minerals they should be sure they get, how to get them, and what these nutrients do to keep women healthy. Good charts on the calcium and iron contents of foods make it easy to monitor your intake of these important nutrients.

Write for:
Please Pass That Woman Some More Calcium and Iron

Cost: Free (postcard requests only)

Send to:
FDA/Office of Consumer Affairs, HFE-88
5600 Fishers Lane
Rockville, MD 20857

A SASE is a self-addressed stamped envelope.

NEW BONES FOR OLD

★★

Have you fed your bones lately? The National Dairy Council invites you to learn more about how important calcium and calcium-rich foods are to good health, no matter your age. Bone tissue is alive, changing every day. New bone is added and old bone is broken down and removed from the body. The body needs calcium, phosphorus, protein, and vitamins A, D, and C to form bone tissue, but calcium is the most important mineral in bone. Two color booklets tell how the body never outgrows its need for calcium, and what to eat or drink to make sure you're getting enough calcium.

Write for:
Calcium: You Never Outgrow Your Need for It
The All-American Guide to Calcium-Rich Foods

Cost: 20¢ each

Send to:
Order Department
National Dairy Council
6300 N. River Rd.
Rosemont, IL 60018-4233

Calcium: You Never Outgrow Your Need for It

The All-American Guide to Calcium-Rich Food

EATING FOR YOUR AGE

★★

Your body's nutritional needs change as you grow older. This booklet describes how to compensate for those changes with the right diet. The different age groups covered are the infant (up to one year), the child (one to ten years), the adolescent, the adult, the pregnant woman, and the aging adult. You'll learn which nutritional needs are crucial at each stage, and which of them you're likely to neglect. There's a list of sources for additional information and a daily food guide that shows the recommended servings of food each age group needs every day from the milk, meat, vegetable/fruit, and bread/cereal categories.

Write for:
Your Age & Your Diet

Cost: $1.00

Send to:
Order Department, OP-031
American Medical Association
P.O. Box 10946
Chicago, IL 60610

DO THE ADS DICTATE YOUR DIET?

★★

Americans are bombarded daily with "food cues"—highly persuasive TV, radio, newspaper, and magazine advertising designed to promote a craving for this food or that. But many of the delectable-looking foods you're tempted to try may fail you nutritionally even while they delight your taste buds. In a series of tip sheets called *Nutrition News,* Roman Meal Co. encourages you to make informed personal choices about food. These single-page newsletters contain valuable information on such subjects as food and health, reducing the risk of heart attack, sensible dieting, and nutrition and alcohol. However, it's a bit disorganized.

Write for:
Nutrition News

Cost: Free with a SASE with two first class stamps

Send to:
Roman Meal Co.
Dept. F
P.O. Box 11126
Tacoma, WA 98411-0126

DON'T PASS THE MEAT

★★

What is a vegetarian? In fact, there are at least three categories of vegetarians: vegans, who eat only plants; lacto-vegetarians, who use dairy products as well; and ovo-lacto-vegetarians, who include both eggs and dairy products in their diets. Some people (who are not, strictly speaking, vegetarians) eat fish and poultry—avoiding only red meats. This information sheet discusses the different kinds of vegetarian diets, the reasons people adopt them (health and religion are the most common), and the importance of maintaining a nutritional bal-

continued

FOOD

ance. The article says there's some justification for vegetarians' wholesomer-than-thou attitude; they seem to have fewer strokes and heart attacks and seem to be less inclined to become overweight than meat-eaters.

Write for:
There's Something To Be Said for Never Saying, 'Please Pass the Meat'

Cost: Free (postcard requests only)

Send to:
FDA/Office of Consumer Affairs, HFE-88
5600 Fishers Lane
Rockville, MD 20857

A DISCUSSION OF VEGETARIANISM
★★

This paper is a review of some of the opinions presented about different vegetarian diets and their nutritional effects and suggests that vegetarianism is "neither salvation nor nonsense." This paper examines the pure vegetarian diet, the ovo-lacto-vegetarian diet, and the lacto-vegetarian diet. It tells when vegetarian diets can be adequate and when they're deficient, reviews clinical findings on vegans (those who eat no animal products of any kind), and reports the pros and cons of an all-plant diet. Excellent references. Good reading for the nutritionally aware.

Write for:
Vegetarianism, A Review

Cost: $1.50

Send to:
United Fresh Fruit and Vegetable Association
727 N. Washington St.
Alexandria, VA 22314

HOW HEALTHY IS HEALTH FOOD?
★★

The material in this booklet is excerpted from consumer writer Sidney Margolius's book of the same name. Here, he traces the origins of the health food movement in America and examines the terms "natural," "organic," and "health" foods, along with some of the hot issues raised by the movement—for instance, the claim that organic fertilizers produce

nutritionally superior foods. He then evaluates certain health food staples as to their true nutritional worth, among them honey, blackstrap molasses, seeds, sprouts, wheat germ, yogurt, and whole wheat bread. All in all, it's a balanced view of the health food craze.

Write for:
Health Foods: Facts and Fakes (No. 498A)

Cost: $1.00

Send to:
Public Affairs Pamphlets
381 Park Ave. South
New York, NY 10016

HI-TECH FOOD
★★★

In the not-too-distant future, American shoppers can expect to buy foods treated with radiation to control insect and bacterial contamination. Although this may make some consumers uneasy, the Food and Drug Administration says the foods will be safe and wholesome to eat. *Irradiation Proposed To Treat Food* is a four-page pamphlet which explores the 30 years of research which have gone into food irradiation and the FDA-proposed regulation that would expand the uses of ionizing radiation on such foods as fresh fruits, vegetables, and spices. Also covered are explanations of how irradiation doses are measured, the worldwide implications of the irradiation of foods, and the safety of the treatment.

Write for:
Irradiation Proposed To Treat Food (No. 532P)

Cost: Free

Send to:
Consumer Information Center
P.O. Box 100
Pueblo, CO 81002

HEALTH FOODS: FACT AND FICTION
★★★

Health foods have to be good for you, right? And if it's organic it must be okay. Not always. Consumers who want to eat right can find that they need help in sorting out the fact from the fiction in the claims made by manufacturers of "health," "organic," and "natural" products. *The Confusing World of Health*

Foods is an excellent guide to making intelligent decisions about these "wonder foods." You'll find the scientific reply to some of the wishful or even fraudulent claims made for some health foods; it's useful information, since health foods are often more expensive than other products. A sidebar on potassium chloride alerts you to the fact that the FDA plans to issue a warning on the use of this salt substitute. This is a clear-eyed look at a timely subject.

Write for:
   The Confusing World of Health Foods

Cost: Free (postcard requests only)

Send to:
   FDA/Office of Consumer Affairs, HFE-88
   5600 Fishers Lane
   Rockville, MD 20857

The Confusing World of Health Foods

What's in the Food You Eat

VITAMINS AND GOOD SENSE
★★

Vitamins are in vogue these days—but what are they, what do they do, and how do they work? *Some Facts and Myths of Vitamins*, a free two-page fold-out from the Food and Drug Administration, explains the real role of vitamins in human nutrition. You'll learn something about each of 13 vitamins, along with how they work to transform foods into

energy and maintain the body in good working order. There's also a look at the problems that can be caused by vitamin deficiency. A brief but pithy section explodes several popular myths about vitamins—such as, "Vitamins give you pep." Not true; they don't.

Write for:
   Some Facts and Myths of Vitamins

Cost: Free (postcard requests only)

Send to:
   FDA/Office of Consumer Affairs, HFE-88
   5600 Fishers Lane
   Rockville, MD 20857

Some Facts and Myths of Vitamins

GETTING THE FACTS ON VITAMINS
★★★

What's a balanced diet? Do we need vitamins and minerals? Do we get enough of them in food or do we need to take supplements? These questions and others are answered in this detailed booklet. You'll also learn, via an easy-to-read chart, what the vitamins are, why we need each one, the symptom(s) of deficiency, good food sources for each one, and how we can lose them in food preparation. There's an example of a nutritionally balanced diet (giving the vitamin content of each food), plus discussion of fat, cholesterol, iron, minerals, and vitamin supplements.

continued

FOOD

Clear-headed advice on a subject that's too often clouded by "fad" treatment.

Write for:
   Vitamins, Food, and Your Health (No. 465)

Cost: $1.00

Send to:
   Public Affairs Pamphlets
   381 Park Ave. South
   New York, NY 10016

MESSAGE ON MINERALS
★★

Although less highly publicized, minerals are not less important than vitamins to a healthy diet. This is the message relayed in *A Primer on Dietary Minerals,* a two-page foldout from the Food and Drug Administration that explains the role played by minerals in maintaining health. It also shows you how to estimate your daily intake of mineral elements. There's an excellent description of the macro-minerals—those that the body requires in relatively large quantities, such as calcium, phosphorus, sodium, potassium, magnesium, and sulphur—with information on their natural sources. There's also a discussion of trace minerals and iron in the diet. The chart giving the RDA (U.S. Recommended Daily Allowances) for minerals in the diet of children, adults, and pregnant women is a plus. The clumsy sketches that illustrate the folder, however, just confuse the issue.

Write for:
   A Primer on Dietary Minerals

Cost: Free (postcard requests only)

Send to:
   FDA/Office of Consumer Affairs, HFE-88
   5600 Fishers Lane
   Rockville, MD 20857

STRAIGHTENING OUT SOME TRICKY WORDS
★★

This is a refreshing, no-nonsense, and straightforward speech given to a sports medicine class at the University of Maryland in 1977. The author takes some of the mystery and magic out of such buzzwords as *energy, protein, vitamins, organic, natural, nutritious, fortified,* and *enriched.* He explains what they actually mean (energy is the exertion of power and force, and in nutrition, that's calories), how they have been misused and misinterpreted, and how the resulting misinformation has been swallowed whole by Americans who are eager to get and stay in shape. There's a lot to think about in this reprint, even if you don't agree.

Write for:
   Energy and Other Tricky Nutrition Words

Cost: $1.50

Send to:
   United Fresh Fruit and Vegetable Association
   727 N. Washington St.
   Alexandria, VA 22314

SODIUM ALERT
★★★

Our bodies need sodium for maintaining blood volume and cellular osmotic pressure and for transmitting nerve impulses, but in many cases our bodies need a lot *less* sodium than we give them. According to the Food and Nutrition Board of the National Academy of Sciences, in fact, our body needs for sodium are not great. Most of the sodium we consume daily comes from the table salt we use, but sodium is also present in many foods, and too much sodium is believed to contribute to high blood pressure or hypertension in some people. Here is a 46-page 5″ × 7″ booklet telling all about sodium and how much is present in what you eat and drink. You also learn how to measure the amount of sodium in salt. For anyone who's serious about healthy eating, this is a very useful booklet.

Write for:
   The Sodium Content of Your Food

Cost: $1.00

Send to:
   Distribution Center
   7 Research Park
   Cornell University
   Ithaca, NY 14850

The Sodium Content of Your Food

FOOD ADDITIVES: THE FACTS

★★★

You've just washed your lunch down with a nice, cool cola—which is actually nothing but water plus a bunch of food additives. Without the coloring, flavoring, sweeteners, or artificial carbonation, your cola is just good old H_2O. This four-page leaflet tells exactly what additives are, why they're used, and what they do. It also explains what the information on the product label means. For instance,"strawberry yogurt" contains all natural strawberry flavor. "Strawberry-flavored" yogurt" contains natural strawberry flavor plus other natural flavorings. You'll learn that the addition of essential vitamins and minerals to everyday foods like milk, flour, cereals, and margarine has helped played a part in removing some "deficiency diseases"—goiter, rickets, pellagra, beriberi—from the vocabulary of most Americans. Available while supplies last.

Write for:
More Than You Ever Thought You Would Know
About Food Additives

Cost: Free (postcard requests only)

Send to:
FDA/Office of Consumer Affairs, HFE-88
5600 Fishers Lane
Rockville, MD 20857

*More Than
You Ever
Thought You
Would Know
About Food Additives*

WHAT ARE YOU EATING?

★★★★

Making food choices is not always easy. In addition to price and nutrient value, many people have questions about certain substances that are added to foods—why they are added and whether they are safe. The concerned shopper-consumer will find this packet of 11 pamphlets must reading. Developed by the Division of Nutritional Sciences faculty at Cornell University, each pamphlet covers a different ingredient or aspect of nutritional shopping—sweeteners, preservatives, caffeine, flavors, advertising claims, food colors, thickeners, and more. You'll learn some of the myths about "natural foods," how to cook with fewer food additives, and how to read product labels and lists of ingredients. There is also a Shopper's Guide to Commonly Used Food Ingredients, with a glossary that explains the chemical names of these substances.

Write for:
11 You Should Know pamphlets

Cost: $1.90

Send to:
Distribution Center
7 Research Park
Cornell University
Ithaca, NY 14850

ALL ABOUT ADDITIVES

★★

Each year we swallow about 2800 different food additives. This includes between five and ten pounds of emulsifiers, preservatives, flavorings, colorings, acids, and vitamins. Salt adds another 15 pounds. Sugar and other sweeteners add another 130 pounds. All told, Americans eat about 150 pounds of additives each year. Read all about what additives do, and which are good and which are questionable, in a new brochure that can help you and your family to a better, healthier diet.

Write for:
Chemical Cookery

Cost: 25¢

Send to:
Center for Science in the Public Interest
1501 Sixteenth St., N.W.
Washington, DC 20036

Chemical Cookery

FOOD

HOW SWEET IT IS!

★★★★

Cave men craved sugar and found it in honey, figs, and dates. Egyptians were keeping bees for honey before 2600 B.C. Sugar in its various forms tastes sweet and most people like it, but how much sugar is good for you? Many nutritionists think Americans eat too much sugar and that over-consumption is detrimental, mainly because sugar's only contribution is taste and calories. If you want to know more about sugar and its place in your diet, and what you can do to reduce your sugar intake, this four-page government brochure can help. It also describes the common sugars and sweeteners and their uses.

Write for:
    Sugar—How Sweet It Is—And Isn't (No. 525P)

Cost: Free

Send to:
    Consumer Information Center
    P.O. Box 100
    Pueblo, CO 81002

Sugar—How Sweet It Is—And Isn't

FAKE FOOD: IMITATIONS AND MYTHS

★★

Many imitation food products are packaged and sold just like traditional foods, and sometimes the consumer can be fooled into believing that because these products look and taste like traditional foods, they're just as nutritious. For instance, imitation cheese may taste something like traditional cheese, but may not be as nutritious. A new brochure tells how you can tell imitation food products from traditional products to get the most for your money and the best for your health. Another brochure tells fact from fancy in myths surrounding foods. If you believe vitamin C can cure the common cold and vitamin E can improve your sex life, check out this information about nutrition and myths. You'll find that you've been "myth-informed" on both counts.

Write for:
    The Limitations of Imitations
    Nutrition Myth-Information

Cost: 20¢ each

Send to:
    Order Department
    National Dairy Council
    6300 N. River Rd.
    Rosemont, IL 60018-4233

The Limitations of Imitations

Nutrition Myth-Information

THE REMARKABLE PROPERTIES OF H₂O

★★

Life appears to have begun in water and seems to be limited to the rather narrow band of temperatures in which water is a liquid. This brief, well-written paper is a clear-cut explanation and description of this fluid that's vital to all life. Water seems commonplace, but it's very complex. You'll learn how it protects against both rising and falling temperatures; the essential role it plays in photosynthesis; how water is needed by all humans (and plants) and what our normal water balance is; and about the special water that comes from food itself and from its cooking water. Finally, you'll learn about hard and soft water and their properties. There's an excellent reference list, too.

Write for:
    Water, The Astounding Nutrient

Cost: $1.50

A SASE is a self-addressed stamped envelope.

Send to:
United Fresh Fruit and Vegetable Association
727 N. Washington St.
Alexandria, VA 22314

CAFFEINE AND YOUR HEALTH

★★★★

People have been consuming caffeine since the origins of tea in China about 4700 B.C. You may believe that only coffee or tea contain caffeine; in fact, many sodas and other drinks, and many foods, contain caffeine. Did you know there is often caffeine in baked goods, frozen dairy products, gelatins, puddings, chocolate, and soft candies? It also is found in many cold, headache, allergy, and stay-awake medications. While some people are not affected by caffeine or are only affected mildly, some people may have serious reactions to the stimulant. Here's a brochure that tells all about caffeine and its use. If caffeine is a problem for you, this publication lets you know what drinks and foods to avoid.

Write for:
The Latest Caffeine Scorecard (No. 519P)

Cost: Free

Send to:
Consumer Information Center
P.O. Box 100
Pueblo, CO 81002

DOES EVERYTHING CAUSE CANCER?

★★

You'll be happy to hear that the answer is no. This booklet answers frequently asked questions about saccharin, nitrites, and the Delaney amendment, which bans the addition to food of chemicals that cause cancer in laboratory animals or humans. Sample questions: If a chemical causes cancer in animals, will it also cause cancer in humans? Are chemicals that do *not* cause cancer in animals always safe for humans? (The answers are yes and no, respectively.) Besides answering the questions in detail and in understandable English, there are some interesting and sensible alternatives to the Delaney amendment and a capsule discussion of carcinogens in beer.

Write for:
Does Everything Cause Cancer?

Cost: $1.50

Send to:
Center for Science in the Public Interest
1501 Sixteenth St., N.W.
Washington, DC 20036

WHAT'S GOOD ABOUT SACCHARIN?

★

Saccharin, the controversial noncaloric, nonsugar sweetener used for 80 years in foods and beverages, has recently been the subject of much debate concerning its safety. Now you can get the facts on saccharin according to the Calorie Control Council, an association of manufacturers and suppliers of dietary foods and beverages. This three-page foldout discusses the sweetener's benefits and risks, and the rat studies that sparked the controversy.

Write for:
Saccharin

Cost: Free

Send to:
Calorie Control Council
Suite 500-D
5775 Peachtree-Dunwoody Rd.
Atlanta, GA 30342

WHAT'S IN WHAT YOU EAT?

★★★

Is everything we eat bad for us? It would seem so, from all the reports we hear about this or that food causing cancer. The American Council on Science and Health has issued a 38-page booklet about carcinogens, substances in food that can cause cancer, and mutagens, substances that can produce hereditary changes or mutations in organisms that could cause cancer. Scientists summarize that we should eat a variety of foods, to minimize the chance that any carcinogen is eaten in large enough quantity to be harmful. This booklet appears to be aimed at the serious nutritionist but can be helpful to anyone concerned about how safe the foods are that we eat.

Write for:
Does Nature Know Best? Natural Carcinogens
in American Food

Cost: $2.00

Send to:
American Council on Science and Health
47 Maple St.
Summit, NJ 07901

FOOD

A HEALTHY MESSAGE

★★

If you're bored with bumper stickers that carry tired old messages like "I love my dog" (even if you *do* love your dog), here are some new thoughts for you, along with an opportunity to advertise a philosophy of healthy eating. One of these stickers proclaims, *Health is the natural high* (No. 10). Another advocates *Live Foods* (No. 8) and has lots of little drawings of veggies along the bottom (this one also has the ubiquitous bright red heart). You may draw the line at *Have you hugged your sprouts today?* (No. 7) or even *Enzymes, Key to Health & Longevity* (No. 12)—you might get rear-ended by someone trying to figure out what enzymes are—but some of these bumper stickers from *The Sproutletter* are really fun. The bumper stickers are 80¢ each and you're asked to order by number. *The Sproutletter* also has buttons and T-shirts with similar messages.

Write for:
Bumper sticker of choice (by number)

Cost: 80¢ each

Send to:
The Sproutletter
P.O. Box 62
Ashland, OR 97520

Sproutletter bumper stickers

A SASE is a self-addressed stamped envelope.

FREE THINGS
for
KIDS

KIDS

Toys, Games, Hobbies, and Collections

BLAST OFF YOUR OWN ROCKETS!

★★

There's an explosion of interest in model rocketry these days, and if you're one of the devotees you'll want to have this catalog of more than 80 different flying model rockets. The kits are coded by skill levels ranging from 1 (very simple) to 4 (extremely challenging). There are diagrams showing how to launch rockets, assurances that these rocket engines are safety tested and certified by national associations and consumer product safety commissions, and "Tech-Tips" on flying model rockets. There's a membership application for the National Association of Rocketry, too, and special offers including the opportunity to secure a free rocket.

Write for:
Estes Flying Model Rocket Catalog

Cost: $1.00

Send to:
Estes Industries
Dept. 95
1295 H St.
Penrose, CO 81240

Estes Flying Model Rocket Catalog

SPACE OUT WITH MODEL ROCKETS

★★★★

What's the perfect space-age hobby? What else but model rocketry? From coast to coast, model rockets of every shape and description are climbing into the skies just like their real-life counterparts at the Kennedy Space Center. If you'd like to know more about this high-flying hobby, write to the National Association of Rocketry for a sample copy of *American Spacemodeling*, the official journal of the NAR. It's packed with information about rockets, diagrams for building your own, and news and views of other space-crazy rocketeers.

For your $2.00 you'll also get a brochure telling you about the National Association of Rocketry, the national organizations (and they are impressive) that support this aerosport, the model rocket safety code, and how this hobby came to be.

Write for:
Sample copy of American Spacemodeling and NAR brochure

Cost: $2.00

Send to:
National Association of Rocketry
182 Madison Dr.
Elizabeth, PA 15037

THE WORLD THROUGH RAINBOW GLASSES

★★★★

Here's a way to see things in a new light—literally. Rainbow glasses are an unusual toy available in a kit from Mr. Rainbows for $1.00. The kit includes two flexible plastic "lenses" that you tape over the cardboard glass frames. An instruction sheet tells you how to attach the lenses to the glasses. When you look at any single light source (preferably not fluorescent and not directly into the sun), the lenses produce a holographic diffraction that separates ordinary white light into all the colors of the rainbow.

Write for:
Rainbow Glasses Kit

Cost: $1.00

Send to:
Mr. Rainbows
P.O. Box 27056 (FT)
Philadelphia, PA 19118

A SASE is a self-addressed stamped envelope.

GLOW-IN-THE-DARK JEWELRY
★★★

Glow-in-the-dark bracelets, necklaces, and earrings? You bet! They're called lightstick jewelry and are made from Cyalume, a safe, nontoxic chemical. All you do is bend, snap, and shake the lightsticks to activate their glow, then attach a connector that comes with the jewelry to form a bracelet or necklace. Earlobe lightstick earrings come with special clip-ons. The glow is supposed to last four to six hours (but the one we tried lasted much longer and was still glowing faintly after 24 hours). The jewelry comes in blue or green. Great fun for the girl with a flare.

Write for:
Lightstick Bracelet
Lightstick Necklace
Lightstick Earrings

Cost: $2.00 each

Send to:
Mr. Rainbows
P.O. Box 27056 (FT)
Philadelphia, PA 19118

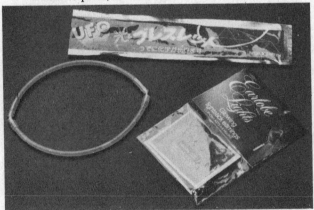
Lightstick Jewelry

JUNQUE JEWELRY
★

Costume jewelry is the "in" accessory today for girls and women of all ages. This offer is for a replica of an oriental tapestry that can be worn as either a pendant or pin. There are several different designs available; yours will be selected at random. One example reflects a tapestry of the Han Kan era (the years 742-756) of the T'ang dynasty. The design shows a groom with two horses. Another, simulating clothwork from the Sung dynasty, shows a man sitting under a tree listening to the wind. Labels on the back of the medallions explain the pictures. These "jewels" are of plastic and paper, so think carefully about parting with $2.00.

Write for:
Pin

Cost: $2.00

Send to:
IMC Management, Inc.
P.O. Box 11-TP
Garnerville, NY 10923

Pin

FUN WITH RAINBOW ROUNDS
★★★

Here's something to liven up a rainy day — Rainbow Rounds. They're shiny, colorful, cut-out circles about the size of a nickel. You can paste or tape them on paper, then draw around them to make a bunch of flowers, balloons, a traffic signal, or a stick figure. Or you can draw something first, then figure out places to add these colorful circles. You'll get 100 Rainbow Rounds for $1.00, but you'll need your own glue.

Write for:
Rainbow Rounds

Cost: $1.00

Send to:
Mr. Rainbows
P.O. Box 27056 (FT)
Philadelphia, PA 19118

PUT RAINBOWS IN YOUR PHOTOS
★★★★

This Rainbow Photography Kit isn't actually a kit — it's a square piece of flexible plastic that you tape

continued

over your camera lens to create a bright rainbow effect on any picture.

The accompanying instruction sheet explains that the Rainbow filter is actually a hologram, shot with a laser beam that produces the rainbow effect from approximately 13,000 lines per inch. Instructions are also given for attaching the filter to your camera and adjusting the exposure. The brighter the light, the more rainbows will appear on the photo. Rainbow ideas are listed on the back of the sheet—a well-lit street at night, a birthday cake with candles, a sunrise or sunset, fireworks, and so on. The kit doesn't look very exciting at first glance—but wait until you see those rainbows.

Write for:
Rainbow Photography Kit

Cost: $1.50

Send to:
Mr. Rainbows
P.O. Box 27056 (FT)
Philadelphia, PA 19118

BOOMERANGS: THEY KEEP COMING BACK
★★★★

Bet you haven't considered *this* gift idea for the person who has everything. It's a boomerang. And if you suspect that you may not want to give a boomerang away once you've got it, you'd better get one for yourself as well. *You Can Do It!* is a 16-page illustrated catalog of handmade boomerangs from all over the world, including the beginner "stick" version; the French MK-1, which is listed as "surely the most accurate returning boomerang;" the Koala Pup, a youth model; and the Mini-Hurricane Hook.

You'll be glad to know that if you order a boomerang you'll also receive instructions on how to throw the thing. And did you know that you can get special boomerangs for left-handed people, or that you can juggle with boomerangs? Clearly, there's more to boomerangs than you expected.

Write for:
You Can Do It! catalog

Cost: Free (postcard requests only)

Send to:
The Boomerang Man
Room CG
1806 North Third Street
Monroe, LA 71201-4222

HOT DOG!
★★★★

"I wish I were an Oscar Mayer wiener. That is what I'd really like to be." So the jingle goes, promoting one of kids' favorite foods. The likelihood of actually becoming a wiener is very slight, but this offer provides a reasonable substitute. It is a three-foot long, inflatable hot dog. Simply blow it up and have lots of fun. The durable plastic is colored to look like the real thing, complete with Oscar's logo in familiar yellow, red, and white. It also comes with instructions for inflation, deflation, and cleaning care. A word of caution from the manufacturer: the wiener is intended for use as a toy, but not as safety support while swimming.

Write for:
Oscar Mayer Inflatable Wiener

Cost: $2.00

Send to:
Oscar Mayer Inflatable Wiener
Department WI
P.O. Box 8940
Madison, WI 53708-8940

Oscar Mayer Inflatable Wiener

GETTING IN THE ACT
★★★★

Juggling apples is one thing, but did you ever consider juggling scarves? It's easy, fun, and the scarves don't roll when they fall on the floor. This teach-yourself Scarf Juggling Kit includes three brightly colored nylon scarves plus a comic-strip illustrated set of directions. Wearing a tuxedo and tennis shoes, "Professor Confidence" leads the way. He'll show you how to "flabbergast your friends in five easy steps." He starts with the basic grip and goes to the toss and the catch. From there he is pictured with two, then three scarves in a continuous throwing pattern. After you know the basic juggling pattern you can use the same steps to juggle balls, rings, or clubs.

Write for:
Scarf Juggling Kit

Cost: $2.00 (U.S. funds only)

Send to:
Jugglebug
Box FT
7506 J Olympic View Drive
Edmonds, WA 98020

Ball Juggling

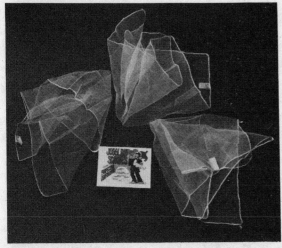

Scarf Juggling Kit

YOU WON'T DROP THE BALL
★★★★

What kid (or adult, for that matter) hasn't attempted his or her own juggling act, only to end up chasing balls or oranges across the room? A fully illustrated poster reveals the secrets of master entertainers. The first thing to learn is how to throw the ball or other object into a basic figure eight pattern. The poster starts out giving directions for one ball, and when the pattern is smooth, adds another. From there you can move onto rings, clubs, multiple objects, and passing to a partner. The pictures are easy to follow and the instructions simple. There is a list of steps for improvement and a gentle reminder to practice, practice, practice.

Write for:
Ball Juggling Poster

Cost: $1.00 (U.S. funds only)

Send to:
Jugglebug
Box FT
7506 J Olympic View Drive
Edmonds, WA 98020

A BRIEF GUIDE TO KITING
★★★

Kiting is the word for it now, the serious art/science/sport of flying and making kites. This small, expert brochure presents some kite history and tells the uses kites have had over the ages—to ward off evil, drop propaganda leaflets, and catch fish. It tells you specifically when to fly (in steady winds from 4 to 18 mph) and where the best places are to fly, and it gives you the Kite Safety Code. You'll also learn about the latest materials for modern kites, options for building your own kite or buying one, and how to fly that kite when the right day arrives. There's a reading list, too, for the serious kiter. Also available (for $1.00) from Kite Lines is *Hundreds of Sleds, Hundreds of Smiles,* which tells group leaders how to prepare for and make sled kites indoors or out.

Write for:
A Brief Guide to Safe and Sure Kiting
Hundreds of Sleds, Hundreds of Smiles

Cost: A Brief Guide: Free with a long SASE
Hundreds of Sleds: $1.00

Send to:
Kite Lines
7106 Campfield Rd.
Baltimore, MD 21207-4699

JUST HUMMIN' ALONG
★★★

Want to start your own band? Want something new to do during vacation? Well, kids, Famous Amos has a suggestion for you—a kazoo. All you have to do is hum into the big end; the music comes out the small

continued

KIDS

end. Whether your taste is for rock, country, pop, or classical, and whether you want to be a one-kid band or recruit the whole block, you can make instant music with the kazoo.

Write for:
Famous Amos Designer Kazoo

Cost: $2.00

Send to:
The Famous Amos Chocolate Chip Cookie
14734 Calvert St.
Van Nuys, CA 91411

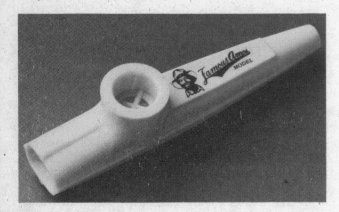

Famous Amos Designer Kazoo

INSTANT MUSIC
★★★★

Those of you who want to learn to play music right away can probably get off to a quicker start with a harmonica than with any other instrument. A harmonica has another advantage—it's so small and compact, you can carry it around in your pocket. The new *How To Play the Hohner Harmonica* is a free 24-page instruction book that teaches the Arrow Method, a simplified technique that will have you playing 20 familiar tunes like "Jingle Bells;" "Good Night Ladies;" "Oh, Susanna;" and "Skip to My Lou" right off the bat. Next, you graduate to the professional tongue blocking method. This neat little booklet also provides tips for making vibrato and tremulo effects.

You can also get a big full-color poster showing 50 different kinds of harmonicas or a little booklet called *A Brief History of the Harmonica.* Be sure to send your request to the right department number.

Write for:
How To Play the Hohner Harmonica (Dept. FT-1)
Harmonica poster (Dept. FT-3)
A Brief History of the Harmonica (Dept. FT-2)

Cost: How To Play the Hohner Harmonica—free with a long SASE
$2.00 for the poster
25¢ and a long SASE for A Brief History of the Harmonica

Send to:
Hohner, Inc.
Dept. FT-1, FT-2, or FT-3
Lakeridge Park
Sycamore Dr.
P.O. Box 15035
Richmond, VA 23227

GETTING THERE IS HALF THE FUN
★★★★

Traveling in the car with your parents, grandparents, aunts, uncles, or friends is always more fun when you play travel games. The miles fly by—and so do the hours—while you try to guess how long a mile is; play word games; try to find one each of every possible kind of car, truck, or jeep on the road; or try to be the first to find a list of special numbers or names on license plates of the cars you pass. These and lots of others are described in *Travel Games.* Once you start playing you'll probably invent more games of your own, and if you send your idea to *Travel Games* and it's printed, you'll get "paid" in free books. This small book is a lot of fun for a dollar—you'll learn all about highway signs, too.

Write for:
Travel Games

Cost: $1.00 (dollar bill, please)

Send to:
The Beavers
Star Route Box 184
LaPorte, MN 56461

Travel Games

A SASE is a self-addressed stamped envelope.

REVOLUTIONARY DICE

★★★

Dice, those small cubes used in games, were found in ancient Egyptian tombs and in the ruins of Babylon. In fact, dice have been popular with game-players up through the centuries. The game of dice was played by Revolutionary War soldiers in America, and was a very popular pastime in Colonial days. Soldiers made their own dice by pounding lead bullets into irregular square shapes and etching the holes with the point of a bayonet. Many authentic 18th-century dice were found near army encampments of 1776-1780. You can send for a replica of a pair of Revolutionary dice that look and feel as if they actually were pounded out of lead bullets. Fun to play with, to use as paperweights, or just as conversation pieces.

Write for:
Revolutionary Dice

Cost: $1.00

Send to:
Historical Documents Co.
8 N. Preston St.
Philadelphia, PA 19104

Revolutionary Dice

OUT OF THIS WORLD STAMPS

★★★★

For the stamp collector who also follows events in worldwide space programs, here is a collection of 100 different stamps of many nations, each celebrating the wonders of modern space adventure. The stamps are brightly colored and depict rockets, space stations, and interplanetary exploration. Just the thing for the young would-be astronaut. A very unusual stamp collection, and a real bargain at $2.00.

Write for:
Space Stamps

Cost: $2.00

Send to:
Space Stamps
P.O. Box 466
Port Washington, NY 11050

Space Stamps

TO TEMPT A BEGINNING STAMP COLLECTOR

★★★

Who could resist embarking on stamp-collecting as a hobby after seeing this sample set of Walt Disney postage stamps? Each is a color reproduction (1½″ × 2″) of a beloved Disney character like Mickey Mouse, Minnie Mouse, Donald Duck, Goofy, and Horace Horsecollar. There are seven stamps in each set. If this particular set isn't available when you write, a similar set will be sent. The quality of these stamps is exceptional, so you're sure to like the ones you get.

Write for:
Set of Full-Color Stamps Honoring Walt Disney

Cost: $1.00

Send to:
International Stamp Collectors Society
P.O. Box 854
Van Nuys, CA 91408

HISTORY ON A POSTAGE STAMP

★★★

Topical Time is a 92-page journal for collectors of topical stamps—stamps featuring a specific subject, such as flags, churches, or musical instruments. It's not a how-to guide for people considering

KIDS

philately as a hobby, but a comprehensive list of sources for topical stamps in all sorts of areas. An interesting look, too, at history and at people and events different countries have considered worthy of the honor of being represented on their postage stamps. You can get a sample copy of this fascinating publication for $1.00.

Write for:
Sample copy of Topical Time

Cost: $1.00

Send to:
American Topical Association.
P.O. Box 630
Johnstown, PA 15907

PARCHMENT MONEY OF THE PAST
★★★★

In Colonial days the colonies issued over $200 million in paper currency, and the Continental Congress issued over $250 million. The rapid depreciation of this paper money led to the well-known phrase, "not worth a Continental." Here are replicas of some of those notes—including a $4 North Carolina bill, a $3 Rhode Island bill, and an $8 Maryland bill. In all, there are 14 different replicas of original currencies in this two-packet set, all printed on parchment that makes them feel and seem old. The quaint wording of each bill makes lively reading, and there's a short history of each bank note, too.

Write for:
14 Different Colonial and Revolutionary Banknotes

Cost: $1.00; please do not send stamps

Send to:
Historical Documents Co.
Dept. E
8 N. Preston St.
Philadelphia, PA 19104

COIN AND STAMP SURPRISE PACKAGE
★★★★

Here's a double surprise package. Jolie Coins, dealers in coins and currency for hobbyists, offers a package of 15 different U.S. commemorative stamps (most of them cancelled) for Christmas mailing, two pieces of genuine foreign paper money (a one-cruzeiro bill from Brazil and a 500-peso bill from

Argentina), and nine different coins from such countries as Uruguay, East Germany, Israel, and the Philippines. Also included in the exciting collection is the beautiful Great Britain Crown, the size of a silver dollar, issued to commemorate the marriage of Prince Charles and Lady Diana. Their pictures are embossed on one side of the coin, and there's a portrait of Queen Elizabeth II on the other. It's all offered in a special 26-piece introductory package that is a fine addition to anyone's stamp or coin collection, or could get you started in the hobbies. You'll like this one a lot.

Write for:
26-Piece Introductory Package

Cost: $2.00

Send to:
Jolie Coins
P.O. Box 68GB
Roslyn Heights, NY 11577

26-Piece Introductory Package

COLONIAL MONEY
★★★★

What kind of paper money and coins did they use back in Colonial days in America, or during the Revolutionary War? The Historical Documents Company has reproduced samples of both a $20.00 U.S. Continental bill from 1778 and a Continental dollar coin from 1776 (both sides), and they're exact replicas of the originals. You may be surprised at the size of the $20.00 bill—it's about half the size of today's paper money. The coin is about the size and weight of a silver dollar. These are two educational, historical, and fun things for collectors. They look and feel 200 years old!

Write for:
Colonial Money

Cost: $1.00

---

150 *A SASE is a self-addressed stamped envelope.*

Colonial Money

BUY OLD MONEY

★★★★

After the Civil War, the money printed by the Southern states—Confederate currency—wasn't worth much. Today it probably isn't worth much, either, in financial terms, but it's certainly fun to see and handle. You can take part in the nation's Civil War history with antiqued reproductions of Confederate paper money that look old and actually feel old. Historical Documents Company will send you either or both of two sets of Confederate currency with interesting old illustrations on them. Each set contains six different paper bills, such as a $100.00 Confederate bill from Virginia, a $5.00 bill from the South Carolina Cotton Growers Association, a $1.00 Arkansas bill, a $2.00 Bank of Chattanooga, Tennessee, bill, or a $500.00 bill issued by the Government of the Confederate States of America. They're yellowed and crispy-crinkly, and you'd think they were over 100 years old.

Write for:
Confederate Currency Set A or B (or both)

Cost: $1.00 each

Send to:
Historical Documents Co.
8 N. Preston St.
Philadelphia, PA 19104

Confederate Currency

FORTY YEARS OF BUTTONS

★★★

There's no telling what will turn a collector on. Some people collect stamps, some collect coins—and some collect buttons. It's not exactly the latest fad, either; button collectors got organized in 1939 and are now celebrating their 46th year as the National Button Society. The *National Button Bulletin* has been published for 40 years now, and if you're intrigued by the idea that there's so much to say about buttons, you can get a sample copy for $1.00. Written in homey, newsletter style, the 96-page bulletin is full of photos of antique or unique buttons, information about button conventions and shows (the 1986 show will be held in San Antonio, Texas), letters from avid collectors, and anecdotes from readers. Even the classified ads in the back are fascinating—you'll find out where to get military buttons, decoupage buttons, handcarved pearl buttons, even Mother Goose nursery rhyme buttons (four to a rhyme).

Write for:
National Button Bulletin

Cost: $1.00

Send to:
National Button Society
Lois Pool, Secretary
2733 Juno Place
Akron, OH 44313

Books to Read or Color

A COLORING BOOK OF ANIMALS

★★★★

Coloring is one of your favorite things to do, and you love animals. Right? Then here's a nice way to combine both these interests. It's a big book—112 pages—of animals to color. Some you see every day, like cats, dogs, and squirrels; some you see in the woods, like deer, owls, and frogs; some you see at the zoo, like hippos, elephants, and giraffes. Alongside the pictures to color are photographs of what the live animals look like, and you'll learn about where they live, what they eat, and how to treat them. And it's got a good message: Respect animals; they've got as much right to life as people. A real bargain for $2.00,

continued

but you'll have to hurry—it's only available to the first 1000 people who write and mention this book. So be sure to state in your letter that you learned about this offer from *Free Things*.

Write for:
The Humane Society Coloring Book

Cost: $2.00

Send to:
Associated Humane Societies
124 Evergreen Ave.
Newark, NJ 07114

BEAUTIFUL HORSES
★★★★

Did you ever wonder why some racehorses are ridden and why some pull buggies? This super 20-page coloring book will give you some of the answers. *The Story of Harness Racing* tells you about harness horses, how they race, and who started the sport. The drawings are simple enough for all but the youngest artist, but the book is detailed and interesting enough for older kids. It's a beautiful book for anyone who loves horses, and you'll find out about an unusual and exciting sport, too. If you like a challenge, there's even a short quiz at the end. One of the nicest coloring books around. And it's free.

Write for:
The Story of Harness Racing

Cost: Free

Send to:
The U.S. Trotting Association
750 Michigan Ave.
Columbus, OH 43215

CRAZY ABOUT HORSES?
★★★★

Learn about harness racing—the exciting world of trotters and pacers—in this puzzle and maze book that is fun and challenging. The games and puzzles are designed for various skill levels and are almost as exciting to work out as a trip to the races. Especially fun for the eight to twelve age group. There are lots of different things to do in this large, 20-page puzzle book and the price sure is right—it's free! This would be a terrific gift for a friend who's crazy about horses.

Write for:
The Harness Racing Puzzle Book

Cost: Free

Send to:
The U.S. Trotting Association
750 Michigan Ave.
Columbus, OH 43215

The Harness Racing Puzzle Book

STEP OUT WITH THE TROTTING HORSES
★★★★

If you love horses, chances are you'll love this big, 100-page magazine about trotting horses. *Hoof Beats* is crammed with articles on the races, the drivers, and the horses—even the classified ads for horses and horse farms are fun to read. The photographs are excellent, and there are regular columns on everything from pedigrees to horseshoeing. A super freebie—especially since this magazine usually costs $2.00. You can also write to the U.S. Trotting Association for free coloring books, brochures, photographs, and posters of trotting horses.

Write for:
Complimentary Copy of Hoof Beats

Cost: Free

Send to:
The U.S. Trotting Association
750 Michigan Ave.
Columbus, OH 43215

KITTENS AND CATS TO COLOR
★★★

Here's a little booklet that you can use two ways. Read it to learn about kittens and cats and how to care for them. Then color the amusing little pictures. You'll get a kick out of lines like, "Each cat wants a kind owner, a steady job (meaning mouse patrol), good food, and warmth." This little book tells you

A SASE is a self-addressed stamped envelope.

what to do if your cat climbs a tree, or if you have a cat who is going to have kittens. It also explains why it's important to have cats spayed or neutered to help stop the pet population explosion that leaves thousands of stray animals without a home.

Write for:
Kittens and Cats

Cost: 25¢ and a long SASE

Send to:
Animal Welfare Institute
P.O. Box 3650
Washington, DC 20007

NATURE ACTIVITY FOR ALL SEASONS

★★★★

This is a very simple book, but it's got lots of charm, and if you're interested in nature and being outdoors you'll love these ideas about collecting leaves in the fall and preserving them or making "leaf people," building a terrarium, adopting a tree, making a 3-D diorama, or exploring a pond.

A Book of Nature Activities has 40 pages of ideas like these, and there are things to do for all four seasons. Study pond life or raise tadpoles and frogs in the spring. Start an insect zoo or make spore prints in the summer. In fall, make leaf people or collect seeds. In the winter, make a suet feeder, a crystal garden, or a planetarium. Sixteen activities in all, and every one's a winner.

Write for:
A Book of Nature Activities

Cost: 75¢

Send to:
The Interstate Printers & Publishers, Inc.
19 N. Jackson
P.O. Box 50
Danville, IL 61834-0050

A Book of Nature Activities

SEYMOUR SAFELY'S ACTIVITY BOOK

★★★★

Seymour Safely is a cartoon character created by the American Optometric Association as a spokesperson for good vision and eye health education. This big, 32-page book—designed for classroom use but a great resource for families, too—contains lots of programs, songs, games, and projects all starring Seymour. Each activity includes background information for teachers or parents, and full directions.

Besides the booklet, you'll receive a pattern for making a paper sack puppet, a window decal that presents eye safety hints, and a color poster (11'' × 17'') in which Seymour repeats eye-saving hints. The kids in your family or those you babysit for will enjoy this cheerful new cartoon friend.

Write for:
Meet Seymour Safely

Cost: $2.00 (check only)

Send to:
Order Department
American Optometric Association
243 N. Lindbergh Blvd.
St. Louis, MO 63141

Meet Seymour Safely

POISON IS NO LAUGHING MATTER

★★★★

Dennis the Menace, that blond little imp who is always getting into (and out of) trouble, warns young people of the dangers of poisons around the home in this free comic book. With his pals, Dennis is on an adventure learning about the dangers of medicines, chemicals, household cleaners, and other potential hazards. Lively color pictures entertain while a child learns about dangers of poisons in the home. One

continued

KIDS

page is a checklist of tips on poison control that you can cut out and put in the bathroom or kitchen. A good way to introduce children to the dangers of poisoning from such substances as oven cleaners and pesticides to furniture polish and cough medicines or tranquilizers. A good reminder to parents, too, to keep potentially hazardous substances away from youngsters—especially adventurous ones.

Write for:
Dennis the Menace Takes a Poke at Poison
(No. 507P)

Cost: Free

Send to:
Consumer Information Center
P.O. Box 100
Pueblo, CO 81002

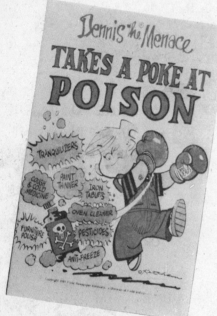

Dennis the Menace Takes a Poke at Poison

COLOR IT SAFETY
★★★

Kids will have a lot of fun with this free coloring book that teaches them how to play safely with their toys. It's a 12-page, 8″ × 11″ coloring book showing boys and girls playing with their toys. Captions tell how to play with the toys safely. Pictures show how kids can shop with their parents for safe toys, put toys where they can't cause an accident, keep tiny toys away from infants who might swallow them, be careful of throwing toys that might hurt someone, and follow other safety measures. A great gift idea for a small brother or sister, or the little kid you babysit for.

Write for:
Toy Safety Coloring Book

Cost: Free

Send to:
U.S. Consumer Product Safety Commission
Office of Information and Public Affairs
Washington, DC 20207

A MESSAGE (ABOUT SHOTS) TO COLOR
★★

This unusual Stay-Well Card contains a message for your parents. It's a small, eight-page coloring booklet that lists seven childhood diseases kids can catch if they don't get their shots. The sad-looking boy shown in bed is sick with measles (color his face red). Kids can also catch mumps, polio, German measles, diphtheria, tetanus, or whooping cough if they aren't immunized. If you color and read this booklet carefully, chances are your parents will get the message too. There's an immunization checklist to keep track of your shots. Nobody *likes* getting shots, but aren't they a lot better than getting sick?

Write for:
Stay-Well Card coloring booklet

Cost: Free

Send to:
Technical Information Services
Center for Prevention Services
Centers for Disease Control
Atlanta, GA 30333

Stay-Well coloring booklet

A SASE is a self-addressed stamped envelope.

COLORING BOOK MAKES IMPORTANT POINT

★★★

The message of this simple coloring book for small children is a vital one: Only moms, dads, doctors, or authorized grown-ups should administer medicine. Kids should *never* help themselves to medicine or take it from anyone else, not even a young friend or brother or sister. While they color the oversize pictures in this book, kids should soak up the urgent message. A great way to teach through play.

Write for:
Tuffy Talks About Medicine

Cost: Free

Send to:
Special Services Librarian
Corporate Communications, DA23
Aetna Life & Casualty
151 Farmington Ave.
Hartford, CT 06156

YES YOU CAN!

★★★

In every elementary school classroom there are a few students who have a learning problem of one kind or another. If you're one of them, you know how lonely a learning disability can sometimes make you feel. *Yes You Can* is a little book just for you. It's written by a teacher who has worked with lots of children with learning problems, and illustrated by a 17-year-old boy who learned to draw because speech problems kept him from communicating freely.

Did you know that geniuses like Thomas Edison, Albert Einstein, Beethoven, Louis Pasteur, and Rodin all had learning problems at one time? You can read about them here. There are also descriptions of the common forms a learning disability can take and ways you can learn to compensate, plus first-person accounts by young people with learning disabilities. Happy reading for you and useful for your parents as well.

Write for:
Yes You Can

Cost: $2.00

Send to:
The National Easter Seal Society
2023 W. Ogden Ave.
Chicago, IL 60612

IT'S ALL IN THE CHEMISTRY

★★★★

What does a person selling perfume in a store have in common with the technician who takes a blood sample for testing in the doctor's office? They're both working with chemistry—the chemicals in perfume, or the chemicals in blood. You're familiar with chemicals like calcium and oxygen. But what about gallium, radon, and xenon? By the time you're through with this lively puzzle book (good for coloring, too) from the American Chemical Society, you'll be able to dazzle your classmates with your chemical vocabulary. You can also try making a Boat Launch and Chemical Rainbows. These brainteasers are geared to elementary grade levels, and come in a friendly 16-page book.

Write for:
Chemistry Brainteasers

Cost: Free

Send to:
American Chemical Society
1155 Sixteenth Street, N.W.
Washington, DC 20036

Chemistry Brainteasers

Flags, Charts, Posters, and Stickers

DOCUMENTING AMERICAN HISTORY

★★★★

It's a great thrill to see these precious documents up close. They're replicas of the Declaration of Independence and the Bill of Rights, and they're on parchment that's been treated so that it really looks

continued

and feels (and smells) old. The quality of the printing is excellent, and you could spend hours studying the exquisite penmanship—not to mention the superb prose—of America's founders. Each document is about 13″ × 16″ and either (or both) would be splendid for framing. These historical documents would make fine gifts for a history buff, or for your favorite schoolchild.

Write for:
Declaration of Independence
Bill of Rights

Cost: $1.00; please do not send stamps

Send to:
Historical Documents Co.
8 N. Preston St.
Philadelphia, PA 19104

AMERICAN PRESIDENTS AND AMERICAN FLAGS

★★★★

Here are two posters (printed on parchment treated in a secret 11-step process to make it look and feel old) that depict important parts of the nation's history. One is a poster showing all the 39 American presidents (in either etchings or photographs), along with the signature of each one and his dates in office. The other poster shows pictures of 16 different flags from various periods of American history, along with a brief description of when and how each one was used. Each document is about 13½″ × 15½″, and the printing is excellent. Super for a wall in your room.

Write for:
Presidents of the U.S.
History of American Flags

Cost: $1.00; please do not send stamps

Send to:
Historical Documents Co.
Dept. E
8 N. Preston St.
Philadelphia, PA 19104

HISTORIC FLAGS

★★★

It's fun and educational to learn more about the flags of the United States, and you can do just that through the National Flag Foundation and the photos and booklets and brochures about flags which they can send you. A new offer is a set of full-color

pictures of three famous flags. They're 8½″ × 11″ prints of the Star-Spangled Banner, the Taunton, and the Grand Union. Each comes with a short history of the flag. You learn how Francis Scott Key came to write the national anthem; that the Grand Union was the first flag of the new American nation; and that the Taunton was the famous English Red Ensign or Meteor Flag to which the people of Taunton, Massachusetts, added the words "Liberty and Union" in 1774 before the American Revolution.

Write for:
Three Flag Scene Prints

Cost: $1.50 and a self-addressed mailing label

Send to:
National Flag Foundation
Flag Plaza
Pittsburgh, PA 15219

Three Flag Scene prints

THE MAKING OF THE STAR-SPANGLED BANNER

★★★★

The flag that flew over Fort McHenry in the War of 1812 and which Francis Scott Key saw in the "dawn's early light" was made by Mary Young Pickersgill. She was carrying on a family tradition: Her grandmother, Rebecca Flower Young, was a professional flagmaker generally credited with making the Grand Union Flag, which General Washington raised over his headquarters on New Year's Day, 1776. In fact, Rebecca Young assisted her granddaughter in making the Star-Spangled Banner. Learn the full story of how the national flag came into being in this packet of information from the Star-Spangled Banner Flag House. You also get the words of the National Anthem and the Pledge of Allegiance, a little leaflet about Mary and the making of her famous banner (which now hangs in the Smithsonian), and a sheet of flag facts. Did you know that Mary's banner was 30 feet hoist (height) by 42 feet fly (span from the flagstaff to the outer edge)—in keeping with the order to make a "flag so large that the British will have no difficulty in seeing it from a distance"?

Write for:
Star-Spangled Banner Packet

Cost: 50¢

Send to:
The Star-Spangled Banner Flag House
844 E. Pratt St.
Baltimore, MD 21202

RAISING THE FLAG

★★★★

You'll find two excellent items in this packet. One is an illustrated foldout brochure on how to honor the American flag, how to display it, how to use it properly in parades and funerals, and when especially to fly it. The second is a booklet, *You Are the Flag.* It's a pictorial history of the many flags used in America from Colonial days to the present. There's a smattering of foreign flags, too, that played their part in American history. Both items are terrific reading for any U.S. student, whatever his or her age.

Write for:
Our Flag
You Are the Flag

Cost: $1.00 and a self-addressed mailing label

Send to:
National Flag Foundation
Flag Plaza
Pittsburgh, PA 15219

FLAG-WAVING FUN

★★★★

A child's own room is special to him, and he likes to personalize it with his own decorative touches. This offer is for a collection of four large colorful pennants which are certain to brighten up any wall. Constructed of heavy-duty felt, the banners depict scenes from places and events such as Washington, D.C., Hawaii, Sesame Street, the Ice Capades, the Statue of Liberty, Mexico, and more. The assortments are randomly selected. This is a good value for $1.00, and will certainly turn a boring wall into a conversation piece. It might even be the start of a new hobby.

Write for:
Pennants

Cost: $1.00

Send to:
IMC Management, Inc.
P.O. Box 11AP
Garnerville, NY 10923

Pennants

TREASURE HUNTS AND PIRATE HORDES

★★★

There are over 40,000 places along the East Coast of the United States and down into the Gulf of Mexico and into the Caribbean that supposedly still have treasure buried onshore or beneath the ocean. Here's a yellowed parchment treasure map showing where to search for 67 of these buried or sunken treasures. The list was made from history, legend, and research. How about looking (or dreaming of looking) off the coast of Delaware for the $4.5 million in gold and jewels that went down into the Atlantic Ocean in 1911 when the liner *Merida* sank about 50 miles off Cape Charles, Virginia? Or imagine checking out the islands off the coast of Wellfleet, Massachusetts, where Pirate Bellamy's ship *Widah* was wrecked in 1717 and sank with $2 million in booty. Another parchment tells about the weapons used by pirates, with illustrations of pistols, cutlasses, and so on. Both these charts measure 14″ × 16″ and would look great on the wall of your bedroom or family room.

Write for:
Treasure Map
Weapons of the Pirates

Cost: $1.00 each; please do not send stamps

continued

KIDS

Send to:
Historical Documents Co.
8 N. Preston St.
Philadelphia, PA 19104

Treasure Map and Weapons of the Pirates

BILLY THE KID WAS A SHORTIE

★★★★

Did you know that Billy the Kid was only 5′3″ tall? That's what it says on this poster. This packet contains "wanted" posters for three of the West's wildest bandits: Billy the Kid, Jesse James, and Jesse's brother Frank. The Billy the Kid poster offers $5,000 reward for the capture dead or alive of the 18-year-old "leader of the worst band of desperadoes the Territory has ever had to deal with." The other poster offers $25,000 for Jesse James, and $15,000 for Frank James, dead or alive. Both posters are about 11″ × 14″ and have photographs of the bandits. They're replicas of authentic documents, and they're reprinted on parchment that looks and feels really old.

Write for:
Billy the Kid Reward Poster
Jesse James Reward Poster

Cost: $1.00; please do not send stamps

Send to:
Historical Documents Co.
Dept. E
8 N. Preston St.
Philadelphia, PA 19104

COLORFUL HANG-UPS!

★★★★

Got a wall that is crying for something colorful and neat to hang on it? If you want a change from pictures of rock or TV or movie stars, how about some patriotic posters? You can send away for a set of three that will put a lot of history and color up on your bedroom, den, or club wall. One is a 14″ × 22″ reprint of cartoonist Milton Caniff's painting and poem, "You Are the Flag," a salute to the American way of life. The second is very timely: a 12″ × 18″ color poster of the Statue of Liberty with a reprint of the entire Emma Lazarus poem that starts, "Give us your tired, your poor...." The third is called "The Rainbow of Hope," an 11″ × 17″ color painting of a rainbow of American flags from different years in the nation's history, all flying in an arch over the head of the Statue of Liberty.

Write for:
Set of 3 Patriotic Posters

Cost: $2.00 and a self-addressed mailing label

Send to:
National Flag Foundation
Flag Plaza
Pittsburgh, PA 15219

WHAT'S THE STATE FLOWER OF PENNSYLVANIA?

★★★

Naturalists, outdoor lovers, and kids, here's a super poster of official Pennsylvania wildlife to add to your collection—if you've got room on your wall. This giant 20″ × 30″ poster features handsome color drawings of Pennsylvania's official state flower, the mountain laurel; the official state tree, the hemlock; the state animal, the white-tail deer; and the state bird, the ruffed grouse. This poster has metal bindings at the top and bottom, plus a hanger.

Write for:
Pennsylvania Official State Flower, Bird, Tree, and Animal poster

Cost: $2.00

Send to:
Pennsylvania Game Commission
P.O. Box 1567
Harrisburg, PA 17120

JUST THE BEAR FACTS

★★★★

This giant color poster (24″ × 32″) stars the black bear of Pennsylvania. One side is a wonderful photograph of a handsome, rather thoughtful-looking bear; the other side is devoted to little-known but interesting bear facts. Did you know that baby bears are born in late January or early February while the

A SASE is a self-addressed stamped envelope.

mother bear is snoozing? And that you estimate the age of a bear by counting the growth rings on his tooth? (How to get the bear to let you examine the tooth is not explained.) Where bears roam in Pennsylvania, what they like to eat, and how to treat them (with respect) make up the rest of the information on this delightful poster.

Write for:
  Bears of Penn's Woods Poster

Cost: Free

Send to:
  Pennsylvania Game Commission
  P.O. Box 1567
  Harrisburg, PA 17120

"BE KIND" MESSAGE TO COLOR

★★★★

Here are all your favorite animals from the zoo ready to color as a picture for your wall. This nice poster from the Massachusetts Society for the Prevention of Cruelty to Animals measures 11″ × 14″ — plenty of room for the elephant, snake, camel, penguin, kangaroo, octopus, and lots more animals. The title is "Be Kind to One and All," a good message for kids and for grown-ups. You can get this happy coloring poster for a quarter.

Write for:
  Be Kind to One and All coloring poster

Cost: 25¢

Send to:
  MSPCA
  Circulation Dept.
  350 S. Huntington Ave.
  Boston, MA 02130

Be Kind to One and All coloring poster

ALL IN HARMONY

★★★

Harmonicas are also known as pocket pianos, blues harps, mouth organs, French harps, and tin sandwiches. But whatever the name, there are probably as many harmonicas in the United States as all other instruments combined. Even President Ronald Reagan plays one. Now, enthusiasts can receive three posters and a booklet of harmonica trivia. The first 22″ × 28″ poster is titled "Get Your Hands On A Hohner And Let The Feelin' Flow," and depicts the part Hohner harmonicas have played in America's history. The second full-color poster is "Get Hot"; it introduces the new Hot Metal Harp and features John Chrisley, Jr., the phenomenal 14-year-old harmonicist from California. The "Harmonica Artist Poster" features ten of today's most popular harmonicists and rounds out the trio. The 16-page booklet, *Easy Reeding*, is free and contains facts, figures, names, and dates. For example, did you know that Frank James, Jesse's older brother, is reputed to have deflected a bullet with the harmonica in his pocket?

Write for:
  EasyReeding
  Desired poster

Cost: EasyReading free with a SASE
  Posters $2.00 each

Send to:
  Hohner, Inc.
  P.O. Box 15035
  Richmond, VA 23227

"Get Your Hands on a Hohner" poster

DO-IT-YOURSELF GROWTH CHART

★★★

Measure your height in centimeters and mark it down on this *Growth Record*. The next time you

continued

measure yourself—say in a couple of months—record the change on the bar graph by coloring in the number of centimeters you've grown. That way you can see how fast you're growing. And you can do the same thing with the weight graph in this same folder. You record how many pounds you've gained since the last weigh-in to see your rate of weight gain. There's also a small chart that tells you what kind of food to eat for good bone growth, to keep your blood healthy, and to help your muscles work and your eyes see better. This is especially for preschoolers and first- and second-graders.

Write for:
  Growth Record

Cost: 10¢

Send to:
  Order Department
  National Dairy Council
  6300 N. River Rd.
  Rosemont, IL 60018

BLIMPS, SKUNKS, AND FROGS
★★★★

Want some jazzy decals to decorate your bike, your schoolbook covers (not the books themselves, remember), or your windows? Here are some super unusual ones that look stunning anywhere light shines or is reflected. These Rainbow Stickers™ are colorful, stick-on decals that reflect light. For $1.00 per sheet you can order eight monkeys, nine cars, six blimps, or, if you don't know where you'd stick six blimps, you can order six skunks, 35 stars, eight frogs, 12 tulips and daisies, nine airplanes, 12 bumble bees, or nine angelfish. Stickers peel off a paper sheet and most are about an inch high. Good for trading, too, or to decorate a birthday gift.

Write for:
  Rainbow Stickers™

Cost: $1.00 per sheet

Send to:
  Mr. Rainbows
  P.O. Box 27056 (FT)
  Philadelphia, PA 19118

COCA-COLA IN EIGHT LANGUAGES
★★★

This unusual postcard features eight square stickers that invite you to drink Coca-Cola soft drinks in

Arabic, French, Japanese, Thai, Spanish, Chinese, Hebrew, and Polish. They're grouped around a large center sticker that says "Coke® Is It!" All the squares are printed in the familiar red and white colors. Did you know that people in more than 155 countries drink Coke? That means it would take 80 stickers—not just eight—to represent all their languages.

Write for:
  International Sticker Postcard

Cost: Free

Send to:
  Coca-Cola USA
  Consumer Information Center
  P.O. Drawer 1734
  Atlanta, GA 30301

International Sticker postcard

Do-It-Yourself Projects and Ideas

A QUARTER-ACRE OF WILDLIFE
★★★★

Kids, this free packet introduces you to the National Wildlife Federation's backyard wildlife program. The program itself tells how you can create a miniature wildlife preserve in your backyard, even if you have only a little space to work with. The packet includes an introductory guide to attracting wildlife, an explanation of the four basic elements of wildlife habitat, and it also tells how to provide for wildlife in suburban and urban settings. You'll learn how to make an inventory of everything in your yard and look at it from an animal's point of view—an old tree, for instance, could be providing a perfect home for a family of birds or a colony of bees. And have you noticed how the brightly colored flowers in the garden attract butterflies and bees? If you get hooked on the idea of having the sort of backyard where birds, butterflies, and small animals are happy to keep you company, you may want to go a step further. Send for a Gardening With Wildlife Kit (it costs $14.95 plus postage) and apply for certification of your yard as an official NWF Backyard Wildlife Habitat. But even with this little free package you'll get lots of delightful ideas about how exciting and attractive a regular old backyard can really be.

Write for:
Backyard Wildlife Habitat Information Packet

Cost: Free

Send to:
National Wildlife Federation
1412 16th St., N.W.
Washington, DC 20036

MAKING WOOD DUCKS FEEL AT HOME
★★

Do you want to build a house for wood ducks? Here's a pamphlet that gives you step-by-step instructions on how to make these feathered friends safe and comfortable in their natural habitat. First, you need a marsh. Nesting houses for the wood duck must be some distance from the shore and completely surrounded by water in order to attract the ducks during the nesting season. This sheet from the Pennsylvania Game Commission gives complete plans for a galvanized pipe nesting house that's bolted to a steel post. The hard part is driving the steel post 30″ into a marsh bottom, best accomplished in the wintertime. Get an adult to help.

Write for:
Predator-Proof Wood Duck Nesting House Plans

Cost: Free

Send to:
Pennsylvania Game Commission
P.O. Box 1567
Harrisburg, PA 17120

BUILD A BIRD FEEDER
★★★★

Birds are not just interesting and beautiful creatures to watch; they can be of great value to us, whether we live in the city or the country. Birds are a part of the balance of nature that helps us live in conditions

of pure air, sun, food, and water. Since birds are so valuable to people, why not do something for them? This striking 26-page booklet, with lots of helpful illustrations, tells all about the value of birds, their habitats, and how to build bird feeders and houses. Birds, like people, don't all like to eat out of the same kind of dish or live in the same kind of house. You'll learn what kind of feeder attracts different birds, and you'll get instructions on how to build a purple martin house, a bluebird house, a screech owl nesting box, a tree swallow house, a wren house, a wood duck nest box, and others. These are feeders and bird houses for birds of Ohio, but many of these winged beauties are common throughout the Midwest and across the country.

Write for:
Attracting Birds in Ohio

Cost: $1.00

Send to:
Ohio Department of Natural Resources
Division of Wildlife
1500 Dublin Rd.
Columbus, OH 43215

Attracting Birds in Ohio

WHAT CATCHES FLIES, BUT ISN'T AN OUTFIELDER?
★★★★

The answer, of course, is a Venus fly trap, a carnivorous plant that lures, captures, and digests insects. The prey is attracted to the plant's bright colors and touches the sensitive trigger hairs; the trap snaps shut, and the victim is caught. Here's a package of Venus fly trap seeds with instructions for growing your own green fly-catchers. You'll also receive a catalog and price list for other carnivorous and woodland terrarium plants, seeds, and books about them. An interesting change from school science projects.

continued

KIDS

Write for:
Venus Fly Trap Seeds and Carnivorous Plants
Brochure

Cost: $2.00 for the seeds and catalog
Catalog only is free

Send to:
Peter Pauls Nurseries
Route 4
Canandaigua, NY 14424

HOW TO BE A (PATIENT) PAPERMAKER
★★★

Papermaking is an ancient art first developed in China in 105 A.D., where it remained a secret for many centuries. Since the beginning of the 19th century, most paper has been machine-made, but if you'd like to try doing it the old-fashioned way, by hand, send for Hammermill Papers' papermaking project.

How To Make Paper by Hand is a 12-page illustrated instruction booklet that divides the process into 17 steps, describing each step in detail. Along with this booklet, you'll also receive a fine-mesh screen for use in the paper mold (which you have to make) and six sheets of ledger paper for use in blotting and drying your paper toward the end of the papermaking process. Though this booklet makes papermaking looks easy as 1-2-3, it could well be a messy and complicated project in the hands of the beginner.

Write for:
How To Make Paper by Hand

Cost: 25¢

Send to:
Hammermill Papers Group
P.O. Box 1440
Erie, PA 16533

How to Make Paper by Hand

MAKE-IT-YOURSELF WATER PUMP
★★★★

Want to know how to make a real, working pump out of old tin cans? Or out of plastic tubing and balloons? The Boston Children's Museum will send you two excellent how-to projects for building water pumps from these simple materials. *A Tin Can Pump* and *A Balloon and Funnel Pump* have large hand-written directions and extra-large drawings that 10- to 12-year-olds can follow step-by-step. Everything you will need for building these projects is probably around the house—nails, a sharp knife, jar lids, a used dishwashing liquid container, and so on. Once you've built your pump, try the experiments suggested on the back of each instruction booklet. For example, what could you do to the parts of the pump so that it might deliver more water per minute?

Write for:
A Balloon and Funnel Pump
A Tin Can Pump

Cost: 50¢ each ($1.00 for both) and a SASE

Send to:
The Museum Shop
Boston Children's Museum
300 Congress Street
Boston, MA 02210

THE SHELL GAME
★★★

If you're a novice shell collector, you'll welcome this brief, beautifully written guide to an absorbing pastime. You'll learn what sea shells are, the difference between a bivalve and a univalve, and the miraculous way the creature produces its shell. There are fine illustrations of some of the more interesting of the 300,000 species of shells on Earth. This introduction to shelling tells where to look for shells (they're experts in camouflage), how to start a collection, and what materials you'll need. There's also a bit about how to clean shells and how to store and display them. Take this little book along on your next trip to the beach.

Write for:
Let's Collect Shells

Cost: $1.00 and a long SASE

Send to:
Benjane Arts
320 Hempstead Ave.
West Hempstead, NY 11552

A SASE is a self-addressed stamped envelope.

GROW MYSTERIOUS CRYSTAL FLOWERS

★★★

You may know from TV advertisements that bluing will help make the laundry whiter and brighter, but did you know you could use it for a far more interesting project—to grow a magic salt crystal garden? You can get the instructions, free, from the makers of Mrs. Stewart's Bluing, who've been showing kids how to do this project for 75 years. They'll send you three copies of the ingenious recipe for growing a salt crystal garden from water, salt, bluing, and other common household products. It will bloom into beautiful rosebuds, coral, and crystal for as long as you like. You can give the extra recipes to your friends.

Write for:
Magic Salt Crystal Garden

Cost: Free with a SASE

Send to:
Luther Ford and Co.
100 N. Seventh St.
Minneapolis, MN 55403

FOR THE SERIOUS KITE BUILDER

★★★

This beautifully written and illustrated booklet is definitely for the serious kitemaker who designs and builds his or her own kites. If that's you, you'll find detailed information here on the different kinds (and coatings) of nylon you can use, and if and how you can color it. You'll learn how to cut on the bias, how to hot and cold cut the material, and how to sew it on whatever machine you have—even down to the right needle and thread to use. There's information on actually sewing the kites (with trouble-shooting data), how to make hems and pockets and reinforce them, piecing, transferring designs, and attaching design pieces. There's a great source list for every possible item you need to build a kite.

Write for:
Mastering Nylon

Cost: $1.75 and a self-addressed mailing label

Send to:
Kite Lines
7106 Campfield Rd.
Baltimore, MD 21207-4699

MAKE YOUR OWN SOAP

★★★

More and more, reasons of ecology and economy are prompting people to make their own soap. Soapmaking is a satisfying hobby, too, and this booklet will tell you how to do it. You have to use lye in the process, so you'll need grown-up supervision unless you're old enough to handle this substance alone. This eight-page foldout about homemade soaps includes selected recipes for several kinds—scented, complexion, and laundry soap—and discusses molds and colorings. It also tells exactly how to make soap safely, step-by-step, and offers recipes for eight different types of soaps, plus a conversion chart for changing liquids to solids.

Write for:
Soapmaking Booklet

Cost: $2.00

Send to:
RASCO, Inc.
P.O. Box 193
Lakeville, CT 06039

FUN FOR WOODWORKERS

★★

If you're skilled with a jigsaw or can get an adult to help you in the workshop, you can make some fun things that are also educational. This company offers full-sized patterns with step-by-step instructions for four 8½″ × 11″ wooden puzzles for little kids. First you learn to cut wooden squares, circles, and triangles, then you progress to more difficult projects like sailboats, rabbits, and more. You can paint the puzzles when you're done. Nice gifts for small children—and educational because they teach children to recognize and put together shapes and colors. You get to practice with a band saw or jigsaw—and, unless you're already experienced enough to use these tools alone, you've got a nice kid-parent project here.

Write for:
Puzzles

Cost: $1.25 and a long SASE

Send to:
Family Educational Assistance
303 S. 34th St.
Tacoma, WA 98408

KIDS

NEEDLE KNACK
★★★★

Whether you have a flair for needlepoint or would like to try your skills for the first time, this craft kit is for you. The offer includes a 4¾'' square canvas printed with a full-color design, yarn to match, complete instructions, and a tapestry needle to get you stitching right along. The patterns are easy to complete, and the finished work can be framed and hung in your room or given as a gift. The manufacturer will pick a design at random and send it to you; all are attractive projects. Beginners and pros alike will find these needlepoint kits easy yet enjoyable.

Write for:
Needlepoint Canvas and Yarn

Cost: $2.00

Send to:
Needlepoint
P.O. Box 11-FR
Garnerville, NY 10923

Needlepoint canvas and yarn

MINI-KNITS FOR BEGINNERS
★★★

Learning to knit can lead you into a wonderful world of creativity and satisfaction. If you can knit, you can learn to make sweaters and mittens, scarves and hats—but everyone has to start out small. You can start *really* small with these little Christmas ornaments: a Scandinavian striped ski hat and a miniature Christmas tree. Patterns include row-by-row instructions; the only materials you'll need are some colored wool and a pair of knitting needles. An easy introduction to knitting.

Write for:
Hat
Christmas Tree

Cost: 50¢ each and a long SASE

Send to:
Emily Ann Creations
303 S. 34th St.
Tacoma, WA 98408

Hat and Christmas Tree

CHRISTMAS DECORATIONS
★★★

Now's the time to get out the cookie cutters and start making decorations for the Christmas tree—no matter if it's mid-July. Here's a simple recipe for salt dough that you can sculpt in the shapes of stars, yule trees, bells, gingerbread people, Santas, hearts, and wreaths. This colorful little brochure tells what you'll need and how to make and decorate your ornaments. You start out making simple ones and then get fancier. A fun way to get into the holiday spirit any time of the year.

Write for:
Salt Sculpture Pamphlet

Cost: Free with a SASE

Send to:
Box FTK
Morton Salt
Consumer Affairs
110 N. Wacker Dr.
Chicago, IL 60606

NICE TO KNIT
★★

Here's how to knit your own Christmas tree ornaments or gift package decorations. Get started right away and when the holiday rush rolls around you'll be able to let it roll right by. These patterns show you how to make two ornaments: a small Christmas bell and a striped mini-stocking. The row-by-row instruc-

A SASE is a self-addressed stamped envelope.

tions are super simple to follow, and all you need for each ornament are scraps of red, green, or white yarn and a pair of knitting needles.

Write for:
   Christmas Bell and Stocking

Cost: 50¢ and a long SASE

Send to:
   Emily Ann Creations
   303 S. 34th St.
   Tacoma, WA 98408

Christmas Bell and Stocking

CHRISTMAS GIFTS ON A SHOESTRING

★★

Want to make a lot of people happy next Christmas but short of cash for gifts? Make your own presents with the help of these 30 creative ideas for solving holiday gift-giving dilemmas. You'll learn how to make pillowcases and baby bibs and homemade jam and bread. You'll also learn how to write your own storybook, put together a gift coupon book and more. Parents and kids can both have a lot of fun with this gift list.

Write for:
   Kids Christmas

Cost: 50¢ and a long SASE

Send to:
   Emily Ann Creations
   303 S. 34th St.
   Tacoma, WA 98408

MAKE YOUR OWN STATIONERY

★★

It's fun to write letters to friends and relatives, and it's even more fun to write on personalized stationery you designed yourself. Here are two offers to help you give the personal touch to your letters. One offer consists of three samples of pastel parchment paper, each with a different drawing in the right top corner—a country farm scene in winter; a goose chasing a farm girl; and a pioneer girl with a bow in her hair.

The other offer (and the more interesting of the two) tells you how to make your own "thumbprint stationery" by inking your thumb and adding details to your thumbprints to make a cat, a boy on skis, a mouse, a devil, etc. Your own thumbprint pictures make your stationery personal in a very special way— a neat idea, and simple even if you think you can't draw.

Write for:
   Stationery Samples
   Thumbprint Instructions

Cost: 50¢ each and a long SASE

Send to:
   Emily Ann Creations
   303 S. 34th St.
   Tacoma, WA 98408

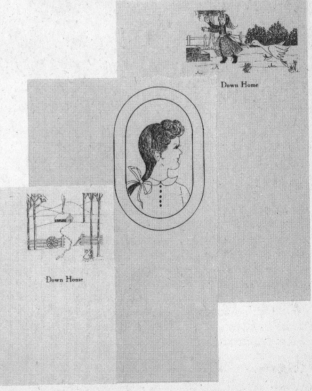

Stationery samples

Prices are for single items only; prices and information are accurate at time of publication.

KIDS

Sports and Outdoor Activities

SOFTBALL: THE OFFICIAL RULES

★★★★

Now you won't be able to say you didn't know if someone says you're not playing by the rules. Here are the *official* rules of the game of softball, as defined by the Amateur Softball Association of America. These include the official rule changes, rule interpretations, and clarifications. There are diagrams and dimensions for official softball diamonds (both 55 ft. and 65 ft.). You'll also learn, by way of text and photographs, how Louisville Slugger aluminum bats are made—from a tube of aluminum to a mighty weapon in the batter's box. And did you know there are four different types of softball games? There are—fast pitch, slow pitch, modified, and 16-inch slow pitch. Nearly 100 pages of information in this pocket-size book.

Write for:
Official Softball Rules

Cost: $1.90

Send to:
H & B Promotions
P.O. Box 18177
Dept. ND
Louisville, KY 40218

Official Softball Rules

IF YOU'RE BATTY ABOUT BASEBALL

★★★★

Batty about baseball? Here are a couple of nice souvenirs of your favorite sport. One is a ballpoint pen shaped like baseball bats and carrying a facsimile of Robin Yount's autograph. You can get the pen for 80¢. The other is a keychain, also shaped like a baseball bat but with Steve Garvey's autograph. This one costs 75¢. They'd make good gifts for your friends who are nuts about baseball too.

Write for:
One Louisville Slugger pen
Louisville Slugger keychain

Cost: 80¢ for the pen
75¢ for the keychain

Send to:
H & B Promotions
P.O. Box 18177
Dept. ND
Louisville, KY 40218

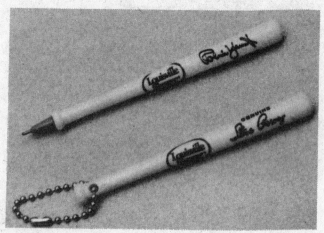

Louisville Slugger pen and keychain

OFFICIAL RULES OF BASEBALL

★★★★

Here they are, 64 pages of official rules governing all play for organized professional baseball. You'll also find official playing equipment standards that manufacturers must follow and the official definition of all the terms of baseball. A large portion of this pocket-size, small-print handbook is devoted to the rules of scoring, and how the official scorer must compile information for permanent statistical records for all the players on a team. There's also an

A SASE is a self-addressed stamped envelope.

application form for applying to the N.B.C. National Association of Umpires. Diagrams of the baseball diamond, too.

Write for:
Official Baseball Rules

Cost: $1.00

Send to:
H & B Promotions
P.O. Box 18177
Dept. ND
Louisville, KY 40218

BASEBALL'S DEFENSIVE PLAYS

★★★★

This knowledgeable little booklet was written by the great Dodger shortstop Pee Wee Reese to help baseball players know what to do with the ball when it is fielded, and to help spectators anticipate defensive plays. There are 30 different diagrams, information on the general strategy of the play, and the moves for each of the other players. Besides the defensive plays, there is biographical information about the author, and a bat selection guide for players according to their height and weight. Nearly 50 pages of good, solid baseball lore.

Write for:
The Louisville Slugger Playmaking Guide

Cost: $1.35

Send to:
H & B Promotions
P.O. Box 18177
Dept. ND
Louisville, KY 40218

The Louisville Slugger Playmaking Guide

STAYING SAFE ON A BICYCLE

★★★

Bike riding is fun, but it can also be dangerous. More than a thousand bike riders are killed each year, and thousands more are injured, in collisions with cars and trucks. Be sure you know how to avoid being a cycling statistic by checking your safety awareness against this brochure from the National Easter Seal Society. It tells why riding the right size of bike is important, what you should know about bicycle accidents, what safety equipment to have on the bike, and what rules to follow for safe cycling. There are also some good tips on bicycle maintenance. Start the wheels rolling for safe biking by sending for this free brochure.

Write for:
Bicycle Safety Tips

Cost: Free with a long SASE

Send to:
National Easter Seal Society
2023 Ogden Ave.
Chicago, IL 60612

Bicycle Safety Tips

GET ON YOUR SOAP BOX AND GO!

★★★

What's a good, old-fashioned summer vacation without watermelon, Fourth of July fireworks, and a soap box derby to enter? Here's lots of information on the last item, and you can get it by writing to the All-American Soap Box Derby. You'll get the Official All-American Soap Box Derby Rule Book for junior and senior divisions — covering everything you'll need to

continued

know to enter the derby, including car dimensions, inspection checklist, grounds for disqualification, and exact specifications for building your car.

Write for:
Official All-American Soap Box Derby Rule Book

Cost: Free

Send to:
All-American Soap Box Derby
P.O. Box 7233
Derby Downs
Akron, OH 44306

MODERN ROBIN HOOD-ERY
★★★

If you know the definition of shafts, nocks, and fletching, you're probably a knowledgeable archer. If you'd *like* to know, this booklet will tell you. It explains different kinds of archery bows and how to choose the best for you, what draw weight your bow should have, and which arrows to choose. You'll learn bow and arrow terms and find out about other necessary shooting equipment. Then you'll read the proper techniques of shooting, step by step. Photographs accompany the text. You'll also learn where you can shoot and the names of the local associations that make up the American Archery Council. A separate brochure describes the basics of hunting with bow and arrow.

Write for:
The ABC's of Archery
The ABC's of Bowhunting

Cost: 75¢ each

Send to:
American Archery Council
200 Castlewood Dr.
North Palm Beach, FL 33408

TAKE ONE CHILD AND ONE FISHING POLE...
★★

Fishing can be highly technical, very complicated, and quite scientific. Or it can be simple and fun. This sheet opts for the latter approach and tells, very basically, how to make your own fishing pole. You take one pole—it needs to be twice as long as you are—add line, bobber, leader, sinker, and bait, and go to it. The simple directions and illustrations are for beginners only. Once you've become skilled at

catching fish with a pole and line, you're ready for a rod and reel.

Write for:
Fishing Fundamentals

Cost: Free

Send to:
Ohio Department of Natural Resources
Division of Wildlife
Fountain Square
Columbus, OH 43224

WOODSY OWL GOES CAMPING
★★

Do you like to go camping or just go walking in the woods? Woodsy Owl is wise in the ways of the outdoors and wants you to have a great time and be sure that others will, too. He tells you to take care of yourself by preparing and storing food properly, to take care of the woods by being careful of the plants and animals that live there, and to take care of others by cleaning up after yourself. Put this bright Woodsy Owl poster on your wall, and take the little folder along on your next trip.

Write for:
Woodsy Owl Poster and Woodsy Owl on Camping (FS-318)

Cost: Free

Send to:
USDA Forest Service
P.O. Box 2417
Washington, DC 20013

HANDY INFO FOR SKIPPER AND FIRST MATE
★★★★

If your folks are keen sailors, but you still keep getting "bow" and "stern" mixed up, or if you just could use an abbreviated boating guide on board, *Don't Make Waves* has easy-to-read information condensed into 24 pages and accompanied by clear line drawings illustrating boating rules, equipment, safety requirements, boarding, weather conditions, navigation tips, rescue procedures—even "hitching up" and driving with a boat on the highway. There's also a handy pre-launch checklist, a chart illustrating the flags and lights used by the Coast Guard to post severe weather warnings, a "channel buoy guide," and a glossary of boating terms. This guide is small and sturdy enough to keep in the nautical equivalent of the glove compartment for quick reference. Useful for sailors, and must reading for first-time passengers.

Write for:
Don't Make Waves

Cost: Free

Send to:
State Farm Insurance Companies
Public Relations Department—DH
One State Farm Plaza
Bloomington, IL 61701

Don't Make Waves

TREAT A BEAR WITH RESPECT

★★★

Here are two brochures about American wildlife. One brochure discusses the American black bear, an interesting but dangerous wild animal. It tells what to do if you encounter one on a hike, and how to store your camp food and garbage to avoid having a bear join you for dinner. It also adds some good house-keeping habits for camp and car. There are also some interesting bear facts. The other brochure discusses the biting trail bugs of the northeast—the mosquito, the ant, the black fly, the punky or "no-see-um," the deer fly, and the bee. It tells which repellant works best on each pest and outlines first aid for serious stings and bites.

Write for:
The Bear Facts
Coping With Trail Bugs of the Northeast

Cost: 15¢ and a long SASE

Send to:
Adirondack Mountain Club, Inc.
172 Ridge St.
Glens Falls, NY 12801

The World Around You

MOUNT ST. HELENS, BEFORE AND AFTER

★★★★

To read the story of Mount St. Helens and study this huge 36″ × 40″ map is to understand the awesome power of nature. On one side of this sheet is a map of the mountain and its vicinity, showing the eruption impact area and where the landslide debris flowed. The other side of the map is a series of breathtaking color photographs showing the mountain before it erupted, as it erupted, and afterward. The text explains the geology of Mount St. Helens, some early legends about the mountain, and the terrible time-table that led to the devastation of May 18, 1980. You'll read about the new topographic features carved by the eruption and what the future of Mount St. Helens is expected to hold. A fascinating story.

Write for:
Mount St. Helens & Vicinity map

Cost: $1.00

Send to:
U.S. Geological Survey
Box 25286
Denver, CO 80225

Mount St. Helens & Vicinity Map

MAKE NEW FRIENDS THROUGH THE MAIL

★★★★

If you're between the ages of 12 and 16 and would like to correspond with someone abroad or in an-

continued

KIDS

other part of the United States, you can order names and addresses with this order blank for student letter exchanges. You can choose a friend-by-mail from any one of 31 countries, and you choose which age and sex you prefer to write to. You can even order names for an entire school, club, or class at one time. All pen pals can correspond in English. The Student Letter Exchange has arranged for pen pals throughout the world for 50 years. A neat way to travel without leaving home.

Write for:
Student Letter Exchange information

Cost: Free

Send to:
Student Letter Exchange
910 4th St., S.E.
Austin, MN 55912

I SPY WITH MY LITTLE EYE
★★

Sight, one of our most important senses, is achieved through a complex photographic process that involves the brain, thousands of nerve endings, and light. An informative two-color poster from the National Society to Prevent Blindness illustrates with clear language and diagrams how this process works. Titled "How We See," the poster names the parts of the eye and outlines the steps which enable the brain to register a three-dimensional image. This is a great educational aid, whether in the classroom or at home.

Write for:
How We See poster

Cost: 50¢ and a long SASE

Send to:
National Society to Prevent Blindness
79 Madison Avenue
New York, NY 10016-7896

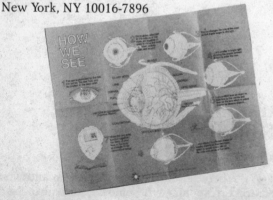

How We See poster

THE AIRPLANE
★★★

For airplane and aviation history buffs, TWA offers *A History of TWA Aircraft*, a free pamphlet that opens into an 18″ × 24″ sheet of fascinating photos and information.

This black-and-white poster-size publication traces TWA's history, beginning with the humble Ford Tri-Motor used from 1929 through 1934 (it had a 77-foot wing span, 50-foot length, and room for 13 passengers). Then read how TWA entered the jet age when its Boeing 707 flew from San Francisco to New York in 4 hours, 40 minutes in 1959. The history concludes with the Boeing 767 and the McDonnell-Douglas MD-80, the most recent additions to the TWA fleet. This brief, very interesting history of TWA's aircraft is accompanied by historical photos.

Write for:
A History of TWA Aircraft

Cost: Free

Send to:
Corporate Communication Department
Trans World Airlines, Inc.
605 Third Ave.
New York, NY 10158

A History of TWA Aircraft

WHAT'S YOUR EYE-Q?
★★★

Half of all blindness is needless and preventable. True or false? The answer is true, and you and your children will learn a lot more about eyesight and eye care with this flyer from the National Society to Prevent Blindness. Illustrated with colorful Walt Disney characters, the true-false quiz is quite informative and fun to read. Did you know that the junior-high-school years bring the greatest risk of accidental injuries to youngsters' eyes? Or that you

A SASE is a self-addressed stamped envelope.

could be headed for serious eye trouble without knowing it? There is also a listing of warning signs for eye problems in both children and adults. This is a good leaflet to read—especially when you realize that half of all blindness can be prevented.

Write for:
Professor Ludwig von Drake's I.Q.

Cost: Free with a long SASE

Send to:
National Society to Prevent Blindness
79 Madison Avenue
New York, NY 10016-7896

LEARNING YOUR WAY AROUND THE LIBRARY

★★

You have to write a school paper on the theory of relativity; you want to know why the dinosaurs died out; you want another book by an author you've just discovered. Maybe your teacher assigned you to write a report on a particular career. You know all this stuff is in the library—somewhere—but how do you find what you want? *The Library—What's In It For You?* and *The Library Reference Aids* will show you your way around the local library. These are delightful, cartoon-style guides to using the card catalog, vertical file, periodical literature, and encyclopedia. You'll learn (painlessly) about author cards, subject cards, title cards, call numbers, and more. These booklets contain "everything you wanted to know about the library but were afraid to ask." Prepared by a librarian, so the info is straight from the top.

Write for:
The Library—What's In It For You?
The Library Reference Aids

Cost: $1.00 for both

Send to:
Interstate Printers & Publishers, Inc.
19 N. Jackson St.
P.O. Box 50
Danville, IL 61834-0050

The Library: What's In It for You?

LEARNING ABOUT LIGHT

★★★

Although the nature of light is still full of mystery, there is a great deal that we do know about it. Find out about light from these three illustrated foldouts, *The Evolution of Light, Radiant Energy,* and *Saving Lighting Energy.* The first is the story of how we have produced light, from cave fires up through the working of the most modern light sources. *Radiant Energy* explains how scientists are developing new medical and industrial uses for infrared, ultraviolet, and laser light. *Saving Lighting Energy* is a bit more technical, comparing the various lamps in common use and how they compare in terms of energy efficiency.

Write for:
Light & Man booklets

Cost: Free

Send to:
GTE Lighting Products
Sylvania Lighting Center
Danvers, MA 01923

SOLAR ENERGY AND YOU

★★

Solar energy is the heat and light that comes from the sun. Thousands of years ago, some people used this energy to heat their homes. Today, solar energy is again helping to heat buildings. You can learn all about solar energy from two free booklets offered by the U.S. Department of Energy. They explain the origins of solar energy and new methods of using the sun's light and heat in both passive and active solar houses. Good educational reading for young people interested in the latest in science and energy.

Write for:
Solar Energy and You
Learning About Renewable Energy

Cost: Free

Send to:
CAREIRS
P.O. Box 8900
Silver Spring, MD 20907

JEWISH HISTORY IN THE HOLY LAND

★★★

This beautifully produced, thoroughly documented, 68-page history book tells the story of Jewish life in

continued

KIDS

the Holy Land, beginning with the first century A.D. It's full of color and black-and-white photographs of ancient documents, archaeological sites, maps, and writings that authenticate the text with visual manifestations of history. The editor of this book, archaeologist Dan Bahat of the State of Israel's Department of Antiquities and Museums, produced the book in order to give a picture of the continuity of Jewish presence in Israel despite thousands of years of foreign conquest.

Write for:
Twenty Centuries of Jewish Life in the Holy Land

Cost: Free

Send to:
Consulate General of Israel in Los Angeles
Suite 1700
6380 Wilshire Blvd.
Los Angeles, CA 90048

THE PASSOVER HAGGADAH
★★★★

This is a deluxe edition of the liturgy of the seder service for the Jewish feast of Passover. It's complete; there are no deletions from either the Hebrew or English traditional versions, and the Hebrew and English texts are printed in parallel columns. You'll also find transliterations of prayers that are supposed to be said in Hebrew.

Write for:
Passover Haggadah

Cost: 75¢

Send to:
Joseph Jacobs Organization, Inc.
60 E. 42nd St.
New York, NY 10165

FOR STARGAZERS
★★★

Maybe you've always been interested in the stars in the skies. Maybe Halley's Comet got you looking into the night sky. Stars are used by sailors to navigate their ships, by farmers to decide when to plant or harvest, and have been studied to win wars or and awaken love in the hearts of men and women. If you want to learn more about the stars in the northern skies, such as Cassiopeia, Andromeda, the Big and Little Dippers, the Corona Borealis and other stars and constellations, send for a neat 24-page booklet, *Stars in Your Eyes*. It tells about the stars in the northern hemisphere and has drawings of the constellations. You also learn where to look in the skies for the various stars.

Write for:
Stars in Your Eyes: A Guide to the Northern Skies (No. 150P)

Cost: $1.50

Send to:
Consumer Information Center
P.O. Box 100
Pueblo, CO 81002

Stars in Your Eyes:

FILL THE BLACK HOLE IN YOUR KNOWLEDGE
★★★★

Are you fascinated or mystified by black holes? Do you wonder what in the universe they are? This packet from the Astronomical Society of the Pacific should help fill the black hole in your knowledge and whet your appetite for learning about other universal mysteries, such as quasars, pulsars, exploding galaxies, and the prospect of life "elsewhere." The packet contains nontechnical articles about black holes that explain what they are (the result of the death of a massive star), where they are, and why they are. There's also a bibliography for further reading.

Write for:
Black Holes packet

Cost: $2.00

A SASE is a self-addressed stamped envelope.

Send to:
Black Holes Packet
Astronomical Society of the Pacific
1290 24th Ave.
San Francisco, CA 94122

EXPLORING THE UNIVERSE

★★★★

The ancient Greeks believed that there were only four different kinds of substances—earth, water, fire, and air. Now we all know that there are more than four—but did you know that a recent computer list of known chemicals had 4,039,907 entries? And did you know that the 92 basic elements that constitute these more than 4 million chemicals can also be found throughout the observable universe? That's just a taste of the fascinating information you can find in this packet of material put together by the Astronomical Society of the Pacific to introduce the beginner to the field of astronomy. Learn the answer to the question, "How fast do you move while sitting?" Find out what the atoms that make up your body were doing eight billion years ago. Read why some stars aren't really where they seem to be. And if this packet doesn't make you more curious about the world beyond the world you live in, you just aren't using your imagination. Super stuff.

Write for:
A Brief Introduction to Astronomy

Cost: $2.00

Send to:
Astronomical Society of the Pacific
Information Packets Dept.
1290 24th Ave.
San Francisco, CA 94122

SETTING YOUR SIGHTS ON A TELESCOPE

★★★★

Thinking of buying a telescope? Then don't leave home on a shopping trip before getting some know-how from the people who *really* know about telescopes—the Astronomical Society of the Pacific. This pamphlet, written in plain English for the non-scientist, tells you how different types of telescopes work and which ones are best for various purposes. You'll learn how telescopes are rated, what sort of mountings are required, and what to do with a telescope once you get it home. There's a handy list of questions to ask *before* you make a purchase— such as whether you live in an urban area where the

night sky is bright with city lights, or in a rural locale with dark night skies. And one tip for the very beginner: start with something easy to find, like the moon. This is a very practical, well-illustrated guide for the first-time buyer who wants to set his or her sights, literally, on the stars.

Write for:
Selecting Your First Telescope

Cost: $2.00

Send to:
Astronomical Society of the Pacific
Telescope Guide Dept.
1290 24th Ave.
San Francisco, CA 94122

LOST IN THE STARS

★★★★

Interested in space and astronomy? The Astronomical Society of the Pacific offers a free list of publications, articles, and record or cassette astronomy programs to interest the budding astronaut. Individual items start at $1.00, but the list is free. A sample of the neat stuff listed here—a black-and-white bumper sticker that says, "Let the Stars Get In Your Eyes." It would look as good on your wall as on a car bumper.

Write for:
Astronomy Information List
"Stars in Your Eyes" Bumper Sticker

Cost: List: Free with a SASE
Bumper Sticker: $1.00 and a long SASE

Send to:
Astronomical Society of the Pacific
1290 24th Avenue
San Francisco, CA 94122

"Stars In Your Eyes" bumper sticker

Prices are for single items only; prices and information are accurate at time of publication.

KIDS

BE YOUR OWN WEATHERPERSON

★★★★

Here's an item you'll really like. This 11″×17″ cloud chart can help you forecast the weather with nearly as much accuracy as the TV weatherperson. There are 35 color photographs of various cloud formations on this cloud chart, with a note on what kind of weather each one predicts. You'll also learn how clouds form, what causes rain, what the different types of clouds are called (those fluffy summer beauties are cumulus), and how to forecast the weather by using this cloud chart. There are also easy-to-understand explanations of weather terms.

There's a simpler version of the chart available, too. It's the same size, but it has 19 pictures, some of which carry traditional weather forecast messages, for instance: "If smoke and birds go high, there's no rain in the sky. If smoke and birds are low, watch out for a blow." Or, "Rainbow in the morning, travelers take warning. Rainbow at night, travelers' delight." If you want the 35-picture chart, ask for Chart B. The 19-picture chart is Chart C.

Write for:
Chart B or Chart C

Cost: $2.00 each and a long SASE

Send to:
Cloud Chart, Inc.
P.O. Box 29294
Richmond, VA 23233

MICHAEL RECYCLE HAS A MESSAGE FOR YOU

★★★

If your school or scout troop is having a recycling drive, or you just want to find out why people think recycling is so important, send for this free comic book from Reynolds Aluminum. *Reynolds Aluminum Presents Michael Recycle* is an eight-page color comic book about kids who learn that they don't have to throw away empty pop cans, pie plates, or aluminum foil—because, for one thing, they can be recycled into something else that's useful, and, for another, sometimes you can actually get cash for trash. Michael Recycle will tell you all about it in this short story.

Write for:
Reynolds Aluminum Presents Michael Recycle

Cost: Free

Send to:
Reynolds Aluminum
Reynolds Metals Co.
Richmond, VA 23261

Reynolds Aluminum Presents Michael Recycle

WHY IS OUR AIR SO BAD?

★★★★

Air pollution stinks. It makes you sick; it makes you cough; it's bad for animals, birds, trees, plants, even fabrics, metal, and rubber. *Don't You Dare Breathe That Air!* is a 16-page, illustrate-it-yourself book about air pollution that will tell you what air pollution is, why our air is so bad, and what you can do to help clean it up. There's space after each section for you to draw *your* pictures of what air pollution means. By the time you've finished, you'll have a better understanding of why clean air matters and how you can help, and you'll have a neat book of pictures you drew yourself.

Write for:
Don't You Dare Breathe That Air!

Cost: Free

Send to:
American Lung Association
P.O. Box 596
New York, NY 10001

Don't you Dare Breathe That Air!

A SASE is a self-addressed stamped envelope.

GOING THE WAY OF THE DINOSAUR?

★★★

Climatic changes or natural selection did away with many species of the past. Today, species are vanishing because they've been hunted out of existence, or because their home or habitat has been bulldozed to make way for roads, housing projects, and shopping centers. You can do your part to save the animals—and proclaim your views on the subject—by sending for the Humane Society's bumper sticker, *Animals...It's Their World Too!* Send a check or money order, not stamps or coins.

Write for:
Animals...It's Their World Too! bumper sticker

Cost: 50¢ (check or money order)

Send to:
The Humane Society of the United States
2100 L St., N.W.
Washington DC 20037

BUILD A BOX, HELP A BLUEBIRD

★★★

Here's a beautiful idea for bird lovers—build a bluebird box. Better yet, build a bluebird trail. A bluebird trail is five or more nesting boxes spaced 100 to 200 yards apart on a farm, park, or golf course, and this brochure from the Ohio Department of Natural Resources gives illustrated directions on how to build and mount the boxes. Be aware that other beneficial birds like the house wren and the Carolina and blackcapped chickadees may take up residence in your box, but no matter. The idea is to slow down the disappearance of one of the nation's most treasured birds. Bluebird boxes and trails should be ready for new tenants by March 15 at the latest. So, plan ahead and get ready for next spring; this could make a fun wintertime project for the family.

Write for:
Hit the Trail for Bluebirds

Cost: Free

Send to:
Ohio Department of Natural Resources
Division of Wildlife
Publications Department
Fountain Square
Columbus, OH 43224

DIDDLEDEE DOG

★★★

Diddledee Dog, the Dirt Digger is a story about a friendly mutt owned by Tommie Wedgewood, who is seven. Everybody loves Diddledee except Tommie's neighbor, Mr. Blurkle. What's the problem? Diddledee has been digging up Mr. Blurkle's lawn. Find out how Diddledee learned to dig somewhere else and how Tommie found out what conservation means from this lively little story. It's written for kids Tommie's age or younger, and will probably not interest older children. Cute cartoon drawings show you what Diddledee, Tommie, and Mr. Blurkle look like.

Write for:
Diddledee Dog, the Dirt Digger

Cost: 85¢

Send to:
The Interstate Printers & Publishers, Inc.
19 N. Jackson
P.O. Box 50
Danville, IL 61834-0050

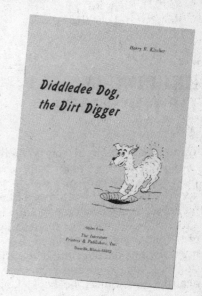

Diddledee Dog, the Dirt Digger

Food and Nutrition

THE CASE OF THE WOBBLING HENS

★★★★

Why did the hens wobble? Because they lacked thiamin—which you probably know as vitamin B_1.

continued

KIDS

This is one of a fascinating series of mysteries that have been solved by food scientists who tracked down vitamins that had been missing in certain people's diets. For instance, sailors who contracted scurvy needed vitamin C; nightblind fishermen were suffering from vitamin A deficiency, and this discovery helped doctors cure the disease beriberi. This well-written, beautifully illustrated 40-page booklet examines all the vitamins and a supporting cast of proteins, carbohydrates, fats, and minerals. It also suggests some good experiments you can do to be a food detective: taking foods "apart," doing chemical tests, and studying your diet. Great reading for kids ten and up. And it's educational too. Maybe it'll remind you not to fuss the next time your mom tells you to eat your vegetables.

Write for:
The Great Vitamin Mystery

Cost: 75¢

Send to:
Order Department
National Dairy Council
6300 N. River Rd.
Rosemont, IL 60018

KEEPING IN TIP TOP SHAPE
★★

Want to do better in sports? Want to have more energy for work or play? Eating right and getting proper exercise can work wonders for your school, sports, and social life. Here is a free 24-page booklet telling what physical fitness is and how you can plan a diet and exercise program to suit your needs. A set of simple exercises is offered to strengthen various muscles and parts of the body. Nutrition information is given, including recommended foods for a healthy diet. Since the booklet is offered by the Sunkist citrus growers, it contains a special section on oranges, lemons, grapefruit, and tangerines, and how to use them in desserts and fruit drinks.

Write for:
Stay in Shape With the Champions

Cost: Free

Send to:
Consumer Services
Sunkist Growers, Inc.
Box 7888
Van Nuys, CA 91409

YOU DON'T *HAVE* TO EAT JUNK
★★★★

No one says *you* have to eat junk just because other kids do. What you eat is your choice. This booklet for teenagers and young people reinforces good eating habits (or introduces some new ones) with facts about food. You'll find all foods divided into four groups: milk, meat, fruits and vegetables, and grains. You'll find out how many servings of each group are recommended each day, and what they'll do for your body. There is sound information on dieting, snacking, meal skipping, fad foods, and regular exercise, and it's all designed to get you started on a lifetime of good eating habits.

Write for:
Your Food—Chance or Choice?

Cost: 45¢

Send to:
Order Department
National Dairy Council
6300 N. River Rd.
Rosemont, IL 60018

NOT FOR POOH BEAR ONLY
★★

If you or someone in your family loves honey as much as Winnie the Pooh, Christopher Robin's bear friend, you'll like this brochure telling of the value of honey and how to use honey. Learn how many bees it takes to make a pound of honey, and how far they must fly to gather enough nectar from flowers. Discover how worker bees and the queen bee create the right hive environment to produce honey. In fact, you'll learn all about the 50-million-year-old miracle that produces one of nature's most important treasures. Types of honey are described—liquid, creamed, comb, and chunk honey—and there are recipes for Honey Raisin Nibbles, Honey Spread, Honey Nut Bars, a frozen honey drink, and a breakfast honey drink. Pooh would love it, except, he'd point out that they've spelled honey wrong ... Pooh spells it "hunny."

Write for:
I Love Honey

Cost: Free

Send to:
California Honey Advisory Board
P.O. Box 265
Sonoma, CA 95476

A SASE is a self-addressed stamped envelope.

I Love Honey

BREAD—BEFORE YOU SLICE IT

★★★

This illustrated booklet tells the story of how bread is made, from growing the wheat to the time you sink your teeth into a fresh, delicious sandwich. Illustrations all along the way show wheat being harvested, wheat at the mill, and wheat packaged with enriched ingredients. The story continues with a visit to a bakery. You'll see dough being mixed in an enormous machine, loaves being formed, baked, and finally packaged for shipment to stores. You can also get a ten-piece jigsaw puzzle in the form of a loaf of bread that shows how bread helps keep you healthy.

Write for:
Bread in the Making
Bread Jigsaw Puzzle

Cost: 50¢ each

Send to:
American Institute of Baking
Communications Dept.
1213 Bakers Way
Manhattan, KS 66502

LUNCH BUNCH

★★★★

For kids who tote their lunch to school every day, this offer is a welcome relief from brown-bag monotony. It is for six brightly colored lunch bags. They're called "Illum-a-Lite" bags, and that gives you an idea of what colors the bags come in—very bright. You'll receive a random selection of colors. The bags are regulation-size lunch bags with lots of room for a sandwich and other treats. Some of the colors are fuschia, lemon yellow, bold green, and sky blue. The decorative bags put extra fun into lunchtime.

Write for:
Lunch Bags

Cost: $1.00

Send to:
Needlepoint Outlet
P.O. Box 11-B
Garnerville, NY 10923

Lunch Bags

CAUGHT ANY GOOD FISH LATELY?

★★

If you love to fish but wonder what to do with a perch, walleye, muskie, northern pike, catfish, or other good eating fish after you've caught it, this brochure is for you. The Wildlife Division of the Ohio Department of Natural Resources offers a free brochure giving tips on handling fish from the time you land it all the way through to the filleting and frying stage. Fishing is fun, but your angling trips can be more enjoyable when a fish you've caught yourself provides a delicious dinner. This helpful instruction booklet has all you'll need to know to get that next whopper you land onto the meal table.

Write for:
Filleting Your Fish

Cost: Free

Send to:
Ohio Department of Natural Resources
Division of Wildlife
1500 Dublin Road
Columbus, OH 43215

KIDS

MAKE PERFECT POPCORN BALLS

★★★

Kids, here's something you'll enjoy—a red plastic mold you can use to turn out dozens of uniform popcorn balls. You'll also receive recipes for two popcorn ball favorites—honey popcorn balls, which are soft ones made with honey, brown sugar, and butter; and caramel popcorn balls made with melted caramels that make them firmer. Your finished balls will be about three inches in diameter. The manufacturer says you won't get burned or sticky fingers if you use this mold.

Write for:
Popcorn Ball Maker

Cost: $1.00 for one
$1.75 for two

Send to:
Jolly Time
P.O. Box 178
Sioux City, IA 51102

Popcorn Ball Maker

HEY KIDS, HERE'S A LOT OF POPCORN!

★★

Feel like a snack? Here are 20 recipes for all kinds of popcorn goodies. You'll learn how to make popcorn balls; a party mix with popcorn, pretzels, cheese curls, and spices; a fruit munch with popcorn; caramel corn; different flavored popcorns; and a lot more—like how to decorate with popcorn. You'll get instructions on how to pop corn perfectly and learn a little about popcorn nutrition and good poppers to use.

Write for:
Smith Family Treasury of Favorite Popcorn Recipes

Cost: 25¢

Send to:
Jolly Time Popcorn Recipes
Box 178
Sioux City, IA 51102

EGGS FOR FUN AS WELL AS FOOD

★★★

This 16-page booklet is designed for children from kindergarten to about the sixth grade. The brochure—featuring Eggory, the Georgia Egg Commission's mascot—includes a variety of craft ideas using eggs, egg shells, and egg cartons. There are also crossword puzzles, games, and coloring sheets. In addition, there are several kid-tested recipes and some good nutritional information.

It's an "eggcellent" way for kids to beat the blahs on a rainy or boring day. If you take care of younger brothers or sisters or if you baby-sit a lot, you could get a good deal of mileage out of these neat ideas. This little book would make a nice stocking stuffer, too. You will get your copy, plus other recipes for kids, for just $2.00. It doesn't look like a lot for $2.00, but it's full of good things.

Write for:
Eggory's Egg Craft Ideas

Cost: $2.00

Send to:
Eggory
Georgia Egg Commission
State Farmer's Market
Forest Park, GA 30050-2082

Eggory's Egg Craft Ideas

A SASE is a self-addressed stamped envelope.

NUTRITION COURSE
★★

We eat about a thousand meals a year, spend a thousand hours eating, spend a thousand dollars on food. Too bad we don't spend more time considering *what* we eat. That's the topic of a new brochure designed to help people learn more about the dangers of too much fat, sugar, and salt in the foods we eat. It also contains a healthy plug for eating more refined grains such as whole wheat bread, whole wheat spaghetti, whole grain cereals, wheat germ, brown rice, and bulgur.

Write for:
A Five-Minute Course in New-trition

Cost: 25¢

Send to:
Center for Science in the Public Interest
1501 Sixteenth St., N.W.
Washington, DC 20036

KIDS CAN COOK, TOO!
★★★★

Cooking can be a lot of fun, and a good way a boy or girl can discover the fun of cooking is through this free 21-page recipe, puzzle, and game book. With this nice book from Ragu—the spaghetti-sauce people—kids can work together or with their parents to learn the principles of cooking. Through the games and puzzles, kids learn safety tips about hot ovens and sharp knives; how to use kitchen gadgets such as graters, shredders, vegetable peelers, and can openers; and how to pan-fry and cook in the oven. Soon young cooks will know how to dice, mince, puree, preheat, simmer, sauté, roast, and bake. You'll find easy-to-follow recipes for making pasta dishes, salads, and desserts, followed by tips on how to set a pretty table and, finally, how to clean up after using the kitchen—someone has to do it. Here's a nice short course in cooking for kids that can be fun for the whole family.

Write for:
Kids Are Cooks Too

Cost: Free

Send to:
Ragu Family Tradition
415 Madison Ave.
New York, NY 10017

PEANUT COLORED
★★★

Which do you like? Crunchy peanut butter or smooth peanut butter? Or both? A four-page coloring booklet published by the Growers Peanut Food Promotions is a fun way to learn more about one of a child's favorite foods—peanuts. *Peanuts, The Fun Food* is geared for kids in kindergarten and first grade. The words are simple and the booklet includes directions for making your own peanut butter from salted or unsalted roasted peanuts and oil. Try it, then spread the result on crackers, bread, celery, or apple slices. The lesson is both nutritious and enjoyable.

Write for:
Peanuts, The Fun Food

Cost: A first-class stamp

Send to:
Betsy Owens, Director
Growers Peanut Food Promotions
P.O. Box 1709
Rocky Mount, NC 27802-1709

WHO DUN-NUT?
★★★★

Sherlock, the peanut detective, has a new assignment—he has to find out all about the peanut. As the animated character researches this question through six pages, your child colors, reads, and learns about this nutritious food. *The Case of the Mysterious Peanut* is designed for grade levels three through five and is published by the Growers Peanut Food Promotions. Sherlock and your child discover how the peanut plant grows and just how healthful this delicious food is. The detective also shares his recipe for homemade old-fashioned peanut butter, made from shelled roasted peanuts and oil. At the end, Sherlock closes his case; he has found out all he had to know.

Write for:
The Case of the Mysterious Peanut

Cost: A first-class stamp

Send to:
Betsy Owens, Director
Growers Peanut Food Promotions
P.O. Box 1709
Rocky Mount, NC 27802-1709

FREE THINGS
for
TEENS

Sex, Drugs, Drink, and Other Tricky Topics

IT'S ABOUT THAT TIME

★★★

Especially geared to preteens and young teens, this pocket-sized, 20-page pamphlet gives the facts of menstruation in an easy-to-read question and answer format. Reassuring young girls that menstruation is normal and a sign of impending womanhood, *Having Your Period* handles many uncertainties. It explains what body changes take place during puberty, how the reproductive system works, menstruation cycles and normalcy, and basic hygiene. Basic care tips are given and old wives' tales dispelled. At the back is a vocabulary and pronunciation of important terms.

Write for:
Having Your Period

Cost: 50¢

Send to:
Planned Parenthood Federation of America, Inc.
810 Seventh Avenue
New York, NY 10019

Having Your Period

GROWING UP PHYSICALLY AND EMOTIONALLY

★★★

This friendly booklet for preteens (and late-blooming teenagers) describes the physical and emotional changes that take place in boys and girls growing up. Easy-to-understand line drawings illustrate the male and female reproductive systems. There's a section on what it means to be a parent, and a

thoughtful discussion about the responsibilities of sex. There's also a suggested reading list, and some thought-provoking questions for teenagers to ask themselves about the emotional aspects of growing up.

Write for:
That Growing Feeling

Cost: 50¢

Send to:
Planned Parenthood Federation of America, Inc./LM
810 Seventh Ave.
New York, NY 10019

SPIDERMAN FIGHTS TEEN PREGNANCIES

★★

This small-sized comic book certainly contains a message against teenage pregnancy, but it's completely obscured by the antics of the cartoon characters in the convoluted plot. The best part is a one-page fact sheet on pregnancy, venereal disease, homosexuality, and teen emotions. There are also suggestions on where teenagers can find counselors to help them come to terms with their developing sexuality. Spiderman and sex education, however, are not really suited to each other in this little tale.

Write for:
The Amazing Spiderman vs. the Prodigy!

Cost: 50¢

Send to:
Planned Parenthood Federation of America, Inc./LM
810 Seventh Ave.
New York, NY 10019

The Amazing Spiderman vs. the Prodigy

TEENS

THE IN-BETWEEN YEARS
★★★★

Adolescence—it's a major crossroad in every person's life. Your body, your mind, and your social life all start making changes at the same time—and there you are, trying to juggle the pieces, while the grown-ups tell you, "It's only a stage; you'll grow out of it." If you read *Coming of Age: Problems of Teenagers*, you'll find your feelings and problems are similar to those that other teens experience. You'll also pick up some useful tips on how to handle big issues like understanding your parents, becoming more independent, dealing with your sexual feelings, and what to do about feelings of inferiority.

Write for:
   Coming of Age: Problems of Teenagers (#234)

Cost: $1.00

Send to:
   Public Affairs Pamphlets
   381 Park Ave. South
   New York, NY 10016

A LITTLE HELP FROM A FRIEND
★★★

There's an old saying that people who talk about suicide won't really do it. Don't believe it. In this little pamphlet, prepared for young people and students, the Suicide Prevention and Crisis Center warns you *not* to ignore suicidal talk. This five-page pamphlet explains a number of ways you can help a suicidal friend. For instance, if someone confides to you or shows any of the warning signs listed, it's best to talk about it, letting that person know you don't condemn him or her for having such feelings. According to this booklet, you don't need to worry that the discussion will encourage your friend to go through with the plan. Rather, it could save a life by proving that there's someone out there willing to be a friend. Good, candid reading at a time when teenage suicide is too often in the news.

Write for:
   Suicide in Youth and What You Can Do About
      It—A Guide for Students

Cost: 50¢

Send to:
   North Wales Press, Inc.
   P.O. Box 1486
   North Wales, PA 19454

A LOOK AT THE CHILDREN'S CHILDREN
★★★★

Statistics show that the problem of teenage pregnancy grows more serious every year. Why does it happen? This booklet attempts to answer that vexing question and to present some new ways that unmarried young women and society can cope with teenage pregnancy. It presents the options now open for a teenage unwed mother, and explores, fittingly, the legal rights and situation of the unwed father—who is equally responsible but usually ignored when decisions are made. There are many sensible suggestions for improved sex education in schools. A thoughtful look at an issue no young person should ignore.

Write for:
   Unmarried Teenagers and Their Children (#537)

Cost: $1.00

Send to:
   Public Affairs Pamphlets
   381 Park Ave. South
   New York, NY 10016

DRUGS: WHY AND WHY NOT
★★★

Drugs and Alcohol: A Handbook for Young People tells you all about the drugs most commonly used today and their short- and long-term effects on the people who use and abuse them. The drugs this booklet covers aren't as simple as aspirin—but some of them are so common that, unfortunately, people forget that they *are* drugs—for instance, caffeine, alcohol, glue, and aerosols. "Hard drugs" like PCP or cocaine are not the only drugs to be concerned about, and all the different kinds are covered here. This little book explains just what these drugs are, what they do to you, and why people use them. The last section, "Who, Why, and Why Not," is excellent—don't miss it. Food for thought for any youngster who is tempted, but not yet hooked, by the drug culture. It might help you or a friend stay away.

Write for:
   Drugs and Alcohol: A Handbook for Young People

Cost: $2.00

Send to:
   Free Things
   Do It Now Foundation
   P.O. Box 21126
   Phoenix, AZ 85026

A SASE is a self-addressed stamped envelope.

Drugs and Alcohol: A Handbook for Young People

IF A PARENT DRINKS

★★★

Alcoholism hurts family members as much as it hurts the alcoholic, and if somebody in your family drinks too much you may be too embarrassed, or too scared, to talk to anyone about it. You can get help, though, through Al-Anon and Alateen Family Groups. *If Your Parents Drink Too Much* is a free booklet for teenagers. The story line shows, in comic-book format, the difficulties faced by three teens whose parents are alcoholics. Although the comic-strip style tends to oversimplify matters, this little booklet does get the message across to teenagers that they are not alone and that help *is* available. Also free are two pocket-size cards, *Alateen Do's and Don'ts* and *Alateen's Just for Today.*

Write for:
    If Your Parents Drink Too Much...
    Alateen Do's and Don'ts
    Alateen's Just for Today

Cost: Free with a long SASE

Send to:
    Al-Anon Family Group Headquarters
    P.O. Box 182
    Madison Square Station
    New York, NY 10159

KICKING THE HABIT

★★★

You probably know as well as the next smoker that smoking is a habit that should be broken. But quitting isn't that easy. This booklet, however, is written especially for teenagers, and puts forward some strong arguments for quitting *now.* You'll learn some of the reasons that teens take up the tobacco habit—with the smoking behavior of other family members high on the list. Girls will find startling facts about women who smoke heightening their susceptibility to heart disease, plus important information on how smoking can adversely affect a pregnant woman's baby. An important section of the booklet offers sensible suggestions on how to quit.

Write for:
    Smoking—A Habit That Should Be Broken
      (#573A)

Cost: $1.00

Send to:
    Public Affairs Pamphlets
    381 Park Ave. South
    New York, NY 10016

TOO YOUNG TO BE AN ALCOHOLIC?

★★★

If you think you're too young to be an alcoholic, ask yourself these questions: Do you drink because you have problems or need to face up to stress? Do you drink when you get mad at other people? Have you begun to drink in the morning, before school? Do you gulp drinks fast, as if to satisfy a great thirst? If the answer is "yes" to any of those questions, this booklet is for you because you may in fact have a drinking problem. It was written to help young alcoholics face up to their problem and get help. It tells about Alcoholics Anonymous, how this organization has helped thousands of people with a similar drinking problem, and how it can help you if *you* want help. *Too Young?* looks like a comic book, but the stories it tells are genuine and scary. The message, however, is a hopeful one: No teenager, whatever the social pressure, needs to become an alcohol abuser just because it's "cool."

Write for:
    Too Young?

continued

TEENS

Cost: 15¢

Send to:
Alcoholics Anonymous World Services, Inc.
P.O. Box 459
Grand Central Station
New York, NY 10163

FOR TEENS WHO DRIINK
★★★

Teenage drinking is a widespread problem—but not in your set, right? Take a look at this questionnaire, all the same. These are some of the questions: Have you lost friends since you've started drinking? Do you hang out with a crowd where stuff is easy to get? Do you drink until the bottle is empty? Do you have to take a drink to go out on a date?

These and other questions are part of a "Score-It-Yourself Quiz" in this 38-page booklet from Alcoholics Anonymous. There's lots of information about young alcoholics, and all the usual excuses for drinking are discussed one by one. There are also ten true stories about young alcoholics who have joined A.A.

Write for:
Young People and A.A.

Cost: 20¢

Send to:
Alcoholics Anonymous World Services, Inc.
P.O. Box 459
Grand Central Station
New York, NY 10163

BUT EVERYBODY DOES IT
★★★★

Today's teenagers are often placed in positions where alcohol is readily available. They must make decisions for themselves whether to partake or abstain and, according to several years' worth of statistics, are choosing to drink. The greatest problems, however, lie not in the use of alcohol but in its misuse. *Teenagers and Alcohol: Patterns and Dangers* takes a comprehensive look at this situation. The 32-page booklet explores factors that can prompt teen drinking, including peer pressure and alcoholic parentage; discusses the dangers of teen drinking and driving; and suggests what a concerned parent can do. Treatment and punishment for the adolescent alcohol abuser are discussed, as is prevention of the problem in the future. A frightening statistic cited in this publication is that each year nearly 10,000 young Americans between the ages of 16 and 24 are killed in accidents involving young people and alcohol.

Write for:
Teenagers and Alcohol: Patterns and Dangers—
Public Affairs Pamphlet No. 612

Cost: $1.00

Send to:
Public Affairs Pamphlets
381 Park Avenue South
New York, NY 10016

Teenagers and Alcohol: Patterns and Dangers

Money Matters

COMING OF AGE FINANCIALLY
★★★

Here's a brief but worthwhile dollar's worth of financial advice for the person on the brink of that important 18th birthday. When you get to be 18, this two-page leaflet points out, you become an adult and lose certain protections you had as a minor—but you also gain new rights, and with them new responsibilities. Among the topics touched on are school requirements, employment (most restrictions on what work you can do are lifted when you reach 18), your Social Security number and income tax status, driver's licenses and permits and auto insurance, and medical treatment and insurance. You'll even find out what you can buy and sell as an adult—as a minor you may only buy and sell personal property in your immediate possession.

A SASE is a self-addressed stamped envelope.

Write for:
Rights & Responsibilities: Age 18

Cost: $1.00

Send to:
Bank of America, Dept. 3120
Box 37128
San Francisco, CA 94137

COMIC BOOK SAYS MONEY ISN'T FUNNY

★★★★

This is the story of money—presented in comic book form. It's an effective way of explaining money, because visual representations are used to demonstrate complex facts. Each bit of text is reinforced with understandable cartoons. You'll learn about the history of money, the "circular" flow of money, and how money is created (and controlled) by the Federal Reserve. You'll also learn about such economic philosophies as mercantilism and monetarism. This should be considered must reading for high school students—and anyone else who uses money without understanding how it "works."

Write for:
The Story of Money

Cost: Free

Send to:
Federal Reserve Bank of New York
Public Information Department
33 Liberty St.
New York, NY 10045

UNDERSTANDING ELECTRONIC BANKING

★★★★

The fascinating history of check-writing and check-paying is presented here in the unlikely format of a comic book, but it works nonetheless. The visual explanations serve to clarify an otherwise complex subject, and the cartoons make it exciting—and funny. You'll learn who wrote the first checks in history (probably the Romans), how checks were used throughout the history of the world and the United States, and how checks work today. Finally, you'll come to understand the Federal Reserve System, and you'll learn about the Reserve's electronic communications network, which settles many banks' accounts. You'll see the flow of checks through the Federal Reserve Bank of New York on a typical day. Unbelievable!

Write for:
The Story of Checks and Electronic Payments

Cost: Free

Send to:
Federal Reserve Bank of New York
Public Information Department
33 Liberty St.
New York, NY 10045

GETTING THE FACTS ON MONEY

★★★

How much do you really know about money? What size is a dollar bill? Where does the serial number appear on paper currency? Whose picture is on the $10,000 bill? This fascinating booklet about money from the Federal Reserve Bank of Atlanta answers these questions—and more. You'll also learn about Federal Reserve notes, what the Great Seal of the United States means, how money gets into circulation, what happens to money when it wears out, and ways to spot counterfeit coin and currency. You'll also learn how coins are designed and minted, and how much money there was in circulation on June 30, 1980 ($127,097,192,148.00!).

Write for:
Fundamental Facts About United States Money

Cost: Free

Send to:
Federal Reserve Bank of Atlanta
Atlanta, GA 30303

WHY THINGS COST MORE

★★★

Two politicians are talking. One says, "Do you know how much it costs to fuel an aircraft carrier today?" The other answers, "Almost as much as it used to cost to build one!" That, briefly, is called inflation. Things generally cost more today than they did a year or several years ago. Why? Learn all about inflation in a free 24-page color comic book from the Federal Reserve Bank of New York. Why do people collect rare coins, jewelry, gold, famous paintings, or antique cars? Because of inflation, items of lasting value such as these become more valuable in relation to money. And inflation makes it harder for your parents to make their work dollars pay for everything the family needs. After reading this, you'll

continued

---

understand better why your mom or dad complains so much about how much things cost.

Write for:
The Story of Inflation

Cost: Free

Send to:
Federal Reserve Bank of New York
Public Information Department
33 Liberty St.
New York, NY 10045

The Story of Inflation

FINANCIAL SUPERMARKETS

★★★★

If you've saved a jar full of pennies, you can take it to your neighborhood bank. A teller will weigh the coins in a little machine and give you dollars or quarters and dimes and nickels for your pennies. You can go to a bank to open a savings and checking account. And if your parents need a loan for a new car or home, they may borrow the money from a bank. Many banks now have machines outside where you can do your money business any hour of any day or night without bothering to step inside or wait in line to see a teller. Learn all about today's banks and their many different functions in this free 24-page color comic book. It's a fun way to learn all about banking.

Write for:
The Story of Banks

Cost: Free

Send to:
Federal Reserve Bank of New York
Public Information Department
33 Liberty St.
New York, NY 10045

THAT'S FOREIGN?

★★★

The camera you use to take your holiday photos may have been made in Japan, and the same may be true of the video recorder you watch movies on at home. Perhaps your mother uses French perfume or owns stock in a German company. If you take a vacation in a foreign country, you may wonder why American money buys more there than it does here. It's all part of a world of finance called foreign trade and exchange. You can learn all about it in a free 24-page comic book that tells about world trade through the centuries and how the foreign exchange market works. It's a fun way to get in on the exciting world of high finance and international trade.

Write for:
The Story of Foreign Trade and Exchange

Cost: Free

Send to:
Federal Reserve Bank of New York
Public Information Department
33 Liberty St.
New York, NY 10045

The Story of Foreign Trade and Exchange

A PLASTIC WORLD

★★★

You know what it means when someone says, "Charge it." And when you start to work full-time or go to college you'll discover that money is almost old-fashioned—people pay their bills with plastic credit cards. Of course, credit cards *are* a form of money, and when the bill for purchases comes in each month, it has to be paid with money—cash or a check. Living with credit cards isn't as simple as it sounds, because it's sometimes easy to forget you have to pay later for what you buy now. And that can get you into all sorts of trouble. Learn about credit and credit cards the easy way by sending for this free 24-page

A SASE is a self-addressed stamped envelope.

full-color comic book that relates a family's adventure using credit cards. The comic book is available free in either English or Spanish.

Write for:
The Story of Consumer Credit
La Historia Del Credito Al Consumidor

Cost: Free

Send to:
Federal Reserve Bank of New York
Public Information Department
33 Liberty St.
New York, NY 10045

DOLLARS DEFINED
★★★

Robinson Crusoe didn't need money on his island. He provided his own food, clothing, and shelter. Even a small colony on his island might have gotten along without money, but in our complex economy people have to deal with one another to get the goods and services they want and need. Money is the medium of exchange. *Money: Master or Servant?* is an interesting, illustrated lesson in basic economics. The 25-page booklet explains supply and demand, how financial institutions operate, and the role the Federal Reserve Bank plays in the overall economy. There are lots of charts and graphs to illustrate the editorial content, but the booklet might be hard for younger teens to understand.

Write for:
Money: Master or Servant?

Cost: Free

Send to:
Public Information Department
Federal Reserve Bank of New York
New York, NY 10045

Money: Master or Servant?

THE STORY OF MONEY
★★★★

The earliest evidence of metal coins has been attributed to about 2500 B.C. when the Egyptians used rings as a medium of exchange. Before that, men had to barter for goods and services, or produce everything that they needed themselves. *Coins and Currency* is a terrific booklet that traces the history of money to the system we know today. You'll learn about the earliest forms of banking and how paper money came into being. In fact, at one time in this country, postage stamps were a widely used form of small change. You'll learn about the establishment of the Federal Reserve Bank and how new coins and currency get into circulation. There are also many great photos of ancient and modern coins, notes, and other forms of currency.

Write for:
Coins and Currency

Cost: Free

Send to:
Public Information Department
Federal Reserve Bank of New York
New York, NY 10045

Coins and Currency

THE MIDAS TOUCH
★★★

Gold has enthralled man since the beginning of history. And speaking of history, gold as a symbol of wealth for both men and nations has played a dramatic role. *Key to the Gold Vault* is an interesting, illustrated booklet by the Federal Reserve Bank of New York; it explains the gold system and how the precious metal has become an international common denominator of exchange. You'll learn where the world's largest known treasure of gold is and how it is stored and secured. You'll learn about

continued

TEENS

the mining of gold and the molding of gold bars. There is also information about customs, traditions, and prohibitions around the world. Good reading for older teens and adults as well.

Write for:
Key to the Gold Vault

Cost: Free

Send to:
Public Information Department
Federal Reserve Bank of New York
New York, NY 10045

THE SUPER BANK
★★★★

From 7 A.M. to 5:30 P.M., this great booklet follows the day of the Federal Reserve Bank of New York, or "Fed" for short. This bank doesn't deal in the day-to-day activities most people rely upon their banks for; the Fed is a bank for banks. It is part of the decentralized system of 12 regional banks supervised by the Washington-based Board of Governors. *A Day at the Fed* is a beautifully illustrated, 32-page booklet that explains our country's economic system using this bank's functions and activities as examples. It discusses credit, currency, the role of the computer, international exchanges, and much more. This is very informative reading for older teens.

Write for:
A Day at the Fed

Cost: Free

Send to:
Public Information Department
Federal Reserve Bank of New York
New York, NY 10045

School and After: Education and Jobs

FALLING ASLEEP OVER YOUR BOOKS?
★★★★

You've got a book in front of you, and you're supposed to be studying. But you find yourself staring out the window, wondering what to have for dinner, leaving your desk for a pencil, a ruler, a glass of water. You just can't seem to study. There is nothing

unique about that, but you could surely use this 48-page booklet called *200 Tips to Students on How to Study*. If you can concentrate on reading it, you'll find that there are good ways and bad ways to study, that you can develop techniques for improving your memory, taking notes, reading a chapter, making an outline, and taking shortcuts to faster study. You'll learn how to handle distractions and set up a regular study schedule, and you'll get comprehensive tips for studying specific subjects—math, English, languages, the arts, and the sciences.

Write for:
200 Tips to Students on How to Study

Cost: $1.75

Send to:
The Interstate Printers & Publishers, Inc.
19 N. Jackson
P.O. Box 50
Danville, IL 61834-0050

200 Tips to Students on How to Study

IDEAS WORTH REPEATING
★★★

What a good idea for a book. Here are 60 short, inspirational messages that focus on individual responsibility and action. The author, George F. Cahill, encourages youth leaders to use them in preparing a speech or talking to a young people's group. Several are written for specific occasions—one is to help restore harmony in a group that's been split by disagreements. Good, thought-provoking quotations from many of the world's great thinkers can provide material to get you started on your own speeches. You'll also find 11 messages prepared especially for this book by well-known youth leaders of America.

Write for:
Big Ideas

Cost: $2.00 and a long SASE

A SASE is a self-addressed stamped envelope.

Send to:
The "Pride In America" Co.
176 Warwick Dr.
Pittsburgh, PA 15241

TEENS AROUND THE WORLD

★★★★

President Reagan has said, "One of the best ways to develop more accurate perspectives on other nations and on ourselves is for more Americans to join, for a time, a family and a community in another land." As part of that spirit, the President's Council for International Youth Exchange was started in 1983. Teenagers around the world learn how to meet via the mails to build mutual understanding, increase their knowledge of the peoples of the world, and to promote peace—one friendship at a time. Teens wanting to know all about the International Youth Exchange and find pen pals around the world can send for this free 64-page booklet.

Write for:
Your Guide to International Youth Exchange
   (No. 501P)

Cost: Free

Send to:
Consumer Information Center
P.O. Box 100
Pueblo, CO 81002

Your Guide to International Youth Exchange

WORKING AND PLAYING IN FARAWAY PLACES

★★★

If you're a high-school junior or senior or college-age student thinking about working, studying, and/or traveling abroad, this catalog will tell you everything you need to know—or where to get further information—on all facets and phases of your project. You'll find basic travel information about pass-

ports, visas, international I.D. cards, student discounts, and insurance. Then there's specific and detailed travel information for Europe, Israel, the U.S.S.R., Egypt, Yukon, Alaska, and South America. The same kind of thorough coverage is devoted to working and studying abroad. This useful catalog is updated every year.

Write for:
Student Work, Study, Travel Catalog

Cost: Free

Send to:
Council on International Educational Exchange
205 E. 42nd St.
New York, NY 10017

HEAD START ON A CHEMISTRY PROJECT

★★★

Here's everything you'll need to know to get a chemistry project off the ground. This booklet tells how to select your idea and research the subject, and it explains the essential but difficult task of how to limit your topic. A hint: Express the project's purpose as a question or series of questions. Then you'll learn how to conduct an experimental project, how to organize a written one, how to give an oral report on the project, and how to prepare an exhibit. A resource list helps locate supplies and equipment, and a reference list guides you to further information.

Write for:
A Chemistry Project From Start to Finish

Cost: Free

Send to:
Career Services Education Division
American Chemical Society
1155 Sixteenth St., N.W.
Washington, DC 20036

A Chemistry Project From Start to Finish

TEENS

BUT WHAT DO YOU *DO* WITH IT?

★★

Here's a little offering from the American Chemical Society. They call it a chemistry awareness piece. It's actually a three-dimensional polygon that carries the message "Chemistry Adds Dimension to Your Life." Pictures and captions on the 14 sides remind you of some of the ways chemical advances contribute to your life: Chemistry makes it possible for you to get your jeans just the way you like them— pre-faded or dark blue, wrinkle-free or wrinkled. And when you watch a movie "you are seeing the magic of chemistry turn a clear sheet of plastic into an adventure". Set this neat little freebie on your desk or dresser and when your friends ask, "What *is* it?" just tell them, "Well, it's a 14-sided three-dimensional polygon, of course." Fortunately, it folds flat for mailing.

Write for:
Chemistry Adds Dimension to Your Life polygon

Cost: Free

Send to:
American Chemical Society
1155 Sixteenth St., N.W.
Washington, DC 20036

Chemistry Adds Dimension to Your Life polygon

IF YOU'RE A SUCKER FOR A LOLLIPOP

★★★

Here's a neat (and sweet) idea for your next school, church, or youthgroup fund-raiser—lollipops with your logo on them. These two catalog sheets show the sort of special logos or imprints you can order, and you get four sample lollipops so you can check them for size, taste, and color. Each lollipop is 2¼ inches across, ⅜ inch thick, and mounted on a 6-inch stick. With a low minimum order, you can have them imprinted with seasonal messages, your name or logo, or special artwork. There are message pops ("We're No. 1," "Go Cougars") and sport pops with sports emblems imprinted. These samples will be sent direct to you. Other ideas galore, too.

Write for:
Fundraising package

Cost: $2.00

Send to:
Rosemary Candy Co.
P.O. Box 189
Springville, NY 14141

Fund-raising Lollipops

BEFORE YOU BABY-SIT

★★★★

Before you let people know you're available as a baby-sitter, take a look at this booklet. It's a good way to learn about the responsibilities a good sitter must undertake. You'll find out, for instance, how to think ahead to ensure the safety of your charges. You'll also learn what first-aid measures to take if there is an accident. How to handle bedtime, diapering, feeding babies and little children—they're all covered here. You'll also find out the kind of play that is appropriate for babies up to two years and kids up to five years old. A friendly, practical booklet.

Write for:
Guide for the First-Time Baby-Sitter (#B-478-English; #B-479-Spanish)

Cost: Free with a long SASE

Send to:
Johnson and Johnson
Dept. FS
Grandview Road
Skillman, NJ 08558

A SASE is a self-addressed stamped envelope.

Guide for the First-Time Baby Sitter

BABY-SITTING: IT'S NOT CHILD'S PLAY

★★★★

Anyone who wants to baby-sit ought to read this complete handbook. It details the qualifications and responsibilities of a sitter and the obligations of parents. One section deals with possible danger zones in the home and gives safety precautions. Another discusses children's behavior, activities for children of various ages, ways to get cooperation from the youngster, and special situations like feeding, bedtime, and arguments. Finally, there is good information on the general characteristics of children in different age groups, hints that will make sitting easier, and a reading list for further information. An excellent publication and must reading for a teenager who wants to baby-sit.

Write for:
So You're Going To Be a Babysitter (71-3)

Cost: 75¢

Send to:
Agricultural Publications
Box U-35
1376 Storrs Rd.
The University of Connecticut
Storrs, CT 06268

KEEPING THE KIDS BUSY

★★

Baby-sitters or big brothers and sisters won't run out of ideas for things for the kids to do if they check the daily calendar sheets offered here. There are suggestions for adventures and activities every day of the month—for instance, visit a park and count

and identify all the trees, or make a leaf collection, or have a home reading night in which you spend time reading with the family. You can send for two different calendars. Send for a one-month sample full of activity ideas for grade-school children, or for the full 12-month calendar.

Write for:
Sample Calendar
1-Year Calendar

Cost: 50¢ and a long SASE for the sample
$2.00 for the full calendar

Send to:
Family Educational Assistance
303 S. 34th St.
Tacoma, WA 98408

HOW TO APPLY FOR FINANCIAL AID

★★★★

If your education will cost more than you and your family can pay, you need financial help. Here is an excellent and necessary piece of literature for anyone who requires financial aid for post-secondary education. This tabloid explains how financial aid works and what you must do to apply. A sample calculation of need is worked out to show you how such applications are figured, though real ones are much more detailed. There's a list of the sources of financial aid available, and information on how to figure your specific needs. The figures in this publication are updated every year.

Write for:
Applying for Financial Aid

Cost: Free

Send to:
American College Testing Program
Student Assistance Services
Educational Services Division
2201 N. Dodge St.
P.O. Box 168
Iowa City, IA 52243

FINDING THE MONEY FOR SCHOOL

★★

With student loans getting tougher to come by these days, kids need all the help they can get. And some

continued

TEENS

help is provided by United Student Aid Funds, a not-for-profit corporation that exists solely to help students obtain loans for school. It is not a lender but an information service, and you can write for its free literature and a toll-free number at which two full-time loan information specialists are on duty to advise students. *USA Funds & Guaranteed Student Loans* is a four-page leaflet describing the corporation, its purpose, its program sponsors, and its various information services. There's also general information on applying for and obtaining loans, and you'll learn about state and corporate programs and how finance charges work.

Write for:
USA Funds & Guaranteed Student Loans

Cost: Free

Send to:
Loan Information Specialist
United Student Aid Funds
P.O. Box 50827
Indianapolis, IN 46250

A LOOK AT TECHNICAL CAREERS
★★★

Teenagers about to enter the job market can learn about new jobs, techniques, and machinery that can bring them up-to-date in the modern working world. This free 74-page book from the National Association of Trade and Technical Schools tells all about more than 100 careers that you can train for in two years or less. Jobs range from computer service technician to electronics specialist to X-ray technician. The book also offers a checklist for the career-seeker, questions on how to choose a trade or technical school, and career questions and answers. Postcards are included for sending to individual schools for information about courses and training programs. Don't job-hunt without this practical reference.

Write for:
Handbook of Trade and Technical Careers and Training

Cost: Free

Send to:
National Association of Trade and Technical Schools
2251 Wisconsin Ave., N.W.
Washington, DC 20007

Handbook of Trade and Technical Careers and Training

CASH FOR COLLEGE
★★★★

If you're planning to attend college but wondering how you can pay for tuition, room and board, you're among 12 million other young Americans hoping to continue their education beyond high school and wondering how they can afford it. The federal government spends almost $12 billion each year on financial assistance to help qualified young people attend college who otherwise might not be able to. To get more imformation on student grants and aids for college, send for the free 46-page booklet offered by the U.S. Department of Education. It could mean the difference between going to college or not.

Write for:
The Student Guide—Five Federal Financial Aid Programs (No. 508P)

Cost: Free

Send to:
Consumer Information Center
P.O. Box 100
Pueblo, CO 81002

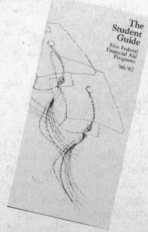

Student Guide

A SASE is a self-addressed stamped envelope.

ALTERNATIVES TO COLLEGE
★★★★

Not everyone wants to or should go to college. Many prefer learning a trade or technical skill, and for those, the answer may be going to a trade or technical school. About two million Americans are currently enrolled in 8000 private trade and technical courses. If you want to join them, this eight-page booklet published by the Better Business Bureau can help you plan for this career decision. The booklet describes typical trade and technical schools, what you should find out about them before deciding which to attend, and what to look out for before signing a contract to take courses. Suggestions, such as study school catalogs, visit several schools, and talk to recent graduates, are summarized in a handy checklist.

Write for:
Tips on Trade and Technical Schools (No. 24-190)

Cost: Free

Send to:
Council of Better Business Bureaus
1515 Wilson Blvd.
Arlington, VA 22209

SKILL TRAINING PAYS OFF
★★★★

Getting Skilled, a 145-page paperback published by the National Association of Trade and Technical Schools, is a valuable guide for both students and their high school counselors. Authors Tom Hebert and John Coyne leave no tough question unanswered in this lively, humorous, well-researched work. The authors, who are educational consultants and career counselors, build a strong case for the reliability and quality of the skill training available through private trade schools—despite some of the scare stories you may have heard from time to time. In this book, prospective students are guided from the initial phase of gathering information on schools right through to graduation and its sequel—job hunting.

Write for:
Getting Skilled: A Guide to Private Trade and
    Technical Schools

Cost: $1.50

Send to:
National Association of Trade and Technical
    Schools
2251 Wisconsin Ave., N.W.
Washington, DC 20007

PREPARING TO MAKE A CAREER CHOICE
★★★★

Selecting a career is not always an easy task. To help you decide on a life's work that is meaningful to you, send for a package of two free leaflets from the American Management Associations. *Sources of Information About Careers* directs you to books on specific careers, books about strategies, methods for seeking jobs, and comprehensive sources of career information. *Career Strategy and Job Search* lists books and audio cassettes that offer help in preparing a resume, advice on interviewing for a job, and dos and don'ts for the job hunter. Teenagers starting to think about careers after high school or college can get a head start toward their future by looking into this free career information.

Write for:
Career Strategy and Job Search
Sources of Information About Careers

Cost: Free

Send to:
Management Information Service
American Management Associations
135 W. 50th St.
New York, NY 10020

JOBS OF TODAY AND TOMORROW
★★★★

What will the jobs of tomorrow be? How many workers will be needed to repair robots or program computers? What about the future of aerospace and medicine? If you're in high school or college and wondering what major will tie in with a wise career plan for the future, a free 32-page publication from the U.S. Department of Labor can be of help. It is an in-depth look at the job market for today and the future. Using information on the demand for goods and services, advances in technology, changes in business practices, and occupational composition of industries, the government has reached some conclusions and predictions about jobs of the future that can help direct you toward a well-paying, meaningful career decision.

Write for:
The Job Outlook in Brief (No. 105P)

continued

TEENS

Cost: Free

Send to:
Consumer Information Center
P.O. Box 100
Pueblo, CO 81002

Job Outlook in Brief

WORKING WITH NATURAL RESOURCES

★★

A forest ranger probably has one of the most misunderstood careers around. A ranger, and not all Forest Service workers are called rangers, is a forester who manages natural resources in forest lands for the benefit of people—including future generations. Rangers are conservationists; they plan reforesting, disease control, use of forest lands, and preservation of wildlife. Ecology and environmental management are responsibilities of the Forest Service also. This 15-page booklet outlines the educational requirements for a career in forestry and its potential rewards.

Write for:
Career Profiles (FS-308)

Cost: Free

Send to:
USDA Forest Service
P.O. Box 2417
Washington, DC 20013

A CAREER UNCOVERING THE PAST

★★★

Archaeologists play a key role in helping to reconstruct and understand the past. If you're contem-plating a career in the field, you may imagine a life of adventure and discovery in foreign lands, or the painstaking research required to piece together the fragments of the past. In a reprint entitled *Archaeology as a Career,* the facts and fallacies are clarified by John Howland Rowe, a UCLA professor and museum curator. In an easy, conversational style, Professor Rowe explains the what, why, and how of an archaeologist's work. His description of the training and temperament that best qualify a person to become an archaeologist should give you a very good idea of whether or not this field is the right one for you. Although the pamphlet is aimed at career-minded students, the article will fascinate all archaeology buffs.

Write for:
Archaeology as a Career

Cost: $1.35

Send to:
Archaeological Institute of America
Dept. CG
Box 1901, Kenmore Station
Boston, MA 02215

HELPING THE HANDICAPPED TO HAVE FUN

★★★★

If you're considering a career in physical education, or if you have a brother or sister who is physically disabled, you'd do well to take a look at this 64-page book of games and other recreational activities designed specially for disabled children and teenagers. It shows that although physically disabled youngsters may need special training and some special equipment, they can take part in and enjoy games with other kids. The book describes games for ages five to seven, eight to eleven, and twelve to eighteen. Besides specially created games such as beanbag jump, pass the ring, wheelchair spin, magic carpets, coffee-can golf, paddle pitch, and floor hockey, there are suggestions on how to adapt more traditional sports such as billiards, shuffleboard, archery, golf, baseball, basketball, and bowling to the needs of physically disabled children. The book was prepared for parents and teachers, but if there's a physically handicapped young person in your life, you can get—and pass on—lots of good ideas from these pages.

Write for:
Let's Play Games!

Cost: $2.00

A SASE is a self-addressed stamped envelope.

Send to:
National Easter Seal Society
2023 Ogden Ave.
Chicago, IL 60612

HOW TO GET ON THE FRONT PAGE

★★★★

The newspaper business employs many people who aren't reporters, and the brochures in this free packet explore some of these other employment opportunities. In *Newspaper Jobs You Never Thought Of* you'll learn about opportunities in marketing research, personnel, advertising, art, and photo direction, as well as jobs for librarians, newspaper lawyers, labor negotiators, and more. *Newspapers, Your Future?* talks about the same opportunities in more general terms, and discusses the special skills you'll need to bring to the different jobs; there's a good resource list for further reading in this one. *Searching for People To Fix the Machines* talks about the shortage of and need for technicians for video display terminals and other computer-based electronics equipment. Also available is *Your Future in Newspapers*, a well-produced 35-page book that gives you the facts you'll need in order to make a most important career decision. It costs a dollar.

Write for:
Your Future in Newspaper packet
Your Future in Newspapers

Cost: Packet: Free
Book: $1.00

Send to:
American Newspaper Publishers Association
Foundation
The Newspaper Center
Box 17407
Washington Dulles International Airport
Washington, DC 20041

CAREER TALK

★★

Most high school students spend a fair amount of time considering for which career they would like to prepare. While it is difficult to predict exactly what the job market will be like in years to come, a number of factors are influencing an increasing demand for speech, language, and hearing professionals. *Careers in Speech-Language Pathology and Audiology*, a colorful brochure published by the American Speech-Language-Hearing Association, explains the job opportunities and requirements for this field. Whether your interest is in the area of research or in working with people, there is employment potential. The pamphlet covers the wide variety of jobs, the outlook for the future, and how to prepare for the profession. It also discusses financial aid, salary, and professional organizations.

Write for:
Careers in Speech-Language Pathology and
Audiology

Cost: Free

Send to:
ASHA Information Resource Center
10801 Rockville Pike
Rockville, MC 20852

Careers in Speech-Language Pathology and Audiology

CAMPING AS A CAREER

★★

Would you enjoy a career that combines the satisfactions of working with people in an outdoor setting? How about professional camping? Few fields require such a variety of backgrounds and disciplines as organized camping, or are as much fun. *Careers in Camping* is an informative brochure you'll want to read if working in fresh air interests you. It gives job descriptions for career positions, from camp director to trip leader, and defines the different types of camping experiences. There is a list of qualifications needed as well as salary information. There is good advice on how to start preparing now for such a career as well as a list of organizations that offer camping programs.

Write for:
Careers in Camping

Cost: Free

continued

TEENS

CAREERS IN ANIMAL CARE
★★★

Both veterinarians and animal technicians are dedicated to protecting the health and welfare of animals. If you enjoy animals and science, a career in veterinary medicine might be for you. These two pamphlets will give you information on what these positions entail and how to prepare for them. *Today's Veterinarian* is a 16-page booklet that covers job opportunities in private practice, research, teaching, public health, and specialized areas such as zoo medicine. It lists the personal abilities required by the animal professional and the educational requirements as well. The pamphlet discusses salaries and the pros and cons of working in this field, and gives a list of colleges of veterinary medicine.

Animal technicians generally begin practicing after two years of college. This information and more is included in *Your Career in Animal Technology*. The small pamphlet also covers the duties, training, salaries, and benefits of this profession.

Write for:
Today's Veterinarian
Your Career in Animal Technology

Cost: Free with a long SASE

Send to:
American Veterinary Medical Association
930 N. Meacham Road
Schaumburg, IL 60196-1074

Today's Veterinarian
Your Career in Animal Technology

CLOWNING AROUND
★★

Okay, *now* you know what you want to be when you grow up—a clown. Information about attending Clown College in Florida (and an application form) is available for the asking. In the ten-week session, would-be clowns, who must be over 17 years old, learn to ride a unicycle, perform magic, pantomine, juggle, do acrobatics, work with animals, make clown costumes, and put on clown-face makeup. Right up your alley? There's one drawback; the competition isn't funny at all—the college receives thousands of inquiries a year, and the maximum enrollment is 60.

Write for:
Clown College information sheet and application form

Cost: Free with a long SASE

Send to:
Ringling Bros. and Barnum & Bailey
Clown College
P.O. Box 1528
Venice, FL 33595

LOOKING GOOD ON THE JOB
★★★

Ready to enter the working world? Are you *really* ready? Do you know what kind of clothes you'll need for an office job? How to keep yourself neat from nine to five? How to get necessary rest and exercise during a busy day? *Reflections on Your Career—A Career Girl's Guide to Grooming and Dress* is a 64-page guide to good looks that gives you all the basics on makeup, hair care, hand care, choosing a wardrobe, health and hygiene—even tips on improving your voice and speech. You'll learn that the well-dressed woman is not necessarily the one who spends the most on clothes, and that no amount of makeup will hide the fact that you didn't get enough sleep last night.

Write for:
Reflections on Your Career—A Career Girl's Guide to Grooming and Dress

Cost: $1.00

Send to:
The Interstate Printers & Publishers, Inc.
19 N. Jackson St.
P.O. Box 50
Danville, IL 61834-0050

A SASE is a self-addressed stamped envelope.

WHAT DID YOU SAY MY NAME WAS?

★★★

Have you ever had your mind go blank at the most inconvenient moment—like when you're filling in a job application? What *was* the name of your last boss? What's the address of your bank? What's your next-door neighbor's phone number? By the time you're done you're not even sure you've got your own name right. This *Personal Information Book* will help you out on your next interview. It's got room for all the names, addresses, and dates you'll need, including your doctor's name and address, school information, past jobs, and personal references. If your mind goes blank next time you stare at an application, all you have to do is consult this pocket-sized booklet. How did you ever manage without it? Especially when it only costs $1.00.

Write for:
Personal Information Book

Cost: $1.00

Send to:
The Interstate Printers & Publishers, Inc.
19 N. Jackson St.
P.O. Box 50
Danville, IL 61834-0050

Personal Information Book

FREE THINGS
for
PARENTS

Pregnancy, Prenatal Care, and Birth

CLEARING OUT THE COBWEBS

★★★★

When you're expecting your first child you may be subject to all kinds of questions, doubts, fears, and concerns that can be quickly cleared up when you know the facts. *Pregnancy and You,* a 28-page booklet from the Public Affairs Committee, could put your mind at rest on a number of issues. It describes the physical and emotional characteristics of each trimester of pregnancy and attempts to dissipate some of the myths and old wives' tales you may have heard. You might save yourself some needless worry for the dollar you spend on this little book. The section on the last months of pregnancy guides you through making hospital arrangements, getting ready for the birth, and your first days back home.

Write for:
Pregnancy and You (No. 482)

Cost: $1.00

Send to:
Public Affairs Pamphlets
381 Park Ave. South
New York, NY 10016

EXPECTATIONS FOR CAREER WOMEN

★★★★

More women, especially professionals who wish to continue working in their fields as long as possible, are delaying having their first child until they are in their thirties. Concerns about work-related hazards, pregnancy disability benefits, and whether age will affect your ability to become pregnant or the health of the baby are addressed in two patient education pamphlets issued by The American College of Obstetricians and Gynecologists. *Pregnancy After 30* encourages women in this age group to discuss their health and timing of conception with their physician before they become pregnant. Even though most women over 30 have uncomplicated pregnancies, the pamphlet explains birth defects, the tests that can detect problems during pregnancy, and the need for genetic counseling. *Pregnancy and the Working Woman* answers questions concerning how long and under what conditions a pregnant woman should work.

Write for:
Pregnancy After 30
Pregnancy and the Working Woman

Cost: Free with a long SASE

Send to:
The American College of Obstetricians and Gynecologists
Resource Center
Suite 300 East
600 Maryland Avenue, SW
Washington, DC 20024

BRINGING UP FATHER

★★

Just learned that you're going to be a father for the first time? This folder contains some excellent ideas and suggestions for you. It concentrates on the tremendous changes that will occur in your life and your spouse's and asks some pertinent questions. Are you ready for additional responsibilities? Will the baby change your relationship with its mother? What about expenses? It tells you what to expect during the pregnancy and how you can lighten the load for the mother-to-be. The booklet also talks about programs for expectant parents and what to expect (and do) when the baby comes home. Lots of information in six small pages.

Write for:
For the Expectant Father

Cost: 40¢

Send to:
Maternity Center Association
48 E. 92nd St.
New York, NY 10128

WHEN YOU'RE PREGNANT

★★

Usually, pregnancy doesn't impose any major restrictions on your daily activities. Although it's always best to talk things over with your doctor, here's a free 10-page booklet that offers a number of pointers that may not come up in talks with your physician. *Pregnancy and Daily Living,* prepared by the American College of Obstetricians and Gynecologists, offers sensible advice on avoiding back strain and keeping up your energy level. There's a look at the latest medical thinking on exercise and pregnancy, and brief hints on comfortable travel, physical changes to expect, and sex during pregnancy.

continued

PARENTS

Write for:
   Pregnancy and Daily Living

Cost: Free

Send to:
   The American College of Obstetricians and
      Gynecologists
   Resource Center
   Suite 300 East
   600 Maryland Ave., S.W.
   Washington, DC 20024

PLANNING FOR THE NEW BABY
★★★

This brief but excellent folder is filled with ideas and tips for making the new baby's arrival as easy as such a life-changing event can be. There's information on budgeting for the new baby, providing for the baby's needs (a simple list with basic, essential equipment only), ways to provide for home management during the mother's hospital stay, and tips on preparing for the all-important homecoming. There are check lists for mother (things to take to the hospital) and dad (things the baby will need to come home in), and reminders to obtain a baby growth and development book to record the progress of the little one.

Write for:
   Preparation for Parenthood

Cost: 25¢

Send to:
   Our Baby's First Seven Years
   Dept. CG
   5841 S. Maryland Ave.
   Chicago, IL 60637

Preparation for Parenthood

BEFORE THE BABY COMES
★★★

The role that genetic disorders play in causing birth defects and the tests performed to determine the fetus' risk are the subjects of three patient education pamphlets published by The American College of Obstetricians and Gynecologists. *Genetic Disorders* explains that just as a baby inherits the color of its eyes and hair from its parents, certain types of birth defects can also be inherited. It outlines the role that dominant, recessive, and X-linked genes play, and how abnormalities in the genes or chromosomes may result in birth defects. It also covers genetic counseling and, for those who believe that genetic problems may exist in their family, suggests tests that can be performed. *Amniocentesis for Prenatal Diagnosis of Genetic Disorders* explains the procedure, possible complications, and results of this type of testing. *Ultrasound Exams in Ob/Gyn* discusses the various methods of ultrasound, the information that is recorded, and how it is used.

Write for:
   Genetic Disorders
   Amniocentesis for Prenatal Diagnosis of Genetic
      Disorders
   Ultrasound Exams in Ob/Gyn

Cost: Free with a long SASE

Send to:
   The American College of Obstetricians and
      Gynecologists
   Resource Center
   Suite 300 East
   600 Maryland Avenue, SW
   Washington, DC 20024

BABIES AT RISK
★★★

Today, both prenatal and newborn care have come a long way toward helping to ensure that women have safe deliveries and healthy newborns. However, a small percentage of newborns do suffer from either minor or major birth defects. *Genetic Disorders: Some Answers, Some Options* sensibly discusses common disorders, both inherited and environmental. You'll learn how those that are inherited, such as Huntington's chorea, are passed through three primary modes of genetic transference. The booklet covers the purpose of genetic screening and counseling, testing before and during pregnancy, and how amniocentesis is performed. Also explored are some options available to couples who are at increased risk of having a child with a birth defect.

A SASE is a self-addressed stamped envelope.

Write for:
Genetic Disorders: Some Answers, Some Options

Cost: 50¢

Send to:
Planned Parenthood Federation of America, Inc.
810 Seventh Avenue
New York, NY 10019

DOES IT RUN IN THE FAMILY?

★★

Here's a practical resource for prospective parents who have concerns that a genetic defect may run in the family and threaten their unborn children. If you know, or suspect, that a hereditary disease or condition exists in your family, write to the National Genetics Foundation for these two free booklets. *How Genetic Disease Can Affect You and Your Family* will get your search for information off to a start, but doesn't go into specific details about hereditary conditions. *For the Concerned Couple Planning a Family* offers good suggestions for preparing a health history of your family for several generations back, to help pinpoint possible tendencies toward genetically transmitted medical problems.

Write for:
How Genetic Disease Can Affect You and
    Your Family
For the Concerned Couple Planning a Family

Cost: $2.00 (check or money order)

Send to:
National Genetics Foundation, Inc.
555 W. 57th St.
New York, NY 10019

DRINKING FOR TWO

★★★★

Every time a pregnant woman drinks an alcoholic beverage, so does the unborn child. Alcohol passes across the placenta to the fetus, reaching its bloodstream in the same concentration as that of the mother. Although research into fetal alcohol syndrome is fairly new, one thing we know for sure— alcohol can cause birth defects. *Alcohol and Pregnancy: Why They Don't Mix* is an enlightening, factual booklet by the American Medical Association; it should be read by every soon-to-be mother. Both fetal alcohol syndrome and fetal alcohol effects are discussed in the 15-page booklet, along with the incidence of miscarriage and stillbirth among pregnant women who consume alcohol. The brochure

also covers habitual, moderate, and spree drinking, and clarifies some of the myths about pregnancy and alcohol.

Write for:
Alcohol and Pregnancy: Why They Don't Mix

Cost: $1.50

Send to:
Order Department, OP-245
American Medical Association
P.O. Box 10946
Chicago, IL 60610

PRACTICAL PREPARATION FOR CHILDBEARING

★★★★

The emphasis here is on practical suggestions and simple techniques for the expectant mother—to promote comfort during pregnancy, to facilitate the process of childbirth, and to ease postpartum adjustment. The father's role is also covered, but to a lesser degree. The best part of this booklet are the diagrams that *show* you how to get out of bed the most comfortable way when you're pregnant and how to lift a toddler or climb stairs; there's an exercise or position to ease most of the discomforts of pregnancy. Other diagrams show what happens during the entire labor process, and they accompany a chart that guides both parents through the stages of labor. There are excellent reading and resource lists. A simple but splendid little book.

Write for:
Preparation for Childbearing

Cost: $2.00

Send to:
Maternity Center Association
48 E. 92nd St.
New York, NY 10128

BABYING YOURSELF

★★★★

So you're going to have a baby. While pregnancy and birth are among life's most natural experiences, there is a great deal you need to know in order to make everything go as smoothly as possible. *Childbirth Today: Where and How to Have Your Baby* is a highly informative 32-page booklet that's loaded with good advice for the expectant mother. You'll learn about

continued

prenatal care and the proper nutritional requirements you'll need to follow to deliver a healthy baby. Each stage of labor is carefully explained as well as popular childbirth methods used today. The book also covers medical professionals from doctors to midwives and the facilities in which they usually practice. A supplementary listing of further reading is in the back of the book.

Send to:
Childbirth Today: Where and How to Have Your Baby (No. 628)

Cost: $1.00

Write for:
Public Affairs Pamphlets
381 Park Ave. South
New York, NY 10016

EXPECTANT EATING
★★

Establish good eating habits early—that's the sensible advice offered to expectant moms in *Food, Pregnancy, and Health.* There's a summary of general rules for planning nutritious meals and a listing of foods in the four major food groups. Perhaps most useful are the friendly hints for assessing your eating habits and commonsense tips for making positive changes if necessary. There are rules of thumb for assuring that you get enough protein, vitamins, and minerals, and suggestions for introducing new, high-nutrition foods into your diet. A small but useful publication from the people who ought to know.

Write for:
Food, Pregnancy, and Health

Cost: Free

Send to:
The American College of Obstetricians and
Gynecologists Resource Center (P001)
Suite 300 East
600 Maryland Ave., S.W.
Washington, DC 20024

NOTES FOR NEW PARENTS
★★★★

This is a gentle, encouraging book about having a baby. In simple terms, with lots of delightful little line drawings, it outlines for the new parents exactly what to expect when the birth is near. It's all explained here—from the first signs of labor to the hospital and its facilities and equipment to the labor and delivery room. There's some especially good advice for the expectant father, and how he can help the new mother at birth and afterwards. Finally, there are some sensible hints about how to integrate the newest member into the family. The moral of the booklet is: Relax, and enjoy one of life's most rewarding experiences. Especially good reading for first-time parents.

Write for:
About Childbirth, a Guide to Maternity Services

Cost: 50¢

Send to:
Planned Parenthood Federation of America, Inc.
810 Seventh Ave.
New York, NY 10019

You and Your Baby

THE NURSING MOTHER
★★★★

Despite plenty of encouragement from medical and social advisers, only two out of five American women breast-feed their babies. *Breastfeeding,* a useful 16-page booklet put out by the Public Affairs Committee, can help you make up your mind about whether you'll breast-feed or not. The booklet outlines the physical advantages nursing offers your baby, as well as how breast-feeding works to help conserve your iron reserves and your energy. There's a presentation of the psychological advantages of nursing for both mother and baby and a discussion of why many women fail to take advantage of an experience that most women who undertake it describe as delightful and rewarding.

Write for:
Breastfeeding (No. 353S)

Cost: $1.00

Send to:
Public Affairs Pamphlets
381 Park Ave. South
New York, NY 10016

A BOOK OF FIRSTS
★★★★

Is a brand new baby coming into your life? Then, of course, you'll want to keep track of all those big important moments in this delightful 16-page, color illustrated booklet. There is room to record the events of that very first day, the family tree, dates and ages of various baby accomplishments, and details of your baby's first birthday party and big holiday. There is an immunization schedule (as recommended by the American Academy of Pediatrics) and space to keep medical information. You'll also find two pages to fill in with current events data to help you remember the state of the world when baby arrived. *It's A New Baby* is a great memoir for the parents—and baby.

Write for:
   It's a New Baby

Cost: 50¢

Send to:
   North Wales Press, Inc.
   P.O. Box 1486
   North Wales, PA 19454

It's a New Baby

SHOPPING FOR BABY EQUIPMENT

★★★

If this is your first baby, you're going to be confronted with an array of items you'll need to buy: a car safety seat, a play yard (playpen is the old name for it), a walker/jumper, various nursery items (crib, dressing table, tub), a high chair, a stroller, child-sized furniture, an infant carrier, and trainers, bed rails, baby backpacks, and so on. Overwhelmed? This guide may help. It gives a list of shopping tips and what to look for in each item. It also tells you how and when the equipment should be used. Baby-equipment manufacturers Cosco/Peterson put this excellent booklet together, but admirably refrained from touting their own products. This is good, straightforward advice.

Write for:
   Ready, Set, Grow

Cost: 50¢

Send to:
   Carol R. Dingledy
   Cosco/Peterson
   2525 State St.
   Columbus, IN 47201

A PRIMER ON BASIC BABY CARE

★★★★

If this is your first baby, this 48-page primer on baby care will help you through some of the new experiences that seem to have no rules. You'll learn about the baby's eating and sleeping habits, how you can best keep the baby clean, and what to do when the baby gets ill. There's an excellent checklist to guide you in explaining your child's symptoms to the doctor, and a good list of things a baby's medicine cabinet should contain. The last section of the booklet deals with ways you can make your world safer for babies and toddlers. There's a reference list of books about toddlers and infants, too. The drawings are a delight.

Write for:
   Baby Care Basics (available in English
      and Spanish)

Cost: Free

Send to:
   Johnson & Johnson
   Consumer and Professional Services-1000
   Grandview Rd.
   Skillman, NJ 08558

Baby Care Basics

PARENTS

BUILDING A FAMILY
★★★★

You know that your baby needs loving care in order to thrive, and the love you give comes naturally. But you'll still appreciate the many ideas and suggestions found in *Your First Months With Your First Baby*. This 28-page booklet talks about the many levels of care your baby needs. You'll find sections on how your life-style will change when the baby comes and some of the individual and temperamental differences you can expect in your baby. New parents will also get a head start with advice on when a small child first needs to learn about discipline, and there's a section on the new father's special role in his family.

Write for:
　Your First Months With Your First Baby (No. 478)

Cost:　$1.00

Send to:
　Public Affairs Pamphlets
　381 Park Ave. South
　New York, NY 10016

BABY TALK
★★★★

The growth of a baby from infancy to childhood is a heartwarming, joyful experience for parents. The first 18 months can also be a fearful time, especially for new mothers and fathers who are novices in the baby business. This 32-page booklet is a great help in telling you what to expect and how to meet the needs of your latest family member. It covers feeding schedules, bottle-feeding versus breast-feeding, weaning, and when to start with solid foods. Bathing, skin care, and diapering are discussed. Several pages of the booklet are devoted to health care and treatment of illness, and a schedule of recommended immunizations is included. You'll also learn about your child's personality formation and physical development. Being a good parent is one of the most demanding jobs in the world. This book is a good start in building a loving relationship with your child.

Send to:
　Caring For the New Baby—the First 18 Months
　　(No. 616)

Cost:　$1.00

Write for:
　Public Affairs Pamphlets
　381 Park Ave. South
　New York, NY 10016

CONVERSATIONS WITH YOUR NEWBORN
★★★★

This charming 18-page booklet describes some of the ways you will get to know your new baby. Her (or his) cries will be one of them, and this primer helps you identify what different kinds of crying mean. You'll learn how quickly your baby responds to touching, smiling, and cuddling, how soon you'll be hearing the first ahs and coos that make up the baby's first vocabulary, and how it *is* possible to have a conversation with your newborn. You'll also find out ways to help your baby build physical skills through exercises and toys. The photographs of parents and children are beautiful, and there's an excellent reference list for further reading on this new, wonderful relationship. The booklet is availabe in both English and Spanish.

Write for:
　Getting To Know Your Newborn (specify English
　　or Spanish)

Cost:　Free

Send to:
　Johnson & Johnson
　Consumer and Professional Services-1000
　Grandview Rd.
　Skillman, NJ 08558

Getting to Know Your Newborn

ENTERTAINMENT FOR THE DIAPER SET
★★★

Is your baby bored? Are you both tired of playing pattycake and knee bouncing? If you need some fresh ideas, *100 Ways to Entertain Your Baby* will give you, yes, 100 of them, for babies from birth to three years old. This 12-page booklet doesn't look fancy, but who cares? It may give you just enough new ideas to enliven your playtime with your baby and encourage the little one to explore, create, and discover the world. It's written by a mother of two—she also has a master's degree in educational media—and most tips are simple to try and inexpensive. Some sound a little messy—tip 32, for example, suggests that you give your baby a raw egg on his high chair and let him finger-paint with it.

Write for:
100 Ways to Entertain Your Baby

Cost: $1.00

Send to:
Nancy Everhart
Baby Book
Tamaqua, PA 18252

BATHING A BABY SAFELY
★

This illustrated instruction sheet, reprinted from a book about babies, shows the correct techniques for bathing a soapy, wiggly, slippery newborn. It's basically a promotion piece for the company's product—an infant bath aid made of sculptured foam rubber that cradles the infant in a reclining position with head above water, leaving both your hands free for the enjoyable job of bathing the baby. Reassuring how-to pictures for nervous new parents.

Write for:
How to Bathe Your Baby in Safety and Comfort

Cost: Free with a long SASE

Send to:
Pansy Ellen Products, Inc.
P.O. Box 720274
Atlanta, GA 30358

How to Bathe Your Baby in Safety and Comfort

PICTURE GUIDE TO BATHING THE BABY
★★★★

On one side of this 22″ × 17″ poster are illustrated instructions on how to give your baby either a sponge bath or a tub bath. Emphasis is on a thorough, safe job using lots of Johnson's baby products, and there's a good list of the items you ought to have on hand for the baby's bath. On the other side of the poster descriptions of how your baby grows from a newborn to a toddler of 24 months are illustrated. In each stage, you see the kind of body, hand, speech, and social development your baby will be gaining. The wealth of good information makes this poster especially valuable for first-time parents. The babies in the illustrations are charmers. This item is available in both English and Spanish.

Write for:
How Your Baby Grows poster (specify English or Spanish)

Cost: Free

Send to:
Johnson & Johnson
Consumer and Professional Services-1000
Grandview Rd.
Skillman, NJ 08558

TWO OF A KIND
★★★

If you're a twin, or there are twins in your family, or you're expecting twins, you'll be glad to know there is a national organization of mothers of twins. It puts out a quarterly newsletter and many booklets that offer helpful hints to twins and parents. The literature talks about such matters as how moms can help twins (or triplets or quadruplets and so on) grow up healthy and happy. For instance, should twins be dressed identically or differently? Should baby twins eat out of the same bowl? Should twins always be taken on outings together? Should they play with the same toys? What special instructions should a babysitter be given if she or he is to look after twins? These and many other questions are answered in the club's newspapers and booklets. Send for a free sample of the newsletter and other literature if twins are coming into your life or are already there.

Write for:
Welcome to the World of Twins

Cost: Free with a long SASE

continued

PARENTS

Send to:
    National Organization of Mothers of Twins Clubs
    5402 Amberwood Lane
    Rockville, MD 20853

NUTRITION IN THE EARLY MONTHS

★★★★

By a baby's first birthday, his or her weight has tripled; he's grown 10 to 11 inches; and his brain, heart, and kidneys have doubled in size. By 18 months, a baby has grown an additional two to three inches and has developed most of the brain cells he will ever have. This 12-page booklet from the Infant Formula Council gives parents vital information on a baby's nutrition needs during the important early months. Discussed in easy-to-understand language are nutrition requirements, iron deficiency, formula and breast-feeding, cow's milk, and the introduction of solid foods. A sensible and informative booklet.

Write for:
    Infant Feeding and Nutrition

Cost: Free

Send to:
    The Infant Formula Council
    P.O. Box 76731
    Atlanta, GA 30358

Infant Feeding and Nutrition

TIMES TWO

★★

You've arrived home with your double blessing—twins—but now what do you do? Certainly two babies at a time is double the pleasure and double the trouble. This small booklet, *Twin Blessed*, is a handy guide for new mothers of multiple newborns, published by a group of women who have been there themselves. You'll find suggested equipment and clothing lists (umbrella strollers and the face-to-face styles are the most popular), and lots of hints for running a household at the same time as mothering (keep it to a minimum, they say). There is advice on feeding and bathing the twins, and on involving older children who may feel left out of the excitement. At the back of the booklet is a bibliography for further reading.

Write for:
    Twin Blessed

Cost: 50¢

Send to:
    Organization of Twin Blessed Mothers
    c/o Ginny Price
    1925 N. 68th Street
    Milwaukee, WI 53213

TEST YOUR BABY'S HEARING

★★★★

How do you test a baby's or toddler's hearing? This *Speech and Hearing Checklist,* from the Alexander Graham Bell Association for the Deaf, gives parents some guidelines on the hearing and speech patterns of children aged three months through five years. The checklist gives questions for you to ask yourself about each stage of your child's development—for example, from three to six months old, "What does he do when you talk to him?" Alongside is the corresponding expected behavior—"He awakens or quiets to the sound of his mother's voice." There's also a shortened version of the checklist called *Can Your Baby Hear?* for babies up to 18 months. Both the checklist and the card are also available in Spanish.

Write for:
    Speech and Hearing Checklist
    Can Your Baby Hear? (specify English or Spanish)

Cost: Free with a long SASE

Send to:
    Alexander Graham Bell Association for the
       Deaf, Inc.
    3417 Volta Place, N.W.
    Washington, DC 20007

THE BABY'S ASLEEP

★★★★

Leave your babysitter important phone numbers on this nifty safety phone card. There's room for your family doctor, a helpful neighbor, the poison control center, the police department, the fire department, and the local hospital. There's even a pad of refillable Postit Self-Stick Notes for those extra instructions you don't want forgotten. On the reverse side of the phone card is a Baby Sleeping Sign to alert visitors to be extra quiet, so as not to wake the baby. Both sides of this colorful card come with velcro fasteners enabling you to mount the card securely near a phone or door bell, or to move it easily when it's not needed. This is a great idea for any new mother—a good shower item, too.

Write for:
Safety Phone Card

Cost: $2.00

Send to:
F & H Baby Products
P.O. Box 2228P
Evansville, IN 47714

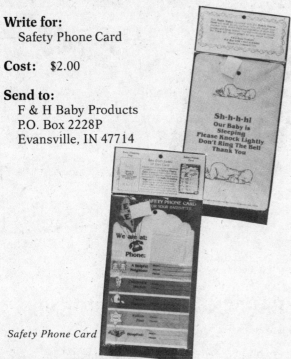

Safety Phone Card

You and Your Growing Child

THE HECTIC YEARS

★★★★

Sooner than it seems possible, your child isn't a baby anymore. At one, two, or three years old, he or she has already entered childhood and left the baby years behind. Although you've probably learned a lot about your youngster by this time, you'll still appreciate the helpful information and advice in *Enjoy Your Child—Ages 1, 2, and 3*. This friendly 28-page booklet from the Public Affairs Committee stresses the young child's two important needs— independence and, at the same time, a grounded feeling of security. Your child wants to try new wings, but wants to stay your baby, too. This can keep a mom or dad on an emotional seesaw, but understanding what's going on can help you handle your child's hectic first, second, and third years of life.

Write for:
Enjoy Your Child—Ages 1, 2, and 3 (No. 141)

Cost: $1.00

Send to:
Public Affairs Pamphlets
381 Park Ave. South
New York, NY 10016

THE RESTLESS YEARS

★★★★

How soon should a child go to school? *Three to Six: Your Child Starts to School*, a 28-page booklet from the Public Affairs Committee, suggests that most kids are ready for school at three or four years of age and will probably drive their parents crazy if they have to stay home much longer. This lively and intelligent little book suggests ways of locating preschool activities, preparing your child for kindergarten, deciding what constitutes a good school, and keeping in touch with the teacher. You'll learn that play is an important part of work in the three to six age group, and how parents can help children acquire that most valuable of skills—reading.

Write for:
Three to Six: Your Child Starts to School (No. 163)

Cost: $1.00

Send to:
Public Affairs Pamphlets
381 Park Ave. South
New York, NY 10016

THE FORGOTTEN YEARS OF CHILDHOOD

★★★★

Some psychologists call the years between ages six and 12 the "forgotten years of childhood," and suggest that parents would do well to learn more about that period of a child's life. *Understand Your Child— From 6 to 12* attempts to portray the inner world of children in this age group, with a view to helping parents get a realistic view of the way the child develops. You'll get the inside story on some of the worries, fears, curiosities, and needs of a child at each stage of the six- to 12-year period, plus suggestions to help you bring out your child's creativity, trust, and sense of responsibility.

Write for:
Understand Your Child—From 6 to 12 (No. 144)

Cost: $1.00

continued

PARENTS

Send to:
Public Affairs Pamphlets
381 Park Ave. South
New York, NY 10016

ADVICE TO NEW PARENTS

★★★★

Fifty parents of grown children over age 21 were asked by the National Institute of Mental Health, "Based upon your personal experiences with your own children, what is the best advice you could give new parents about raising children?" Their answers, in a free four-page publication, can be of help to parents in raising their youngsters today. The most frequent responses of the parents are classified under ten basic principles about which there is general agreement among those surveyed. The advice can also be helpful to teachers, day care workers, and others who care for children.

Write for:
Plain Talk About Raising Children (No. 505P)

Cost: Free

Send to:
Consumer Information Center
P.O. Box 100
Pueblo, CO 81002

CHAT ABOUT CHILDREN

★★

You'll find chatty, easy-to-read information on children in this free sample newsletter addressed to parents. *Growing Child* is "designed to bring you up-to-date information on the growth and development of your child." When you write, include your child's birthdate; you'll receive a sample newsletter all about children the same age as yours. The six-page sample on newborns, for instance, talks about the natural nervousness of first-time parents, communicating with your doctor, breast-feeding and bottle-feeding, and information about newborns—birthmarks, movement, brain development, intelligence, even appearance.

You can also ask for the *Growing Child Toy Catalog*, a free 48-page listing of the company's developmental toys, books, and records.

Write for:
Growing Child Newsletter
Growing Child Toy Catalog

Cost: Free (include your child's birthdate when you write for the newsletter)

Send to:
Growing Child Newsletter
22 N. 2nd St.
P.O. Box 620 CG
Lafayette, IN 47902

Growing Child Newsletter and Catalog

LEARNING TO BE A FRIEND

★★★★

Everybody needs friends, but friendships need nurturing, and learning to be a friend is an important part of growing up. This enlightening 28-page booklet, *Playmates: The Importance of Childhood Friendships,* stresses the ways in which a child's friendships help him or her learn the ways, beliefs, values, and standards of society. It also gives you, the parent, some sound advice on how to cope with your little ones and their friendships—how to keep your sense of perspective when yesterday's best friend is today's worst enemy, how to handle (or not handle) children's fights, and what to do if Johnny won't share his toys. You'll also find suggestions for helping your child survive the ending of a special friendship and some helpful words on quality versus quantity in friendships.

Write for:
Playmates: The Importance of Childhood Friendships (No. 525)

Cost: $1.00

Send to:
Public Affairs Pamphlets
381 Park Ave. South
New York, NY 10016

A SASE is a self-addressed stamped envelope.

IS MY CHILD NORMAL?

★★

How much hinges on this question. And how much in that question hinges on the meaning of one word—a word too easily used and easily abused. For any parent who has worried about how "normal" his or her child is, this article reprint will allay fears. It was written by a professor of speech pathology at the University of Iowa and is constructed in letter format to a set of parents whose daughter suffered from polio. Dr. Wendell Johnson addresses the issue of normalcy by defining the many meanings and applications of the term. He suggests the child's abilities be measured against her own capabilities rather than someone else's. The letter is warm and reassuring, and offers suggestions to the parents to bring about improvement. Even though the article was written in the 1950s, the information is still viable today.

Write for:
Is My Child Normal? (No. 453)

Cost: 65¢

Send to:
Interstate Printers & Publishers, Inc.
19 N. Jackson St.
P.O. Box 50
Danville, IL 61834-0050

WHAT MAKES A CHILD WANT TO DO WELL

★★★★

It's easy enough to observe what people do. Understanding *why* they do it is not so simple. Motivation is the fuel of achievement; in children, it's what makes them want to do well, and if a teacher tells you your child is "unmotivated" panic sets in. Here's a helpful little book that explains the experiences that shape your child's ability to give direction to his or her life. In *Motivation and Your Child* you'll learn about the building blocks of motivation and how to encourage a healthy self-image in your child. Also included are a variety of practical, usable concepts and how-to hints for helping children develop positive motivation toward their goals. There's also a useful section that makes the distinction between healthy and misplaced aggression.

Write for:
Motivation and Your Child (No. 523)

Cost: $1.00

Send to:
Public Affairs Pamphlets
381 Park Ave. South
New York, NY 10016

THE ANGRY CHILD

★★★★

Handling children's anger can be puzzling, draining, and distressing for parents, babysitters, teachers, and anyone else who deals with children. A free four-page publication from the National Institute of Mental Health suggests how to deal with and react to a child's anger. Ideas are then given for how adult skills can be directed toward showing children acceptable ways of expressing their anger as well as other feelings. The booklet suggests that in dealing with angry children, an adult's actions should be motivated by the need to protect and to teach, not by a desire to punish. Good information here for parents, teachers, counselors, and administrators working with children.

Write for:
Plain Talk About Dealing with the Angry Child
(No. 504P)

Cost: Free

Send to:
Consumer Information Center
P.O. Box 100
Pueblo, CO 81002

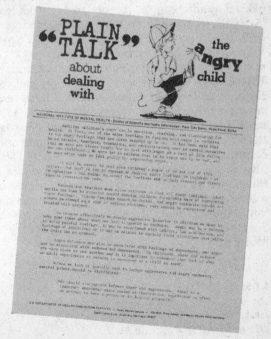

Plain Talk About Dealing With an Angry Child

PARENTS

NEW WAYS OF DISCIPLINE
★★★★

Most parents will agree on one thing: Kids need disciplining from time to time. And most parents worry about the right way to discipline. This 28-page booklet called *How To Discipline Your Children* suggests new ways of disciplining and points out that it's never too early—or too late—to begin. You'll learn to understand underlying feelings that often prompt naughty behavior in children and how to use this understanding to avoid disciplinary problems. You'll also like the sensitive section on helping a child admit hurt, anger, and sad feelings as a way to learning self-acceptance.

Write for:
 How To Discipline Your Children (No. 154)

Cost: $1.00

Send to:
 Public Affairs Pamphlets
 381 Park Ave. South
 New York, NY 10016

NEVER TOO YOUNG
★★★★

One of the best things you can do for a child is help him, or her, develop dependability and reliability. (These qualities make it more pleasant for you to live with your children, too.) Get some ideas on how to achieve this goal from *Your Child's Sense of Responsibility*, one of the fine publications on child-rearing put out by the Public Affairs Committee. This 28-page booklet tells you how to help your children understand what it means to be a responsible person and how to encourage them to seek responsibility within the family. There are suggestions for starting children early on becoming orderly, helpful, and capable of making decisions. There's also first aid for the irresponsible child and a cautionary note on the dangers of trying to make a child too responsible too soon. This booklet is available while supplies last.

Write for:
 Your Child's Sense of Responsibility (No. 254)

Cost: $1.00

Send to:
 Public Affairs Pamphlets
 381 Park Ave. South
 New York, NY 10016

CONTENTED KID OR SPOILED BRAT?
★★★★

There's a fine line, many parents discover to their dismay, between raising a child who feels loved, cherished, and important, and raising a spoiled brat. Kids need to learn that privileges are earned through responsibility, and coddling can be just as damaging to a child as neglect. How do you draw that fine line between flexibility and firmness? This booklet offers answers to this and many similar parental mind-benders. You'll learn what it means to be a flexible parent, as well as how to motivate your children to accomplish assigned chores, help with meals, care for their rooms and personal effects, take responsibility for pets, handle the family car, and learn financial responsibility. Included are solutions worked out by a number of thoughtful parents that you may be able to adapt to your own family's situation. Good family discussion material here.

Write for:
 What Should Parents Expect From Children?
  (No. 357)

Cost: $1.00

Send to:
 Public Affairs Pamphlets
 381 Park Ave. South
 New York, NY 10016

SPEAKING EASY
★★★

Approximately 70 percent of the average person's waking day is related to communication. Therefore, the importance of effective communication must be emphasized—first at home during early childhood and later both at home and in the classroom throughout the school years. Two pamphlets contain suggestions and illustrations for parents, teachers, and others to improve the child's oral and listening skills. They present basic information related to normal communication development, as well as communication disorders and speech correction. Practical ways of identifying and helping children with speech, hearing, and/or language problems are provided. By helping the child to listen and talk, we are helping him or her to succeed in later educational, occupational, and interpersonal settings.

Write for:
 Helping the Child to Listen and Talk (No. 2355)
 Your Child's Experience in Speech Correction
  (No. 851)

A SASE is a self-addressed stamped envelope.

Cost: $1.00 each

Send to:
Interstate Printers & Publishers, Inc.
19 N. Jackson St.
P.O. Box 50
Danville, IL 61834-0050

Your Child's Experience in Speech Correction

PATIENCE AND PRACTICE FOR STUTTERERS

★★★

Is your child's speech not as fluent as you think it should be? Are you fearful he is beginning to stutter? This collection of literature is written for the parents, because so much can be done to help the child who stutters. Understanding, persistence and patience, developed over a period of time, go a long way. *Is Your Child Beginning to Stutter?* is an authoritative, 20-page booklet that discusses the causes of stuttering, clears up misconceptions, and offers specific suggestions you can carry out to help the nonfluent child. *For Parents of a Child Beginning to Stutter* answers many commonly asked questions and gives practical advice on preventing the communication disability. Both booklets include reference lists for further reading. Also available is an article reprint of an open letter to a concerned mother, written by a professor of speech pathology and psychology in a warm, caring style. The letter offers case histories and the practical methods used to help these children.

Write for:
Is Your Child Beginning to Stutter? (No. 542)
For Parents of a Child Beginning to Stutter
 (No. 401)
An Open Letter to the Mother of a "Stuttering"
 Child (No. 156)

Cost: $1.00 for Is Your Child?
 75¢ for For Parents of a Child
 50¢ for Open Letter

Send to:
Interstate Printers & Publishers, Inc.
19 N. Jackson St.
P.O. Box 50
Danville, IL 61834-0050

THE SHY CHILD

★★★★

The shy youngster can suffer acutely in the rambunctious world of childhood, and shy children may find themselves in a vicious circle of rebuff and retreat. Understanding the way a timid child views the world can be the parent's key to breaking this cycle of withdrawal. If you're the parent of a painfully shy child, read this booklet. It explains the root causes of shyness and how they express themselves; once you recognize the causes, you may be able to help your youngster find some way, other than retreating into a shell of timidity, to cope with conflicts, physical illness, or other fearful situations.

Write for:
The Shy Child (No. 239)

Cost: $1.00

Send to:
Public Affairs Pamphlets
381 Park Ave. South
New York, NY 10016

YES, YOU CAN HELP

★★★

Few things can frustrate parents more than watching their child struggle with tasks that are vital to progress in learning. Parents want to know why Susie has good vision, but cannot read; why Johnny's hearing is adequate, but he can't follow directions or misinterprets them. Children who are functioning well in many areas, but unaccountably underachieve in specific tasks, may be identified as having learning disabilities. *Helping the Child with a Learning Disability* is an informative 16-page pamphlet that offers both comfort and advice to baffled parents. It discusses how school subjects are "learned" and explains how certain children may have difficulties with this learning process. It also contains many suggestions that may enable parents to stimulate the child and help him become more aware of the world about him. The suggestions are simple, practical, and easy to follow.

Write for:
Helping the Child with a Learning Disability
 (No. 2247)

continued

PARENTS

Cost: 75¢

Send to:
Interstate Printers & Publishers, Inc.
19 N. Jackson St.
P.O. Box 50
Danville, IL 61834-0050

FIRST DAY IN SCHOOL
★★★★

Is your boy or girl about ready to start school? It's a big day, not only in a child's life, but in a parent's. Your understanding of this turning point is important to your child's future attitude toward school and to his or her healthy growth and development, says the National Institute of Mental Health in a two-page publication free to parents. It offers advice on teaching children to enjoy school and learning, how to prepare them for their new experience at school, talking over transportation plans—in fact, how to become involved in your child's entire school adventure.

Write for:
Plain Talk About When Your Child Starts School
(No. 506P)

Cost: Free

Send to:
Consumer Information Center
P.O. Box 100
Pueblo, CO 81002

Plain Talk About When Your Child Starts School

HOW TOYS TEACH
★★★★

Here's an authoritative guide for parents who want to encourage a child's mental, social, and emotional development long before the first day of school. There's a fascinating list of toys for children in various age groups, plus information on how children learn from toys. For instance, rubber squeeze toys that bend or stretch easily help develop muscular coordination; and a four-year-old stringing necklaces from beads or macaroni is learning the small muscle control so vital for the future development of reading and writing skills.

Write for:
How Can I Help My Child Get Ready To Read?

Cost: 50¢

Send to:
International Reading Association
800 Barksdale Rd.
P.O. Box 8139
Newark, DE 19714-8139

BOOKS MAKE GOOD FRIENDS
★★

Very young kids, just like adults, love a good story with an interesting plot and plenty of action. Add suspense, humor, a bit of repetition, and a happy ending, and you've got the perfect book for your youngster. This booklet points out that infants love to be read to or sung to softly while they're being held, and that this early experience prepares a child to feel comforted by and familiar with the world of books and music later on. Perhaps the most valuable information here is a selected list of books suited to children from infancy to six years.

Write for:
What Books and Records Should I Get for My Preschooler?

Cost: 50¢

Send to:
International Reading Association
800 Barksdale Rd.
P.O. Box 8139
Newark, DE 19714-8139

READING LIST FOR KIDS
★★★★

What are some of the best books your child can read? The Library of Congress' Children's Literature Center has compiled a list of recommended reading for children that can be helpful to parents, teachers,

A SASE is a self-addressed stamped envelope.

librarians, and others interested in guiding young people to the best books. A 16-page booklet divides into age level lists from preschoolers' picture and game and song books to early reader folklore, Bible story and verse, easy-reading stories and nonfiction for six- to eight-year-olds, and tales of mystery, humor and adventure for children aged eight to eleven. For older readers there are books about plants, people, poetry, and adventure; science fiction; humor; biographies; mysteries; etc. A handy reference book that can serve as a springboard to the best in children's literature.

Write for:
Books for Children (No. 108P)

Cost: Free

Send to:
Consumer Information Center
P.O. Box 100
Pueblo, CO 81002

TURN THE TABLES ON TV
★★★

It's been estimated that many children spend as much as 34 to 53 hours a week in front of the television set, and many parents are very unhappy about these figures. What can you do, short of dumping the set in the garbage, to teach a child sensible viewing habits? One theory is to let TV work for you, and the International Reading Association believes you can use television to stimulate your child's reading habits. This excellent foldout, written by a reading expert, points out that it's possible for TV to enlarge your child's vocabulary, expand his or her horizons, and encourage hobbies. To turn TV into a teaching tool instead of a drug, you can follow some of the sensible guidelines suggested here. For instance, devise a program rating scale to teach your child selectiveness. The pamphlet is available in English, French, or Spanish.

Write for:
You Can Use Television To Stimulate Your
    Child's Reading Habits (specify English,
    French, or Spanish)

Cost: Free with a long SASE

Send to:
International Reading Association
800 Barksdale Rd.
P.O. Box 8139
Newark, DE 19714-8139

You Can Use Television to Stimulate Your Child's Reading Habits

CHOOSING BOOKS FOR CHILDREN
★★★

It's never too early to introduce a child to the magic of books. Even babies respond to brightly colored pictures, touchable textures, and the rhythms of storytelling. This excellent folder advises adults on the books children like best, broken down by age groups. It also lists the best resources for finding children's books. Good for parents and other grown-up gift givers.

Write for:
Choosing a Child's Book

Cost: Free with a long SASE (one 22¢ stamp)

Send to:
Children's Book Council
67 Irving Place
New York, NY 10003

Choosing a Child's Book

Prices are for single items only; prices and information are accurate at time of publication.

PARENTS

HEY, MOM, I CAN READ!
★★★

Reading is an activity not merely to be learned, but one which your child should come to enjoy and look upon as both useful and pleasurable. Schools are making great efforts to use attractive and interesting books in reading instruction, but your encouragement at home also plays an important role. This pamphlet from the International Reading Association explores the factors which influence interest in reading and offers suggestions for parents to stimulate that interest. Preschoolers, for example, like rhymes, bright colors and characters their own age, while the primary-aged child seeks further depth to a story. Children who embrace reading skills while they are young often carry their interest into adulthood. Parents can encourage their child's reading through trips to the library and by setting an example as readers themselves. The pamphlet is also available in French and Spanish.

Write for:
You Can Encourage Your Child to Read (specify English, French, or Spanish)

Cost: Free with a long SASE

Send to:
International Reading Association
800 Barksdale Road
P.O. Box 8139
Newark, DE 19714-8139

ADD READING TO RELAXATION
★★★

Don't you wish you, like your kids, had the whole summer vacation to catch up on your reading? How come, you wonder, kids don't take advantage of it? In fact, it's easy to motivate them to add reading to their fun activities, and this free foldout has some very good ideas for relating a child's everyday activities and interests to books. For instance, let a younger child help you plan family outings, and give him or her a chance to read the maps, tour guides, and menus. Or have your child help you cook—it takes reading skills to follow a recipe. Available in English or French.

Write for:
Summer Reading Is Important (specify English or French)

Cost: Free with a long SASE

Send to:
International Reading Association
800 Barksdale Rd.
P.O. Box 8139
Newark, DE 19714-8139

Summer Reading Is Important

CREAM OF THE CROP
★★★★

Read up on what your kids should be reading in *Parent's Choice*, a fascinating guide for parents, librarians, and teachers to the best books, television programs, movies, music, story records, toys, computer programs, and home videos for children. For $1.50, the Parents' Choice Foundation will send you a sample issue of this 20-page tabloid, which welcomes suggestions from parents about books and so on that are worth review. The articles and reviews are intelligent and thoughtful. One reviewer, for instance, notes the absence of positive feminine models in the rock opera *Tommy* by The Who. Another notes that poets who write for children need "the eye of a hawk and the ear of a dolphin."

Write for:
Sample copy of Parent's Choice

Cost: $1.50

Send to:
Parent's Choice Foundation
Box 185
Waban, MA 02168

A CHANCE FOR EVERY CHILD
★★★★

This booklet discusses a way in which Aid to Families With Dependent Children and social security payments to children would be abolished in favor of a children's allowance—a specified payment for each child in a family, regardless of the family's income.

A SASE is a self-addressed stamped envelope.

The system is used in 62 countries all over the world; no country ever abandoned the allowance once it began. The pros and cons of children's allowances are listed on a chart. An interesting idea, especially in light of the current economic climate.

Write for:
A Chance for Every Child—the Case for Children's Allowances (No. 444)

Cost: $1.00

Send to:
Public Affairs Pamphlets
381 Park Ave. South
New York, NY 10016

HANGING IT UP

★★★★

One of the minor frustrations of being a parent of a small child is organizing his or her wardrobe. Those tiny clothes just don't fit on standard-sized hangers. Sometimes they have to be pinned on or clipped on, and still the little dresses and shirts fall off. Child-sized hangers will do the trick, quickly and easily. This offer is for 12 hangers, each eight inches wide. The hooks are big enough to hang on a regular closet rod. These mini-hangers have clip-tabs to hang skirts and pants, and shoulder grooves to hook straps. You'll receive a random assortment of a dozen colorful plastic hangers—just the right size.

Write for:
Hangers

Cost: $1.00

Send to:
Needlepoint Outlet
Box 11-H
Garnerville, NY 10923

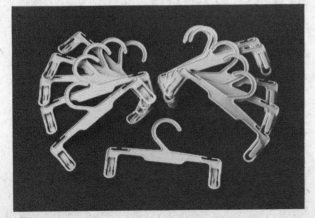

Hangers

SELF-HELP CLOTHING

★★★

Parents of children with physical disabilities will be glad to learn there is a new booklet with help on buying clothing or altering or making new clothing for such children and teenagers. The 64-page booklet starts with suggestions for how to cope with a child's physical disability and how to help the child. It goes on to focus on clothing and discusses such things as sizes, fabric, wearability, and special needs in everything from underwear to footwear to school clothing. A concluding section offers helpful guides to use in teaching dressing skills to disabled children.

Write for:
Self-Help Clothing

Cost: $2.00

Send to:
National Easter Seal Society
2023 Ogden Ave.
Chicago, IL 60612

Self-Help Clothing

THE "ASKABLE" PARENT

★★★★

As pregnancy among school-age children reaches crisis proportions, concerned parents are looking for more effective ways to help kids understand the realities of sex. *Sex Education: The Parents' Role* is a no-nonsense, practical 28-page booklet designed, as the title suggests, to help parents provide sound guidance for their children in the sensitive area of sex. If you're a parent, you'll spend a dollar wisely on this publication. You'll find a list of some of the questions most frequently asked by preschoolers, preteens, and teenagers concerning their bodies and their sexuality. There are also excellent suggestions to help you become an "askable" parent—or to take advantage of "teachable moments" if your child

continued

PARENTS

doesn't ask questions. The final message is clear: It's the parents' responsibility to provide adequate sex education in view of the ample evidence that what children don't know *can* hurt them.

Write for:
Sex Education: The Parents' Role (No. 549)

Cost: $1.00

Send to:
Public Affairs Pamphlets
381 Park Ave. South
New York, NY 10016

DELICATE DISCUSSIONS
★★★★

If you're the parent of a preteen—the nine to 13 age group—you'll appreciate the information and the authoritative suggestions contained in *Talking to Preteenagers About Sex*. You'll get an insight into the emotional changes that accompany your child's physical changes, as well as what kids want to know but may not tell you they want to know about menstruation, sexual relations, pregnancy, birth, and heredity. There's also a useful list of books and pamphlets (some written for parents, some for kids) and a brief look at the role the school ought to play in sex education.

Write for:
Talking to Preteenagers About Sex (No. 476)

Cost: $1.00

Send to:
Public Affairs Pamphlets
381 Park Ave. South
New York, NY 10016

You and Your Teenager

GROWING PAINS
★★★★

Questioning authority, testing the rules, and experimenting with adult behaviors are all a natural part of adolescent growth. Youngsters want freedom, yet freedom is frightening. There are new feelings to contend with and decisions to be made. Making responsible decisions is a skill that is best learned with the help of someone more experienced. Shared

decision making begins with good communication between parent and child. It is the objective of this 20-page, color-illustrated booklet to help family members better understand each other, talk more easily and effectively to each other, and make more responsible decisions that are more agreeable to both parent and child. *Helping Youth Decide* is divided into three parts. Part I discusses what's involved for you and your child during the adolescent years. Part II suggests methods to develop more open lines of communication with your teenagers and ways to guide them in decision making. Part III includes materials designed to help you implement the ideas presented previously—homework for both you and your child.

Write for:
Helping Youth Decide

Cost: Free

Send to:
National Association of State Boards of Education
P.O. Box 1176
Alexandria, VA 22313

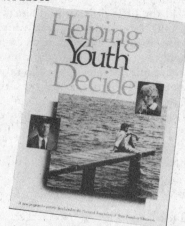

Helping Youth Decide

ROOM TO GROW
★★★★

Negotiating the adolescent years can be a trying business for teenagers and parents alike. But teenagers need room to grow, and finding ways to give everyone the necessary elbow room is one of the topics covered in *Parents and Teenagers*. This pamphlet gives a good account of how the changes a youngster experiences in adolescence result in behavior that is sometimes hard for parents to accept or understand. Knowing the meaning behind the moods, the stubbornness, and the self-assertion of the teen years can help parents open up ways to enhance, rather than frustrate, a teenage child's quest for self. If there's a teenager in the family, maybe you should have this little book in the family too. It's written for parents, but teens will find it good reading as well.

Write for:
Parents and Teenagers (No. 490)

Cost: $1.00

Send to:
Public Affairs Pamphlets
381 Park Ave. South
New York, NY 10016

BETWEEN GENERATIONS
★★★★

It's the old story: Teens think their parents don't understand; parents feel they can't get through to their teens. *Parent-Teenager Communication: Bridging the Communication Gap* insists that it's not so difficult to open up the lines of communication. This is an excellent guide, with commonsense advice for parents about respecting a child's need for individuality and a fine section on learning to listen. Because parent-child conflicts erupt so frequently over sex, money, and religion, these issues get special treatment. Ask your teen to take the self-test; it will let you know how he or she views your level of communication. An excellent publication for $1.00, and definitely one you and your teenage son or daughter can work with together.

Write for:
Parent-Teenager Communication: Bridging
the Generation Gap (No. 438)

Cost: $1.00

Send to:
Public Affairs Pamphlets
381 Park Ave. South
New York, NY 10016

KEEPING THE KIDS OFF DRUGS
★★★★

A recent University of Michigan study of seniors in 130 high schools across the country showed that six or seven out of every 10 students reported some form of illicit drug use. This booklet is an excellent attempt to arm parents with knowledge, both about why youngsters use drugs and about the drugs they use. A glossary explains each drug, how it's used, and what it does. There's also information about drug paraphernalia, signs that warn of drug use, treatments available to addicts, and advice on what

parents can do in the community to help combat the drug problem. In addition, good hints on where to go for help. There's lots of good reading in these 28 small pages.

Write for:
Children and Drugs (No. 584)

Cost: $1.00

Send to:
Public Affairs Pamphlets
381 Park Ave. South
New York, NY 10016

DRUGS—USE, MISUSE, ABUSE
★★★★

This is one of several excellent booklets on drugs put out by the Public Affairs Committee. This one is a 28-page publication that addresses the subject in general terms and concentrates on how to build the kind of family life that discourages drug use. In fact, there's a very good list of suggestions from teens on how parents can help their children stay away from the drug scene. There's specific information on right and wrong ways to educate your children about drugs, and points to remember when dealing with a drug-dependent person are presented. A family decision sheet on drugs will help you decide if using any drug—medical or nonmedical—is valid. This is a levelheaded resource for the whole family.

Write for:
Drugs—Use, Misuse, Abuse (No. 515A)

Cost: $1.00

Send to:
Public Affairs Pamphlets
381 Park Ave. South
New York, NY 10016

TALK IT OUT
★★★★

Growing up—a time of searching, questioning, and discovering. Perhaps there is no area more intensely personal to a youngster than developing and understanding his or her own sexuality. Yet the information gleaned by most children is subject to distortion and ignorance. *How to Talk to Your Teenagers About the Facts of Life* will help you deal intelligently with this sensitive, important issue. A recent nationwide study showed that more than five in ten young people aged 15 to 19 reported sexual activity, but only a third of them had always used contraception. The

continued

PARENTS

excellent, clearly written 24-page booklet tells you the intimate concerns of various children's age groups and will help you talk comfortably about these matters. In a question and answer format, it covers common inquiries, including male and female reproductive systems, childbirth, and birth control. Contraceptive techniques that don't work are listed, and venereal disease, abortion, and "normalcy" are also covered.

Write for:
How to Talk to Your Teenagers About the Facts of Life

Cost: 50¢

Send to:
Planned Parenthood Federation of America, Inc.
810 Seventh Avenue
New York, NY 10019

How to Talk to Your Teenagers About the Facts of Life

HEALTH CARE FOR THE ADOLESCENT
★★★★

Think of this: The growth spurt of adolescence is the second most rapid in life—second only to that of the first year. Yet most pediatricians usually stop treating their patients at age 12 or 13. This 28-page booklet focuses on a new specialty among some farsighted physicians: adolescent medicine. It discusses the physiological changes of the teen years—health problems like acne; infections; bone and joint complaints; menstruation and sexuality; and emotional turmoil. There's information on some of the centers in the country that maintain special adolescent units and a good reading list for further study on the subject. An intelligent guide for parents.

Write for:
Health Care for the Adolescent (No. 463)

Cost: $1.00

Send to:
Public Affairs Pamphlets
381 Park Ave. South
New York, NY 10016

TEENS WITH SPECIAL NEEDS
★★★★

Almost by definition all teenagers have inner conflicts and emotional problems; handicapped teenagers, however, may have special difficulty coming to terms with growing up. *Helping the Handicapped Teenager Mature* is a 28-page booklet from the Public Affairs Committee designed to help parents or teachers guide handicapped teens toward self-acceptance, independence, and confidence. There are sympathetic but clear-headed sections on the steps a handicapped teenager must take toward adulthood, and discussions of common sex problems, special schooling, learning problems, and job possibilities. A straightforward look at an important subject that can catch parents of handicapped children off guard.

Write for:
Helping the Handicapped Teenager Mature
(No. 504)

Cost: $1.00

Send to:
Public Affairs Pamphlets
381 Park Ave. South
New York, NY 10016

NOT MY CHILD
★★★

In most countries throughout the world, suicide in adolescence has doubled over the past ten years and now ranks between second and third among the leading causes of death during the teenage to young adult years. Today we recognize that young people live under a great variety of pressures, including the stresses that result from the phenomena of adolescence, from the high expectancies of early adulthood, and from those strains of competition and achievement that are unique in young people. A factual 12-page booklet, *Suicide in Young People,* explains why adolescents are committing suicide, characteristics to look for in determining a potential suicide victim, and what to do to prevent the crisis. The booklet includes a selected bibliography for further reading.

Write for:
Suicide in Young People

Cost: 50¢

A SASE is a self-addressed stamped envelope.

Send to:
North Wales Press, Inc.
P.O. Box 1486
North Wales, PA 19454

Suicide in Young People

THE BOOK OF THE MOVIE
★★★

Thousands of American teenagers are below-average readers. If your teenager is one of them, this booklet is for you. It suggests that you can help break through the block by giving your youngster books from which popular movies have been made. Since the youngster already knows the plot, reading difficulties are minimized and pleasure in the story enhanced. This little publication also reminds you that parents who read are the best advertisement for books, but that you can also help a child who has "no time to read" by being sure your youngster's schedule of schoolwork, social activities, and household chores leaves him or her with some quiet time when settling down with a book would be a neat thing to do.

Write for:
How Can I Get My Teenager To Read?

Cost: 50¢

Send to:
International Reading Association
800 Barksdale Rd.
P.O. Box 8139
Newark, DE 19711-8139

Playing With Your Child

HOW TO GROW GRASS HAIR
★★★

Whether you're running a preschool group or entertaining your own tots at home, *Totline* will give you lots of fresh ideas for working with young children. It's a 24-page newsletter, published bimonthly, that provides activity ideas, a feature article, a short story, art ideas, language games, musical lyrics, snack ideas, and a list of resources for parents and preschool teachers. Find out about engrossing activities like growing grass hair in a styrofoam cup with a face painted on it, making rain paintings, and making a kite from a plastic garbage bag. You can get a sample newsletter for $1.00.

Write for:
Totline Newsletter

Cost: $1.00 for newsletter

Send to:
Warren Publishing House, Inc.
P.O. Box 2255
Everett, WA 98203

Totline Newsletter

SHAPING CREATIVITY
★★

This is the shape of things to come. A small plastic bag contains flat pieces of colorful paper and cardboard, precut into interesting shapes and designs. The whole bag goes under the name of "Good Stuff," and the idea is that the shapes stimulate the imagination. They may be used in art projects, games, and other activities, or to teach children counting and sorting. The shapes are all cut from recycled materi-

continued

als; you can probably supplement the kit, or even make your own, by cutting up leftover paper (from magazines, shopping bags, shoe boxes, greeting cards, gift wrap) you have at home. A small ideas sheet comes in the 4'' × 6'' package. Two more comprehensive activity sheets are available, but they cost another 50¢. It's a cute idea by the Neighborhood Workshop.

Write for:
Good Stuff Kit
Good Stuff Extra Activities Sheets

Cost: $1.00 plus a long SASE for Good Stuff Kit
50¢ plus a long SASE (same one is fine if ordering both) for Extra Activities Sheets

Send to:
The Neighborhood Workshop
P.O. Box 15
Wynnewood, PA 19096

Good Stuff Kit

A SHARED PLEASURE
★★★

If somebody in the family read to you often as a child, chances are you're a book lover to this day. You can do the same for your children by making reading a family activity. *Why Read Aloud to Children* suggests ways to transform reading from a private to a shared activity and points out that storytelling is one of the most pleasurable reading-related activities of all. For example, Dad can tell about some unusual sign he noticed on the way home; children can dramatize something they studied in school. And by reading to very young children, you're teaching them what reading is all about: that a book should be held in a certain way, that the reader's eyes move back and forth, that the story proceeds from line to line, and that signals on the page tell the reader when to start, pause, and stop.

Write for:
Why Read Aloud to Children?

Cost: 50¢

Send to:
International Reading Association
800 Barksdale Rd.
P.O. Box 8139
Newark, DE 19714-8139

PONY BASEBALL FOR KIDS
★★★★

If you think the neighborhood kids need something more than sandlot baseball or softball in the streets, why not organize a Pony Baseball League? *The Blue Book of Pony Baseball* will tell you how. Pony Baseball, Inc. is a nonprofit corporation in charge of all the leagues for different age groups from Pinto (ages 7 and 8) all the way up to Thorobred (ages 19 to 21). This book is a special free offer to *Free Things* readers—it usually costs $4.00. It's complete with photos, poems, and inspirational sayings and stories, and gives all the official information on membership, playing schedules, costs, organizing a league, managing, coaching, fund raising, and more. The group's constitution and bylaws are spelled out, and diagrams of the playing fields for each age group are included.

Write for:
Blue Book of Pony Baseball

Cost: Free

Send to:
Pony Baseball Headquarters
Box 225
Washington, PA 15301

RULES OF LITTLE LEAGUE, A-Z
★★★★

Here, in 65 pages of information, is all you need to know about Little League baseball, including the official regulations and playing rules. You'll also find information about Little League, its structure, purpose, federal charter, and administration. The 65 pages tell what qualifications a team must have in order to become chartered in the Little League; age bracket, eligibility, tryouts, and selection of potential players; and what leagues youngsters who graduate from Little League may enter. You'll also learn about the role of adults in this league and how you can become a volunteer. The Little League Safety Code is here, too.

Write for:
Little League Baseball Official Regulations

Cost: $1.25

Send to:
H & B Promotions
P.O. Box 18177
Dept. ND
Louisville, KY 40218

Little League Baseball Official Regulations

How to Teach a Youngster to Water Ski

WATER SKIING FOR SMALL FRY

★★★★

Here's how to turn your youngster into a real water baby. It's a booklet from the American Water Ski Association that tells how to teach a youngster to water ski. You'll learn how to select the proper site and equipment, what your attitude as instructor should be, and how to ensure the safe, careful driving of the tow boat. You'll discover the right size skis for kids as small as three or four years old and what older kids over 10 should wear. The booklet describes how you begin with dry-land instruction and then transfer the maneuvers to water (your first lesson should not be too long or try to cover too much, but it will cover getting up and stopping). Special tips, too, for teaching a student who fears the water or who is a bit uncoordinated.

Write for:
How To Teach a Youngster To Water Ski

Cost: 45¢

Send to:
American Water Ski Association
P.O. Box 191
Winter Haven, FL 33880

AN ATVENTURE IN SAFETY

★★★★

Riding an ATV (All-Terrain Vehicle) is lots of fun, but remember ATV's are not toys. Just as bicycles handle differently than automobiles or motorcycles, ATV's handle differently, too. Your youngster's safety will depend on your commitment to taking a "Safety First" attitude, and that's what this booklet is about. *Parents, Youngsters and ATV's* is a good education in proper riding techniques, starting with proper protective riding gear. The 40-page illustrated booklet discusses learning areas, exercises to help in mastering the controls, and getting used to the vehicle in motion. There is a pre-ride safety checklist, and a guide to help the parent to determine the child's readiness. There are also games and puzzles to aid in learning about ATV safety, parts, and controls.

Write for:
Parents, Youngsters, and ATV's

Cost: Free

Send to:
Specialty Vehicle Institute of America
Public Affairs
3151 Airway Avenue
Building K-107
Costa Mesa, CA 92626

Parents, Youngsters, and ATV's

PARENTS

Helping Your Child Learn

YOUR CHILD'S FIRST SCHOOL
★★★

Parents are their children's first teachers. Since the first five years of your child's life are probably spent at home—a time when he or she learns more than during any other span of life—you can be considered the most important teacher your child will ever have. In this pamphlet, *Your Home Is Your Child's First School*, parents learn how they can have a positive influence on their children's educational future. Activities are suggested for aiding in the development of physical, intellectual, and communication skills, and for encouraging reading readiness. You'll learn how almost anything in the child's day-to-day environment can be used to broaden horizons and stimulate learning. There is also reassurance for parents whose children do not mature as quickly as their playmates. The pamphlet is also available in French and Spanish.

Write for:
    Your Home Is Your Child's First School
    (specify English, French, or Spanish)

Cost: Free with a long SASE

Send to:
    International Reading Association
    800 Barksdale Rd.
    P.O. Box 8139
    Newark, DE 19714-8139

Your Home Is Your Child's First School

DEVELOPING A CHILD'S CREATIVITY
★★★

A set of books designed to help children in grades one through five learn how to use their minds more creatively is offered by a company called 120 Creative Corner. Three "Fun Books" cover basic creative living and thinking skills, for $5 or $6 each. You can send for a less expensive introduction to the series, an 8-page booklet called *Developing Creative Thinking With Your Child*. It describes specific thinking skills, followed by an activity that helps the child practice that skill. The child is invited to find other opportunities to use each of the skills presented. The exercises are presented in a simple style, but they may interest parents or teachers.

Write for:
    Developing Creative Thinking With Your Child

Cost: $1.50

Send to:
    120 Creative Corner
    4175 Lovell Rd.
    Suite 140, Box 18
    Circle Pines, MN 55014

Developing Creative Thinking With Your Child

LEARNING WHILE PLAYING
★★

The home is a child's first school and a parent is the child's first teacher. There is much a parent can do to prepare a child for formalized education and to strengthen the skills he will need in the classroom. This booklet suggests games to help develop and improve the perceptual skills of the preschooler. Each game falls into a specific category, or learning area. There are games designed to build auditory skills, visual skills, touch-awareness skills, and articulation skills. The 8-page

A SASE is a self-addressed stamped envelope.

booklet also contains formulas, or recipes, for concocting further fun—play dough, soap bubbles, colored bath water. The author reminds the reader that the major occupation of pre-schoolers is play, and much can be accomplished when learning can be effectively combined with playing.

Write for:
Games to Improve Perceptual Skills of Pre-Schoolers (No. 2049)

Cost: $1.00

Send to:
Interstate Printers & Publishers, Inc.
19 N. Jackson St.
P.O. Box 50
Danville, IL 61834-0050

SUSIE DOESN'T TALK YET
★★★

Delayed speech is a serious problem for the child who has difficulty in communicating and for the family who tries to understand. Speech is, after all, the most important avenue to social adjustment. A child who cannot express himself is often a lonely, frustrated, and sometimes resentful child. If your child is having difficulties with oral communication, these two great booklets are for your family to read. The first, *For Parents of a Child Whose Speech is Delayed*, traces speech patterns and the possible causes of delayed speech, from home conflict to hearing loss. It also gives many helpful suggestions for helping babies learn to talk and for assisting the child whose speech is delayed to talk. *Enrich Your Child's Speech and Language Development* is good companion reading, filled with activities to develop the child's auditory, visual, and tactile reception; auditory-vocal and visual-motor associations; memory and more.

Write for:
For Parents of a Child Whose Speech is Delayed (No. 2137)
Enrich Your Child's Speech and Language Development (No. 1726)

Cost: 75¢ for For Parents of a Child Whose Speech is Delayed
$1.00 for Enrich Your Child's Speech and Language Development

Send to:
Interstate Printers & Publishers, Inc.
19 N. Jackson St.
P.O. Box 50
Danville, IL 61834-0050

SMART KIDS
★★★

Your child's education never stops—and it should *start* as soon as possible. Parents who wish to give their children an educational advantage are confronted with a wealth of options that include everything from preschools to the right sorts of toys. How do you sort it all? The National Association for the Education of Young Children (NAEYC) offers a series of informative brochures that will answer many of your questions and put your options into perspective. Topics include how to plan and start a good early childhood educational program, how to choose an existing program, and career opportunities in early childhood education. Other subjects include reading and appropriate toys. The brochures are brief but informative and written in clear, straightforward language. They're a good place to begin your child's educational program.

Write for:
Beginner's Bibliography
Business Incentives for Providing Child Care as a Benefit to Employees: Sources for Further Information
Careers in Early Childhood Information
Choosing Good Toys for Young Children
Helping Children Learn About Reading
How to Choose a Good Early Childhood Program (also available in Spanish)
How to Plan and Start a Good Early Childhood Program
What Are the Benefits of Quality Child Care for Preschool Children?

Cost: Each free with a SASE

Send to:
National Association for the Education of Young Children
1834 Connecticut Ave., N.W.
Washington, DC 20009

HELP YOUR CHILD TO BETTER SPEECH
★★★★

You may not look on speech as a skill that you can teach your children—like using the toilet, dressing and feeding themselves, or putting toys away. But parents can and should help their children speak correctly. This 28-page booklet tells how to teach speech sounds, build larger vocabularies, and teach a child self-correction. It briefly covers the causes of some speech problems, explains what a speech

continued

---

therapist does (and where to find qualified ones), and sums up the parents' responsibilities in such therapy. A sound and sensible little publication.

Write for:
Helping Your Child Speak Correctly (No. 445)

Cost: $1.00

Send to:
Public Affairs Pamphlets
381 Park Ave. South
New York, NY 10016

SPEECH LORE
★★★★

Speech Chief is a therapy workbook that can be used to correct or strengthen the production of any articulation sound of the elementary school child. Cleverly illustrated with cartoon-style Indians and Indian artifacts, the 62-page booklet is comprised of speech therapy assignments that allow you to include words from textbooks the child is using. The exercises give children practice in correctly pronouncing their problem sound in isolation, syllables, words, sentences, and conversational assignments. The exercises can be done as part of the speech lesson or as homework. This is a very useful tool for developing your child's communication skills, and its fun approach will make speech lessons more enjoyable for everyone involved—children, parents, and teachers.

Write for:
Speech Chief (No. 2108)

Cost: $2.00

Send to:
Interstate Printers & Publishers, Inc.
19 N. Jackson St.
P.O. Box 50
Danville, IL 61834-0050

Speech Chief

HELPING THE CHILD WHO STUTTERS
★★★★

Speech handicaps can be most demoralizing, especially for children. *If Your Child Stutters* is an authoritative and understandable guide for parents of three- to six-year-old children. This excellent handbook describes eight signs that give warning that a child may become a stutterer—since the problem can be prevented if action is taken early enough, this is vital information. If you're the parent of a child who stutters, you'll welcome the section on how you can help your child. You'll learn to listen with "all ears" and to talk *with* your child rather than *at* him. You'll also learn to find ways to avoid frustration and negative feelings and to make speech experiences rewarding for the child. A most helpful publication from the Speech Foundation of America.

Write for:
If Your Child Stutters: A Guide for Parents

Cost: $2.00

Send to:
Speech Foundation of America
P.O. Box 11749
Memphis, TN 38111

"GOOD" AND "BAD": WHAT DO THEY MEAN?
★★

How much can children learn in the classroom about morals, values, and ethics? A lot, according to the man who wrote this single-sheet essay—but only if there's a distinction made between the teaching of values and indoctrination, and only if children understand ethical language. *A Way of Teaching Values in the Schools,* written by Warren Shibles, sets forth this philosophy professor's thoughts on current misuse of ethical language, especially the terms "good" and "bad," both of which, as he points out, can have any number of meanings.

Write for:
A Way of Teaching Values in the Schools

Cost: Free with a long SASE

Send to:
The Language Press
Box 342
Whitewater, WI 53190

A SASE is a self-addressed stamped envelope.

HOW A CHILD LEARNS TO STUDY

★★★

You can send your child to the best school in the neighborhood, but it will be a total waste of time if the child won't study. This free foldout reminds parents that the study habit doesn't come naturally to most people but that there are ways they can encourage its development in children. You can encourage the study habit even before your child starts school, just by setting aside a daily quiet time for activities like drawing, painting, coloring and reading books together. For a school-age child, this quiet time becomes study time, and you can make sure that the supplies needed for homework are on hand. Lots of sensible, practical suggestions here for any parent.

Write for:
Studying: A Key to Success . . . Ways Parents Can Help

Cost: Free with a long SASE

Send to:
International Reading Association
800 Barksdale Rd.
P.O. Box 8139
Newark, DE 19714-8139

Studying: A Key to Success . . . Ways Parents Can Help

CROPS IN THE CLASSROOM

★★★★

This teaching guide is designed to bring the green world into the classroom, with numerous activities and explorations. Whether your school project is small plants growing on a window sill or cultivating an outdoor garden, children attain the joys of gardening. The 54-page *A Child's Garden* describes the transformation of a California elementary school's asphalt playground into an ecological learning center. There are botanically oriented projects which coordinate with art, social studies, science classes, songs, and worksheets. Simple experiments demonstrate scientific principles. Parents and teachers will also find good information to share with children on plant propagation, soil enrichment, and cultivation. A planting chart and chapter on how to grow popular vegetables are special helps. There's even a resource list for additional information in the back of the book.

Write for:
A Child's Garden

Cost: 50¢; free to teachers

Send to:
Chevron Chemical Company
Educational Materials
Public Affairs Department
P.O. Box 7144
San Francisco, CA 94120-7144

A Child's Garden

TEACHING CHILDREN ABOUT MONEY

★★★★

Should you pay your child for doing chores? Should you expect a youngster to do chores in exchange for an allowance? This realistic, practical, 25-page booklet covers these and other prickly questions parents face in teaching children about money. Among the subjects under discussion: allowance guidelines for all ages and incomes, when and how to review allowances, teaching your child how to save *and* spend, borrowing, and what parents can reasonably expect from working teenagers. An excellent, sensible aid to parenting.

Write for:
Teaching Children About Money (No. 593)

Cost: $1.00

continued

PARENTS

Send to:
Public Affairs Pamphlets
381 Park Ave. South
New York, NY 10016

MOMMY—HOW DO CHECKS BOUNCE?

★★★★

This is a godsend for any parent whose children are convinced that money grows in a checkbook. *Children and Money Management* is 28 pages of solid common sense, addressed to parents and concerned with teaching children the value of a dollar. This illustrated guide offers sound advice on setting limits, making rules, being honest about money matters, and generally guiding kids in such basics as handling allowances and cash gifts, attending family finance sessions (much encouraged), shopping, saving, being paid for work both inside and outside the home, and, for older children, checking accounts, credit, employment—even stock ownership.

Especially helpful is a good section on common money problems that have probably kept many a parent awake nights. What if a child steals? What if a child hoards (or loses) money? What if you can't afford to meet your children's extra expenses?

Write for:
Children and Money Management

Cost: $1.00

Send to:
Money Management Institute
Household International
2700 Sanders Rd.
Prospect Heights, IL 60070

Children and Money Management

HEADLINERS

★★★

Teachers have known for years to use the daily newspaper to develop communication skills and enrich the reading of children. As a parent, you, too, can help your child increase his or her levels of accomplishment and enjoyment. Newspapers are a good tool because they broaden the variety of material a child reads and help children become aware of the daily events happening around them. This pamphlet gives parents good ideas for getting involved. It suggests discussion questions to prompt your child's interest in newspapers, and lists child-parent activities. One such project might be asking your child to clip food coupons for the family's grocery shopping. Another is to ask your child to read aloud to you. Reading becomes a family affair. The pamphlet is also available in French.

Write for:
You Can Help Your Child in Reading by Using the Newspaper (specify English or French)

Cost: Free with a long SASE

Send to:
International Reading Association
800 Barksdale Rd.
P.O. Box 8139
Newark, DE 19714-8139

You Can Help Your Child in Reading by Using the Newspaper

CREATE A READING ATMOSPHERE

★★★

As you read nursery rhymes to your children, engage them in conversation—even when they're infants. Talk about what's going on during everyday activities like shopping or watching TV. By doing so, you're helping your child build positive attitudes toward reading. These and other excellent suggestions are to be found in these two booklets. They're

A SASE is a self-addressed stamped envelope.

written especially for parents and tell how to teach children through make-believe, how to develop a family reading time, and how to increase your enjoyment of reading.

Write for:
How Can I Help My Child Build Positive Attitudes Toward Reading?
How Can I Encourage My Primary-Grade Child to Read?

Cost: 50¢ for each title

Send to:
International Reading Association
800 Barksdale Rd.
P.O. Box 8139
Newark, DE 19714-8139

READING READINESS EXPLAINED

★★★

The growing number of kids who can't read is a matter of grave concern to parents and teachers, and "reading readiness" is a term you hear a lot when educators get together. What does it mean? It's a term coined in the past 40 years to indicate the age at which a child will find success, rather than anxiety and frustration, in his or her efforts to read. This booklet explains the factors involved—from a child's mental and emotional development to the physical skills necessary for the complex task of reading. You can use the information gathered here to evaluate your own child's reading readiness. There's also information on problems with motor control, hearing, vision, or learning disabilities that may delay reading skills.

Write for:
What Is Reading Readiness?

Cost: 50¢

Send to:
International Reading Association
800 Barksdale Rd.
P.O. Box 8139
Newark, DE 19714-8139

HOOKED ON BOOKS

★★★

Early, enjoyable experiences with books are powerful proof to young children that it's worth the time and effort it takes to learn to read. Here's an eight-page foldout from the International Reading Associ-

ation written for parents of young children, and it's full of tips and suggestions to help you get your little ones hooked on books. Listening to the rhythm of nursery rhymes prepares a child to delight in poetry, for instance. And when your child graduates to picture books, ask him questions about what's going on in the pictures—you'll be helping him learn to listen to and appreciate a story. Available in English or French.

Write for:
Good Books Make Reading Fun for Your Child (specify English or French)

Cost: Free with a long SASE

Send to:
International Reading Association
800 Barksdale Rd.
P.O. Box 8139
Newark, DE 19714-8139

Good Books Make Reading Fun For Your Child

SPEAKING TWO LANGUAGES

★★★

A child who speaks one language in school and another at home can have a hard time dealing with the two cultures every day. But there's a bright side, too, because being bilingual expands a child's horizons and opens up new job possibilities later on. This valuable pamphlet, available in both Spanish and English, suggests many ways for helping develop a bilingual child's vocabulary, interest in reading, and verbal confidence. Even if you always speak to your child in your native tongue, you'll find that what a child understands in one language, he will transfer to another.

Write for:
How Can I Help My Child Learn To Read English As a Second Language? (specify English or Spanish)

continued

PARENTS

Cost: 50¢

Send to:
International Reading Association
800 Barksdale Rd.
P.O. Box 8139
Newark, DE 19714-8139

SOCIAL STUDIES BOOKS FOR CHILDREN

★★★★

The books selected for this bibliography were chosen with five criteria in mind: They are written for children in grades K through 8; they emphasize human relations; they present an original theme or a fresh slant on a traditional topic; they're highly readable; when appropriate, they include maps or illustrations. Reading levels are indicated (primary, intermediate, and advanced) and some of the categories are: American heritage, native Americans, world history, biography and autobiography, other places and cultures, legends, traditions and religions, and contemporary concerns. A good reference if you're interested in having your youngsters read intelligent stuff instead of junk.

Write for:
Notable Children's Trade Books in the Field of Social Studies

Cost: Free with a long SASE (three 22¢ stamps)

Send to:
The Children's Book Council
67 Irving Place
New York, NY 10003

SEX ED—AT HOME OR AT SCHOOL?

★★★★

Where should kids learn about sex—at home or at school? The title of this publication succinctly expresses its philosophy: *Schools and Parents— Partners in Sex Education*. This well-written 28-page booklet is for parents who want to improve the quality of sex education in their children's schools. It briefly summarizes current trends in sex education and then presents a comprehensive discussion of the topics that should be included in a good sex education program. It even lays out model curricula for students in the early grades (K-3), middle grades (4-6), junior high (7-9), and senior high school. There are also useful hints on how parents can best support a sex education program and how they can

evaluate the personal qualities that make for a good teacher of sex education—an ability to be "cool" is essential and so is a sense of humor.

Write for:
Schools and Parents—Partners in Sex Education (No. 581)

Cost: $1.00

Send to:
Public Affairs Pamphlets
381 Park Ave. South
New York, NY 10016

HELPING THE SLOW LEARNER

★★★★

One out of every six children in America is a slow learner—a child whose measured intelligence is about 75 to 90 percent of the average child's. This excellent booklet distinguishes between true slow learners and pseudo slow learners who may be either retarded or "late bloomers." It tells how parents and teachers can recognize, identify, understand, and work with the slow learning child. Tips for parents concentrate on accepting the situation, then building success experiences, fostering self-confidence and independence, and working continually with the school.

Write for:
Helping the Slow Learner (No. 405)

Cost: $1.00

Send to:
Public Affairs Pamphlets
381 Park Ave. South
New York, NY 10016

HOPE AND HELP FOR LEARNING PROBLEMS

★★★★

An estimated 7.5 million American children are affected by learning disabilities. If your child is one of them, you'll find some hopeful and helpful information in *Learning Disabilities: Problems and Progress*. This 28-page booklet explains some of the causes of learning disabilities, and discusses prevention and treatment of these conditions that formerly doomed many children to be inaccurately labeled "slow learners" or "behavior problems."

Parents are alerted to the early warning signals that may indicate possible learning problems and

228

A SASE is a self-addressed stamped envelope.

are made aware of the special tests administered by schools to help identify learning disabled children.

Write for:
Learning Disabilities: Problems and Progress (No. 578)

Cost: $1.00

Send to:
Public Affairs Pamphlets
381 Park Ave. South
New York, NY 10016

SPECIAL EDUCATION FOR THE RETARDED

★★★★

A great deal of progress has been made in the field of education for mentally retarded children. Today, the goals of both parents and educators are to help retarded children and adults develop their capabilities to the maximum so they can live as independently as possible. *Mental Retardation — A Changing World* defines mental retardation and explains some of the causes. The major part of the booklet covers what can be done to help retarded persons make the normal transitions into adulthood — to leave home and live apart from their parents, to hold jobs, and to manage their daily lives successfully. There's also a section on the legal rights of mentally retarded people. Twenty-eight sensible and compassionate pages, and worthwhile reading for parents of mentally handicapped youngsters or for anyone with an interest in the field.

Write for:
Mental Retardation — A Changing World (No. 577)

Cost: $1.00

Send to:
Public Affairs Pamphlets
381 Park Ave. South
New York, NY 10016

GOOD THINGS FOR THE GIFTED CHILD

★★★

Here's how to keep up with your bright kid. It's a packet of materials for parents from the National Association for Gifted Children. You'll find information on characteristics of the gifted child, ways parents can help the child, and books that will interest a particularly bright youngster. There's a bibliography

of background reading for parents, an article titled "What If Your Child Is Gifted?" and a rundown on what the gifted child needs from parents: acceptance, understanding, and time to talk and be listened to. Above all, advises the Association, permit time for thinking and daydreaming — just because a child isn't doing anything doesn't mean his mind isn't busy.

Write for:
Parent Packet

Cost: $2.00

Send to:
National Association for Gifted Children
4175 Lovell Rd. Suite 140
Circle Pines, MN 55014

RAISING A GIFTED CHILD

★★★★

This is an award-winning monthly with a prestigious editorial advisory board, and it's directed to the parents of gifted children. In it you'll find reviews of books that your gifted child will enjoy. There's challenging advice for parents on ways to deal with a gifted child, and news of parent groups all over the country. There's a buyer's guide — one recent issue discussed video games — and a regular four-page activity section aimed at the child. Plenty of good ideas and resources conveniently arranged.

Write for:
Sample copy of Gifted Children Monthly

Cost: $1.00

Send to:
Gifted Children Monthly
P.O. Box 115
Sewell, NJ 08080

Sample copy of Gifted Children Monthly

PARENTS

Keeping Your Child Healthy

JUST TO MAKE SURE
★★

Because of the miracle of vaccines, the risk of your child catching measles, rubella, and other diseases is a lot lower than it used to be. But too many children still suffer from these illnesses and the serious problems that sometimes go with them. Why? Because many children were never vaccinated. Two handy pamphlets tell all the whats, whys, and whens. *Because You Care* explains the dangers of and the differences between measles and rubella, and answers many commonly asked questions about these diseases. It discusses the recommended frequency and the possible side effects of the vaccines. This eight-page brochure is also available in Spanish. *Help Protect Your Baby* is an informative four-page pamphlet that covers seven of the most common childhood diseases. It tells you when to start your child's vaccination program and gives a useful immunization schedule as recommended by the American Academy of Pediatrics.

Write for:
  Because You Care
  Help Protect Your Baby

Cost: 50¢ each

Send to:
  North Wales Press, Inc.
  P.O. Box 1486
  North Wales, PA 19454

Help Protect Your Baby

HANDLING CHILDHOOD ILLNESS
★★★

If you're a parent, you recognize that sinking feeling you get when a child gets sick. This informative, sensible booklet should give you the knowledge and moral support to handle most childhood sickness. The 28 pages include a guide to when to call the doctor, advice on what to do about fever, a new evaluation of the words "bed rest," and some down-to-earth advice about *your* emotional reaction to your child's illness. You'll find remedies and advice for most common childhood ailments and special information about going to the hospital, accidents, and long-term illnesses. A reassuring reference to have on hand.

Write for:
  When Your Child Is Sick (No. 441A)

Cost: $1.00

Send to:
  Public Affairs Pamphlets
  381 Park Ave. South
  New York, NY 10016

A HEALTHY CURRICULUM
★★

The overall purpose of public education is to prepare students to live successful, fulfilling lives. Health instruction is a vital part of this total system, according to the American Medical Association's pamphlet *Why Health Education in Your School?* A well-planned school health instruction program can provide children with accurate information about growth and development, physical and mental fitness, safety and first aid, and sexuality and family life. The 10-page booklet describes qualifications of an effective program and the multiple benefits received by the schoolchild. It answers the questions about where health education fits into school curriculum and how health program goals have changed over the years.

Write for:
  Why Health Education in Your School?

Cost: $1.50

Send to:
  Order Department, OP-331
  American Medical Association
  P.O. Box 10946
  Chicago, IL 60610

A SASE is a self-addressed stamped envelope.

ALLERGIES EXAMINED
★★★

In this oversized (8½″ × 11″) illustrated booklet, a doctor talks to parents and kids about allergies—what they are, why some children have them, and how you can try to make your home and your child's room allergy-proof. The author talks, too, about food allergies and the foods that cause them and about allergic conditions like hay fever, asthma, hives, eczema, and certain insect bites. Good news—for children, anyway—is that even a child who's allergic to other animals can still have a lizard, a snake, or an alligator for a pet. There's a checklist for allergy-proofing your home, definitions of terms, and a list of books for further reading. This booklet is available in English or Spanish.

Write for:
    Sneezing, Wheezing, and Scratching
       (specify English or Spanish)

Cost: $1.99 (no cash or stamps)

Send to:
    The ECR Collection
    P.O. Box 615
    Los Altos, CA 94022

ENVIRONMENTAL HAZARDS TO CHILDREN
★★★★

Industrialized societies like ours produce increasing quantities of hazardous substances each year. These substances pose a risk to everyone, but children are especially vulnerable because their developing bodies are less resistant than those of adults. This excellent 29-page report describes the most common toxic materials in our atmosphere, food, and water, and what they can do to human beings. It also describes the physical effects of smoking, alcohol, food additives, and common household substances on children, and emphasizes the steps parents can take to spare children from these hazards. You'll find a good reading list, too, but this little book itself is must reading for concerned parents.

Write for:
    Environmental Hazards to Children (No. 600)

Cost: $1.00

Send to:
    Public Affairs Pamphlets
    381 Park Ave. South
    New York, NY 10016

WELL IN SIGHT
★★★★

It is estimated that one in every 20 preschool-age children in the U.S. has a vision problem. A child thinks everyone sees the way he does. If he doesn't see well, he probably won't complain. He doesn't know he has a vision problem. Two aids from the National Society to Prevent Blindness will assist the parent in watching for visual deficiencies in the child. The first, *Home Eye Test for Pre-Schoolers*, is a step-by-step chart with directions on giving the test. It is available in both English and Spanish. The second is a pamphlet on common eye problems, illustrated with Charlie Brown comic strips; after all, Sally suffered from amblyopia. The pamphlet also lists signals which may indicate possible vision trouble in your child.

Write for:
    Home Eye Test for Pre-Schoolers (specify English
       or Spanish)
    Charlie Brown Detective

Cost: Free with a long SASE

Send to:
    National Society to Prevent Blindness
    79 Madison Avenue
    New York, NY 10016-7896

Home Eye Test for Pre-Schoolers

Charlie Brown Detective

PARENTS

NOT FOR ADULTS ONLY
★★★

A cataract is a cloudy area inside the eye that interferes with vision. Cataracts generally are found in the elderly, but sometimes they are present in the newborn infant, or they may develop in young children. This booklet about childhood cataracts has been prepared in nonmedical terms to explain why the ophthamologist may recommend an operation as the best treatment for your infant or child. The illustrated 10-page pamphlet precisely defines cataracts and the effect they have on vision, discusses when surgery should take place, and what the operation entails. What to expect after the operation and during recovery is also covered.

Write for:
About Cataract Surgery in Infants and Children

Cost: Free

Send to:
American College of Surgeons
Office of Public Information
55 East Erie Street
Chicago, IL 60611-2797

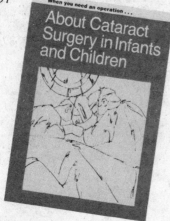

About Cataract Surgery in Infants and Children

DOES VISION AFFECT READING?
★★★

How well does your child see? This booklet reminds parents that a slight vision problem can easily go unnoticed by both parent and child, but that poor vision will definitely show up as a problem when a child starts reading. This thorough, illustrated booklet from the International Reading Association explains vision impairments, with photographs that simulate how scenes and objects appear to a child with astigmatism or crossed eyes. You'll also find a list of symptoms—like headaches, dizziness, sensitivity to light, sties, squinting, and frequent rubbing of the eyes—that can help you identify visual problems early.

Write for:
How Does My Child's Vision Affect His Reading?

Cost: 50¢

Send to:
International Reading Association
800 Barksdale Rd.
P.O. Box 8139
Newark, DE 19714-8139

CHILDREN'S HEARING PROBLEMS
★★★★

According to the Alexander Graham Bell Association for the Deaf, hearing loss is the most common handicap in the United States today, affecting an estimated 13 million adults and three million children. This useful publication is for parents of hearing-impaired (deaf or hard-of-hearing) children. There's advice on detecting a hearing problem, hearing aids, creating a "hearing environment" by making the child more aware of sounds and speech, and more. Also available is a card that asks *Doctor, Is My Baby Deaf?* It lists danger signs to look for at various ages and steps to take if a hearing problem is suspected. The association points out that no child is too young to be tested, and that it's never too early to consult a doctor about a hearing problem.

Write for:
Listen! Hear! For Parents of Hearing-Impaired Children
Doctor, Is My Baby Deaf? (specify English or Spanish)

Cost: Free with a long SASE

Send to:
Alexander Graham Bell Association for the Deaf, Inc.
3417 Volta Place, N.W.
Washington, DC 20007

THE ROAD TO CLEAR COMMUNICATION
★★★

The ability to communicate is our most human characteristic, and one that is essential to learning, working, and social interaction. Impaired communication can affect every aspect of a person's life. Because communication disorders and skills become

A SASE is a self-addressed stamped envelope.

apparent very early in a child's development, the parents are usually the first to detect any problems. Three pamphlets from the National Association for Hearing and Speech Action will help you detect hearing, speech, and language disorders; work with your child's communication skills; and seek professional help if necessary. *How Does Your Child Hear and Talk?* is written in useful chart form and cites the progression level of various age ranges. *Recognizing Communication Disorders* lists symptoms of common speech, language, and hearing problems. *The Speech-Language Pathologist in the Schools* explains the services these professionals can offer.

Write for:
How Does Your Child Hear and Talk?
 (specify English or Spanish)
Recognizing Communication Disorders
The Speech-Language Pathologist in the Schools

Cost: Free

Send to:
The National Association for Hearing and
 Speech Action
10801 Rockville Pike
Rockville, MD 20852

Communication brochures

COMMUNICATION ANSWERS

★★

The first years of life are important for learning speech and language. It is during this time that the child learns to comprehend the words of others, and to express his own desires and thoughts. For many reasons, some children do not progress as naturally as others. Four question-and-answer pamphlets from the National Association for Hearing and Speech Action give factual information and reassurance to parents worried about their children's speech and hearing development. The small flyers define various communication disorders and help you find professional help. You'll learn about otitis media and the hearing loss which can result, articulation

patterns, and how to help the stutterer. Good general reading.

Write for:
NAHSA Answers Questions About Child Language
NAHSA Answers Questions About Otitis Media
 and Language Development
NAHSA Answers Questions About Articulation
 Problems
NAHSA Answers Questions About Stuttering

Cost: Free

Send to:
The National Association for Hearing and
 Speech Action
10801 Rockville Pike
Rockville, MD 20852

NAHSA Answers Questions pamphlets

HELPING CHILDREN COPE

★★★★

Children react to a crisis just like adults do—it can bring out the best in them or leave them feeling quite unable to cope. Whichever way they react, children need special help during crisis periods—like when a parent, brother, or sister dies, or during a divorce. *Helping Children Face Crises* will give you an understanding of some of the reactions your child may experience in the face of a crisis and help you find ways to teach your child the coping skills he or she needs. Among the crisis situations discussed are the death of a parent or sibling, separation and divorce, moving, being ill, starting school, and going away from home. This sympathetic 28-page booklet is one of the Public Affairs Committee's publications on subjects of common concern to people today.

Write for:
Helping Children Face Crises (No. 541)

Cost: $1.00

continued

PARENTS

Send to:
Public Affairs Pamphlets
381 Park Ave. South
New York, NY 10016

WHEN A CHILD CALLS FOR HELP

★★★★

When a child becomes troubled, lonely, isolated, it's a signal to the adults in his or her life that some kind of help is needed. *Help for Your Troubled Child* is a valuable 28-page booklet that can guide you in making a decision as to whether or not your child needs special help. It also has solid advice on how to get psychotherapeutic assistance, how to prepare your child for therapy, and the course you and the child can expect the therapy to follow. You'll also learn how parents and therapist can work together to give the child his or her best chance of benefitting from the treatment. This is a comforting, commonsense look at a subject that can scare a parent half to death. A case where knowledge dispels fear.

Write for:
Help for Your Troubled Child (No. 454)

Cost: $1.00

Send to:
Public Affairs Pamphlets
381 Park Ave. South
New York, NY 10016

WHY CHILDREN WORRY

★★★★

For all the wishful thinking grown-ups express about the carefree days of childhood, children suffer stresses and strains just as adults do. High parental expectations put pressure on children, as do circumstances like poverty, sibling rivalry, or having to take on too much responsibility too young. *Pressures on Children* is an excellent 28-page booklet that will help parents understand the pressures children can experience at every stage of their lives, from preschool through high school years. There are also suggestions for recognizing when a child is under too much stress, and how grown-ups in his or her life can help ease the pressure. This is a valuable resource that deals with a facet of child development that is currently receiving a lot of serious attention.

Write for:
Pressures on Children (No. 589)

Cost: $1.00

Send to:
Public Affairs Pamphlets
381 Park Ave. South
New York, NY 10016

HOSPITAL VISITS: THE PARENT'S RIGHTS

★★★

This is not a cheery, lighthearted folder about what to say and do to prepare your child for a hospital stay. It's a serious, thoughtful piece of information to put you in the right frame of mind for your child's upcoming trip to the hospital. You're advised to trust your instincts—you have the right to stay with your child at any time if you think he needs you, no matter what the official visiting hours are; to shop around for a doctor who is sympathetic to your being with your child in the hospital as much as you feel is necessary; to shop for a hospital with cooperative visiting and rooming-in privileges; to prepare yourself thoroughly by asking questions, reading, and talking with other parents; and to be honest with your child. Eight small pages.

Write for:
Children in Hospitals

Cost: 25¢ and a long SASE

Send to:
Children in Hospitals
31 Wilshire Park
Needham, MA 02192

Keeping Your Child Safe

CHARTING FIRST AID TREATMENTS

★★★★

When you need easy-to-read first aid information, and need it fast, consult this handy slide chart. With symptoms of and treatment for 23 baby ailments, from seizures to diaper rash, you'll quickly know what to do to give comfort and relief. There is a lot more information on this convenient chart, too. It tells you when to call your doctor, how to manage a fever, and what to do in event of a serious accident. There are step-by-step directions for giving mouth to

A SASE is a self-addressed stamped envelope.

mouth resuscitation, an immunization schedule, and spaces to fill in emergency phone numbers. You'll want to hang this chart inside a cupboard near the telephone, just in case. This offer also includes a household safety booklet.

Write for:
Baby First Aid Guide and Household Safety Booklet

Cost: $1.00

Send to:
F & H Baby Products
P.O. Box 2228P
Evansville, IN 47714

Baby First Aid Guide slide chart

DON'T EAT THE POINSETTIA
★★★★

It's scary to think about, but one leaf of a poinsettia plant can kill a child who eats it. *All* parts of those glorious azaleas and rhododendrons are poisonous and can cause death if eaten. This pamphlet describes 38 garden and forest plants (often with line illustrations or photos) that are poisonous. It gives several rules for teaching little children to avoid poisonous plants and an excellent guide telling what to do if *you* are accidentally poisoned. If you spend a lot of time outdoors, the reading list that's included can help you explore the subject further.

Write for:
Some Plants Are Poison!

Cost: Free

Send to:
Game News
Pennsylvania Game Commission
P.O. Box 1567
Harrisburg, PA 17120

FOR SAFEKEEPING
★★

On the average, 25 million reported injuries occur in the home each year in the United States. Of these, approximately 10 million involve children under the age of 16. Accidents involving falls, fire, suffocation, poisoning, and drowning are the leading sources of injury and death to children in the home. Fortunately many of these accidents are preventable with proper adult supervision and instruction. This eight-page safety guide from Aetna Life and Casualty shows you how to protect your children. The booklet leads you through every room of the house, pinpointing danger spots such as stairs, spills, and scattered toys. There are also tips for outdoor and automobile safety. Every home should be inspected for these potentially hazardous conditions.

Write for:
Keeping Danger Out of Reach

Cost: Free

Send to:
Resources
Aetna Life & Casualty
151 Farmington Avenue
Hartford, CT 06156

SHOCKPROOF YOUR HOME
★★★★

When your baby gets old enough to start exploring, household safety becomes a priority. Electrical outlets are particularly tempting to prying fingers, but you can prevent electrical shocks and burns by using these special safety caps—plastic plugs to insert in each outlet in your home that is not in use. You can remove the plugs when you want to plug in an appliance, but the design makes it virtually impossible for a baby or toddler to remove them. For $2.00 this company will send you 20 shockproof safety plugs, plus a booklet on child-proofing your home against all the hazards that are so easy to overlook. You'll learn how to make a safety tour through your home, and there's a good safety checklist, too.

Write for:
20 Safety Caps
Protect Your Baby With F & H Safety Products

continued

PARENTS

Cost: $2.00

Send to:
F & H
Box 2228P
Evansville, IN 47714

20 Safety Caps

HAVE A SAFE JOURNEY
★★★★

The purpose of this excellent little booklet is to impress on adults the hazards of driving with a child who is not restrained in a car seat. That message forcefully expressed, the booklet goes on to explain federal safety standards and which kinds of car seats meet those standards. Finally, there's some good, practical advice for traveling with babies and children on both short and long trips, and special advice about auto trips for the mother-to-be. This booklet is put out by a company that makes car seats, but there's lots of good general information and minimal promotion of the company's products. Well worth your 50¢.

Write for:
Travel With Baby

Cost: 50¢

Send to:
Cosco/Peterson
Subsidiary of Kidde Inc.
2525 State St.
Columbus, IN 47201

Travel With Baby

For Single and Adoptive Parents

FOR PARENTS GOING IT ALONE
★★★★

Parents without partners know that it can be lonely raising children alone; their children may also feel "different" or insecure. *One-Parent Families*, a 28-page booklet from the Public Affairs Committee, addresses some of the concerns that single parents encounter and discusses topics like child care, problems faced by the working parent, dating, and the grief that accompanies divorce or the death of a spouse. There are good suggestions to help single parents explore all their options, as well as a discussion of governmental agencies and mutual help groups. If you're struggling with being a single parent, this little book will reassure you that you and your children are not alone and that the world is wider than you think.

Write for:
One-Parent Families (No. 543)

Cost: $1.00

Send to:
Public Affairs Pamphlets
381 Park Ave. South
New York, NY 10016

SELECTED, NOT EXPECTED
★★★★

In a number of ways, raising a child who is adopted differs from raising a child who is born into the family. This 28-page pamphlet addresses many of the issues that confront families formed by adoption. *Raising an Adopted Child* is illustrated with case histories and covers whether and when to tell the child he is adopted, dealing with an older child or one of another race, and raising handicapped children. The controversial issue of searching for biological family is also discussed. There is a selected bibliography for further reading and a list of national adoption organizations.

Write for:
Raising an Adopted Child (No. 620)

Cost: $1.00

A SASE is a self-addressed stamped envelope.

Send to:
Public Affairs Pamphlets
381 Park Ave. South
New York, NY 10016

Raising an Adopted Child

CHOOSING YOUR CHILD

★★★★

Adopting a child is a momentous step, requiring much careful thought on the part of prospective adoptive parents. *Adopting a Child,* a valuable 29-page booklet from the Public Affairs Committee, is a good place to start. It offers an overview of the adoption process itself and covers the steps involved in both agency and nonagency adoption. Brief but frank discussions explore the legal and emotional implications of adopting older children, handicapped children, and foreign children, and crossing racial lines.

Write for:
Adopting a Child (No. 585)

Cost: $1.00

Send to:
Public Affairs Pamphlets
381 Park Avenue South
New York, NY 10016

LIVING IN STEP

★★★★

Becoming a stepfamily takes longer than the ceremony that creates one. It requires adjustment to the new situation by all who are involved, and depends on the commitment of the husband and wife to the marriage and each other. Communication and compromise are necessary. *Stepfamilies — A Growing Reality* should be read by everyone contemplating remarriage or already in such a union. The 32-page booklet is both warm and factual, dealing

with many of the myths and surprising realities of a ready-made family. Feelings and fears of each family member are explored, along with actual case histories. You'll read about combining two families, the differences when the first parent has died, visitation, and finances. The book discusses step-sibling relationships and the decision to have more children. A recommended reading list for both children and adults is given.

Write for:
Stepfamilies — A Growing Reality (No. 609)

Cost: $1.00

Send to:
Public Affairs Pamphlets
381 Park Avenue South
New York, NY 10016

Stepfamilies — A Growing Reality

ENFORCING CHILD SUPPORT LAWS

★★★★

The Child Support Enforcement program is a federal/state/local effort to collect child support from parents who are legally obligated to pay it. Its goals are to ensure that children are supported by their parents, to encourage family responsibility, and to reduce the costs of welfare to the taxpayer. The U.S. Department of Health and Human Services' Office of Child Support Enforcement offers a free 40-page booklet explaining child support laws and how to make sure they work. A single parent who's having difficulty with support payments will find tips here on how to collect from a spouse who is under a legal order to make child support payments but is reluctant to do so.

Write for:
Handbook on Child Support Enforcement (No. 503P)

Cost: Free

Send to:
Consumer Information Center
P.O. Box 100
Pueblo, CO 81002

FREE THINGS
to
HELP
YOU STAY
HEALTHY

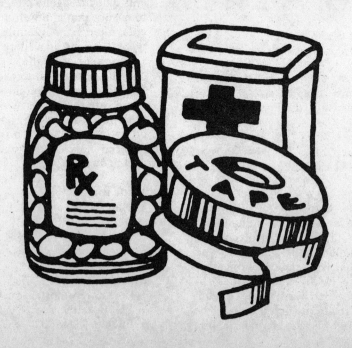

Routine Health Care and Preventive Medicine

MINI-LESSONS IN HEALTH CARE

★★★

From depression to angina to arthritis, Pfizer Pharmaceuticals has published a series of one-page flyers covering a variety of ailments. The seventeen sheets that make up this series contain a wealth of information on symptoms, physiology, and working with your doctor. You'll learn the dangers and tendencies of high blood pressure, how stomach cramps can indicate heart trouble, and the causes and cures of depression. Other pages cover diabetes, cancer, and overall healthful living. A great deal of useful information is contained in the Healthcare Series, along with reminders that the individual plays a strong role in his or her physical condition.

Write for:
The Pfizer Healthcare Series

Cost: Free

Send to:
Pfizer Pharmaceuticals
Post Office Box 3852
Grand Central Station
New York, NY 10163

THIS WON'T HURT A BIT

★★

All children should receive proper immunization levels to avoid infectious diseases that might affect them. All adults need to maintain their immunization levels to further avoid such illnesses. Vaccines have been developed for many of the diseases that years ago often meant death or disfigurement. This pamphlet describes the types of vaccines available for immunization of all family members. From diptheria to small pox to tetanus, 10 major immunization procedures and their boosters are discussed, as well as who should receive the treatment and when. There is also advice for the foreign traveler and for keeping a record of your family's immunizations. A handy chart provides immunization schedules for the infectious diseases discussed. This pamphlet is available while supplies last.

Write for:
Immunization

Cost: 75¢

Send to:
Order Department, OP-19
American Medical Association
P.O. Box 10946
Chicago, IL 60610-9968

Immunization

WHEN DID MARY HAVE THE MUMPS?

★★★★

How many times have you needed to provide basic facts about the health of members of your family—for school records, for insurance forms, or for a doctor's medical history? Up-to-date notations on family health—kept current—can be of permanent value, and this booklet is an easy way to keep track of the information. It contains space for important medical information on immunization, injuries, and physical examinations, plus removable medical identification cards—each family member can complete one and carry it in pocket or purse. If you or someone in your family are unable to tell your medical story after an accident or in the case of an illness, the card could save your life. A sensible buy.

Write for:
Family Health Record

Cost: $1.50

Send to:
Order Department, OP-016
American Medical Association
P.O. Box 10946
Chicago, IL 60610-9968

continued

STAY HEALTHY

Family Health Record

THE AIR WE BREATHE

★★★★

Anyone who has trouble breathing because of a chronic lung condition should read this informative full-size booklet, *Help Yourself to Better Breathing*. The 28-page illustrated handbook starts out with a diagrammed explanation of how our lungs work and how they malfunction. It's full of suggestions to make breathing easier for you. There are case histories from other sufferers, and lots of questions and answers. There is advice on how to control coughing, how to breathe more relaxedly, and how to clear your lungs. You'll find a recommended diet and exercise plan, and warnings of potential trouble-making situations. A description of medicines and breathing aids is given, as is a listing of good lifestyle hints.

Write for:
Help Yourself to Better Breathing

Cost: Free

Send to:
American Lung Association
P.O. Box 596
New York, NY 10001

Help Yourself to Better Breathing

SIGHT TO BEHOLD

★★★

Two pamphlets from the National Society to Prevent Blindness offer lots of interesting information on how our eyes work and should be cared for. The first is an illustrated chart that explains the sense of sight. Illustrations show the muscles that attach to the outside covering of the eye, and how the amount of light entering the eye changes the size of the pupil. A cross-section diagram labels the various parts, and a vocabulary defines pertinent terminology. The second pamphlet, *Television and Your Eyes*, explains how to watch television with greatest comfort to your eyes. Room lighting, distance, and picture focus all play a part. It also answers questions concerning color versus black-and-white television viewing, wearing tinted glasses, and danger of x-ray radiation.

Write for:
The Eye and How We See
Television and Your Eyes

Cost: 50¢ and a long SASE for The Eye and How We See
Free with a long SASE for Television and Your Eyes

Send to:
National Society to Prevent Blindness
79 Madison Avenue
New York, NY 10016-7896

The Eye and How We See
Television and Your Eyes

FOR SUN LOVERS

★★★

Sunglasses, now worn by many people throughout the year, are available in a vast array of shapes, sizes, colors, and prices. Though often regarded as a fashion accessory, they should be selected with care to provide visual comfort and adequate protection from the sun's rays. This factual 12-page booklet

A SASE is a self-addressed stamped envelope.

tells you how. You'll learn what construction materials are the best and how to tell good quality from bad. There is good advice on choosing lens color and size and how to determine correct fit. A simple test is described for you to apply to any pair you are considering buying. You'll also find a list of general helpful hints concerning when to wear sunglasses, medical considerations, and recommendations for athletes.

Write for:
Sunglasses pamphlet

Cost: Free with a long SASE

Send to:
National Society to Prevent Blindness
79 Madison Avenue
New York, NY 10016-7896

Sunglasses pamphlet

GLAUCOMA BLINDNESS: A PREVENTABLE TRAGEDY

★

Though the cause of glaucoma is unknown, early and sustained treatment can prevent blindness. That's the urgent message of this small pamphlet that also explains just what glaucoma is—excess eye fluid that elevates pressure within the eye—the four kinds of glaucoma, warning signs of the disease, who may be at high risk, and the importance of regular eye examinations to check for glaucoma.

Write for:
Saving Your Sight From Glaucoma

Cost: 50¢

Send to:
North Wales Press, Inc.
P.O. Box 1486
North Wales, PA 19454

WATCHING OVER YOUR EYES

★★★★

Glaucoma has been called the well-hidden disease of the eye because it works so silently. In many cases, there are no pain signals to warn you that something's amiss, and the disease can go undetected for a long time. Since glaucoma can lead to blindness if untreated or not caught early enough, it makes sense to be aware of the symptoms that may indicate a problem. *Keeping an Eye on Glaucoma*, a free booklet from the FDA, suggests that knowing that the symptoms can often be sneaky and easy to dismiss could one day save your vision. It also discusses the many excellent treatments that have been developed.

Write for:
Keeping an Eye on Glaucoma

Cost: Free (postcard requests only)

Send to:
FDA Office of Consumer Affairs
5600 Fishers Lane (HFE-88)
Rockville, MD 20857

SPEAKING UP

★★★

Your voice, like your fingerprints, is unique to you. And just as parts of your body (such as your eyes, ears, legs, and back) can be damaged, so can your voice. Vocal damage can be present at birth, or it can occur during childhood, the teenage years, mid-life, or the senior years. This 23-page booklet was written to help you understand more about the causes of and the treatments for disorders of the voice—that very critical, unique, and human vehicle of communication. This publication answers some of the questions most frequently asked in an easy-to-read Q & A format. The replies are somewhat general, but if you are interested in reading more, there is a selected bibliography in the back. You'll also find a list of practical guidelines for protecting your voice throughout your lifetime.

Write for:
Voice Problems: Questions & Answers for
    Persons with Voice Disorders

Cost: $1.25

Send to:
The Interstate Printers & Publishers, Inc.
19 N. Jackson
P.O. Box 50
Danville, IL 61834-0050

Prices are for single items only; prices and information are accurate at time of publication.

STAY HEALTHY

VERDICT: HEARING LOSS
★★

An inability to hear speech and other sounds clearly is referred to as a hearing loss. There are conductive hearing losses, sensorineural hearing losses, and central auditory impairments. Hearing loss may or may not be an indication of a current disease. Three question-and-answer pamphlets from the National Association for Hearing and Speech Action address the concerns of the hearing impaired. You'll learn about types of hearing loss, how excessive noise can cause hearing loss, and how to protect yourself if you work near exposure to damaging noise. You'll also learn about the different hearing aids available today and how an audiologist can help the hearing impaired.

Write for:
NAHSA Answers Questions: About Hearing Loss
NAHSA Answers Questions: About Noise and Hearing Loss
NAHSA Answers Questions: About Assistive Listening Devices

Cost: Free

Send to:
National Association for Hearing and Speech Action
10801 Rockville Pike
Rockville, MD 20852

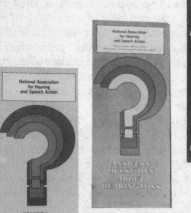

NAHSA Answers Questions series

THE TIME OF THE MONTH
★★

After separating the old wives' tales from modern medical facts, the truth is that more than half and perhaps as many as 90 percent of all women have experienced discomfort related to menstruation. For some it is lower backache and abdominal cramping; for others it is unexplainable mood swings or water retention. *Doing Something About Menstrual Discomforts* is a four-page reprint from the FDA Consumer, which addresses this issue. You'll learn about some of the over-the-counter and prescription remedies available today, and FDA findings as to their effectiveness. Causes and treatment for premenstrual syndrome (PMS) are discussed, as well as drug combinations which are viewed to be safe.

Write for:
Doing Something About Menstrual Discomforts (No. 565P)

Cost: Free

Send to:
Consumer Information Center
P.O. Box 100
Pueblo, CO 81002

A WOMAN'S PROBLEMS
★★★

One of the most common, and most irritating, of all problems affecting a woman's reproductive system is vaginitis. Discharge, burning, and itching are the most typical symptoms of any of several infections prone to inhabit the female body. *On Yeast Infections and Other Female Irritations* is a three-page article reprinted from the *FDA Consumer* magazine which addresses this issue. You'll learn about the symptoms and causes of trichomoniasis and candidiasis and other forms of vaginitis, and the effectiveness of various drugs prescribed to treat them. You'll learn about some of the patterns of recurrence and how some groups of women are particularly susceptible. There is also a list of suggestions for alleviating the problem and for preventing future attacks.

Write for:
On Yeast Infections and Other Female Irritations (No. 572P)

Cost: Free

Send to:
Consumer Information Center
P.O. Box 100
Pueblo, CO 81002

A SASE is a self-addressed stamped envelope.

EARLY DETECTION SAVES LIVES

★★★★

Breast cancer is the most common form of cancer among American women, with approximately 111,000 cases occurring a year. Two-thirds of the women who are diagnosed with this cancer will be over the age of 50, but the disease does occur in younger women and in a small percentage of men. Breast cancer is most treatable and curable when the tumor is small, and that is what this booklet is about. Early detection of breast tumors saves lives and limits disfiguration. *Breast Exams: What You Should Know* discusses the risks of breast cancer, who is especially susceptible, and the importance of regular examinations. The pros and cons of mammography are also covered in this 14-page illustrated booklet. A foldout chart with instructions for breast self-examination are included.

Write for:
Breast Exams: What You Should Know (No. 559P)

Cost: Free

Send to:
Consumer Information Center
P.O. Box 100
Pueblo, CO 81002

Breast Exams

CONTRACEPTIVE CHOICES

★★★★

If having a baby doesn't fit in with your plans right now, a number of contraceptive methods are available. Some can be obtained without a doctor's prescription; others require medical consultation and follow-up. When choosing a method there are several factors to consider, among them personal preferences, psychological or religious attitudes, and individual medical history. But there is more. *Contraception: Comparing the Options* is a foldout chart that discusses how various methods work, how effective they are, what side effects they may have, and what health problems may be related to their use. Advantages and disadvantages of each are also explored. Of course, no method is 100 percent effective, but the more informed you are, the better choice you will make for your own needs.

Write for:
Contraception: Comparing the Options (No. 544P)

Cost: Free

Send to:
Consumer Information Center
P.O. Box 100
Pueblo, CO 81002

CHARTING THE PROS AND CONS OF BIRTH CONTROL

★★★★

According to a Gallup Poll commissioned by The American College of Obstetricians and Gynecologists (ACOG), a large proportion of Americans underestimate the effectiveness of and overestimate the health risks of contraception. A slide chart, "Benefits, Risks and Effectiveness of Contraception," has been developed by ACOG to help people judge the advantages and disadvantages of 10 methods of contraception, from no method to sterilization. The slide chart shows the effectiveness rates, mortality rates, and yearly costs of birth control methods. This will help you distinguish the strengths and weaknesses of each method and determine which is right for you.

Write for:
Benefits, Risks and Effectiveness of
Contraception Slide Chart

Cost: Free with a long SASE

Send to:
The American College of Obstetricians and
Gynecologists
Public Information
600 Maryland Avenue, S.W.
Washington, DC 20024

*Benefits, Risks and Effectiveness
of Contraception Slide Chart*

STAY HEALTHY

CALCIUM DEFICIENCY IN WOMEN

★★★★

It is no coincidence that at the age many women switch from milk to some other drink, like diet soda or white wine, eight out of ten may start to develop a serious calcium deficiency. In fact, calcium deficiency now rates with iron deficiency as one of the biggest nutritional problems among Americans. Over time, lack of calcium can result in weakening of your body's bone structure and can cause bones to age before their time. For $1.00 you can receive this calcium information kit from Lederle Laboratories. You'll receive a copy of a colorful eight-page booklet, *The Calcium Crisis in the American Woman's Diet*, which describes your body's vital need for calcium and explains the benefits of supplementing your diet with Caltrate 600, a calcium counter to help you chart your daily intake and achieve a positive balance in your body, a four-tablet sample, and a coupon worth 50¢ toward the purchase of Caltrate 600.

Write for:
Caltrate 600 Information Kit

Cost: $1.00

Send to:
Caltrate 600 Information Kit
Lederle Promotional Center
2200 Bradley Hill Road
Blauvelt, NY 10913

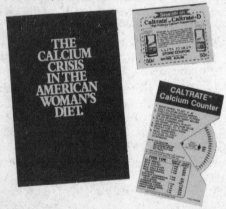

Caltrate 600 Information Kit

HOW ARE YOUR BONES?

★★

More and more Americans, an estimated 15 million in fact, have some degree of osteoporosis, a painful and eventually crippling bone disease. The disease develops slowly, and you may not realize you have it until it's too late and you have a cracked hip or wrist bone. There is no cure for osteoporosis, but you can do a lot to prevent it. A new brochure tells how proper diet, exercise, and control of stress can help prevent osteoporosis. Women, who tend to live longer than men and have thinner and less dense bones, are prime targets for the disease. They are also less likely to eat enough of the calcium-rich foods needed to build their bones and keep them strong. Milk, cheese, ice cream, and yogurt are some of the best sources of calcium, which you'll learn more about in this helpful brochure.

Write for:
Are You at Risk for Bone Disease?

Cost: 20¢

Send to:
National Dairy Council
6300 N. River Rd.
Rosemont, IL 60018-4233

ATTACK ON PLAQUE

★★

Periodontal disease wipes out more teeth from our heads every year than any other major dental disease, including tooth decay. The disease costs the American public an estimated $4 billion a year for repair of its ravages. Periodontal disease, which begins with a buildup of plaque on the teeth, crowds, irritates, and eventually pushes back the gumline; the bone in which the tooth is set shrinks away and the teeth loosen and deteriorate. *The Dental Plaque Battle is Endless but Worth it* is a two-page magazine reprint from the *FDA Consumer* which warns against the dangers of tartar deposits and how to prevent periodontal disease. There is good advice on proper dental hygiene, and information on the treatment of periodontitis is both early and advanced stages.

Write for:
The Dental Plaque Battle is Endless but Worth it (No. 564P)

Cost: Free

Send to:
Consumer Information Center
P.O. Box 100
Pueblo, CO 81002

PLAQUE ATTACK

★★★

When it comes to good oral health, there is one major villain—plaque. Plaque builds up on teeth and causes cavities and gum disease. It's a cinch that most of us are out to get this villain and rub him out of our lives and mouths forever, but plaque doesn't go away that easily. It doesn't stay away, either, unless we exercise constant vigilance. The Plakadent Tooth Scrubber is a new kind of toothbrush, shaped differently from what you are accustomed to. The scrubber has a wide, U-shaped head with two brushes facing into the middle. It's supposed to help you get rid of plaque because, as you brush against the top of your tooth, the scrubber is also reaching down toward the gumline, where some of the worst dental problems are located. It is a novel idea, but one which should still be used in conjunction with other good habits, such as flossing regularly and avoiding sugar.

Write for:
Plakadent Tooth Scrubber

Cost: $1.00

Send to:
IMC Management, Inc.
P.O. Box 11-TS
Garnerville, NY 10923

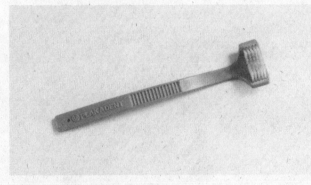

Plakadent Tooth Scrubber

KEEPING YOUR MOUTH HEALTHY

★★★★

Mouth and canker sores don't leave scars, but they can be very painful—and annoying—while they last. Here's an opportunity to try, free, a medicated formula designed to ease the discomfort of mouth or canker sores and promote healing. It's called Kank•a and comes from the Blistex people, who will send you a trial-size phial of the liquid medication and a report explaining why the sores occur and how to treat them. You'll learn that there are all sorts of reasons for canker sores, ranging from eating too many spicy foods, to irritation from dentures or braces, to inner stress from financial or marital

troubles. There's also an explanation of the difference between canker sores and cold sores—the latter are caused by the herpes simplex virus.

Send to:
Kank•a sample and pamphlet: Canker and
   Mouth Sores: The Inside Story

Cost: Free with a long SASE

Send to:
Blistex Inc.
1800 Swift Drive
Oak Brook, IL 60521

Kank-a sample and pamphlet

KEEPING OUT OF HEART TROUBLE

★★★★

Can heart attacks be prevented? This important question is addressed in a readable and informative manner in *Understand Your Heart*, a 28-page booklet from the Public Affairs Committee. You'll learn how the normal heart functions and repairs itself and what some of the major heart afflictions are. Although a common misconception would have you believe that heart attacks are most likely to hit high-powered executives, the truth is that heart disease can affect anyone—risk factors such as overweight, lack of exercise, high blood pressure, high cholesterol levels, smoking, heredity, and tension can all lead to heart disease. This booklet helps you to assess your chances of heart disease and suggests some practical steps to decrease any risks you find lurking in your lifestyle.

Write for:
Understand Your Heart (No. 514)

Cost: $1.00

continued

STAY HEALTHY

Send to:
Public Affairs Pamphlets
381 Park Ave. South
New York, NY 10016

THE EBBS AND FLOWS OF BLOOD PRESSURE

★★★

It is important to know that blood pressure changes in every person: When you are sleeping it is lower, when you are smoking it rises, it is different if you are sitting or standing. People with hypertension, high blood pressure, have too much blood pressure most of the time. It is almost always elevated. There are an estimated 23 million Americans with hypertension, with fewer than 15 percent of these receiving adequate treatment. Yet, this condition can be readily detected, and certain types can be cured and others controlled. *Protect Your Lifeline! Fight High Blood Pressure* is a 24-page booklet designed to help you find out what high blood pressure is, what it can do to you and your body, and how you can help control it.

Write for:
Protect Your Lifeline! Fight High Blood Pressure
(No. 124P)

Cost: $2.00

Send to:
Consumer Information Center
P.O. Box 100
Pueblo, CO 81002

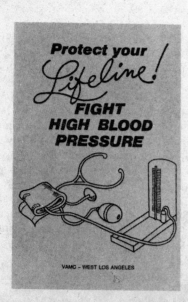

Protect Your Lifeline! Fight High Blood Pressure

THE WAR ON COLDS (YOU'RE LOSING)

★★★★

It's like winning the battle but losing the war; you can subdue a cold's symptoms but you can't prevent, cure, or shorten it. This eight-page booklet from the Food and Drug Administration tells you how to relieve the symptoms of a cold with nonprescription drugs, preferably single-ingredient products—if you only have a sore throat, it doesn't make sense to take drugs for sniffles and congestion too. The booklet lists the ingredients that go into the common cold remedies and the FDA's evaluation of their safety and effectiveness. Good information for the sufferer or the person in charge of stocking the medicine chest. Entertaining graphics.

Write for:
The Common Cold: Relief But No Cure

Cost: Free (postcard requests only)

Send to:
FDA Office of Consumer Affairs
5600 Fishers Lane (HFE-88)
Rockville, MD 20857

The Common Cold: Relief But No Cure

THE SAME, BUT DIFFERENT

★★★

Coughing, sneezing, fever, headache, chills—how can you tell whether you've got a cold or the flu? The symptoms are so similar they are often lumped together as one ailment. Yet colds and flus are very different, as you will see in this four-page article, *Flu/Cold—Never The Strain Shall Meet*. Reprinted from the FDA Consumer magazine, the article differentiates between the two as having distinctly separate sources; also, influenza can be prevented by vaccination. Neither colds nor flu attacks have known cures but their symptoms can be alleviated. The article also discusses the various strains of flu viruses and the seriousness of the illness.

Write for:
Flu/Cold—Never The Strain Shall Meet (No. 567P)

Cost: Free

Send to:
Consumer Information Center
P.O. Box 100
Pueblo, CO 81002

OH, MY ACHING HEAD!
★★★

Some 40 million Americans experience chronic headaches. Besides being painful or discomforting, headaches are costly. Headache sufferers make over 8 million visits a year to their doctor. Migraine victims alone lose over 64 million workdays because of headache pain. The National Institutes of Health offer a 36-page booklet about headaches and how to get relief from them. It tells what you can do yourself to relieve headache pain and also when to see a doctor. Headaches can serve as warning signals of more serious disorders, and the booklet describes what these might be and what to do about them.

Write for:
Headache: Hope Through Research (No. 123P)

Cost: $2.00

Send to:
Consumer Information Center
P.O. Box 100
Pueblo, CO 81002

Headache: Hope Through Research

SHAKE HANDS WITH YOUR FEET
★★★

Each of your feet contains 26 bones. Together, the 52 bones of the feet make up one fourth of all the bones in the body. This lighthearted (but down-to-earth) booklet explains the foot's physical structure and tells you why, after taking 8,000 to 10,000 steps a day, your feet tend to hurt. You'll learn what causes corns, calluses, foot odor, bunions, athlete's foot, "hammer-toe," blisters, chilblains, and plantar's warts. There are shoe-buying tips, and advice on ways to take care of your feet—including some limbering up exercises.

Write for:
Meet Your Feet

Cost: Free with a long SASE

Send to:
American Podiatric Medical Association
20 Chevy Chase Circle, N.W.
Washington, DC 20015

A PAIN IN THE BACK
★★

Although theories vary as to what causes backs to hurt, most experts would agree that the most common causes are gradual wear and tear, stress, and lack of proper exercise. Most authorities agree that the key to a pain-free back is strong muscles, particularly abdominal muscles. *Back Pain: Ubiquitous, Controversial* is a four-page magazine reprint from *FDA Consumer* which addresses the problems and treatments of aching backs. The article discusses worn facet joints, herniated discs, pinched nerves, and more, as well as the difficulty of diagnosis. You'll learn about a variety of treatments, from drugs to manipulation to surgery, along with possible side effects. You'll also read about the spine and its components—a mini-lesson in physiology of the back.

Write for:
Back Pain: Ubiquitous, Controversial (No. 558P)

Cost: Free

Send to:
Consumer Information Center
P.O. Box 100
Pueblo, CO 81002

STAY HEALTHY

ON YOUR FEET
★★

The human foot is a biological masterpiece, but it needs good care if it's going to give you its best work. *Your Podiatrist Talks About Foot Health* explains the fascinating and complex combination of 26 bones, muscles, ligaments, and blood vessels in the foot, and the causes of corns, calluses, warts, bunions, athlete's foot, and ingrown nails. Most important are the basic rules of foot care—you can follow them with minimum expense or effort. This informative leaflet will help you prevent foot problems before they occur by treating your feet with the respect they deserve.

Write for:
　Your Podiatrist Talks About Foot Health

Cost:　Free with a long SASE

Send to:
　American Podiatric Medical Association
　20 Chevy Chase Circle, N.W.
　Washington, DC 20015

MY ACHING BACK
★★★★

About 75 million Americans are believed to suffer continuing low back problems. So if you have lower back pain, you aren't alone. That won't make you feel better, but perhaps this booklet will. *Low Back Pain—What It Is, What Can Be Done* is informative reading on the subject. It discusses the spinal structure and the stressors that affect its smooth function. Causes of back pain, from arthritis to muscle strain, are covered, and so are treatments. There is lots of good advice as to what you might try when you are inflicted with a backache, and warnings about what *not* to do. There are also ideas for altering your life-style to prevent future strain on the spine. An illustrated suggested exercise program is included, along with a supplemental reading list.

Write for:
　Low Back Pain—What It Is, What Can Be Done
　　(No. 601)

Cost:　$1.00

Send to:
　Public Affairs Pamphlets
　381 Park Ave. South
　New York, NY 10016

Low Back Pain—What It Is, What Can Be Done

GOOD NEWS ABOUT CANCER
★★★★

The news is getting better all the time. In the past few years, scientists have identified many causes of cancer, and today it is known that about 80 percent of cancer cases are tied to the way people live—the food they eat, the work they do, and whether or not they smoke. This booklet tells you some things you can do every day to help protect yourself and your family. In an easy-to-read question-and-answer format, this informative booklet discusses causes and risk factors, from X-rays to cigarettes. Good, solid advice is given on nutritional eating, vitamins, suntanning, and alcohol consumption. There are lists of cancer prevention tips and a quiz to identify your own personal risks of developing cancer. At the back of the 24-page booklet is a glossary.

Write for:
　Good News, Better News

Cost:　Free

Send to:
　Department of Health and Human Services
　Public Health Service
　National Institutes of Health
　Bethesda, MD 20205

YOU CAN COMBAT CANCER
★★★

Today the outlook for cancer is more hopeful than it used to be. For many cancers, cure rates are better than ever before, and they continue to improve. Although three out of 10 Americans may develop some form of cancer within their lifetimes, scientists have learned a great deal about how people can increase their chances of being among those who will *not*

A SASE is a self-addressed stamped envelope.

develop this feared disease. This illustrated 16-page brochure seeks to answer some common questions about the causes and prevention of cancer and about the laboratory animal tests that identify cancer-causing substances. It's written in an easy-to-follow question and answer format to show you that, contrary to what may seem to be the case, not everything causes cancer.

Write for:
Everything Doesn't Cause Cancer (No. 566P)

Cost: Free

Send to:
Consumer Information Center
P.O. Box 100
Pueblo, CO 81002

Everything Doesn't Cause Cancer

THE COLON CONNECTION

★★★

Although it is relatively short—only a fifth of the total length of the intestinal canal—the colon is the site of a surprising variety of discomforting and sometimes life-threatening disorders. Virtually no part of this organ is immune from disease, ranging from appendicitis at the point where the colon begins to hemorrhoids at the point where it ends. In between, the colon is beset by inflammatory and infectious diseases, polyps and, of course, cancer. *The Colon Goes Up, Over, Down and Out* is an eight-page collection of three articles reprinted from the FDA Consumer magazine. You'll learn about many of the disorders which affect the lower digestive tract, along with the available treatments and cures known today. You'll also learn about the anatomy of the colon and how the use of enemas can be detrimental to your overall health.

Write for:
The Colon Goes Up, Over, Down and Out (No. 562P)

Cost: Free

Send to:
Consumer Information Center
P.O. Box 100
Pueblo, CO 81002

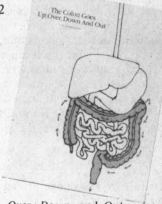

The Colon Goes Up, Over, Down, and Out

TAN TERRIFIC?

★★

The pursuit of sun-kissed skin leads many of us to bask long hours under summer skies, or to flee to southern climates during winter snows. Love, sex appeal, and popularity are all promised to those who sport deep golden suntans. Although a suntan is temporary, the undesirable side effects that come with it are longer lasting. Most dermatologists consider excessive sunbathing downright foolhardy. *Tan Now, Pay Later?* is the question posed in this two-page article reprinted from the *FDA Consumer* magazine, which discusses many of the perils that can develop from exposure to ultraviolet rays. The article discusses how different types of skin react differently to sun exposure, types of skin cancer, and ultraviolet radiation devices such as sunlamps. You'll also learn about the sun protection factor (SPF) and how it relates to over-the-counter suntan and sunscreen products, as well as the ingredients which have been found to be safe and effective in these products.

Write for:
Tan Now, Pay Later? (No. 570P)

Cost: Free

Send to:
Consumer Information Center
P.O. Box 100
Pueblo, CO 81002

STAY HEALTHY

DON'T EAT THE DAFFODILS
★

The stated purpose of this leaflet is not to alarm the reader, but to be used as reference by parents, teachers, doctors (and other health professionals), camp counselors, scoutmasters and 4-H leaders as a source of knowledge. It tells some rules to follow about eating plants (*don't,* until you're certain of their identity), how plant poisons affect people, and what to do if poisoning occurs, and then lists common Connecticut plants that possess poisonous properties and what the symptoms of toxicity are. You'll learn that even plants with such lovely names as star-of-Bethlehem and snow on the mountain can make you sick. So can daffodil bulbs and the leaves of your tomato plants. No antidotes are given; no photos or drawings are included. A good short reading list, though.

Write for:
   Plants With Poisonous Properties (81-9)

Cost: 50¢

Send to:
   Agricultural Publications
   Box U-35
   The University of Connecticut
   Storrs, CT 06268

POISON PREVENTION TIPS
★★★★

Every three minutes, the Food and Drug Administration's Poison Control Division gets a report of a serious case of poisoning. Most poisoning accidents happen between 4 P.M. and 6 P.M. and on weekend mornings. Over a quarter of a million potential poisons are offered for sale at stores where you shop. These range from pesticides to vitamins and laxatives which can be fatal if taken in large quantities. Learn all about poison dangers and prevention in *Tips on Poison Prevention in the Home,* a free 14-page booklet from the Better Business Bureau.

Write for:
   Tips on Poison Prevention in the Home
      (No. 24-167)

Cost: Free

Send to:
   Council of Better Business Bureaus
   1515 Wilson Blvd.
   Arlington, VA 22209

Emergency Care and First Aid

IN CASE OF EMERGENCY
★

An emergency medical identification card is your protection in any emergency. If you are not able to tell your medical story after an accident or sudden illness, the information entered on this card could save your life. A wallet-sized stub detaches from the Emergency Medical Identification card and should be carried with you at all times. Fill in your name and address, persons to be notified in case of an emergency, and your doctor's name. On the other side is space for a compact medical history—immunization dates, present medical problems, medicines taken regularly, and dangerous allergies. The recommendation is also made that persons with medical problems wear a small signal device around the neck or arm with identification and warnings for further protection. Available while supplies last.

Write for:
   Emergency Medical Identification Card

Cost: 75¢

Send to:
   Order Department, OP-002
   American Medical Association
   P.O. Box 10946
   Chicago, IL 60610-9968

FIRST AID FOR ATHLETES
★★★

Every field house, gymnasium, and locker room should be equipped with this first aid poster for athletic injuries. The brightly colored, illustrated chart gives important information on what to do in an emergency before the doctor arrives. There are instructions for mouth-to-mouth resuscitation and external cardiac massage. Also covered are bruises, fractures and dislocations, impact blows, and heat illnesses. There is a list of pre-first-aid precautions you can take, as well as general recommendations for care and treatment of injured athletes. The immediate and temporary care offered to the stricken athlete until the services of a physician can be obtained minimizes the aggravation of injury and enhances the earliest possible return of the athlete to peak performance. Available while supplies last.

A SASE is a self-addressed stamped envelope.

Write for:
First Aid for Athletic Injuries poster

Cost: 75¢

Send to:
Order Department, OP-307
American Medical Association
P.O. Box 10946
Chicago, IL 60610-9968

*First Aid for
Athletic Injuries poster*

POISON PREVENTION

★★★

This wall chart could be a lifesaver in your own home. By referring to this poster, which contains authoritative information on what to do in the event of a poisoning emergency, you might be able to prevent an accident from becoming a tragedy. There are instructions for administering aid to victims who have swallowed or inhaled poisons, come in contact with plant poisons, or received insect stings. You'll know when not to induce vomiting and how to do it when you should. There is also information on handling eye injuries and snake bites. A list of general first aid actions gives good advice on keeping the victim comfortable before professional help arrives. Adhesive edges allow you to attach the chart in a handy location, such as inside a cupboard or near the telephone. Space for important emergency phone numbers is also included. Available while supplies last.

Write for:
Danger Lurks . . . Prevent Poisoning poster

Cost: $1.50

Send to:
Order Department, OP-304
American Medical Association
P.O. Box 10946
Chicago, IL 60610-9968

FIRST AID FOR POISON IVY

★★★★

Among more than 60 plants that can cause an allergic reaction, poison ivy, poison oak, and poison sumac are by far the most common—and the most severe. Here's a little sample of a poison ivy treatment that you can tuck in your backpack or picnic basket next time you venture into the great outdoors. This ⅛-ounce sachet of Ivarest medicated cream comes from the people who make Blistex, and is accompanied by a leaflet, prepared by a dermatologist, about poison ivy (its botanical name is Rhus toxicodendron) and its symptoms and effects. It's best, of course, to avoid the plant, but if you've stumbled into it by accident, you should wash the affected skin as soon as possible to remove the plant oil, and then treat with a nonprescription remedy such as Ivarest to reduce the rash and relieve itching. Ivarest works, say the makers, for eight hours or more. The pamphlet points out that severe poison ivy dermatitis should be treated by a doctor. Along with the cream and pamphlet, you also get a 15¢ coupon toward a store purchase of Ivarest.

Write for:
Ivarest cream and coupon

Cost: Free with a SASE

Send to:
Blistex Inc.
1800 Swift Drive
Oak Brook, IL 60521

Ivarest creme and coupon

STAY HEALTHY

ONE FOR THE MEDICINE CABINET

★★★★

Always looking for something new and effective for your medicine chest? The people who make Blistex lip salve offer this free sample of Foille medicated first aid ointment, which is recommended for temporary relief of pain from minor burns, sunburn, and scratches. The makers say it also protects against skin infection. With the ⅛-ounce sample, you get a 25¢ coupon good toward any purchase of a Foille brand medicated first aid product.

Send to:
Foille sample and coupon

Cost: Free

Write for:
Blistex Inc.
1800 Swift Drive
Oak Brook, IL 60521

Foille sample and coupon

SPRING CLEANING YOUR MEDICINE CHEST

★★★

When is the last time you cleaned out your medicine chest? What is in there, anyway? Do you still have leftover prescription drugs from 1975 and free samples of stuff whose purpose you've forgotten? Is the dog's medicine kept along with the aspirin and antacid remedies? This one-page leaflet will help you sort out what you should and should not have on hand. Although each household's needs vary, *Does Your Medicine Chest Need First Aid?* cautions against overstocking. Sometimes buying the large economy size turns out to be more expensive in the long run. You'll find a list of suggested drug and non-drug products to equip your shelves as well as recommendations for optimum storage.

Write for:
Does Your Medicine Chest Need First Aid?
(No. 545P)

Cost: Free

Send to:
Consumer Information Center
P.O. Box 100
Pueblo, CO 81002

Nutrition, Diet, and Exercise

VIVE LA DIFFERENCE?

★★★

It seems unfair that the man in your life can eat baked potatoes with all the trimmings, second helpings of everything, and then dessert while you seem to gain weight although you eat far less. Even in this age of equality, there is a broad difference in the calorie needs of men and women. The answer lies in differences in body size and in body composition. The amount of energy expended through physical activity also plays a major role. These differences are discussed in a somewhat technical eight-page pamphlet, *The Gender Gap at the Dinner Table.* Research studies on caloric intake and output are explored, as well as eating disorders and fad diets. Tables demonstrate suggested desirable weights for heights, and mean heights and weights. Energy expenditures for men and women performing similar tasks are also given.

Write for:
The Gender Gap at the Dinner Table (No. 521P)

Cost: Free

Send to:
Consumer Information Center
P.O. Box 100
Pueblo, CO 81002

Gender Gap at Dinner Table

A SASE is a self-addressed stamped envelope.

NUTRITIONAL WEALTH

★★

You can make sure you have an adequate intake of vitamins and minerals by eating a variety of foods in sufficient amounts. But sometimes it just isn't possible to eat regular balanced meals. In that case, supplements are useful. *Vitamin-Mineral Supplements and Their Correct Use* is an informative little pamphlet that gives you solid information. It tells you the suggested minimum daily servings of the basic food groups and the recommended daily allowances of vitamins and minerals. It discusses the special nutritional needs of the elderly, alcoholics, dieters, pregnant women, and nursing mothers. Infants and children also have exceptional nutritional needs. You'll also learn the dangers of overindulging in high-potency supplements and to beware of questionable sales pitches touting fancy, ineffective products. A bibliography of additional reading is included. This publication is available while supplies last.

Write for:
Vitamin-Mineral Supplements and Their
Correct Use

Cost: $1.50

Send to:
Order Department, OP-107
American Medical Association
P.O. Box 10946
Chicago, IL 60610-9968

Vitamin-Mineral Supplements and Their Correct Use

PASS THE SALT

★★★

Sodium is a nutrient that is essential for maintaining fluid balance and normal function of the heart and other muscles. Although table salt is the most common sodium compound added to foods, there are many others. Most of us get much more than the amount needed for normal growth, development, and maintenance of health. Too much can be harmful, causing hypertension, or high blood pressure. *Sodium and Your Health* is an informative little pamphlet which discusses the dangers of excess sodium as well as what amount of sodium can be considered safe and adequate. It lists the sodium content of many foods, organized according to basic food groups. Canned and frozen vegetables are compared. Sodium content of condiments, beverages, and seasonings are also cited. This is a good pamphlet for anyone who wants to plan a safe, nutritious diet. A supplemental reading list is included.

Write for:
Sodium and Your Health

Cost: 75¢

Send to:
Order Department, OP-145
American Medical Association
P.O. Box 10946
Chicago, IL 60610-9968

DANGEROUS DIETING

★★★★

Trying to take off excess pounds is one thing, but an obsession with thinness is another. Anorexia nervosa and bulimia are two eating disorders that take irrationality regarding food to the breaking point. In extreme cases, both have been known to lead to starvation and death. This authoritative 32-page pamphlet takes an intelligent look at these two ailments which are sadly affecting our society's young women and, occasionally, men. Both disorders and their symptoms are thoughtfully defined along with the major known causes and factors which prompt them. You'll learn how cultural influences and psychological development play their roles. Also discussed are various methods of treatment and psychotherapeutic approaches used by eating disorder professionals. There is a chart which profiles normal and abnormal eating habits. Resource listings are included for further information.

Write for:
Anorexia Nervosa and Bulimia: Two Severe
Eating Disorders (No. 632)

Cost: $1.00

Send to:
Public Affairs Pamphlets
381 Park Ave. South
New York, NY 10016

continued

STAY HEALTHY

Anorexia Nervosa and Bulimia: Two Severe Eating Disorders

ANOTHER NEW (FAD) DIET

★★★

What does it take to lose weight? Millions of dieters who try to starve it off, melt it off, and sometimes even sleep it off would like to know. And of those who are successful at losing, fewer than 20 percent are able to keep off the pounds they shed. There is a secret to losing weight and keeping it off, but the answer lies in a few easily understood scientific principles, not in another new fad diet. *How to Take Weight Off (And Keep it Off) Without Getting Ripped Off* is a four-page article that demystifies the dieter's dilemma. It exposes some of the popular diets for the gimmicks they are, as well as various miracle pills, potions, and devices. A sensible approach to dieting is also discussed, with lots of healthy tips for getting started on the road to a new you.

Write for:
How To Take Weight Off (and Keep it Off) Without Getting Ripped Off (No. 1554P)

Cost: Free

Send to:
Consumer Information Center
P.O. Box 100
Pueblo, CO 81002

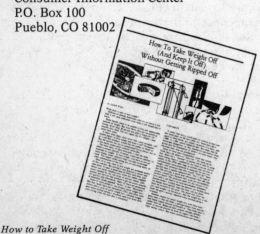

How to Take Weight Off

OVERWEIGHT: PROBLEM OF CIVILIZATION

★★★★

Only civilized man and a few tame animals suffer from overweight. This informative booklet tells what causes overweight in adults and children, the specific dangers it presents, and the principles of reducing. You'll learn about exercise and diet (if you're more than 10 to 15 percent overweight, you should consult your doctor before beginning to diet) and why you should not use amphetamines to lose weight. This sensible booklet from the Public Affairs Committee also discusses hospitalization and psychological support for extreme cases of overweight.

Write for:
Overweight—A Problem for Millions (No. 364A)

Cost: $1.00

Send to:
Public Affairs Pamphlets
381 Park Ave. South
New York, NY 10016

WHY THAT PUDGE WON'T BUDGE

★★★

Herbal pills, lotions, loofah scrubs: They're all "guaranteed" to remove cellulite, yet you could spend a small fortune on them without losing that "hard to budge pudge." Obesity experts insist that cellulite is just plain fat and there's only one way to get rid of it—diet and exercise. Next time you're tempted to buy anti-cellulite products, take along a copy of *Cellulite: Hard to Budge Pudge.* This free two-page folder from the Food and Drug Administration will remind you of the difference between fact and fiction. There's a good summary of what doctors and scientists have to say about what cellulite is and what goes into some of the "miracle" products. One lotion contained irritating hot red pepper to fool the gullible user into thinking the stuff was "working."

Write for:
Cellulite: Hard to Budge Pudge

Cost: Free (postcard requests only)

Send to:
FDA Office of Consumer Affairs
5600 Fishers Lane (HFE-88)
Rockville, MD 20857

A SASE is a self-addressed stamped envelope.

EAT BETTER, PLAY BETTER
★★★

The diet of both athletes and nonathletes must supply adequate quantities of water, carbohydrates, fats, protein, vitamins, and minerals. Athletes, however, have additional nutritional needs to compensate for their greater energy output. *Nutrition and Exercise for the Athlete* is a detailed little pamphlet full of good information for the sports enthusiast. It recommends what to eat (and in what proportions), and when to eat, outlines basic nutritional principles, and explains how the body works during exercise. Weight loss and gain programs are discussed, as well as the role various major nutrients play in an athlete's performance. A supplemental reading list is also included.

Write for:
   Nutrition and Exercise for the Athlete

Cost: 35¢

Send to:
   Distribution Center
   7 Research Park
   Cornell University
   Ithaca, NY 14850

BEFORE YOU START AN EXERCISE PROGRAM
★★★

The decision to carry out a physical fitness program cannot be taken lightly. It requires a commitment of time and effort, and, especially in the beginning, a dose of patience—you can't regain in a few days what you have lost in years of watching reruns on television. *Fitness Fundamentals* gives basic information you need to begin and maintain a personal physical fitness program. The eight-page pamphlet covers the four components of physical fitness, designing a proper exercise program, measuring your heart rate, and controlling your weight. Appropriate clothing for your chosen sport and when to exercise are also discussed. After reading this, the rest is up to you.

Write for:
   Fitness Fundamentals (No. 121P)

Cost: $1.00

Send to:
   Consumer Information Center
   P.O. Box 100
   Pueblo, CO 81002

Fitness Fundamentals

FIT AS A FIDDLE
★★★★

Exercise isn't a panacea for all mental and physical ills, but it can be a big help—millions of people can vouch for the way healthy exercise boosts vim, vigor, and vitality. No matter how old or young you are, there's an exercise program for you, and *Listen to Your Body*, a 28-page booklet from the Public Affairs Committee, is a handbook for those who want sensible advice and information before they choose a fitness program. The well-written booklet summarizes all the latest findings on physical fitness, with a special emphasis on running. Would-be joggers will welcome down-to-earth tips on deciding goals, warming up, setting a pace, and determining where, when, and how long to run. Dance, yoga, tennis, walking, and many other activities are also covered briefly.

Write for:
   Listen to Your Body: Exercise and Physical
      Fitness (No. 599)

Cost: $1.00

Send to:
   Public Affairs Pamphlets
   381 Park Ave. South
   New York, NY 10016

TAKING A HIKE
★★

Once dismissed as being "too easy" to be taken seriously as exercise, walking recently has gained new respect as a means of improving physical fitness. Studies now show that, when done briskly on a regular schedule, walking can improve the body's ability to consume oxygen during exertion, lower the

continued

STAY HEALTHY

resting heart rate, reduce blood pressure, and burn excess calories. It is a slower route to fitness than more strenuous activities, but the difference is not as great as you might believe. *Walking for Exercise and Pleasure* is a 16-page booklet that will get you started on the right path. You'll learn the benefits of walking and the correct posture to maintain. There is good advice on what to wear, along with illustrated directions for warm-up exercises. There is also information on how you can qualify for the Presidential Sports Award.

Write for:
   Walking for Exercise and Pleasure (No. 122P)

Cost: $1.00

Send to:
   Consumer Information Center
   P.O. Box 100
   Pueblo, CO 81002

Walking for Exercise and Pleasure

EXERCISE FOR YOUR GOOD HEALTH

Millions of Americans are checking into self-improvement centers such as health spas or weight-loss clinics each year. Many of these centers provide legitimate, quality services, but some are disreputable operations that not only take your money under false pretenses, but can be detrimental to your health. If you're thinking of joining a health spa or weight-loss clinic, check out this free six-page booklet from the Better Business Bureau. It tells the differences between health spas and weight-loss clinics and offers practical advice on how to choose a reputable facility. It tells you what to expect in services and what to look for in a contract before you sign it. This is good commonsense advice.

Write for:
   Tips on Health Spas (No. 24-188)

Cost: Free

Send to:
   Council of Better Business Bureaus
   1515 Wilson Blvd.
   Arlington, VA 22209

Tips on Health Spas

Understanding Medications

KEEPING TRACK OF YOUR MEDICINES
★★★

If you're taking more than one medicine, you may find this four-week medication calendar very useful. You fill in the name of the medicine, its color and shape, the conditions you must take it under (on an empty stomach, for example, or with food or milk), and how much to take. Then, you put a check in the appropriate box after you've taken each dose. Ask also for a blood pressure wallet card, which you can keep in your wallet or purse and bring with you to doctor appointments to record your blood pressure. The card also has space for a number of emergency phone numbers. Two useful items.

Write for:
   Keeping on Schedule with Your Medicines
   Blood Pressure Wallet Card

Cost: 50¢

Send to:
   North Wales Press, Inc.
   P.O. Box 1486
   North Wales, PA 19454

256   *A SASE is a self-addressed stamped envelope.*

Keeping on Schedule with Your Medicines

TAKE TWO AND CALL IN THE MORNING

★★★

Aspirin and acetaminophen are similar commonly ingested pain relievers, but there are some important differences between them. Most people know that aspirin can have unpleasant side effects, such as stomach irritation or nausea, but it does offer some benefits that acetaminophen doesn't. Acetaminophen, for example, has no effect on the inflammation from which arthritis victims suffer. *Aspirin vs. Acetaminophen* is a three-page article that discusses the differences, the advantages, and the side effects of the two over-the-counter drugs. You'll learn some of the history of both, special precautionary measures to take, and how to diagnose an overdose of each. Regardless of the medication taken, smart consumers always read the labels carefully.

Write for:
Aspirin vs. Acetaminophen (No. 542P)

Cost: Free

Send to:
Consumer Information Center
P.O. Box 100
Pueblo, CO 81002

TAKE TWO ASPIRIN...

★★★★

Aspirin is the world's most widely used medication; an average rate of 150 tablets are taken per person each year in the United States. Though generally regarded as harmless, aspirin is a drug and can have bad as well as good results. Not everyone can take aspirin safely. *Aspirin: Current Knowledge About an Old Medication* is a beneficial pamphlet which discusses this common medical treatment. The 28-page booklet covers the history of aspirin and its common uses today. You'll learn about the dangers of the drug and how it can irritate the stomach and the asthma sufferer. Types of aspirin and its alternative medications are covered, as well as research into potential capabilities of the drug. There is also a list of rules for taking aspirin which every household member should read.

Write for:
Aspirin: Current Knowledge About an Old Medication (No. 614)

Cost: $1.00

Send to:
Public Affairs Pamphlets
381 Park Ave. South
New York, NY 10016

Aspirin: Current Knowledge About an Old Medicine

THE HOUSEHOLD PAIN RELIEVER

★★★★

Americans consume more than 20 tons of aspirin a day. Aspirin is the drug most widely used in this country, but it's only in recent years that scientists have begun to understand how it works and what some of the risks of overuse are. Most people are aware that aspirin can sometimes cause a little stomach upset; it's now known, however, that its effects can be severe enough to cause gastrointestinal hemorrhage. If aspirin is your family's favorite cure-all, now you can educate yourself, and them, through this well-written free booklet. You'll learn how to use this valuable drug carefully instead of casually.

continued

STAY HEALTHY

Write for:
Aspirin: America's Favorite Drug

Cost: Free (postcard requests only)

Send to:
FDA Office of Consumer Affairs
5600 Fishers Lane (HFE-88)
Rockville, MD 20857

UNDERSTANDING PRESCRIPTION DRUGS
★★★

You see your doctor, get a prescription, have it filled, and take the medicine. But that's not the end of the matter. Drugs are powerful chemicals. Along with their benefits, they also have a potential for harm and must be handled correctly. *Here Are Some Things You Should Know About Prescription Drugs* is a three-page article that will help you use medication correctly. You'll learn about some possible adverse reactions you might experience from prescription drugs as well as effects of combining two or more drugs, or combining drugs and certain foods. Drugs taken with alcoholic beverages can also cause problems. The article also talks about how to work with your doctor, and discusses brand name versus generic products.

Write for:
Here Are Some Things You Should Know About Prescription Drugs (No. 551P)

Cost: Free

Send to:
Consumer Information Center
P.O. Box 100
Pueblo, CO 81002

Here Are Things You Should Know About Prescription Drugs

YOUR HEALTH IS YOUR CONCERN
★★★★

Don't leave it all to your doctor; you can take an active role in your own health care program. One way to participate is by being informed about the medications you take. This four-page foldout, free from the Food and Drug Administration, has lots of useful advice on using prescription drugs effectively and safely. *Prescription Drugs* offers guidelines on what your doctor needs to know about your health history before prescribing a drug and the questions you should ask your doctor before taking the medication—like does it have any side effects, can you drink alcohol while you're taking it, and can you save money by asking for the generic equivalent.

Write for:
Prescription Drugs

Cost: Free (postcard requests only)

Send to:
FDA Office of Consumer Affairs
5600 Fishers Lane (HFE-88)
Rockville, MD 20857

USING MEDICINES WISELY
★★★★

How much do you really know about the medications you take? You'll know more if you read *Know Your Medication: How To Use Over-the-Counter and Prescription Drugs*. Use this booklet as a guide to supplement your doctor's advice on how, when, and when not to take medications. There are suggestions for how (and how not) to mix food, drink, and medications; dos and don'ts for using over-the-counter analgesics, cough and cold remedies, sleeping pills, antacids, hemorrhoidal preparations, and so on; and advice for wise use of prescribed drugs, such as antibiotics, fungus fighters, heart and blood pressure drugs, painkillers, and tranquilizers. When you realize that all drugs have potential side effects, and that the number of available over-the-counter and prescription drugs increases constantly, it makes sense to do a little homework.

Write for:
Know Your Medication: How To Use Over-the-Counter and Prescription Drugs (No. 570)

Cost: $1.00

Send to:
Public Affairs Pamphlets
381 Park Ave. South
New York, NY 10016

A SASE is a self-addressed stamped envelope.

DANGEROUS REACTIONS

★★★

Would it occur to you not to swallow a tetracycline capsule with a glass of milk? Or to eat more green leafy vegetables if you are on the Pill? If you're taking a drug, the food you eat could make it work faster or slower or even prevent it from working at all. Eating certain foods while taking certain drugs can be dangerous, and some drugs can affect the way your body uses food. *Food and Drug Interactions* is a four-page article that discusses many of the problematic reactions that can occur, often quite innocently, while you are under medication. It explains how drugs may act in various ways to impair proper nutrition, how foods enhance or impede absorption of drugs into the bloodstream, and how even over-the-counter drugs can cause adverse reactions.

Write for:
   Food and Drug Interactions (No. 546P)

Cost: Free

Send to:
   Consumer Information Center
   P.O. Box 100
   Pueblo, CO 81002

A VERSATILE DRUG

★★★

Antihistamines are remarkable for their multiplicity of uses, from hay fever relief to easing motion sickness. But they also have a multiplicity of side effects, and even though they are available in both over-the-counter and prescription drug products, should be taken with care. Antihistamines do exactly what the name suggests—counteract the effect of histamine, a chemical substance found in almost all the body's tissues. When released, histamine causes some very uncomfortable reactions. *Antihistamines Wear Many Therapeutic Hats* is a three-page article that explores, in somewhat technical language, both the positive and negative effects of the drug as well as its many uses. It discusses the various types of antihistamines, offers a chart of trade and generic names, and gives a list of suggestions for using your medication in the safest and most effective manner.

Write for:
   Antihistamines Wear Many Therapeutic Hats
      (No. 514P)

Cost: Free

Send to:
   Consumer Information Center
   P.O. Box 100
   Pueblo, CO 81002

WHAT'S IN A (BRAND) NAME?

★★★★

With very few exceptions, the Food and Drug Administration has found that generic drugs are as safe and effective as their brand name counterparts. Since they're often produced by the same major drug manufacturer, this is hardly surprising. Some people, however, still feel that a product bearing a well-known brand name has to be better. To dispel this misconception that brand name drugs are superior to generics, the Food and Drug Administration has prepared an excellent two-page booklet that they'll send to you at no charge. *Generic Drugs: How Good Are They?* includes results of recent tests that compare generics and brand name drugs, and a list of the 14 most-prescribed drugs that are available generically. It also points out that many consumers, particularly those who take prescription drugs for prolonged periods, can save money by choosing generics.

Write for:
   Generic Drugs: How Good Are They?

Cost: Free (postcard requests only)

Send to:
   FDA Office of Consumer Affairs
   5600 Fishers Lane (HFE-88)
   Rockville, MD 20857

Generic Drugs:
How Good Are They?

STAY HEALTHY

HERBS: NOT A MAGIC CURE

★★★

Before the days of modern medicine and processed foods, herbs were the primary drugs and food additives. Today, with the popularity of natural foods and holistic health, use of herbs is on the rise, with many people growing and hunting their own. The problem is that some of these plants can be dangerous. Our ancestors used herbs to make poison and weapons. *Herbs Are Often More Toxic Than Magical* is an eight-page article that explains some of these toxicants. You'll learn about the history of herbal usage, research studies that have been done, and how toxic plants often resemble harmless ones. You'll also find a list compiled by the Food and Drug Administration of unsafe food herbs, their botanical and common names, and why they should be avoided.

Write for:
Herbs Are Often More Toxic Than Magical
(No. 549P)

Cost: Free

Send to:
Consumer Information Center
P.O. Box 100
Pueblo, CO 81002

Understanding Your Medical Care

JUST WHAT THE DOCTOR ORDERED

★★★★

Time was, you saw the family doctor for any health problem. Today you can see a wide variety of specialists for various health concerns. You can choose a doctor in private practice or one who belongs to a Health Maintenance Organization (HMO). If you need surgery, it can be performed in a hospital or in an outpatient surgical center or clinic. What all this amounts to is that today our medical care options are much more varied than they once were, and they can be confusing, too. A free booklet from the Better Business Bureau can help you sort out the various medical services and choose the ones you need and feel comfortable with.

A second booklet, *Tips on Medical Quackery,* can help protect you from being deceived and taken advantage of by unscrupulous manufacturers of certain "medical" treatments. It offers warnings about possible quackery, including diets that may be dangerous, arthritis products that may be worthless, and everything from baldness cures to so-called "youth prolongers."

Write for:
Tips on Choosing Medical Services (No. 24-214)
Tips on Medical Quackery (No. 24-194)

Cost: Free

Send to:
Council of Better Business Bureaus
1515 Wilson Blvd.
Arlington, VA 22209

THAT'S A GOOD QUESTION

★★★

The decisions you make about which health services and products to purchase are some of the most important and expensive decisions you make as a consumer. Yet, like many people, you may spend less time choosing a health professional than you would choosing a new television set. *Healthy Questions* is an eight-page guide that encourages you to take an active part in your health care. It includes sections on how to select and use the services of health professionals: physicians, dentists, vision care specialists, and pharmacists. There are lists of questions to ask each one, along with answers you might expect to hear. The booklet also discusses health maintenance organizations and building comfortable relationships with the professionals you select.

Write for:
Healthy Questions (No. 537P)

Cost: Free

Send to:
Consumer Information Center
P.O. Box 100
Pueblo, CO 81002

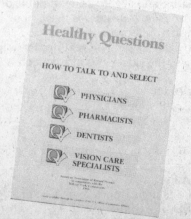

Healthy Questions

A SASE is a self-addressed stamped envelope.

MEDICALLY SPEAKING . . .

★★★★

The purpose of a medical examination is to diagnose illness in time to cure it, and to detect potential illness in time to prevent it. A good doctor, a thorough examination, well-maintained records, and your cooperation as a patient make it all possible. But even though we know it's necessary, sometimes an exam can cause anxiety. *Understanding Your Medical Examination* tells you what to expect. It answers questions of how often and how thorough your exams should be and explains the importance of your medical history. You'll learn what signals and symptoms your physician is looking for and how he will study various systems within your body. Various laboratory tests are described as well as how they are useful in diagnosing ailments. The 28-page booklet also covers the importance of your role as a patient.

Write for:
Understanding Your Medical Examination
(No. 630)

Cost: $1.00

Send to:
Public Affairs Pamphlets
381 Park Ave. South
New York, NY 10016

Understanding Your Medical Examination

WHY THOSE LAB TESTS?

★★★

The main purpose of those lab tests your doctor ordered is to give him a diagnosis of what's happening inside your body. Tests can help determine what's really wrong with you, or point to the need for an operation, or tell your doctor how you're reacting to a medication. This informative pamphlet from the College of American Pathologists thoroughly explains why lab tests are necessary, who does the testing, how samples are taken for which tests (and why),

and what you have to do to prepare for the tests. It also explains some common tests such as BUN (blood urea nitrogen); CBC (complete blood count); and tests for uric acid, glucose, and cholesterol. This sensible, low-key aid takes some of the mystery out of medical care.

Write for:
The Laboratory Connection

Cost: Free with a long SASE

Send to:
Department of Communications
College of American Pathologists
7400 N. Skokie Blvd.
Skokie, IL 60077

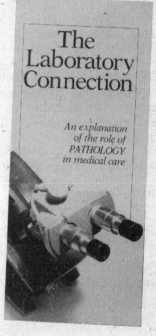

The Laboratory Connection

BASICS OF BIOFEEDBACK

★★

Biofeedback is a treatment technique in which people are trained to improve their health by using signals from their own bodies. Scientists cannot yet explain how biofeedback works; most patients who benefit from the treatment are trained to relax and modify their behavior. Migraine headaches, cardiac abnormalities, paralysis, and many other ailments can be treated clinically. *Biofeedback* is a three-page article that explores this treatment and traces its history. It discusses the many practical applications of biofeedback, especially in disorders that are stress-related. There is information to consider in determining whether you might be a candidate for the treatment, and a list of professional organizations.

Write for:
Biofeedback (No. 550P)

continued

Prices are for single items only; prices and information are accurate at time of publication.

STAY HEALTHY

Cost: Free

Send to:
Consumer Information Center
P.O. Box 100
Pueblo, CO 81002

UNKNOWNS OF ULTRASOUND

★★

Is diagnostic ultrasound a perfectly safe procedure, especially in pregnant women? Probably, but it is too soon to tell, says this three-page article. The electronic technology involved is fairly uncomplicated—a device that transforms electrical energy into sound energy is passed over a patient's body in contact with the skin. High-frequency, inaudible sound waves travel into the body and bounce back as they encounter hard and soft tissue, bones, and organs. The procedure is used to detect injuries, abnormalities, and disease. Ultrasound is also used in surgery, dentistry, and physical therapy. Yet in spite of its many benefits, we know very little about the long-term ramifications of the procedure.

Write for:
The Unknowns of Ultrasound (No. 552P)

Cost: Free

Send to:
Consumer Information Center
P.O. Box 100
Pueblo, CO 81002

MORE THAN BEAUTIFUL SMILES

★★★

Everyone knows braces straighten crooked teeth, but the scope and purpose of orthodontics is much broader than just creating beautiful smiles. Orthodontic treatment also plays an important role in improving overall oral health. In this pamphlet, illustrated with color photographs, you'll discover how and why the dental specialty of orthodontics can benefit you or your child. *Orthodontics* discusses who needs treatment, when to begin treatment, and what treatment costs; impressive before-and-after photos demonstrate some of the possibilities of treatment. While you're at it, ask for another free leaflet, *Orthodontic Insurance*, which answers questions about costs and coverage, and how to go about implementing such an insurance plan at your place of employment.

Write for:
Orthodontics
Orthodontic Insurance

Cost: Free

Send to:
American Association of Orthodontists
460 North Lindbergh Boulevard
St. Louis, MO 63141

Orthodontic Insurance

FINDING AN ORTHODONTIST

★★

Orthodontic treatment usually occurs once in a life time. It is important that the diagnosis and treatment be properly managed to achieve the best result. But if you're new in town, or if orthodontia is a new experience for your family, you may not know where to call for services. Members of the American Association of Orthodontists (AAO) are dentists who have the advanced education or qualifications and experience necessary to be identified as specialists by the American Dental Association. By writing to the AAO, you can receive a list of practitioners in your immediate area. It's a lot better than finding your orthodontist in the Yellow Pages.

Write for:
AAO Member List (specify geographic area)

Cost: Free

Send to:
American Association of Orthodontists
460 North Lindbergh Boulevard
St. Louis, MO 63141

IF YOU'RE HAVING AN OPERATION

★★

Who should perform your operation? What will it cost? Should you seek a second opinion? What does

A SASE is a self-addressed stamped envelope.

giving your informed consent mean? This series of four brochures answers these four questions. The series is designed to educate the prospective surgical patient on the importance of being well informed before consenting to an operation. The brochures are well written and easy to understand, and underscore the importance of asking questions and getting answers from a prospective surgeon. Sensible words from the American College of Surgeons.

Write for:
When You Need An Operation
brochure series

Cost: Free

Send to:
Office of Public Information
American College of Surgeons
55 E. Erie St.
Chicago, IL 60611

When You Need An Operation

A WOMAN'S SURGERY

★★

Hysterectomy is the surgical removal of the uterus; there are a number of conditions that may lead your doctor to recommend this operation. This booklet has been prepared to tell you about the operation and why this procedure might be necessary. The eight-page illustrated pamphlet explains the functions of the uterus and describes the symptoms and conditions which can lead to hysterectomy. Fibroid tumors, excessive uterine bleeding, precancerous and cancerous conditions, and postdelivery problems are discussed. You'll also learn what happens during the operation and what to expect during your recovery.

Write for:
About Hysterectomy

Cost: Free

Send to:
Office of Public Information
American College of Surgeons
55 East Erie Street
Chicago, IL 60611-2797

SPECIAL SURGERIES

★★

When your doctor tells you that you may need an operation, chances are you feel apprehensive. Many worries begin floating through your mind. This is only natural. But if you are an informed patient, you'll face the prospect of surgery with greater confidence and peace of mind. The American College of Surgeons has published several small pamphlets, each pertaining to a different operation. Hernias, cataracts, and lower back problems are three of the specific disorders that are explained using illustrations and nonmedical text. You'll learn the physiology of the affected body area, causes of the disorder, what the operation entails, and what to expect during recovery. The eight- and ten-page pamphlets are filled with solid information for anyone facing the scary prospect of surgery.

Write for:
About Hernia Repair
About Cataract Surgery in Adults
About Low-Back Pain

Cost: Free

Send to:
Office of Public Information
American College of Surgeons
55 East Erie Street
Chicago, IL 60611-2797

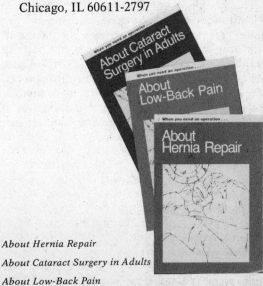

About Hernia Repair

About Cataract Surgery in Adults

About Low-Back Pain

STAY HEALTHY

UNDERSTANDING YOUR OPERATION
★★★

Three of the brochures in this packet discuss frequently performed operations: appendectomy, tonsillectomy, adenoidectomy, and cholecystectomy (removal of the gall bladder). In each case you learn what the organ is and what the symptoms of the disease are. You'll also learn how the diagnoses are made, what each operation involves, and the length of time you'll spend recovering. The fourth brochure deals with childbirth by Caesarean section. You'll learn the specific conditions that indicate that the procedure is necessary, and how it is performed.

Write for:
Four Brochures About Frequently Performed Operations

Cost: Free

Send to:
Office of Public Information
American College of Surgeons
55 E. Erie St.
Chicago, IL 60611-2797

HOME OR HOSPITAL: SENSIBLE CHOICES
★★★

Even the American Medical Association and the American Nurses' Association now endorse home health care for patients who do not require intensive care, constant supervision, or complex medical treatment. This booklet points out who should *not* have home health care, which services home health care personnel can provide, and the psychological and practical implications of home health care for the family who'll be caring for the patient. The booklet also tells how to explore the home health care options in your community, suggests facts to investigate *before* you engage a caregiver, and alerts you to the necessity of checking whether your health insurance covers home health care.

Write for:
A Guide to Home Health Care

Cost: Free with a long SASE

Send to:
Upjohn Health Care Services
2605 S. Kilgore
Kalamazoo, MI 49002

A Guide to Home Health Care

OUT OF COMMISSION
★

So you've broken your leg, and there's nothing to do except wait for it to heal. Not exactly. There are steps you can take to keep yourself comfortable now and when the cast comes off. *So You're Out on a Limb* repeats suggestions that your doctor or physical therapist may already have made, but it's a useful reminder that tells you how to make sure that crutches fit properly, how to keep from getting too stiff during a spell of forced inactivity, and how isometric exercises can help you regain full use of the limb after the cast comes off. Use it as a bookmark to remind you of this limited but sound advice.

Write for:
So You're Out on a Limb

Cost: Free with a long SASE

Send to:
Communications Dept.
The National Easter Seal Society
2023 W. Ogden Ave.
Chicago, IL 60612

NO MIRACLE CURES
★★

It doesn't make any difference whether the product being touted is snake oil or a pill to cure cancer—there are no miracles that will bring about better health and longer lives. All the same, every year Americans spend billions of dollars on pills, devices, and potions that do nothing at all—or may even be harmful. The ads are hard to resist; many people would like to grow taller, build a bigger bust, or say good riddance to baldness. *Quackery— The Billion Dollar Miracle Business* is a small foldout leaflet that will help you separate facts from

A SASE is a self-addressed stamped envelope.

fantasy. You'll learn about the high price of health fraud, and today's most common targets for quack attack. You'll also learn how to read between the lines of the enticing advertisements and how to protect yourself from being preyed upon by the charlatans.

Write for:
Quackery—The Billion Dollar Miracle Business

Cost: Free

Send to:
Consumer Information Center
P.O. Box 100
Pueblo, CO 81002

Quackery—
Billion Dollar Miracle Business

THINK TWICE
★★★★

"Miracle" gadgets that promise the way to bigger biceps or slimmer thighs get lots of advertising space in popular newspapers and magazines. They may sound amusing—or, maybe, secretly tempting—but there's a dark side to this medicine show. According to the Food and Drug Administration, most of these health ads are false or misleading, and this is the message of *The Big Quack Attack: Medical Devices*. This illustrated booklet is an invaluable weapon against being bamboozled by products that may be not only a waste of your hard-earned money, but direct or indirect health hazards. In 23 pages of sound common sense, *The Big Quack Attack* offers a questionnaire that helps you assess the claims of medical devices, information on how to report "quack device" problems, and a run-down on some of the questionable products now on the market.

Write for:
The Big Quack Attack: Medical Devices

Cost: Free (postcard requests only)

Send to:
FDA Office of Consumer Affairs
5600 Fishers Lane (HFE-88)
Rockville, MD 20857

THE FDA GOES AFTER QUACK ADS
★★★

Will somebody's marvelous new technique really halt your receding hairline or make you slim in a few days? Probably not. But every year, thousands of people are taken in by fraudulent advertising that makes unjustified health claims. Now the Food and Drug Administration offers free reprints of an article describing the problem of quack advertising and suggesting ways for consumers to steer clear of quackery. Before you send money to try a health product that may claim better results than you think possible, it might be a good idea to read this report. Single copies are free as long as supplies last. Incidentally, California—the most populous state in the U.S.—is the happiest hunting ground for the quack. Of the 435 advertisements studied for this report, 84 were published in California. More than half the ads were for weight-loss products (mostly diet pills), with hair restoration schemes next in number.

Write for:
Critiquing Quack Ads

Cost: Free (postcard requests only)

Send to:
FDA/Office of Consumer Affairs, HFE-88
5600 Fishers Lane
Rockville, MD 20857

THESE BEAUTY GAMES ARE NO FUN
★★★★

Watch out for those newspaper and magazine testimonials that feature a smiling, shapely creature who claims delightedly that she lost unwanted inches—or added curves where none were previously—just through a few days' use of a simple device. In a six-page illustrated booklet called *In Only Four Weeks . . .* the Food and Drug Administration takes a look at some of these wonders—and finds them not so wonderful after all. Some, for example a vibrating face mask or highly touted skin cream, may only hurt your pocketbook and your pride when you realize that you've thrown away good money. Others, like body wraps or silicone injections, may be potential health hazards.

continued

STAY HEALTHY

Write for:
In Only Four Weeks . . .

Cost: Free (postcard requests only)

Send to:
FDA Office of Consumer Affairs
5600 Fishers Lane (HFE-88)
Rockville, MD 20857

ARTHRITIS QUACKERY
★★★★

If you suffer from arthritis you can't be blamed for getting excited about any news of a new "cure," but the sad truth is that the copper bracelets, vibrating chairs, hormone treatments, and unapproved drugs currently being peddled aren't going to help. In *Hocus-Pocus as Applied to Arthritis,* the Food and Drug Administration exposes an astounding variety of quack devices aimed at arthritis sufferers. Although some of these products may do you no harm (beyond wasting your money), others could actually be dangerous. If recent publicity about certain arthritis cures has made you want to try them, be sure to read what the FDA has to say about their efficacy.

Write for:
Hocus-Pocus as Applied to Arthritis

Cost: Free (postcard requests only)

Send to:
FDA Office of Consumer Affairs
5600 Fishers Lane (HFE-88)
Rockville, MD 20857

Staying Healthy in Your Senior Years

STAYING HEALTHY LONGER
★★★★

The premise of this positive booklet is that you *can* keep your health as you age. There's a brief discussion on the aging process followed by advice on the best ways to keep fit. You'll learn how and what to eat, the value of judicious exercise, the importance of sufficient rest, and how you can relax and sleep well. Other subjects discussed include alcohol (in moderation, it's *friendly)* and accidents (they don't have to happen if you take some simple precautions). And there are ways to preserve and enhance your vision and hearing, too. A good feature is the

list of special resources for older people in the fields of continuing education, employment, and counseling.

Write for:
Better Health in Later Years (No. 446)

Cost: $1.00

Send to:
Public Affairs Pamphlets
381 Park Ave. South
New York, NY 10016

HOW SENIORS STAY HEALTHY
★★★★

By learning about normal age-related changes and techniques of preventive care, older people can take an active role in maintaining a healthy, independent life-style for as long as possible. Several national agencies on aging and health have pooled their information resources to offer a free 62-page booklet containing fact sheets on a number of common health problems among those aged 50 and older. Subjects discussed include arthritis, cancer, constipation, diabetes, dietary supplements, exercise, foot care, hearing, high blood pressure, osteoporosis, prostate problems, senility, sexuality in later life, skin care, teeth care, and urinary problems. A fact-filled, handy, and helpful health guide for anyone 50 or older.

Write for:
Help Yourself to Good Health

Cost: Free

Send to:
Pfizer, Inc.
230 Brighton Rd.
Clifton, NJ 07012-1498

Help Yourself to Good Health

EATING WHEN YOU'RE OVER 50

★★★

This large-size, easily legible booklet presents nutrition information for people over 50. In *To Your Health, In Your Second Fifty Years* you'll learn how nutrients work for you and how many servings to eat daily from each of the four food groups. There's good advice about low-calorie meals, shopping hints, warnings to avoid food fads and cults, and tips on planning an emergency shelf for bad weather days when you can't travel to the local grocer. You'll also find good information on how to shop for and store foods if you lack refrigeration or cooking facilities, or if you live alone. *For Mature Eaters Only: Guidelines for Good Nutrition* explains the importance of fiber and calcium-rich foods in the diet and how to manage low-cost, high-nutrient meals.

Write for:
　　To Your Health, In Your Second Fifty Years
　　For Mature Eaters Only: Guidelines for Good
　　　Nutrition

Cost:　45¢ for To Your Health
　　　　　20¢ for For Mature Eaters Only

Send to:
　　Order Department
　　National Dairy Council
　　6300 N. River Rd.
　　Rosemont, IL 60018-4233

DIET FOR THE ELDERLY

★★★★

Most experts on aging agree that nutrition is a factor in the aging process. As one gets older, the chances of suffering a chronic illness increase, and health experts believe that poor eating habits contribute to some of them. Also, changing bad eating habits to improve nutrient intake can be a possible therapy for some health conditions. A free four-page folder from the Department of Health and Human Services offers information and suggestions on diet and the elderly. A list of recommended foods is given, and there is discussion of medicines, drugs, and alcohol. Good advice here for older people to live longer and healthier through better dietary habits.

Write for:
　　Diet and the Elderly (No. 517P)

Cost:　Free

Send to:
　　Consumer Information Center
　　P.O. Box 100
　　Pueblo, CO 81002

Diet and Elderly

LIVING WITH PRESSURE

★★★

Of the more than 60 million Americans today who have high blood pressure, more than 40 percent are people age 60 and over. When it is not brought under control, high blood pressure can cause heart attack, stroke, and heart and kidney failure. As you will learn in this brochure, prompt medical treatment, including prescribed medication, proper diet, and exercise, can help bring high blood pressure under control. This booklet provides basic information on controlling high blood pressure and offers suggestions for solving those day-to-day problems that can make it difficult to follow the doctor's instructions. You'll learn how to interpret your blood pressure reading, modify your diet and weight, and build an exercise program. Guidelines for keeping track of your medication and working with your doctor are also included.

Write for:
　　Feelin' Fine: Living With High Blood Pressure
　　　as We Grow Older

Cost:　50¢

Send to:
　　North Wales Press, Inc.
　　P.O. Box 1486
　　North Wales, PA 19454

continued

STAY HEALTHY

Feelin' Fine:
Living With High Blood Pressure as We Grow Older

FOR YOUR MEDICAL LIBRARY
★★

Anyone over the age of 50 is especially susceptible to a wide range of illnesses and physical troubles. As you grow older, it is wise to be aware of this tendency and to do what you can to maintain optimum health. Two small pamphlets alert you to potential problems. The first, *Guard Against Flu/Pneumonia*, discusses this special threat to the elderly. It tells you how vaccinations can help, and it describes the possible side effects of immunization. There is also a list of additional recommendations for maintaining good health in the winter. The second pamphlet, *High Blood Pressure*, covers the causes of this condition and describes ways to control it. It discusses how you can work with your doctor to beat high blood pressure and prolong your life.

Write for:
Guard Against Flu/Pneumonia
High Blood Pressure: Your Doctor's Advice Could
Save Your Life

Cost: 50¢ each

Send to:
North Wales Press, Inc.
P.O. Box 1486
North Wales, PA 19454

High Blood Pressure
Guard Against Flu/Pneumonia

HYPOTHERMIA: A WINTER HAZARD
★★★★

Exposure to the cold is risky for anyone, but especially for the elderly. Even mildly cool temperatures of 60° to 65°F can trigger accidental hypothermia, a drop in deep body temperature that can be fatal if not detected promptly and treated properly. The National Institute on Aging offers a 12-page brochure on hypothermia, telling what it is, who is at risk, how it can be detected, and how the elderly can protect themselves against accidental hypothermia. A helpful booklet for senior citizens and those attending to their health.

Write for:
Hypothermia—A Winter Hazard for the Old
(No. 595P)

Cost: Free

Send to:
Consumer Information Center
P.O. Box 100
Pueblo, CO 81002

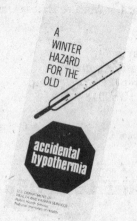

Hypothermia—A Winter Hazard for the Old

COMMUNICATION DISORDERS AND AGING
★★

Disorders of speech, language, and hearing are more frequently found among older adults than at any other age level. These individuals often find themselves at a distinct disadvantage on social, economic, and personal levels. With the number of older adults growing rapidly, and with the increased number of survivors of illnesses and accidents which can result in disorders of speech, language, and hearing, more older adults with communications problems will be encountered. This small leaflet from the

National Association for Hearing and Speech Action discusses this issue, and explains the causes and symptoms of common problems. You'll learn what a speech-language pathologist and audiologist can do to help and where to find the services you need.

Write for:
Communication Disorders and Aging

Cost: Free

Send to:
National Association for Hearing and Speech Action
10801 Rockville Pike
Rockville, MD 20852

Communication Disorders and Aging

MEDICARE IS NOT ENOUGH

★★★★

Medicare pays a large part of older people's health care expenses, but not all of them. There are limits on some covered services and Medicare recipients must pay certain amounts as deductibles or co-payments. Medicare doesn't cover some medical services at all. If you're shopping for insurance to supplement Medicare for yourself or a senior citizen, a free government booklet can answer a lot of your questions and lead you to an appropriate decision. The booklet explains what Medicare is, what it does and doesn't cover, and what it covers in part. Hints are offered for shopping for supplemental private health insurance and various types of private policies are described.

Write for:
Guide to Health Insurance for People with Medicare (No. 536P)

Cost: Free

Send to:
Consumer Information Center
P.O. Box 100
Pueblo, CO 81002

WHEN IT'S TIME TO CHOOSE A NURSING HOME

★★★

Ideally, a nursing home is a facility which provides good nursing care in an environment as physically and psychologically like home as possible. Yet nursing homes differ vastly in the services they are prepared to offer. How do you choose? This booklet, *What to Look for in a Nursing Home*, will guide you as you make this important decision for a relative, friend, or possibly yourself. The 12-page pamphlet tells you about general care, and the differences between a long-term health care facility and a residential one. There is a list of questions you should ask when you visit a nursing home—and the answers you should receive. There is advice as to what you should check for yourself while you are on the tour. Costs and Medicare are also discussed.

Write for:
What to Look for in a Nursing Home

Cost: $1.00

Send to:
Order Department, OP-61
American Medical Association
P.O. Box 10946
Chicago, IL 60610

What to Look For in a Nursing Home

MEDICAL AND HOUSING CARE FOR SENIORS

★★★★

Longer lifespans for many Americans mean new problems in housing and medical needs for older or disabled people. Is a nursing or retirement home the answer? The Better Business Bureau's 14-page booklet on long-term care facilities presents typical problems of caring for the elderly and disabled, and it

continued

STAY HEALTHY

offers possible solutions. Learn about the three basic types of long-term care facilities—skilled nursing facilities, intermediate care facilities, and residential care facilities. This brochure offers tips that can help you in your search for the right long-term care facility, and it gives you a list of questions to ask that can guide you to a satisfactory choice. There's also a section that summarizes Medicare and Medicaid.

Write for:
Tips on Choosing a Long-Term Care Facility (No. 24-176)

Cost: Free

Send to:
Council of Better Business Bureaus
1515 Wilson Blvd.
Arlington, VA 22209

Taking Care of Your Mental Health

SUCCESSFUL STRESS MANAGEMENT
★★★★

Absorbing and applying the information in this pamphlet will help you manage the stress in your life more effectively while enhancing a health-oriented life-style. Few people realize that their minds and bodies send out signals that often are reactions to stress; nor do they know that stress can be positive as well as negative. *How to Handle Stress: Techniques for Living Well* is a great self-help booklet. It discusses psychological and physical stress symptoms, causes, and responses, and it reminds of how we often push ourselves into stressful living. There are strategies for managing stress, relaxation techniques, and tips for taking care of yourself. There are also worksheets and assignments to get you thinking about realigning your priorities and goals, and a scale of known stressors so you can estimate the amount of tension you may be under.

Write for:
How to Handle Stress: Techniques for Living Well (No. 622)

Cost: $1.00

Send to:
Public Affairs Pamphlets
381 Park Ave. South
New York, NY 10016

How to Handle Stress: Techniques for Living Well

STRESS: IT'S NOT ALL BAD
★★★★

Emotional stress is not all bad. Without some stress, life would be dull and unexciting. Stress brings challenge and opportunity to life. Too much stress, however, can seriously affect physical and mental well-being, and a major challenge in today's stress-filled society is to make the stress in your life work for you instead of against you. A free two-page leaflet from the National Institute of Mental Health suggests how to react to stress, and how to handle it when it does occur. Good advice here for anyone experiencing anxiety, depression, or other symptoms of too much stress.

Write for:
Plain Talk About Handling Stress (No. 578P)

Cost: Free

Send to:
Consumer Information Center
P.O. Box 100
Pueblo, CO 81002

Plain Talk About Handling Stress

A SASE is a self-addressed stamped envelope.

STRESS AND DISTRESS

★★★★

Stress is a word that has very negative connotations in today's language, but stress isn't always bad. Stress is the body's natural reaction to events or situations it perceives as either extremely good or extremely threatening, and the stress response is essential to life. Learn to understand stress and to cope with its negative aspects by reading this interesting study. It explains that what we call stress is inherited from our prehistoric ancestors' "fight or flight" survival mechanism. There are also readable explanations of the anatomy of stress, how chronic stress can lead to illness and disease, and how you can begin to practice simple steps to avoid the damaging effects of too much stress.

Write for:
Understanding Stress (No. 538)

Cost: $1.00

Send to:
Public Affairs Pamphlets
381 Park Ave. South
New York, NY 10016

TENSION: THE MODERN MALAISE

★★★★

Americans today may live in less fear of bodily danger than their ancestors did, but psychologically they may not be so secure. If you, like so many modern people, suffer anxiety and stress, you'll find this little book useful reading. *Tensions — And How to Master Them* enumerates some of the causes of stress and tension in modern life and suggests a step-by-step method for controlling tension. There's a self-test to help you determine whether the level of your stressful feelings is slight or severe. There are also some good, time-honored suggestions for relieving stress by a change of scene, letting go of unrealistic expectations, and not striving so hard for perfection. Sensible and timely advice.

Write for:
Tensions — And How to Master Them (No. 305)

Cost: $1.00

Send to:
Public Affairs Pamphlets
381 Park Ave. South
New York, NY 10016

ROLLING WITH THE PUNCHES

★★★★

Sooner or later, most people have to deal with distressing events — and crises often happen without warning. Although you can't prevent crises (the death of a loved one, loss of a job, news of a serious illness, the end of a love affair) you can learn to roll with the punches as best you can. You'll learn about major crisis situations, and how each stressful situation evokes normal human emotions that should be acknowledged and accepted in *How to Cope with Crises*. This 28-page booklet suggests positive ways of coping and explains how to let other people help you through a crisis.

Write for:
How to Cope with Crises (No. 464)

Cost: $1.00

Send to:
Public Affairs Pamphlets
381 Park Ave. South
New York, NY 10016

A HANDLE ON GUILT

★★★★

Nobody knows how much suffering, even tragedy, has been triggered by needless feelings of guilt. Guilt is a common and powerful emotion, and it can easily get out of control. Unjustified, excessive guilt can sour your enjoyment of living, hobble your social and business life, and dishearten and humiliate the person who feels guilty. Fears and anxieties stemming from feelings of guilt can bring on emotional ills. A free four-page publication from the National Institute of Mental Health discusses guilt and how to handle it, suggesting that guilt can be tamed and used to advantage as you go on with the business of living.

Write for:
Plain Talk About Feelings of Guilt (No. 575P)

Cost: Free

Send to:
Consumer Information Center
P.O. Box 100
Pueblo, CO 81002

Plain Talk About Feelings of Guilt

STAY HEALTHY

FEELING BLUE

★★★

In its milder forms, depression is a natural reaction to everyday stress and frustration. Everyone goes through times when life is marked by sadness. Normally, the intensity and duration of a person's response relates to a life event, a loss of some kind. And even though the loss may be severe, time brings recovery from the setback and resumption of a normal life. Not everyone however, is this fortunate. Some individuals become overwhelmed by their feelings of depression and find it difficult to function. But depression can be overcome, as this pamphlet shows. In eight helpful pages, it discusses the causes and effects of depression; how to recognize the signs and symptoms; suicide; antidepressant drugs; professional help; and tips for living with the depressed person. If you're depressed and feel that you're at the end of your rope you should probably read this.

Write for:
Depression: It Can Be Overcome

Cost: 50¢

Send to:
North Wales Press, Inc.
P.O. Box 1486
North Wales, PA 19454

Depression: It Can Be Overcome

HOW TO DEAL WITH DEPRESSION

★★★★

Clinical depression is a medical disorder that can seriously harm people and families, and according to the National Institute of Mental Health it affects at least one in 10 Americans at some point in their lives. Yet most people fail to recognize it in themselves or their loved ones. A free 66-page booklet describes clinical depression and gives the good news that it is highly treatable. Mental health ex-

perts say nearly 90 percent of those afflicted can be helped successfully. This booklet lifts the veils that have made clinical depression a mystery to so many people. Read it and learn what clinical depression is, how to recognize it, and what to do about it.

Write for:
Depression—What We Know (No. 574P)

Cost: Free

Send to:
Consumer Information Center
P.O. Box 100
Pueblo, CO 81002

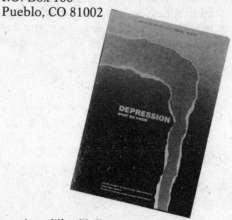
Depression—What We Know

WHEN THE BLUES WON'T GO AWAY

★★★★

Everyone gets depressed at one time or another. What's important is the degree of depression and how long it lasts. This excellent booklet examines the subject extensively, discussing who gets depressed (even babies do), what depression *is*—an emotional state of dejection and sadness ranging from mild discouragement to utter hopelessness and despair—and the various kinds and degrees of depression. There's also a discussion of mood-elevating medications and other remedies, such as behavior or psychotherapy and the cost of such treatment. There's a short reading list, too, and suggestions for several ways that you can help yourself or someone who's depressed.

Write for:
Depression: Causes and Treatment (No. 488)

Cost: $1.00

Send to:
Public Affairs Pamphlets
381 Park Ave. South
New York, NY 10016

A SASE is a self-addressed stamped envelope.

DRUGS AND DEPRESSION

★★★★

One day, Abraham Lincoln wrote his law partner saying, "I am now the most miserable man living. Whether I shall ever be better, I cannot tell. To remain as I am is impossible. I must die or be better ..." Lincoln, like as many as 11 million Americans today, suffered from clinical depression. Depression goes back to the earliest ages of mankind, but the bright side of the picture is that today depression can be treated. The National Institute of Mental Health offers a free four-page brochure describing depression and the drugs and other medications and therapies that can lessen the oppressive load that depressed people have to carry.

Write for:
Anti-Depressant Drugs (No. 540P)

Cost: Free

Send to:
Consumer Information Center
P.O. Box 100
Pueblo, CO 81002

SUICIDE: A CALL FOR HELP

★★

Most people experience periods of melancholy and gloom from time to time. But when depression becomes exaggerated, a person may attempt suicide as a drastic call for help. Although all kinds of people may think about taking their own lives, and for many different reasons, there are definite warning signals or clues that can alert you to the fact that a loved one's mental condition is approaching the suicidal. Learn what the warning signs are from these two booklets from the American Association of Suicidology. *Before It's Too Late* is aimed especially at the family and friends of someone who has survived a suicide attempt. *Suicide—It Doesn't Have to Happen* goes into greater depth on the kinds of professional and personal help available to troubled individuals so that they can find their way through crises without getting to the point of self-destruction.

Write for:
Before It's Too Late
Suicide—It Doesn't Have to Happen

Cost: 50¢ each

Send to:
North Wales Press, Inc.
P.O. Box 1486
North Wales, PA 19454

Before It's Too Late

Suicide—It Doesn't Have to Happen

SOMEONE WHO UNDERSTANDS

★★★★

There are no easy answers or cures for many human problems, but they don't have to be suffered alone. Millions of people whose problems and needs are not met through formal health care, social services, and counseling programs can find hope and personal support through mutual help groups. Members share common concerns and benefit from the understanding and help of others who have gone through similar experiences. A free four-page leaflet from the National Institute of Mental Health tells what mutal help groups are and how they work, and offers a list of names and addresses of various help groups.

Write for:
Plain Talk About Mutual Help Groups (No. 576P)

Cost: Free

Send to:
Consumer Information Center
P.O. Box 100
Pueblo, CO 81002

REACHING OUT: THE SELF-HELP MOVEMENT

★★★★

One of the classic ways of coping is to talk over a problem with someone who can say "I understand" and mean it because he or she has been through the same thing. That's the key to the blossoming in recent years of self-help groups for people feeling pain from causes that range from drug addiction and widowhood to the problems of people on wel-

continued

fare or those coping with a life-threatening illness. *Partners in Coping: Groups for Self and Mutual Help* probes how the depersonalization of many human services agencies has fostered this self-help movement. There are summary descriptions of how a number of these groups function.

Write for:
   Partners in Coping: Groups for Self and Mutual
      Help (No. 559)

Cost: $1.00

Send to:
   Public Affairs Pamphlets
   381 Park Ave. South
   New York, NY 10016

MENTAL HEALTH HELP
★★★★

From time to time most people suffer from some degree of depression or anxiety, or experience some other form of psychological or emotional distress. It may be caused by losing a job, ending a relationship, experiencing the death of a loved one, or by a physical health problem. Mental health is as important to well-being as physical health, and should be considered just as objectively. The National Institute of Mental Health offers a free 20-page booklet answering questions about mental health. It suggests agencies to contact for help with mental health problems, how to pay for assistance, and how to get free or inexpensive treatment for children, adults, and senior citizens. Treatment methods are also discussed.

Write for:
   A Consumer's Guide to Mental Health Services
      (No. 573P)

Cost: Free

Send to:
   Consumer Information Center
   P.O. Box 100
   Pueblo, CO 81002

Consumer's Guide to Mental Health Services

WHEN PROBLEMS OVERWHELM
★★★★

Most people are able to handle life's everyday challenges and changes as well as the different stages that everyone has faced or will face in life—school problems, marriage difficulties, loss of loved ones, retirement. But for those who are emotionally disturbed or mentally ill, minor difficulties are often exaggerated. If you or someone you know is having trouble coping, you may get some help from the National Institute of Mental Health's 12-page booklet. Types of mental disorders and illnesses and their causes are described and suggested treatments are explained. Agencies are listed that can help provide services to those experiencing mental or emotional stress.

Write for:
   You Are Not Alone (No. 127P)

Cost: $1.00

Send to:
   Consumer Information Center
   P.O. Box 100
   Pueblo, CO 81002

You Are Not Alone

GETTING YOUR HEAD STRAIGHT
★★★★

In recent years, psychotherapy has become more widely accepted—and accessible—as an option for people in every walk of life. So many kinds of therapies are now available that it can be difficult to know which one might work for you, but there's some sound information on the subject in *The Psychotherapies Today*, a 28-page booklet from the Public Affairs Committee. This useful little book discusses in nontechnical terms the various modern techniques that might help you or someone close to you resolve

A SASE is a self-addressed stamped envelope.

psychological difficulties. Although the approach is necessarily oversimplified at times, this booklet succeeds in summarizing the basics of 14 major "schools" of therapy, including Freudian, Jungian, and Gestalt therapies; transactional analysis; biofeedback; and behavior modification.

Write for:
   The Psychotherapies Today (No. 596)

Cost: $1.00

Send to:
   Public Affairs Pamphlets
   381 Park Ave. South
   New York, NY 10016

KEEPING IN SHAPE
★★★★

If you feel good about yourself and the world around you, you're probably both physically and mentally fit. If you're overweight, don't get enough exercise, and feel out of sorts with yourself and the world, chances are you need to take another look at the role physical fitness plays in good mental health. A free four-page publication from the National Institute of Mental Health examines the correlation between exercise, health, and physical and emotional fitness. It tells how to start a regular exercise program for children, adults, or senior citizens. Whether you decide on an exercise program, jogging, swimming, tennis, golf, or any other activity, this booklet is a good place to start taking care of your physical and mental health.

Write for:
   Plain Talk About Physical Fitness and Mental
      Health (No. 577P)

Cost: Free

Send to:
   Consumer Information Center
   P.O. Box 100
   Pueblo, CO 81002

COMPULSIVE GAMBLING
★★★★

It's estimated that 1.1 million Americans are compulsive gamblers and another 3.3 million are headed that way. What causes compulsive gambling? Who is a compulsive gambler? What treatment is available to help break the habit? Answers to these questions make up the nitty-gritty of this excellent study of a serious national problem. You'll also find sources of

help for compulsive gamblers and an intelligent discussion of legalized gambling. A 20-question checklist prepared by Gamblers Anonymous suggest some warning signs that indicate gambling is getting out of hand.

Write for:
   Compulsive Gambling (No. 598)

Cost: $1.00

Send to:
   Public Affairs Pamphlets
   381 Park Ave. South
   New York, NY 10016

Health Hazards:
Drinking, Smoking, Drugs

TO YOUR GOOD HEALTH
★★★★

If you're lucky enough to enjoy good health you can give some of the credit to the genes you inherited. But the secret to maintaining good health lies in yourself and your life-style. What you eat, what you weigh, how much you exercise, and similar factors can positively or negatively influence your health. Find out if you're doing right by your body with the help of this booklet. *Health Hazard Appraisal: Clues for a Healthier Lifestyle* includes self-tests on exercise, nutrition, alcohol, drugs, tobacco, safety, personal health, and leisure habits to help you determine problem areas in your own life-style. Once you've identified any of these self-imposed hazards, you can begin to make commonsense changes.

Write for:
   Health Hazard Appraisal: Clues for a Healthier
      Lifestyle (No. 558)

Cost: $1.00

Send to:
   Public Affairs Pamphlets
   381 Park Ave. South
   New York, NY 10016

TAKE YOUR LAST PUFF
★★★★

You *can* quit smoking. Many smokers have quit "cold turkey," without first cutting down, planning a spe-

continued

cial program, or seeking professional help. But many others have successfully given up cigarettes by replacing them with new habits or by using some gimmick. A free 32-page booklet from the National Institutes of Health tells how to quit smoking by trying various techniques such as doing it with someone else with a smoking habit, switching brands of cigarettes, cutting down on the number of cigarettes smoked, and how to keep from being tempted back into smoking. It tells what to expect after you quit smoking and how to handle aftereffects such as possible weight gain or smokers' "crazies," and gives other tips on kicking the smoking habit.

Write for:
Clearing the Air: Guide to Quitting Smoking (No. 561P)

Cost: Free

Send to:
Consumer Information Center
P.O. Box 100
Pueblo, CO 81002

Clearing the Air

HAVEN'T YOU QUIT YET?
★★★★

Research studies strongly indicate that tobacco smoking, and particularly cigarette smoking, is linked to a shortened life expectancy. About 300,000 Americans die prematurely each year from diseases related to smoking including lung cancer, heart disease, emphysema, and chronic bronchitis. If you still smoke and would like to quit, read *Smoking: Facts You Should Know.* This important 12-page pamphlet covers the harmful effects on the respiratory and circulatory systems, on unborn children, and on nonsmokers. Cigars, pipes, and low-tar cigarettes are also dangerous. There is good advice for female smokers, and suggestions for anyone who would like to give up the habit. A resource list for further information is included. The pamphlet is available while supplies last.

Write for:
Smoking: Facts You Should Know

Cost: 75¢

Send to:
Order Department, OP-42
American Medical Association
P.O. Box 10946
Chicago, IL 60610

Smoking: Facts You Should Know

HOW TO QUIT SMOKING
★★★★

If you don't smoke, chances are you have a friend or relative who does. If you do smoke, you've probably heard about how health-damaging smoking is and would like to quit. In the last 15 years, 33 million Americans have kicked the smoking habit. If you want to know how you can stop smoking, check out the new 36-page booklet on smoking cessation techniques from the American Council on Science and Health. It tells about various plans for stopping smoking and discusses products which claim to help you quit. Curious about nicotine chewing gum, stop smoking diets, hypnosis, or acupuncture to kick the smoking habit? This booklet tells about these methods and more.

Write for:
Searching for a Way Out

Cost: $2.00

Send to:
American Council on Science and Health
47 Maple St.
Summit, NJ 07901

A SASE is a self-addressed stamped envelope.

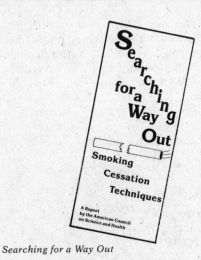

Searching for a Way Out

MEET THE MISOCAPNISTS

★★

Women have always used tobacco in this country. The wives of colonial New England smoked pipes while they baked and cooked. It's only fairly recently that studies were made of women who smoked and the true health risk story surfaced. This booklet, written by a science writer for the *New York Times,* particularly stresses the studies made on smoking and pregnancy, illness, and disability, and how women influence their children's smoking patterns. There's a discussion on quitting and how misocapnists (tobacco haters) are fighting back. Though the statistics cited are alarming, they're 10 years old. Statistics resulting from current studies would tell the story better.

Write for:
 Women and Smoking (No. 475)

Cost: $1.00

Send to:
 Public Affairs Pamphlets
 381 Park Ave. South
 New York, NY 10016

COCAINE CONCERNS

★★★★

Cocaine is not "just" a recreational drug. It is a poison which can be abused and which can lead to ruined lives, and premature death. *The Cocaine Epidemic* is an informative booklet on the dangers of this substance, and it explores the extent of the widespread problem. It covers what cocaine is and where it comes from, how the drug affects the body, and the harmful effects of use. You'll learn about the addictive powers of cocaine, how to identify users, where the user can go for help, and what treatments are available. The 28-page booklet discusses the link between cocaine and crime, and what the government and other agencies are doing to prevent the influx of the substance into this country. A source list for further information is in the back of the book.

Write for:
 The Cocaine Epidemic (No. 633)

Cost: $1.00

Send to:
 Public Affairs Pamphlets
 381 Park Ave. South
 New York, NY 10016

The Cocaine Epidemic

DON'T TAKE A PILL

★★★★

Misuse and abuse of prescription drugs is a special problem today, especially for women, but there is lots of help available. This authoritative 28-page pamphlet explores drug dependencies as a growing societal concern. It explains why women are more vulnerable than men and how the problem covers all socioeconomic groups. You'll learn how misuse begins and can eventually lead to abuse and addiction, and about the phenomenon of tolerance and the dangers of combining drugs with alcohol. The booklet describes many commonly abused prescription drugs, their intended purposes, and their effects. There is also a section devoted to the pregnant woman; a list of signals which may indicate a person is abusing prescription drugs; and discussion of a variety of treatments.

Write for:
 Women and Abuse of Prescription Drugs
 (No. 604)

Cost: $1.00

continued

Prices are for single items only; prices and information are accurate at time of publication.

STAY HEALTHY

Send to:
    Public Affairs Pamphlets
    381 Park Ave. South
    New York, NY 10016

Specialized Health Care

ALLERGY TEST ALERT
★★★

Cytotoxic testing is touted as a way of tracking down and curing ills by on-the-spot examination of the blood for food allergies. The evidence of such allergies is then used to explain a variety of symptoms patients may have or think they have. While the idea may sound plausible, there is no proof it works. The test, which combines blood with nearly 200 commonly eaten foods and additives, is not currently approved by either the Food and Drug Administration or the American Academy of Allergists. In a free pamphlet, *The Flaw in Cytotoxic Testing,* the FDA warns the consumer to beware of spending hundreds of dollars for these tests. Claims made by operators of cytotoxic testing clinics are usually not modest; many promise deliverance from excess weight and a wide range of physical symptoms. In addition, clinics are not always licensed or staffed by medical personnel.

Write for:
    The Flaw in Cytotoxic Testing (postcard
        request only)

Cost: Free

Send to:
    FDA/Office of Consumer Affairs, HFE-88
    5600 Fishers Lane
    Rockville, MD 20857

GETTING TO GRIPS WITH ALLERGIES
★★★★

What do you really know about allergies? You'll know more after reading this extensive booklet written by a doctor who explains what allergies are, what causes them, and who is affected. He explains asthma, hay fever, perennial allergic rhinitis, dermatitis, hives, certain kinds of headache, and some reactions to insect bites—all conditions caused by allergies. He briefly covers food allergies (and why skin tests are generally of little value in diagnosing them), drug allergies, and the susceptibilities of various age groups. What can you do if you have an allergy? You can stay away from food that triggers allergy, have desensitization treatments, and/or use medications—they're all explained in the booklet. You'll also learn what research is being done, and where you can go for more information about this insidious problem.

Write for:
    What Do We Know About Allergies? (No. 486)

Cost: $1.00

Send to:
    Public Affairs Pamphlets
    381 Park Ave. South
    New York, NY 10016

PARDON MY ACHOO!
★★★★

Few things can spoil an otherwise great time faster than hay fever. Many people sneeze their way through autumn with red eyes, stuffy nose, scratchy throat, and other agonies of hay fever, while others suffer from these and other symptoms at other times of the year as well. A new report by the American Council on Science and Health offers help for hay fever sufferers. It discusses the kinds of medical treatments available to treat the malady (antihistamines, sympathomimetics, and others), and gives information on allergy shots which can reduce or eliminate hay fever symptoms. A new medication, cromolyn sodium, also is described. Included is a helpful guide describing hay fever drugs, their brand names, and their primary side effects.

Write for:
    Hay Fever

Cost: $2.00

Send to:
    American Council on Science and Health
    47 Maple St.
    Summit, NJ 07901

Hay Fever

A SASE is a self-addressed stamped envelope.

EASING
ASTHMA ATTACKS

★★★★

Asthma sufferers rarely die from an asthma attack, but the feeling of suffocation that occurs as the airways begin to close can make sufferers fear they've already gasped their last breath. Asthma is a chronic disease involving a reversible obstruction of the airways, especially the bronchi and bronchioles, the large and small tubes that carry air into the lungs. A free four-page publication from the National Institutes of Health explains the two basic types of asthma and describes various drugs along with steps asthmatics can take to relieve their condition.

Write for:
   Asthma Is All in the Chest (No. 557P)

Cost: Free

Send to:
   Consumer Information Center
   P.O. Box 100
   Pueblo, CO 81002

WHEN YOU CAN'T
BREATHE . . .

★★★★

People with asthma, particularly children, can be helped to accept their condition calmly, gain confidence in what they can do to control it, and avoid falling into traps of invalidism or feeling different from others. The thing to remember is that not only can asthma attacks be treated, but many can be prevented. *Asthma—Episodes and Treatment* takes an informative look at this chronic respiratory condition and is good reading for anyone involved with the ailment. The 28-page booklet covers what happens during an episode, how it starts, and how it can be triggered. It deals with allergens and the all-important factor of attitude. You'll learn what can be done for an asthma attack, both medically and psychologically, as well as how to prevent future episodes.

Write for:
   Asthma—Episodes and Treatment (No. 608)

Cost: $1.00

Send to:
   Public Affairs Pamphlets
   381 Park Ave. South
   New York, NY 10016

Asthma—Episodes and Treatment

UNDERSTANDING ASTHMA

★★★★

If you sometimes have trouble breathing because of asthma, this handbook from the American Lung Association is for you and your family. In 28 full-size pages, the illustrated book describes what happens in the body during an asthma episode and the factors, or "triggers," which can set off the attack. A question-and-answer format and worksheets enable the asthma sufferer to think about his or her own triggers and follow the advice given for each possibility. There is information for smokers and non-smokers, and case histories from fellow sufferers. The person who has asthma will learn how to control episodes and how to work effectively with the doctor. There's a recommended diet plan, and a glossary of asthma medicines.

Write for:
   The Asthma Handbook

Cost: Free

Send to:
   American Lung Association
   P.O. Box 596
   New York, NY 10001

The Asthma Handbook

STAY HEALTHY

KEEP ON RUNNING
★★★★

This pamphlet is written primarily for the young athlete with diabetes and for those who share the responsibility of management of the disorder, including family, friends, coaches, and involved professionals. *Diabetic Athlete* is a comprehensive look at this baffling disease and how the sports enthusiast can enjoy his or her recreation and accommodate his or her physical needs simultaneously. The 20-page booklet answers many questions, such as how exercise affects the diabetic and how to prepare for the rigors of competition. Hypoglycemia and its symptoms and prevention are also discussed. The athlete learns to guard against low blood sugar, and how to control the condition to allow participation in athletic events. This publication is available while supplies last.

Write for:
Diabetic Athlete

Cost: $2.00

Send to:
Order Department, OP-084
American Medical Association
P.O. Box 10946
Chicago, IL 60610

Diabetic Athlete

ACNE—IT'S A FOUR-LETTER WORD
★★★

Acne—for many teens it's the worst four-letter word in the vocabulary. If you're one of the sufferers, take a look at *Stubborn and Vexing, That's Acne,* an excellent, and free, four-page booklet from the Food and Drug Administration. The booklet will tell you what causes acne and what you can do to avoid or control it. Illustrations of normal and acne-afflicted skin show you how plugged sebaceous glands result in the condition known as acne. This is a good rundown on available commercial products that can help, and it gives guidelines for their use. This booklet's suggestions can help you decide whether your case of acne needs a doctor's care rather than a nonprescription remedy.

Write for:
Stubborn and Vexing, That's Acne

Cost: Free (postcard requests only)

Send to:
FDA/Office of Consumer Affairs, HFE-88
5600 Fishers Lane
Rockville, MD 20857

NOW HEAR THIS!
★★★★

Impaired hearing is considered to be the most common handicapping health problem in the United States, affecting millions of people. Many who suffer hearing loss can be helped by medical or surgical treatment and countless others are helped by using a hearing aid. A new booklet put out by the Better Business Bureau offers help to those with hearing disorders who may be considering seeking medical help or buying a hearing aid. Types of hearing loss are described, signs of hearing loss are indicated, and suggestions are given for what to do for various signs of hearing loss. The four types of hearing aids are explained and suggestions are given for how to select the right hearing aid for your needs.

Write for:
Facts About Hearing Aids (No. 03-250)

Cost: Free

Send to:
Council of Better Business Bureaus
1515 Wilson Blvd.
Arlington, VA 22209

HELP FOR SPEECH AND HEARING DISORDERS
★★★

Do you suspect that someone in your family has a speech or hearing problem? The American Speech-Language-Hearing Association offers a number of excellent brochures that deal with common disorders and tell you how to get help. *Hearing Aids and Hearing Help* explains how an audiologist trains someone with a hearing problem to speech-read and pick up clues from a speaker's facial expression,

A SASE is a self-addressed stamped envelope.

hand gestures, and body posture. *Hearing Impairment and the Audiologist* provides an overview of the causes and treatments of hearing disorders.

Write for:
    Hearing Aids and Hearing Help
    Hearing Impairment and the Audiologist

Cost: Free

Send to:
    American Speech-Language-Hearing Association
    10801 Rockville Pike
    Rockville, MD 20852

Hearing Aids and Hearing Help
Hearing Impairment and the Audiologist

HELP FOR THE LARYNGECTOMEE

★★★

You or someone in your family has cancer of the larynx and has had to have an operation to remove the voice box. After recovering from the initial shock and fear of that diagnosis and surgery, there are probably many questions that you want to ask. This booklet is an attempt to answer some of the questions frequently asked by the laryngectomee and persons close to him or her. In nontechnical language the 24-page booklet discusses laryngeal cancer, post-surgical care, relearning to speak and communicate, physical limitations of the patient, and more. There is also a bibliography and suggested reading list for further information.

Write for:
    Questions & Answers for the Laryngectomee
    and the Family

Cost: $1.25

Send to:
    Interstate Printers & Publishers, Inc.
    19 N. Jackson St.
    P.O. Box 50
    Danville, IL 61834-0050

UNDERSTANDING COMMUNICATION DISORDERS

★★

Speech and language disorders affect the way people talk and understand. These disorders may range from simple sound substitutions to not being able to use speech and language at all. Some of the more common ones are stuttering, articulation disorders, voice disorders, aphasia, and delayed language. Three helpful pamphlets from the National Association for Hearing and Speech Action will help you understand these problems and explain what the speech-language pathologist can do to help. You'll learn some of the causes and symptoms, as well as some good advice for preventive care of the voice. The information given is general and nontechnical.

Write for:
    Speech and Language Disorders and the
      Speech-Language Pathologist
    NAHSA Answers Questions About Voice Problems
    NAHSA Answers Questions About Adult Aphasia

Cost: Free

Send to:
    National Association for Hearing and
      Speech Action
    10801 Rockville Pike
    Rockville, MD 20852

Speed and Language Disorders

INDEPENDENCE AGAINST THE ODDS

★★★★

Some 11 million Americans are physically disabled or handicapped in some way, and more and more of them are breaking through the barriers that formerly excluded them from the mainstream of life. *Independent Living: New Goal for Disabled Persons* is a 28-page booklet that compares the "old" institu-

continued

STAY HEALTHY

tionalized approach to handicapped people with the dynamic new approaches that are being developed on the principle of self-help. If you're handicapped, you will want to read this little book. It describes a wealth of options, alternatives, and suggestions for learning skills, group living, special equipment, home health aides, etc., that can help you become as independent as possible. An encouraging publication from the Public Affairs Committee.

Write for:
Independent Living: New Goal for Disabled Persons (No. 522)

Cost: $1.00

Send to:
Public Affairs Pamphlets
381 Park Ave. South
New York, NY 10016

ARTHRITIS AND YOU
★★★★

Arthritis is not a specific disease but a symptom that can occur in over 100 conditions. The word itself means "joint inflammation." Today a variety of drugs are available to treat arthritis and provide relief from the pain, and to slow and maybe halt the potentially crippling effects of rheumatoid arthritis. A free four-page publication by the National Institutes of Health tells all about arthritis and discusses various possible pain relievers and cures. It includes a list of commonly prescribed arthritis drugs but also suggests rest, programmed exercise, physical therapy, splints and other home-help devices, and a well-balanced diet, all of which can be part of a total treatment program.

Write for:
For Treating Arthritis, Start with Aspirin (No. 547P)

Cost: Free

Send to:
Consumer Information Center
P.O. Box 100
Pueblo, CO 81002

HELP FOR HERPES
★★

Genital herpes is the third most common form of venereal disease in the United States today. No drug, diet, vaccine, or other product has been shown to be effective in preventing or curing the disease. Be-cause genital herpes is caused by a virus rather than a bacteria, antibiotics do not help. *Herpes: Drug Eases Symptoms but Still No Cure* is a three-page article that discusses the herpes virus, the symptoms, the transmission of the disease, and its recurring outbreaks. It discusses the special concerns posed to women by infection during pregnancy. The drug acyclovir is available in oral, intravenous and ointment forms, and this article explores what relief can and cannot be expected from it. Although other drugs are being studied, at this time acyclovir is the only one approved by the FDA and it, too, has side effects.

Write for:
Herpes: Drug Eases Symptoms but Still No Cure (No. 568P)

Cost: Free

Send to:
Consumer Information Center
P.O. Box 100
Pueblo, CO 81002

COUNTING SHEEP
★★

Insomnia is the triumph of mind over mattress, as one joke has it. But for many people, not being able to sleep is no laughing matter. Americans spend about $25 million a year on over-the-counter sleep aids, and several million more on prescription drugs. *On Making It Through The Night* examines the safety of some of those drugs as well as coping with the problem without chemicals. The various sleep stages are discussed in this three-page article, along with how sleeping pills can interfere with these stages. You'll learn about some common sleep disorders and the differences gender can play in your ability to sleep tight. You'll also learn how sleep clinics and biofeedback may be able to help.

Write for:
On Making It Through the Night (No. 569P)

Cost: Free

Send to:
Consumer Information Center
P.O. Box 100
Pueblo, CO 81002

A STROKE OF HOPE
★★★

Because of medical advances, more stroke victims than ever are surviving. Over the past 20 years,

A SASE is a self-addressed stamped envelope.

stroke deaths have dropped 40 percent. Many survivors, even those with severe handicaps, are learning to walk again, to talk again, and to lead independent lives. If you or someone close to you is a victim of this paralyzing ailment, read *Stroke: Hope Through Research,* prepared by the U.S. Department of Health and Human Services. The informative, illustrated 32-page booklet answers many questions you may have about the causes of stroke, the importance of immediate attention, and diagnostic tests. You'll learn about treatment and rehabilitation, surgery, and prevention. Pending research studies are also covered. The booklet contains a supplemental reading list and glossary.

Write for:
Stroke: Hope Through Research (No. 125P)

Cost: $1.75

Send to:
Consumer Information Center
P.O. Box 100
Pueblo, CO 81002

Stroke: Hope Through Research

INFORMATION ABOUT ULCERS
★★★

About 12 percent of U.S. males and four to eight percent of females will develop one or more ulcers during their lifetimes. An estimated four million Americans suffer from peptic ulcer disease at any given time. If you are a victim, or suspect you might be, you'll want to read *When Digestive Juices Corrode, You've Got an Ulcer.* The four-page article, reprinted from *FDA Consumer* magazine, gives factual information on types of ulcers, susceptibility, and causes. You'll learn about common irritants of the ulcer (including diet and stress), and the effects of antacids. Diagnosis and treatment, drugs, and surgery are also discussed. Many ulcers clear up

without drug therapy or with only occasional use of antacids, but others become severe, leading to perforation of the stomach or obstruction of the intestinal tract.

Write for:
When Digestive Juices Corrode, You've Got an Ulcer (No. 571P)

Cost: Free

Send to:
Consumer Information Center
P.O. Box 100
Pueblo, CO 81002

FACTS ON VARICOSE VEINS
★★

Varicose veins, those swollen bluish veins found most frequently on the inner side and back of the calf and inner side of the thigh, are both unsightly and uncomfortable to live with. Superficial veins, those lying just under the skin, are most commonly affected. Deeper veins are surrounded and supported by muscle tissue. *Varicose Veins: What Can Be Done About Them* is a 12-page pamphlet which addresses many of the questions and concerns of the sufferer. You'll learn what causes varicose veins, who is most commonly afflicted, and how pregnancy contributes to their development. The booklet also discusses types of therapy, from support hose to exercise to surgery. The good news, you'll find, is that varicose veins usually do respond to treatment.

Write for:
Varicose Veins: What Can Be Done About Them (No. 126P)

Cost: $1.00

Send to:
Consumer Information Center
P.O. Box 100
Pueblo, CO 81002

Varicose Veins: What Can Be Done About Them

FREE THINGS
to
HELP YOU LOOK GOOD

Clothes Care and Accessories

ARGYLE SOCKS AND ALLIGATOR SHOES

★★★★

Don't waste time sighing over the fashion pages or dreaming in front of the display window; come down to earth and take a look at *Your Clothing Dollar,* the Money Management Institute's 40-page guide to budgeting, shopping, and caring for your wardrobe. Amid colorful fashion sketches, you'll find practical information on planning a wardrobe; prices; retail credit and how to apply for it; and comparison shopping in department, specialty, and discount stores as well as through factory outlets and catalogs. There are detailed explanations of fibers, fabric construction, dyes, finishes, nonfibrous materials and furs; tips on judging quality; pointers on getting a good fit for jackets and coats, skirts, men's suits, and undergarments; information on buying and caring for shoes, boots, hosiery, accessories, and children's apparel; and advice on sewing, laundering, and dry cleaning. Good reading that will help you put together a good-looking wardrobe.

Write for:
Your Clothing Dollar

Cost: $1.00

Send to:
Money Management Institute
Dept. PI
Household International
2700 Sanders Rd.
Prospect Heights, IL 60070

Your Clothing Dollar

WHEN THE LABEL SAYS "DRY CLEAN ONLY"

★★★

Dry cleaning is the use of solvents with little or no water to remove soil and stains from fabric. Some natural fibers such as wools and silks have to be dry cleaned rather than laundered in order to avoid shrinkage or other damage. Your local dry cleaning establishment can help make your clothes look and feel better and extend the life of your wardrobe, so it's a good idea to know more about dry cleaning. This ten-page booklet from the Better Business Bureau tells about the dry cleaning process, care labels, fabrics, colors, decorative trims, and other important factors involved in clothing manufacture, use, and cleaning. You get advice, too, on how to get the most out of your dry cleaning dollars and how to treat your garments after they are dry cleaned.

Write for:
Tips on Dry Cleaning (No. 311-02221)

Cost: Free

Send to:
Council of Better Business Bureaus
1515 Wilson Blvd.
Arlington, VA 22209

FIFTH EDITION LAUNDRY ENCYCLOPEDIA

★★★★

Here's everything you ever wanted to know about home laundry. The Maytag people claim that this is the most comprehensive discussion of laundry and related topics ever available, and there's no reason to doubt them. The 208-page paperback (now in its fifth edition) contains a wealth of material on home laundry planning, laundry equipment, fibers, fabric finishes, spot removal, energy conservation, and laundering products. It's an invaluable practical reference for any home — read it yourself and pass it on to the younger members of the family.

Write for:
Maytag Encyclopedia of Home Laundry

Cost: $1.25

Send to:
Consumer Information Center
Encyclopedia, Dept. FT
The Maytag Co.
Newton, IA 50208

continued

LOOK GOOD

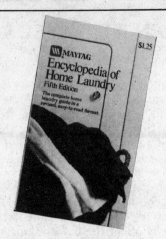

Maytag Encyclopedia of Home Laundry

LAUNDRY ROOM GUIDE
★★★★

Which clothes should you wash and which should you send to the dry cleaners? Which fabrics can you bleach? Which garments require low-heat drying? You won't ruin your best clothes if you check the Clorox Company's handy cardboard guide to reading care labels. Color drawings illustrate washing and drying tips that can be hung by or taped onto the washer or dryer. On the back is a very helpful glossary of standard terms you see on garment care labels. This could be a "must" for the laundry room, especially if you've got youngsters who need to learn how to do their own laundry.

Write for:
Care Labels Are Important!

Cost: 25¢

Send to:
The Clorox Company
Corporate Communications Dept.
P.O. Box 24305
Oakland, CA 94623

Care Labels Are Important!

WHAT CARE LABELS MEAN
★★★★

Do you tend to ignore the care labels found in the collars of shirts, blouses, or sweaters, or sewn into the seams of other garments? If you do, and if you clean the garments yourself, you're making a mistake. Care labels tell you things you need to know. New care labels contain more specific directions for cleaning clothing, but the terms used may be confusing. The Federal Trade Commission takes the mystery out of care labels in a free 10-page booklet telling how to follow instructions for washing, cleaning, and dry cleaning garments. There's a handy glossary of standard terms that you can keep by the washer and dryer to help you get maximum good looks and wear from your clothing.

Write for:
What's New About Care Labels

Cost: Free

Send to:
Federal Trade Commission
Room B-3
6th and Pennsylvania Ave., N.W.
Washington, DC 20580

FOR THE ACTIVE SET
★★★

Runners, joggers, bikers, swimmers, and others who like to be active can learn a lot from this series of six brochures on clothing for fitness. The series has been put together by Cornell University researchers. One brochure suggests what to wear for running and jogging, another is on bicycle wear, and a third is on swimwear. Other brochures discuss sport bras and socks for active people. A sixth suggests ways to be more visible while jogging or biking, both in the daytime and at night. Good advice here for sports-minded individuals and physical education instructors. The six brochures come in a packet and are not available individually.

Write for:
Actionwear: Clothing for Fitness

Cost: $1.50 for the packet

Send to:
Distribution Center
7 Research Park
Cornell University
Ithaca, NY 14850

A SASE is a self-addressed stamped envelope.

SOCKS APPEAL

★★★★

Colored and textured hosiery is a number one fashion accent right now. Match with shoes, match with pants, or contrast with everything, but have fun with your socks. These days skin-toned hosiery simply seems drab. One thing that should certainly be a basic staple in your stocking wardrobe is a pair of white knee-hi's, and that's where this offer comes in. Three pairs of white knee-hi's are yours for $1.00. In translucent nylon, the knee-hi's are sized to fit everyone. What a bargain! Wear them with jeans or dress trousers, the look is great and contemporary.

Write for:
Nylon Knee Hi's

Cost: $1.00

Send to:
IMC Management, Inc.
P.O. Box 11 KH
Garnerville, NY 10923

Nylon Knee Hi's

AN AIR OF SCENT-UALITY

★★★★

Elegant and old-fashioned, potpourris are making a comeback into our homes, closets, and dresser drawers. What a nice touch it is, to catch aromatic whiffs of outdoor freshness throughout the day. This offer is for two special potpourri mixtures, the Greenfield or the Christmas blend. There is enough in each package to make two or three sachets or one large closet ball. The Greenfield is a springtime mix of flowers and spices. For those of you who love the smell of a winter forest, the Christmas blend combines bayberry, pine needles, orange peel, and spices. At a bargain price of $1.00 each, maybe you should order both.

Write for:
Greenfield Potpourri
Christmas Potpourri

Cost: $1.00 each

Send to:
IMC Management, Inc.
P.O. Box 11-P
Garnerville, NY 10923

Greenfield Potpourri

Christmas Potpourri

A GIRL'S BEST FRIEND

★★★

Diamonds may be a girl's best friend, but (as with friends) she should be able to tell a real one from a fake. Read up on this fascinating subject in one of these five brochures offered free from the Jewelers of America. Others are on cultured pearls, karat gold jewelry, platinum jewelry, and colored gemstone jewelry. Diagrams in the diamond brochure show the different cuts of stones. The gemstones brochure tells what factors determine the value and price of gemstones. The brochure on cultured pearls tells about the different types of pearls and how to care for them. The brochure on karat gold jewelry explains how to tell if something is real gold and talks about collecting gold coins.

Write for:
What You Should Know About Buying a Diamond
What You Should Know About Colored Gemstones
What You Should Know About Cultured Pearls
What You Should Know About Platinum Jewelry
What You Should Know About Karat Gold Jewelry

Cost: Free

Send to:
Jewelers of America
Consumer Information Dept. PI
1271 Avenue of the Americas
New York, NY 10020

continued

LOOK GOOD

THINGS OF BEAUTY

★★★

Many men, as well as women, buy jewelry for themselves or as gifts. Whether you regard a piece of good jewelry as a fashion accessory or an investment, it is a major expenditure that should be thought out carefully before making a purchase. This booklet from the Better Business Bureau offers tips on buying jewelry and covers gemstones, diamonds, pearls, emeralds, rubies, sapphires, and other precious stones. Gem substitutes—synthetic gems—also are described, as well as precious metals, gold, silver, platinum and palladium, and costume jewelry. The information in this booklet can help you shop wisely for jewelry gifts or jewelry as an investment.

Write for:
   Tips on Buying Jewelry (No. 24-172)

Cost: Free

Send to:
   Council of Better Business Bureaus
   1515 Wilson Blvd.
   Arlington, VA 22209

Tips on Buying Jewelry

DOING JUSTICE TO FINE JEWELRY

★★

The Jewelers of America offer two free brochures to help you care for and clean your fine jewelry and find out how much it's worth. One brochure tells how to care for diamonds (diamonds are tough, but you still shouldn't wear them when doing rough chores), colored gemstones, karat gold jewelry, and cultured pearls. The other tells how to have jewelry appraised, and who should appraise new jewelry— an unethical appraiser may distort the value of your pieces, so it's important to be careful. Lots of useful tips here.

Write for:
   What You Should Know About the Care and
      Cleaning of Your Fine Jewelry
   What You Should Know About Jewelry Appraisals

Cost: Free

Send to:
   Jewelers of America
   Consumer Information Dept. PI
   1271 Avenue of the Americas
   New York, NY 10020

THE COLOR OF YOUR FEELINGS

★★★★

Now this is a novel way to get in touch with yourself— the psychic mood ring measures your emotions. The stone changes color as your feelings vary. Black forecasts tension, topaz means anxiety, jade represents tranquility, aqua stands for feeling free, and sapphire is ecstasy. The ring knows before you do. Two dollars gives you a choice of either silver or goldtone finish. Be sure to specify your ring size and the finish you prefer. The company making this offer states that although they have limited quantities available they will try to comply with requests. The mood ring is fun and would make a great icebreaker at parties. Kids will love it, too.

Write for:
   Ring

Cost: $2.00

Send to:
   IMC Management, Inc.
   P.O. Box 11R
   Garnerville, NY 10923

Mood Ring

DESIGNER APPEAL
★★

If your costume jewelry collection could use some pepping up, this offer is for you. This attractive multicolored beaded necklace was designed by the international couturier Hattie Carnegie, and was sold in major department and specialty stores throughout the country. The 18-inch strand is strung with small plastic Indian-style beads and attaches with a screw-back clasp. The necklace originally sold for $4.00. Our sample was composed of dark brown and turquoise beads, one style of an assortment.

Write for:
Necklace

Cost: $1.00

Send to:
IMC Management, Inc.
P.O. Box 11N
Garnerville, NY 10923

Necklace

AS TIME GOES BY
★★★

If a watch is more to you than just a way to tell time, and you appreciate quality craftsmanship, the Jewelers of America have a neat, free brochure for you. *What You Should Know About Buying a Fine Watch* tells you about the different types of watches, discusses price (you could pay up to $100,000) and style, suggests where to buy a fine watch, and what to look for when deciding on your purchase. Also included are tips on how to care for fine watches and what to do if they need repair or cleaning. You'll even learn who owns the first known wristwatch—Elizabeth I of England, who was presented with the historic timepiece in 1571. Unfortunately though, it didn't do her much good—it kept terrible time. This is an unassuming little leaflet, but it's quite fascinating.

Write for:
What You Should Know About Buying a Fine Watch

Cost: Free

Send to:
Jewelers of America
Consumer Information Dept. PI
1271 Avenue of the Americas
New York, NY 10020

Beauty Care and Cosmetics

NATURAL SKIN TREATMENT
★★★

Active Moisture Formula, the makers claim, will dramatically improve the look and feel of every skin type by regulating the skin's optimum moisture balance. You can test the claim by sending for a ¼-oz. sample, just the right size for traveling, in a durable plastic container. According to the manufacturers, Active Moisture Formula is blended with natural oils and a special amino acid protein which aids in maximizing skin hydration and maintaining skin elasticity; is lightweight; and is designed to smooth, soothe, and help restore youthful skin tone.

Write for:
Active Moisture Formula Trial Size ¼-oz.

Cost: $1.75

Send to:
Orjene Natural Cosmetics
5-43 48th Avenue
Long Island City, NY 11101

Active Moisture Formula Trial Size

LOOK GOOD

BECAUSE YOU CARE
★★★

Does dry skin have you feeling you've got scales instead of skin? Are moisturizers simply not moist enough for you? Here is an offer you may want to try. For $1.00, you'll receive a 1½-oz. trial bottle of Cococare Oils & Aloe Beauty Lotion, along with a 50¢ coupon toward the purchase of a full-size bottle. The formula is a true balance of vitamin E oil and aloe vera gel, claim the manufacturers, who say that it is blended for daily use and designed to gently protect your face and neck from drying out. The manufacturers describe this as a rich, non-greasy lotion that makes a perfect makeup base and an ideal all-night moisturizer.

Write for:
Cococare Oils & Aloe Beauty Lotion sample

Cost: $1.00

Send to:
Cococare Products, Inc.
175 LeGrand Avenue
P.O. Box 111
Northvale, NJ 07647

Cococare Oils & Aloe Beauty Lotion sample

ELASTIN CREME SAMPLE
★★★

Orjene has made natural cosmetics and personal care products since 1928. This is a sample jar (¼ oz.) of the company's Elastin, a color-free, fragrance-free restorative made of elastin protein, collegen protein, PABA (a sunscreen), and vitamins A, D, and E. Orjene's claim is that Elastin will help maintain your skin's elasticity; help restore firmness and tone to sagging skin—under eyes, chin, and arms; help prevent or decrease the appearance of stretch marks, and help ease out crow's feet, laugh lines, and wrinkles. You'll also get a brochure on Orjene's complete line of products.

Write for:
Elastin Creme Trial Size

Cost: $1.50

Send to:
Orjene Natural Cosmetics
5-43 48th Ave.
Long Island City, NY 11101

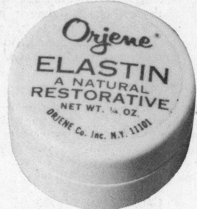

Elastikn Creme Trial Size

LIGHT AND MOIST
★★★

The makers of a light and creamy moisturizer that contains no oils would like you to try their product. Their Na PCA Creme, they say, contains a special natural ingredient which helps hydrate the complexion by coaxing water from the atmosphere into the skin, replacing the moisture that is lost during both the aging process and exposure to harsh elements. Na PCA Creme has no colorings added, and is offered for use on all skin types. For $1.50 you can receive a ¼ oz. trial sample of the whipped-light moisturizer.

Write for:
Na PCA Creme Trial Size ¼ oz.

Cost: $1.50

Send to:
Orjene Natural Cosmetics
5-43 48th Avenue
Long Island City, NY 11101

Na PCA Creme Trial Size

A SASE is a self-addressed stamped envelope.

LIP SALVE SAMPLE

★★★★

If you greet the winter with dismay, knowing you'll suffer from chapped, cracked lips clear through until spring, cheer yourself up with this free sample of Blistex lip ointment. It comes with a five-page leaflet advising on all-year lip care and explaining some of the reasons why lips get dry and chapped. Some of the most common causes are the herpes simplex virus, which causes cold sores; cosmetic dermatitis in people who are allergic to certain ingredients used in beauty products; photosensitivity; or cheilitis, which refers to persistent inflammation of one or both lips. There's a list of "tips for great-looking lips," too, along with a warning that dry, chapped lips are not only unappealing but are more prone to bacterial and other infections and allergies. A 10¢ coupon for Blistex comes with the sample and leaflet.

Write for:
Blistex sample and pamphlet: Smooth Moist Lips Are Healthy Lips

Cost: Free with a long SASE

Send to:
Blistex Inc.
1800 Swift Drive
Oak Brook, IL 60521

Blistex sample and pamphlet

GOOD LOOKS FOR GUYS AND GIRLS

★★★

The key to good looks is not simply conforming to a current fashion trend, claims this 14-page booklet. Nobody has to try to look like everyone else, but everyone *can* look clean and groomed, especially if they follow the few simple suggestions given here. Girls and boys learn how to keep their skin healthy and problem-free and their hair looking good. A special section gives tips on getting clean after working on a job or hobby that involves dirt or grime. The booklet covers everything from solving perspiration problems to relieving aches from sore muscles brought on by sports or heavy workouts.

Write for:
Grooming Hints for Girls and Guys (B-391)

Cost: Free with a long SASE

Send to:
Johnson & Johnson
Dept. FS
Grandview Road
Skillman, NJ 08558

VEGETABLE COMBO FOR YOUR HAIR

★★★

If you love spinach and broccoli, and believe firmly in the value of vegetables, here's a chance to go one step further and try a vegetable on your hair. Algin (sea kelp) is incorporated in these two products that the Freeman Cosmetic Corporation offers in sample sizes costing $1.50 per pair. A one-ounce packet of Sea Kelp Vegetable Protein Pack is designed, according to the makers, to add body to hair and repair tensile strength with kelp, soy protein, and vitamins A, D, and E. Sea Kelp Shampoo, offered in a two-ounce bottle, is hypo-allergenic, contains vitamins A, D, and E, and is said to be formulated with actual sea kelp.

Write for:
Sea Kelp Vegetable Protein Pack
Sea Kelp Shampoo

Cost: $1.50

Send to:
The Freeman Cosmetic Corp.
P.O. Box 17
Hollywood, CA 90078

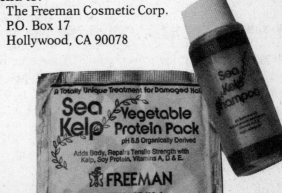

Sea Kelp Vegetable Protein Pack

Sea Kelp Shampoo

LOOK GOOD

YOUR CROWNING GLORY
★★★

Healthy hair is beautiful hair, and healthy hair depends on your understanding of the basic principles of hair care. At the top of the list are proper brushing and combing, which stimulates scalp circulation, and cleaning both hair and scalp when you wash your hair. Some of the best tips in this 20-page booklet tell you what makes a good haircut, how often you need one, and how to find a hairstyle that's flattering to the shape of your face. There are also sections on coloring your hair, perming, straightening, and what causes dandruff, split ends, and hair discoloration. Lots of good information, attractively presented.

Write for:
  Hair Care

Cost: Free (postcard requests only)

Send to:
  Johnson Wax
  Consumer Education
  P.O. Box 567, Dept. T-85
  Racine, WI 53403

BALD ISN'T BAD
★★★★

There's good news and bad news for people who are bald. First, the bad news. A panel of medical scientists and dermatologists has concluded that over-the-counter hair-growth products don't work. Hair growth is cyclical, not continuous, and the growth pattern also reverses, leaving a full head of hair nothing but a memory. But the good news, presented in a free two-page government publication, is that baldness need not be considered bad. The Bald-Headed League, a national organization with 4,000 members including former President Gerald Ford, Sen. Henry Jackson, actor Telly Savalas and others, suggests taking pride in being bald. The brochure can help you with answers to baldness and how to develop a positive self-image.

Write for:
  Balding Is Forever, Experts Say (No. 543P)

Cost: Free

Send to:
  Consumer Information Center
  P.O. Box 100
  Pueblo, CO 81002

SHAMPOO NATURALLY
★★★

You'll be delighted with the looks and performance of your hair after just one cleansing, say the manufacturers of Orjene Pure Herbal Shampoo. They claim that their special formulation of herbal extracts blended in a coconut base is right for any hair type, and that the pH-balanced product cleans the scalp of loose dandruff and helps restore the hair's natural highlights and lustre. The fragrance, barely perceptible but quite pleasing, is a mix of chamomile, rosemary, thyme, sage, fennel, hops, balm, mint, mistletoe, yarrow, and chlorophyll. For $1.00 you get a 2 oz. travel-sized sample in an unbreakable plastic bottle with pull-open, push-close top.

Write for:
  Pure Herbal Shampoo Trial/Travel Size 2 oz.

Cost: $1.00

Send to:
  Orjene Natural Cosmetics
  5-43 48th Avenue
  Long Island City, NY 11101

Pure Herbal Shampoo Trial/Travel Size 2 oz.

HELP FOR DAMAGED HAIR
★★★

If damaged, undernourished hair is your problem, don't hang your head in shame. The Freeman Cosmetic Corporation offers samples of two products that they claim will repair split ends and treat damaged hair. For $1.50 you can get a two-ounce bottle of Presto Amino Shampoo, which, according to the instructions, will help eliminate split ends, and a one-ounce packet of Presto Amino Ultimate Protein Paque. This is "formulated to help restructure damaged hair" and to "insulate hair from heat of curling irons, hot rollers, and blow dryers."

Write for:
> Presto Amino Shampoo
> Presto Amino Ultimate Protein Paque

Cost: $1.50

Send to:
> The Freeman Cosmetic Corp.
> P.O. Box 171
> Hollywood, CA 90078

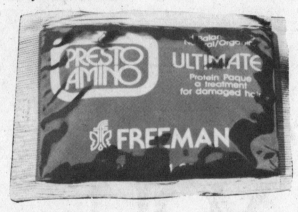

Presto Amino Ultimate Protein Paque

Send to:
> Essential Products Co., Inc.
> 90 Water St.
> New York, NY 10005

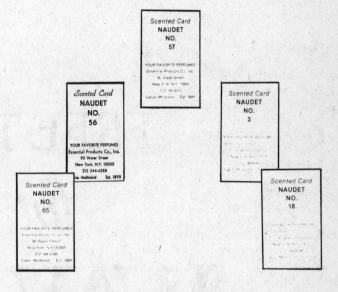

Five Scented Fragrance Cards

FOR THE JOY OF IT

★★★

Does the price of your favorite perfume knock you out of the leagues of luxury? Does the price tag of $175 an ounce take the joy out of Joy? If so, you'll be interested in comparing the scents on these five sample cards with the real thing. Then you can tuck them in your lingerie drawer or under your pillow for an extra hint of scent. This company, in business since 1895, manufactures essential flavors and fragrances at a fraction of the cost of imported perfumes. Would you believe $18 an ounce for women's perfume and $9 for 4 oz. for men's fragrance? Now compare that to what you'll find at your local cosmetics department. The company offers interpretations of such top-name fragrances as Giorgio, Opium, Paco Rabanne, Polo and many more—58 of them, in fact. You'll receive five scented cards, order form, and fragrance list.

Write for:
> Five Scented Fragrance Cards

Cost: Free with a long SASE

MIRROR ON THE WALL . . .

★★★★

Last year, more than $10 billion was spent on hair preparations, mouthwash, makeup, shaving cream, and perfume. Cosmetics can make you look good, but the Food and Drug Administration's free two-page brochure on cosmetics cautions that it's necessary to consider the safety of cosmetic products. The publication is for those who are concerned about what's in the cosmetics they use, with answers to typical questions posed by the public to the Food and Drug Administration. Experts talk about using eye liners, facial foundation powders and lotions, cosmetic creams, hair coloring, permanent waves, and other popular aids to good looks.

Write for:
> Questions Concerning Cosmetics (No. 539P)

Cost: Free

Send to:
> Consumer Information Center
> P.O. Box 100
> Pueblo, CO 81002

FREE THINGS
for the
WAY YOU LIVE

Education and Jobs

STUDY AT HOME

★★★★

Many people who are unable to attend regular classes at a school or college consider enrolling in home study courses to learn new skills or increase their knowledge. Home study courses can let you learn at your own pace and schedule without interfering with your job or home life. The Better Business Bureau's free eight-page brochure, *Tips on Home Study Schools,* tells what types of home study schools there are and suggests how you can check them out to be sure they're legitimate and deliver all they promise. The booklet cautions to be aware of "degree mills" that sell phony diplomas for a price, and tells how to select a reputable home study school.

Write for:
Tips on Home Study Schools (No. 311-02229)

Cost: Free

Send to:
Council of Better Business Bureaus
1515 Wilson Blvd.
Arlington, VA 22209

Tips on Home Study Schools

COLLEGE FOR ADULTS: WHY NOT?

★★★★

Why not go back to school as an adult? The means are diverse; the costs need not be excessive. This excellent booklet explains how colleges have changed their requirements in order to give adults a second chance at a degree, and describes some of the options that are open—often they don't even require going to a campus. You'll read about contract learning (a new wrinkle), college in your living room,

learning without teachers, and correspondence courses. Some non-collegiate learning opportunities are presented too, and there's good information on education "brokers" who can help you find the right program, financial aid, and where to go for further information.

Write for:
New Paths to Learning: College Education for Adults (No. 546)

Cost: $1.00

Send to:
Public Affairs Pamphlets
381 Park Ave. South
New York, NY 10016

CURRENT READING

★★★★

Lots of people feel there's never enough time to catch up on their reading—the latest bestsellers, professional treatises, or even the daily newspaper. Many haven't been inside a library since their last year of school. If you'd like to brush up on your reading techniques, these one-sheet publications may help. They will give you some pointers to more efficient reading so you can keep up with current events and find time to explore new areas of learning. Each is written by a noted educator, journalist, or media personality. *How to Read Faster,* by Bill Cosby (who has a doctorate degree in education) gives tips on previewing, skimming, and clustering to increase reading speed and comprehension. *How to Use the Library,* by James A. Michener, clues you in to the wealth of information you can find in the "stacks" and how to look for it. *How to Read a Newspaper,* by Walter Cronkite, tells how to make the most of the time you spend with your city's print media.

Write for:
How to Read Faster
How to Use a Library
How to Read a Newspaper

Cost: Free

Send to:
Power of the Printed Word
International Paper Co.
P.O. Box 954
Madison Square Station
New York, NY 10010

continued

THE WAY YOU LIVE

How to Read Faster

How to Use a Library

How to Read a Newspaper

READ A GOOD BOOK LATELY?

★★★★

Do you feel trapped in the land of soap operas and trashy novels? That you don't have the time or energy to concentrate on anything that seems to require an effort? Here's a way out. Just because you're out of school is no reason to stop learning, and if you've decided that this is your year to do some "great reading," these one-sheet publications may spur you on. *How to Enjoy the Classics* and *How to Enjoy Poetry* will guide even the most latent scholar down the path to learning—pleasantly. There are tips on how to increase your understanding, examples taken from recognized works of literary art, and suggestions for getting started. You'll find greater pleasure in anything you read from now on. Also ask for *How to Encourage Your Child to Read,* by Erma Bombeck—and start your kids out early.

Write for:
   How to Enjoy the Classics
   How to Enjoy Poetry
   How to Encourage Your Child to Read

Cost: Free

Send to:
   Power of the Printed Word
   International Paper Co.
   P.O. Box 954
   Madison Square Station
   New York, NY 10010

WRITE WHAT YOU MEAN

★★★★

Many people are terrified by the sight of a blank sheet of paper. Fill it with words? Impossible! But *How to Write Clearly, How to Write With Style, How to Improve Your Vocabulary, How to Spell,* and *How to Punctuate* are short, clear sets of guidelines intended to see you through to that very end. *Reader's Digest* editor-in-chief Edward Thompson gives advice on how to organize your thoughts, write clearly and briefly, and avoid unnecessary words; novelist Kurt Vonnegut gives tips on putting style into your style; actor Tony Randall gives exercise lessons on building your vocabulary and increasing your understanding of what words really mean; novelist and former bad speller John Irving gives his tricks and tips on learning how to spell; Pulitzer Prize-winning essayist Russell Baker gives a course on how to use the ten most important punctuation marks. These single-sheet pieces are suitable in style and content for anyone from the sixth grade on up who wants to (or has to) write.

Write for:
   How to Write Clearly
   How to Write With Style
   How to Improve Your Vocabulary
   How to Spell
   How to Punctuate

Cost: Free

Send to:
   Power of the Printed Word
   International Paper Co.
   P.O. Box 954
   Madison Square Station
   New York, NY 10010

SECRETS OF BUSINESS COMMUNICATION

★★★★

Your job doesn't require writing ability? Are you sure? Chances are you had to present yourself on paper, in your resume, in order to get hired in the first place. And sometimes in the course of your job you have to write to a business for service, or to air a complaint. You probably have to use other communication skills, too—make a speech, perhaps, or make sense of the annual report, cutting through all the bureaucratic jargon to discover what's happening in the company or what needs to be done next. These four single-sheet publications are good quick-reference guides to business communication. Something for everyone.

Write for:
   How to Write a Resume
   How to Write a Business Letter
   How to Make a Speech
   How to Read an Annual Report

A SASE is a self-addressed stamped envelope.

Cost: Free

Send to:
Power of the Printed Word
International Paper Co.
P.O. Box 954
Madison Square Station
New York, NY 10010

THE PINK SLIP

★★★★

You heard rumors about layoffs, but you didn't really believe them. Or maybe being fired was a complete surprise to you. Nevertheless, after all these years you're out of a job. You can expect to be preoccupied with concerns about survival for you and your family, staying afloat financially, and keeping your head emotionally until you find another job. This publication outlines some of the specific problems you face when you're out of a job and, more important, some specific solutions. *What to Do When You Lose Your Job*, a 28-page booklet by the Public Affairs Committee, has good advice on job-hunting strategies and how to keep busy while you're waiting. There is good financial advice, too, on tightening your budget, and what to do if you're in danger of losing your home.

Write for:
What to Do When You Lose Your Job (No. 617)

Cost: $1.00

Send to:
Public Affairs Pamphlets
381 Park Ave. South
New York, NY 10016

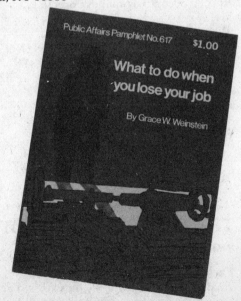

What to Do When You Lose Your Job

ALL ABOUT EMPLOYMENT AGENCIES

★★★★

Finding the right job at the right time can be no easy trick. Searching the "help wanted" ads in the newspaper may find you "a" job, but not "the" job. One way to get help in job-hunting is to get an employment service working for you. A free 16-page booklet from the Better Business Bureau describes the various types of employment services, tells what they do and offer, what they cannot do, and how to choose the employment agency that can do the most for you. Types of employment agency fees are discussed as well as cautions on "employer paid fees" and service agreements.

Write for:
Tips on Employment Services (No. 24-178)

Cost: Free

Send to:
Council of Better Business Bureaus
1515 Wilson Blvd.
Arlington, VA 22209

MARKETING YOURSELF

★★

When it is time to make a major career change, you and your family members alike are affected. There are many decisions to make, and some of them are confusing and difficult. It may help to know about the Catalyst network, a national not-for-profit organization that works with corporations and individuals to develop career and family options. Local independent affiliates provide career and educational counseling and programs for those who wish to advance their careers, change fields, or re-enter the job market. The *National Network of Career Resource Centers* brochure lists nearly 200 centers across the country that offer career guidance. The *Publications* booklet is a complete listing of Catalyst's current materials on career and family choices and development for women and men of all ages.

Write for:
National Network of Career Resource Centers
Publications

Cost: Free

Send to:
Catalyst
250 Park Ave. South
New York, NY 10003

continued

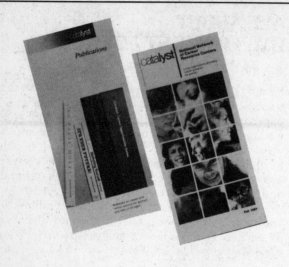

National Network of Career Resource Centers Publications

WOMEN IN BUSINESS

★★★★

The latest figures of the Census Bureau (1980) indicate that almost three million American women owned their own businesses—about 22 percent of all sole proprietorships—and generated $6.2 billion in net income. If you're a woman thinking of starting your own business, you'll find helpful information in a free 16-page publication from the U.S. Small Business Administration. It outlines the current state of small business in America, and offers tips on agencies that can provide specific help, federal assistance, banking, loan applications, procurement assistance, and other aspects of starting a business. Also included is a list of materials for further reading.

Write for:
Women's Handbook: How SBA Can Help You Go Into Business (No. 502P)

Cost: Free

Send to:
Consumer Information Center
P.O. Box 100
Pueblo, CO 81002

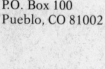

Women's Handbook: How SBA Can Help

CAREER SHOPPING

★★

The recent years have brought a torrent of books offering advice on getting a job, advancing in a career, or starting a small business. Now there's a mail-order catalog devoted specifically to books on these and related topics. The first issue of *The Whole Work Catalog* describes books in the categories of career development, self-employment, and better ways of working. Short articles and news items are interspersed with the book descriptions. Lots of positive thinking accompanies each issue along with general tips and info on career satisfaction.

Write for:
The Whole Work Catalog

Cost: $2.00 for two-issue trial subscription

Send to:
The New Careers Center
6003 N. 51st Street
Boulder, CO 80301

BEWARE OF BUSINESS FRAUDS

★★★★

Every day you read about get-rich-quick schemes that sound good, at first. "You can make big dollars working at home." "Mail order business for sale, cheap." "Pyramid your investment into a fortune." The Better Business Bureau says many such work or investment offers are frauds, and offers this series of three booklets to caution you against falling victim to such deceptive business practices.

Write for:
Tips on Work-At-Home Schemes (No. 204)
Tips on Mail Order Profit Mirages (No. 311-02219)
Tips on Multi-Level Marketing (No. 02-239)

Cost: Free

Send to:
Council of Better Business Bureaus
1515 Wilson Blvd.
Arlington, VA 22209

THE DISABLED EMPLOYEE

★★★★

Each year, hundreds of thousands of men and women have accidents or illnesses that permanently limit their ability to function in some way or ways important to work. They and their employers seri-

A SASE is a self-addressed stamped envelope.

ously question whether returning to employment is feasible, or even possible. Yet it can be done, and often is. *Jobs for Disabled People* challenges old myths about disabled persons and gives good advice for building new dreams and fulfilling them. The 28-page booklet explores the rights and responsibilities of the handicapped. It covers many accommodation aids and devices, and special programs that are available. At the back of the book is a lengthy compilation of federal and private organizations that promote education and careers for the disabled.

Write for:
Jobs for Disabled People (No. 631)

Cost: $1.00

Send to:
Public Affairs Pamphlets
381 Park Ave. South
New York, NY 10016

Jobs for Disabled People

OWN YOUR OWN BUSINESS

★★★★

One way to own your own business is to operate a franchise. Many Americans are finding happiness and financial success in operating a local outlet of a national business, whether it be a product like a fried chicken business or a service such as an instant print shop. The Better Business Bureau's 14-page booklet on franchises tells how to select a safe franchise company, what possible pitfalls to look out for, what your rights are in a contract, how to negotiate a franchise purchase, and tips on being aware of franchise frauds and schemes. A franchise could be a lucky career decision or a disaster. This booklet helps you to make a smart decision.

Write for:
Facts on Selecting a Franchise (No. 02-255)

Cost: Free

Send to:
Council of Better Business Bureaus
1515 Wilson Blvd.
Arlington, VA 22209

Facts on Selecting a Franchise

THINGS AREN'T GOING SO WELL

★★★★

People with personal problems are not likely to be full of bounce and energy on their jobs. On the contrary, they may show symptoms of depression and anxiety, which can affect work performance dramatically. In recognition of this reality, thousands of corporations and unions are sponsoring what are generally called employee assistance programs, or EAP's, which offer confidential help. *Help for the Troubled Employee* discusses various types of problems and, using case histories, shows how EAP's have proved beneficial. The 28-page booklet discusses the effectiveness and confidentiality of such programs, how to identify a troubled employee, and the perspective of the unions. After all, employees who have worked out their difficulties very often regain their past level of productivity.

Write for:
Help for the Troubled Employee (No. 611)

Cost: $1.00

Send to:
Public Affairs Pamphlets
381 Park Ave. South
New York, NY 10016

Help for the Troubled Employee

THE WAY YOU LIVE

THE ABCs OF SLIDE PRESENTATIONS

★★★★

Scared to death of that audiovisual presentation you're supposed to give? Need some basic tips on using audiovisual equipment and preparing slides? Here's a helping hand. *Basic Tips on Preparing for a Meeting That Uses Slides* may not be the slickest title you've ever heard, but it introduces a helpful four-page foldout that gives step-by-step instructions on making slides, using projectors, even arranging the room for the most effective presentation. *Basic Tips on Producing and Using Overhead Transparencies* is a two-color guide to setting up the room and equipment, preparing, masking, and mounting transparencies, and running a smooth presentation. There is lots of information packed into these two leaflets.

Write for:
    Basic Tips on Preparing for a Meeting That Uses Slides
    Basic Tips on Producing and Using Overhead Transparencies

Cost: Free with a long SASE

Send to:
    International Communications Industries Association (ICIA)
    3150 Spring St.
    Fairfax, VA 22031-2399

ARE COMPUTER VIDEO SCREENS SAFE?

★★★

More than 12 million Americans spend part of their work or leisure day in front of a computer, and in recent years questions have arisen over how safe it is to work at a computer video display terminal. This new 36-page report by the American Council on Science and Health answers some of the questions on video display terminal health and safety hazards. Subjects include radiation, computer use by pregnant women, possible X-ray emissions, problems of light and glare, eyestrain, heat, noise, and physical and emotional stress. If you are one of the people who spend long stretches of time at a video display terminal, you will be especially interested in the findings of the Council.

Write for:
    Health and Safety Aspects of Video Display Terminals

Cost: $2.00

Send to:
    American Council on Science and Health
    47 Maple St.
    Summit, NJ 07901

WRITING FOR KIDS: IT'S NOT CHILD'S PLAY

★★

Don't let anyone fool you that writing children's books is a snap—or illustrating them, either. Here are two pamphlets from The Children's Book Council that explain what prospective writers and illustrators face in publishing a book for children. Competition is rough—3,000 new books for children are published each year. Still, the pamphlets do give some encouragement to new, publishable writers, and there's some practical advice on how and where writers and illustrators can present their work.

Write for:
    Writing Books for Children and Young Adults
    Illustrating Children's Books

Cost: Free with a long SASE (two 22¢ stamps)

Send to:
    The Children's Book Council
    67 Irving Place
    New York, NY 10003

Especially for Seniors

GO FOR IT IN YOUR GOLDEN YEARS

★★★★

Getting the most out of life is an individual quest, regardless of age. However, as one grows older barriers to full living may arise more frequently. But even if the senior citizen's quest for a satisfying life becomes restricted, it's definitely not halted. *How the Older Person Can Get the Most Out of Living* is a great booklet filled with ideas and encouragement. It covers the importance of employment and gives suggestions for part-time or volunteer work; participation in family activities and recreation; and ways to make a contribution to the world around you. There is a list of "don'ts" for the older person who wants to have vital, happy relationships, and another list of questions and answers about making the best use of the retirement years. This publication is available while supplies last.

A SASE is a self-addressed stamped envelope.

Write for:
   How the Older Person Can Get the Most Out
   of Living

Cost: $1.25

Send to:
   Order Department, OP-312
   American Medical Association
   P.O. Box 10946
   Chicago, IL 60610-9968

How the Older Person Can Get the Most Out of Living

RETIREMENT, YOUR WAY

★★★★

You want your retirement years to be rewarding, active, and rich in new experiences. Unfortunately, too many people end up bored, lonely, and poor, but it doesn't have to be that way, if you plan right. *And One Day You Retire* is a great, magazine-size book to help you plan your leisure years, whether retirement is presently a dream or a reality. It will help you manage your financial matters, plan your new unstructured time, and make living arrangements. One chapter assists the retiree in building a second career. There is lots of good advice on insurance, physical fitness, sex, and death. You'll find a re-source list for housing alternatives and a list of senior citizens' clubs and organizations. The book is authoritative and well worth the price.

Write for:
   And One Day You Retire

Cost: $2.00

Send to:
   Resources
   Aetna Life & Casualty
   151 Farmington Avenue
   Hartford, CT 06156

NEW HORIZONS, OR OVER THE HILL?

★★★★

This excellent booklet stresses the resources that the elderly can use to foster self-reliance with the goal of leading spirited, free lives, and enjoying their later years. It covers different housing arrangements, meal services, transportation, and legal assistance. It tells about adult education, opportunities for volunteer service, and even paid jobs. You'll learn how entire families can help aging members, and where to find out about resources in your own community.

Write for:
   After 65: Resources for Self-Reliance (No. 501A)

Cost: $1.00

Send to:
   Public Affairs Pamphlets
   381 Park Ave. South
   New York, NY 10016

THE ABUSED SENIOR

★★★★

Abuse and neglect of the elderly by family members is certainly not a new problem, but it is a serious societal concern. Whatever the motive—whether mis-treatment is the result of malice or ignorance—abuse is cruel and inhumane. *Family Neglect and Abuse of the Aged: A Growing Concern* studies this sad prob-lem which affects people in every income range. The 32-page booklet is illustrated with case histories; defines the differences between neglect and abuse; and charts the patterns which lead to abuse. It also discusses strategies for intervention, legal consider-ations, and protective services which might alleviate the abuse. Recommendations are given for preven-tion of senior citizen abuse, as is a source list of agencies and organizations which offer additional help.

Write for:
   Family Neglect and Abuse of the Aged:
   A Growing Concern (No. 603)

Cost: $1.00

Send to:
   Public Affairs Pamphlets
   381 Park Ave. South
   New York, NY 10016

Family Neglect and Abuse of the Aged: A Growing Concern

THE WAY YOU LIVE

MEDICARE: WHAT IT WILL (AND WON'T) DO

★★

This pamphlet discusses what Medicare does and doesn't pay, and what this might mean to you. You'll find out if you need private health insurance in addition to Medicare (if you qualify for Medicaid, chances are you don't). There are a lot of excellent hints for shopping around for private health insurance, and you'll learn about the different types available and exactly what you should look for in the policy. Finally, the pamphlet spells out exactly what Medicare (Parts A and B) will and won't pay. It also tells you where you can go for additional help or advice on Medicare benefits. Read it carefully—you need to know.

Write for:
  Guide to Health Insurance for People With
    Medicare

Cost: Free

Send to:
  Office of Beneficiary Services
  Health Care Financing Administration
  6325 Security Blvd.
  Baltimore, MD 21207

PINPOINT HAZARDS IN THE HOME

★★★★

Each year, many older Americans are injured in and around their homes. In 1981, more than 622,000 people over 65 were treated in hospital emergency rooms for home-related injuries. The U.S. Consumer Product Safety Commission's free 32-page booklet suggests that many of these injuries result from hazards that are easy to overlook, but also easy to fix. The publication lists common household hazards and how to take simple steps to correct them and prevent injuries. Room by room, you learn potential home hazards to look out for.

Write for:
  Safety for Older Consumers (No. 443P)

Cost: Free

Send to:
  Consumer Information Center
  P.O. Box 100
  Pueblo, CO 81002

Safety for Older Consumers

ALTERNATIVE HOUSING FOR SENIORS

★★★★

Most older Americans live on their own, often staying in the same home and neighborhood for years. But the day may come when circumstances suggest a move. Running a house may become physically difficult or financially draining; or an alternative living arrangement may become a necessity because of health or other reasons. You, or a senior citizen you know who is faced with the prospect of moving into a more satisfactory living arrangement, can find lots of answers in this free 32-page booklet from the American Association of Retired Persons and the Federal Trade Commission. Among the alternative housing solutions described here are nursing homes, retirement homes, house sharing, and apartments.

Write for:
  Your Home, Your Choice (No. 582P)

Cost: Free

Send to:
  Consumer Information Center
  P.O. Box 100
  Pueblo, CO 81002

Your Home, Your Choice

A SASE is a self-addressed stamped envelope.

HOME EQUITY INCOME

★★★★

Many senior citizens who own their own homes but are short on ready cash consider turning their home equity into income. Eighty percent of those over 65 own their own homes free and clear, without any mortgage. The equity they have accumulated in their homes may represent their largest single financial asset, but they find it difficult to meet their monthly bills because of low cash flow. Home equity loans by elderly Americans now total more than $600 billion. To learn how to turn your home ownership into monthly income, or how to finance needed home repairs, send for this free 16-page booklet from the government's Special Committee on Aging.

Write for:
Turning Home Equity Into Income for Older Homeowners (No. 130P)

Cost: Free

Send to:
Consumer Information Center
P.O. Box 100
Pueblo, CO 81002

PROBLEMS OF OLDER CONSUMERS

★★★★

Older people who have been wise consumer shoppers all their lives can still find themselves falling victim to fraudulent transactions in their later years. Some unscrupulous businessmen prey on older people who may not be as alert as they once were, to take advantage of their weaknesses and fears in older age. The Better Business Bureau offers a free 12-page booklet, *Consumer Problems of the Elderly*, which helps identify the needs of older consumers and suggests ways to avoid fraudulent practices. The discussion covers such topics as physical safety needs, housing, health care, and investments. This is a good guide for older consumers or family members concerned about their protection.

Write for:
Consumer Problems of the Elderly (No. 24-171)

Cost: Free

Send to:
Council of Better Business Bureaus
1515 Wilson Blvd.
Arlington, VA 22209

Consumer Problems of the Elderly

Your Relationships

NEW LIGHT ON LOVE

★★★★

Songs, novels, poems, and movies—so many of them are devoted to that universal human phenomenon, love. Yet love is still always full of surprises. Lovers who want to broaden their understanding of this complex topic—and parents who want to answer some of their children's questions—will want to read what psychologists have to say in *Men and Women—What We Know About Love*, a 24-page booklet from the Public Affairs Committee. There are interesting discussions on how humans learn to love as infants, how parents teach about loving, what creates attraction between individuals, and how people can give and receive love fully. A fascinating dollar's worth.

Write for:
Men and Women—What We Know About Love (No. 592)

Cost: $1.00

Send to:
Public Affairs Pamphlets
381 Park Ave. South
New York, NY 10016

COMMUNICATION: LEARN BEFORE YOU WED

★★★★

Communication—everyone's talking about it, but not everyone knows how to do it. And communication in marriage is a special art. *Talking It Over*

continued

THE WAY YOU LIVE

Before Marriage: Exercises in Premarital Communication is an excellent primer in the arts of listening, sharing, and exchanging feelings and ideas. There's an inventory to help you and your partner understand how you come across to one another, followed by practical exercises to build communication skills in the areas of trust, safety of expression, listening for understanding, empathy, expectations, and reassurance. The booklet suggests you talk about each exercise after doing it, and provides guidelines for the discussion. An excellent book that will really make you think . . . and talk about what you're thinking. Just as valuable for established couples as for new ones.

Write for:
Talking It Over Before Marriage: Exercises in Premarital Communication (No. 512)

Cost: $1.00

Send to:
Public Affairs Pamphlets
381 Park Ave. South
New York, NY 10016

GREAT EXPECTATIONS

★★★★

When the first blush of romance wears off and reality takes over, newly married couples can take advantage of this discouraging, even scary period to deepen their understanding of the marriage bond. *The Early Years of Marriage,* according to this 28-page booklet, is the time to lay the foundation of a lasting partnership. This booklet offers the newly married, or those about to be married, a thoughtful discussion of what makes marriage rewarding and worth the effort. Among the topics covered are communication, finding the determination to succeed in marriage, changing expectations, sexual harmony, money concerns, and problem solving. Securely married couples will appreciate this little book as much as newlyweds.

Write for:
The Early Years of Marriage (No. 424)

Cost: $1.00

Send to:
Public Affairs Pamphlets
381 Park Ave. South
New York, NY 10016

MARRIAGE: MAKE IT LAST

★★★★

Getting married is easy. Staying married is a different matter. Although marriage is basically a legal contract, you need a lot more than legality to make it through strains and stress to your golden anniversary. This little book tries to help. Here's straight talk and sound advice on what couples can do to create an enduring, loving bond. There's a thoughtful look at what makes love last, as well as discussion of more down-to-earth matters such as money, in-laws, sharing pleasures, settling differences, and where to go for help if your marriage does hit a rough spot. Incidentally, this booklet is in its 44th printing — and the advice is still sound as ever.

Write for:
Building Your Marriage (No. 113)

Cost: $1.00

Send to:
Public Affairs Pamphlets
381 Park Ave. South
New York, NY 10016

MARRIAGE ENRICHMENT PROGRAMS

★★★★

Modern marriages call for modern methods of communication—and in many cases the modern method that couples choose is a marriage enrichment program. *New Ways to Better Marriages* offers an overview of some of the most successful of these programs, and describes the Quaker model, Marriage Encounter Groups, and Marriage Communication Labs along with many of the techniques and structures the programs offer. You can adapt some of these techniques to your own situation or use the guidelines to evaluate a marital therapy program that you're interested in. An interesting look at a fairly new aid to marital communication.

Write for:
New Ways to Better Marriages (No. 547)

Cost: $1.00

Send to:
Public Affairs Pamphlets
381 Park Ave. South
New York, NY 10016

A SASE is a self-addressed stamped envelope.

WHAT MAKES MARRIAGE HAPPY?

★★★★

A happy marriage: for the majority it is still the ideal commitment. But the divorce statistics are a relentless reminder of how many marriages never achieve that ideal. *What Makes a Marriage Happy?* is a thoughtful 28-page booklet that gives you the opportunity to measure your experiences against the way other couples describe their marriages. You'll also get an angle on whether you may be expecting too much from your partner, or looking for the wrong things in married life. You'll find suggestions for making decisions jointly, learning to be more flexible, and allowing your mate "room to breathe." There are also some thought-provoking words on how children can positively or negatively affect a marriage.

Write for:
   What Makes a Marriage Happy? (No. 290)

Cost: $1.00

Send to:
   Public Affairs Pamphlets
   381 Park Ave. South
   New York, NY 10016

WHAT YOU BELIEVE: THE COMMON GROUND

★★★★

Maybe what the two of you believe isn't so different, after all; if you're contemplating an interfaith marriage you'll find that message, along with other helpful information, suggestions, and guidance, in *Building a Marriage on Two Altars*. There's an especially good section in which religions are compared for their similarities rather than for their differences. You and your partner will find surefire points of agreement in these brief analyses of the Protestant common ground, the Catholic-Protestant common ground, the Jewish-Christian common ground, as well as religious and nonreligious common ground. This thoughtful booklet could help clarify your thinking if your decision to marry outside your faith is causing you problems. It could also give you answers to some of the questions you may have to field from both families.

Write for:
   Building a Marriage on Two Altars (No. 466)

Cost: $1.00

Send to:
   Public Affairs Pamphlets
   381 Park Ave. South
   New York, NY 10016

WHY MARRIED PEOPLE FIGHT

★★★★

More than 100,000 couples a year seek help from ministers, counselors, psychiatrists, and social work agencies in order to learn how to get along with each other. *What Can You Do About Quarreling?* a commonsense 28-page guide from the Public Affairs Committee, points out that it's normal to fight once in a while, but that chronic quarreling can be a marriage destroyer. This booklet examines early life experiences that can make it difficult for couples, no matter how much they love one another, to get along harmoniously. You'll also learn some of the danger signals that will enable you to sidestep or neutralize potential quarrels, as well as some practical guidelines for smoother handling of marital conflicts.

Write for:
   What Can You Do About Quarreling? (No. 369)

Cost: $1.00

Send to:
   Public Affairs Pamphlets
   381 Park Ave. South
   New York, NY 10016

SMOOTHING THINGS OVER

★★★★

When the signals break down, family communication gets difficult. But it's never too late to work toward more effective understanding, according to *Talking It Over at Home: Problems in Family Communication.* This excellent booklet offers clearly written counsel for improving husband-wife communication as well as building a family communications network. It points out that learning to listen is often the key to effective rapport and gives suggestions for listening "between the lines," listening with "the inner ear," and listening calmly. There are also pointers to help family members give one another positive and negative criticism, and special hints for tuning in to preschoolers and teenagers.

Write for:
   Talking It Over at Home: Problems in Family Communication (No. 410)

continued

THE WAY YOU LIVE

Cost: $1.00

Send to:
Public Affairs Pamphlets
381 Park Ave. South
New York, NY 10016

MORE THAN TWO
★★★★

Marriage unites two individuals—and creates a flock of in-laws on both sides of the new family. Parents-in-law and other relatives by marriage can enrich the lives of the married couple, yet frequently these relationships don't work out quite so well. Hurt feelings, misunderstandings, and failed expectations are common, particularly in the early, sensitive years of a marriage. *You and Your In-Laws: Help for Some Common Problems* may help smooth such a situation. This 28-page booklet tactfully discusses many of the problems and analyzes how they can occur. It covers special troubles, such as holidays, live-in arrangements, and divorce, and gives good advice for coping.

Write for:
You and Your In-Laws: Help for Some Common Problems (No. 635)

Cost: $1.00

Send to:
Public Affairs Pamphlets
381 Park Ave. South
New York, NY 10016

You and Your In-Laws: Help for Some Common Problems

Your Community

THE COUNTING OF AMERICA
★★★★

America has taken a census every 10 years since 1790. In 1980, the 20th census was taken, and a 16-page publication by the Bureau of the Census tells us the results. America is growing more slowly in terms of population and will grow even more slowly in the next decades. We're still moving farther west; we're getting older; and we're better educated. If you want to know more about America and its people today, this is a valuable reference guide. It will interest students, educators, market analysts, and the public.

Write for:
We, the Americans (No. 157P)

Cost: $1.00

Send to:
Consumer Information Center
P.O. Box 100
Pueblo, CO 81002

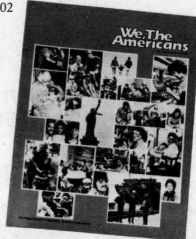

We, the Americans

AMERICAN WOMEN
★★★★

On Census Day in 1980, there were almost 117 million American women, about 12 million more than a decade earlier, and today, women outnumber men in this country by more than six million. American women are growing in more than numbers—they're better educated, gaining more voting power, becoming a greater force in the workplace, owning their own businesses, and owning their own homes. The Bureau of the Census offers a 16-page booklet summarizing the results of the 1980 census as it pertains to women. It's valuable reference material for all

A SASE is a self-addressed stamped envelope.

women, especially students, educators, and market analysts.

Write for:
We, the American Women (No. 158P)

Cost: $1.00

Send to:
Consumer Information Center
P.O. Box 100
Pueblo, CO 81002

We, the American Women

CHILD ABUSE: A NATIONAL DISGRACE
★★★★

Everyone who cares about kids recognizes that the phenomenon of battered children is a national problem of frightening dimensions. This 28-page booklet from the Public Affairs Committee attempts to define the broad range of situations covered by the term "child abuse," probes the causes of maltreatment by parents, and explains legal measures that have been developed to deal with this complex problem. An important section of this concise booklet deals with treatment programs for parents, and suggests possible ways of preventing child abuse. Important reading for everyone in the community who has dealings with children—which, in fact, means virtually everyone in the community.

Write for:
To Combat and Prevent Child Abuse and Neglect (No. 588)

Cost: $1.00

Send to:
Public Affairs Pamphlets
381 Park Ave. South
New York, NY 10019

A GOOD SENSE GUIDE
★★

How do you feel when you meet someone who has a disability? Embarrassed, nervous, tongue-tied? The other person probably feels the same way. You'll find it easier to be friendly and natural if you follow the suggestions in *Points to Remember,* a small sheet of simple advice from the Easter Seal Society. It's based on plain common sense, tact, and friendliness. Also available from the Easter Seal Society is a bookmark for students called *When You Meet a Classmate Who Has a Disability.* Again, it gives sensible, friendly advice.

Write for:
Points to Remember
When You Meet a Classmate bookmark

Cost: Free with a long SASE

Send to:
National Easter Seal Society
2023 W. Ogden Ave.
Chicago, IL 60612

ADVICE FOR ABUSED WIVES
★★★★

Between two and four million incidents of domestic violence occur every year in American homes. Wife abuse is one kind of family violence that occurs far more than most people imagine, and many women suffer this abuse for years without getting help. A free four-page flyer from the National Institute of Mental Health explores the subject of wife abuse and offers advice on what women can do to prevent the problem, or how they can seek help if it does occur. A list of agencies for further help is given, and a list of publications for additional information and guidance is provided.

Write for:
Plain Talk About Wife Abuse (No. 579P)

Cost: Free

Send to:
Consumer Information Center
P.O. Box 100
Pueblo, CO 81002

THE WAY YOU LIVE

SEXUAL ASSAULT: THE FACTS

★★★★

Sexual assault is one of the subjects few people like to think about. You hope it will never happen to you, but you'll be safer if you realize that it *could*. The U.S. Department of Justice offers a 16-page booklet with facts and tips on sexual assault. It contains facts about rape; how to reduce the risk of being assaulted; what you should do if you are attacked; and what happens if you have become a victim, including medical and court procedures to take. Special programs to help rape victims are described, and names and addresses of help groups are given.

Write for:
How to Protect Yourself Against Sexual Assault (No. 155P)

Cost: $1.00

Send to:
Consumer Information Center
P.O. Box 100
Pueblo, CO 81002

How to Protect Yourself Against Sexual Assault

CALLING THE MEETING TO ORDER

★★★★

Do your 4-H club meetings go on forever? Are the Rotarians getting rowdy? Is the PTA board meeting a free-for-all you wouldn't want the kids to see? Bring the meeting to order by enforcing the rules laid down in *The 'How' in Parliamentary Procedure*, a comprehensive, 74-page booklet that will tell you exactly how an efficient meeting should be organized. This no-nonsense booklet explains parliamentary procedure and its many facets in simple terms. Electing officers, introducing new business, enforcing rules, using the gavel, stopping a discussion,

interrupting or ending a meeting—all of the fine points are considered. Good stuff. And you'll save on aspirin.

Write for:
The 'How' In Parliamentary Procedure

Cost: $2.00

Send to:
The Interstate Printers & Publishers, Inc.
19 N. Jackson
P.O. Box 50
Danville, IL 61834-0050

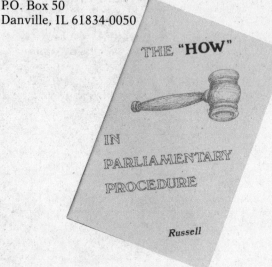

The 'How' In Parlimentary Procedure

HOW CHARITABLE ARE THE CHARITIES?

★★★

Seems like someone's always asking for money—ringing your doorbell, collecting for some charity, asking you to sponsor a race participant, or making a plea through the latest in a seemingly endless series of TV marathons. How ethical are these practices? And where does the money go? Does it go to the needy, or is it swallowed up in administrative costs? *Standards for Charitable Solicitations* lists the standards set by the Council of Better Business Bureaus "... in the belief that both the general public and soliciting organizations will benefit by full and accurate disclosure of all information. ..." Covered in these eight pages are 22 voluntary standards that refer to charities' public accountability, use of funds, solicitations and informational materials, fund-raising practices, and governance.

Write for:
Standards for Charitable Solicitations

Cost: free with a long SASE

A SASE is a self-addressed stamped envelope.

Send to:
Philanthropic Advisory Service
Council of Better Business Bureaus, Inc.
1515 Wilson Blvd.
Arlington, VA 22209

IT'S FOR A GOOD CAUSE

★★★

When you're asked to open your pocketbook to donate to a charitable organization, it isn't always possible to know whether your dollars are going to be used as you intended. *Give But Give Wisely* is a bimonthly review of charitable, educational, and religious organizations that solicit nationally or conduct national or international programs. It's published by the Philanthropic Advisory Service of the Council of Better Business Bureaus, Inc., which keeps files and collects inquiries on such groups. You'll find a list of CBBB Standards for Charitable Solicitations and reports on organizations which adhere to or vary from those standards, a list of groups who are currently being asked for further information, and another list of groups who have not disclosed the requested data. About 300 charitable organizations are listed in each issue, but the CBBB adds the disclaimer that inclusion or omission of any group does not signify approval or disapproval. There are also guidelines for intelligent philanthropic giving.

Write for:
Give But Give Wisely

Cost: $1.00 and a long SASE

Send to:
Philanthropic Advisory Service
Council of Better Business Bureaus, Inc.
1515 Wilson Boulevard
Arlington, VA 22209

Your Government

YOU AND SOCIAL SECURITY

★★★★

Nine out of 10 American workers are earning protection under Social Security, and one out of every six persons receives a monthly Social Security check. A free 36-page booklet tells all about Social Security—how you earn protection under the system, the kinds of benefits you and your family can receive, how Social Security is financed, and other information to help you in planning for your future and your retirement. The booklet also explains Medicare, and how much work credit you need to build up before you are eligible for retirement benefits under Social Security. This is a valuable guide to help you understand what's coming to you.

Write for:
Your Social Security (No. 510P)

Cost: Free

Send to:
Consumer Information Center
P.O. Box 100
Pueblo, CO 81002

Your Social Security

A WOMAN'S FUTURE

★★★

Almost all Americans have Social Security protection, either as workers or as dependents of workers. But certain aspects of the program are particularly relevant to women. Whether a woman interrupts her career to care for her family, never works, or becomes divorced, this booklet can help answer her questions. *A Woman's Guide to Social Security* is not intended as a complete explanation of the program, but is a useful handbook of Social Security provisions which are or can be of interest to women. The 16-page booklet covers elegibility under a variety of circumstances, retirement and death benefits, and widow's benefits. You'll learn how remarriage can affect your benefits, and how public pension plans can reduce your monthly entitlement.

continued

THE WAY YOU LIVE

Write for:
    A Woman's Guide to Social Security (No. 509P)

Cost: Free

Send to:
    Consumer Information Center
    P.O. Box 100
    Pueblo, CO 81002

A Women's Guide to Social Security

ABOUT MY SOCIAL SECURITY . . .
★★★★

Social Security was born in the economic despair of the Great Depression and first signed into law in 1935. It is a contract between generations whereby today's workers pay taxes to aid today's beneficiaries. It has been this country's most widely accepted social program since the first checks were mailed in 1940, but what is the future of Social Security? How secure is Social Security? *Social Security: Crisis, Questions, Remedies,* holds some of the answers. In 32 pages it discusses the long- and short-term problems, and gives an interesting history of the program and the reforms along the way. You'll learn how earnings are taxed, what changes are anticipated, and how the American public is committed to upholding this program.

Write for:
    Social Security: Crises, Questions, Remedies
    (No. 621)

Cost: $1.00

Send to:
    Public Affairs Pamphlets
    381 Park Ave. South
    New York, NY 10019

Social Security: Crises, Questions, Remedies

IN HONOR OF YOUR SERVICE
★★★

If you have served your country in the active military, naval, or air forces, you and your dependents are entitled to a wide range of benefits from the government. This 36-page booklet, *A Summary of Veterans Administration Benefits* is designed to introduce and highlight the various programs available. The information given is not regulatory and should not be interpreted as such, but gives a good overview and tells you where to get further advice to determine your eligibility. You'll learn about overseas benefits, educational assistance and job training, medical care, loans, insurance, and death benefits. Note that benefits are available without discrimination on the basis of race, color, national origin, sex, handicap, or religion.

Write for:
    A Summary of Veterans Administration Benefits
    (No. 413P)

Cost: Free

Send to:
    Consumer Information Center
    P.O. Box 100
    Pueblo, CO 81002

MAIL CALL
★★

When you're waiting for a check to be delivered or have to mail a birthday gift to a distant friend, you know it's the post office whose services you need. But how informed are you about the other dozens of programs offered by the U.S. Postal Service? They do much more than sell stamps, as you will discover in *A Consumer's Directory of Postal Services and Prod-*

 A SASE is a self-addressed stamped envelope.

ucts. The colorful 24-page guide lists and describes the many services available to both individuals and businesses, from Collect-On-Delivery (COD) to the international INTELPOST. You'll learn about purchasing stamps by mail, applying for passports, and collecting stamps as a hobby. There is also good advice about addressing your mail efficiently, and minimum and nonstandard sizes of mailing pieces.

Write for:
A Consumer's Directory of Postal Services and
Products (No. 587P)

Cost: Free

Send to:
Consumer Information Center
P.O. Box 100
Pueblo, CO 81002

Consumer's Directory of Postal Services and Products

FINDING OUT WHAT YOU WANT TO KNOW

★★★★

Have you ever tried to find an answer to a simple question about the federal government but gotten on a merry-go-round of referrals? A free brochure tells about the Federal Information Center, which can answer your questions quickly and efficiently—or help you find the person who's got the answer. It contains a state-by-state list of addresses and phone numbers. A companion brochure, the *Consumer Information Catalog,* is a 16-page catalog of selected federal publications of consumer interest. Many of the publications are either free or cost less than $2.00.

Write for:
Federal Information Centers
Consumer Information Catalog (No. 591P)

Cost: Free

Send to:
Consumer Information Center
P.O. Box 100
Pueblo, CO 81002

Federal Information Centers/Consumer Information

YOUR RIGHT TO KNOW

★★★★

To help fulfill its reponsibility to inform the public on policies and programs of the Federal Government, Congress established the Depository Library Program. This program is based upon three principles: 1) all government publications, with certain exceptions, be made available to depository libraries; 2) depository libraries be located in each state and congressional district in order to make government publications widely available; and 3) these publications shall be available for the free use of the general public. As of last year, 1389 libraries have accepted the designation as depositories. A 46-page guide to these libraries is available for the asking. Each is listed by city and state for easy reference. There is also a copy of the present law which governs these libraries.

Write for:
A Directory of U.S. Government Depository
Libraries

Cost: Free

Send to:
Consumer Information Center
P.O. Box 100
Pueblo, CO 81002

THE WAY YOU LIVE

BUT WHERE ARE THE PAPERS?

★★★★

Lost your birth certificate and can't prove your age or place of birth? Need to know when and where your parents were married? Can't find your divorce or annulment papers? If you've mislaid or lost any of your vital records, or need to have information on someone else's vital records and are qualified to obtain that information, you can contact the state, county, or city health department, which may be able to provide a copy of the document or the information you seek. A 24-page booklet tells how to obtain copies of lost vital records or information on them, with a state-by-state list of agencies to contact, cost of a copy, and important information on when each agency started keeping records.

Write for:
    Where to Write for Vital Records (No. 159P)

Cost: $1.50

Send to:
    Consumer Information Center
    P.O. Box 100
    Pueblo, CO 81002

Where to Write for Vital Records

A CURRENT VIEW OF THE BILL OF RIGHTS

★★★★

This splendid booklet should be required reading for every citizen of the United States. It does an extraordinary job of explaining a complex document in readily understandable language. It first reviews the Bill of Rights' history, and then states its primary function: "to protect 'minority members of society' who are in such a position because they are poor or powerless, because they hold unorthodox ideas, or belong to a minority religious, racial, political, or cultural group." The booklet then documents some of the major historical challenges to the Bill of Rights and the role that the Supreme Court played in each, and explains what the interpretations have meant to our society. Some clear and present dangers to the Bill of Rights provide food for thought.

Write for:
    The Bill of Rights Today (No. 489A)

Cost: $1.00

Send to:
    Public Affairs Pamphlets
    381 Park Ave. South
    New York, NY 10016

CRIMINAL JUSTICE: HOW IT WORKS

★★★★

"An uninformed public may accept an inefficient criminal justice system out of ignorance." This booklet's praiseworthy purpose is to shed light on such ignorance. It traces and defines American law, and tells how laws can be changed. There's a good discussion of law enforcement and the key concept of "probable cause" in making arrests. There is also a large section on prosecution and plea bargaining. The booklet thoroughly covers the judicial and correctional systems and briefly touches on the question, do prisons work? The major elements of the criminal justice system have been put in outline form to make the system easier to understand. There are excellent resource and reading lists for further study. Must reading for every concerned citizen.

Write for:
    Understanding the Criminal Justice System
        (No. 574)

Cost: $1.00

Send to:
    Public Affairs Pamphlets
    381 Park Ave. South
    New York, NY 10016

CALLED TO JUDGE

★★★★

The jury system is the basis for democratic justice. Because the jury represents society, it is the eyes and ears of the whole community. Almost no other institution requires people to examine their biases so seriously, and then try to put them aside for the greater good of society. *Understanding the Jury*

A SASE is a self-addressed stamped envelope.

System is a very informative 32-page booklet by the Public Affairs Committee which explains how the system works. You'll learn some history of how the jury system came to be, how juries are selected, and, once chosen, what responsibilities and rights jurors have. Also covered are the questions of sentencing, interpretation of the law, grand juries, and how the jury system might be changed to society's benefit.

Write for:
Understanding the Jury System (No. 619)

Cost: Free

Send to:
Public Affairs Pamphlets
381 Park Ave. South
New York, NY 10016

Understanding the Jury System

Your Environment

WATER, WATER, NOT EVERYWHERE
★★★★

Most people take the safety of their drinking water for granted. In general, this is justifiable, true, for water in this country is as free of bacterial and viral disease organisms as any in the world, but the supply is threatened nonetheless. Chemical contamination of water sources is a very real hazard. *Our Drinking Water: A Threatened Resource* is a factual, 28-page booklet which deals with this issue. You'll learn how dangerous chemicals enter the water system and the extent of the problem. The Safe Drinking Water Act and the role of the Environmental Protection Agency are discussed, as well as what the individual citizen and homeowner can do. There is a description of various drinking water pollutants and a listing of all EPA Regional Offices throughout the country.

Write for:
Our Drinking Water: A Threatened Resource
(No. 613)

Cost: $1.00

Send to:
Public Affairs Pamphlets
381 Park Ave. South
New York, NY 10016

Our Drinking Water: A Threatened Resource

STASHING THE TRASH
★★

Keep America Beautiful is a national, nonprofit, public service organization dedicated to promoting proper waste handling through voluntary action. Litter reductions of up to 80 percent have been realized in many KAB System cities and counties. Cities interested in the KAB System must complete an application for certification and send a Project Team to be trained. Communities clean up their own environments and compete for awards. If you, too, would like to help keep America trash-free, you'll be interested in the KAB *Bulletin*. This quarterly newsletter features the most recent program developments, case studies of programs and projects undertaken in various areas, and general news and announcements of local-level events of KAB cities and counties. A fact sheet gives you more info about KAB's philosophy, methods, and special programs.

Write for:
KAB Bulletin sample copy
KAB Fact Sheet

Cost: Free

Send to:
Keep America Beautiful, Inc.
99 Park Avenue
New York, NY 10016

THE BIG CLEANUP
★★

If everyone picked up just a bit of trash regularly, much progress would be made toward maintaining

continued

THE WAY YOU LIVE

the country's beauty and cleanliness. That's what the "Keep America Beautiful System" is all about. This environmental improvement program involves individual communities across the country, each promoting its own proper waste management. Your city or town can be a part of this campaign, too, and *Your Community and the Keep America Beautiful System* is a 12-page pamphlet that tells you how. It discusses benefits to the community, responsibilities to the program, and service awards your area can win for pulling together in the fight against litter and unsanitary conditions. Ask also for two one-page flyers, *You Take the First Step* and *Community Cleanup Campaign Checklist*, so you can get started.

Write for:
Your Community and the Keep America Beautiful
    System
You Take the First Step
Community Cleanup Campaign Checklist

Cost: Free

Send to:
Keep America Beautiful, Inc.
99 Park Avenue
Ncw York, NY 10016

AMERICA UNDONE— LITTER-ALLY
★★

Keep America Beautiful, Inc., lists three special offers which promote volunteer efforts to clean up and enhance the natural beauty of our individual communities. The first is an attractive, high-quality patch which is a great idea for scout or youth groups involved in local campaigns. A U.S. flag encircled with the words "Keep America Beautiful" is reproduced on a white background three inches in diameter. The other two are colorful posters. One features Iron Eyes Cody, the "crying Indian" in Keep America Beautiful's public service ads, and carries the slogan, "Pollution: It's a Crying Shame." The other, also with Iron Eyes Cody and another Indian scene, reads, "In the Fight Against Litter and Pollution We Still Have So Far to Go."

Write for:
KAB Patch
Pollution: It's a Crying Shame Poster
In The Fight Against Litter and Pollution Poster

Cost: $1.50 for patch
            $2.00 each for posters

Send to:
Keep America Beautiful, Inc.
99 Park Avenue
New York, NY 10016

Keep America Beautiful patch

Pollution posters

FOR BETTER AIR
★★★

The air in your home may be more polluted than the air you breathe outdoors. In addition, the average American spends at least 90 percent of his or her time indoors, of which 65 percent is at home. How clean is the air in your house? Two leaflets from the American Lung Association will help you become aware of and take responsibility for air quality. The first, *Air Pollution in Your Home?*, lists many precautions you can take. It also lists the major indoor air pollutants, from household and personal care products to fungi to formaldehyde. Harmful effects of each of these pollutants is given along with major sources. The second leaflet is a home indoor air quality checklist. Test yourself for sources and strength of indoor contaminants, and then implement the suggested control measures.

Write for:
Air Pollution in Your Home?
Test Your I.A.Q.

Cost: Free

Send to:
American Lung Association
P.O. Box 596
New York, NY 10001

IS WOOD GOOD?

★★★

In the last decade, wood-burning stoves have come back into popular use, partly because wood can be a more economical fuel source than gas or electricity, and partly in response to the "back to nature" movement. An 18-page booklet from the American Council on Science and Health tells of the merits and drawbacks of wood as a home fuel, including its negative side as a source of air pollution. The report tells what pollutants are produced by burning wood in stoves and fireplaces, what health hazards they pose both indoors and outdoors, and what other dangers they create—such as potential fire hazards and causes of carbon monoxide poisoning.

Write for:
Wood as Home Fuel

Cost: $2.00

Send to:
American Council on Science and Health
47 Maple St.
Summit, NJ 07901

NATURE AT ITS BEST

★★★

The National Wildlife Refuge System is a collection of lands and waters which was begun in 1903 when Theodore Roosevelt established tiny Pelican Island refuge in Florida. Now more than 400 National Wildlife Refuges enable you to catch a glimpse of a unique wildlife heritage, and provide you with a yardstick against which you can contrast the quality of your own environment. Over 88 million acres of land and water afford opportunities for discovering nature, naturally. *National Wildlife Refuges: A Visitor's Guide* is a colorful foldout map of the United States with designations of the refuges which invite interested tourists. A detailed locations and facilities chart lists refuges by state and indicates best viewing times along with recreational activities and accommodations available.

Write for:
National Wildlife Refuges: A Visitor's Guide
(No. 149P)

Cost: $1.00

Send to:
Consumer Information Center
P.O. Box 100
Pueblo, CO 81002

National Wildlife Refuges

EXTINCT POSSIBILITIES

★★

Since life began eons ago, thousands of creatures have come and gone like the dinosaur, sometimes rendered extinct by naturally changing ecological conditions but more recently by humans and their activities. Many of our plant and animal populations are declining because of exploitation, habitat alteration or destruction, and pollution. The Endangered Species Act of 1973 mandates protecting endangered species and restoring them to the point where their existence is no longer jeopardized. *Endangered Species* is a free foldout leaflet from the U.S. Department of the Interior which explains the problem and describes some of the recovery efforts going on today. There are also suggestions on what you can do to help.

Write for:
Endangered Species (No. 589P)

Cost: Free

Send to:
Consumer Information Center
P.O. Box 100
Pueblo, CO 81002

Endangered Species

THE WAY YOU LIVE

WITH ENERGY TO SPARE
★★

Conservation of precious natural resources is a serious concern to consumers and environmentalists alike. It should be, as this country's population in the year 2000 is projected to be 300 million. *Earthbeats* addresses the problem. The small newspaper is based on stories from *Earthwatch*, a daily Wisconsin environmental radio program. Some ideas for future energy sources are quite innovative, or seem so today. A recent issue explored the uses of ice, water, and garbage power. Another article focused on how the 19th century farmer took most of his energy supplies from his own land, and the great degree to which future farmers could do the same. The Household Energy Game illustrates how much energy your family uses, how your comsumption compares to today's average household, and where you might be able to conserve.

Write for:
Earthbeats Sample Copy

Cost: Free

Send to:
Sea Grant Institute
University of Wisconsin
1800 University Avenue
Madison, WI 53705

A REALISTIC LOOK AT GREEN BAY
★★★★

This is a fascinating look at a community. What's so great about Green Bay, Wisconsin? Well, in the mid-19th century it was known as the "shingle capital of the world"; in 1923, it was the world's leading producer of toilet paper (it still retains a huge papermaking industry); its "bay of bad odors," the name of its polluted lakeshore, is improving. This and lots more information on the town is included in *Green Bay: Portrait of a Waterway*, a large-format (11½″ × 14″) booklet published by the University of Wisconsin Sea Grant College Program. It's not a tourist guide that paints a rosy-colored picture of the place, but a collection of newspaper articles, originally published in the *Green Bay Press Gazette*, about the town's heritage and industrial growth, its fishing industry and port, its deteriorating marshes and wetlands, its clean-up successes in recent years, and its plans for a new marina in the future.

Write for:
Green Bay: Portrait of a Waterway

Cost: $1.00

Send to:
Sea Grant Institute
University of Wisconsin
1800 University Ave.
Madison, WI 53705

CONSERVING OUR NATURAL RESOURCES
★★★★

Scrap iron and steel represent a vast source of energy and mineral reserves that we've only barely begun to tap. To reinforce awareness of this fact, the Institute of Scrap Iron and Steel has prepared a free booklet that reveals how a deeper national commitment to recycling iron and steel could save energy, reduce the drain on natural resources, and help clean up—as well as protect—the environment. Did you know, for instance, that it requires four times as much energy to make steel from virgin iron ore as it does to make the same steel from scrap? Not to mention the fact that recycling protects dwindling mineral resources. This 36-page, elegantly designed book also details the history of the scrap processing industry, how scrap metal is collected and processed, and its importance as an international commodity. It's good reading for the energy-conscious consumer.

Write for:
Metallic Scrap—The Manufactured Resource

Cost: Free

Send to:
Institute of Scrap Iron and Steel, Inc.
1627 K St., N.W.
Washington, DC 20006

Metallic Scrap: The Manufactured Resource

A SASE is a self-addressed stamped envelope.

PLANNING FOR THE UNTHINKABLE

★★

If you believe that worldwide food crises lie ahead—and quite a few thoughtful people do—you'll want to read this prudent, rather alarming booklet that thoroughly examines the potential problem of food shortages. The booklet outlines the best foods to store (wheat, legumes), how and where to buy grain in bulk, how much to store per person, the storage containers to use, and how to preserve grain and water. The booklet also touches briefly on the emotional aspects of surviving, hoarding, and dependence on the community.

Write for:
Fat Years/Lean Years

Cost: $2.00

Send to:
Creative Living Center
Box 478
San Andreas, CA 95249

Fat Years/Lean Years

FREE THINGS
for Your
FREE TIME

Crafts, Hobbies, and Do-It-Yourself Projects

A QUILT FOR BABY

★★★

Emily Ann's baby quilt is soft, fluffy, and full of lace and bows. It may be the only quilt you'll ever want to make for that special baby in your life. The fast, easy instructions are full of diagrams to make this a quick one-evening project that could become a family heirloom. You can make this quilt on your sewing machine, so the minimum of hand stitching is necessary, and the batting is held in place with knotted threads, so you don't even have to do any actual quilting. With your "Sew-Sweet Baby Quilt" pattern you will also receive Emily Ann Creation's newest craft brochure and a coupon for $1.00 off your first purchase over $6.00 on Emily Ann's Sew-Sweet Baby and Baby-Knit patterns. Crafters are always on the lookout for new ideas; this one's worth investigating.

Write for:
Sew-Sweet Baby Quilt pattern

Cost: 50¢ and a long SASE

Send to:
Emily Ann Creations
303 S. 34th St.
Tacoma, WA 98408

STAR-SPANGLED NEEDLEPOINT

★★★★

Celebrate the Centennial Anniversary of the Statue of Liberty (1886 to 1986) with a seven-color 8″ × 10″ Collector's Edition needlepoint design from the NeedleCraft Club of America. This striking needlepoint canvas is perfectly timed to coincide with the commemorative and restorative festivities that will be taking place throughout the U.S. this year. Along with the canvas you will also receive a free copy of *Needlecraft News* and information on the Needle-Craft Club of America. The $2.00 investment will provide you with hours of stitching pleasure as well as a beautiful hanging for your home.

Write for:
Statue of Liberty Needlepoint

Cost: $2.00

Send to:
The NeedleCraft Club of America
352 Route 59
Dept. TFT-1
Monsey, NY 10952

Statue of Liberty Needlepoint

A POLITICAL STATEMENT

★★★★

No matter on which side of the political fence your loyalty lies, you can stand up and be counted—in needlepoint. This complete craft kit comes in your choice of Democratic or Republican motif, and would make a perfect gift for your favorite elected official, or for anyone involved in party activities. A 5″ × 7″ stylized Democratic donkey or Republican elephant pattern is stitched in patriotic red, white, and blue yarn. In your kit you will receive printed canvas, quality orlon yarn, a tapestry needle, and easy-to-follow fully illustrated stitching instructions. You would pay much more than $2.00 in a craft or hobby shop.

Write for:
Democratic Needlecraft Kit
Republican Needlecraft Kit

Cost: $2.00 each

Send to:
IMC Management, Inc.
P.O. Box 11Q
Garnerville, NY 10923

Democratic Needlecraft Kit
Republican Needlecraft Kit

FREE TIME

STITCH A UNICORN
★★★★

The mythological unicorn is a popular and beloved motif for most handcrafters today, whatever the medium. For $2.00, needlepointers can receive this lovely prancing unicorn pattern with multi-colored ribbons streaming from its hooves and horn. The finished wall hanging measures 8″ × 10″ and is made with seven colors of yarn. The legendary creature makes a fine addition to your home or an attractive gift for someone special you know. It would make a super stocking stuffer for Christmas, too. For your $2.00 you will also receive a copy of *Needlecraft News* and information on the NeedleCraft Club of America.

Write for:
Unicorn Needlepoint Canvas

Cost: $2.00

Send to:
The NeedleCraft Club of America
352 Route 59
Dept. TFT-2
Monsey, NY 10952

Unicorn Needlepoint Canvas

TRY OUT YOUR CREATIVITY
★★★

Are you looking for a small but nifty craft project for your Girl Scout troop, church group, or other organization? This design-your-own needlepoint kit from IMC Management, Inc. could end your search. For $1.50 you will receive an 8″ × 10″ blank needlepoint canvas, a selection of yarn in assorted colors, graph paper, a needle, and complete instructions for the basic continental stitch. Your group could easily make coasters, patches, wall decorations, and more. Stitch your logo or club name in needlepoint—all the necessary materials are right here.

Write for:
Design Your Own Needlepoint

Cost: $1.50

Send to:
IMC Needlecraft
P.O. Box 109N
Stony Point, NY 10980

DESIGN IT YOURSELF
★★★

These two needlepoint offers will certainly spur your imagination on to greater heights of creativity. Order the raw materials of your craft and design your own patterns. Perhaps you've seen a photograph or print and have thought it could easily be translated into needlepoint. IMC Management, Inc. makes it easy and inexpensive. For $2.00 you can receive a half-pound package of needlepoint yarn in assorted rainbow colors and plys; each strand is of manageable working length. For another $2.00, you'll get a generous cut of canvas in a choice of assorted sizes and meshes.

Write for:
Mixed Colors Needlepoint Yarn
Needlepoint Canvas

Cost: $2.00 each

Send to:
IMC Management, Inc.
P.O. Box 11
Garnerville, NY 10923

NEEDLEWORK FROM THE HEART
★★★

Here are two new handicraft patterns from Emily Ann Creations, both super ideas for your Valentine or anytime sweetie. The first is for a counted cross-stitch "Here's My Heart" patterned bookmark; it comes with complete illustrated and charted instructions. The heart pattern can also be adapted to kitchen, bath, and baby accessories. For the bookmark, all you need is a leftover scrap of fabric and a small amount of cotton embroidery thread. It's an easy craft project to carry in a zip-lock bag in your purse to do during all those spare moments that might otherwise be wasted. The second "Here's My Heart" craft is for an afghan. This is an easy panel-knit project with knit hearts that you appliqué into the "frames" for a three-dimensional look. Each proj-

A SASE is a self-addressed stamped envelope.

ect includes a current catalog and a $1.00 coupon good on certain items.

Write for:
Here's My Heart Bookmark
Here's My Heart Afghan

Cost: 25¢ and a long SASE for the bookmark
50¢ and a long SASE for the afghan

Send to:
Emily Ann Creations
303 S. 34th St.
Tacoma, WA 98408

STITCHING IN TIME
★★★

The secret to those delicate designs of counted cross-stitch is starting out with a quality fabric backing. This offer is for Even Weave polyester/cotton fabric—a high quality, washable permanent press fabric woven especially for counted cross-stitch projects. You'll receive a 16″ × 16″ piece of this 65/35 blend, which has a count of 18 "squares" per inch. You can make pillows, sachets, wall hangings, and even blouses with the softness of combed cotton and the convenience of a wrinkle-free fabric. The package costs $2.00, a bargain when compared to the prices you would expect to pay elsewhere.

Write for:
Aida Cloth for Counted Cross-Stitch

Cost: $2.00

Send to:
IMC Management, Inc.
P.O. Box 11 CCS
Garnerville, NY 10923

BUDDING ARTISTRY
★★★

Now this is a potpourri of a different kind. For $1.00 you'll receive a grab-bag of various needlecraft supplies which are sure to appeal to your imagination and creativity. Our sample kit included the basic materials for embroidery, latch hook, and needlepoint projects—all you need is the idea. There is multi-colored and multi-weight yarn, fabric for backings, a needle, and a metal frame. You'll also receive illustrated instructions for many of the stitches you'll be using. This a great rainy day activity for children, or surprise for an arty friend who is always creating new craftwork.

Write for:
Creativity Pack

Cost: $1.00

Send to:
IMC Management, Inc.
P.O. Box 11 CP
Garnerville, NY 10923

Creativity Pack

CREATIVE HOOKING
★★

Unleash the hidden creativity and inventiveness buried inside you with two latch hook offers from IMC Management, Inc. If hooking is your bag, or if you have children with nothing to do some rainy afternoon, read on. You'll receive the bare essentials, each priced at $2.00. The first is a one-pound bag of pre-cut yarn snippets, the perfect length for latch hooking. The colors are assorted rainbow hues. The second is the canvas, pre-cut into assorted sizes. There are no instructions or directions—just canvas and yarn so you can put your talents to work designing your own projects.

Write for:
Mixed Colors Latch Hook Yarn
Latch Hook Canvas

Cost: $2.00 each

Send to:
IMC Management, Inc.
P.O. Box 11
Garnerville, NY 10923

HOOKING YOUR HERITAGE
★★★

If you've always wanted to learn to hook rugs, or if you're an old hand looking for a new project, you'll

continued

FREE TIME

want to get your hooks on this simple do-it-yourself craft kit. You can make your own family crest, complete with initials, and the finished project will measure approximately 13″ × 16″. Included is everything you need except the actual hooking tool—canvas, pre-cut yarn in two colors, and complete directions for making your wall hanging. The illustrated instructions explain how to set up your work, how to loop each strand, how to bind edges, and suggestions for displaying the finished piece. Purchasing this novelty decoration in a craft store would certainly cost more than $2.00.

Write for:
  Family Crest Latch Hook Kit

Cost: $2.00

Send to:
  Needlepoint Outlet
  P.O. Box 11-F
  Garnerville, NY 10923

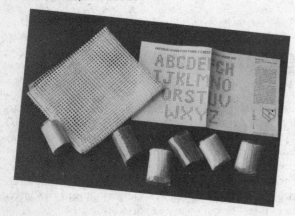

Family Crest Latch Hook Kit

SPINNING A YARN
★★

Whether you crochet, weave, or knit by hand or on a knitting machine, you know that success depends in part on your choice of yarn. Here are some that you can appraise at home. For 50¢ this Maine company will send you a sample packet of wool yarns—fisherman's yarns (good for sweaters and mittens because the natural lanolin oils have been left in), tweeds, homespuns, sport yarns and soft spuns for use with knitting machines, and unspun yarn for a handspun look. The accompanying catalog gives tips on washing wool with JEN-TIL; all these yarns need to be washed, not dry cleaned. There's also a handy yardage chart for figuring how much you'll need.

Write for:
  Bartlettyarns Yarn Samples

Cost: Free

Send to:
  Bartlettyarns, Inc.
  P.O. Box 36, Dept. CG
  Harmony, ME 04942

Bartlettyarns Yarn Samples

ZIP IT UP
★★★

A Swede named Gideon Sundback perfected the modern zipper in 1913. Since then, we've found zillions of uses for the slide closure in home, clothing, and hobby work. As a handicrafter yourself, you know how often you use zippers for your projects. Now you can receive five zippers for just $1.00. You'll get a random selection of different colors and types, ranging in size from 7 to 24 inches. There are nylon and metal zippers, as well as skirt, dress, pants, and jacket styles. In addition, there are zipper closers for handbags, totebags, pillows, and slip covers. Some are close-end and others open-end.

Write for:
  Zippers

Cost: $1.00

Send to:
  IMC Management, Inc.
  P.O. Box 11-Z
  Garnerville, NY 10923

Zippers

A SASE is a self-addressed stamped envelope.

A LOOK AT LIVING HISTORY
★★★★

Native American arts and crafts are much prized by collectors today, and the *Source Directory of Indian, Eskimo and Aleut Owned and Operated Arts and Crafts Businesses*, published by the U.S. Department of the Interior, can give you a lead to some of the finest examples. This free, 48-page directory lists 223 shops, co-ops, cultural centers, and individual craftsmen, grouped alphabetically by state. Each listing includes the tribal affiliation, name, and address of the owner or manager; business hours; and phone number. There is also a description of products offered for sale, price list and catalog, and mail order information when applicable. Beautiful black-and-white photos of Native American arts and crafts illustrate the pages.

Write for:
Source Directory of Indian, Eskimo and Aleut Arts and Crafts Businesses

Cost: Free

Send to:
Indian Arts and Crafts Board
Room 4004-Main Interior
U.S. Department of Interior
Washington, DC 20240

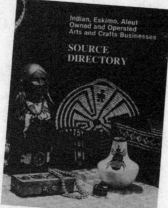

Source Directory of Indian, Eskimo and Aleut Arts and Crafts Businesses

GOURDSMANSHIP
★★★★

Hardshelled gourds are relatives of such common garden vegetables as cucumbers, squash, pumpkins, and melons. Gourds take 3½ months to mature and an additional three to six months to dry. Then they can be fashioned into dozens of useful and artistic objects. This 20-page booklet is a primer on creating with gourds. You'll learn about dozens of different kinds of gourds, how you can grow them and train them into the right shape for future proj-

ects, how to harvest and cure them, and then how to make them into everything from lamp bases, animals, and birds to toys and objects of art. You'll also learn about the special techniques, tools, and tricks you'll need to work with gourds. An intriguing handbook.

Write for:
Creativity With Gourds

Cost: $1.75

Send to:
American Gourd Society
Box 274C
Mount Gilead, OH 43338

THE FINISHING TOUCH
★★★★

Many long hours, filled with love, go into your priceless handicraft. Whether your nimble fingers produce crewel, embroidery, or candlewicking, your plaques and wallhangings are beautiful to look at and delightful to receive as gifts. The finishing touch is always the frame. Sometimes this is the most expensive part of your work. IMC Needlecraft has a special offer for you: Take your choice of a 5″ × 5″ or 5″ × 7″ wooden frame for only a dollar. The frames are lightweight, nicely finished, and perfect for bordering any needlework. You'd expect to pay much more in the local hobby shop.

Write for:
Wooden Picture Frame (specify size)

Cost: $1.00

Send to:
IMC Needlecraft
1 Bridge Street
Garnerville, NY 10923

Wooden Picture Frames

FREE TIME

DO-IT-YOURSELF PICTURE FRAMES
★★★★

Are some of your favorite photographs, pictures, oil paintings—not to mention your child's first masterpiece—stowed away out of sight because you never got them framed? This splendid little booklet is a minicourse in do-it-yourself framing and might tempt you to bring those treasures out of the closet. Here's a concise explanation of everything you need to know about framing a picture: how to choose a frame and select a moulding, and the tools you'll need to work with. Excellent line drawings take you step by step through making the frame, then show you how to finish, mat, mount, and back your picture. You'll get ideas for attractive picture groups, and straight data on hanging your work. You'll spend 60¢ well on this well-produced booklet.

Write for:
How To Make Picture Frames

Cost: 60¢

Send to:
Western Wood Moulding and Millwork Producers
P.O. Box 25278
Portland, OR 97225

How to Make Picture Frames

MAKE A WOOD WINE RACK
★★★★

You've probably found that keeping even a modest selection of wine on hand can turn an ordinary family meal or the arrival of unexpected guests into a festive occasion. And the best way to store your new or older vintages is in a wine rack. This booklet of design ideas and detailed construction plans for a number of ingenious and practical wine racks comes from Louisiana-Pacific. It includes suggestions for cylindrical racks, drawer racks, portable racks, lattice racks, and designs that hold anywhere from six to 48 bottles of wine. The company says that the California redwood they supply is traditional "wine wood"—it's used by many of the state's wineries for production vats and storage tanks.

Write for:
Redwood Wine Rack Construction Plans

Cost: 50¢

Send to:
Redwood-Louisiana Pacific
Louisiana Pacific
1300 S.W. 5th Ave.
Portland, OR 97201

TOY WITH A GIFT IDEA
★★★

For a special birthday or holiday gift this year, why not give your child a dollhouse that you've built yourself? If you're tempted, Louisiana-Pacific has a free instruction booklet for this project, and includes step-by-step directions and detailed plans for layout, cutting, and assembly. The illustrated plan is printed on a single sheet that opens up flat for convenient reference while you work. An attractive project with good, clear illustrations of assembly details—a plus for the less experienced woodworker.

Write for:
Waferwood® Dollhouse

Cost: Free

Send to:
Waferwood-Lousiana Pacific
Louisiana Pacific
1300 S.W. 5th Ave.
Portland, OR 97201

Waferwood® Dollhouse

A SASE is a self-addressed stamped envelope.

WOODCRAFTING FOR FAMILY AND FUN

★★

Making your own toys and home furnishings can pave the way to hours of entertainment and satisfaction for you and your family. In fact, you may enjoy the hobby so much that it becomes a second source of income. The *Blueprints* catalog shows wooden pull toys, puzzles, wall plaques, desk or shelf organizers, birdhouses, planters, bookracks, and more. You can write for full-scale blueprints with step-by-step instructions. The manufacturer stresses that the blueprints are easy to read, and because they are full-scale, they don't need to be enlarged or reduced. A materials list and finishing suggestions are also given. The catalog is $1.00 and pattern prices start at $1.00. The catalog also contains a list of books on do-it-yourself crafts.

Write for:
Blueprints by Design Group

Cost: $1.00

Send to:
Design Group
P.O. Box 514-PL
Miller Place, NY 11764

Collections

HISTORICALLY SPEAKING

★★★★

This is an offer which combines two neat hobbies: coin collecting and American history. Jolie Coins presents a collection of three old United States coins, each at least 75 years old. You will receive a 1910 Lincoln Head Cent, an Indian Head Cent from 1907 or earlier, and a Liberty-V Nickel dated 1911 or earlier. The three coins can be obtained for $2.00. Also included in the package is a price list for other coin and money offers. Collecting old coins is like owning pieces of the country's history.

Write for:
75 Year Old Coin Collection

Cost: $2.00 (U.S. funds only)

Send to:
Jolie Coins
P.O. Box 68 US
Roslyn Heights, NY 11577

75 Year Old Coin Collection

COLLECTOR'S GUIDE

★★★

How much is that old porcelain figurine of a sparrow that you found in the attic really worth? Is that old Hummel Goose Girl doll your Aunt Maggie left you worth anything as an antique? How about that Blue Boy plate someone gave your mother as a wedding present? You'll find out what limited edition plates, figurines, bells, graphics, steins, and dolls are worth to collectors in the latest edition of the Collectors' Information Bureau Price Index. It's a 40-page magazine listing issue price and what collectors might pay for an item today (usually many times more than it originally sold for). Prices are based on interviews with dealers all over the U.S. The Bureau calls it the most comprehensive and up-to-date index of its kind.

Write for:
Price Index to Limited Edition Plates, Figurines, Bells, Graphics, Steins, and Dolls

Cost: $1.00

Send to:
Collectors' Information Bureau
187 Ridge Ave.
Winnetka, IL 60093

A HISTORICAL PERSPECTIVE

★★★

A great way to explore the country's heritage is through this historical stamp collection from the U.S. Stamp Collector's Society. Whether this is a starter set for you or someone you know, or an addition to an existing collection, you'll enjoy the 101-stamp offer. Each one is different. There are commemoratives, definitives, and airmails, includ-

continued

FREE TIME

ing one of the first commemorative issues — the Columbian Exposition stamp of 1893. Although each collection is slightly different, a recent compilation honored the 1984 Olympics, New York's Metropolitan Opera, Roanoke Villages, Andrew Jackson, and the locomotives of the 1870's. All are cancelled, and of high quality.

Write for:
Collection of 101 U.S. Stamps

Cost: $2.00

Send to:
U.S. Stamp Collector's Society
P.O. Box 480655
Los Angeles, CA 90048

Collection of 101 U.S. Stamps

IN THE DOLL HOUSE
★★★

Doll Castle News is a pocketbook-size magazine for doll collectors and people interested in dollhouses and miniatures. It's full of delightful information on the history of dolls, dressing dolls, making dolls that may be antiques one day, dollhouses and furnishings, and a finders' corner through which to identify the antique doll you inherited from Great-Aunt Fanny. You'll be captivated by the range of collectors and the ingenious means they find to clothe and furnish these "small treasures." If you've always had a secret conviction that dolls shouldn't be just for children, you'll enjoy this remarkable list of sources and information.

Write for:
Sample copy of Doll Castle News

Cost: $2.00

Send to:
Doll Castle News
P.O. Box 247
Washington, NJ 07882

UP-TO-THE-MINUTE STAMPS
★★★★

The Philatelic Catalog, put out by the U.S. Post Office, is updated and sent out to customers six times a year. It tells which commemorative stamps are available (with illustrations), and which mint sets you can get. You'll also find regular issues, booklets, precanceled stamps, and special stamps on certain subjects, and you'll learn which stamps will be removed from sale and on what date. It's fascinating, but so detailed that only experienced stamp collectors will be able to understand its significance.

Write for:
Philatelic Catalog

Cost: Free

Send to:
Philatelic Catalog
Philatelic Sales Division
Washington, DC 20265-9998

Philatelic Catalog

Video and Audio Entertainment

ELECTRONIC TOYS FOR ADULTS
★★★★

The wonders of electronics are here to stay and are fast becoming affordable to more and more people. This excellent user's guide explains the intricacies of television, component television, projection television, and videocassette recorders. Those persons owning videodisc players, video games and computers will learn what the advantages of each system are. There are tips on cable service, wireless remote control units, advice on caring for your new equipment, notes on antennas, and information on safety, warranties, and servicing.

Write for:
Video: Your New Window on the World

Cost: Free with a long SASE (39¢ postage)

Send to:
Electronic Industries Association
Consumer Electronics Group
P.O. Box 19100
Washington, D.C. 20036

Video: Your New Window on the World

SAFETY TIPS FOR VIDEO PRODUCTS
★★

With many Americans owning at least two television sets, it's easy to forget that a TV, like any other electronic product, must be handled safely. Learn how from the Electronic Industries Association, which has just updated this video safety pamphlet. The pamphlet informs the viewer on installation, use, and service of video products, and lists 40 tips to make you more aware of safety factors. It also diagrams the installation and grounding of an antenna system for the home, and offers simple commonsense tips—like keeping liquids away from your electronic products.

Write for:
Video Products Safety—A Guide for Consumers

Cost: Free with a long SASE

Send to:
Electronic Industries Association
Consumer Electronics Group
P.O. Box 19100
Washington, D.C. 20036

GETTING TO KNOW YOUR VCR
★★★

If you've decided that now is the time to buy a VCR, welcome to the VCR party. This helpful pamphlet answers all sorts of questions typically asked by the first-time purchaser of a VCR, and discusses video cameras and tapes as well. This pamphlet also presents a diagram of VCR hookup with cable systems. Good information, too, on camcorders—the new combination of camera and recorder.

Write for:
How to Buy, Use, and Care for VCRs, Cameras and Tape

Cost: Free with a long SASE (39¢ postage)

Send to:
Electronic Industries Association
Consumer Electronics Group
P.O. Box 19100
Washington, D.C. 20036

TLC FOR THE BOOB TUBE
★★

This helpful pamphlet reminds you not to take your TV for granted, and lists 21 safety tips to keep in mind when you install your set and when you use it. You'll learn where to install your set, and to be cautioned to let a professional put up the outdoor antenna because it can be hazardous to do it yourself. There are tips for safe operation and use of the set (don't place liquids on top of the set; don't let small children play with it), and a diagram for proper antenna grounding according to National Electrical Code instructions. Good, practical words for the viewer to take to heart.

Write for:
A Consumer Guide to Television Safety

Cost: Free with a long SASE

Send to:
Electronic Industries Association
Consumer Electronics Group
P.O. Box 19100
Washington, D.C. 20036

VIDEO VENTURES
★★★

Video is unique as a communications tool. It is immediate, direct, flexible, intimate, mobile, and alive. There are no hard and fast rules on when to

continued

FREE TIME

use this medium for your message (each project should be evaluated on its own merits) but *Basic Tips On Video* is a concise guide for new video users. You'll get good advice on selecting, purchasing, and caring for your equipment. Before going into production, there are many factors to consider: your audience, your budget, presentation of your story. Next you'll learn about the production process and get suggestions for low-budget productions. There is also a list of tips on choosing outside producers. This publication contains good beginner's information and includes ideas to help you expand your knowledge.

Write for:
Basic Tips on Video

Cost: Free with a long SASE

Send to:
International Communications Industries Association
3150 Spring Street
Fairfax, VA 22031-2399

Basic Tips on Video

WOW! IT'S STEREO TV!
★★★★

Since its arrival as a consumer product in the late 1940s, the television set has remained basically the same, while manufacturers concentrated on improving the picture quality. If you shop for a TV set today, you'll discover a wide variety of options, such as sets with flatter and squarer picture tubes, larger screens, and more jacks so you can use your TV set with video cassette recorders and home computers. Many new TV sets also are equipped to receive stereo TV broadcasts, and this free 8-page booklet from the Electronic Industries Association tells all about stereo TV broadcasting; TV sets that can receive stereo signals; and how to buy stereo TV sets that will be compatible with your stereo system, VCR, or computer.

Write for:
Consumers Should Know—All About Stereo Television

Cost: Free with a long SASE

Send to:
Electronic Industries Association
Consumer Electronics Group
P.O. Box 19100
Washington, DC 20036

UNTANGLING CABLE TV QUESTIONS
★★

Has the cable boom caused confusion in your life? If so, send for this straightforward fact sheet prepared to answer questions about cable service. It gives you the basics concerning TV and cable and outlines the options you have when purchasing a television with or without the capability of cable hookup. The fact sheet talks about remote control compatibility with cable systems. You should also know that using cable services without paying for them can subject you to fines and civil damages. No-nonsense information for TV viewers.

Write for:
Facts About Television and Cable Systems

Cost: Free with a long SASE

Send to:
Electronic Industries Association
Consumer Electronics Group
P.O. Box 19100
Washington, D.C. 20036

IS CABLE TV FOR YOU?
★★★★

Cable television, the transmission of television program signals by a cable TV company to subscribers through underground or aerial wires, has brought TV to many rural parts of the country that otherwise wouldn't be able to receive television signals. In recent years, cable TV also has come to cities, offering a wide choice of pay movie channels. You can see dozens of movies for a moderate monthly fee. If cable TV is offered in your area and you are thinking about subscribing, a free 8-page booklet from the Better Business Bureau can be helpful in making a decision. It tells what cable TV is, how it works, what satellite TV is, and what subscription TV is. The booklet also offers tips on how to decide which service will do the most for you.

A SASE is a self-addressed stamped envelope.

Write for:
Tips on Cable TV and Other Options (No. 24-177)

Cost: Free

Send to:
Council of Better Business Bureaus
1515 Wilson Blvd.
Arlington, VA 22209

WHEN THINGS GO ON THE FRITZ

★★★★

You probably seldom appreciate how much you enjoy your television, stereo, or VCR until they give you trouble, and you have to think about getting them fixed. The more you add to your home entertainment system, the more likely you are going to experience trouble with one or more of the components. The Electronic Industries Association offers a free 16-page booklet with advice on what to look for *before* you call for service if you have trouble with audio or video equipment. If you can't solve the problem yourself and need to take the equipment in for service, the booklet offers suggestions on how to find a reputable repair technician and deal with estimates and service contracts.

Write for:
Consumer Service Guide for Audio and Video
    Products

Cost: Free with a SASE

Send to:
Electronic Industries Association
Consumer Electronics Group
P.O. Box 19100
Washington, DC 20036

THE WORLD OF ELECTRONIC SOUND

★★★★

If you're a bit baffled and bewitched by component systems, consoles, compacts, compact discs, microsystems, single-brand and rack-mounted systems in the world of sound, you're going to welcome this guide. It explains all of the above in detail, covers personal portable and car audio systems, and touches on the subject of add-on accessories for your component system. There are tape basics and eight tips on taping that will ensure quality recordings. There's a glossary of audio terms, too. Ask also for the free mini-leaflet on "Audio Headset Safety."

Write for:
Audio: Your New World of Listening

Cost: Free with a long SASE (39¢ postage)

Send to:
Electronic Industries Association
Consumer Electronics Group
P.O. Box 19100
Washington, D.C. 20036

AUDIO EQUIPMENT SAFETY TIPS

★★★

Incorrectly installed, used, or serviced audio products present the threat of electrical shock or fire, and here are 17 suggestions for the correct use of your audio equipment from a safety standpoint. One of them: Never place equipment in a built-in enclosure unless proper ventilation is provided. Another: Never leave your set on when leaving the house, and unplug it during a lightning storm or if you're going to leave it unattended for an extended period of time. Above all, let your dealer or service technician attend to all service adjustments.

Write for:
A Consumer Guide to Audio Products Safety

Cost: Free with a long SASE (39¢ postage)

Send to:
Electronic Industries Association
Consumer Electronics Group
P.O. Box 19100
Washington, D.C. 20036

A GREAT NEW SOUND!

★★★★

If you're still playing records on a phonograph recorder or tapes on a tape recorder, you're missing a lot of great sound. The hottest development in audio today, the compact disc and compact disc player, is opening the ears of even the most uncritical music lover and is being hailed as the greatest step forward in audio since the cylinder gave way to the flat wax record at the start of this century. The Electronic Industries Association offers a free 12-page booklet describing compact discs and players so you can make wise shopping decisions if you decide to get in on the compact disc revolution.

Write for:
Consumers Should Know—All About Compact
    Discs and Players

continued

FREE TIME

Cost: Free with a long SASE

Send to:
Electronic Industries Association
Consumer Electronics Group
P.O. Box 19100
Washington, DC 20036

Special Interests

POST SCRIPT
★★★★

Keeping in touch is easy and inexpensive with this impressive collection of 12 beautifully illustrated postcards. Whether postcards are your hobby or simply a way to let someone know you care, this offer is worth much more than the 50¢ asked for here. These cards depict precious moments of friendship, romance, and humor through photographs and headlines such as "Being together," "Have a nice day," "Our warm love," and more. The packets are compiled from the manufacturer's overstock, which is good news for you.

Write for:
Postcard Offer

Cost: 50¢

Send to:
IMC Management, Inc.
P.O. Box 11
Garnerville, NY 10923

Postcards

WRITE ON!
★★★★

Do you have thank-you notes to write, long overdue? Is there someone you owe a long, chatty letter, but until you get around to it would like to send a few lines to say you haven't forgotten? Are you losing the battle of trying to get your kids to write to Grandma? You need Little Letters—the convenient, fun-to-use stationery that folds over and seals. No fuss, no envelopes. IMC Management, Inc. offers a set of 12 colorful notecards and 12 seals. The inside is blank for you to write your message, and the outside is adorned with decorative designs with room for address and stamp. This offer would make a great stocking stuffer, too.

Write for:
Little Letters

Cost: $1.00

Send to:
IMC Management, Inc.
55 Railroad Avenue
Garnerville, NY 10923

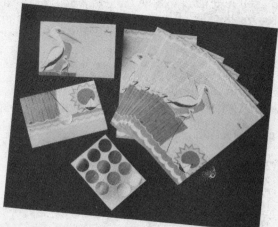

Little Letters

CHECK IT OUT
★★

If you're a chess buff, you probably know about *Chess Life*, the monthly magazine published by the United States Chess Federation. If you're on the way to becoming an enthusiast, send a dollar for a sample copy. You can examine 60 or more pages of chess news, chess theory, personality profiles, and articles on the history, psychology, and art of chess. Your sample issue may also contain a special section of products sold by the United States Chess Federation—like computer opponents, chess sets, and books. There are monthly features by chess masters on techniques, great moves, and secret strategies

A SASE is a self-addressed stamped envelope.

that may improve your game. Some of the more interesting positions are diagrammed. The Federation also offers a copy of the official rules of chess. Both these items are a must for anyone who takes the game seriously.

Write for:
Rules brochure and sample issue of *Chess Life*

Cost: $1.00

Send to:
United States Chess Federation
186 Rte. 9W
New Windsor, NY 12550

CHECKERS, ANYONE?

★★★

No, the game of checkers is not only for little children or old men sitting around the general store, as you will quickly learn from these three leaflets from the American Checker Federation. *Basic Rules of Checkers* gives rules regarding the checkerboard, pieces, methods of play, and won and drawn games. *Beginners' Corner* lists a dozen detailed pointers on checker strategy, and eight elementary positions.

The third pamphlet provides information on the Federation, its goals and functions, history (it was organized in 1948, though the first tournament ever was in 1907), membership, tournaments, and matches. The casual checker player will be surprised at the amount of information available here.

Write for:
Basic Rules of Checkers
Beginners' Corner—A Dozen Pointers and Some
    Elementary Positions
A Description of the American Checker Federation

Cost: Three first-class stamps

Send to:
American Checker Federation
W.B. Grandjean, Secretary
3475 Belmont Ave.
Baton Rouge, LA 70808

FIX UP THAT OLD CHEVY

★★★

If you own a Chevrolet automobile vintage 1955-1957, including Corvettes or trucks, or just love them, you're eligible to join the exclusive Classic Chevy Club, which has been in operation since 1974. The Club offers prospective members a reduced price on

its latest monthly magazine, which has articles about the club and several Chevy models as well as information on parts available to restore old Chevys. Membership in the club includes the monthly magazine, which can help classic Chevy owners with tips on repairing and rebuilding their cars.

Write for:
Sample issue, Classic Chevy World

Cost: $2.00

Send to:
Classic Chevy Club International
P.O. Box 17188
Orlando, FL 32860

Classic Chevy World

ASTRONOMICAL BUMPER STICKERS

★★★

If you've had it with boring, unfunny bumper stickers that make jokes about the same old things, you'll probably enjoy the astronomical point of view of this set, which uses the stars and other galaxy-spanning phenomena as the springboard for some unexpected humor. Here are some examples: "Astronomy is Looking Up," "Interstellar Matter is a Gas," and "Quasars Are Far Out." The stickers are also ideal for notebooks, bulletin boards, or your office door.

Write for:
Astronomical Bumper Stickers

Cost: $1.00 each

Send to:
Astronomical Society of the Pacific
1290 24th Ave.
San Francisco, CA 94122

FREE TIME

STAR HACKING
★★★

This pamphlet is a listing of computer programs that deal with astronomy. Published by the Astronomical Society of the Pacific, the list includes 45 programs available on disk or cassette for such popular home computers as Apple, IBM, Commodore, Atari, and TRS-80. Each listing contains a brief description of what the software does and the full address of the manufacturer. Prices have not been listed because they change frequently. The publishers state they have not tested all of these programs or verified the claims made for them, but the comprehensive listing is a good place to start exploring the universe. A selected reading list is also included.

Write for:
Astronomy Computer List

Cost: $1.00

Send to:
Astronomical Society of the Pacific
1290 24th Ave.
San Francisco, CA 94122

THOSE PUZZLING QUASARS
★★★

Of all the wonders revealed by the science of astronomy, among the most perplexing are quasars, the most distant and most energetic objects known in the universe. They resemble stars (their name is a contraction of "quasi-star"), but their distances from Earth are astonishingly vast. A typical quasar might be so far away that its light has taken ten billion years to reach us. Because quasars can be detected at all means that they are producing energy on a scale so massive as to be incomprehensible. No satisfactory explanation for this energy potential has yet been reached. If you'd like to learn more about this fascinating phenomenon, this illustrated information packet describes quasars in interesting but somewhat technical terms that will have special appeal for people with a serious interest in astronomy and natural science.

Write for:
Quasar Information Packet

Cost: $2.00

Send to:
Astronomical Society of the Pacific
Quasars Packet Department
1290 24th Ave.
San Francisco, CA 94122

SUN SIGNS
★★★

Are you a Leo? A Capricorn, perhaps? It doesn't matter, claims the Astronomical Society of the Pacific, which has compiled a packet of information that debunks the popular superstition called astrology. Included are reprints of several articles explaining dozens of careful scientific tests that have now shown that astrology simply does not work. Designed to provide students, teachers, librarians, and the public with specific information on this controversial subject, the packet also includes a bibliography for further reading, and an interview with astronomer George Abell, who has spent considerable time examining and exposing the tenets of astrology.

Write for:
Astrology and Astronomy

Cost: $2.00

Send to:
Astronomical Society of the Pacific
1290 24th Ave.
San Francisco, CA 94122

Astrology Packet

SHORTWAVE LISTENERS' BULLETIN
★★★

If you're a shortwave listener hobbyist, you'll want to look at a sample newsbulletin of the American Shortwave Listeners club, which has news of monthly programming from all over the world. You'll learn what's being beamed from North and Central America, South America, USSR, Asia and the Middle East, Europe, and Africa, and at what time and on what day. There are also articles on forthcoming programs, news, and reports from ASWLC chapters. The ASWLC motto is "World Friendship Thru Shortwave." A fascinating way to widen your horizons.

A SASE is a self-addressed stamped envelope.

Write for:
Sample issue of ASWLC Newsbulletin

Cost: $2.00

Send to:
American Shortwave Listeners Club
16182 Ballad Lane
Huntington Beach, CA 92649-2202

FOR AMATEUR RADIO BUFFS

★★★★

Tens of thousands of Americans are "ham radio" enthusiasts—part of a growing network of amateur radio buffs. They are licensed to operate two-way radio stations from their homes and cars, talking with other hams across town or across the world. If you want to learn how to become an amateur radio operator, the American Radio Relay League offers a free "Dear Friends" package to get you started. It contains League membership information; an article about how to master the Morse code so you can obtain your amateur radio license; a brochure telling of many varied uses of amateur radio such as in natural disasters and outer space; and an order form for purchasing booklets and cloth patches or bumper stickers. For instance, you can get a five-inch diamond-shaped patch for $2.00, or a variety of decals for 25¢ or 50¢.

Write for:
"Dear Friends" Package

Cost: Free

Send to:
American Radio Relay League
225 Main St.
Newington, CT 06111

American Radio Relay League patches, bumper stickers, and decals

NO TRIVIAL MATTER

★★★

What was Ronald Reagan's first job in show business? Who invented the transatlantic cable? What is Paul McCartney's middle name? If Trivial Pursuit is your sport of choice, this book is for you. *Trivia Masters* is a magazine-size soft-cover book chock full of quizzes that test your knowledge of "little information." There are fill-in-the-blank and mix-and-match questions about movie, television, music, and soap opera celebrities, literature, history, and more. Play each trivia game, then check your answers at the end of each chapter. Add up all your points and compare them with the master scoring key to see how well you've done. The book is fully illustrated with black-and-white photos of your favorite stars. It originally sold for $3.95, but is available to readers of *1000s of Free Things* for $1.00.

Write for:
Trivia Masters

Cost: $1.00

Send to:
IMC Management, Inc.
P.O. Box 11
Garnerville, NY 10923

Trivia Masters

WANT TO OWN A SPA
OR HOT TUB?

★★

Do you picture yourself lounging for hours with a favorite drink in a hot tub or spa? Forget it! Safety rules say you shouldn't drink anything alcoholic while soaking in a spa or hot tub, and you shouldn't soak for more than 15 minutes at high water temper-

continued

atures. If you're thinking of buying a hot tub or spa, or if you already own one, you can learn more about how to get the most out of it the safe way from this 14-page booklet put out by the National Spa and Pool Institute. Besides tips on soaking safely, the booklet describes exercise programs you and the family can enjoy in a spa or hot tub, gives suggestions for entertaining, and details equipment needed in and around the spa or hot tub.

Write for:
The Sensible Way to Enjoy Your Spa or Hot Tub

Cost: $1.00

Send to:
Dept. PI
National Spa and Pool Institute
2111 Eisenhower Ave.
Alexandria, VA 22314

ENJOY YOUR SWIMMING POOL SAFELY
★★★

Having a swimming pool is a lot of fun—but it also involves a lot of responsibility. For instance, as a pool owner, you may be legally liable for the safety of anyone who uses your pool. This well-put-together booklet tells you just about all you need to know about operating and maintaining a pool and making sure family and guests have a good time without taking risks.

Write for:
The Sensible Way to Enjoy Your Pool

Cost: $1.75

Send to:
Dept. PI
National Spa and Pool Institute
2111 Eisenhower Avenue
Alexandria, VA 22314

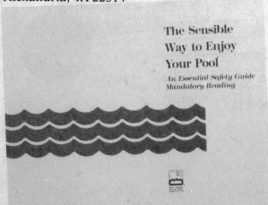

The Sensible Way to Enjoy Your Pool

Sports and Outdoor Activities

TENNIS, EVERYONE?
★★★★

This is not a beginner's book nor a learner's manual. It's the official USTA rule book and the last word for people who play without an official but who want official answers to questions arising during play. The United States Tennis Association publishes this 14-page booklet on the *Rules of Tennis and Cases and Decisions,* so you'll know the information is coming straight from the people who know.

Write for:
Rules of Tennis and Cases and Decisions

Cost: 50¢

Send to:
United States Tennis Association
Education and Research Center
729 Alexander Road
Princeton, NJ 08540

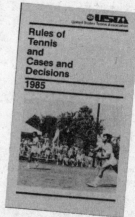

Rules of Tennis and Cases and Decisions

A GOOD SPORT
★★

Lots of people have played ping pong at some time or another, without having thought about it seriously as a sport. If that's your experience, you can now discover the sport in its own right. If you're ready to take ping pong seriously, write for *How to Start a Table Tennis Club* and get the basic ground rules for setting up a steering committee, assigning important functions to the officers of the club, detailed specifications for the nets, balls, table, barriers, rackets, and lighting you need to consider, as well as hints for finding a good location for establishing your club. This useful booklet also covers operating

A SASE is a self-addressed stamped envelope.

expenses, income, club activities, and ways to generate publicity about your group. The 30-page illustrated booklet even tells you exactly *when* to form a club: "when the cross beams of the low ceiling become a part of your special rules . . . you realize that your love for the sport requires different action."

Write for:
How to Start a Table Tennis Club

Cost: $1.50

Send to:
United States Table Tennis Association
Olympic House
1750 E. Boulder St.
Colorado Springs, CO 80909

BIG MONEY IN BOWLING

★★★

If you haven't been keeping up with the sport of professional bowling, you're going to be surprised at the top money prizes awarded at 30-plus annual national tournaments on the Professional Bowlers Association Tour — approximately $6 million. This is the official program for the tour; it lists the players, gives information on past winners, shows records tumbling under new ones, tells who has been inducted into the Hall of Fame, and gives tournament highlights. Lots of photographs, ads, and news of this widespread U.S. sport.

Write for:
Official Program

Cost: $1.50

Send to:
Professional Bowlers Association
P.O. Box 5118
1720 Merriman Rd.
Akron, OH 44313

Official Program PBA

POCKET BOOK OF GOLF RULES

★★★★

Any golfer, whatever his or her skill level, would be happy to have this illustrated, simplified, clearly written pocket book of golf rules. They've all been checked for accuracy by the United States Golf Association, and there are several pages of golf terms and definitions as well. For those golfers who may be changing their status, the strict requirements for retaining amateur status are declared. You'll also find a list of National Golf Foundation publications and their prices. A tiny book, but handy.

Write for:
Easy Way To Learn Golf Rules

Cost: 30¢

Send to:
National Golf Foundation
200 Castlewood Dr.
North Palm Beach, FL 33408

RUN FOR FUN AND FITNESS

★★★★

Is jogging for you? To find out, read *Successful Jogging*, a four-page illustrated tabloid from the American Running & Fitness Association. It explains the advantages of jogging and how aerobic activity improves your heart and circulation. Beginners will like the 12-week schedule for getting started, and the recommended program is one that can be used by men and women of all ages and adapted to whatever pace or mileage you choose for yourself. You'll learn to give yourself a pulse test that will show you if you're overdoing things, and how to use alternating periods of workouts and rest to build your stamina.

Write for:
Successful Jogging

Cost: 75¢ and a long SASE

Send to:
American Running & Fitness Association
2001 S Street, NW #540
Washington, DC 20009

PITY YOUR POOR FEET

★★

Jogging can put a special strain on the complex structures that are your feet, so heed the suggestions

continued

in *Jogging Advice From Your Podiatrist.* This foldout from the American Podiatric Medical Association is a good memo on elementary foot care for joggers or runners. You'll pick up some simple tricks, such as wearing soft, thick socks to reduce friction and irritation and pedicuring your feet to protect your toes from injury. There's also a 30-week running timetable to guard the beginning jogger against going too far, too fast, too soon.

Write for:
Jogging Advice From Your Podiatrist

Cost: Free with a long SASE

Send to:
American Podiatric Medical Association
20 Chevy Chase Circle, N W
Washington, DC 20015

RUNNING PAINS
★★★

"Runner's knee" is a catchall term for the knee problems associated with running. Achilles tendinitis, shin splints, and runner's heel are other common injuries that plague runners. *Aches and Pains of Running* is a three-page foldout from the American Running & Fitness Association that can help you prevent or treat some of these minor complaints yourself. It's written by a podiatrist and explains causes of these conditions and simple measures you can take to avoid them. Proper stretching or working with weights, for instance, can go a long way toward preventing running injuries, and this flyer explains which exercises can be most effective. A sensible guide that summarizes much of the information found in more expensive publications.

Write for:
Aches and Pains of Running

Cost: 75¢ and a long SASE

Send to:
American Running & Fitness Association
2001 S Street NW #540
Washington, DC 20009

HOSPITALITY FOR HIKERS
★★★

There is always something for hikers to discover, and in New Hampshire's White Mountains they can share their experiences in a special way. The Huts of the Appalachian Mountain Club make it all possible.

Spaced a day's hike apart along the famed Appalachian Trail, the eight AMC Huts offer a unique—and uniquely accessible—chance to see and understand the heart of New England's most popular backcountry region. *The Friendly Huts* brochure lists the lodgings maintained by the club, along with a hiking map and information about reservations, guides, food, and accommodations. There is also a list of equipment and clothing you will need. If you're seeking a rustic vacation, this could give you some new ideas.

Write for:
The Friendly Huts

Cost: Free

Send to:
Appalachian Mountain Club
5 Joy Street
Boston, MA 02108

A DAY HIKER'S GUIDE
★★★

This excellent brochure underscores the importance of thorough planning for an enjoyable, safe, and comfortable day hike. You'll learn how to lay out your route, how many people to take with you (never hike alone), and some pre-hike preparations. You'll learn to pace yourself and follow trails on the hike. You'll find out what kind of footgear, food, and clothing is best for a hike and there's a checklist for the equipment you'll need—23 necessary items. There's also a list of safety precautions, reminders about not picking plants and steering clear of wild animals, and information on where you can write for trail guides and maps of Adirondack Park in New York.

Write for:
For the Day Hiker

Cost: 15¢ and a long SASE

Send to:
The Adirondack Mountain Club, Inc.
172 Ridge St.
Glen Falls, NY 12801

THE CONSIDERATE CAMPER
★★★

With the rapidly increasing public awareness of the outdoors and the expanding use of public and private lands everywhere, it is critical to ensure that the backcountry is not degraded or even destroyed through misuse or abuse. Many areas are

A SASE is a self-addressed stamped envelope.

"camped out" due to the popularity of hiking, camping, and climbing. The Appalachian Mountain Club has published a small but excellent pamphlet on "low impact" camping to promote the wise and safe recreational use of our lands. "Be thoughtful and be protective" is the primary advice. The pamphlet recommends leaving no traces of your use, not reusing someone else's site, and camping at least 200 feet from a lake or stream to minimize pollution. Most of it is pretty much based on common sense but it's a good approach to enjoying Mother Nature as she intended.

Write for:
Low Impact Use

Cost: Free

Send to:
Appalachian Mountain Club
5 Joy Street
Boston, MA 02108

IS IT A GREBE OR A COOT?
★★

Beginning birdwatchers who still need help distinguishing a pied-billed grebe from a coot or a whistling swan from a Canada goose will welcome this sheet on identifying waterfowl. Major characteristics are listed first. You identify those, and then by a process of elimination of physical colorings you should be able to name the waterfowl you've seen. An illustration sheet diagrams wing features, foot and hind toe characteristics, and bill differences that will aid in the identification.

Write for:
Waterfowl Identification Key

Cost: Free

Send to:
Ohio Department of Natural Resources
Division of Wildlife
Fountain Square
Columbus, OH 43224

Waterfowl Identification Key

THE WOODSY LOOK
★★★

Wilderness lovers can go public with a decal or patch from the Adirondack Mountain Club, or with a variety of (more expensive) apparel and accessories. Whether you're interested in hiking, canoeing, backpacking, camping, or just having a good time in the wild, the club catalog offers a variety of books and products that you'll probably enjoy.

Write for:
ADK Decal
ADK Patch
Publications Brochure

Cost: 50¢ for Decal; 75¢ for Patch; Brochure is Free

Send to:
Adirondack Mountain Club, Inc.
172 Ridge St.
Glens Falls, NY 12801

ADK decal, patch, and Publications brochure

KNIFE KNOWLEDGE
★★

This foldout pamphlet tells you what to look for when you're buying a pocket or hunting knife. It explains about stainless steel vs. carbon steel or chrome vanadium, diagrams the parts of a pocket knife, and tells what the terms "walking" and "talking" mean when applied to a knife. There are diagrams of the different blade shapes, the correct way to close a locking knife, how to care for your knife, and exactly how to sharpen it.

Write for:
How to Choose and Care for Pocket Knives and
Hunting Knives *continued*

FREE TIME

Cost: 25¢

Send to:
W.R. Case & Sons Cutlery Co.
Bradford, PA 16701

GOIN' FISHIN'?

★★★★

If fishing is your sport, don't miss the *Mepps® Fishing Guide*. It's a catalog of lures, hooks, and other fishing accessories, combined with dozens of down-home snapshots of amateur anglers who made the big catch. The guide, which has lots of full-color illustrations, is updated annually. You can read about spinners, squirrel tail hooks, striper spoons, and killer hooks, and you'll be inspired by the fishing stories and photos of adults and kids who caught all kinds of enormous fish. Good tips from readers on how to make fishing easier, illustrated directions for things like filleting fish, and tips on taking photos of your own big catch.

Write for:
Mepps® Fishing Guide

Cost: Free

Send to:
Sheldons, Inc.
CS 508
626 Center St.
Antigo, WI 54409

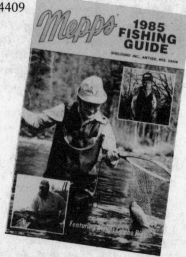

Mepps® Fishing Guide

FISHING FOR ANSWERS

★★★

Many experienced fishermen agree that they get far more personal satisfaction and enjoyment from catching fish with fly rod equipment than with any other type of gear. Still, anglers everywhere are constantly looking for the edge that will help them perfect their technique. Two question-and-answer booklets from Cortland Line Company offer loads of tricks and advice. *Fly Fishing Questions & Answers* gives information on the how-tos and wheres, as well as on equipment and casting fundamentals. *Questions about Fly Fishing Leaders and Their Answers* covers tapered leaders, tippet size and strength, attaching the leader to the fly line, and what to do for problems such as sinking leaders. Both illustrated pamphlets give directions for tying the knots you'll need.

Write for:
Fly Fishing Questions & Answers
Questions About Fly Fishing Leaders and
   Their Answers

Cost: Free with a long SASE

Send to:
Cortland Line Company, Inc.
3736 Kellogg Rd.
P.O. Box 5588
Cortland, NY 13045-5588

VITAL STATISTICS ON LAKE SUPERIOR FISH

★★★★

Lake Superior, once fished by Chippewa fishermen and French explorers, still supports a large fishing industry, and this is the subject of *Fish of Lake Superior*, a 36-page booklet from the University of Wisconsin Sea Grant College Program. Designed in modern style with good line drawings, the book first gives a history of the region, and provides description of 23 different species of fish populating the waters of Lake Superior. There's a line drawing of each variety of fish, along with vital statistics such as length, weight, coloring, and common names, and a discussion of the fish's diet and breeding habits. Learn about the lake herring, several types of trout, the alewife, and the unwelcome, predatory sea lamprey. Good reading for all environmentalists, not just fishermen.

Write for:
Fish of Lake Superior — Revised

Cost: $1.00

Send to:
University of Wisconsin
Sea Grant Institute
1800 University Avenue
Madison, WI 53705

A SASE is a self-addressed stamped envelope.

MEET THE FISH OF LAKE MICHIGAN

★★★★

The lake herring, the chinook salmon, the white sucker, the walleye, the sea lamprey, the rainbow smelt—these varieties and more (21 in all) are portrayed in detail in this striking 32-page booklet. *Fish of Lake Michigan*, from the University of Wisconsin Sea Grant College Program, describes the fish found in Lake Michigan, their vital statistics (length, weight, coloring, and common names), eating and breeding habits, population sizes, and histories. The booklet opens with a history of the fishing industry in Lake Michigan, from its alewife population explosion to its recent imports of chinook salmon and rainbow trout. Modern graphic design and detailed line drawings make this an attractive publication.

Write for:
Fish of Lake Michigan

Cost: $1.00

Send to:
University of Wisconsin
Sea Grant Office
1800 University Ave.
Madison, WI 53705

Fish of Lake Michigan

COLD BUT FUN!

★★★

When winter comes, you don't have to put away your fishing tackle or lures just because the lakes have frozen over. People who fish on the ice say the fish bite more in winter than in any other season. This 24-page booklet introduces you to the world of ice fishing. It's illustrated with sketches of fish to catch in winter and what tip-ups and other ice fishing gear and shelters look like. You learn what clothing to wear, what gear and gadgets to take along, and how to fish through the ice. Safety tips round out the instruction. Ice fishing may not make long winters any shorter, but it can help them go by faster.

Write for:
Ice Fishing

Cost: 50¢

Send to:
University of Wisconsin Sea Grant Institute
1800 University Ave.
Madison, WI 53705

Ice Fishing

JITTERBUG, HAWAIIAN WIGGLER, OR MUD-BUG?

★★★★

Should you use a jitterbug, Hawaiian wiggler, or mud-bug? It depends on the depth of water in which you're fishing. They're all fishing lures designed for different water conditions. The jitterbug is a surface lure, the Hawaiian wiggler a mid-depth lure, and the mud-bug a deep-running lure. This small fishing hint booklet tells exactly how to fish with each kind of lure. With it you get a colorful sew-on patch of a bass snapping at a lure. A pocket catalog completes this package.

Write for:
Patch, Fishing Hints Booklet, and Mini-Catalog

Cost: $2.00

Send to:
Fred Arbogast Company, Inc.
313 W. North St.
Akron, OH 44303

RAISING A CROP OF WORMS

★★★★

If you fish, you may have wondered if you could raise bait in your own backyard rather than dig for

continued

FREE TIME

worms or buy bait. Here's the answer. *Backyard Fish Bait* tells you all you need to know to breed your own minnows, worms, and crickets on a small scale. Presented in question-and-answer form in a three-page foldout is information on how long it takes to produce a crop of worms (six months); what kinds of crickets can be produced (two species—the common black field cricket and the Australian grey cricket); and which minnow is best (the golden shiner). Also included are diagrams of a cricket brood pen and of a worm bed that you can construct yourself.

Write for:
Backyard Fish Bait

Cost: Free with a SASE

Send to:
Department of Wildlife Conservation
1801 N. Lincoln Blvd.
Oklahoma City, OK 73105

KIDS AND OTHER FISHING BEGINNERS
★★★★

The premise of this racy little booklet is that fly rod fishing is more productive, more intriguing, and offers more direct contact with the fish than plain old fishing where you drop a line, a hook, bait, and sinker into water and wait for a fish to bite. This booklet explains casting in five simple steps, and discusses the equipment you'll need and some new sinking fly lines that let you fish under the surface. You'll also learn about bucktails and streamers that lure trout, how to tie several good knots, and a bit about fly tying. There are plenty of tips on techniques, and what to do when you land your fish.

Write for:
Fly Rod Fishing Made Easy

Cost: 50¢ and a long SASE

Send to:
Cortland Line Co.
3736 Kellogg Rd.
P.O. Box 5588
Cortland, NY 13045

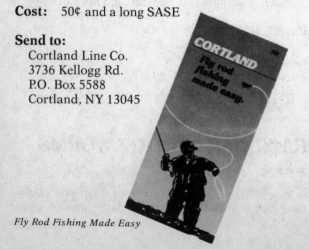

Fly Rod Fishing Made Easy

WHITEWATER THRILLS
★★★

Few thrill-seekers are disappointed by the excitement of taking a canoe down a whitewater rapid. The spray, the movement, the rush of blood to your cheeks—it's an experience that's hard to beat. Experienced whitewater canoeists and novices alike will enjoy this 22″ × 28″ sepia-tone wall poster featuring an action photograph, a glossary of terms, and a helpful diagram of the parts of a whitewater canoe. Attractive calligraphy adds to the poster's appeal. Unless a mailing tube is requested, the poster will be mailed folded.

Write for:
Poster: The Complete Whitewater Canoeist

Cost: Free

Send to:
The Blue Hole Canoe Company
Sunbright, TN 37872

A CANOE AND YOU
★★★

Of all styles of boating, canoeing is probably the most economical, and is certainly among the most fun. If you're planning to paddle your way through nature's splendor, you'll find this 34-page booklet of considerable interest. Inside you'll find tips on canoe and kayak safety, national sources of paddling information, and a detailed state-by-state compilation of where to write for free information about canoeing/kayaking waters, trails, preserves, and parks.

Write for:
Canoe America

Cost: 20¢

Send to:
National Marine Manufacturers Association
401 North Michigan Ave.
Chicago, IL 60611

NOW YOU CAN CANOE DOWN MAIN STREET
★★★★

Are you into canoes? You can tell the world about it with this bright blue and white bumper sticker that says: *Warning! This Car Stops at All River Crossings.* It is illustrated with a drawing of a car with a canoe on top.

A SASE is a self-addressed stamped envelope.

Write for:

This Car Stops at All River Crossings bumper sticker

Cost: 50¢

Send to:

The Blue Hole Canoe Co.
Sunbright, TN 37872

BOATS IN A BAG
★★★

Inflatable boats are a fun and economical way for people to take to the water. If you're a scuba diver, skier, camper, or fisherman, an inflatable boat makes good sense. This handy, photo-illustrated pamphlet offers brief but informative discussions of the safety, performance, portability, and versatility of inflatable boats. There's also a special section on purchase tips.

Write for:

Inflatables—Those Versatile Boats in a Bag

Cost: 25¢

Send to:

National Marine Manufacturers Association
401 North Michigan Ave.
Chicago, IL 60611

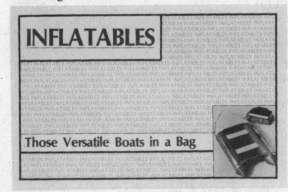

Inflatables-- Those Versatile Boats in a Bag

BOATING FUN ... AND SAFETY
★★★

Thinking about getting a boat? Already have one? Bet you can't wait to get on the water, right? Well, be sure you've taken all the standard safety precautions first, because boating isn't as easy as it looks. This handy, illustrated pamphlet includes valuable safety tips, quizzes, checklists, and descriptions of necessary equipment such as life vests and fire extinguishers. Boating is great fun, and you'll enjoy it all the more if you're prepared for any eventuality.

Write for:

(Almost) Everything You Ever Wanted to Know About Boating

Cost: 10¢

Send to:

National Marine Manufacturers Association
401 North Michigan Ave.
Chicago, IL 60611

(Almost) Everything You Ever Wanted to Know About Boating

GET TO KNOW YOUR POWER BOAT
★★★★

Power boating means fun—it also means responsibility, and taking care to see that you've followed all the standard safety precautions. This well-illustrated, 42-page booklet is a detailed (but not exhaustive) guide to power boat operation and maintenance. You'll find valuable hints on registration, equipment, and proper procedure for different types of waters and situations. There's also useful information about power boat engines and other mechanical things, as well as a troubleshooter's guide. In all, this is a helpful preliminary guide.

Write for:

You and Your Boat

Cost: 20¢

Send to:

National Marine Manufacturers Association
401 North Michigan Ave.
Chicago, IL 60611

LOOK, NO SKIS!
★★★

It sounds easy. It looks easy. But is it easy? There are plenty of photographs in this folder from the Ameri-

continued

can Water Ski Association to show you *how* easily you can get up on your two bare feet and water ski. There's even one of a six-year-old who is barefooting. However, you must be an accomplished water skier before you try it, because the maneuver of stepping out of your skis and onto water is a tricky one. Two ingredients that make this unbelievable sport successful are proper speed and calm waters—no more than a few inches of chop. You'll also learn two beach and deepwater starts. Ask also for the association's brochure on safe water skiing.

Write for:
Footin' Fundamentals
AWSA Guide to Safe Water Skiing

Cost: 65¢

Send to:
American Water Ski Association
P.O. Box 191
Winter Haven, FL 33880

Water Skiing pamphlets

LONG-DISTANCE, ON HORSEBACK
★★

The American Endurance Ride Conference is a national organization with more than 2,000 members. It's been in existence for more than 10 years, and its main purpose is the sanctioning and recording of endurance horse races. This newsletter, called the *Endurance News,* is filled with articles and news on endurance riding and trails. There are lists of the current rides (and where they are), and photographs of the race winners. Rides—which are really races—range from 50 miles to 150 miles at a time. The newsletter is published monthly, and you can get a sample copy free. A challenge for serious—and energetic—riders.

Write for:
Sample copy of Endurance News

Cost: Free

Send to:
American Endurance Ride Conference
Suite 216
701 High St.
Auburn, CA 95603

HAPPY TRAILS
★★★

Share the great outdoors and your favorite recreation —your all-terrain vehicle, or ATV— with your friends by forming an ATV Club. All the hows-tos are discussed in this great 20-page booklet from the Specialty Vehicle Institute of America. Clubs can hold rider skills and education courses, find new places to ride, and publicize this adventurous pastime in a positive way. *How to Form an ATV Club* tells you how to get started and how to conduct your meetings. You'll learn how to work harmoniously within your community, too. You'll read about one particular club's success story. There is a sample set of bylaws your group may want to adopt, and a listing of other materials available from the SVIA.

Write for:
How to Form an ATV Club

Cost: Free

Send to:
Specialty Vehicle Institute of America
Public Affairs
3151 Airway Ave.
Bldg. K-107
Costa Mesa, CA 92626

How to Form an ATV Club

A SASE is a self-addressed stamped envelope.

FREE THINGS
for
PET OWNERS

PET OWNERS

Caring for Your Dog

CANINE CLUBS AND KENNELS
★★★

If you are planning to buy a dog at a kennel, looking for a reputable kennel to board your dog, or planning to have your dog trained for obedience, hunting, or showing, consult this 48-page booklet. It's a national directory of kennels, breed clubs, and obedience clubs and also contains helpful tips on how to choose a dog—what breed, large vs. small, short- vs. long-haired, male vs. female, etc. There's also a list of breeds that are good with children. Pedigrees are explained and tips are given on showing purebred dogs in competition. And if you have to find a place to keep your dog while you're away on vacation, advice is given on boarding establishments.

Write for:
Where to Buy, Board, or Train a Dog

Cost: $1.50

Send to:
Gaines Booklets
P.O. Box 8177
Kankakee, IL 60902

Where to Buy, Board, or Train a Dog

AREN'T THEY CUTE!
★★★★

Dogs are wonderful pets, but the hard fact is there are too many unwanted and stray dogs in the United States today. Veterinarians suggest that dog owners think more than twice before deciding to let a female have pups. If you do decide to let your dog have a litter, here is a pair of free 16-page booklets that can advise you on the breeding process and how to prepare for the arrival of a litter of puppies. Topics covered include care of the pregnant dog, preparation for the birth of the litter, what to do during the birthing process, the nursing period, and weaning. The booklet on new pups tells about caring for a new puppy, first feedings, first steps in house training, and obedience training.

Write for:
The Brood Bitch and Puppies
Welcoming Your New Puppy

Cost: Free

Send to:
Gaines Booklets
P.O. Box 8177
Kankakee, IL 60902

The Brood Bitch and Puppies

Welcoming Your New Puppy

NICE DOG!
★★★★

Puppies and dogs can be wonderful pets, but not when they do their thing in the wrong places or generally misbehave. Gaines Foods offers three free 16-page booklets to help puppy and dog owners train their pets to do their thing in the proper place at the proper time. When accidents do happen, here's how to react and train the pup or dog not to repeat them. Despite what they say about how old dogs can't learn new tricks, older dogs can be taught housebreaking habits that may be different from those learned from a previous owner. Three very helpful booklets for any dog owner and lover.

Write for:
Housebreaking: What Is a Puppy Owner to Do?
House Training Puppies and Dogs
Eliminating Behavior Problems in Dogs

Cost: Free

A SASE is a self-addressed stamped envelope.

Send to:
Gaines Booklets
P.O. Box 8177
Kankakee, IL 60902

YOUR DOG AND YOUR NEW BABY

★★★★

Your dog is used to being the center of attention and getting lots of treats and petting, but now a new member is coming into the family—a baby. How will your dog react? Will it be jealous and try to harm the infant? If you're not sure how to handle the situation, this free eight-page booklet from Gaines Foods may help. It reassures you that introducing your old pet to your new baby doesn't have to be a problem. Dogs have natural instincts that help them learn to accept infants as part of the family. You'll learn how to monitor your dog's behavior, how to introduce your dog to the baby, and what to do the first few days the dog and the baby are in the house together. With a new baby coming you have enough to think about and plan for, and this booklet can help ease your mind.

Write for:
Introducing Your Dog to Your New Baby

Cost: Free

Send to:
Gaines Booklets
P.O. Box 8177
Kankakee, IL 60902

Introducing Your Dog to Your New Baby

PUPPY DOG TALES

★★★

Canine companions give love, friendship, and years of enjoyment; in turn, the responsible pet owner must care for their needs. The well-cared-for dog will be better behaved and a more welcome member of the family and neighborhood. This 12-page pamphlet will give you some basic information that will help you keep your dog healthy and happy. You'll learn about licensing and leashing, altering, and housebreaking. *Dogs* covers what to feed your best friend and whether to keep him indoors or out. You'll learn how to groom your dog and how to break him of bad habits. One section discusses diseases and ailments and the suggested preventive and first aid measures.

Write for:
Dogs

Cost: Free with a long SASE

Send to:
Animal Rescue League of Boston
P.O. Box 265
Boston, MA 02117

Dogs

WHAT (AND HOW MUCH) TO FEED YOUR DOG

★★★★

Nutritionists specializing in dog care agree that certain elements are essential in what you feed your dog, and that correct feeding is more important than any other factor in keeping healthy dogs. This free 16-page booklet outlines the values of the three basic types of dog foods—dry meal, soft-moist foods, and canned dog foods—and comments on "extras" such as fresh or frozen meat, eggs, vegetables, and bones. You learn how, and how much, to feed your dog. If your dog is overweight, send for another brochure that offers advice on how to reduce the animal's diet and exercise him more, to get his weight under better control and avoid the danger of obesity.

Write for:
Feeding Your Dog Right
Is Your Dog Overweight?

continued

PET OWNERS

Cost: Free

Send to:
Gaines Booklets
P.O. Box 8177
Kankakee, IL 60902

Feeding Your Dog Right

Is Your Dog Overweight?

GROOMING: THE GOOD-LOOKING DOG
★★★★

Your dog doesn't have to be a pedigree poodle or wolf hound to need grooming. Every dog should be brushed regularly and his eyes, ears, toenails, and teeth cared for. In this free 16-page booklet you learn how to care properly for a dog's grooming needs. The booklet includes sections on special grooming equipment for certain breeds that require more attention than usual to look their best. If you plan to show your dog in competition, this booklet is a definite help. Special sections tell how to groom poodles and terriers.

Write for:
Guide to Grooming

Cost: Free

Send to:
Gaines Booklets
P.O. Box 8177
Kankakee, IL 60902

BEAUTIFUL BEASTS
★★★

In order to enjoy a dog show, first you have to understand what's going on. This well-written foldout pamphlet explains what happens at a dog show, and why. You'll discover what a licensed, sanctioned AKC dog show is (a huge elimination contest) and in what classes you can enter a dog—

puppy, novice, bred-by-exhibitor, American bred, and open. This pamphlet tells how to enter your pedigree pooch in a dog show, how champions are made (a diagram shows the steps a dog must achieve to become Best in Show), and all about ring stewards, judges, and professional handlers. Charts list seven groups of dogs that are recognized by the American Kennel Club. Interesting even for the dog owner whose best friend is a mutt.

Write for:
How to Understand and Enjoy a Dog Show

Cost: Free

Send to:
Ralston Purina Co.
Office of Consumer Affairs
Checkerboard Square
St. Louis, MO 63188

THE WELL-BEHAVED DOG
★★★★

How do you train your dog to be obedient? According to this helpful 16-page booklet, common sense, consistent commands, gentle firmness, enthusiastic praise, and, above all, patience are the fundamentals of effective dog training. It teaches how to get your dog's attention during training; where to train, how to get your dog to "walk at heel," sit, sit-and-stay, stand-stay, lie down, come when called, and other obedience lessons. A companion booklet tells how to train a dog to catch a frisbee. It contains delightful photos of dogs leaping high to catch the flying discs.

Write for:
What Every Good Dog Should Know
Teaching Your Dog to Catch a Flying Disc

Cost: Free

Send to:
Gaines Booklets
P.O. Box 8177
Kankakee, IL 60902

HOW TO KEEP FIDO HEALTHY
★★★★

A healthy child is a happy child. So, too, with dogs. A series of three 16-page free booklets tells how to keep your dog healthy with tips on first aid, vaccination, and controlling worms. Your dog may love you and family members and be gentle as a lamb when healthy, but when injured or ill may become fright-

A SASE is a self-addressed stamped envelope.

ened and act quite differently. First-aid tips for injured dogs include how to apply a pressure bandage, give a dog medicine, and treat such emergencies as broken bones, burns, and heatstroke. You learn what vaccinations a dog should have and how to prepare the animal for shots that can prevent the risk of dangerous diseases.

Write for:
First Aid for Dogs
The Vaccination Story
How to Control Worms in Dogs

Cost: Free

Send to:
Gaines Booklets
P.O. Box 8177
Kankakee, IL 60902

TRAVELING WITH YOUR DOG
★★★

If you travel with your dog or take him along on vacation with the rest of the family, problems can arise. Be prepared by reading this 62-page publication that tells how to travel with your dog and offers suggestions on how to prepare for a trip, what to bring along for the dog, how to handle a dog in a car, and what to do if you ship a dog by rail or air. A directory lists the hotels and motels in the United States that accommodate guests with dogs. Also included are four 50¢ discount coupons for Gaines dog food.

Write for:
Touring with Towser

Cost: $1.50

Send to:
Gaines TWT
P.O. Box 8172
Kankakee, IL 60902

DOGS OF ALL KINDS
★★★

Here's an attractive offering for you or a young dog-lover of your acquaintance. This handsome, full-sized color poster shows dozens of the most common breeds of dogs, with short descriptions of each. You see how dogs are divided into herding breeds, ter-

riers, toy breeds, hounds, working breeds, and sporting and non sporting breeds. This could make a nice surprise gift for a kid who loves dogs. The poster comes folded.

Write for:
Gaines Dog Chart

Cost: $1.50

Send to:
Gaines Dog Chart
P.O. Box 8177
Kankakee, IL 60902

Gaines Dog Chart

Caring for Your Cat

HERE, KITTY, KITTY
★★★

No other pet will ever satisfy a cat lover. No other animal is as easy to care for, as simple to house train, or as much an individualist as a feline. But remember, despite his independent attitude, your cat does rely on you as his owner for care, love, and guidance. Your cat can be a perfect pet if you are a responsible cat owner, and this 12-page booklet on cat care is filled with good advice on how to be just that. You'll learn about feeding and training, altering, and collars. A section on health care covers common cat diseases and ailments as well as many first aid measures.

Write for:
Cats

continued

PET OWNERS

Cost: Free with a long SASE

Send to:
Animal Rescue League of Boston
P.O. Box 265
Boston, MA 02117

Cats

CAT CARE FOR THE NEW OWNER
★★★

You succumbed. You have a new kitten. If this is your first experience as a cat owner, this free pamphlet from the American Feline Society will give you lots of basic information about caring for this new creature in your life. For one thing, don't turn your cat out at night to roam the streets. You'll learn what and how to feed your cat, how to train a kitten to use a litter pan, and what health precautions to take. You'll also learn that some house plants are poisonous to cats—(philodendron, for one)—and what to do if your cat is accidentally poisoned. There's information on catnip (which cats adore), grooming, spaying or neutering, and traveling with your cat.

Write for:
Cat Care and Feeding

Cost: Free with a long SASE

Send to:
The American Feline Society, Inc.
204 West 20th Street
New York, NY 10011

BASIC CARE FOR A NEW KITTEN
★★★

This simple card lists 14 basic things to remember if you're bringing a new kitten into your life and home. Post it where everyone in the family can refer to it during the getting-to-know-you period with your new pet. The card tells what a new kitten needs in the way of food, water, sand or litter box, toys, and a special "break-away" elastic identification collar. A short section deals with training and housebreaking—a very easy process with a cat. Enjoy your pet.

Write for:
Paws for Thought Kitty Letter

Cost: Free

Send to:
MSPCA
Circulation Dept.
350 S. Huntington Ave.
Boston, MA 02130

TRAINING YOUR CAT (OR VICE VERSA)
★★★★

Cats have fascinated humans for centuries. Today Americans accept them as delightful, if rather inscrutable, pets. If you're planning to adopt a cat but your knowledge of the species is limited, read *Cat Care,* the Massachusetts Society for the Prevention of Cruelty to Animals' 16-page handbook. It answers the questions most frequently asked by new cat owners, so don't expect comprehensive coverage. But you will find an affectionate and realistic view of what to expect when you adopt a cat. There's a guide to choosing a healthy cat as well as tips on grooming, health care, and breeding. There's also an intriguing section on training a cat by reinforcing natural behavior with praise and reward.

Write for:
Cat Care

Cost: $1.00

Send to:
MSPCA
Circulation Dept.
350 S. Huntington Ave.
Boston, MA 02130

Cat Care

A SASE is a self-addressed stamped envelope.

More Free Things for Animal Lovers

COMPATIBLE HOUSEMATES
★★★

Guinea pigs, gerbils, hamsters, mice, rabbits, birds, fish, and reptiles are animals the entire family can enjoy as pets. They are inexpensive to maintain and care for, and don't require lots of food or a large housing space. All the same, it is important to provide your small pets with the proper care—they are fragile, and should be handled gently. This 12-page booklet, *Small Pets*, describes the temperaments, habits, and housing and feeding requirements of many small animals. There is advice about adoption, and a caution against bringing wild animals into the home.

Write for:
Small Pets

Cost: Free with a long SASE

Send to:
Animal Rescue League of Boston
P.O. Box 265
Boston, MA 02117

Small Pets

SMALL PETS HAVE SPECIAL NEEDS
★★★★

Small mammals make sensitive, intelligent pets, but only for owners who understand their special needs and limitations. *Small Mammal Care*, a 16-page handbook put out by the Massachusetts Society for the Prevention of Cruelty to Animals, is designed to provide the inexperienced pet owner with a general overview of each of the popular small mammal pets. You'll learn, for example, that rabbits, gerbils, guinea pigs, hamsters, mice, and rats must have a means

for wearing down their teeth (which grow all the time), that cages must have a nest box for privacy, and that there's an art to handling small mammals so they don't get frightened. For each of the common small mammals there's a brief historical and biological description plus specific information on housing, feeding, care, and handling.

Write for:
Small Mammal Care

Cost: $1.00

Send to:
MSPCA
Circulation Dept.
350 S. Huntington Ave.
Boston, MA 02130

HORSE SENSE
★★★

With the increase in many people's leisure time and the growing popularity of horseback riding as a sport, many riding stables and riding academies have sprung up throughout the country. This booklet, *So You Want to Ride a Horse!*, furnishes the occasional riding enthusiast with basic horsemanship information and guidelines. It is no substitute, of course, for training and practice, but it has some good advice. You'll learn how to choose a stable, what to look for in a healthy horse, and basic safety and mounting tips. The 12-page booklet also covers trail manners, dismounting procedures, and stable fire safety.

Write for:
So You Want to Ride a Horse!

Cost: Free with a long SASE

Send to:
Animal Rescue League of Boston
P.O. Box 265
Boston, MA 02117

SO HARD TO SAY GOODBYE
★★★

Perhaps the kindest thing you can do for a pet that is so sick or severely injured that it will never recover normal health is to have your veterinarian induce its death quietly and humanely. Your decision to have your pet euthantized is a serious one, never easy to take. A small brochure by the American Veterinary Medical Association discusses the grief and emotion that follow the loss of a family pet. It describes
continued

PET OWNERS

the euthanasia procedure and when it should best be implemented. Saying goodbye, and making a decision about whether to get another pet are also discussed in *Pet Loss and Human Emotion*. A supplemental reading list is given.

Write for:
Pet Loss and Human Emotion

Cost: Free with a long SASE

Send to:
American Veterinary Medical Association
Public Information Division
930 N. Meacham Road
Schaumburg, IL 60196-1074

Pet Loss and Human Emotion

ATTRACT FEATHERED (AND FURRY) TENANTS
★★★★

Two pamphlets are offered here. One contains plans for an array of birdhouses, nesting boxes, feeding stations, and squirrel den boxes you can build out of lumber, plain logs, tin cans, or galvanized metal. It also illustrates how you can provide food and cover crops for wildlife. The other pamphlet explains why birds are good neighbors and which food and water facilities will attract them; it also presents an annual calendar of activity for most birds and an excellent chart that shows which trees, shrubs, and flowers appeal to which creatures, and why.

Write for:
Nesting Boxes
Wings Out Your Window

Cost: 50¢ for both

Send to:
Pennsylvania Game Commission
P.O. Box 1567
Harrisburg, PA 17120

DO SOME HOMEWORK ON DUCKS
★★★

This pictorial duck identification guide is great for birdwatchers. It illustrates the shape of duck bills, wing markings, feet or head crest color, and the different markings on the male and female birds. By checking for the specific marking or characteristic in prescribed order, you can identify each species of duck. For identifying ducks in flight or sitting on the water, there are other illustrations showing typical flock formations and relative sizes of different wild ducks.

Write for:
Duck Identification Guide for the Hunter

Cost: Free

Send to:
Pennsylvania Game Commission
P.O. Box 1567
Harrisburg, PA 17120

VACATIONING WITH YOUR POOCH
★★★

Taking your pet pooch on vacation? This little brochure is filled with general tips about traveling with your pet and some good specific information about air and car travel. It points out that most states prohibit animals on buses, and new rules prohibit them on trains. You'll get useful reminders of the importance of proper pet identification and why you should take along a rabies vaccination certificate. Packing your pet's favorite toys, food, and dishes will also make your trip go more smoothly. *Traveling With Your Pet* is also available in Spanish.

Write for:
Traveling With Your Pet

Cost: Free with a long SASE

Send to:
American Veterinary Medical Association
930 N. Meacham Rd.
Schaumburg, IL 60196

SELECTING A KENNEL
★★★★

Knowing that your pet is being well cared for in your absence means you can have a relaxed vacation. And here's one way to make sure your pet will enjoy his

A SASE is a self-addressed stamped envelope.

stay in the boarding kennel you choose. Use this guide from the American Boarding Kennels Association to help you find a suitable kennel, make a reservation, and prepare your pet for boarding. *How To Select a Boarding Kennel* tells you how to evaluate a kennel, including safety and health considerations, and what to do if a problem occurs. A must for any pet owner—and remember, when you go on vacation is only one of the times when you may need to board your pet; unexpected trips or family emergencies may also mean you need to find good care in a hurry.

Write for:
How To Select a Boarding Kennel

Cost: $2.00

Send to:
American Boarding Kennels Association
311 N. Union
Colorado Springs, CO 80909

PLANNED PARENTHOOD FOR PETS
★★★

This informative folder from the American Veterinary Medical Association lays out the pros and cons of having your pet neutered. It points out the physical demands that parenthood lays on your pet and the alarming statistic that only one or two of every 10 animals in shelters ever get placed in homes—the others are destroyed. Also discussed are the mechanics of surgical neutering for male and female animals, the effect it may have—yes, she may have a tendency to put on weight, but she may also get more affectionate—and the alternatives to neutering. The engaging color illustrations will probably entice children into reading this, too . . . a useful step toward responsible pet ownership.

Write for:
Choose for Your Pet . . . Pethood or Parenthood

Cost: Free with a long SASE

Send to:
American Veterinary Medical Association
930 N. Meacham Rd.
Schaumburg, IL 60196

NOTHING TO SNEEZE ABOUT
★★★★

Do your eyes burn at certain times of the year? Does your nose run a lot and get clogged up? Do you sneeze all the time? If so, you may have an allergy. Many people are allergic to dust, pollens, mold, and pets. If you do have an allergy, don't assume it's caused by your pet dog or cat. But if you know for sure your pet *is* causing your allergy, you can probably solve the problem without giving up your pet. Here's a booklet from the Associated Humane Societies that tells how you and your allergy-causing pet can live under the same roof. It suggests medication you can take, how to keep your pet's dander (humans call it dandruff) under control, and how to de-allergize your pet by bathing it, brushing it, and other methods. The booklet also tells about foods, types of clothing, and other things around the house that can cause allergies and how to deal with them. Instructions and diagrams are included on reducing mold in and around the house, and desensitizing a car and a room.

Write for:
Allergy-Proofing Your Pet

Cost: $1.00

Send to:
Associated Humane Societies
124-F Evergreen Ave.
Newark, NJ 07114

HANDY CARD FOR PET OWNERS
★★★

If you have pets and live alone, this is a useful item for you. It's a card to carry along with the identification cards you keep in your wallet to tell strangers what to do if you're ever involved in an accident. This *Pet Alert Card,* available free from the Animal Rescue League of Boston, has room for your name and address, and the names and addresses of two people who will care for your pet. After detaching the wallet-size insert from the larger card, you post the larger card in your kitchen to tell your helpful friends how to feed and care for your pet if they ever do have to take over unexpectedly. You might also like to have the League's free *Operation Identification* folder. It's a form to fill out and display if your pet runs away. You can fill in the form, make copies, and post it around the neighborhood until your pet is found.

Write for:
Pet Alert Card
Operation Identification

Cost: Free with a long SASE

continued

PET OWNERS

Send to:
Animal Rescue League of Boston
P.O. Box 265
Boston, MA 02117

Operation Identification

Especially for Children

ANIMAL ACTIVITIES FOR PEOPLE
★★★★

How would you like to start a "Be Kind to Animals Club" with your friends? Or make an animal scrapbook, or a present for your pet? Here's a book that tells you how to do these and lots of other projects. *Animals and You* is a 16-page handbook of "animal activities for people" available from the Massachusetts Society for the Prevention of Cruelty to Animals. There are things you can do by yourself, with your pets, or with your family and friends. There are more than 60 illustrated projects, plus ideas to help you understand the sort of animals you don't keep as pets, like farm animals. How about setting up a visit to a farm, an agricultural show, or even a fish hatchery? The section on wildlife tells you about the many endangered species of animals, and why it's so important to protect them.

Write for:
Animals and You

Cost: $1.00

Send to:
MSPCA
Circulation Dept.
350 S. Huntington Ave.
Boston, MA 02130

POPULATION CONTROL FOR PETS
★★

Kittens are cute, but they grow up into cats and cats have to be fed, they need to have their litter changed, and they must be taken to the veterinarian now and again (and make a fuss of). And those are the lucky ones. Lots of kittens don't have comfortable homes and loving owners but have to find their own way in a world that can be very cruel to unwanted animals. That's why the Associated Humane Societies advise people to have female cats spayed so they don't have litter after litter of kittens that may not be able to find homes. You could help spread the message with these three litter bags offered by the Associated Humane Societies for a dollar (the dollar helps their work for animals). The plastic bags are 12" × 8½" with a hole so you can hang them on the wall or in a closet to hold odds and ends. Nice for the car, too, so you don't get candy wrappers all over the floor and get your parents mad. Each bag features a charming puppy and kitten carrying cards that say, "Don't Litter, Spay." A good way to remind people that pet population control begins with responsible pet owners.

Write for:
3 litter bags

Cost: $1.00

Send to:
Associated Humane Societies
124-F Evergreen Avenue
Newark, NJ 07114

Litter Bag

DOG PRIMER FOR KIDS
★★★

Here's a nice, simple coloring-type booklet that explains the basics of being a good dog owner. There

352

are some funny scenes—like what would happen if all the kids who own dogs let their pets come to school—and some sensible information every young dog owner should know about tags and licenses, where dogs should stay when kids aren't home, and what kind of shelter and water a dog needs when he's alone. There's also a funny (but sensible) warning about meeting strange dogs and waiting for a proper introduction. There's a bit about spaying female dogs, and calling the Humane Society when you can't care for your pet.

Write for:
You and Your Dog

Cost: 25¢ and a long SASE

Send to:
Animal Welfare Institute
P.O. Box 3650
Washington, DC 20007

HORSE CARE FOR BEGINNERS

★★★★

Naturally, you've told your family that you'll take care of the horse all by yourself, but do you realize how much care a horse will need? It's a lot easier to get a horse than to look after it—it takes a lot more time, energy, and money than owning a cat or dog. To answer the questions most often asked by would-be horse owners, the Massachusetts Society for the Prevention of Cruelty to Animals puts out an excellent 16-page starter manual called *Horse Care*. Although you'll need to talk with experienced horse owners, trainers, and veterinarians for more information, this guide will help you find out if you *really* want to own a horse. If you do, there's good advice on selecting, stabling, and equipping the animal.

Write for:
Horse Care

Cost: $1.00

Send to:
MSPCA
Circulation Dept.
350 S. Huntington Ave.
Boston, MA 02130

Horse Care

KIDS' GUIDE TO BIRDWATCHING

★★★

Did you ever watch a beautiful bird fly above you and wonder what its name was? Perhaps you've heard a strange birdcall and tried to identify the owner. If either has happened to you, you have the makings of a life-long birdwatcher. One of these reprints from *Ranger Rick's Nature Magazine* talks about the fun and the how-to of birdwatching. You'll need a field guide and some binoculars to get you started, but chances are you'll be better at it than lots of adults—kids often are more observant than grown-ups. The other reprint in this packet is an interesting article on recycling and how you can start some recycling activities in your neighborhood for glass, aluminum, and paper.

Write for:
Birdwatching
Recycle for the Birds (Order #79258)

Cost: $1.00

Send to:
National Wildlife Federation
1412 16th St., N.W.
Washington, DC 20036

Birdwatching

WHY WILD CREATURES SHOULDN'T BE PETS

★★★★

Did you ever wish you had a pet skunk or some other wild thing? There's a story in this book about what it's really like to have a wild pet, and it may surprise you. There's also a kind of scary story about a beautiful dog, Jessa, and her owner, Greg, who disobeyed his mom and let Jessa off her leash. You'll also find out some interesting things about whales, what a

continued

PET OWNERS

habitat is and which animals live in the many kinds of habitats. There's a good animal puzzle, too. This story and activity book makes you *think* about animals, not just enjoy them. A lot of good pictures to color while you're thinking. A super (and different) animal book.

Write for:
The Best of Animalia

Cost: $1.25

Send to:
MSPCA
Circulation Dept.
350 S. Huntington Ave.
Boston, MA 02130

The Best of Animalia

FROM TWO MICE TO MILLIONS OF MICE

★★★★

Did you know that a pair of field mice can produce six baby mice 17 times a year? The young are soon ready to raise their own families, and in just a few months two mice could become millions. This fascinating information comes from a *Ranger Rick's Nature Magazine* reprint, which explains why the world is not overrun with field mice or other creatures that reproduce very rapidly. You'll learn here about the scientific and natural laws that keep populations in check. The other reprint in this packet is a scary tale about a world where the children can't find any beaches or mountains because the adults have ruined the land. Both the reprints in this packet give a kid a lot to think about. Super color illustrations, too.

Write for:
Populations
A Place for the Children (Order #79329)

Cost: $1.00

Send to:
National Wildlife Federation
1412 16th St., N.W.
Washington, DC 20036

Populations

A Place for the Children

FOR WILDLIFE LOVERS

★★★

If you love to watch or study animals, birds, or fish in their natural habitats, you'll be glad to know about dozens of brochures and publications offered by the Ohio Division of Wildlife. A free brochure tells you about publications you can send for that are free or cost from 25¢ to $1.00. Free brochures include those on animal orphans, conservation concepts, and bird banding and feeding. Others are on deer, dog training, endangered wild animals, falconry, fish identification, fishing instruction, hunting and trapping, pheasant rearing, and wildlife habitat information. You can also send for life histories of bald eagles, brook trout, bluebirds, great horned owls, gray fox, raccoons, red fox, white-tailed deer, and other animals, birds, and fish of Ohio. Lots of good stuff for anyone interested in the great outdoors and the wonderful creatures that inhabit it.

Write for:
Division of Wildlife Publication List

Cost: Free

Send to:
Ohio Department of Natural Resources
Division of Wildlife
1500 Dublin Road
Columbus, OH 43215

ENDANGERED WILDLIFE

★★★★

If you care about furry animals and birds, seals and whales, you'll be interested in sending for the book-

A SASE is a self-addressed stamped envelope.

lets offered by Elsa Clubs. You first met Elsa the lion as a cub in the famous movie *Born Free,* and she symbolizes the work Elsa Clubs do to help save endangered animals. You can get acquainted with the clubs' work by sending for a set of six eight-page booklets describing the lives of 12 endangered animals, including the ocelot, California condor, Ivory-bill woodpecker, Texas Blind Salamander, red wolf, Florida Key Deer, and others. The booklets are illustrated with drawings of the animals which you can color according to color information in the text that describes them. There are puzzle and quiz pages, too. Or send for the 16-page *Save the Whales* booklet, which tells how and why the world's great whales are faced with extinction and what you can do to help save them. You'll also get information on how to join the Elsa Clubs.

Write for:
America's Endangered Wildlife
Whale Packet

Cost: $2.00 each

Send to:
Elsa Clubs
3210 Tepusquet Rd.
Santa Maria, CA 93454

A WILDLIFE GUIDE
★★★★

Nature lovers young and old will cherish this super guide to 50 wild creatures. Though the title specifies that these animals inhabit Pennsylvania, chances are you can encounter most of them in whatever state you live. The exceptional illustrations are finely done black-and-white drawings. They accompany well-written, informative paragraphs about each wild thing. There's a wildlife crossword puzzle, too.

Write for:
50 Birds and Mammals of Pennsylvania

Cost: Free

Send to:
Pennsylvania Game Commission
P.O. Box 1567
Harrisburg, PA 17120

HELPING WILD CREATURES
★★★★

Did you ever bring a baby bird home and ask your parents if you could keep it? Maybe its wing was broken, or it seemed to be an orphan. These two beautiful booklets are reprints from *Ranger Rick's Nature Magazine,* and they tell about wild creatures and how humans can best help them. In one you'll learn "first bird-aid" for birds with broken wings, legs, or feet. And you'll learn how necessary it is for wild things to be free after you've done your best to help them. In the other booklet you're going to read about some of nature's liveliest, cutest, and most destructive mischief-makers, the raccoons. Both booklets have good stories and wonderful color photographs.

Write for:
Let It Be Wild and Free
Mischief Makers (Order #79356)

Cost: $1.00

Send to:
National Wildlife Federation
1412 16th St., N.W.
Washington, DC 20036

Let It Be Wild and Free

Mischief Makers

FREE THINGS
for Your
CAR

Buying a New
or Used Car

TO BUY OR NOT TO BUY: DRIVING HOME THE POINT

★★★★

Americans have a traditional love for their cars. But it's getting harder by the minute to maintain that affection as sticker prices and running costs skyrocket and some unscrupulous auto mechanics bring a whole new meaning to the phrase, "nickel and dime ya to death." *Your Automobile Dollar,* a 40-page guide from the Money Management Institute, is full of sober advice on how to keep your nickels and dimes from being sunk into bad investments, inadequate or excessive insurance, or unnecessary repairs. Livened by cheerful cartoon drawings, this booklet discusses whether you really need or can afford a car, what depreciation really means, renting and leasing options, and preparing your present car for selling or trading. There are 14 pages on buying new and used cars, as well as tips on insurance, reducing maintenance costs, dealing with winter weather, and handling service and repairs. Several helpful charts include a full-page price comparison chart to take along to the showrooms, an insurance cost chart, and charts on owning and operating costs. For less than the price of a gallon of gas this booklet can provide a bundle of information on the care and feeding of your car.

Write for:
Money Management — Your Automobile Dollar

Cost: $1.00

Send to:
Money Management Institute
Household International
2700 Sanders Rd.
Prospect Heights, IL 60070

WANT TO BUY A GOOD USED CAR?

★★★★

A good buy in a used car is a well-maintained, reliable brand in a popular model, economical to operate, with repair or replacement parts readily available, says the Better Business Bureau. In fact, a car that was a good buy when it was new is more likely to be a good buy after use, too. To learn the ins and outs of buying a used car, check out this 10-page booklet from the Bureau. Information includes advice on how to choose a reliable used car dealer, how

to buy from a private owner, and how to compare prices. Tips also are given for making an on-lot inspection and what to look for when taking the car on a road test. Need to finance the sale? There are helpful tips on finding the most advantageous place to finance your car.

Write for:
Tips on Buying a Used Car (No. 311-02247)

Cost: Free

Send to:
Council of Better Business Bureaus
1515 Wilson Blvd.
Arlington, VA 22209

Tips on Buying a Used Car

GUIDELINES FOR BUYING A USED CAR

★★★

Though buying a used car is taking a chance on someone else's problems, the new Federal Trade Commission's Used Car Rule will relieve you of some of the guesswork. The rule requires all used car dealers to place a large sticker, called a Buyers Guide, in the window of each used vehicle they offer for sale. *Buying a Used Car* explains the information the Buyers Guide contains. It discusses warranties, spoken promises, service contracts, prepurchase independent inspection, and more. The six-page article includes a reproduction of the Buyers Guide so you'll know what to look for. There are also suggestions for purchasing a used car from a private owner.

Write for:
Buying a Used Car (No. 445P)

Cost: 50¢

Send to:
Consumer Information Center
P.O. Box 100
Pueblo, CO 81002

CARS

BUYING A USED RENTAL CAR

★★★

Each year, car rental companies sell current model used cars and replace them with newer models. Some companies that keep large fleets of cars, such as leasing companies, do the same. So most cars offered for sale by rental or leasing companies are only one year old and have low mileage, which means they can be good buys. Two free booklets from National Car Rental explore this option. *Used Cars: Where to Buy, How to Buy*, offers general tips on buying used cars, and specific information on buying from rental agencies. The second booklet is a directory of National Car Rental used car locations across the United States where you can inquire about buying used rental cars.

Write for:
Used Cars: Where to Shop, How to Shop
Directory of National Car Rental Used Car Locations

Cost: Free

Send to:
Public Relations
National Car Rental System
7700 France Ave., S.
Minneapolis, MN 55435

Used Cars: Where to Shop, How to Shop

Directory of National Car Rental Used Car Locations

HOW MUCH IS TOO MUCH?

★★★★

The ALA Auto and Travel Club updates this excellent car cost study pamphlet every two or three years. *What It Costs to Run a Car* shows how you can estimate your costs, stack them up against the averages, and do something about them. It takes a typical new car and averages the running expenses, taxes and fees, depreciation, insurance, gas, and maintenance. A worksheet is included for you to calculate your own auto expenses, which you can then compare to the averages provided. There is also good advice on buying a new car and how to keep your own transportation costs to a minimum. It is a handy, informative guide with figures that may surprise you.

Write for:
What It Costs to Run a Car

Cost: Free

Send to:
ALA Auto and Travel Club
888 Worcester St.
Wellesley, MA 02181

What it Costs to Run a Car

Routine and Do-It-Yourself Maintenance

GET SMART ABOUT AUTO REPAIRS

★★★★

You don't have to know all about your car or its engine in order to be a smart consumer when it comes time for having auto repair work done. This free 14-page booklet from the Better Business Bureau tells what to do for car trouble before calling for service. If repair is needed and you can't do it yourself, tips are offered on how to find a reputable auto repair shop and what to look for there. A special section advises on emergency and out-of-town repairs. A companion brochure tells specifically what to do if you have car trouble on a trip away from home.

Write for:
Tips on Car Repair (No. 311-03246)
Consumer Tips on Car Care on the Road (No. 292)

Cost: Free

Send to:
Council of Better Business Bureaus
1515 Wilson Blvd.
Arlington, VA 22209

A SASE is a self-addressed stamped envelope.

KEEP YOUR CAR IN TIP-TOP SHAPE

★★★★

Four simple five-minute checks can keep your car running better and longer. A major national car rental company has its mechanics follow these four steps each week to keep its fleet in good running order. The checkups include oil level, automatic transmission fluid, electric fan, engine cooling system, tires, shock absorbers, lights, seat belts, and brakes. A free 18-page booklet describes these checkups and offers tips on how to approach common problems you might be able to solve yourself, saving a call to the auto repairman or tow company.

Write for:
Guide to Preventive Maintenance

Cost: Free

Send to:
Public Relations Department
National Car Rental
7700 France Ave., S.
Minneapolis, MN 55435

TUNING UP IN THREE EASY LESSONS

★★★★

One of the best things you can do for your car (and your wallet) is make sure it has a regular tune-up. Besides avoiding costly breakdowns, tune-ups prevent wasteful consumption of fuel. An average tune-up will pay for itself in 7000 miles—2500 miles if you do the work yourself. *The Three-Part Gasoline Engine Tuneup* is an 18-page booklet which, through pictures and step-by-step instructions, takes you through the tune-up procedure. You'll learn exactly what to do, how to do it, what to look for, and what you need to get the job done. After reading this informative manual, you may still decide that you don't care to tune your own car, but you'll be better informed when you take it to the garage to have the work done.

Write for:
The Three-Part Gasoline Engine Tuneup (No. 153P)

Cost: $1.50

Send to:
Consumer Information Center
P.O. Box 100
Pueblo, CO 81002

The Three-Part Gasoline Engine Tuneup

WHAT GOES ON UNDER A CAR HOOD

★★★

If you don't know a spark plug from a radiator cap, but wish you did, improve your knowledge about what goes on under the hood of your car with the help of this booklet from the Car Care Council. It offers a quick and easy guide to preventive maintenance, and it could help you keep your car in better running order and avoid expensive repair bills. A companion booklet on keeping your car in tune also tells how a car's electrical system works and how you can keep it working smoothly.

Write for:
How to Find Your Way Under the Hood and Around the Car
How to Keep Your Car in Tune

Cost: 25¢ and a long SASE for each

Send to:
Car Check and/or Tune-Up
Car Care Council
600 Renaissance Center
Detroit, MI 48243

DO-IT-YOURSELF CAR REPAIRS

★★★

You've probably noticed that the "service" is rapidly disappearing from many service stations. Gas station attendants don't routinely check under your hood anymore when you pull up to the pumps; at many stations, they don't even pump the gas. The times are changing, but that doesn't mean your car doesn't need the attention it once received. Minor servicing can keep your car running better and more

continued

safely. As a responsible automobile owner, you can simply and easily learn to make these quick checks— and even minor repairs—by yourself. *Simple Self-Service* can help show you how. In nontechnical language, the six-page pamphlet explains the various car components, where they are, what they do, and what they need to keep running smoothly. It also offers a list of the tools and equipment you'll need to do your own checkups.

Write for:
Simple Self-Service (No. 154P)

Cost: $1.00

Send to:
Consumer Information Center
P.O. Box 100
Pueblo, CO 81002

CAR CARE MADE EASY
★★

What happens when you hear a grinding noise when you apply the brakes on your car? What does it mean if you have to pump the brakes to stop? The Car Care Council offers a brochure with advice on brake care with cartoons illustrating various brake problems and solutions. Other brochures tell how to keep your car's filters in good order and the cooling system running efficiently. These are three helpful booklets for the do-it-yourself motorist and could help save on big auto repair bills.

Write for:
How to Keep Your Brakes from Letting You Down
Keep an Eye on Your Car's Filters
How to Help Your Car Keep Its Cool

Cost: 25¢ and a long SASE for each

Send to:
Brakes, Filters, and/or Cooling
Car Care Council
600 Renaissance Center
Detroit, MI 48243

TRANSMISSION AND TIRE CARE
★★★★

One of the hardest tasks most car owners have is being able to say just what the nature of their car's transmission troubles are. A free 10-page brochure from the Better Business Bureau tells in simple language what a car's automatic transmission is, how it works, and how to care for it. Typical symp-

toms of transmission trouble are described and what has to be done to correct the problems. A companion booklet on tires tells how to take care of your car's tires for maximum mileage and tire life. You get tips on buying new tires, and on alignment and tire rotation.

Write for:
Tips on Automatic Transmissions (No. 02-139)
Tips on Tires (No. 24-176)

Cost: Free

Send to:
Council of Better Business Bureaus
1515 Wilson Blvd.
Arlington, VA 22209

ALL ABOUT MOTOR OIL
★★★★

The American Petroleum Institute publishes this booklet to highlight the functions of automotive lubricating oils and the way they protect your car's engine. You'll find out why today's engines have demanding lubrication requirements. You'll learn how oils protect engines from extremes of heat and cold, pressure, corrosion, oxidation, contaminants, and foaming. You'll learn also about different additives to oil and the importance of changing the oil in your car regularly. There's a good list of the different types of oils and which work best for which cars, and another list of tips to help you prolong the life of your engine. Good information.

Write for:
Know Your Motor Oil

Cost: $1.00

Send to:
American Petroleum Institute
1220 L St., N.W.
Washington, DC 20005

Car Safety

SEAT BELTS OR AIR BAGS?
★★★

Automobile seat belts similar to those used today were first installed in "horseless carriages," and have been used in airplanes since 1910. Barney Oldfield began using them in racing cars in 1922. Yet controversy persists about which type of car safety

A SASE is a self-addressed stamped envelope.

device is best, the seat belt or the air bag restraint. A 34-page booklet from the American Council on Science and Health tells the history of seat belt and air bag study, describes the uses of each type of restraint, and analyzes the conflicts in the debate over auto occupant restraint systems. There's good information for any motorist concerned about safety, but this publication is especially useful for driver education students, teachers, and others interested in driver safety.

Write for:
Automobile Occupant Restraint Systems

Cost: $2.00

Send to:
American Council on Science and Health
47 Maple St.
Summit, NJ 07901

SAFE JUMP-STARTING

★★★★

A dead battery is certainly one of life's petty annoyances, but fortunately, a jump-start can often put you back on the road quickly. It is simple to do, but can be quite dangerous if not handled correctly. This offer from the National Society to Prevent Blindness is for an adhesive-backed set of directions for proper jump-starting. Every car should have one affixed in the glove compartment or some other clean, dry location. There are general cautions for positioning the two cars, wearing eye protection, and avoiding sparks. Step-by-step illustrated directions are given for connecting and disconnecting the battery terminals, and should be followed in the order in which they are given.

Write for:
How to Jump-Start a Car Safely

Cost: 25¢ and a long SASE

Send to:
National Society to Prevent Blindness
79 Madison Avenue
New York, NY 10016-7896

AUTO THEFT PREVENTION

★★★

There are no ready-made solutions to the spiraling auto theft problem, but daily precautions are an essential first step. Take them consistently and you'll significantly reduce the odds of becoming a victim of one of the two auto thefts which occur each

minute in the United States. These two pamphlets from Aetna Life & Casualty will help you protect your vehicle. The first, *Auto Theft,* gives surprising information about this widespread crime. For example, did you know over half of all auto thefts occur in residential areas? It also tells how you can recognize possible stolen cars and what to do if you spot one. *Fifty Ways to Foil a Car Thief* is a handy wallet-sized tip sheet with lots of ideas for making your car difficult to steal, insuring identification if it is stolen, and avoiding the purchase of a stolen vehicle.

Write for:
Auto Theft
Fifty Ways to Foil a Car Thief

Cost: Free

Send to:
Resources
Aetna Life & Casualty
151 Farmington Avenue
Hartford, CT 06156

Auto Theft pamphlets

ONE DRIVER, ON THE ROCKS

★★

Three volunteers mixed drinking and driving to show how the average driver performs under the influence of alcohol, and the results are reported in this frightening brochure. The three drivers were tested on a stationary simulator car, and their performance demonstrated how driving skills deteriorate with each drink. Had they actually encountered the conditions presented by the simulator, two of the drivers tested would have died in accidents and the other one would have been seriously injured. A chart shows the estimated blood alcohol level that results from the consumption of various drinks in a given time. This brief publication effectively highlights the dangers of mixing even "social" drinking and driving.

Write for:
Under the Influence . . .

Cost: Free

Send to:
Aetna Life & Casualty
151 Farmington Ave.
Hartford, CT 06156

FREE THINGS
about
MONEY

Budgeting and Money Management

MORE THAN A MATTER OF MONEY

★★★★

Almost every family has problems with money. Most of these problems are very real, and legitimate money worries such as these can throw family relationships off balance. But practical problems are often compounded by emotional factors. Even when money is plentiful, differing attitudes toward it can strain relationships. *Handling Family Money Problems* explores not only how to make the available dollars go around the budget, but also how to recognize the emotions that fiscal matters arouse. The 28-page booklet discusses money as a control issue and a symbol of love and security, methods of money management, spending, and saving. You'll learn about using credit wisely and financing college educations. There is also lots of good advice on planning for the future.

Write for:
Handling Family Money Problems (No. 626)

Cost: $1.00

Send to:
Public Affairs Pamphlets
381 Park Ave. South
New York, NY 10016

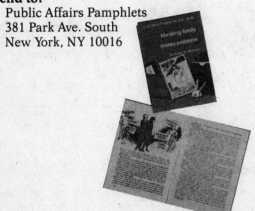

Handling Family Money Problems

BE A BETTER SHOPPER

★★★★

Do you shop for groceries when you're hungry? Or wander through shopping malls, buying shoes on impulse? Do you spend more time and energy on choosing a greeting card than on buying a washing machine? If so, send off right away for *Your Shopping Dollar*. It can help you plan expenditures, decide where to shop, develop purchasing skills, decide how to pay for purchases (everyone needs help *there*), even make complaints.

This pleasantly illustrated 32-page book from the Money Management Institute covers shopping for food, clothing, home furnishings, appliances, and medicine, and discusses services you buy—from beauty shops to doctors and lawyers. Get the straight facts on advertising, seals of approval, guarantees, and warranties. Find out how to spot a fraud. There's even a sample complaint letter that might come in handy. A discussion on high-, medium-, and low-quality buys is worth reading; so is the advice on sales, coupons, and trading stamps.

Write for:
Money Management—Your Shopping Dollar

Cost: $1.00

Send to:
Money Management Institute
Dept. PI
Household International
2700 Sanders Rd.
Prospect Heights, IL 60070

GETTING OUT FROM UNDER

★★★

Never really understood the implications of the term "that sinking feeling" until the grisly moment when you realized that you're up to your ears in debt? Here's a down-to-earth four pages of advice. *What to Do When Debts Pile Up* takes a cool look at what to do to get out from under, and recommends confrontation rather than avoidance. These days, it points out, you don't have to be an irresponsible spender in order to get into debt. A major change—losing your job, having a baby, getting divorced—can throw a hefty wrench into your financial works. But whatever the reason you're in hock, the wise thing to do is consider the situation rationally and take steps to get out of it. And first, suggests this publication, you should confront your creditors—if you've been responsible in the past, most creditors will appreciate your taking the initiative and will try to help you arrange a payment plan. The advice given here covers extensions, loan rewrites, credit insurance, and consolidation loans, as well as the rights of creditors, sources of help for you in the form of financial counseling, and hints on what to do about home loan problems.

Write for:
What to Do When Debts Pile Up

continued

MONEY

Cost: $1.00 (U.S. check or money order only)

Send to:
Bank of America, Dept. 3120
Box 37128
San Francisco, CA 94137

MAKING ENDS MEET

★★★★

What does it cost to live today? How can you plan a household budget and shop wisely? These and other questions about money matters are answered in a compact 32-page booklet called *Making Ends Meet*. It's written by Grace W. Weinstein, author of seven books on money management and psychology, and is published by the Public Affairs Committee, a non-profit educational organization. You'll get tips on smart shopping for food, clothing, appliances, automobiles, apartments, and insurance. Suggestions for saving and wise use of credit also are included. It's a practical and helpful guide to managing a family or personal budget.

Write for:
Making Ends Meet

Cost: $1.00

Send to:
Public Affairs Pamphlets
381 Park Ave. South
New York, NY 10016

Making Ends Meet

MAKING A MONEY PLANNER

★★★

A money plan can help you get more satisfaction from your hard-earned dollars by directing them where they're needed most. This four-page brochure tells how to start a money plan, provides work sheets, and offers ideas for putting your plan into action. It helps you plan for both short- and long-term goals such as paying all bills on time, keeping credit card and charge account spending within predetermined limits, establishing a savings account for emergencies,

and saving up for major items such as a car or home. It also has some good words on setting up an investment program for additional income in retirement.

Write for:
Personal Money Planner

Cost: $1.00 (U.S. check or money order only)

Send to:
Bank of America, Dept. 3120
Box 37128
San Francisco, CA 94137

EASY COME, EASY...

★★★★

Where does all the money go? Could you make better use of your cash in the future? The importance of planning *before* spending is emphasized in *Your Financial Plan*. This attractive, 32-page guide, nicely designed with modern line illustrations and graphics, discusses living in today's economy — setting short- and long-range financial goals, determining your present financial situation and net worth, and establishing a financial plan. There are pointers on how to manage the plan once you've gotten it down on paper, including record keeping, choosing a money manager, paying bills, handling money in checking and savings accounts, credit, and — ah, yes — living with inflation. There are plenty of charts to clarify options, including a four-page chart for figuring your total plan.

Write for:
Your Financial Plan

Cost: $1.00

Send to:
Money Management Institute
Household International
2700 Sanders Rd.
Prospect Heights, IL 60070

Your Financial Plan

A SASE is a self-addressed stamped envelope.

MONEY MANAGEMENT MAGAZINE

★★★

This small magazine, published by the Credit Union National Association, is filled with articles and news about personal finance and consumer affairs. It covers topics like the types of mortgages currently available to home buyers, teaching kids the value of money, new estate laws, and clothing sizes that don't always measure up. There's a list of useful publications for consumers and a question-and-answer forum on financial matters. Interesting and easy to read. For 50¢ you can get the issue that's current at the time you write. If you like it, you can subscribe for a year for $2.00.

Write for:
Everybody's Money

Cost: 50¢

Send to:
Everybody's Money
Credit Union National Association, Inc.
P.O. Box 431
Madison, WI 53701

Everybody's Money

HOW TO BALANCE YOUR CHECKBOOK

★★

Balancing your checking account is an important monthly task and you should do it regularly. A new four-page report from the Bank of America tells you how to balance your checkbook and helps you keep accurate records of your deposited funds. A special section tells how to track down errors that may keep you from accurately balancing your account. Samples of typical checking account statements and checkbooks help you visualize the forms you must fill out and check in order to balance your checkbook.

Write for:
How to Balance Your Checkbook

Cost: $1.00 (U.S. check or money order only)

Send to:
Bank of America, Dept. 3120
Box 37128
San Francisco, CA 94137

ALL ABOUT CHECKS AND CHECKING ACCOUNTS

★★★

The ins and outs of checks and checking accounts can be complicated. With the information in a new four-page report from the Bank of America you will be able to handle checking transactions with ease and confidence, and you'll know where to turn if problems arise. It tells about personal checks, customized checks, counter checks, universal checks, domestic and international money orders, cashier's checks, and traveler's checks. It tells about cashing and depositing checks, covers special situations such as what to do about lost or stolen checks, and how to arrange for stop payments on checks. A handy list of checking tips is included.

Write for:
A Guide to Checks and Checking

Cost: $1.00 (U.S. check or money order only)

Send to:
Bank of America, Dept. 3120
Box 37128
San Francisco, CA 94137

ALICE AND THE MONEY MACHINES

★★★★

Just got around to controlling your credit card spending? Financial officers say that credit cards will be out of date soon, anyhow. EFTs (Electronic Fund Transfer) and ATMs (Automated Teller Machines) are the payment centers of the future. Many people already use preauthorized payments to take care of mortgages or auto payments, but this is only the beginning. *Alice in Debitland* takes you through the wonders of computerized transactions, lists their pros and cons, and tells you how to protect yourself from human and computer error, what your rights and obligations are, and how to protest an error. Good basic information. The Alice-style illustrations are very clever.

continued

MONEY

Write for:
Alice in Debitland

Cost: Free

Send to:
Federal Reserve System
Publications Services
Division of Support Services
Washington, DC 20551

Alice in Debitland

WHERE DID YOU PUT
THE PAPERS?

★★★

Do you know where your marriage certificate is? How about your mother's naturalization papers? Can you locate (quickly) your college diploma, the deed to your house, or the stock certificates for your three shares in IBM? This bulletin will help you inventory your important papers and locate them when you need them. In an emergency, it will direct others to where they are. The eight-page inventory covers information on family birth records, whom to notify when serious emergencies occur, names of family advisers, and where your important papers are kept. There's space for banking information, real estate and business information, stocks and bonds, all types of insurance data, retirement and employment history, and debts owed. No excuse for being disorganized with such a handy helper.

Write for:
Do You Know Your Valuable Papers?

Cost: 85¢

Send to:
Distribution Center
7 Research Park
Cornell University
Ithaca, NY 14850

KEEPING THE RECORD
STRAIGHT

★★★

Maybe you've got all the data on your financial affairs stored safely in your head—which is fine except that in an emergency nobody else will have access to that information. Sometimes a death in the family leaves the surviving members completely in the dark about bank accounts, outstanding bills, insurance policies, and where the will is kept—or even if there *is* a will. To avoid this happening to your family, send for this very practical guide, fill it out as completely as possible, keep it up-to-date, and store it in a convenient, safe place where your family can find it immediately if the need arises.

Write for:
Locator Guide of Personal Records

Cost: $1.00

Send to:
National Association of Mature People
2212 NW 50
P.O. Box 26792
Oklahoma City, OK 73126

FINANCIAL ADVICE FOR
THE WIDOWED

★★★

If you've had the sort of marriage where your partner handled the money matters, the death of your spouse may leave you not just emotionally bereft but at a loss as to just how to take over your financial responsibilities. This four-page publication from the Bank of America takes a necessarily brief but still comprehensive look at the issues you'd have to deal with in such a situation. It points out that many financial matters will be handled by the executor or administrator of your spouse's will—the person named in the will or by the court to do most of the actual work involved in putting your financial house in order. But you'll still be responsible for some tasks yourself, and your best starting point may be with your files at home. This pamphlet discusses important papers you'll need, the situations where you may want to get good legal advice, how to handle taxes, and what to do about credit responsibilities. Lots of clear-headed information to help at a time when you're likely to be anything but clear-headed yourself.

Write for:
Financial Transactions for the Widowed

Cost: $1.00 (U.S. check or money order only)

A SASE is a self-addressed stamped envelope.

TO YOUR CREDIT

★★★

Money management is like a game; play it right and you'll come out the winner. However, this is one game that you'll play for an entire lifetime, so if you seem to be on the losing end, it may be a good move to heed these two pamphlets from Associated Credit Bureaus, Inc. *How to Manage Your Money Cleverly* is a 12-page compilation of useful budget information, from wise shopping to figuring the cost of credit. You'll learn how to get the least expensive credit when you need it, and how to take care of your creditors. There is also a personal budget worksheet. *Consumers, Credit Bureaus and the Fair Credit Reporting Act* answers questions about your credit file and how to keep it in your favor. You'll learn how to correct errors and just how much personal information is maintained in this report.

Write for:
How to Manage Your Money Cleverly
Consumers, Credit Bureaus and the Fair Credit
    Reporting Act

Cost: Free

Send to:
Associated Credit Bureaus, Inc.
16211 Park Ten Place
P.O. Box 218300
Houston, TX 77218

How to Manage Your Money Cleverly

Credit and How to Use It

GIVE YOURSELF SOME CREDIT

★★★

If you ever apply for a charge account, a credit card, a car loan, or a mortgage, your credit experience—or lack of it—will be a major factor considered by the creditor in reviewing your request. It may even affect your ability to get a job or buy life insurance. Buying on credit has become such an accepted way of life that it is difficult to make some major purchases without it. Two small pamphlets, *Your Credit Rating* and *How to Establish and Use Credit,* will help you take care of this privilege. You'll learn how to build a good credit rating, how to determine the amount of credit your budget can handle, and what credit bureaus do and what information they keep in your file. Correcting misinformation is also covered, as well as other ways to protect your financial reputation.

Write for:
Your Credit Rating
How to Establish and Use Credit

Cost: Free

Send to:
Federal Reserve Bank of New York
Public Information Department
New York, NY 10045

Your Credit Rating

How to Establish and Use Credit

UNDERSTANDING CREDIT

★★

In today's marketplace nearly everyone uses credit at one time or another, for charging merchandise at a department store, buying gas, or taking a personal

continued

MONEY

loan at a local bank. Because the use of credit generally results in the use of forms, responsible consumers should watch for meaningful information in the contracts they sign. If you use credit, two small booklets from the Federal Reserve Bank of New York will help you understand what you are reading before you agree to contract stipulations. *Consumer Credit Terminology Handbook* is a pocket-sized directory of phrases and words you will encounter in the world of buy now, pay later. *If You Use a Credit Card* discusses your protections under Federal law. Now you'll know what you can do about unsolicited credit cards, defective goods and services, or stolen cards—and you can rectify these situations in the correct language.

Write for:
Consumer Credit Terminology Handbook
If You Use a Credit Card

Cost: Free

Send to:
Federal Reserve Bank of New York
Public Information Department
New York, NY 10045

IN MONTHLY INSTALLMENTS
★★★

"Only 36 easy monthly payments," the advertising reads. The promises of buying on time aren't hard to take, especially when there is a car, boat, furniture, or wardrobe you want to have today. Don't be fooled—there is much more to borrowing or leasing than easy payments. Three small pamphlets from the Federal Reserve Bank of New York give straight talk about the cost of doing business with other people's money. *Truth in Lending Simplified* explains your rights as a borrower and the information that must be disclosed to you at the time of the transaction. *Truth in Leasing* discusses the Consumer Leasing Act, costs and terms, open-end leases, and balloon payments. *The Rule of 78's* covers why prepayment of a loan will cost more than you anticipated.

Write for:
Truth in Lending Simplified
Truth in Leasing
The Rule of 78's

Cost: Free

Send to:
Federal Reserve Bank of New York
Public Information Department
New York, NY 10045

HOW TO HANDLE CREDIT
★★★★

Establishing credit is an important step in building a sound financial future, but wise handling of credit once established may be even more important. The proper use of consumer credit is based on an understanding of how credit works and, equally, on a realistic budget plan for the individual and family. The Better Business Bureau offers a free 10-page brochure that describes the two basic types of consumer credit—installment sales credit and direct loans. It tells how to shop for credit and what your rights are in a retail installment contract or in revolving credit. The Bureau also suggests what to do if you can't meet your credit obligations on time.

Write for:
Tips on Consumer Credit (No. 24-157)

Cost: Free

Send to:
Council of Better Business Bureaus
1515 Wilson Blvd.
Arlington, VA 22209

ADJUSTABLE CREDIT RATES
★★★

Shopping for the best credit rates? Adjustable-rate credit is something to consider, but don't rush into it. Traditional loans have fixed rates of interest and you always know how much your monthly payment will be. Adjustable-rate loans for home mortgages or other major purchases offer lower initial interest rates and monthly payments. But they will rise over the course of the loan. Learn more about adjustable-rate credit from this four-page publication from the Bank of America National Trust and Savings Association.

Write for:
Shopping for Adjustable-Rate Credit

Cost: $1.00 (U.S. check or money order only)

Send to:
Bank of America, Dept. 3120
Box 37128
San Francisco, CA 94137

WILL THAT BE CASH OR CHARGE?
★★★★

Now that it's more common to pay with credit than with cold, hard cash, it does no harm to take a cold, hard look at credit every now and then. A good place to start is *Managing Your Credit*, 44 readable pages giving thorough coverage of the definition and role of consumer credit in our economy, its costs, pros and cons, and much more. There's practical information and advice on credit bureaus, women and credit, and credit agreement—even how to shop for it and how to understand congressional legislation on the subject.

Write for:
  Managing Your Credit

Cost: $1.00

Send to:
  Money Management Institute
  Dept. PI
  Household International
  2700 Sanders Rd.
  Prospect Heights, IL 60070

A GUIDE TO CREDIT PROTECTION LAWS

★★★★

You and your husband apply for a mortgage on your dream home. Your joint incomes are more than enough to make the payments, but you're turned down by the lender because he thinks you might become pregnant and leave your job. That turndown is illegal. This booklet is filled with this kind of information that will make you a better informed user of credit. Some of the things you'll learn about are the cost of credit, applying for credit and what lenders look for, credit histories and records, how to correct credit mistakes, transferring funds electronically, and—most important—how to complain about credit practices. There's a short glossary and a list of federal enforcement agencies for consumers.

Write for:
  Consumer Handbook to Credit Protection Laws

Cost: Free

Send to:
  Federal Reserve System
  Publication Services
  Division of Support Services
  Washington, DC 20551

TO THE COMPLAINT DEPARTMENT

★★★

"Charge it." What magic words these are, at least until an error shows up on your bill. If you've ever been hassled by the credit department's computer, you'll be pleased to learn you have rights when you think your bill is wrong. Fair Credit Billing, an addition to the Truth in Lending law, requires prompt correction of billing mistakes. Three small but informative pamphlets explain how to resolve disputes while protecting your credit rating. *Fair Credit Billing* defines the types of errors you may challenge and gives step by step instructions for obtaining satisfaction. If yours is a problem with a bank, follow the directions in *How to File a Consumer Credit Complaint* and the Federal Reserve will help. *Fair Debt Collection Practices* explains this law in simplified language, and discusses locating and contacting debtors and prohibited tactics in attempting to collect.

Write for:
  Fair Credit Billing
  How to File a Consumer Credit Complaint
  Fair Debt Collection Practices

Cost: Free

Send to:
  Federal Reserve Bank of New York
  Public Information Department
  New York, NY 10045

Home, Car, Life, and Health Insurance

FACTS ON HOMEOWNER'S INSURANCE

★★★★

To protect against heavy financial loss if your home is jeopardized by fire, theft, or natural disaster, you should have an up-to-date homeowner's insurance policy that adequately covers both your home and the possessions therein. Homeowner's insurance policies vary widely and can be confusing. To learn all about homeowner's insurance, send for a free 10-page brochure from the Better Business Bureau. It tells about the types of policies available, how much protection you need, how to make an inventory to decide what coverage you should take, and how to shop around for the best policy.

Write for:
  Tips on Homeowners Insurance (No. 24-197)

Cost: Free

continued

MONEY

HOME INSURANCE BASICS
★★★

This little leaflet's designed to help you get maximum value for your insurance dollar. It's especially good if you're buying homeowner's insurance for the first time because it explains basic terms. You'll learn the four different kinds of homeowner's policies and the specific losses they cover; how to estimate the cost of rebuilding your house at current prices; how to take a home inventory; what a homeowner's policy does not cover; how to shop and compare to get the best insurance plan; and what you must do after you buy insurance.

Write for:
Home Insurance Basics

Cost: Free with a long SASE

Send to:
Insurance Information Institute
Publications Service Center, Dept. HiB
110 William St.
New York, NY 10038

ABOUT TITLE INSURANCE
★★★

What is title insurance? Is it as important as fire insurance? What is a title defect? If the person I'm buying my home from has title insurance, why do I need it too? These and 27 other questions are answered in this booklet. There's also a brief glossary of terms used in the title insurance context. It is interesting to note that not all titles are insurable. Some are "sick," and it's as important to find out this as it is to learn that a title is clear. By the way: Title means you have a legal right to possess certain property and use it (within restrictions imposed by authorities), superimposed on the basic right to possession by previous owners.

Write for:
Questions & Answers About Title Insurance
for Prospective Homeowners

Cost: Free

Send to:
Lawyers Title Insurance Corp.
P.O. Box 27567
Richmond, VA 23261

TITLE INSURANCE: WHAT IT MEANS
★★★

This glossary is designed to acquaint people with the terms commonly used in the title insurance business, in that context only. It's important to understand that the same term often has an entirely different meaning if it's used in another context. The definitions are clearly written and easy to understand, for example: *Deed: Written instrument duly executed and delivered by which the title to land is transferred from one person to another.* Over 170 terms are defined. A useful freebie.

Write for:
Title Insurance Glossary

Cost: Free

Send to:
Lawyers Title Insurance Corp.
P.O. Box 27567
Richmond, VA 23261

WHY TENANT'S INSURANCE?
★★

Why tenant's insurance? The reason is simple. Though your landlord probably has insurance to cover the house or apartment building, it does not include coverage for your personal belongings. Nor does it cover your liability to others—if a visitor trips and falls in your apartment, for instance. This leaflet outlines Tenant's Form Insurance (HO-4), what it covers, how you can determine exactly how much insurance you need with an inventory and photographs, and how to shop for the best buy.

Write for:
Tenant's Insurance Basics

Cost: Free with a long SASE

Send to:
Insurance Information Institute
Publications Service Center, Dept. TiB
110 William St.
New York, NY 10038

Tenants Insurance Basics

A SASE is a self-addressed stamped envelope.

TEST YOUR A.I.Q.

★★★

There's more to this brochure than its useful discussion of the six kinds of basic auto insurance coverage. There's also a reasoned discussion of your financial responsibility as a driver, what "no-fault" insurance means and what some of the variations are in different states, and how rates are determined for automobiles. There's a good section on youthful drivers, driver education credit, and student discounts. You'll also find a test that measures your "A.I.Q.— Auto Insurance Quotient." Good information, clearly set down.

Write for:
Insurance for the Car

Cost: Free with a long SASE

Send to:
Insurance Information Institute
Publications Service Center, Dept. IC
110 William St.
New York, NY 10038

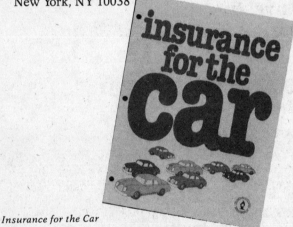

Insurance for the Car

YOUR AUTO INSURANCE

★★

Quick—name the six basic auto insurance coverages. If you can't, you need to study this leaflet that explains what they are, which coverages you need, and how you can get the best insurance plan for your money by carefully shopping around and comparing policies. In case you're stumped about the six basic coverages, they are: bodily injury liability, property damage liability, medical payments insurance, uninsured motorist's protection, collision insurance, and comprehensive physical damage insurance. Chances are you still don't know what each covers. This slim leaflet tells you.

Write for:
Auto Insurance Basics

Cost: Free with a long SASE

Send to:
Insurance Information Institute
Publications Service Center, Dept. AiB
110 William St.
New York, NY 10038

FOR YOUR FAMILY'S FUTURE

★★★

Life insurance is primarily purchased to provide an immediate estate. It protects your family's financial resources when you die, and the income your family will need to pay household bills. It's a contract between you and an insurance company requiring the company to pay your beneficiaries a certain amount of money on your death. Life insurance takes many forms, as you will learn in *A Consumer's Guide to Life Insurance.* The 24-page booklet discusses the three basic types of policies and weighs the advantages and disadvantages of each. There is advice on which type to purchase and how to determine the amount of protection your family needs. There is a worksheet to help you calculate your net worth and a glossary of pertinent terminology.

Write for:
A Consumer's Guide to Life Insurance (No. 514P)

Cost: Free

Send to:
Consumer Information Center
P.O. Box 100
Pueblo, CO 81002

HOW TO BUY LIFE INSURANCE

★★★★

Life insurance can protect a family against financial want in case of the death of a family provider. Because there are so many kinds of life insurance policies, with different protection and benefits, terms and conditions, the subject can be complicated and confusing. A free 10-page booklet from the Better Business Bureau tells what life insurance is, how it works, who should have it, the kinds of insurance policies available, and how much insurance you ought to have. It also discusses life insurance and savings and investment plans. Suggestions are given for selecting a reliable insurance representative and insurance company.

Write for:
Tips on Life Insurance (No. 24-155)

continued

MONEY

Cost: Free

Send to:
Council of Better Business Bureaus
1515 Wilson Blvd.
Arlington, VA 22209

Tips on Life Insurance

INSURING YOUR FAMILY'S FUTURE

★★★

Life insurance does more than provide financial protection for your family if you should die prematurely. Proper coverage can help you meet personal, family, and business financial needs and objectives. These two free pamphlets can help you plan wisely for the futures of you and your loved ones. The first is *Some Guidelines for Deciding What Kind of Life Insurance is Your Best Buy*. The 12-page booklet gives sound advice on understanding your life insurance, the service of your life underwriter, the differences between term and whole life insurance, and more. The second, *Your Life Underwriter and You*, tells you how to select a qualified underwriter and how he or she can help you to meet your goals.

Write for:
Some Guidelines for Deciding What Kind of
Life Insurance Is Your Best Buy
Your Life Underwriter and You

Cost: 25¢ for Guidelines
Your Life Underwriter is free

Send to:
The National Association of Life Underwriters
Attn: Consumer Education Dept.
1922 F Street, N.W.
Washington, DC 20006-4387

HOW MUCH HEALTH INSURANCE IS ENOUGH?

★★★★

With high and rising medical costs, most individuals and families agree that health insurance is a necessity. But few purchases are as complicated and confusing as choosing a good health insurance program. A 24-page booklet from the Better Business Bureau, *Facts About Health Insurance*, helps clear up some of the confusion. You learn what health insurance is and what it can do for you and your family, and about the five types of health insurance—hospital expense insurance, surgical expense insurance, physician's expense insurance, major medical insurance, and disability insurance. How much and what kind of insurance do you and your family need? This booklet can help you make these important decisions.

Write for:
Facts About Health Insurance (No. 238)

Cost: Free

Send to:
Council of Better Business Bureaus
1515 Wilson Blvd.
Arlington, VA 22209

Investing and Estate Planning

SMART SAVING AND INVESTING

★★★★

If you have money in a savings account, fine. But there are other important ways to save and invest your money, too. A free 14-page booklet from the Better Business Bureau explores many of the various alternatives to saving accounts. It describes commercial banks, savings and loan associations, mutual savings banks, and credit unions; tells how savings accounts work and what interest they yield; and defines money market accounts, certificates of deposit, and IRAs (Individual Retirement Accounts). Ways to invest, such as stocks and bonds, mutual funds, Treasury bills, and U.S. savings bonds are described. This is an easy-to-understand short course in saving and investment that can be helpful to almost anyone.

Write for:
Tips on Saving and Investing (No. 24-174)

Cost: Free

Send to:
Council of Better Business Bureaus
1515 Wilson Blvd.
Arlington, VA 22209

A SASE is a self-addressed stamped envelope.

Tips on Savings and Investing

MAKING MONEY GROW

★★★

How can you get a better return on your money? This booklet discusses one way: mutual funds. It tells what a mutual fund is (a practical and efficient way for people with similar goals to pool their money to achieve these goals), how they have increased in value over the years, and the different kinds of funds there are: growth, income, or combination growth-income fund; balanced fund; bond fund; money market fund; and municipal bond fund. The booklet also discusses the special services offered by mutual funds, and there's a seven-question quiz to help you zero in on your financial goals. Brief— 21 pages—but useful.

Write for:
A Translation: Turning "Investment-ese" into Investment Ease

Cost: Free

Send to:
Investment Company Institute
1600 M St., N.W.
Washington, DC 20036

MAKING THE MOST OF SAVINGS

★★★★

If you can manage—after paying the bills, buying the groceries, and filling the gas tank—to scrape up some money to *save*, you'll want to make those savings work for you. *Your Savings and Investment Dollar* presents the alternatives open to you. Forty pages of detailed information, accompanied by simple drawings and helpful charts, advise consumers on establishing and achieving financial objectives.

Different savings programs are discussed in detail: bank accounts, savings and loan associations, government savings bonds, credit union shares, life insurance policies, and annuities. Social security plans and other pension and retirement plans are discussed. The section on investment deals with investing in yourself (education), durable goods (home, car, and other possessions), and income-producing assets (securities, real estate, and business investments). Lots of practical information here, presented in a very readable style.

Write for:
Your Savings and Investment Dollar

Cost: $1.00

Send to:
Money Management Institute
Household International
2700 Sanders Rd.
Prospect Heights, IL 60070

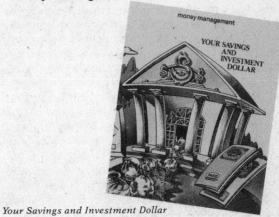

Your Savings and Investment Dollar

INVESTING IN SAVINGS BONDS

★★★

U.S. savings bonds are one of the safest and securest places you can invest your money, but it's still wise to learn more about them before you make up your mind to invest. The Department of the Treasury offers a 12-page booklet explaining what U.S. savings bonds are, what types are available, what interest rates you can get, and how to purchase savings bonds. One section is devoted to the redemption and exchange of savings bonds and another covers taxes and "final maturity" of savings bonds. This is a valuable guide if you're interested in investing in savings bonds.

Write for:
50 Q & A on U.S. Savings Bonds (No. 417P)

Cost: 50¢

continued

MONEY

UNDERSTANDING IRA ACCOUNTS

★★★

An Individual Retirement Account is a program that lets you set up your own retirement plan and save on taxes at the same time. This booklet answers every question you may have about IRA accounts, and some you may not have thought of. It also tells about the different ways you can contribute to an IRA account—through savings accounts, certificates of deposit at a bank, an insurance annuity, individual stocks and bonds, or government retirement bonds. It tells when to invest, and how you can "roll-over" lump-sum payments from employers to IRA accounts. The options are many, and this 28-page booklet briefly explains them all.

Write for:
Plan Tomorrow Today

Cost: Free

Send to:
Investment Company Institute
1600 M St., N.W.
Washington, DC 20036

ALL ABOUT IRAS

★★★

One way to plan and save for your retirement and the financial well-being of your family is to contribute to an individual retirement account (IRA). With an IRA you pay less federal income tax now, and you build a nest egg for the future. But IRAs are a complicated subject, and choosing a high-yielding, safe IRA investment isn't something you should decide without careful study. You can learn more about investing in IRAs by sending for this 10-page booklet prepared by the Special Committee on Aging of the United States Senate. It tells how IRAs work, offers tips on making an IRA investment, and explains the federal income tax aspects of IRAs. It's a useful guide and a good introduction to a sometimes confusing subject.

Write for:
A Guide to IRAs (No. 112P)

Cost: $2.00

HOW TO PLAN FOR RETIREMENT

★★★

To get the maximum income during retirement, you need to start planning now, whether you're 30 or 60. A new four-page report examines investments and stategies to help you reach your retirement goals. Making a sound financial plan can help ensure that your retirement income is large enough to cover your expenses. The publication tells how to choose investments with an eye to return, risk, diversification, liquidity, your tax bracket, and your age. It describes various types of retirement investments such as U.S. savings bonds, money market securities, stocks, and mutual funds. Also mentioned are other prospects such as life insurance, tax-deferred annuities, and individual retirement accounts (IRAs).

Write for:
Planning for Retirement Income

Cost: $1.00 (U.S. check or money order only)

Send to:
Bank of America, Dept. 3120
Box 37128
San Francisco, CA 94137

Planning Your Retirement Income

UNDERSTANDING AND WRITING YOUR WILL

★★★

It's possible, in theory, to write a one-sentence will. Most people's circumstances—and the complexities of tax laws—make that unadvisable. You write a will to make sure that your property is distributed the way you want with as little delay

A SASE is a self-addressed stamped envelope.

and expense as possible, and *What You Should Know About Wills* tells you how to do it. This six-page reprint leads you through choosing an executor, a trustee, and guardians for the children, and lists the costs involved—immediate and ongoing. You may be surprised how much you're worth when you fill out the net worth statement form included. The clear language and step-by-step instructions here should take some of the mystique out of legalese.

Write for:
  What You Should Know About Wills

Cost: $1.00

Send to:
  National Resource Center for Consumers of Legal
    Services
  3254 Jones Ct. N.W.
  Washington, DC 20007

Consumer Services: Your Rights and Responsibilities

WISE BUYS
★★★★

Careful shopping saves money and forestalls problems, and it means knowing as much as you can about products and services before you buy. It also applies to how you make your purchases. It isn't difficult to be an informed shopper, but you do have to know what to look for. *The Informed Shopper: A Guide to Consumer Rights* is a good place to start. The 28-page pamphlet from the Public Affairs Committee helps you understand advertising claims, credit rights, credit bureaus, and collection agencies. You'll learn about your rights as a consumer when it comes to warranties, lemon laws, and shopping by mail. You'll also learn how to complain effectively when you have a problem.

Write for:
  The Informed Shopper: A Guide to
    Consumer Rights (No. 627)

Cost: $1.00

Send to:
  Public Affairs Pamphlets
  381 Park Ave. South
  New York, NY 10016

The Informed Shopper: A Guide to Consumer Rights

BE YOUR OWN CONSUMER EXPERT
★★★★

Even in today's complex marketplace, you should expect quality products and services at fair prices. When something goes wrong, however, you need to let the company know about your problem and try to resolve it with them. Not only is this the fastest way to get your complaint resolved, but it also gives the company a chance to keep you as a satisfied customer. *Consumer's Resource Handbook* should be in every home. Published by the U.S. Office of Consumer Affairs, the 90-page book contains a directory listing the name, address, and phone number of hundreds of manufacturers and corporations, as well as federal and state agencies and commissions who might be able to give you additional help or with whom you can register a complaint. There is lots of information on shopping wisely, complaining effectively, and writing a complaint letter. You won't ever have to be stuck with a lemon again.

Write for:
  Consumer's Resource Handbook

Cost: Free

Send to:
  Handbook
  Consumer Information Center
  Pueblo, CO 81009

ARE ALL SALES FINAL?
★★★★

Many stores have policies that say "All sales are final," but the fact is that most will put customer relations before a slogan. If you buy something in a
continued

store or from a mail order catalog and later decide it isn't what you want or expected, chances are good you can get a refund or exchange it for something else you do want. Here, the Better Business Bureau offers two short brochures explaining about refunds, exchanges, and returns. They tell how you can best go about getting your money back or exchanging an item. If you can't resolve a consumer dispute yourself, you can contact your local Better Business Bureau for help. Both brochures offer good advice for shoppers who later change their minds.

Write for:
Refunds, Exchanges, and Returns—
   a Customer Service (No. 24-175)
Tips on Refunds and Exchanges (No. 311-02207)

Cost: Free

Send to:
Council of Better Business Bureaus
1515 Wilson Blvd.
Arlington, VA 22209

SHOPPING BY PHONE
★★★

Shopping at home using the telephone can save time, energy, and the gas you use driving from store to store. It's also easy on your nervous system—especially in a pre-holiday crush. If you favor telephone shopping, check out this free booklet offered by the Direct Marketing Association. It tells you how to "comparison shop" by phone, how to get complete information from salespeople, and how to order products by phone that may not be readily available from stores or service organizations where you live. Tips also cover use of toll-free 800 numbers. You are encouraged to keep records of your calls and orders, and given cautions for use of credit cards over the telephone.

Write for:
Guidelines for Telephone Shopping

Cost: Free

Send to:
Telephone Guidelines
Direct Marketing Association
6 E. 43rd St.
New York, NY 10017

SOLVING THE MAILING LIST MYSTERY
★★★

How do you get on (and off) mailing lists of companies you've never heard of? This low-key pamphlet from the Direct Marketing Association tells you how. It tells you how you got on the list in the first place, explains list rentals, attempts to explain their rationale, and offers hope. It tells how people who want to can have their names removed from most future list rentals, but points out that the only way not to be on some kind of mailing list is to become a hermit. This sensible pamphlet explains the marketing psychology of direct mail companies in a friendly manner and ends with the question "Do you really want to get off all lists?" Think about it.

Write for:
How Did They Get My Name?

Cost: Free with a long SASE

Send to:
Direct Marketing Association, Inc.
6 E. 43rd St.
New York, NY 10017

SHOP WISELY BY MAIL
★★★★

Ten tips for wise mail-order shopping make up this small, informative booklet from the Direct Marketing Association. You'll learn the Federal Trade Commission's mail order rules on cancellation of orders, credits for such cancellations on your monthly bill, and negative option clubs (you have a minimum of 10 days in which to decide if you want to receive a selection). Tip #10 is a good one: If you ever get something in the U.S. mail that you didn't order, and you're not a member of a negative option or club plan, it's your legal right to keep it without paying for it. This little book is a must for anyone who does a lot of shopping by mail.

Write for:
Make Knowledge Your Partner in Mail Order
   Shopping

Cost: Free with a long SASE

Send to:
Direct Marketing Association
6 E. 43rd St.
New York, NY 10017

A SASE is a self-addressed stamped envelope.

FREE THINGS
about
TRAVEL

TRAVEL

Planning and Packing
for a Trip

THAT ONCE-A-YEAR TIME

★★★★

Ah, it won't be long now. Two weeks to get away from it all. No work, no worries. It's almost vacation time. But wait! Have you decided where to go and how you'll get there? What will it be this year, back to the beach or to the golf course? National Car Rental offers a free 14-page booklet of vacation ideas and suggestions on planning your next—and maybe best—vacation. What do you want, rest and relaxation or adventure? Cultural enrichment or a shopping trip? Romance or self-improvement? This booklet can help you think ahead to your next vacation so it can be the best ever.

Write for:
Vacations: Making the Most of a Good Thing

Cost: Free

Send to:
Public Relations Department
National Car Rental
7700 France Ave. S.
Minneapolis, MN 55435

Vacations:

THE COSTS OF HAVING
A GOOD TIME

★★★★

Ah, leisure! Americans are supposed to have lots of it. But having a good time can be an expensive business and figuring a "leisure budget" can be hard work. *Your Recreation Dollar*, a 40-page guide from the Money Management Institute, gives leisurely advice on managing your money so you can afford a little R&R. Its easy-to-read style and cute, colorful cartoon drawings pass along information on handling your free time; considering the costs, work, and energy involved in recreating (*that's* depressing); setting goals; and planning expenses. There's good advice on the costs of clothing and equipment for a new-found hobby or sport, a discussion of health club memberships, and four pages on renting or buying a recreation vehicle. A substantial section on vacation and travel covers travel agents, lodging alternatives (camping, house swapping, and hostels, to name a few), foreign travel, methods of payment, and getting from A to B by every imaginable means of travel short of camel-back. Also included are a full-page chart for managing your monthly and annual recreation expenses and a pre-vacation checklist.

Write for:
Your Recreation Dollar

Cost: $1.00

Send to:
Money Management Institute
Household International
2700 Sanders Rd.
Prospect Heights, IL 60070

TRAVELING RIGHT

★★★

This 25-page booklet can make your trip more enjoyable by helping you preplan. Choosing lodging to suit your needs and budget, choosing a time of year to travel, finding travel package plans, healthy travel eating habits, safety hints—they're all included here. If you're one of those people whose vacations never seem to turn out quite right this could be just what you need.

Write for:
Tips for Travelers

Cost: $1.00 and a long SASE (39¢ postage)

Send to:
American Hotel and Motel Association
888 Seventh Ave.
New York, NY 10106

Tips for Travelers

A SASE is a self-addressed stamped envelope.

GOING IN STYLE

★★★

When you go on a trip you invariably overpack—no matter how firm your resolve to travel light this time. Or you're experienced at traveling light, but always forget to carry along your umbrella, a raincoat, or a flashlight for emergencies. Brush up on your packing know-how with *See America in Style*, a handy guide to what and how to pack for fun, convenience, and flexibility. There's a great Pack 'n' Go Checklist to remind you of the necessities, and some really super suggestions for women on "double-duty" lingerie—gaily patterned undies that double as bikinis, or elegantly printed pajamas that go to evening parties as well as to bed. (Could revolutionize your shopping habits at home as well as away.) There's an art to dressing comfortably while you're en route, too, so check out the section on what to wear on a plane, train, bus, or car trip. Good tips for men, women, and kid travelers.

Write for:
   See America in Style: A Travel and Fashion Guide

Cost: Free with a long SASE

Send to:
   Union Label Department, ILGWU
   Dept. CGP
   275 7th Ave.
   5th Floor
   New York, NY 10001

FLYING IN A WHEELCHAIR

★★★★

Just because you're one of 35 million Americans who are physically handicapped doesn't mean you don't have the freedom to fly around the world. *Access Travel: Airports* is designed to encourage disabled and elderly citizens to take full advantage of transportation opportunities available today. The 40-page compilation lists design features, facilities, and services at 519 airport terminals in 62 countries which can be important to the handicapped traveler. From Aberdeen, Scotland to Zurich, Switzerland, you will be able to determine where to find elevator controls with raised lettering for the blind, telecommunications devices for the deaf, and much more. There are also suggestions for working with airport and airline personnel so they can best meet your needs.

Write for:
   Access Travel: Airports (No. 585P)

Cost: Free

Send to:
   Consumer Information Center
   P.O. Box 100
   Pueblo, CO 81002

WISH YOU WERE HERE

★★★★

Whether you are traveling overseas for business, pleasure, or study, the best way to ensure a carefree and relaxing trip is to prevent problems before they happen. The more you know about passports, visas, customs, immunizations, and other travel basics, the less likely you are to incur any difficulties while you are abroad. *Your Trip Abroad* is a great 40-page booklet which discusses these issues and much more. You'll learn about driver's licenses, handling of money, drug arrests, and what the American consulate can and cannot do. There is also a source list for obtaining additional information. This booklet is must reading for anyone anticipating a trip out of the country.

Write for:
   Your Trip Abroad (No. 151P)

Cost: $1.00

Send to:
   Consumer Information Center
   P.O. Box 100
   Pueblo, CO 81002

Your Trip Abroad

BON VOYAGE—SPEND WISELY

★★★

Stretching your travel dollars is an important consideration when you vacation abroad, and this little pamphlet is designed to simplify some of the complexities of handling money in a foreign country. *Money Sense Overseas* warns both first-timers and seasoned travelers against carrying cash and advises all travelers to do their own translating. There's also information on shopping for a good converter, budgeting, and buying foreign currency. First-time travelers will like the travel checklist of items to take along and tasks to complete at home and at work

continued

before leaving on vacation. Tipping guidelines are also included.

Write for:
Money Sense Overseas

Cost: Free with a long SASE

Send to:
Travel Enterprises
3602 W. Glen Branch
Peoria, IL 61614

Money Sense Overseas

BUT HOW MUCH IN DOLLARS?

★★★★

Now you won't have to gaze in total bewilderment at the Parisian waiter who's trying to explain the finer points of your restaurant check. You can convert and exchange foreign money easily with the help of the *Foreign Currency Rate Guide*. This handy guide provides a currency table for 36 countries throughout the world. You'll also receive a brochure entitled *Travelling With Foreign Currency* which explains why you should purchase foreign currency and travelers checks before leaving on your trip. It also answers questions about foreign currency travelers checks and what to do about leftover currency. Nice freebies to make your traveling easier from Deak-Perera, the foreign exchange people.

Write for:
Foreign Currency Rate Guide

Cost: Free with a long SASE

Send to:
Deak-Perera U.S., Inc.
29 Broadway
New York, NY 10006

THE ABC'S OF TRAVEL

★★★

APEX, MAP, EP, FIT—do you know what these abbreviations stand for? How about lido, rack rate, or tender? You'll find their meanings, along with other expressions and jargon commonly used in the travel industry, in this handy glossary published by the Institute of Certified Travel Agents. These are the terms that are good to know in order to plan your next vacation or business trip efficiently. Almost a hundred definitions are given in this small pamphlet. Just for your information, the answers to the above questions are: Advance Purchase Excursion Fare, Modified American Plan, European Plan, Foreign Independent Travel. A lido is a swimming pool and the area surrounding it, rack rate refers to the official posted rate for hotel rooms, and a tender is a boat used to transport passengers to and from shore when docking is not possible.

Write for:
Let's Talk Travel

Cost: Free with a long SASE

Send to:
Institute of Certified Travel Agents
148 Linden Street
P.O. Box 56
Wellesley, MA 02181

Let's Talk Travel

HOW TO SELECT A PACKAGE TOUR

★★★★

More vacationers are learning the many benefits of package tours, a combination of travel services which includes hotel accommodations, land and/or air transportation, sightseeing tours, etc., that are carefully integrated and offered at a "package" price which may be considerably less than you'd spend if you planned a similar vacation yourself. By contracting in bulk over scheduled periods for hotels, accommodations, ground transportation, sightseeing tours, tour escorts, meals and other services, the tour operator can achieve substantial savings which can be passed on to the traveler. To learn more about package tours, send for the free eight-page booklet offered by the United States Tour Operators Association.

Write for:
How to Select a Package Tour

Cost: Free

Send to:
U.S. Tour Operators Association
211 E. 51st St., Suite 4B
New York, NY 10022

Camping and RV-ing

YOU AND YOUR RV
★★★

If you're into RV-ing, here's a useful reference for you. This pack of three information sheets gives you the names and addresses of national camping clubs, and the "brand name" camping clubs restricted to owners of particular types of RVs. There is a toll-free number that you can use for making campground reservations anywhere in the country, and a list of companies offering RV rentals. Serious RV campers will also appreciate knowing where to write for magazines and newspapers devoted to articles on trailer camping life, and travelers' guides to parks and campgrounds. Trade periodicals and RV trade associations are listed.

Write for:
RV Clubs, Associations, and Magazines

Cost: Free with a long SASE

Send to:
Recreation Vehicle Industry Association
Dept. ACG
P.O. Box 2999
Reston, VA 22090

CAMPING MADE EASY
★★★★

The good ideas in this little book begin on the cover—the model is wearing a camper's grooming apron: a nifty terry cloth pullover with lots of pockets sewn into the front to hold shampoo, toothbrush, hairbrush and so on; a loose-fitting front to protect clothing; and a long towel attached at the waist. This is only one of many truly original, do-it-yourself camping ideas from the company that makes Ziploc bags. The bags themselves have the most intriguing uses—as mixing bowls, drinking cups, gloves, even inflated as makeshift pillows. Learn how to make a hanging water jug from a plastic bleach bottle or a raincoat from a garbage bag, and how to start a fire with two flashlight batteries and some fine steel wool. Also included are cooking tips and snack ideas (try the Walking Salad or, if you're daring, the Gorp).

Write for:
Camping With Ease

Cost: 25¢

Send to:
Dow Chemical U.S.A.
P.O. Box 68511
Indianapolis, IN 46268

Camping With Ease

ESCAPING THE RAT RACE IN AN RV
★★★★

Have you dreamed of giving up the rat race, leaving the house that requires more and more of your free time, to travel the country with your mate? This 22-page booklet asks the question *Is Full-Time RV-ing for You?* (RV = recreational vehicle). You'll find sensible advice and important things to think about if you're considering full-time RV-ing. If you have fears about personal safety, think you can't handle the rig with ease, believe high prices limit travel, and worry about the tiny living spaces, this booklet by a full-time RV-er will answer your questions, tell you how it's possible to travel *and* save money as you go, and suggest how to satisfy that yearning for permanent roots even when you live on the move.

continued

TRAVEL

Write for:
Is Full-Time RV-ing for You?

Cost: $1.95

Send to:
Escapees
Route 5 Box 310
Livingston, TX 77351
(409) 327-8873

SETTING UP YOUR RV

★★★★

One of the pleasures of traveling in a recreation vehicle is that you can take along some of the comforts of home. This little book offers 12 pages of helpful hints on making the most of storage space in your RV, packing clothing and bedding, setting up the RV kitchen, and controlling the water and sanitary systems. Many of the hints in this attractive pamphlet from Dow Chemical center on using Ziploc bags (the company's product) not only for storing equipment and personal items, but also for such unusual uses as a miniature "washing machine" or a mixing bowl. There are recipes for easy-traveling foods — muffins, cookies, granola mix, hot chocolate mix, muffin pizzas, and noodle dishes.

Write for:
Traveling With Ease

Cost: 25¢

Send to:
Dow Chemical U.S.A.
P.O. Box 68511
Indianapolis, IN 46268

How to Find Out About Where You're Going

INSIDE INFORMATION ON FOREIGN TRAVEL

★★★★

When it comes to planning a trip abroad no one can be more helpful than the foreign tourist offices for the countries you plan to visit. These organizations provide literature plus a whole range of other services — usually free of charge. They'll give you information on climate and clothing, health regulations and entry requirements, currency and exchange rates, and the history and geography of the land. You'll often get maps, hotel information, shopping guides, calendars of events, and all kinds of other good stuff as well. This useful *Directory of Government Tourist Offices* lists all foreign tourist offices in the United States and Canada. You'll learn where to find tourist information for places from American Samoa to Zimbabwe, and 145 destinations in between. Countries that have their own offices or other representation in over 25 major metropolitan areas in the United States are listed alphabetically, along with 339 individual office locations. Each entry includes name, address, and telephone number (including toll-free numbers). At $2.00 this convenient 24-page directory is a must for anyone planning to travel abroad.

Write for:
Directory of Government Tourist Offices

Cost: $2.00

Send to:
Travel Insider
P.O. Box 66323
O'Hare International Airport
Chicago, IL 60666

LET THE STATE TRAVEL OFFICES HELP PLAN YOUR VACATION

★★★★

If you're planning a trip in the United States you'll find that some of the best freebies around come from each state's travel or tourist organization. Wherever you plan to go, write ahead of time to the travel office of the state or states you want to visit for free maps, guides, calendars of events, information on historical and geographical landmarks, and other traveler's aids. In many cases you'll also get thorough information on sports or activities that are popular in that state — skiing, sailing, fishing, hunting, exploring wildlife, hiking, camping, and so on. Some tourist offices will even send you bumper stickers, decals, and other freebies in your information package. The quantity and type of material you'll receive varies from state to state, but you can be sure you'll be getting good, current information to help you plan your vacation. Listed below are the addresses of the office state travel offices throughout the United States. They're in alphabetical order. Happy traveling.

Write for:
Travel Information

Cost: Free

Send to:

ALABAMA
Bureau of Tourism and Travel
532 S. Perry St.
Montgomery, AL 36104

ALASKA
Division of Tourism
Department of Commerce and
Economic Development
State Office Bldg.
333 Willoughby Avenue
P.O. Box E
Juneau, AK 99811

ARIZONA
Office of Tourism
Office of the Governor
1480 E. Bethany Home Rd.
Phoenix, AZ 85014

ARKANSAS
Department of Parks and Tourism
1 Capitol Mall
Little Rock, AR 72201

CALIFORNIA
Office of Tourism
Department of Commerce
1121 L St., Suite 103
Sacramento, CA 95814

COLORADO
Colorado Tourism Board
5500 S. Syracuse Circle, Suite 267
Englewood, CO 80111

CONNECTICUT
Tourism Division
Department of Economic
Development
210 Washington St.
Hartford, CT 06106

DELAWARE
Delaware State Travel Service
Delaware Development Office
Executive Office of the Governor
99 Kings Hwy.
P.O. Box 1401
Dover, DE 19903

DISTRICT OF COLUMBIA
Executive Office of the Mayor
210 District Bldg.
1350 Pennsylvania Avenue, N.W.
Washington, DC 20004

FLORIDA
Division of Tourism
Department of Commerce
505 Collins Bldg.
107 W. Gaines St.
Tallahassee, FL 32301

GEORGIA
Tourist Division
Department of Industry and
Trade
P.O. Box 1776
Atlanta, GA 30301

HAWAII
Office of Tourism
Department of Planning and
Economic Development
Kamamalu Bldg.
250 S. King St.
P.O. Box 2359
Honolulu, HI 96804

IDAHO
Idaho Department of Commerce
108 State Capitol Bldg.
700 W. Jefferson St.
Boise, ID 83720

ILLINOIS
Tourism Office
Community and Industrial
Development Division
Department of Commerce and
Community Affairs
620 E. Adams St.
Springfield, IL 62701

INDIANA
Indiana Tourism Division
One N. Capitol St., Suite 700
Indianapolis, IN 46204-2288

IOWA
Visitors and Tourism Division
Iowa Development Commission
600 E. Court Avenue
Des Moines, IA 50309

KANSAS
Travel and Tourism Division
Department of Economic
Development
400 W. 8th St., 5th Floor
Topeka, KS 66603

KENTUCKY
Travel
Capital Plaza Tower
Frankfort, KY 40601

LOUISIANA
Office of Tourism
Department of Culture,
Recreation, and Tourism
666 N. Foster Dr.
P.O. Box 94291
Baton Rouge, LA 70804-9291

MAINE
Division of Tourism
State House, Station 59
Augusta, ME 04333

MARYLAND
Office of Tourist Development
Department of Economic and
Community Development
45 Calvert St.
Annapolis, MD 21401

MASSACHUSETTS
Division of Tourism
Department of Commerce and
Development
100 Cambridge St., 13th Floor
Boston, MA 02202

MICHIGAN
Michigan Travel Bureau
333 S. Capitol Ave.
Lansing, MI 48909

MINNESOTA
Minnesota Office of Tourism
240 Bremer Bldg.
419 N. Robert St.
St. Paul, MN 55101

MISSISSIPPI
Mississippi Department of
Economic Development
Division of Tourism
P.O. Box 849
Jackson, MS 39205

continued

TRAVEL

MISSOURI
Division of Tourism
Department of Economic
    Development
301 W. High St.
P.O. Box 1055
Jefferson City, MO 65102

MONTANA
Montana Promotion Division
Department of Commerce
1424 9th Ave.
Helena, MT 59620

NEBRASKA
Division of Travel and Tourism
Department of Economic
    Development
State Office Bldg.
301 Centennial Mall, S.
P.O. Box 94666
Lincoln, NE 68509

NEVADA
Commission on Tourism
600 E. Williams St., Suite 207
Carson City, NV 89710

NEW HAMPSHIRE
New Hampshire Office of
    Vacation Travel
Department of Resources and
    Economic Development
105 Loudon Rd.
P.O. Box 856
Concord, NH 03301

NEW JERSEY
Division of Travel and Tourism
Department of Commerce and
    Economic Development
New Jersey National Bank Bldg.
1 W. State St.
C.N. 826
Trenton, NJ 08625

NEW MEXICO
Tourism and Travel Division
Economic Development and
    Tourism Department
Bataan Memorial Bldg.
Santa Fe, NM 87503

NEW YORK
Division of Tourism
Department of Commerce
One Commerce Plaza, 3rd Floor
99 Washington Ave.
Albany, NY 12245

NORTH CAROLINA
Travel and Tourism Division
Department of Commerce
430 N. Salisbury St.
Raleigh, NC 27611

NORTH DAKOTA
North Dakota Tourism Promotion
Liberty Memorial Bldg.
State Capitol Grounds
Bismarck, ND 58505

OHIO
Office of Travel and Tourism
P.O. Box 1001
Columbus, OH 43216-1001

OHLAHOMA
State of Oklahoma Tourism and
    Recreation Department
500 Will Rogers Bldg.
Oklahoma City, OK 73205

OREGON
Tourism Division
Department of Economic
    Development
595 Cottage St., N.E.
Salem, OR 97310

PENNSYLVANIA
Bureau of Travel Development
Department of Commerce
416 Forum Bldg.
Walnut St. and Commonwealth
    Avenue
Harrisburg, PA 17120

RHODE ISLAND
Tourist Promotion Division
Department of Economic
    Development
7 Jackson Walkway
Providence, RI 02903

SOUTH CAROLINA
Division of Tourism
Department of Parks, Recreation,
    and Tourism
Edgar A. Brown Bldg.
1205 Pendleton St.
Columbia, SC 29201

SOUTH DAKOTA
Division of Tourism
Department of State Development
Capital Lake Plaza
711 Wells Ave.
P.O. Box 6000
Pierre, SD 57501

TENNESSEE
Department of Tourist
    Development
State of Tennessee
P.O. Box 23170
Nashville, TN 37202

TEXAS
Tourist Development Agency
200 E. 18th St.
P.O. Box 12008, Capitol Sta.
Austin, TX 78711

UTAH
Utah Travel Council
Council Hall
Capitol Hall
Salt Lake City, UT 84114

VERMONT
Vermont Travel Division
Agency of Development and
    Community Affairs
134 State St.
Montpelier, VT 05602

VIRGINIA
Virginia Division of Tourism
Department of Economic
    Development
202 N. 9th St., Suite 500
Richmond, VA 23219

WASHINGTON
Tourism Development Division
Department of Commerce and
    Economic Development
101 General Administration Bldg.
11th Ave. and Columbia St.
Mail Stop AX-13
Olympia, WA 98504

WEST VIRGINIA
Department of Commerce
1900 Washington, St., E.
Charleston, WV 25305

WISCONSIN
Division of Tourism
Department of Development
123 W. Washington Ave.
P.O. Box 7970
Madison, WI 53707

WYOMING
Wyoming Travel Commission
Frank Norris, Jr., Travel Center
I-25 at Etchepare Circle
Cheyenne, WY 82002